THE OXFORD HANDBO

CREDIT
DERIVATIVES

OXFORD HANDBOOKS IN FINANCE

SERIES EDITOR: MICHAEL DEMPSTER

THE OXFORD HANDBOOK OF BANKING
Edited by Allen N. Berger, Philip Molyneux, and John O.S. Wilson

THE OXFORD HANDBOOK OF CREDIT DERIVATIVES
Edited by Alexander Lipton and Andrew Rennie

THE OXFORD HANDBOOK OF

CREDIT DERIVATIVES

Edited by
ALEXANDER LIPTON
and
ANDREW RENNIE

OXFORD
UNIVERSITY PRESS

OXFORD

UNIVERSITY PRESS

Great Clarendon Street, Oxford, OX2 6DP,
United Kingdom

Oxford University Press is a department of the University of Oxford.
It furthers the University's objective of excellence in research, scholarship,
and education by publishing worldwide. Oxford is a registered trade mark of
Oxford University Press in the UK and in certain other countries

First published in paperback 2013
First Edition published in 2011

Impression: 1

British Library Cataloguing in Publication Data
Data available

Library of Congress Cataloging in Publication Data
Data available

ISBN 978-0-19-954678-7 (hbk)
ISBN 978-0-19-966948-6 (pbk)

Printed in Great Britain on acid-free paper by
Ashford Colour Press Ltd., Gosport, Hampshire

SERIES EDITOR'S PREFACE

Recently two series of Oxford Handbooks covering financial topics have been merged into one under a single editorship – those in Finance found under Business and Economics and those in Quantitative Finance found under Mathematics. This is as it should be, for in spite of all the accusations regarding their role in the recent crisis and recession, financial services are both necessary and critical to the successful development of a global economy facing environmental and pension crises on top of the current one. It can also be argued that banking, insurance and fund management are the last post war industries to go "high tech" and that the esoteric topics involved need exposition to a more general audience than simply that of their creators. The aim of this handbook series is therefore to cover recent developments in financial services, institutions and markets in an up to date, accurate and comprehensive manner which is clear and comprehensible to the interested reader. This will be achieved by careful choice of editors for, and exacting selection of contributors to, each handbook.

It is my hope that over time the volumes in this series will help to create a better understanding of financial topics by the educated public, including financial services managers, regulators and legislators. Such an understanding appeared to be lacking in the run-up to the recent crisis, but it will be crucial to successful management of the global economy in the future.

Michael Dempster

Contents

PART I INTRODUCTION

PART II STATISTICAL OVERVIEW

PART III SINGLE AND MULTI-NAME THEORY

PART IV BEYOND NORMALITY

PART V SECURITIZATION

LIST OF FIGURES

LIST OF TABLES

LIST OF CONTRIBUTORS

Edward Altman is the Max L. Heine Professor of Finance at the Stern School of Business, New York University, and Director of the Credit and Fixed Income Research Program at the NYU Salomon Center. Dr Altman has an international reputation as an expert on corporate bankruptcy, high yield bonds, distressed debt, and credit risk analysis. He was named Laureate 1984 by the Hautes Études Commerciales Foundation in Paris for his accumulated works on corporate distress prediction models and procedures for firm financial rehabilitation and awarded the Graham & Dodd Scroll for 1985 by the Financial Analysts Federation for his work on Default Rates and High Yield Corporate Debt. He was inducted into the Fixed Income Analysts Society Hall of Fame in 2001 and elected President of the Financial Management Association (2003) and a Fellow of the FMA in 2004, and was amongst the inaugural inductees into the Turnaround Management Association's Hall of Fame in 2008. In 2005, Dr Altman was named one of the '100 Most Influential People in Finance' by Treasury & Risk, Management magazine and is frequently quoted in the popular press and on network TV. Dr Altman is an adviser to many financial institutions including Citigroup, Concordia Advisors, Paulson and Company and Investcorp, as well as on the Boards of the Franklin Mutual Series Funds and, until recently, Automated Trading Desk, Inc. He is also Chairman of the Academic Advisory Council of the Turnaround Management Association.

Élie Ayache was born in Lebanon in 1966. Trained as an engineer at l'École Polytechnique of Paris, he pursued a career of option market maker on the floor of MATIF (1987–1990) and LIFFE (1990–1995). He then turned to the philosophy of probability (DEA at la Sorbonne) and to derivative pricing, and co-founded ITO 33, a financial software company, in 1999. Today, ITO 33 is the leading specialist in the pricing of convertible bonds, in the equity-to-credit problem, and more generally, in the calibration and recalibration of volatility surfaces. Élie has published many articles in the philosophy of contingent claims. He is the author of The Blank Swan: the End of Probability, forthcoming.

Alexander Batchvarov, Ph.D., CFA has headed the international structured finance effort for Merrill Lynch since 1998, having prior to that worked in Moody's structured finance and sovereign teams in New York and London, in the emerging markets group of Citibank in New York, and in academia. He has worked extensively in both developed and emerging markets of Europe and North America, Latin America and

Asia, Eastern Europe, and the Middle East. He has authored and edited several books on mortgage markets and mortgage finance in Europe, Asia, and Latin America, on hybrid products and has contributed numerous chapters to publications on structured finance. He holds an M.Sc. Economics, an MBA in Finance, and a Ph.D. in Economics and is a CFA Charter holder.

Arthur Berd is the Head of OTC and Macro Vol Strategies at Capital Fund Management, a hedge fund with offices in Paris and New York, specializing in systematic investment strategies. Prior to that, he was the Head of Quantitative Market Strategies at BlueMountain Capital Management, a leading credit hedge fund in New York. Earlier, Arthur was a Senior Vice President at Lehman Brothers where he was responsible for a variety of quantitative credit models and strategies across corporate bonds and credit derivatives. Before joining Lehman Brothers in 2001, he was a Vice President at Goldman Sachs Asset Management, focusing on fixed income risk management and quantitative portfolio analysis for cash and CDO products. Dr Berd is a member of the editorial board of the Journal of Credit Risk, and is the founding coordinator of the quantitative finance section of www.arXiv.org, a global electronic research repository. Dr Berd is a charter member of the CFA Institute, the New York Society of Securities Analysts, and Risk Who's Who. He holds a Ph.D. in physics from Stanford University. He is an author of more than thirty publications and a frequent invited speaker at major industry conferences.

Tomasz R. Bielecki is a Professor of Applied Mathematics at the Illinois Institute of Technology and the Director of the Master of Mathematical Finance programme at IIT. He has previously held academic positions in the Warsaw School of Economics, University of Kansas, University of Illinois at Chicago, Northeastern Illinois University, and visiting positions in the New York University and the Argonne National Laboratory. He is an author of numerous research papers in the areas of stochastic analysis, stochastic control, manufacturing systems, operations research and mathematical finance. He is a co-author, with Marek Rutkowski, of the monograph 'Credit Risk: Modeling, Valuation and Hedging', which was published by Springer-Verlag in 2002. He is also a co-author, with Monique Jeanblanc and Marek Rutkowski, of the monograph 'Credit Risk Modeling,' which was published by Osaka University Press in 2009. He has been a recipient of various research grants and awards.

Valérie Chavez-Demoulin is lecturer in the Department of Mathematics at the Swiss Federal Institute of Technology in Lausanne (EPFL). Her research on Quantitative Risk Management at the Risklab of the Swiss Federal Institute of Technology in Zurich (ETHZ) consists of statistical methods applied to insurance and finance, mainly concentrating on the impact of extremal events. Aside from her research, she has been the Quantitative Analyst for a Hedge Fund for three years and Head of Statistics at the Direction of Education at the EPFL over the past two years.

Stéphane Crépey obtained his Ph.D. degree in Applied Mathematics from École Polytechnique at INRIA Sophia Antipolis and the Caisse Autonome de Refinancement (group 'Caisse des Dépôts'). He is now an Associate Professor at the Mathematics Department of Evry University. He is director of the Master programme M.Sc. Financial Engineering of Evry University. His current research interests are Financial Modelling, Credit Risk, Numerical Finance, as well as connected mathematical topics in the fields of Backward Stochastic Differential Equations and PDEs. Stéphane Crépey also had various consulting activities in the banking and financial engineering sector.

Mark Davis is Professor of Mathematics at Imperial College London, specializing in stochastic analysis and financial mathematics, in particular in credit risk models, pricing in incomplete markets, and stochastic volatility. From 1995 to 1999 he was Head of Research and Product Development at Tokyo-Mitsubishi International, leading a front-office group providing pricing models and risk analysis for fixed-income, equity and credit-related products. Dr Davis holds a Ph.D. in Electrical Engineering from the University of California Berkeley and an Sc.D. in Mathematics from Cambridge University. He is the author of three books on stochastic analysis and optimization, and was awarded the Naylor Prize in Applied Mathematics by the London Mathematical Society in 2002.

Youssef Elouerkhaoui is a Managing Director and the Global Head of Credit Derivatives Quantitative Research at Citi. His group is responsible for model development and analytics for all the credit businesses at Citi, this includes: Flow Credit Trading, Correlation Trading, ABS, Credit Exotics and Emerging Markets. Prior to this, he was a Director in the Fixed Income Derivatives Quantitative Research Group at UBS, where he was in charge of developing and implementing models for the Structured Credit Derivatives Desk. Before joining UBS, Youssef was a Quantitative Research Analyst at Credit Lyonnais supporting the Interest Rates Exotics business. He has also worked as a Senior Consultant in the Risk Analytics and Research Group at Ernst & Young. He is a graduate of École Centrale Paris, and he holds a Ph.D. in Mathematics from Paris-Dauphine University.

Paul Embrechts, Department of Mathematics, RiskLab, ETH Zurich. Paul Embrechts is Professor of Mathematics at the ETH Zurich specializing in actuarial mathematics and quantitative risk management. Previous academic positions include the Universities of Leuven, Limburg, and London (Imperial College). Dr Embrechts has held visiting professorships at numerous universities. He is an Elected Fellow of the Institute of Mathematical Statistics, Actuary-SAA, Honorary Fellow of the Institute and the Faculty of Actuaries, Corresponding Member of the Italian Institute of Actuaries, Member Honoris Causa of the Belgian Institute of Actuaries, and is on the editorial board of several scientific journals. He belongs to various national and international research and academic advisory committees. He co-authored the influential books 'Modelling of Extremal Events for Insurance and Finance', Springer, 1997 and 'Quantitative Risk Management: Concepts, Techniques, Tools', Princeton UP, 2005. Dr Embrechts consults on issues in quantitative risk management for financial institutions, insurance companies, and international regulatory authorities.

Jon Gregory is a consultant specializing in counterparty risk and credit derivatives. Until 2008, he was Global Head of Credit Analytics at Barclays Capital based in London. Jon has worked on many aspects of credit modelling over the last decade, being previously with BNP Paribas and Salomon Brothers (now Citigroup). In addition to publishing papers on the pricing of credit risk and related topics, he was in 2001 co-author of the book '*Credit: The Complete Guide to Pricing, Hedging and Risk Management*', shortlisted for the Kulp-Wright Book Award for the most significant text in the field of risk management and insurance. He is author of the book '*Counterparty Risk: The Next Challenge for the Global Financial Markets*' published by Wiley Finance in December 2009. Jon has a Ph.D. from Cambridge University.

Alexander Herbertsson is at present employed as researcher at Centre for Finance and Department of Economics at the School of Business, Economics and Law, belonging to University of Gothenburg. He holds a Ph.D. in Economics (Quantitative Finance) from University of Gothenburg, and has a Licentiate degree in Industrial mathematics from Chalmers University of Technology and an M.Sc. in Engineering Physics from the same university. During 2008 he was a postdoc at the Department of Mathematics at the University of Leipzig, Germany. His main research field is default dependence modelling with a view towards pricing and hedging portfolio credit derivatives. Alexander has also done practical work in option pricing (implied volatility tree models) as a programmer and quantitative analyst in the Financial Engineering and Risk Management group at Handelsbanken Markets, Stockholm. He has taught maths courses at Chalmers University of Technology, in stochastic calculus for Ph.D. students at the Department of Economics, and also given courses in credit risk modelling as well as financial risk.

Vladimir Kamotski, gained an M.Sc. from St Petersburg State University (1999) and Ph.D. from Steklov Institute of Mathematics (2003). He was a postdoc at University of Bath (BICS) and worked on multi-scale problems in PDEs. Since 2007 he has been quantitative analyst at Merrill Lynch, and is the author of five papers in major scientific journals.

Alexander Levin is Director of Financial Engineering at Andrew Davidson & Co., Inc. He is responsible for developing new efficient valuation models for mortgages, derivatives, and other financial instruments and related consulting work. Alex has developed a suite of interest rate models that can be instantly calibrated to swap rates and a swaption volatility matrix. He proposed and developed the Active-Passive Decomposition (APD) mortgage model facilitated by a backward induction OAS pricing. In a joint effort with Andrew Davidson, Alex developed a new concept of prepay risk-and-option-adjusted valuation. This approach introduced a new valuation measure, prOAS, and a notion of risk-neutral prepay modelling that explained many phenomena of the MBS markets. Alex's current work focuses on the valuation of instruments exposed to credit risk ('Credit OAS'), home price modelling, and projects related to the ongoing MBS crisis. Prior to AD&Co, Alex worked as the Director of Treasury Research and Analytics at The Dime Bancorp (the Dime) in New York, taught at The City College of NY, and worked at Ryan Labs, a fixed income research and money management company. Alex is a frequent speaker at the Mathematical Finance Seminar (NYU, Courant Institute), AD&Co client conferences, and has published a number of papers. He holds an MS in Applied Mathematics from Naval Engineering Institute, Leningrad, and a Ph.D. in Control and Dynamic Systems from Leningrad State University.

Alexander Lipton is a Managing Director and Co-Head of the Global Quantitative Group at Bank of America Merrill Lynch, and a Visiting Professor of Mathematics at Imperial College London. Prior to his current role, he has held senior positions at Citadel Investment Group, Credit Suisse, Deutsche Bank, and Bankers Trust. Previously, Dr Lipton was a Full Professor of Mathematics at the University of Illinois at Chicago and a Consultant at Los Alamos National Laboratory. He received his MS and Ph.D. from Lomonosov Moscow State University. His current interests include applications of Levy processes in finance and technical trading strategies. In 2000 Dr Lipton was awarded the first Quant of the Year Award by Risk Magazine. He has published two books and edited three more. He has also published numerous research papers on hydrodynamics, magnetohydrodynamics, astrophysics, and financial engineering.

Julian Manzano holds a Ph.D. in Theoretical Physics from the Faculty of Physics, University of Barcelona, Spain, and a Master in Financial Derivatives from the Faculty of Statistics and Mathematics, Universitat Politècnica de Catalunya. After completing a postdoc at the Department of Physics and Measurement Technology, Linköping University, Sweden, in 2004 he joined HSBC Bank in New York working as a structured credit quant. In 2006 he joined Merrill Lynch in London and currently he is working for Bank of America Merrill Lynch on the area on algorithmic trading focusing on the FX market.

Richard Martin is Head of Quantitative Credit Strategies at AHL, the largest part of Man Group PLC, where he works on the development of credit trading strategies. Before that he was a Managing Director in Fixed Income at Credit Suisse in London. In the last few years his interests have been CDO correlation trading, credit-equity trading, and pricing and hedging of credit derivatives. One of the leading authorities on portfolio modelling, he introduced to the financial community the saddle-point method as a tool for assisting in portfolio risk calculations. He was awarded Quant of the Year by *Risk* Magazine in 2002.

Umberto Pesavento, a native of Padova, Italy, graduated from Princeton University with a BA in Physics. He received a Ph.D. in Physics from Cornell University where he also worked as a postdoctoral associate and lecturer in the Theoretical and Applied Mechanics Department conducting research in fluid dynamics and computational physics. Since 2008 he has been working at Merrill Lynch and Bank of America Merrill Lynch as a quant in the credit and interest rates groups.

Andrew Rennie has spent sixteen years on large-scale modelling projects in the financial sector, working on exotic interest rate products at UBS before moving to be Global Head of Financial Engineering at Rabobank International and most recently, Global Head of Quantitative Analytics at Merrill Lynch responsible for all modelling of derivatives across interest rates, foreign exchange, credit, commodities, and equities. He studied Mathematics, and after graduating, Philosophy at Cambridge University, as well as publishing papers on the mathematical and chemical properties of one-dimensional inclusion compounds. He co-authored one of the standard textbooks on derivative pricing—*Financial Calculus*, Cambridge University Press, 1996—and has written various papers on quantitative modelling. He is currently a consultant advising on derivative pricing and risk management.

Lutz Schloegl is a managing director in the fixed income quantitative research group of Nomura International, co-heading the modelling efforts for credit, commodities, and ABS. From 2000 to 2008 he was a quant at Lehman Brothers International, specializing in credit derivatives, and has been global head of credit correlation product modelling since 2006. He studied mathematics at the University Bonn, where he was also awarded a Ph.D. in financial economics in 2001.

Artur Sepp is a Vice President in the equity derivatives analytics at Bank of America Merrill Lynch in London, where he is developing quantitative models for equity volatility and structured products. Prior to joining the equity group in 2009, he worked with the credit derivatives group at Merrill Lynch in New York focusing on quantitative models for multi- and single-name credit derivatives and hybrid products. He holds a Ph.D. in Mathematical Statistics from University of Tartu (Estonia).

David Shelton, Director, is co-head of Credit Derivatives Research at Bank of America Merrill Lynch. Within Credit Research David's main interests are pricing and hedging of CDOs and correlation products counterparty risk and dynamic models of credit risk. Since 1998, David has worked as a quantitative analyst on FX, hybrid FX interest rate, and Credit products. Prior to his current role, David worked at Natwest, Citigroup and Barclays Capital. Before that he was a postdoctoral theoretical physicist in Canada and Oxford for two years, after receiving a D.Phil. in Theoretical Physics from the University of Oxford.

Gillian Tett is currently an assistant editor of the *Financial Times* who oversees the newpaper's global coverage of the financial markets. In addition to shaping the strategic direction of the coverage, she writes commentary and analysis pieces and runs the global team. In 2007 she was awarded the Wincott prize, the premier British award for financial journalism, for her capital markets coverage. In 2008 she was named Business Journalist of the Year in the British Press Awards for her coverage of the credit turmoil. In 2009 she was named Journalist of the Year, in all categories. She joined the *FT* in London in 1993 and initially worked as a foreign reporter in the former Soviet Union and Europe, and then joining the economics team where she covered the UK and

European economies. In 1997 she went to Tokyo, where she was *FT* Bureau Chief. In 2003 she became deputy head of the Lex column of the *FT*, writing comment pieces about international economics and finance. She has published a book about Japanese and US finance: *Saving the Sun: How Wall Street Mavericks Shook up Japan's Financial System and Made Billions* (HarperCollins and Random House). In 2009 she published *Fool's Gold; How the Bold Dream of a Small Tribe at J. P. Morgan was corrupted by Wall Street Greed and Unleashed a Catastrophe* (Simon and Schuster and Little Brown). It was awarded the Spears Prize for best business book in 2009. Gillian Tett has a Ph.D. in Social Anthropology from Cambridge University, based on research conducted in the former Soviet Union in the early 1990s. She speaks French, Russian, and moderate Japanese.

Zhen Wei is currently a Vice President in Bank of America Merrill Lynch covering Equity Investment Strategies across the Asia Pacific Region. Prior to joining Merrill Lynch, Mr Wei was a Strategist at Nomura International (HK) and Lehman Brothers (Asia), covering Fixed Income products including Bond Portfolio, Credit Derivatives, Interest Rate and FX Derivatives, and Commodities. He received his Ph.D. degree in Statistics and Masters of Science degree in Financial Mathematics from Stanford University, California. He graduated from Peking University, China, with a Bachelor's degree in Statistics and a minor in Computer Science. Mr Wei was born in China and is currently based in Hong Kong.

PART I

INTRODUCTION

CHAPTER 1

NON-TECHNICAL
INTRODUCTION

GILLIAN TETT

BACK in the mid 1990s, a regulator working for America's Office of the Comptroller of the Currency (OCC) encountered some marketing literature from J. P. Morgan bank which described the concept of credit derivatives. Back then, the idea seemed extraordinarily novel. However, this particular regulator was both surprised and thrilled. 'It seemed to me that this was one of the most important innovations that had occurred for years,' he later recalled, adding that he immediately called the J. P. Morgan bankers to express his enthusiasm. 'The whole concept of credit derivatives seemed wonderful—such a clever way to reduce systemic risk!'

These days, this particular American financial official is now wondering, as he says, 'how it all just went so wrong'. So are many other investors, bankers, and government officials. In the fifteen years since the credit derivatives concept was first developed by groups such as J. P. Morgan, Bankers Trust, Credit Suisse—and others—this product has expanded with dizzying speed. At the start of the decade, official data from ISDA suggested that barely $1 trillion of these contracts had been written in the global markets when measured in terms of gross outstanding amount (i.e. without netting off contracts which offset each other). By 2008, that sum had swelled above $60 trillion. More striking still, the original concept of credit derivatives had mutated into numerous new forms, breeding a host of acronyms along the way covering corporate, sovereign, and mortgage debt.

But as the concept has taken root, it has become increasingly controversial. Most notably, during the banking crisis of 2007 and 2008, some regulators, bankers, and investors blamed credit derivatives instruments for contributing to the financial woes. More specifically, these products are perceived to have exacerbated the credit bubble on the 'way up' by concealing the scale of leverage in the system and amplifying risk taking. Worse still, credit derivatives also made it harder for policy makers to contain the shock when the bubble burst, because the opacity of the sector made it hard to identify developing risks—and these contracts had interwoven different institutions in a complex mesh of exposures, creating the so-called 'too interconnected to fail' woes. Thus, during 2009 there has been a plethora of hand-wringing about credit derivatives—and a new global drive to subject these instruments to new regulatory controls.

Some bankers insist that these criticisms of credit derivatives are grossly unfair. After all, they argue, the real source of the credit bubble during the early years of this decade was not the credit derivatives technology per se, but the flood of cheap money, as a result of excessively loose monetary policy, and poor regulation of sectors such as the mortgage industry. Moreover, these defenders would add, it was not the credit derivatives market alone which created the 'too interconnected to fail' headache (or the idea that it was impossible for governments to let any big bank collapse, since it would have repercussions for everybody else, due to counterparty risk). The structure of the tri-party repurchase market, for example, also played a key role in the financial panic of 2008. So did accounting rules.

Nevertheless, such pleading by the banking industry has not deterred the criticism. Consequently, as the debate about the culpability of credit derivatives rages on, the one thing that is crystal clear is that the whole concept of credit derivatives has now become more high profile than most bankers ever dreamt. Whereas the details of this market used to only arouse interest among financial experts, they have now been splashed across newspapers and prime-time television shows in America and the UK. The topic has even provoked political debate in Washington and Brussels. And that in turn has prompted observers both inside and outside the banking world to ask new questions about the product; most notably about where the idea first erupted from. And where it might now be heading, after the recent controversy.

Identifying the source of the credit derivatives idea is not easy. After all, finance is not a field of activity swathed with patents or intellectual copyrights: instead, ideas tend to swirl around the markets, to be endlessly copied, improved, and advanced, making it hard for any one individual—or bank—to ever claim true 'authorship' of an idea. Arguably the first place where credit derivatives deals appeared was at Bankers Trust bank in New York, where a small team of bankers, including Peter Freund and John Crystal, first cut a couple of rudimentary deals in 1991. These essentially took the concept that had been central to the previous derivative products—namely using tailor-made contracts to 'swap' exposures, say, to fixed and floating rates or currencies—and applied it to the field of credit risk. Essentially, that meant that one party promised to compensate another party if a bond (or loan) went into default—in exchange for a predetermined fee. What was being 'swapped', in other words, was a fixed fee and an exposure to default risk, in a private, off-exchange deal between two parties.

Initially, this brainchild did not appear to cause much of a splash, either inside or outside Bankers Trust. Freund's team did not immediately see any way to make the concept yield significant profits or fees for their bank (or not, at least, compared to the plethora of innovative interest rate products which were being developed in the market at the time). And that, coupled with personnel changes, deterred them from allocating too many resources to the idea, leaving the field clear for other rivals.

One of those—and the most important early player in the credit derivatives field—was J. P. Morgan bank. During the 1980s and early 1990s, the bank had developed a large interest and foreign exchange derivatives business, and by the mid-1990s it was seeking ways to expand this. Under the leadership of men such as Peter Hancock and Bill Demchak, long-time employees of J. P. Morgan, the bank decided it would be worthwhile to pursue the credit derivatives idea, even if it did not appear to be an immediate source of client or proprietary profits. This was partly because J. P. Morgan, as a large corporate lender, had a natural expertise in corporate debt, and a large stable of corporate clients. The bank also had a huge regulatory incentive: in the early 1990s, the bank's top management had realized that they needed to remove credit risk from J. P. Morgan's book and to use its economic and regulatory capital more efficiently. However, they did not wish to do this through 'simple' loan sales that could undermine client relationships. Developing synthetic swaps thus appeared to be an attractive way to remove credit risk, while preserving a lending franchise.

The young bankers at J. P. Morgan also argued that there could also be wider systemic benefits to the idea, beyond anything that pertained to their bank. If banks such as J. P. Morgan started shedding credit risk, they suggested, that would enable them to reduce the type of risk concentrations that had hurt commercial lenders in previous economic cycles, such as during the Savings and Loans crisis of the late 1980s. A new era of banking would dawn, where banks were diversified and hedged in a way that would make the financial system stronger; or so the theory went. And for the most part the theory was one that was enthusiastically accepted by regulators, not just at the OCC, but by the US Federal Reserve as well as their European counterpart. That, in turn, helped to create a benign regulatory climate for the new instruments.

The first set of products that the J. P. Morgan group developed in the early and mid-1990s were fairly ad hoc credit derivatives, based on contracts that traded the credit risk on individual companies or sovereign entities, ranging from Exxon to the Korean Development bank. Other banks quickly copied the contracts, which were mostly arranged in the form of credit default swaps (CDS). But then, bankers started to bundle multiple different credit risks together, in a variety of different structures, to enable participants to shift credit risk on a larger scale (and investors to further diversify their exposures). By 1997, Swiss Bank, Chase Manhattan, Merrill Lynch, and Credit Suisse, for example, were all playing around with variants of this idea, using leveraged loans, corporate bonds, and sovereign credit. Then in late 1997, the J. P. Morgan team in London launched a particularly eye-catching product that came to be known as 'Bistro'. This scheme, which was technically short for 'Broad Secured Trust Offering'—but was also known as 'BIS total rip off' on the J. P. Morgan desk, since it appeared to run rings around the bank capital rules devised by the Bank of International Settlements—essentially bundled together dozens of corporate credits into a single structure, and removed these from the balance sheet of J. P. Morgan. It did this by transferring the risk to a special purpose vehicle, funded through the sale of bonds to third party investors, carrying different tranches of risk. In some respects that reflected similar structures created by groups such as Swiss Bank, but what made the Bistro scheme path-breaking was that the SPV did not fund itself fully; on the contrary, barely $700million of funds were raised, to support a $10-odd billion credit portfolio. This made it significantly cheaper to arrange than previous schemes. The scheme was still able to get a top-notch rating from the credit rating agencies, since these presumed that the loans were of such good quality that it was extremely unlikely that there would be enough defaults to wipe out the $700m-odd cushion. The net result was that J. P. Morgan could to dance more effectively around the BIS rules.

The concept quickly caught on, spawning dozens of similar offerings, which subsequently came to be known as 'synthetic collateralized debt obligations'. As the ratings agencies spotted a lucrative new line of business, they supported these new products by providing the all-important 'triple A' stamp for the deals, thus enabling the banks to keep dancing around the Basel rules on a growing scale. Then, in the early years of the new decade, bankers took the 'Bistro' concept a step further, developing so-called 'single tranche' collateralized debt obligations (CDOs)(deals where one tranche was funded, but not necessarily the most senior tranche). The practice of trading single-name CDS—or those written on individual companies, rather than bundled together—rapidly expanded too, particularly in Europe, as events such as the 1998 Asian financial crisis and collapse of the internet boom sparked more investor interest in the idea of hedging credit risk. Then in the early years of the new decade, bankers at the newly merged JPMorgan Chase, along with those at Deutsche Bank, Morgan Stanley, and elsewhere, launched so-called tradeable credit derivatives indices. These essentially offered a price for a basket of credit default swaps—but also provided a contract that could be traded in its own right. Since these products were more liquid and transparent than single name CDS, they attracted a wider pool of investors. These items also provided crucial reference points for structures such as single tranche CDOs. These innovations turbo-charged the market: between 2000 and 2003, ISDA estimated that the gross notional outstanding value of trades more than tripled to around $3 trillion, and then increased fivefold in the next two years.

The other reason why the market exploded was the wider macroeconomic climate. After the collapse of the telecoms bubble in 2001, Alan Greenspan, chairman of the US Federal Reserve, slashed short-term interest rates. At the same time, a savings surplus in Asia helped to drive long-term yields down in the government bond market too. Taken together, that spurred investors to seek new ways to increase their returns, most notably by turning to derivatives, increasing credit risk, and using dramatically higher levels of leverage. Banks also expanded the scope of products involved in the credit derivatives business. Back in the mid-1990s, when the CDS concept had first sprung to life, bankers at J. P. Morgan had not generally sought to apply the idea to residential mortgages, since that was not an area of the bank's expertise. Furthermore, some J. P. Morgan bankers were wary of trying to model the risk in the housing market, since they feared that there was not enough reliable data on what might happen in a house price crash to give good calculations for the price of the tranches of a CDO linked to mortgage risk.

From the late 1990s onwards, however, other banks started to play around with the concept of using mortgage risk. That was partly because there was strong investor appetite for mortgage debt in the wake of the telecoms crash, since the housing markets—unlike the corporate sector—had not generally been hurt by that crash. Some bankers and investors were also attracted by the idea of using derivatives technology in the mortgage world since it appeared to offer more flexibility than the traditional practice of bundling mortgage bonds together via cash CDOs. More specifically, by 2005 there was strong investor demand for products composed of sub-prime mortgage securities, which paid (relatively) good returns—but not enough sub-prime loans to meet that demand. Thus, instead of building CDOs from tangible mortgage bonds, bankers increasingly turned to derivatives instead, to overcome the shortage. And those endeavours were given a big boost when a tradeable index of mortgage derivatives was launched at the start of 2006. This new index, run by Markit, was known as the 'ABX' series and designed to complement the other corporate and loan credit derivatives indices, known respectively as iTraxx (European corporate credit), CDX (American corporate credit), and LCDX (leverage loans.)

The net result of all these trends was a further boom in the scale and complexity of the credit derivatives world. As the product expanded, a subtle—but crucially important—shift occurred in the nature of the market. Back in the early 1990s, when concepts such as Bistro or single-name CDS had first emerged, these instruments had generally been presented and perceived as hedging tools, rather than having a purpose that was primarily speculative. In reality, of course, speculation always played a role; it is impossible to have hedging in any market, unless somebody is willing to take a risk. The key reason why groups such as the OCC—and other regulators—initially backed the idea of credit derivatives so enthusiastically was that they believed this hedging incentive was dominant, hence their enthusiasm for viewing credit derivatives as a tool to mitigate systemic risk.

However, by the middle of the new decade, this 'hedging' function of the market became overwhelmed by speculative practices and motives. Surveys by the OCC, for example, showed that banks were no longer simply writing CDS to hedge against the default risk of credits which they held on their books, but taking net short positions in credits they did not hold, either for themselves or clients. Numerous other investors were doing the same. Conversely, investors, such as hedge funds, were writing protection as a way to get long in booming markets, such as sub-prime securities. In reality, it was far from clear that all those new investors had sufficient resources to actually honour all those insurance claims, if there was a massive wave of defaults. But, the hedge funds were happy to take the fees for writing insurance, via credit derivatives; and banks (and others) often seemed almost indifferent to the quality of their counterparties, since CDS contracts were increasingly being used to gain regulatory relief, rather than provide genuine economic protection. The product, in other words, was becoming more and more of a tool for speculation and regulatory arbitrage, than a genuine source of credit hedging.

These subtle shifts alarmed some regulators. The Bank for International Settlements, for example, started warning other banking officials as early as 2003 that the explosive pace of growth in the CDS sector, coupled with its opacity, could pose a systemic risk. They also pointed out that these instruments could create moral hazard: since instruments such as CDS appeared to provide such an easy way for banks to hedge their risks, there was no less incentive for lenders to restrict credit or monitor credit quality. However, it was hard for the BIS, or other naysayers, to argue their case in a truly compelling manner, since there was a paucity of data—not least because these contracts were being concluded via private, Over-The-Counter deals, not on the exchange. Meanwhile, groups such as the US Federal Reserve tended to brush off concerns, since men such as Greenspan strongly believed that the credit derivatives boom had made the system far safer than before, as it enabled banks to diversify their credit risks. Greenspan (and others) also tended to assume that free markets were self-correcting and market participants would have a rational incentive to demand rational systems for trading risks; thus even if some excesses were developing in the CDS space, the argument went, bankers themselves should be able to correct them—precisely because the innovation had enabled credit risk to be traded in a more purely free-market manner than ever before.

In many respects, the Fed (and others) appeared to have history firmly on their side, as they presented those arguments. From 2000 onwards, financial markets were beset by a series of shocks, including the bursting of the telecoms bubble, the attack on the World Trade Centre, Enron scandal, failure of WorldCom, Parmalat scandal, the credit ratings agency downgrade of Ford and General Motors—and then the implosion of Amaranth hedge fund. Between 2000 and 2007, the banking system absorbed these blows relatively smoothly, without any large collapses. Regulators generally attributed that to the fact that banks had successfully hedged their credit exposures, using CDS (alongside other tools such as loan sales). Credit derivatives thus seemed to have produced a safer system—just as the J. P. Morgan bankers had once claimed (and the OCC regulators hoped).

In reality, there were two terrible paradoxes sitting at the very heart of the system. One was the fact that while credit derivatives had been developed under the mantra of 'market completion' (or to promote liquid free markets for credit and credit risk), by the middle of the new decade many of the products had quietly become so complex that they were not actually being traded at all. Single-name CDS contracts often traded, and the index products were generally very liquid, but bespoke tranches of synthetic CDOs generally did not trade freely. Consequently, when banks and investors tried to value these instruments in their own books they were forced to use models to extrapolate prices from other reference points, since there was no true 'market' price available.

That pattern was not, of course, unique to CDS: cash bonds are often illiquid too, but the scale of the CDS boom, and its opacity, created huge opportunities for canny traders not just to engage in forms of economic arbitrage, but to arbitrage their own banks' accounting systems and the wider regulatory framework too. One tactic used by traders at some banks during 2005 and 2006, for example, was to enter a relatively low 'model' price for a synthetic product at the start of the year, and to then revalue it at a higher price later in the year—meaning that the difference could be booked as profit for the desk (and thus counted towards the bonus). Observers outside those trading desks (such as risk officers) often found it difficult to challenge this, since the sector was so complex and opaque, and there were no easily tradeable reference points. And that, in turn, had another crucial implication: since banks were relying on 'model' prices, and not market prices, there was a lack of the type of true price signals that would have allowed the sector to adjust to changing circumstances—or 'self-correct'—as men such as Greenspan presumed it should.

The case of super-senior tranches of CDOs was a case in point. The idea of 'super-senior' piece of debt first cropped up in the original J. P. Morgan Bistro trade, when the phrase was used to refer to the unfunded portion of the structure which was supposed to be so extraordinarily safe that it could never default (and thus, by implication, even safer than triple A debt). But by the middle of the next decade, the phrase was being used in a loose manner to refer to the safest, and most highly rated chunk of a synthetic CDO, or a credit derivatives contract offering protection against the default of an ultra-safe chunk of debt. Initially, during the early years of the synthetic boom, banks had tried to sell that piece of super-senior debt to other investors, particularly when they were assembling bundles of debt for a third party. Insurance groups such as AIG, for example, were often willing to buy super-senior credit derivatives (or write protection), since, while the yield was low, AIG did not have to hold much capital against these positions. The deals thus provided a reasonably stable source of income.

By the middle of the decade, however, spreads in the credit market were collapsing so far that it was becoming extremely difficult for bankers to find a way to make all the different tranches of a CDO 'pay their way'. If they structured the deal to ensure that the junior pieces of debt carried enough yield to be attractive to investors, then the returns on super-senior were so paltry they were was hard to sell. To make matters worse, the scale of CDO activity was rising so fast, that there was a glut of super-senior debt on the market. If a fully fledged, transparent secondary liquid market had existed for the tranches, this problem might have been apparent relatively quickly; but, as the price signals were so distorted, it was not—and the CDO boom simply became more, not less intense. So, partly as a result—and for lack of alternative buyers—banks started to stockpile CDO tranches on their own balance sheets. At some banks (such as Merrill Lynch) this was viewed as merely a temporary tactic, to ensure that a pipeline of deals could be completed; at other groups (such as UBS) this stockpiling came to be regarded as a deliberate strategy. (UBS bankers were able to arbitrage the internal risk and pricing models and use cheap sources of capital to keep 'booking' profits on the super-senior structures, even as the risk in these exposures disappeared from management reports.)

This pattern then produced a second, even more important paradox: namely that as banks stockpiled CDOs, or super-senior exposures, risks started to be concentrated back onto the banks' books—rather than dispersed across the system, as the original supports of the credit derivatives revolution had expected. As AIG acquired vast quantities of seemingly safe super-senior mortgage risk, for example, it was also becoming increasingly exposed to a highly correlated book of systemic risk. So were banks such as UBS, Merrill Lynch, and Citi, to name but a few. And, just to make matters worse, large banks were often acting as counterparties to each others' deals—and the reference names in these deals were often large financial institutions too.

Moreover, as banks started concentrating the risks back on their own books, another, more subtle form of concentration was occurring inside the deals as well. When the J. P. Morgan bankers had first created synthetic CDOs back in the late 1990s, they had done so assuming that the baskets of credits were diversified, and thus that the level of correlation between corporate defaults was not too high. Those assumptions had also been baked into the approaches used by rating agencies to model the deals. However, as bankers started to use mortgage credit instead of corporate credit for these deals, the pattern of correlation changed. Most notably, although many analysts presumed that the deals would provide diversification, because they included mortgages from different regions of America or mortgage pools; in practice the mortgages tended to be structured in such a similar manner that default correlations were relatively high. If the cost of servicing a mortgage rose above a certain threshold, or the house prices fell, then borrowers were apt to default wherever they lived. Worse still, when bankers started to create CDOs of CDOs, these concentrations tended to be intensified. The ratings agencies generally continued to provide high ratings for these deals, since they lacked the resources—and the incentives—to track the way the mortgage market was changing, and the impact this was having on potential default correlations.

From time to time during 2005 and 2006, as the credit boom grew wilder, some regulators expressed unease in general terms about the nature of the credit boom. In the spring of 2007, for example, the Bank of England observed in a half-yearly financial stability report that it seemed odd that banks' balance sheets were growing—even though they claimed to be shedding credit risk. Timothy Geithner, then head of the New York Federal Reserve, warned on several occasions that some market participants appeared excessively complacent about so-called 'tail risks', or the danger that losses could occur which would be so extreme that they would hurt even 'safe' debt, and activate credit derivatives. However, the main focus of the regulatory community during this period in relation to credit derivatives was on trading and settlement processes. By 2005, men such as Geithner had realized that the speed of expansion in the CDS sphere had overwhelmed the banks' back offices due to a dire lack of resources. That was leaving deals uncompleted for days, if not weeks, which threatened to create a dangerous legal quagmire if any counterparties ever failed. Thus, from 2005 onwards, British and American regulators exhorted the banks to overhaul their back office procedures, and threatened to impose sanctions on the banks if they did not comply. And the campaign paid off: by 2007, the back office systems at most banks and hedge funds had been radically upgraded. But—ironically enough—amid all the debate about trading systems, there was minimal discussion about the tangible impact of all the new CDS contracts that were being cut through these systems. Thus very few observers noticed that a tool which was supposed to mitigate systemic risk had now spread a whole new range of risks. Even fewer realized that beneath the mantra of risk dispersion, the sector was becoming marked by a growing risk concentration and correlation.

The deadly consequences of this pattern became clear during 2007 and 2008. In early 2007, a bubble in sub-prime lending started to burst. Ironically—or perhaps appropriately—one of the first places where this shift was signalled was in the ABX index: from early 2007, this started to move in a manner that implied that the cost of purchasing protection against a default of a sub-prime bond was rising sharply. Until mid-2007 relatively few non-specialists had ever paid much attention to the ABX (not least since it had only been launched in early 2006), but the price swings had a stealthy domino effect: during 2005 and 2006, many banks and investment groups had used the ABX index and credit ratings as key inputs for the models that they were using to value CDOs and complex derivatives. Thus, as the ABX began to move, financial institutions were forced to start revaluing their assets downwards. Around the same time, the rating agencies started—belatedly—to cut their ratings for mortgage-linked products. That caused prices to fall further. And since many institutions had taken on huge levels of leverage in 2006, that downward revaluation had a devastating impact.

Two highly leveraged hedge funds linked to Bear Stearns were one of the first visible casualties: in midsummer 2007, they both imploded, largely due to swings in the ABX index and other CDO products. Within months a host of other institutions came under pressure too, ranging from hedge funds to major Wall Street banks, and European groups, such as IKB. As share prices in the financial sector tumbled, that sowed panic. That sense of fear was exacerbated by a second, more subtle development: counterparties rushed to hedge their exposures to banks, by using single-name credit derivatives, which then caused the price of those CDS contracts to swing. On one level, this appeared to be an entirely encouraging development, since it reaffirmed the original 'hedging' function of the instrument. In another sense, though, the development worsened the panic, since the CDS spread provided a readily available way to gauge the level of investor concern about default risk, and also provided an easy way for investors to bet on a potential bank collapse. Moreover, since it had become common practice from the middle of the decade onwards to use CDS spreads as a way to decide the price of bank debt, the rising CDS spreads also pushed up funding costs—creating a vicious circle of pressure for the banks.

Of course, the CDS market was not the only place where these signs of stress were emerging, and being exacerbated: the slump in the equity markets and the rising cost of finance in the interbank sector were also playing key roles. What made the patterns in the CDS sector particularly notable—and controversial—was the relatively level of opacity in this sphere. Ever since it had first sprung to life, the CDS market had been a private, over-the-counter market. As a result, by 2007, it was still hard for regulators (or anybody else) to get accurate data on trading volumes, counterparties, or even intra-day prices—in notable contrast to the situation in, say, the equity markets. Until

2007, that state of affairs had not prompted much comment, since regulators had generally appeared content to leave the sector as a lightly regulated, OTC business. During the 1990s, the Commodities and Futures Exchange had made a few attempts to pull the sector into its regulatory net, and force it onto exchanges, as part of a wider move to take control of the OTC derivatives sector. This was firmly rebuffed by Greenspan and others, and during the first seven years of the new century there was a widespread consensus—in keeping with the dominant free-market ideology of the times—that CDS should be left lightly regulated, in the OTC sphere.

As the swing in CDS prices began to have wider implications in the autumn of 2007, regulatory scrutiny started to rise. Politicians started to question the way that ratings agencies had rated products during the credit boom, and call for reform of the ratings sector. Concerns were voiced about the way that, say, the ABX sector was managed, since the movements in the index were having a big impact on banks— but it was unclear just how deep the market was, or whether there was any scope for market manipulation, or not. Then a second issue emerged, which further provoked regulatory unease: banks (and other investors) began to worry about counterparty risk. Most notably, since CDS trades were typically settled via bilateral deals, without a centralized counterparty, investors did not have any third party involved in the market to settle trades if one counterparty failed. Since the late 1990s, groups such as ISDA had sought to mitigate that risk by demanding that counterparties post collateral to cover any potential losses if a counterparty did fail—in much the same way that collateral was used in a range of other OTC derivatives deals. Credit derivatives, though—unlike interest rates swaps—have a binary nature: either an entity has gone into default, or not. Thus, whereas counterparties to an interest swap might be able to adjust collateral positions in a gradual manner to reflect changing risks, some market players feared this would prove harder for CDS contracts.

The implosion of Bear Stearns in the spring of 2008 then dramatically raised the level of market concern about those two issues. In the run-up to the dramatic crisis at the broker, the cost of buying default protection for Bear Stearns via the CDS sector suddenly surged. Some investors argued that this simply reflected tangible, rational investor concerns; but some of the Bear Stearns management insisted that rivals were spreading rumours to destabilize the bank, and manipulating thin, murky markets. Whatever the truth, as confidence in Bear crumbled, banks, hedge funds, and investors became extremely fearful about counterparty risk for any contracts where Bear was a counterparty—and rushed to sell them on, or mitigate those risks in other ways. Those moves further fuelled the sense of alarm about the way that CDS was exacerbating systemic risk.

In the event, much of this concern appeared to be ill-founded, since JPMorgan Chase stepped in to rescue Bear, with government backing. A crunch was thus averted. Nonetheless, the events left regulators on both sides of the Atlantic convinced that they urgently needed to reform the way that the CDS market operated and to put it on more robust and transparent footing. So, in the weeks after the implosion of Bear Stearns, the New Federal Reserve and British FSA held a series of meetings with bankers, at which they exhorted the industry to start using centralized clearing platforms, develop more standardized systems for reporting and pricing, and to provide more transparent reporting of deals. Some voices in the industry appeared reluctant to embrace that. Senior officials at ISDA, for example, had previously been very wary of imposing a centralized clearing platform on the industry, and at the body's annual conference in Vienna in the summer of 2008, ISDA made it clear that it was extremely reluctant to embrace more scrutiny or regulation, but as the pressure mounted, ISDA was forced to modify its stance. And by the late summer efforts were accelerating to launch a clearing house—albeit one partly controlled by the sell-side banks themselves.

Controversy about CDS then exploded further in the autumn of 2008. One trigger was the collapse of Lehman Brothers in mid-September. In the days leading up to the failure of the broker, the CDS spread on Lehman—like that of Bear Stearns six months before—swung dramatically. That exacerbated the sense of market unease, and prompted allegations about market manipulation. Then, when the US Fed decided to let Lehman Brothers collapse, concern about counterparty risk resurfaced again, in relation to the numerous deals which Lehman Brothers had written with other banks. In a frantic effort to contain that systemic risk, the New York Fed called all senior CDS traders on Wall Street into its office on the Sunday afternoon, just before it announced Lehman Brothers' collapse, and urged them to cancel offsetting deals. However, that initiative was a failure: the web of deals that linked the banks to Lehman (and each other) proved to be so complex and opaque it was hard to match up the offsetting trades in a hurry, without the presence of a central party, such as a clearing house.

That prompted concerns, once again, about the systemic risk created by the opacity of the CDS contracts. There was also widespread fear about the potential impact of unwinding CDS contracts in which Lehman Brothers was a reference entity: in the days after the collapse of the broker, rumours circulated around the market that banks and hedge funds would need to find around $400bn of cash—or Lehman bonds—to actually honour these deals. In reality many of those fears later proved to be false. In the weeks that followed Lehman's collapse, most of the broker's counterparties managed to unwind contracts which they had concluded with Lehman Brothers without too much difficulty. That was largely because the shock of the Bear Stearns event had already prompted senior managers of banks to debate the issues and to improve their collateral practices. Meanwhile, it also proved far easier to settle deals written on Lehman's credit that had been feared. In the year before the Lehman failure, ISDA had introduced an auction mechanism to settle the price at which a CDS contract should be settled after default, and to allow banks to net off their exposures, without needing to find bonds. In the weeks after the Lehman collapse this system was used, with good results, and the total volume of money that changed hands to settle the CDS was a minute fraction of the gross notional value of all contracts using Lehman as a reference entity.

But even if those events helped to ease some of the systemic concerns, in the days after the Lehman collapse another event crystallized the sense of controversy: the Fed announced that AIG, the insurance group, was all but bankrupt, and it announced a massive rescue package, which initially totalled some $85bn, but later swelled well above $100bn. Once again, credit derivatives appeared to have played a role in this debacle. Most notably, a key reason for AIG's problems was that since the late 1990s, AIG Financial Products had been quietly acquiring the super-senior tranches of CDOs, or writing protection for CDO tranches held by other institutions, using credit derivatives. Few observers outside AIGFP were aware of the size of this activity, but by 2007, the outstanding value of these trades had swelled above $450bn. These left AIGFP exposed to a deadly concentration of risks, which the insurance group had not reserved against, since it was not required to post much capital against these trades, under its regulatory regime. Worse still, many of these CDS contracts stipulated that AIG needed to post more collateral with its counterparties if its credit rating deteriorated. Thus, when credit quality deteriorated in the autumn of 2008 and AIG's own rating was slashed, the insurance group suddenly found itself facing a black hole—for which it was utterly unprepared.

As that news trickled out, in the weeks after the AIG debacle, it unleashed a new wave of criticism of credit derivatives. Some bankers involved in the industry insisted that this was unfair, since the 'super-senior' instruments that AIG held on its balance sheet were so specialized that they did not really meet the classic definition of 'credit derivatives'. This hair-splitting did not convince regulators or politicians: in the aftermath of the AIG collapse, pressure intensified for a thoroughgoing overhaul of the credit derivatives world, to make it radically more transparent, standardized, and robust. There was also a drive to prevent the use of the regulatory arbitrage practices which had been widespread before 2007, and which AIG's business exemplified to a particularly startling degree. For while few regulators believed that credit derivatives per se had actually created the bubble, many were convinced that these instruments had exacerbated the excesses—while the sheer opacity of the sector had made it harder to see the risk concentrations and price distortions. The interconnectivity created by the contracts had also intensified the sense of panic, as groups such as AIG or Lehman ailed. Thus, by late 2008, there was a widespread consensus among Western governments that the credit derivatives market had to change.

By late 2009, these pressures had left the credit derivatives sector at a crossroads. During the course of 2009, a wave of potentially significant changes occurred: efforts got underway to create half a dozen new clearing houses in Europe and the US, to clear a wide range of CDS trades; the level of transparency rose, as groups such as Markit and Bloomberg began to publish prices and the Depository Trust and Clearing Corporation started to publish information about trading volumes and outstanding contracts. Regulators also began to use DTCC figures to create more detailed pictures of counterparty exposures (albeit not for public consumption). Meanwhile, the banks embarked on a big ISDA-lead initiative to tear up offsetting, redundant contracts, with a view to streamlining their exposures. That slashed the gross nominal value of the sector by half, from $62,000bn at the end of 2007, to nearer $31,000bn in 2009. Standardized coupons were also introduced in the US, and industry participants expressed a hope that they would be soon introduced in Europe too. The ISDA-led settlement procedure that was used—so successfully—to deal with the CDS contracts linked to Lehman, in the autumn of 2008, was used for almost two dozen other bankruptcy cases, with smooth results. Last but not least, regulators on both sides of the Atlantic started a crackdown on insider trading in the market, in an effort to dispel long-running rumours that some unscrupulous players were manipulating prices, due to the sector's opacity.

Nevertheless, by late 2009, even amid this plethora of change, some fundamental questions about the sector's future remained. Some American and European politicians remained unconvinced by the scope of the changes, and continued to press for more radical action, such as mandatory efforts to force all activity onto exchanges, or to place the sector under the control of insurance regulators. Some insurance regulators also called for a ban on so-called 'naked shorting' (i.e. buying protection without owning the underlying credit), and a few politicians even called for an outright closure of the sector, as a whole. These demands to curb 'naked shorting' were further fuelled by allegations that the presence of credit derivatives contracts had complicated efforts to restructure troubled companies after the credit bubble burst. These were rejected by groups such as ISDA, but by 2009, some bankers and lawyers claimed that creditors who had managed to hedge their exposure to a troubled company, or even take net short positions, had no incentive to place a cooperative role in any corporate restructuring, making the process more costly and time consuming.

Such demands for a truly radical clampdown appeared unlikely to gain traction at present, since they were opposed by the US Treasury, European Commission, and most central banks. Inside the largest institutional investors however—and even in the ranks of some sell-side banks—there was a growing acceptance that it might be wise to place at least a few index contracts onto an exchange in the future. Taking that step, some financiers and investors argued, would at least ensure that the industry had a visibly transparent and standardized benchmark—in much the same way that other sectors, such as the equity, foreign exchange, interest rate, or commodities worlds, also had visible, publicly accessible benchmarks that carried wider credibility.

Separately, some central banks remained concerned about the continued opacity in some parts of the market and the threat that CDS contracts could still produce concentrations of risk, rather than dispersion. In August 2009, for example, the European Central Bank released an extensive report on the sector, which pointed out that one of the biggest shortcomings in the market was that non-financial groups had never really adopted the product in any significant manner (in sharp contrast to the situation in, say, commodity, foreign exchange or interest rate derivatives). As a result, the ECB pointed out, most trading in the market continued to take place among a limited number of counterparties, such as banks and hedge funds—and that group had shrunk during 2008, because so many hedge funds (and some banks) had exited the market. As a result, by 2008, data from the OCC data suggested that JPMorgan Chase accounted for around a third of CDS activity in the US market—comparable to the position it held in the late 1990s, when the market was dramatically smaller. Moreover, since many outstanding CDS deals were written on large financial institutions, this was further fuelling a sense of circularity in the market, as a small pool of counterparties offered protection to each other in relation to financial credits.

Nevertheless, these potential shortcomings did not appear to deter market participants. By late 2009, most banks recognized that it was unlikely that the most complex products—such as single-tranche CDOs—would return soon, but they insisted that overall demand for credit derivatives remained strong, at least in their simpler form. That was partly because the events of 2008 had raised concerns about credit risk, not just in relation to companies, but sovereign entities too. Indeed, during the course of 2009, one notable new trend in the market was a rising level of demand for so-called sovereign CDS, both in relation to emerging market debt, but also that of the developed world. That trend threatened to raise the level of regulatory scrutiny of the sector even higher, particularly when spreads started to rise in late 2009; however, it also promised to provide a whole new engine of growth for the CDS world as a whole.

So by late 2009, some fifteen years after the CDS market first sprung to life, the world of credit derivatives essentially looked like the financial equivalent of a teenager: gangly, and a touch unruly, it had grown at stunning speed, producing its fair share of accidents, which had repeatedly dashed the hopes of those who had first created this product; but in the wake of the banking crisis, the CDS world was finally—albeit belatedly—being forced to 'grow up' into a more mature, reliable player. Just how long that would take remained critically unclear; so too did the most central question of all, namely whether the CDS market would ultimately end up being able to truly disperse credit risk in a beneficial and rational manner, as a force for good—as its original creators first hoped, before their dreams were so rudely shaken.

CHAPTER 2

TECHNICAL INTRODUCTION

ANDREW RENNIE AND
ALEXANDER LIPTON

'Modern man drives a mortgaged car over a bond-financed highway on credit-card gas'

EARL WILSON 1907–1987

'*Et in Arcadia ego*'

Traditionally ascribed to DEATH

1 INTRODUCTION

WE write this introduction as a deep and global credit crisis continues to unfold, following years where spectacular growth in the credit markets coupled with benign conditions convinced many that we had permanently entered a new paradigm of plentiful cheap credit. The cyclical nature of credit is nothing new; the struggle between borrowers and lenders is documented throughout recorded history and each generation adds new examples of lenders led by transient periods of good behaviour into extending credit until they collapse as borrowers' conditions abruptly change for the worse. For a story that has repeated itself many hundreds of times with the same outcome, perhaps the only useful observation is how quickly it is forgotten. This time is always different.

There is, however, one way in which this current crisis does differ. Not in its inevitability, but in the form of the underlying relationship between borrowers and lenders. In the past, the credit risk embedded in this relationship was analysed and managed in traditional ways. Lenders performed detailed examinations of the business models, assets, and liabilities of particular obligors as well as the characteristics and quality of collateral offered up as security for loans. After terms were agreed and loans extended, they were then carried to term on the books of the lender, usually a commercial bank. Corporate debt and other subordinated debt were also carried to term in institutions such as banks, mutual and pension funds. Secondary trading was limited and markets effectively non-existent. The concept of price as the *sine qua non* of credit quality was almost unknown.

In the late nineties, another complementary approach to credit began to appear in which derivatives-inspired ideas allowed spectacular growth in the size and liquidity of secondary markets. The derivative counterpart of the corporate bond, the credit default swap (CDS), appeared first and rapidly achieved dominance in the market. In its simplest form, the CDS is an over-the-counter agreement between a protection buyer (PB) and a protection seller (PS) in which the PB agrees to pay fees in a regular periodic schedule to the PS in exchange for the PS paying a lump sum in the event of the default of a reference entity (RE). The size of the lump sum—effectively the insurance payout compensating for the RE defaulting—is determined by agreement on the recovery level for the appropriate subordination of debt. Though during the current credit crisis the high level of risk led the fees to be paid up-front, conventionally these periodic fees were quoted as a spread in basis points. And as so often when a single numerical measure emerges, this spread became reified and arguably supplanted more complex and subtle traditional measures. Price and the market became increasingly important.

Following on from the CDS came the introduction of synthetic collateral debt obligations (CDOs). These derivative-style contracts were imitative of the much older subordination rules that govern equity and debt claims over the assets and liabilities of a conventional corporation. However, instead of claims over real assets and liabilities, the arranger of a CDO defined a basket of reference entities (often a hundred or so) and provided periodic payments to investors in exchange for compensation in the event of losses being incurred by the basket of entities, calculated in a similar manner to the synthetic losses in CDSs. The CDO structure came from the fact that all investors were not equally liable for losses (and principal payments)—instead, as in a standard capital structure, they fell into categories each subordinate in turn to the previous one. Each class of investors would make payments only when the basket's total loss reached a particular trigger (the attachment) and ceased payments as the basket loss passed another, higher, trigger (the detachment). These classes are often referred to by terms from the language of corporate debt—equity, mezzanine, senior, super-senior—and the CDO structure determined by a set of attachment and detachment points, $a_\theta, \beta_\theta, \theta = e, m, s, ss$, which described the percentage of losses attributed to each tranche and formed a disjoint cover of the capital structure—i.e. $a_e = 0$, $a_m = \beta_e$ etc. If N is the total notional of the basket and L the sum of calculated losses from inception to maturity, then the total payment demanded from an investor in a θ tranche would change, as L increased, from 0 for $L \leq a_\theta N$ to $(\beta_\theta - a_\theta) \times N$ for $L \geq \beta_\theta N$, with the rise linear between the two levels. As with CDSs, a liquid market developed for these tranches, though given the many thousand possible REs and basket sizes in the hundreds, combinatorics alone rapidly led to massive standardization with just two main investment-grade (IG) baskets achieving dominance—DJ CDX and iTRAXX—representing respectively agreed-upon sets of 125 American and European BBB corporates. A few other baskets were less liquid but also traded—High Vol (HV), Crossover (XO), and High Yield (HY).

Unlike the single reference entity CDSs, single tranches of CDOs represent exposure to the decorrelation or otherwise of many reference entities. Thus instead of a quoted spread becoming totemic, a form of correlation derived from the first and most popular model of joint defaults of obligors, the Gaussian copula, became the quoted number that represented the markets. Its relatively low value became symbolic of the period before the current crisis when systemic risk was believed abolished.

Other, more complex, derivative products also thrived in this period, but the notable feature of the times was the rise of mathematical modelling of credit and the primacy of the act of pricing via increasingly sophisticated algorithms calculated on ever larger arrays of computer processors. Thousands of technical papers were devoted to the new discipline of credit risk modelling and in the case of the most popular models such as Gaussian copulae, their parameters became real features of day-to-day markets.

This growth of mathematical modelling is the main impetus behind this handbook. We aim to provide an overview of this complex and relatively novel area of financial engineering. There is also another motivation. Given the fact that mathematics entering into the analysis of credit risk was contemporaneous with unprecedented growth in the credit markets and thus preceded the crash, it is not surprising that many view mathematics as the cause of the crisis. We believe strongly that despite the inevitable shortcomings of each mathematical model used, mathematics was not the cause of the current difficulties. That is not to say that it was completely innocent—before the current crisis broke we argued, along with others, that Gaussian copula modelling was oversimplistic and structurally underplayed system risks. Many models struggled to adapt as the weather changed from good to bad. Yet this credit crisis bears striking similarities to earlier ones, each achieved without the current mathematical framework. Moreover, the widely acknowledged worst culprits—sub-prime mortgages securitized into so-called ABS CDOs—were primarily analysed with traditional methods, often involving zipcode by zipcode examination of borrower behaviour. Until recently, there were almost no mathematical papers on ABS CDOs and the two chapters included in this book on house price modelling and pricing ABS CDOs are post-crisis attempts to introduce mathematics into this area. We can only hope that our attempt to describe the mathematics of credit risk, dealing openly with its successes and deficiencies, is timely, necessary, and useful.

2 EMPIRICAL ANALYSIS OF OBLIGORS

Before we can focus on theoretical aspects of modelling, we introduce a set of chapters that deal directly with either empirical analysis of actual markets or the statistical tools required to do so.

In Chapter 3, Altman considers the relationship between the probability of default of an individual obligor (PD) and the recovery rate in the event of default (RR). He surveys a number of models (whose theoretical bases are described in subsequent chapters) and categorizes the resulting implied relationships between PD and RR before turning to empirical analysis of corporate defaults. Previous statistical attempts to link PD and RR via joint observation of default rates, and corresponding recovery values of bonds have led to contradictory results, sometimes showing little correlation, sometimes negative correlation. Altman argues that this is due in large part to credit showing 'regime'-like behaviour with quite different behaviours between 'good' periods and 'bad'. In contrast to good times, during downturns there is significant negative correlation between PD and RR. This should be taken into account when designing regulatory frameworks or implementing VaR-like schemas.

In Chapter 4, Berd also considers the behaviour of recovery rates, but this time from the perspective of corporate bond valuation. Arguing from empirical grounds that the most realistic approach to recovery is to treat it as a fraction of the par value of the bond, he observes that this assumption rules out the traditional approach of stripping of bonds into risky zeros. Instead he lays out a different approach to the valuation of bonds via survival probabilities and recovery fractions and shows how survival probabilities can be derived from credit default swap spreads and recovery swap prices or by estimating survival probabilities via regression on the observed prices of bonds of similar type. For completeness, he surveys a number of other simpler bond valuation measures as well as deriving suitable risk measures.

In Chapter 5, Wei also analyses default, but from the theoretical perspective of Cox's model of proportional hazard rates (Cox 1972). Just as Altman stresses the importance of considering different regimes for default intensity or hazard rates, Wei considers a Cox model for hazard rates $h(t)$ of the form:

$$h_t = h_0(t) \exp\left(\mathbf{x}^T \beta\right) \tag{1}$$

for some fundamental baseline function $h_0(t)$ where $\mathbf{x}$ represents some state vector and β provides the weighting between this state and the resulting hazard rate shocks. A comprehensive range of algorithms are described for estimation of β via various forms of maximum or partial likelihood functions before the author demonstrates a concrete example in the form of a spline basis for a trading strategy on credit indices.

3   THEORY OF INDIVIDUAL OBLIGORS

The second set of chapters deals first with the theory of single obligors before extending to deal with the theory of many and the behaviour of obligors in aggregate. In general there are two approaches to describing the default of individual obligors—the reduced form model pioneered by Lando (1998) and Jarrow and Turnbull (1995) and the older firm-value model originated by Merton (1974) and extended by Black and Cox (1976), Leland (1994), and Longstaff and Schwartz (1995). Traditionally, they have represented quite different approaches to the problem of individual default. The reduced form model focuses carefully on forming a sub-filtration devoid of default time information, whilst the firm-value model explicitly includes default times. In its original form, with continuous behaviour of asset value, the firm-value model had no choice—default was completely predictable given knowledge of the asset process and indeed instantaneously was either impossible or inevitable. Having said this, recent extensions to include discontinuous behaviour have clouded this distinction—default can now be unpredictable in the firm-value model and the differences are less pronounced than before. It remains, however, constructive to compare and contrast the formalism.

We start with the reduced-form model—the inspiration comes from extending the short-rate formulation of interest rate modelling to the intensity λ_t of a Cox process whose first jump represents the default of the obligor. Recent practice has emphasized the careful separation of filtration between a background $\mathcal{F}_t$ containing all information available except for the explicit observation of default and a default filtration $\mathcal{D}_t$ which merely observes the default indicator. The combined filtration $\mathcal{G}_t = \mathcal{F}_t \vee \mathcal{D}_t$ represents the full market but in order to avoid technical difficulties such as risky numeraires becoming zero-valued, the theory aims to recast as much as possible of the pricing in terms of conditioning on $\mathcal{F}_t$ rather than $\mathcal{G}_t$. Conditioned on $\mathcal{F}_t$, default is unpredictable.

A simple concrete example is the following—given a short rate r_t adapted to the filtration $\mathcal{F}_t$ produced by Brownian motion $W_1(t)$ and described by the stochastic differential equation (SDE)

$$dr_t = \mu_1(t, \mathcal{F}_t)dt + \sigma_1(t, \mathcal{F}_t)dW_1(t) \tag{2}$$

we can invoke a numeraire $B_t = \exp\left(\int_0^t r_s\, ds\right)$ and a pricing equation for a $\mathcal{F}_T$-adapted claim X_T, given by the usual

$$X_t = B_t \mathbb{E}_{\mathbb{Q}}\left[B_T^{-1} X_T \,\middle|\, \mathcal{F}_t \right] \tag{3}$$

where $\mathbb{Q}$ represents the appropriate pricing measure.

We then have the value of a risk-free zero coupon bond $D(t, T)$ corresponding to the claim $X_T = 1$ given by

$$X_t = B_t \mathbb{E}_{\mathbb{Q}}\left[B_T^{-1} | \mathcal{F}_t \right] = \mathbb{E}_{\mathbb{Q}}\left[\exp\left(-\int_t^T r_s\, ds \right) \middle| \mathcal{F}_t \right] \tag{4}$$

Other more complex interest rate claims follow similarly and the model parameters μ_1 and σ_1 could be calibrated to the yield curve and chosen vols from the swaption market. We now consider the extension to risky claims by increasing the filtration $\mathcal{F}_t$ to include a second Brownian motion $W_2(t)$ and driving the stochastic intensity λ_t via the SDE:

$$d\lambda_t = \mu_2(t, \mathcal{F}_t)dt + \sigma_2(t, \mathcal{F}_t)dW_2(t) \tag{5}$$

Note that within $\mathcal{F}_t$, we have no explicit knowledge of the default time—indeed conditioned on $\mathcal{F}_t$, the event of default in any finite interval has probability strictly less than 1.

Within the extended filtration $\mathcal{G}_t = \mathcal{F}_t \vee \mathcal{D}_t$, the pricing equation for the $\mathcal{G}_T$-adapted risky claim of the form $\mathbf{1}_{\tau > T} X_T$ is the usual

$$X_t = B_t \mathbb{E}_\mathbb{Q}\left[B_T^{-1} \mathbf{1}_{\tau > T} X_T | \mathcal{G}_t \right] \tag{6}$$

However, if we wish to work entirely conditioned on sub-filtration $\mathcal{F}_t$, this becomes

$$X_t = \frac{\mathbf{1}_{\tau > t}}{\mathbb{E}_\mathbb{Q}\left[\mathbf{1}_{\tau > t} | \mathcal{F}_t \right]} B_t \mathbb{E}_\mathbb{Q}\left[B_T^{-1} \mathbf{1}_{\tau > T} X_T \middle| \mathcal{F}_t \right] \tag{7}$$

Thus the value of the risky zero coupon bond Qt, T is

$$Q(t, T) = \mathbf{1}_{\tau > t} \exp\left(\int_0^t (\lambda_s + r_s) \, ds \right) \mathbb{E}_\mathbb{Q}\left[\exp\left(-\int_0^T (\lambda_s + r_s) \, ds \right) \middle| \mathcal{F}_t \right] \tag{8}$$

$$= \mathbf{1}_{\tau > t} \mathbb{E}_\mathbb{Q}\left[\exp\left(-\int_t^T (\lambda_s + r_s) \, ds \right) \middle| \mathcal{F}_t \right]$$

Again more complex claims can be valued, and with appropriate recovery assumptions μ_2 and σ_2 can be calibrated to the CDS term structure and CDS options.

In contrast, in the firm-value model we consider the evolution of a process representing an abstract firm value where default occurs because this value hits a down-and-out barrier representing the point at which the firm is no longer solvent. Typically, the firm value v_t might be governed by an SDE of the form:

$$dv_t = r_t v_t dt + \sigma_t v_t dW_t \tag{9}$$

with the firm defaulting if and when v_t crosses a time-dependent barrier H_t, with $H_0 < v_0$.

In this framework, we have the value of a risky claim $\mathbf{1}_{\tau > T} X_T$ given by

$$X_t = \mathbf{1}_{v_s > H_s \forall s \in [0,t]} B_t \mathbb{E}_\mathbb{Q}\left[B_T^{-1} \mathbf{1}_{v_s > H_s \forall s \in [t,T]} X_T \middle| \mathcal{F}_t \right] \tag{10}$$

where this time the filtration $\mathcal{F}_t$ contains the default indicator and often (but not necessarily) the numeraire $B_t = \exp\left(\int_0^t r_s \, ds \right)$ is derived from a non-stochastic short rate r_t.

If we hold all parameters constant, and choose a barrier $H_t = H_0 \exp(rt)$, then the risky zero-recovery discount bond becomes

$$Q(t, T) = \mathbf{1}_{v_s > H_s \forall s \in [0,t]} B_t B_T^{-1} \left[\Phi\left(\frac{\ln(\frac{v_t}{H_t}) - \frac{1}{2}\sigma^2(T - t)}{\sqrt{\sigma^2(T - t)}} \right) \right. \tag{11}$$

$$\left. - \frac{v_t}{H_t} \Phi\left(\frac{\ln(\frac{H_t}{v_t}) - \frac{1}{2}\sigma^2(T - t)}{\sqrt{\sigma^2(T - t)}} \right) \right]$$

However, as is obvious from the construction of the model, if $v_t > H_t$, the continuity of Brownian motion prevents any possibility of default in the interval $[t, t + dt]$. Until default becomes inevitable, the instantaneous CDS spread s_t is always zero. Specifically, $s_0 = 0$ which is emphatically not an observed feature of the market. Introduction of curvilinear barriers such that $v_t - H_t \downarrow 0$ as $t \downarrow 0$ improves calibration to the short end of the CDS curve, but the problem simply re-emerges when conditioned on future firm values. This has led to suggesting uncertain barriers (Duffie and Pan 2001) or, more naturally, adding discontinuous Levy behaviour such as Poisson jumps into the firm-value process. Introducing such discontinuities clearly allows default to become unpredictable even when $v_t > H_t$ and thus allows more natural calibration to the initial CDS term structure and more natural evolution of that curve. It also has another useful consequence when the theory is extended to multiple reference entities: allowing simultaneous jumps in firm values can dramatically increase the amount of coupling between defaults allowing necessary freedom when calibrating to markets.

In Chapter 6, Schloegl lays out the detailed theoretical basis for CDS market models—reduced-form models that define the stochastic properties of market observables such as forward CDS spreads. He lays out the theoretical underpinning of the filtration separation $\mathcal{G}_t = \mathcal{F}_t \vee \mathcal{D}_t$ implicit in reduced-form models before describing the necessary change of numeraires away from the standard rolling $B_t = \exp\left(\int_0^t (r_s)\,dt\right)$ towards risky numeraires. He demonstrates that a numeraire such as a risky annuity allows a model in which options on CDSs have Black-Scholes type price solutions. Extending these ideas further, Schloegl shows how Libor-market models (where the behaviour of forward Libor rates is controlled) can be extended to include carefully defined forward default intensities. With IR and credit correlated, the coupling between CDS spreads and the IR and intensity processes prevents forward CDS spreads being treated in a similar manner. However, as Schloegl shows, if interest rates and intensities are independent, this coupling becomes unimportant and a full CDS market model can be constructed.

Within Chapter 7, Lipton and Shelton extend the toy reduced-form model above to consider the following

$$dX_t = \kappa\,(\theta_t - X_t)\,dt + \sigma\sqrt{X_t}\,dW_t + J\,dN_t \tag{12}$$

where in addition to W_t as Brownian motion, we have N_t as a Poisson process with intensity v_t and J a positive jump distribution with jump values occurring in the set $\{0, 1, \ldots, M\}$, all processes and distributions mutually independent. This forms an affine jump diffusion process capable, with careful parameter choice, of remaining strictly positive. From this the authors derive prices for coupon and protection legs for CDSs as well as describing practical extensions to market instruments such as index default swaps. This affine jump diffusion model extends very naturally to multiple obligors but this, as well as further description of multiple obligor theory, we will describe in the next section.

4 THEORY OF MULTIPLE OBLIGORS

Just as reduced-form and firm-value modelling emerged to analyse the default of single obligors, a series of models have arisen to analyse the joint default of multiple obligors. And just as the spectacular growth of the CDS market drove the first, the growth of CDO issuance, and specifically the challenge of warehousing single-tranche CDOs, has driven the second.

To motivate the modelling discussion, consider pricing a single CDO tranche, covering the losses between the two thresholds $0 \le \alpha < \beta \le 1$. If R_i is the recovery associated with the default of obligor i, the portfolio loss process L_t is given by

$$L_t = \frac{1}{n} \sum_{i=1}^{n} (1 - R_i) \, \mathbf{1}_{\tau_i < t} \tag{13}$$

and the loss on the tranche (α, β), $M_t^{\alpha, \beta}$ is then given by

$$M_t^{\alpha, \beta} = \min \left(\max \left(L_t - \alpha, 0 \right), (\beta - \alpha) \right) \tag{14}$$

Note that L_t and $M_t^{\alpha, \beta}$ are both jump processes, with the payments on the CDO protection leg corresponding to the jumps of $M_t^{\alpha, \beta}$.

Given a numeraire B_t and associated pricing measure $\mathbb{Q}$, we have the value of the protection leg V_1 given by

$$V_1 = \mathbb{E}_{\mathbb{Q}} \left[\int_0^T B_t^{-1} \, dM_t^{\alpha, \beta} \right] \tag{15}$$

and the value of the corresponding premium leg V_2 given by

$$V_2 = \mathbb{E}_{\mathbb{Q}} \left[s_i \sum_{i=1}^{n} B_{T_i}^{-1} \left((\beta - \alpha) - M_{T_i}^{\alpha, \beta} \right) \right] \tag{16}$$

where $(0 = T_0, T_1, \ldots, T_N = T)$ represent the schedule of dates associated with the premium leg and s_i the (full) premium associated with the period $[T_{i-1}, T_i]$.

If we assume deterministic numeraire B_t, then it is clear that the value of the premium leg is fully determined by knowledge of $\mathbb{E}_{\mathbb{Q}} \left[M_t^{\alpha, \beta} \right]$. The protection leg is superficially less clear, but integration by parts yields

$$V_1 = B_T^{-1} \mathbb{E}_{\mathbb{Q}} \left[M_T^{\alpha, \beta} \right] - \int_0^T \frac{dB_t^{-1}}{dt} \mathbb{E}_{\mathbb{Q}} \left[M_t^{\alpha, \beta} \right] dt \tag{17}$$

and again, we have the value only dependent on $\mathbb{E}_{\mathbb{Q}} \left[M_t^{\alpha, \beta} \right]$. Knowledge of the marginal distribution for loss is sufficient to price a single-tranche CDO.

Given this simplification, it is unsurprising that an early and subsequently dominant model used for pricing single-tranche CDOs was the (in)famous Gaussian copula model. Sklar's theorem (1959) shows that given a known multivariate cumulant $F(x_1, \ldots, x_n)$, with corresponding individual cumulants $F_1(), \ldots, F_n()$, we can manufacture a multivariate cumulant $G(y_1, \ldots, y_n)$ from individual cumulants $G_1(), \ldots, G_n()$ via

$$G(y_1, \ldots, y_n) = F\left[F_1^{-1}(G_1(y_1)), \ldots, F_n^{-1}(G_n(y_n))\right] \tag{18}$$

Thus for arbitrary $G_1, \ldots, G_n$, we can construct a coherent joint distribution via the scaffolding provided by F. Though it can be argued that subsequent history has shown it to be a poor choice, the initial scaffolding chosen was the familiar multivariate Gaussian $\Phi_\rho^n[.]$ with constant pair-wise correlation ρ.

Given the simple correlation structure, the multivariate Gaussian $X_1, \ldots, X_n$ can be rewritten in terms of $n + 1$ IID Gaussians $Y_0, Y_1, \ldots, Y_n$ via

$$X_i = \sqrt{\rho}Y_0 + \sqrt{1-\rho}Y_i \tag{19}$$

and thus the joint cumulant of default times

$$\mathbb{P}(\tau_1 \leq T_1, \ldots, \tau_n \leq T_n) = \Phi_\rho^{(n)}\left[\Phi^{-1}(\mathbb{P}_1(\tau_1 \leq T_1)), \ldots, \Phi^{-1}(\mathbb{P}_n(\tau_n \leq T_n))\right] \tag{20}$$

can be written as

$$\mathbb{P}(\tau_1 \leq T_1, \ldots, \tau_n \leq T_n) = \int_0^\infty \prod_{i=1}^n \Phi\left(\frac{\Phi^{-1}(\mathbb{P}_i(\tau_i \leq T_i)) - \sqrt{\rho}y}{\sqrt{1-\rho}}\right)\phi(y)\,dy \tag{21}$$

where Φ, Φ^{-1} and ϕ are the standard Gaussian cumulant, its inverse and density respectively.

In this way, we can construct a coherent joint distribution for default times, with a single parameter ρ which by inspection plays a plausible role in inducing coupling between obligors. If, for example, all the $\mathbb{P}_i$ are identical, then as $\rho \to 1$, the default times of the obligors on any sample path coincide. And from this distribution of default times, numerical methods such as FFT or convolution coupled with 1D quadrature can produce effective estimates for $\mathbb{E}_{\mathbb{Q}}\left[M_t^{a,\beta}\right]$.

As discussed earlier in this introduction, this single correlation ρ became totemic in the markets replacing other measures of diversification inherent in baskets of obligors. And as with any simplification, it has its dangers. Though some (see Salmon 2009) have gone as far as blaming the Gaussian copula for the current crisis—its simplicity inducing complacency in those warehousing increasing levels of risk in CDO form—it is worth noting again the inevitability of the credit cycle and the perhaps surprising fact that the analysis of ABS CDOs often involved no stochastic model whatsoever, let alone a Gaussian copula.

Indeed, as a model, it successfully weathered the 'correlation crisis' of May 2005 and continued dominant as the model of choice for single-tranche CDOs. Yet its disadvantages should not be understated. The first and most obvious is that the single correlation parameter ρ, or its variant base correlation the ρ_θ corresponding to tranches with attachment point 0, is far from constant across either detachment point or maturity. Models in other markets also demonstrate 'skew' and 'term structure', of course, but it is sufficiently pronounced in the CDO market to render extrapolating the Gaussian copula to other products perilous. Moreover, the choice of the multivariate Gaussian as scaffolding means that the model inherits its distinctive and unusually weak tail dependence. Specifically for multivariate Gaussian $X_1, \ldots, X_n$ with pairwise correlation $\rho < 1$,

$$\lim_{k \to \infty} \mathbb{P}\left[X_i > k \mid X_j > k \right] = 0, \quad i \neq j \tag{22}$$

This inability for the multivariate Gaussian to give weight to simultaneous extremes impacts the ability for the Gaussian copula to price super-senior tranches. This effect also brings into doubt the model's general capacity to cope with less benign credit conditions.

In recognition of this, much has been suggested in the form of extensions to the Gaussian copula—different choices of the scaffolding multivariate with improved tail dependence such as multivariate t-copula (or indeed non-parametric formulations) as well as introducing explicit states corresponding to 'Doomsday' scenarios via additional Poisson processes. In addition to the purely static approach of copulae, there has also been substantial focus on multivariate extensions to reduced-form or firm-value models. One such interesting extension to the reduced form approach is the Marshall-Olkin framework (Marshall and Olkin 1967), where coupling between obligors is induced in a particularly natural way. Instead of a one-to-one mapping, the framework proposes a more complex mapping between m Poisson processes with intensity λ^j and n obligors, with $m > n$. The mapping of defaults is intermediated via {0,1}-valued Bernoulli variables with probabilities $p^{i,j} \in [0, 1]$ which decide whether obligor i can default given a jump in Poisson process j. More formally, this can be thought of as a set of independent Poisson processes $(N^\pi)_{\pi \in \Pi_n}$ associated with all possible subsets of the obligors $\pi \in \Pi_n$ with intensities λ^π given by

$$\lambda^\pi = \sum_{j=1}^m \left(\prod_{i \in \pi} p^{i,j} \prod_{i \notin \pi} (1 - p^{i,j}) \right) \lambda^j \tag{23}$$

The default of individual obligor i then becomes the first jump across all N^π with $i \in \pi$. This framework is simultaneously rich enough to induce many different types of coupling and also analytically tractable.

These approaches, known as 'bottom-up' models because of their focus on modelling the obligors individually have proved a rich source for understanding the range of possible aggregate loss distributions. In contrast, there is also activity in the form of 'top-down' modelling where the loss distribution is tackled directly. The motivation behind these models is the desire to use couplings such as contagion where one default changes the likelihood of others, but to avoid working with the 2^n sized filtration arising when the defaults of individual obligors are tracked. Given suitable homogeneity assumptions, top-down modelling can often use a filtration of size $O(n)$ and then apply results from continuous-time Markov chains.

Consider such a Markov chain C_t, defined on $K = \{0, 1, \ldots, n\}$ with time-homogeneous transition probabilities $p_{ij}(t)$ given by

$$\mathbb{P}(C_{s+t} = j \,|\, C_s = i) = p_{ij}(t) \quad \forall i, j \in K \tag{24}$$

Then imposing sufficient conditions for it to exist, we can define a transition intensity λ_{ij} given by

$$\lambda_{ij} = \lim_{t \to 0} \frac{p_{ij}(t) - p_{ij}(0)}{t} \tag{25}$$

and then form the *generator matrix* $\Lambda = [\lambda_{ij}]$

This generator matrix uniquely determines the behaviour of the Markov chain—the probability density of states at time t being given by the solution to the linearly coupled ODEs

$$\frac{d}{dt} \boldsymbol{p}(t) - \Lambda \boldsymbol{p}(t) = 0 \tag{26}$$

where $\boldsymbol{p}(t) = (p_0(t), \ldots, p_n(t))$ is the row vector representing the density of states at time t and $\boldsymbol{p}(0)$ is set appropriately. This or the corresponding backwards equation can be solved either via conventional ODE techniques or by directly approximating the matrix exponential $e^{\Lambda t}$ via Padé approximants.

Both approaches are relatively efficient and allow respectable calculation times for state spaces several hundred in size. Given the typical basket size for single-tranche CDOs of a hundred or so, this allows a reasonable range of models including, as mentioned before, contagion models with filtrations of $2n + 1$ or similar.

There are consequences, however, to reducing the state space to $O(n)$. Strict homogeneity assumptions are often needed—all obligors, for example, might be forced to be interchangeable. And this is in many ways a significant shortcoming compared to the 'bottom-up' approach. Not only is it not true in practice that baskets contain identically behaving obligors—indeed during crises it is not unknown for the spreads of obligors in a single basket to diverge by two orders of magnitude—but this variation of behaviour has significant effect on the relative value of junior and senior tranches. More significantly, perhaps, if the identity of individual obligors is lost, it remains an outstanding, non-trivial problem to derive hedging strategies.

Returning to Chapter 7, Lipton and Shelton provide a comprehensive overview of topics in multiple obligor modelling which this introduction only touches upon. They demonstrate a multivariate extension of their example affine jump-diffusion model which induces a wide range of correlations between defaults of obligors and gives a concrete example of pricing first- and second-to-default baskets within a two-factor model.

The authors also devote considerable attention to calculation of portfolio loss distributions for multiple obligors giving a comparison of FFT, recursion and various analytic approximations. For homogeneous portfolios, there is a surprising result attributed to Panjer (1981), but likely to date back to Euler. For the restricted class of distributions on the non-negative integers m such that

$$p_m = p_{m-1}\left(a + \frac{b}{m}\right) \tag{27}$$

where p_m can be thought of as the probability of m defaults, then given a distribution for individual losses $f(j)$ discretized onto the positive integers $j \in \mathbb{Z}^+$ we have the remarkable result that the probability $p^n(i)$ of the sum of n obligors resulting in loss i is

$$p^n(0) = p_0 \tag{28}$$

$$p^n(i) = \sum_{j=1}^{i}\left(a + \frac{bj}{i}\right) f(j)p^n(i-j), \quad i = 1, 2, 3\ldots$$

which is $O(n^2)$ compared to the more usual $O(n^3)$.

In Chapter 8, Elouerkhaoui gives details of a Marshall-Olkin model where for n obligors a number $m > n$ of Poisson processes are coupled to the default of the obligors by Bernoulli variables which decide for the rth jump of a given Poisson process which, if any, of the obligors default. By careful specification of the probabilities of these Bernoulli variables, the Poisson jumps become categorized into inducing patterns of default ranging from idiosyncratic, through enhanced defaulting in sectors, to group 'Doomsday' style defaults. Elouerkhaoui shows a range of efficient numerical techniques, including the Panjer recursion detailed above, before demonstrating the properties of a particular choice of Marshall-Olkin model. As he observes, suitable choices for the Poisson intensities and corresponding sets of Bernoulli variables can result in a relaxed, natural calibration to single-tranche CDOs and have fewer of the term-structure and skew issues of Gaussian copulae.

In Chapter 9, Davis sets out a taxonomy of continuous-time Markov modelling, giving three main categories—*factor*, *frailty*, and *contagion* models. In a factor model, the intensity of a given obligor is driven by a (common) multivariate process X_t often representing the macro-economy via a finite-state Markov chain. As usual, suitable homogeneity assumptions for the obligors renders the filtration manageable. In frailty models, this is extended to include additional random variables corresponding to 'hidden' unobservable features which further modify, usually multiplicatively, the factor-driven intensities. In contagion models, as described above, the intensities are altered not by exogenous factors or frailties but by the events of defaults of the obligors themselves.

Davis showcases an elegant example of a contagion model with an $O(n)$ filtration in which homogeneous obligors shuttle back and forwards spontaneously between a 'normal' state and an 'enhanced' risk state (with higher intensities) augmented by forced transition into the enhanced state if defaults occur. A filtration of size $2n + 1$ again allows fast computation.

In Chapter 10, Bielecki, Crépey, and Herbertsson provide a comprehensive overview of continuous-time Markov chains, before reviewing a number of Markovian models for portfolio credit risk. They give examples of both 'top-down' and 'bottom-up' modelling with the corresponding divergence in size of filtration. They detail Monte Carlo methods for large filtrations and compare and contrast a range of matrix exponential and direct ODE solvers for models with smaller filtrations. Focusing on the latter, they introduce a contagion model for intensities with interesting properties. Inevitably homogeneity is a critical assumption with all obligors interchangeable and the default times of individual obligors $\{\tau_1, \tau_2, \ldots, \tau_n\}$ replaced by the portfolio default times $\{T_1, T_2, \ldots, T_n\}$ representing the ordering of the individual τ_i. The obligors' intensities are specified by

$$\lambda_t = a + \sum_{k=1}^{n-1} b_k \mathbf{1}_{(T_k \leq t)} \tag{29}$$

where a is the common base intensity and $\{b_k\}$ are the increments to the obligors' intensities caused by the number of defaults in the portfolio rising to k.

Given that a typical index such as iTraxx or CDX has $n = 125$, but provides far fewer market observed tranche prices, the model induces further parsimony by grouping the b_k into partitions $\{\mu_1, \mu_2, \ldots, \mu_6 = n\}$ via

$$b_k = \begin{cases} b^{(1)} & 1 \leq k < \mu_1 \\ b^{(2)} & \mu_1 \leq k < \mu_2 \\ \cdot & \\ \cdot & \\ \cdot & \\ b^{(6)} & \mu_5 \leq k < \mu_6 = n \end{cases} \tag{30}$$

This grouping into blocks allows tuning of different tranche values via the $b^{(i)}$ producing a natural calibration; the relatively low filtration of $n + 1$ gives respectable computation times.

5 COUNTERPARTY CREDIT

So far we have focused on the default of reference entities, this being the most obvious source of credit risk in products such as CDSs and CDOs. There are, however, two other obligors in a derivative transaction that should be considered—the buyer and the seller. The fact that a derivative represents an exchange of (generally) contingent cash flows, some owed by buyer to seller, some owed by seller to buyer, exposes the risk that non-payment might occur. This risk, known as counterparty risk, can have a sizeable effect on the value, particularly if the reference entity or entities and one or other counterparty have coupled likelihoods of default. This exposes the other counterparty to the risk of non-payment precisely when the amount owed is large—this 'wrong-way' risk is not uncommon in real-world trades.

Models used for counterparty risk valuation have to be rich enough to deal not only with the relative order of defaults of reference entities and counterparties but also the conditional value of the contracts at the time of default of a counterparty. This requirement arises through the natural asymmetry caused by a counterparty in default being unable to make full payment if net monies are owed, but nonetheless still demanding full payment if net monies are due. Specifically, given just one risky counterparty with default time τ and recovery rate R entered into a contract with value at time t of V_t, we can integrate across the time of default of the counterparty to give the difference in value now, ΔV_0, caused by the possibility of default as

$$\Delta V_0 = \mathbb{E}_\mathbb{Q}\left[\int_0^T B_t^{-1}(1-R)V_t^+\mathbf{1}_{\tau=t}\,dt\right] \tag{31}$$

Multivariate firm-value or stochastic reduced-form models are capable of a filtration rich enough to capture the joint dependency on V_t^+ and $\mathbf{1}_{\tau=t}\,dt$ but simpler marginal default distribution models such as copulae require careful extension to allow calculation of the necessary conditioned V_t^+.

In Chapter 11, Gregory takes up the challenges posed by marginal default distribution models—for illustrative purposes he chooses a straightforward Gaussian copula—and details counterparty risk corrections for CDSs, index CDSs, and CDOs. As he points out, the static copula approach fixes the expected value of the product conditional on counterparty default, but not its distribution. As a consequence, he provides only bounds for the value of the correction, but in many cases these are tight enough to be useful. He provides a number of numerical examples including a timely reminder that 'risk-free' super-senior tranches are particularly prone to counterparty risk.

In Chapter 12, Lipton and Sepp provide a multivariate time-inhomogeneous firm-value model where the coupling between firms is driven not only by the familiar correlative coupling between Brownian diffusive components $W_i(t)$ but also by inducing jumps in the firm values via Poisson processes $N_i(t)$ which are also coupled together by a Marshall–Olkin inspired common 'systemic' Poisson process. The authors consider two different distributions for the jump sizes—one with a single value $-\nu$ and the other an exponential distribution with mean $-1/\nu$. The first induces strong coupling, the second weaker since though the likelihood of jumps is correlated, the sizes of the jumps remain independent. This choice allows the model to fit both regimes where the default correlations are low and regimes where they are high.

One attraction of a firm-value model is the capacity to model equity as well as credit and the authors exploit this. Formally, given a firm value $v(t)$, they assume a down-and-out barrier

$$H_t = H_0 \exp\left(\int_0^t (r_s - \zeta_s)\,ds\right) \tag{32}$$

where r_t is the deterministic short rate and ζ_t the deterministic dividend rate for the firm's assets. They can then regard the equity price as $v_t - H_t$ prior to default; the resulting displaced diffusion with jumps being a realistic model for equity derivative valuation.

Concluding that the current market state with relatively high default correlations favours the discrete jump model, the authors choose a suitable level of default correlation and via analytic and numerical results for CDSs, CDS options, and equity options demonstrate a detailed calibration to the market with realistic skews for equity and CDS options.

6 BEYOND NORMALITY

In much of the preceding discussion, it is apparent that restricting modelling to Gaussian marginals or Brownian processes fails to capture the 'fat-tailed' nature of credit. The probability of large events in a Gaussian framework seems too low to fit the observed frequency of extremes in credit and the strong restrictions on local structure that result from pricing with just the continuous Brownian part of generic Lévy processes similarly hamper attempts to match actual market prices. To some extent, this is an inevitable consequence of a popular and not unreasonable philosophy of pricing. This philosophy views limiting the number of parameters and imposing a restrictive structure via process choice such as Brownian as *essential* to safely pricing claims outside the linear span of liquidly observed market instruments. As a market fragments during a crisis, it is not surprising that such a stiff model struggles to fit but, more positively, it forces acknowledgement that the safety of pricing 'difficult' claims depends on a well-behaved market.

There are, however, different responses. One, as described in provocative fashion by Ayache in Chapter 13, is to abandon the philosophy altogether and instead of a process-based model which underfits reality, move to an overfitted 'regime'-based model with many parameters. With such a model, the calibration net can be spread wide enough to both fit difficult conditions and to increase the linear span of calibrated instruments large enough to reduce extrapolation in pricing. Arguably the non-parametric regime model which Ayache describes is one of the few ways to allow a market to speak freely, unencumbered by artificial restrictions. But it remains controversial amongst those who doubt that pricing can ever fully escape extrapolation and that without an a priori justifiable structure underpinning a model, extrapolation is lethal.

A second less controversial approach remains. The Gaussian distribution and Brownian motion may be limiting but they are far from inevitable. Within the framework of Lévy processes, Brownian motion is just one sub-species of process—coherent discontinuous processes with both finite (i.e. Poisson) and infinite (i.e. Gamma) activity also exist providing much greater access to extreme behaviour. And Gaussian distributions are distinctively 'thin-tailed' compared to almost any other choice without finite support. More formally, given $X_1, X_2, \ldots$ IID, and following Fisher and Tippett (1928), if there exist norming constants $c_n > 0, d_n \in \mathbb{R}$ such that

$$\frac{\max(X_1, \ldots, X_n) - d_n}{c_n} \xrightarrow{d} H \text{ as } n \to \infty \tag{33}$$

for some non-degenerate H, then H must be of the following type

$$H_\xi(x) = \begin{cases} \exp\left(-(1 + \xi x)^{-\frac{1}{\xi}}\right) & \text{if } \xi \neq 0, (1 + \xi x) > 0 \\ \exp\left(-\exp(-x)\right) & \text{if } \xi = 0 \end{cases} \tag{34}$$

These extreme value distributions—*Weibull* for $\xi < 0$, *Gumbel* for $\xi = 0$, and *Fréchet* for $\xi > 0$—represent a universe of non-degenerate distributions for $\max(X_1, \ldots, X_n)$ that far exceed the restricted behaviour of Gaussians. Indeed if $X_1, \ldots, X_n$ are Gaussian, the corresponding H_ξ is the Gumbel with $\xi = 0$, the thinnest-tailed distribution in the family that still retains infinite support.

As Chavez-Demoulin and Embrechts detail in Chapter 14, the existence of a pre-scriptive family H_ξ has two critical implications.

The first, as already observed, raises awareness of a much larger fat-tailed world outside the familiar Gaussian. Ten or twenty standard-deviation sized events are not necessarily as 'impossible' as the Gaussian predicts and it is hard to overstate the importance of this observation for anyone such as regulators interested in the extremes of distributions. The Gaussian distribution is commonplace when modelling the 'middle' of distributions—the not unlikely events—but it forces a very particular and aggressive reduction of probability as the size of observations increase. This is far from inevitable, indeed empirical study suggests a $\xi > 0$ across much of financial markets and for applications such as VaR, a Gaussian choice can lead to massive understatement of risk.

The second is that though there is more freedom to extremes than Gaussians would suggest, this freedom is not without limit. Indeed for large enough values, tails have a surprisingly restricted structure, which opens up the possibility of meaningful parameter estimation from data and thus investigation of tails empirically. Chavez-Demoulin and Embrechts provide an overview of some of the relevant statistical techniques.

The first implication is uncontroversial; the second, as the authors themselves warn, should be treated with more caution. By its nature, extreme-value theory deals with events that are rare and thus only marginally present (if at all) in any data; any estimation will almost inevitably involve alarmingly few data points. Moreover, the theory itself is silent on how far out in the tails we must go for convergence to happen; some base distributions for X_i involve extremely slow convergence into H_ξ.

In Chapter 15, Martin continues with this theme with results that provide good approximations for the tail of the sum of n i.i.d. random variables even in non-Gaussian cases. Specifically, if $X_1, X_2, \ldots, X_n$ are i.i.d. with cumulant $K_X(\omega) = \ln \mathbb{E}\left[\exp(i\omega x)\right]$ valid for $\omega \in \mathbb{C}$ in some band around the real axis, then the density f_Y of $Y = \sum_{i=1}^{n} X_i$ is given by

$$f_Y(y) = \frac{1}{2\pi i} \int_C e^{nK_X(\omega)} e^{-i\omega y} \, d\omega \tag{35}$$

for any contour C equivalent to integration along the real axis.

With careful choice of $\mathcal{C}$, specifically one that lies along the path of steepest descent, the integrand is well behaved and Watson's Lemma provides a high-quality approximation, namely

$$f_Y(y) \approx \frac{e^{nK_X(\hat{\omega})-i\hat{\omega}y}}{\sqrt{2\pi n K_X''(\hat{\omega})}} \tag{36}$$

where $\hat{\omega}$ is such that $nK_X(\omega) - i\omega y$ is stationary, indeed forming a saddlepoint.

Given analytic knowledge of $K_X(\omega)$ for a useful range of distributions, plus the ability to induce coupling in models via conditional independence thus preserving the above conditional on one (or more) variable(s), Martin shows how the saddlepoint method can be a computationally efficient technique for VaR and other tail-related values that avoids the use of Gaussian approximation.

7 SECURITIZATION

The final part of the book is devoted to the asset backed securities (ABS) which played (and continue to play) such a pivotal role in the recent banking crisis. This part consists of three chapters discussing ABS from several complementary viewpoints.

In Chapter 16, Alexander Batchvarov describes the rise and fall of the parallel banking system based on securitization. In essence, the parallel banking system emerged as a result of de-regulation and disintermediation and led to in a period of very high and, in retrospect, unsustainable leverage. Its development was facilitated by the creation of new financial instruments (notably CDSs and CDOs). Instead of keeping loans on their books, banks and other financial players were originating them, bundling them together, slicing into tranches, and selling these tranches to other investors, such as pension funds, insurers, etc., with different and complementary risk appetites. While this system supported the real economy for a long time—especially consumer, real estate, and leveraged finance—it contributed to the build-up of leverage in the global capital markets and subsequent worldwide crisis.

Batchvarov convincingly demonstrates that the collapse of the parallel banking system was precipitated by an asset/liability mismatch which could not be avoided due to the absence of a lender of last resort (central bank)—a critical role in the traditional banking system. This collapse, which led to a severe systemic crisis, has been extremely traumatic for both the real and financial economy and resulted in re-regulation and re-intermediation. As of this writing, both governments and private investors are looking for a better structure of the markets based on lower leverage levels and more sensible regulations.

Batchvarov makes another interesting point, which is the 'fallacy of the historical data series'. Specifically, he points out that during the boom of the parallel banking system market participants (especially and disastrously rating agencies) worked with historical data, which, by their very nature, did not account for the effects of the leverage facilitated by the creation of the parallel banking system. By the same token, in the future, financial data series are going to incorporate effects created by the parallel banking system, while the system itself is no longer in place. Thus, blind reliance on historical data is dangerous and has to be avoided; instead, one should augment historical information with a healthy dose of common sense.

Undoubtedly, residential and commercial mortgages form the most important class of financial instruments which are used as building blocks of ABS. In Chapter 17, Alexander Levin discusses the nature of the housing prices and their dynamics. More specifically, he presents a qualitative and quantitative overview of the formation of the housing price bubble in the United States and its subsequent collapse. Levin argues that home prices are stochastic in nature and proposes their modelling in two complementary ways: (a) based on pure empirical considerations; (b) based on general risk-neutral arguments using the fact that several purely financial home price indices (HPI) are traded at various exchanges. He starts with a detailed overview of financial indices such as the Case-Shiller futures and Radar Logic (RPX) forwards. Next, Levin introduces the so-called equilibrium HPI, HPIeq, which he determines using a simple postulate: a mortgage loan payment has to constitute a constant part of the household income. While the corresponding constant is difficult to determine, it turns out that one can build a meaningful dynamic model without knowledge of it, since the real quantity of interest is changes in the HPI, i.e. $\delta \ln \left(HPIeq\right) / \delta t$ rather than $\ln \left(HPIeq\right)$ itself.

In order to describe the evolution of HPI in quantitative terms, Levin introduces the so-called home price appreciation measure (HPA) which represents the rate of return on HPI (in recent times, home price depreciation might be a more accurate term) and proceeds to model it as a mean-reverting stochastic process. By its nature, it is convenient to view HPA as a quantity defined on discrete time grid with, say, a quarterly time step. Then one can model the evolution for $x_k = x(t_k)$, $t_k = kh$, in the well-known Kalman filter framework as follows

$$x_k = X_{1k} + \text{iinf}_k + v_k \tag{37}$$

$$\mathbf{X}_k = \mathbf{F}\mathbf{X}_{k-1} + \mathbf{u}_k + \mathbf{w}_k \tag{38}$$

where $\mathbf{X}_k = (X_{1k}, X_{2k})^T$ is the vector of unobservable state variables, iinf_k is the income inflation, and $\mathbf{u}_k = h\left(k_1, k_3\right)^T \delta \ln \left(HPIeq\right) / \delta t$, and $v_k, \mathbf{w}_k$ are appropriately normalized normal variables. The corresponding transition matrix $\mathbf{F}$ has the form

$$\mathbf{F} = \begin{pmatrix} 1 & h \\ -bh & 1 - ah \end{pmatrix} \tag{39}$$

where constants a, b are chosen in such a way that the matrix $\mathbf{F}$ possesses stable complex conjugate roots $-a \pm i\beta$. Levin analyses the corresponding system in detail and decomposes HPA into rate-related, non-systematic volatility, and system volatility due to other economic and social factors. He then develops an HPI forecast with an emphasis on the growth of the real estate bubble and its subsequent crash. The key observation is that the bubble was caused to a large degree by the very big discrepancy between the nominal mortgage rate and the effective mortgage rate attributable to the proliferation of cheap financing in the form of Option ARMs (adjustable-rate mortgages), IO (interest-only) ARMs, and the like. Next, Levin considers HPI futures and forwards and develops a traditional risk-neutral model for their dynamics based on the classical (Health-Jarrow-Morton) HJM premisses. Overall, Levin provides a detailed description of housing prices and their dynamics.

Finally, in Chapter 18, Manzano et al. develop a pricing model for ABS CDO tranches backed by mortgage collateral (including prime, sub-prime, and other property types) via the Monte Carlo method. Traditional pricing of such tranches is done along the following lines. First, a very small set of possible scenarios describing the future evolution of collateral is chosen (often this set is reduced to a single scenario). These scenarios are characterized by different levels of CPR (Constant Prepayment Rate), CDR (Constant Default Rate), and Severity S (100% minus the price at liquidation as a percentage of the loan balance) for prime properties. Base case parameters are adjusted as appropriate for other property types. Each scenario is run through INTEX subroutines that model waterfall rules applied to prepayment, delinquency, loss, and IR scenarios specified by the user, and appropriate cash flows are generated. (INTEX is a software provider used as a de facto market standard; applying INTEX subroutines is very computationally costly.) Finally, the corresponding cash flows are averaged with (somewhat arbitrary) weights assigned to different scenarios and the tranche under consideration is priced.

It is clear that this approach has many deficiencies, mainly due to the small number of scenarios used and their arbitrary weighting. Manzano et al. develop an alternative approach. First, they generate a much larger number of scenarios (about 10,000) while taking particular care to correctly model the behaviour of all the relevant property types (from prime to sub-prime). Next, they use INTEX to generate cash flows for the tranche under consideration and a set of other instruments with known market prices which are used for calibration purposes. Using an entropy regularizer, Manzano et al. find the probability distribution for the set scenarios that best describes the corresponding market quotes. Once the weights for individual scenarios are found, the model is used to price the target ABS CDO tranche and compute fast price sensitivities to all the calibration instruments.

REFERENCES

Black, F., and Cox, J. (1976). 'Valuing corporate securities: some effects of bond indenture provisions'. *Journal of Finance*, 31: 351–67.

Cox, D. R. (1972). 'Regression models and life tables'. *Journal of the Royal Statistical Society*, Series B 34/2: 187–220.

Duffie, D., and Lando, D. (2001). 'Term structures of credit spreads with incomplete accounting information'. *Econometrica*, 69/3: 633–64.

Fisher, R., and Tippett, L. (1928). 'Limiting forms of the frequency distribution of the largest or smallest member of a sample'. *Proceedings of Cambridge Philosophical Society*, 24: 180–90.

Jarrow, R., and Turnbull, T. (1995). 'Pricing derivatives on financial securities subject to credit risk'. *Journal of Finance*, 50/1: 53–85.

Lando, D. (1998). 'On Cox processes and credit risky securities'. *Review of Derivatives Research*, 2: 99–120.

Leland, H. (1994). 'Risky debt, bond covenants and optimal capital structure'. *Journal of Finance*, 49: 1213–52.

Longstaff, F., and Schwartz, E. (1995). 'A simple approach to valuing risky fixed and floating rate debt'. *Journal of Finance*, 50: 789–819.

Marshall, A. W., and Olkin, I. (1967). 'A multivariate exponential distribution'. *Journal of the American Statistical Association*, 2: 84–98.

Merton, R. (1974). 'On the pricing of corporate debt: the risk structure of interest rates'. *Journal of Finance*, 29: 449–70.

Panjer, H. (1981). 'Recursive evaluation of a family of compound distributions'. *ASTIN Bulletin*, 12: 22–6.

Salmon, F. (2009). 'Recipe for disaster: the formula that killed Wall Street'. *Wired*, 17/03.

PART II

STATISTICAL OVERVIEW

CHAPTER 3

DEFAULT RECOVERY RATES AND LGD IN CREDIT RISK MODELLING AND PRACTICE

EDWARD I. ALTMAN

1 INTRODUCTION

THREE main variables affect the credit risk of a financial asset: (i) the probability of default (PD), (ii) the 'loss given default' (LGD), which is equal to one minus the recovery rate in the event of default (RR), and (iii) the exposure at default (EAD). While significant attention has been devoted by the credit risk literature on the estimation of the first component (PD), much less attention has been dedicated to the estimation of RR and to the relationship between PD and RR. This is mainly the consequence of two related factors. First, credit pricing models and risk management applications tend to focus on the systematic risk components of credit risk, as these are the only ones that attract risk premia. Second, credit risk models traditionally assumed RR to be dependent on individual features (e.g. collateral or seniority) that do not respond to systematic factors, and therefore to be independent of PD.

This traditional focus only on default analysis has been reversed by the recent increase in the number of studies dedicated to the subject of RR estimation and the relationship between the PD and RR (Fridson, Garman, and Okashima 2000; Gupton, Gates, and Carty 2000; Altman et al. 2002; Altman et al. 2003/2005; Frye 2000a, 2000b, 2000c; Hu and Perraudin 2002; Hamilton, Gupton, and Berthault 2001; Jarrow 2001; Jokivuolle and Peura 2003; Acharya, Bharath, and Srinivasan, 2007). This is partly

This is an updated and expanded review of E. I. Altman, A. Resti, and A. Sironi, 'Default Recovery Rates: A Review of the Literature and Recent Empirical Evidence', *Journal of Finance Literature* (Winter 2006), 21–45.

the consequence of the parallel increase in default rates and decrease of recovery rates registered during a substantial part of the 1999–2009 period. More generally, evidence from many countries in recent years suggests that collateral values and recovery rates can be volatile and, moreover, they tend to go down just when the number of defaults goes up in economic downturns. Indeed, first half results in 2009 (8.0% year-to-date) indicate that the default rate on high-yield bonds will reach a record high level in 2009 and recovery rates will fall to perhaps the lowest level in history, at least in the modern high yield bond era (22.5% year-to-date, Altman and Karlin (2009) and Keisman and Marshella Moody (2009).

This chapter presents a detailed review of the way credit risk models, developed during the last thirty years, have treated the recovery rate and, more specifically, its relationship with the probability of default of an obligor. These models can be divided into two main categories: (a) credit pricing models, and (b) portfolio credit value-at-risk (VaR) models. Credit pricing models can in turn be divided into three main approaches: (i) 'first generation' structural-form models, (ii) 'second generation' structural-form models, and (iii) reduced-form models. These three different approaches together with their basic assumptions, advantages, drawbacks, and empirical performance are reviewed in sections 2, 3, and 4. Credit VaR models are then examined in section 5. The more recent studies explicitly modelling and empirically investigating the relationship between PD and RR are reviewed in section 6. In section 7, we discuss BIS efforts to motivate banks to consider 'downturn LGD' in the specification of capital requirements under Basel II. Section 8 reviews the very recent efforts by the major rating agencies to provide explicit estimates of recovery given default. Section 9 revisits the issue of procyclicality and section 10 presents some recent empirical evidence on recovery rates on both defaulted bonds and loans and also on the relationship between default and recovery rates. Section 11 concludes.

2 First generation structural-form models: the Merton approach

The first category of credit risk models are the ones based on the original framework developed by Merton (1974) using the principles of option pricing (Black and Scholes 1973). In such a framework, the default process of a company is driven by the value of the company's assets and the risk of a firm's default is therefore explicitly linked to the variability of the firm's asset value. The basic intuition behind the Merton model is relatively simple: default occurs when the value of a firm's assets (the market value of the firm) is lower than that of its liabilities. The payment to the debtholders at the maturity of the debt is therefore the smaller of two quantities: the face value of the debt or the market value of the firm's assets. Assuming that the company's debt is entirely represented by a zero-coupon bond, if the value of the firm at maturity is greater than the face value of the bond, then the bondholder gets back the face value of the bond. However, if the value of the firm is less than the face value of the bond, the shareholders get nothing and the bondholder gets back the market value of the firm. The payoff at maturity to the bondholder is therefore equivalent to the face value of the bond minus a put option on the value of the firm, with a strike price equal to the face value of the bond and a maturity equal to the maturity of the bond. Following this basic intuition, Merton derived an explicit formula for risky bonds which can be used both to estimate the PD of a firm and to estimate the yield differential between a risky bond and a default-free bond.

In addition to Merton (1974), first generation structural-form models include Black and Cox (1976), Geske (1977), and Vasicek (1984). Each of these models tries to refine the original Merton framework by removing one or more of the unrealistic assumptions. Black and Cox (1976) introduce the possibility of more complex capital structures, with subordinated debt; Geske (1977) introduces interest-paying debt; Vasicek (1984) introduces the distinction between short-and long-term liabilities which now represents a distinctive feature of the KMV model.[1]

Under these models, all the relevant credit risk elements, including default and recovery at default, are a function of the structural characteristics of the firm: asset levels, asset volatility (business risk), and leverage (financial risk). The RR is therefore an endogenous variable, as the creditors' payoff is a function of the residual value of the defaulted company's assets. More precisely, under Merton's theoretical framework, PD and RR tend to be inversely related. If, for example, the firm's value increases, then its PD tends to decrease while the expected RR at default increases (*ceteris paribus*). On the other side, if the firm's debt increases, its PD increases while the expected RR at default decreases. Finally, if the firm's asset volatility increases, its PD increases while the expected RR at default decreases, since the possible asset values can be quite low relative to liability levels.

Although the line of research that followed the Merton approach has proven very useful in addressing the qualitatively important aspects of pricing credit risks, it has been less successful in practical applications.[2] This lack of success has been attributed to different reasons. First, under Merton's model the firm defaults only at maturity of the debt, a scenario that is at odds with reality. Second, for the model to be used in valuing default-risky debts of a firm with more than one class of debt in its capital structure (complex capital structures), the priority/seniority structures of various debts have to be specified. Also, this framework assumes that the absolute-priority rules are actually adhered to upon default in that debts are paid off in the order of their seniority. However, empirical evidence, such as in Franks and Torous (1994), indicates

---

[1] In the KMV model, default occurs when the firm's asset value goes below a threshold represented by the sum of the total amount of short-term liabilities and half of the amount of long-term liabilities.

[2] The standard reference is Jones, Mason, and Rosenfeld (1984), who found that, even for firms with very simple capital structures, a Merton-type model is unable to price investment-grade corporate bonds better than a naive model that assumes no risk of default.

that the absolute-priority rules are often violated. Moreover, the use of a lognormal distribution in the basic Merton model (instead of a more fat tailed distribution) tends to overstate recovery rates in the event of default.

3 SECOND-GENERATION STRUCTURAL-FORM MODELS

In response to such difficulties, an alternative approach has been developed which still adopts the original Merton framework as far as the default process is concerned but, at the same time, removes one of the unrealistic assumptions of the Merton model; namely, that default can occur only at maturity of the debt when the firm's assets are no longer sufficient to cover debt obligations. Instead, it is assumed that default may occur anytime between the issuance and maturity of the debt and that default is triggered when the value of the firm's assets reaches a lower threshold level.[3] These models include Kim, Ramaswamy, and Sundaresan (1993), Hull and White (1995), Nielsen, Saà-Requejo, and Santa-Clara (1993), Longstaff and Schwartz (1995), and others.

Under these models, the RR in the event of default is exogenous and independent from the firm's asset value. It is generally defined as a fixed ratio of the outstanding debt value and is therefore independent from the PD. For example, Longstaff and Schwartz (1995) argue that, by looking at the history of defaults and the recovery rates for various classes of debt of comparable firms, one can form a reliable estimate of the RR. In their model, they allow for a stochastic term structure of interest rates and for some correlation between defaults and interest rates. They find that this correlation between default risk and the interest rate has a significant effect on the properties of the credit spread.[4] This approach simplifies the first class of models by both exogenously specifying the cash flows to risky debt in the event of bankruptcy and simplifying the bankruptcy process. The latter occurs when the value of the firm's underlying assets hits some exogenously specified boundary.

Despite these improvements with respect to the original Merton's framework, second generation structural-form models still suffer from three main drawbacks, which represent the main reasons behind their relatively poor empirical performance.[5] First, they still require estimates for the parameters of the firm's asset value, which is non-observable. Indeed, unlike the stock price in the Black and Scholes formula for valuing equity options, the current market value of a firm is not easily observable. Second, structural-form models cannot incorporate credit rating changes that occur quite frequently for default-risky corporate debts. Most corporate bonds undergo credit

---

[3] One of the earliest studies based on this framework is Black and Cox (1976). However, this is not included in the second-generation models in terms of the treatment of the recovery rate.

[4] Using Moody's corporate bond yield data, they find that credit spreads are negatively related to interest rates and that durations of risky bonds depend on the correlation with interest rates.

[5] See Eom, Helwege, and Huang (2001) for an empirical analysis of structural-form models.

downgrades before they actually default. As a consequence, any credit risk model should take into account the uncertainty associated with credit rating changes as well as the uncertainty concerning default. Finally, most structural-form models assume that the value of the firm is continuous in time. As a result, the time of default can be predicted just before it happens and hence, as argued by Duffie and Lando (2000), there are no 'sudden surprises'. In other words, without recurring to a 'jump process', the PD of a firm is known with certainty.

4 REDUCED-FORM MODELS

The attempt to overcome the above-mentioned shortcomings of structural-form models gave rise to reduced-form models. These include Litterman and Iben (1991), Madan and Unal (1995), Jarrow and Turnbull (1995), Jarrow, Lando, and Turnbull (1997), Lando (1998), Duffie (1998), and Duffie and Singleton (1999). Unlike structural-form models, reduced-form models do not condition default on the value of the firm, and parameters related to the firm's value need not be estimated to implement them. In addition to that, reduced-form models introduce separate explicit assumptions on the dynamic of both PD and RR. These variables are modelled independently from the structural features of the firm, its asset volatility and leverage. Generally speaking, reduced-form models assume an exogenous RR that is independent from the PD and take as basics the behaviour of default-free interest rates, the RR of defaultable bonds at default, as well as a stochastic process for default intensity. At each instant, there is some probability that a firm defaults on its obligations. Both this probability and the RR in the event of default may vary stochastically through time. Those stochastic processes determine the price of credit risk. Although these processes are not formally linked to the firm's asset value, there is presumably some underlying relation. Thus Duffie and Singleton (1999) describe these alternative approaches as reduced-form models.

Reduced-form models fundamentally differ from typical structural-form models in the degree of predictability of the default as they can accommodate defaults that are sudden surprises. A typical reduced-form model assumes that an exogenous random variable drives default and that the probability of default over any time interval is non-zero. Default occurs when the random variable undergoes a discrete shift in its level. These models treat defaults as unpredictable Poisson events. The time at which the discrete shift will occur cannot be foretold on the basis of information available today.

Reduced-form models somewhat differ from each other by the manner in which the RR is parameterized. For example, Jarrow and Turnbull (1995) assumed that, at default, a bond would have a market value equal to an exogenously specified fraction of an otherwise equivalent default-free bond. Duffie and Singleton (1999) followed with a model that, when market value at default (i.e. RR) is exogenously specified, allows for closed-form solutions for the term structure of credit spreads. Their model also allows for a random RR that depends on the pre-default value of the bond. While this model assumes an exogenous process for the expected loss at default, meaning that the RR does not depend on the value of the defaultable claim, it allows for correlation between the default hazard-rate process and RR. Indeed, in this model, the behaviour of both PD and RR may be allowed to depend on firm-specific or macroeconomic variables and therefore to be correlated.

Other models assume that bonds of the same issuer, seniority, and face value have the same RR at default, regardless of the remaining maturity. For example, Duffie (1998) assumes that, at default, the holder of a bond of given face value receives a fixed payment, irrespective of the coupon level or maturity, and the same fraction of face value as any other bond of the same seniority. This allows him to use recovery parameters based on statistics provided by rating agencies such as Moody's. Jarrow, Lando, and Turnbull (1997) also allow for different debt seniorities to translate into different RRs for a given firm. Both Lando (1998) and Jarrow, Lando, and Turnbull (1997) use transition matrices (historical probabilities of credit rating changes) to price defaultable bonds.

Empirical evidence concerning reduced-form models is rather limited. Using the Duffie and Singleton (1999) framework, Duffee (1999) finds that these models have difficulty in explaining the observed term structure of credit spreads across firms of different credit risk qualities. In particular, such models have difficulty generating both relatively flat yield spreads when firms have low credit risk and steeper yield spreads when firms have higher credit risk.

A recent attempt to combine the advantages of structural-form models—a clear economic mechanism behind the default process—and the ones of reduced-form models—unpredictability of default—can be found in Zhou (2001). This is done by modelling the evolution of firm value as a jump-diffusion process. This model links RRs to the firm value at default so that the variation in RRs is endogenously generated and the correlation between RRs and credit ratings reported first in Altman (1989) and Gupton, Gates, and Carty (2000) is justified.

5 CREDIT VALUE-AT-RISK MODELS

During the second half of the nineties, banks and consultants started developing credit risk models aimed at measuring the potential loss, with a predetermined confidence level, that a portfolio of credit exposures could suffer within a specified time horizon (generally one year). These were mostly motivated by the growing importance of credit risk management especially since the now complete Basel II was anticipated to be proposed by the BD. These value-at-risk (VaR) models include J. P. Morgan's *CreditMetrics*® (Gupton, Finger, and Bhatia 1997 now provided by the Risk Metrics Group), *Credit Suisse Financial Products' CreditRisk*⁺® (1997), McKinsey's

CreditPortfolioView® (Wilson 1998), Moody's KMV's *CreditPortfolioManager*®, and Kamakura's *Risk Manager*®.

Credit VaR models can be gathered in two main categories: (1) default mode models (DM) and (2) mark-to-market (MTM) models. In the former, credit risk is identified with default risk and a binomial approach is adopted. Therefore, only two possible events are taken into account: default and survival. The latter includes all possible changes of the borrower creditworthiness, technically called 'credit migrations'. In DM models, credit losses only arise when a default occurs. On the other hand, MTM models are multinomial, in that losses arise also when negative credit migrations occur. The two approaches basically differ for the amount of data necessary to feed them: limited in the case of default mode models, much wider in the case of mark-to-market ones.

The main output of a credit risk model is the probability density function (PDF) of the future losses on a credit portfolio. From the analysis of such a loss distribution, a financial institution can estimate both the expected loss and the unexpected loss on its credit portfolio. The expected loss equals the (unconditional) mean of the loss distribution; it represents the amount the investor can expect to lose within a specific period of time (usually one year). On the other side, the unexpected loss represents the 'deviation' from expected loss and measures the actual portfolio risk. This can in turn be measured as the standard deviation of the loss distribution. Such a measure is relevant only in the case of a normal distribution and is therefore hardly useful for credit risk measurement: indeed, the distribution of credit losses is usually highly asymmetrical and fat tailed. This implies that the probability of large losses is higher than the one associated with a normal distribution. Financial institutions typically apply credit risk models to evaluate the 'economic capital' necessary to face the risk associated with their credit portfolios. In such a framework, provisions for credit losses should cover expected losses,[6] while economic capital is seen as a cushion for unexpected losses. Indeed, Basel II in its final iteration (BIS, June 2004) separated these two types of losses.

Credit VaR models can largely be seen as reduced-form models, where the RR is typically taken as an exogenous constant parameter or a stochastic variable independent from PD. Some of these models, such as *CreditMetrics*®, treat the RR in the event of default as a stochastic variable—generally modelled through a beta distribution—independent from the PD. Others, such as *CreditRisk*[+®], treat it as a constant parameter that must be specified as an input for each single credit exposure. While a comprehensive analysis of these models goes beyond the aim of this review,[7] it is important to highlight that all credit VaR models treat RR and PD as two independent variables.

---

[6] Reserves are used to cover expected losses.

[7] For a comprehensive analysis of these models, see Crouhy, Galai, and Mark (2000) and Gordy (2000).

6 RECENT CONTRIBUTIONS ON THE PD-RR RELATIONSHIP AND THEIR IMPACT

During the last several years, new approaches explicitly modelling and empirically investigating the relationship between PD and RR have been developed. These models include Bakshi, Madan, and Zhang (2001), Jokivuolle and Peura (2003). Frye (2000a, 2000b), Jarrow (2001), Hu and Perraudin (2002), and Carey and Gordy (2003), Altman, Resti, and Sironi (2002), Altman, et al. (2003/2005), and Acharya, Bharath, and Srinivasan, (2007).

Bakshi, Madan, and Zhang (2001) enhance the reduced-form models presented in section 4 to allow for a flexible correlation between the risk-free rate, the default probability, and the recovery rate. Based on some evidence published by rating agencies, they force recovery rates to be negatively associated with default probability. They find some strong support for this hypothesis through the analysis of a sample of BBB-rated corporate bonds: more precisely, their empirical results show that, on average, a 4% worsening in the (risk-neutral) hazard rate is associated with a 1% decline in (risk-neutral) recovery rates.

A rather different approach is the one proposed by Jokivuolle and Peura (2003). The authors present a model for bank loans in which collateral value is correlated with the PD. They use the option pricing framework for modelling risky debt: the borrowing firm's total asset value triggers the event of default. However, the firm's asset value does not determine the RR. Rather, the collateral value is in turn assumed to be the only stochastic element determining recovery.[8] Because of this assumption, the model can be implemented using an exogenous PD, so that the firm's asset value parameters need not be estimated. In this respect, the model combines features of both structural-form and reduced-form models. Assuming a positive correlation between a firm's asset value and collateral value, the authors obtain a similar result as Frye (2000a, 2000b), that realized default rates and recovery rates have an inverse relationship.

The model proposed by Frye draws from the conditional approach suggested by Finger (1999) and Gordy (2000). In these models, defaults are driven by a single systematic factor—the state of the economy—rather than by a multitude of correlation parameters. These models are based on the assumption that the same economic conditions that cause defaults to rise might cause RRs to decline, i.e. that the distribution of recovery is different in high-default periods from low-default ones. In Frye's model, both PD and RR depend on the state of the systematic factor. The correlation between these two variables therefore derives from their mutual dependence on the systematic factor.

---

[8] Because of this simplifying assumption the model can be implemented using an exogenous PD, so that the firm asset value parameters need not be estimated. In this respect, the model combines features of both structural-form and reduced-form models.

The intuition behind Frye's theoretical model is relatively simple: if a borrower defaults on a loan, a bank's recovery may depend on the value of the loan collateral. The value of the collateral, like the value of other assets, depends on economic conditions. If the economy experiences a recession, RRs may decrease just as default rates tend to increase. This gives rise to a negative correlation between default rates and RRs.

While the model originally developed by Frye (2000a) implied recovery to be taken from an equation that determines collateral, Frye (2000b) modelled recovery directly. This allowed him to empirically test his model using data on defaults and recoveries from US corporate bond data. More precisely, data from Moody's Default Risk Service database for the 1982–97 period were used for the empirical analysis.[9] Results show a strong negative correlation between default rates and RRs for corporate bonds. This evidence is consistent with US bond market data, indicating a simultaneous increase in default rates and LGDs for the 1999–2002 period.[10] Frye's (2000b, 2000c) empirical analysis allows him to conclude that in a severe economic downturn, bond recoveries might decline 20–25 percentage points from their normal-year average. Loan recoveries may decline by a similar amount, but from a higher level. In all cases, Frye, and others, compare defaults and recoveries just after default, not the ultimate recovery after the restructuring, or recovery period.

Jarrow (2001) presents a new methodology for estimating RRs and PDs implicit in both debt and equity prices. As in Frye, RRs and PDs are correlated and depend on the state of the macroeconomy. However, Jarrow's methodology explicitly incorporates equity prices in the estimation procedure, allowing the separate identification of RRs and PDs and the use of an expanded and relevant dataset. In addition to that, the methodology explicitly incorporates a liquidity premium in the estimation procedure, which is considered essential in light of the high variability in the yield spreads between risky debt and US Treasury securities.

Using four different datasets (Moody's Default Risk Service database of bond defaults and LGDs, Society of Actuaries database of private placement defaults and LGDs, Standard & Poor's database of bond defaults and LGDs, and Portfolio Management Data's database of LGDs) ranging from 1970 to 1999, Carey and Gordy (2003) analyse LGD measures and their correlation with default rates. Their preliminary results contrast with the findings of Frye (2000b): estimates of simple default rate-LGD correlation are close to zero. They find, however, that limiting the sample period to 1988–98, estimated correlations are more in line with Frye's results (0.45 for senior debt and 0.8 for subordinated debt). The authors postulate that during this short period the correlation rises not so much because LGDs are low during the low-default years 1993–96, but rather because LGDs are relatively high during the high-default years 1990 and 1991. They therefore conclude that the basic intuition behind Frye's model may not adequately characterize the relationship between default rates and

[9] Data for the 1970–81 period have been eliminated from the sample period because of the low number of default prices available for the computation of yearly recovery rates.

[10] Hamilton, Gupton, and Berthault (2001) and Altman et al. (2003/2005), provide clear empirical evidence of this phenomenon.

LGDs. Indeed, a weak or asymmetric relationship suggests that default rates and LGDs may be influenced by different components of the economic cycle.

Using defaulted bonds' data for the sample period 1982–2002, which includes the relatively high-default years of 2000–2, Altman et al. (2003/2005), following Altman, Resti, and Sironi (2002), find empirical results that appear consistent with Frye's intuition: a negative correlation between default rates and RRs. However, they find that the single systematic risk factor—i.e. the performance of the economy—is less predictive than Frye's model would suggest. Their econometric univariate and multivariate models assign a key role to the supply of defaulted bonds (the default rate) and show that this variable, together with variables that proxy the size of the high-yield bond market and the economic cycle, explain a substantial proportion (close to 90%)of the variance in bond recovery rates aggregated across all seniority and collateral levels. They conclude that a simple market mechanism based on supply and demand for the defaulted securities drives aggregate recovery rates more than a macroeconomic model based on the common dependence of default and recovery on the state of the cycle. In high default years, the supply of defaulted securities tends to exceed demand,[11] thereby driving secondary market prices down. This in turn negatively affects RR estimates, as these are generally measured using bond prices shortly after default. During periods of low defaults, as we have observed in the 2004–6 cycle, recoveries increase.

The coincident relationship between high-yield bond default rates and recovery rates is shown in Figure 3.1. This graph shows the association of weighted average default rates and recovery rates over the period 1982–2009, using four bivariate regression specifications. The actual regressions are based on data from 1982 to 2003 and the subsequent five years (2004–9) are inserted to show the regressions estimate compared to the actual. Note that the degree of explanatory power is excellent with as much as 65% of the variation in aggregate bond recovery rates explained by just one variable—the aggregate default rate. These regressions include linear (53.6%), quadratic (61.5%), log-linear (62.9%), and power function (65.3%) structures. The clear negative relationship between default and recovery rates is striking with periods of excess supply of defaults relative to demand resulting in unusually low recoveries in such years as 1990, 1991, 2001, and 2002.

One can also observe, however, that the most recent years, 2005 and 2006, which are part of an extremely low default cycle, show estimates which are far below the actual results. For example, our model would have predicted an above average recovery rate of about 56% in 2006. Instead, the actual rate was almost 73% as of the end of the third quarter. And the 2005 estimate of about 45% compares to the actual recovery rate of over 60%. Either the model has performed poorly or the default market has

---

[11] Demand mostly comes from niche investors called 'vultures', who intentionally purchase bonds in default. These investors represented a relatively small (perhaps $100 billion) and specialized segment of the debt market. This hedge-fund sector grew considerably, however, in the 2003–6 period, perhaps more than doubling in size (author estimates).

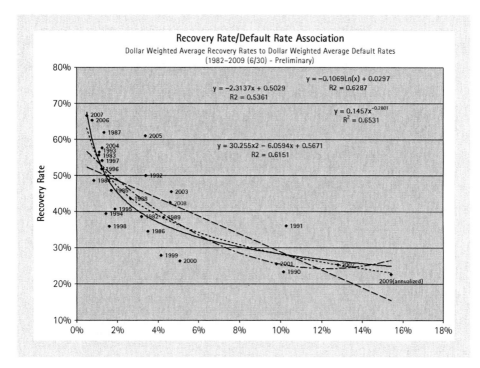

FIGURE 3.1 Recovery Rate/Default Rate Association.

Source: Altman et al. (2003/2005) and Altman and Karlin (2009).

been influenced by an unusual amount of excess credit liquidity, and perhaps other factors, which have changed, perhaps temporarily, the dynamics in the credit markets.

A recent article (Altman 2007) argues that there was a type of 'credit bubble' causing seemingly highly distressed firms to remain non-bankrupt when, in more 'normal' periods, many of these firms would have defaulted. This, in turn, produced an abnormally low default rate and the huge liquidity of distressed debt investors bid up the prices of both existing and newly defaulted issues. As we had predicted, a regression to the long-term mean, i.e. lower recoveries, and a huge increase in default rates began in 2008 and culminated in record high first-half 2009 defaults and near record low recovery rates (Altman and Karlin 2009).

Using Moody's historical bond market data, Hu and Perraudin (2002) also examine the dependence between recovery rates and default rates. They first standardize the quarterly recovery data in order to filter out the volatility of recovery rates due to changes over time in the pool of rated borrowers. They find that correlations between quarterly recovery rates and default rates for bonds issued by US-domiciled obligors are 0.22 for post-1982 data (1983–2000) and 0.19 for the 1971–2000 periods. Using extreme value theory and other non-parametric techniques, they also examine the impact of this negative correlation on credit VaR measures and find that the increase is statistically significant when confidence levels exceed 99%.

7 CORRELATION RESULTS' IMPACT AND DOWNTURN LGD

The impact of the Altman et al. studies of 2002, 2003, as well as the Hu and Per-raudin (2002) and Frye (2000a, 2000b, and 2000c) studies, was almost immediate, resulting in suggested changes in Basel II's pillar I's guidelines. Specifically, the final BIS (Bank for International Settlement) Accord (2004) suggested, via its paragraph 468 declaration, a 'downturn' or 'stressed' LGD for banks. According to this document, Internal Ratings-based (IRB) banks are required to use estimates of LGD parameters, where necessary, to capture the relevant risks. The guidelines were in general terms only and left specific details of the quantification process to supervisors to develop in collaboration with the banking industry. The underlying theory was that recovery rates on defaulted exposures may be lower during economic downturns than during more normal conditions and that a capital rule be realized to guarantee sufficient capital to cover losses during these adverse circumstances. Paragraph 468 also stated that loss severities may not exhibit such cyclical variability, especially if based on ultimate recoveries, and therefore LGD estimates of downturn LGD may not differ materially from the long-run weighted average.

Many banks reacted negatively to this conservative approach and proposed more modest adjustments. Indeed, Araten, Jacobs, and Varshny (2004) suggested that cor-relations are not usually material. All of this discussion and debate resulted in a set of more explicit guidelines and principles in the BIS (Basel Commission 2005) 'Guidance on paragraph 468 of the Framework Document'. In this report, the BIS found (1) that there is a potential for realized recovery rates to be lower than average during times of high default rates and failing to account for this could result in an understatement of the capital required to cover unexpected losses; (2) that data limitations pose a difficult challenge to the estimation of LGD in general and particularly in downturns; and (3) there is little consensus with respect to appropriate methods for incorporating downturn conditions in LGD estimates. The BIS was careful to state that any principles be flexible enough to allow for a range of sound practices and to encourage continued refinements. In other words, while requiring analysis and reports about 'downturn LGD' amongst its members, banks appear to be free to specify if there should be any penalty or not to their average assessments of LGD parameters.

The principles (2005) were that banks must have a rigorous and well-documented process for assessing, economic downturn's impact if any, on recovery rates and that this process must consist of (1) the identification of appropriate downturn condi-tions for each asset class, (2) identification of adverse dependencies, if any, between default and recovery rates, and (3) incorporating them to produce LGD estimates. The recovery cash flows should utilize a discount rate that reflects the costs of holding defaulted assets over the workout period, including an appropriate risk premium. These costs should be consistent with the concept of economic loss, not an accounting concept of economic loss (e.g. not the interest rate on the old loan). This can be accomplished either with a discount rate based on the risk-free rate plus a spread appropriate for the risk of recovery and cost of cash flows or by converting the cash flows to certainty equivalents (described in footnote 3 in (Basel Commission 2005) and discounting these by the risk-free rate, or, by a combination of these adjustments to the discount rate.

By specifically referring to the stream of cash flows over the restructuring period, the BIS, and banks, are embracing the use of ultimate recoveries and not recoveries at the time of default. As such, the correlation between default and recovery rates observed in the bond markets by several researchers, discussed earlier, may not imply a negative correlation between default and ultimate recovery rates. Indeed, there is a timing disconnect which may be important, especially if the distressed loan market is not efficient and the discounted values of ultimate recoveries are materially different from the recovery values at the time of default. Finally, the BIS principles refer to the possibility that stress tests performed under normal expected values of recoveries will not produce different results from downturn LGD estimates under paragraph 468. It remains to be seen how bank regulators will respond to efforts by banks to assess downturn LGD estimates.

One regulator in the United States, the Federal Reserve System, has suggested that IRB banks in the US use a simple formula to specify downturn LGD, of the form:[12]

$$\text{LGD in downturn} = .08 + .92\ \text{LGD},$$

Where LGD = long-term LGD average. So, where the long-term LGD equals, for example, 0.3 (i.e. recovery rates of 0.7), the downturn LGD would increase modestly to 0.33 (about 10%). If this modification were applied to Foundation Basel II banks, not possible in the US, then the downturn LGD = 0.494 on unsecured exposure, (.08 + .92 (.45) = .494), again an increase of about 10% of the normal conditions' expected recovery. For secured loans, the analysis requires a stress test on the collateral itself.

Miu and Ozdemir (2006) analyse this downturn LGD requirement and suggest that the original LGD assessment by banks, without considering PD and RR correlation, can be appropriately adjusted by incorporating a certain degree of conservatism in cyclical LGD estimates within a point-in-time modelling framework. They find even greater impacts on economic capital than even Altman, Resti, and Sironi (2001) did— with as much as an increase of 35–45% in corporate loan portfolios and 16% for a middle-market portfolio to compensate for the lack of correlations. Altman et al. had found, through simulations of loan portfolios that about 30% needed to be added. Both studies, however, suggest that banks determine these penalties, if any, without abandoning the point-in-time, one-year perspective as to estimating LGD.

---

[12] From <http://federalreserve.gov/GeneralInfo/Basel2/NPR_20060905/NPR/>.

7.1 Some final references

A number of related studies on LGD can be found in Altman, Resti, and Sironi's (2006) anthology. These include Chabane, Laurent, and Salomon's credit risk assessment of stochastic LGD and correlation effects, Friedman and Sandow's conditional probability distribution analysis of recovery rates, Laurent and Schmit's estimation of distressed LGD on leasing contracts, DeLaurentis and Riani's further analysis of LGD in the leasing industry, Citron and Wright's investigation of recovery rates on distressed management buyouts, and Dermine and Neto de Carvalho's empirical investigation of recoveries' impact on bank provisions. Schuermann provides an overview on what we know and do not know about LGD, as well, in the volume.

Gupton and Stein (2002) analyse the recovery rate on over 1,800 corporate bond, loan, and preferred stock defaults, from 900 companies, in order to specify and test Moody's LossCalc® model for predicting loss given default (LGD). Their model estimates LGD at two points in time—immediately and in one year—adding a holding period dimension to the analysis. The authors find that their multifactor model, incorporating micro-variables (e.g. debt type, seniority), industry, and some macroeconomics factors (e.g. default rates, changes in leading indicators) outperforms traditional historic average methods in predicting LGD.

Using data on observed prices of defaulted securities in the United States over the period 1982–99, Acharya, Bharath, and Srinivasan (HBH) (2007) find that seniority and security are important determinants of recovery rates. While this result is not surprising and in line with previous empirical studies on recoveries, their second main result is rather striking and concerns the effect of industry-specific and macroeconomic conditions in the default year. Indeed, industry conditions at the time of default are found to be robust and important determinants of recovery rates. They show that creditors of defaulted firms recover significantly lower amounts in present-value terms when the industry of defaulted firms is in distress and also when non-defaulted firms are rather illiquid and if their debt is collateralized by specific assets that are not easily redeployable into other sectors. Also, they find that there is little effect of macroeconomic conditions over and above the industry conditions and the latter is robust even with the inclusion of macroeconomic factors. ABH suggest that the linkage, again highlighted by Altman et al. (2003/2005), between bond market aggregate variables and recoveries arises due to supply-side effects in segmented bond markets, and that this may be a manifestation of Schleifer and Vishny's (1992) industry equilibrium effect. That is, macroeconomic variables and bond market conditions may be picking up the effect of omitted industry conditions. The importance of the 'industry' factor in determining LGD has been recently highlighted by Schuermann (2004) in a survey of the academic and practitioner literature.

Frye (2000a), Pykhtin (2003), and Dullmann and Trapp (2004) all propose a model that accounts for the dependence of recoveries on systematic risk. They extend the single factor model proposed by Gordy (2000), by assuming that the recovery rate follows a lognormal (Pykhtin 2003) or a logit-normal (Dullmann and Trapp 2004) one. The latter study empirically compares the results obtained using the three alternative models (Frye 2000a; Pykhtin 2003; Dullmann and Trapp 2004). They use time series of default rates and recovery rates from *Standard and Poor's Credit Pro* database, including bond and loan default information in the time period from 1982 to 1999. They find that estimates of recovery rates based on market prices at default are significantly higher than the ones obtained using recovery rates at emergence from restructuring. The findings of this study are in line with previous ones: systematic risk is an important factor that influences recovery rates. The authors show that ignoring this risk component may lead to downward biased estimates of economic capital.

8 RECOVERY RATINGS

There has been a debate in the practitioner literature about how recovery rates impact bond ratings ascribed to default risk estimates from the various major rating agencies. One agency, Moody's, has always maintained that it explicitly considered recoveries in the bond rating of a particular corporate issue. Others (S&P and Fitch) typically adjusted, through 'notching', the senior unsecured issuer rating based on whether the particular issue was investment grade or speculative grade given a certain seniority priority. For example, a subordinated issue of an investment grade company was typically 'down-notched' by one notch and a speculative grade issue was penalized by two notches if subordinated. The Moody's assertion was questionable since prior to the 1990s there simply was no reliable database on recoveries available.

Regardless of the 'ancient' approaches used, all three rating agencies have recently recognized the heightened importance of recoveries for a number of applications including Basel II, structured products, the credit default swap market, as well as traditional default analysis, and have introduced 'Recovery Ratings' as a complementary risk rating indicator.

Table 3.1 reviews these 'Recovery Ratings', first introduced by S&P on US senior bank loans in December 2003 and discussed by Chew & Kerr in Altman et al. (2003/2005). Fitch then introduced, in late 2005, their recovery analysis on all highly speculative grade issues rated B or below. Finally, Moody's in September 2006 introduced their rating of US non-financial speculative grade issues and expected to do the same in Europe in 2007. We expect that all of the rating agencies will expand their coverage if the market deems this information valuable.

As shown in Table 3.1, each of the recovery rating classes, six in each case, has a quantitative estimate of the proportion of the issue that can be expected to be recovered given a default. These range from as high as 100% down to estimates of 0–10%. In addition to the recovery percentage estimates, Table 3.1 reviews each rating agency's methodology for arriving at their estimate. Fundamental valuation techniques are employed followed by priority analysis of each issue under consideration.

Table 3.1 Recovery Ratings from the Rating Agencies

Agency	Moody's	Standard & Poor's	Fitch
Ratings Type	Loss Given Default Ratings	Recovery Ratings	Recovery Ratings
Ratings Scale	LGD1 0–9% LGD2 10–29% LGD3 30–49% LGD4 50–69% LGD5 70–89% LGD6 90–100%	1+ 100% 1 100% 2 80–100% 3 50–80% 4 25–50% 5 0–25%	RR1 91–100% RR2 71–90% RR3 51–70% RR4 31–50% RR5 11–30% RR6 0–10%
Assets Rated	Non-financial corporate speculative-grade issuers in the US	US and Canadian secured bank loans to which it assigns bank loan ratings, to senior secured loans in Europe, and to any secured bonds issued along with rated bank loans	All corporate, financial institutions and sovereign issuers rated in the single B category and below
Methodology	1. Establish priority of claim a. Jr bonds are subordinated to Sr bonds, but may or may not be subordinated to other unsecured obligations b. Prioritize clamis across affiliates 2. Assume a beta probability distribution for potential Enterprise Value(EV) outcomes a. For most issuers, assume a beta distribution of EV relative to total liabilities	1. Review transaction structure 2. Review borrower's projections 3. Establish simulated path to default 4. Forecast borrower's free cash flow at default based on our simulated default based on our simulated default scenario and default proxv 5. Determine valuation	1. Estimate the enterprise value(EV) a. Establish the level of cash flow upon which it is most appropriate to base the valuation b. Apply a multiple reflecting a company's relative position within a sector based on actual or expected market and/or distressed multiples 2. Estimate the coeditor mass, i.e. identify existing claims a. Claims taken on as a company's fortunes deteriorate

b. Corporate LGD distribution will have 50% mean and 26% standard deviation	6. Identify priority debt claims and value	b. Claims necessary to the reorganization process
3. For each EV outcome, calculate LGDs for each security class implied by absolute priority	7. Determine collateral value available to lenders	c. Claims that have priority in the relevant bankruptcy code
4. Expected LGD equals the probability-weighted averages of LGDs across EV outcomes	8. Assign recovery rating	3. Distributing the EV
	9. Convey the recovery analytics to the issuer and investment community	a. The resulting value is allocated to creditors according to jurisdictional practice

Source: Moody's, S & P, and Fitch (New York).

In all cases, the recovery ratings are available in addition to the traditional default ratings. It remains to be seen as to the market's acceptance of this second set of ratings and whether they will form a material part of their investment decisions.

9 RECOVERY RATES AND PROCYCLICALITY

Altman et al. (2003/2005) also highlight the implications of their results for credit risk modelling and for the issue of procyclicality[13] of capital requirements. In order to assess the impact of a negative correlation between default rates and recovery rates on credit risk models, they run Monte Carlo simulations on a sample portfolio of bank loans and compare the key risk measures (expected and unexpected losses). They show that both the expected loss and the unexpected loss are vastly understated if one assumes that PDs and RRs are uncorrelated.[14] Therefore, credit models that do not carefully factor in the negative correlation between PDs and RRs might lead to insufficient bank reserves and cause unnecessary shocks to financial markets.

As far as procyclicality is concerned, they show that this effect tends to be exacerbated by the correlation between PDs and RRs: low recovery rates when defaults

---

[13] Procyclicality involves the sensitivity of regulatory capital requirements to economic and financial market cycles. Since ratings and default rates respond to the cycle, the new IRB approach proposed by the Basel Committee risks increasing capital charges, and limiting credit supply, when the economy is slowing (the reverse being true when the economy is growing at a fast rate).

[14] Both expected losses and VaR measures associated with different confidence levels tend to be underestimated by approximately 30%.

are high would amplify cyclical effects. This would especially be true under the so-called 'advanced' IRB approach, where banks are free to estimate their own recovery rates and might tend to revise them downwards when defaults increase and ratings worsen. The impact of such a mechanism was also assessed by Resti (2002), based on simulations over a twenty-year period, using a standard portfolio of bank loans (the composition of which is adjusted through time according to S&P transition matrices). Two main results emerged from this simulation exercise: (i) the procyclicality effect is driven more by up- and downgrades, rather than by default rates; in other words, adjustments in credit supply needed to comply with capital requirements respond mainly to changes in the structure of weighted assets, and only to a lesser extent to actual credit losses (except in extremely high default years); (ii) when RRs are permitted to fluctuate with default rates, the procyclicality effect increases significantly.

10 FURTHER EMPIRICAL EVIDENCE

This section focuses on different measurements and the most recent empirical evidence of default recovery rates. Most credit risk models utilize historical average empirical estimates, combined with their primary analytical specification of the probability of default, to arrive at the all-important loss-given-default (LGD) input. Since very few financial institutions have ample data on recovery rates by asset type and by type of collateral, model builders and analysts responsible for Basel II inputs into their IRB models begin with estimates from public bond and private bank loan markets. Of course, some banks will research their own internal databases in order to conform to the requirements of the Advanced IRB approach.

10.1 Early empirical evidence

Published data on default recovery rates generally, but not always, use secondary market bond or bank loan prices. The first empirical study, that we are aware of, that estimated default recovery rates was in Altman, Haldeman, and Narayanan's (1977) ZETA® model's adjustment of the optimal cut-off score in their second generation credit scoring model. Interestingly, these bank loan recovery estimates did not come from the secondary loan trading market—they did not exist then—but from a survey of bank workout-department experience (1971–75). The general conclusion from this early experience of these departments was a recovery rate on non-performing, unsecured loans of only about 30% of the loan amount plus accrued interest. The cash inflows for three years post-default was not discounted back to default date. We will refer to this experience as the 'ultimate nominal recovery' since it utilizes post-default recoveries, usually from the end of the restructuring period.

In later studies, ultimate recovery rates refer to the nominal or discounted value of bonds or loans based on either the price of the security at the end of the reorganization period (usually Chapter 11) or the value of the package of cash or securities upon emergence from restructuring. For example, Altman and Eberhart (1994) observed the price performance of defaulted bonds, stratified by seniority, at the time of the restructuring emergence as well as the discounted value of these prices. They concluded that the most senior bonds in the capital structure (senior secured and senior unsecured) did very well in the post-default period (20–30% per annum returns) but the more junior bonds (senior subordinated and subordinated) did poorly, barely breaking even on a nominal basis and losing money on a discounted basis. Similar, but less extreme, results were found by Fridson et al. (Merrill Lynch (2000) when they updated (1994–2000) Altman and Eberhart's earlier study which covered the period 1981–93.)

Other studies that analysed bank loan recovery rates were by Asarnow and Edwards (1995) and Eales and Bosworth (1998). The first study presents the results of an analysis of losses on bank-loan defaults based on twenty-four years of data compiled by Citibank; their database comprises 831 commercial and industrial (C&I) loans, as well as 89 structured loans (highly collateralized loans that contain many restrictive covenants). Their results (based on 'ultimate' recoveries) indicate a LGD of about 35% for C&I loans (with larger loans, above US$ 10 million, showing a somewhat lower loss rate of 29%); unsurprisingly, the LGD for structured loans is considerably lower (13%), due to the role played by collateral and covenants in supporting the early default-detection and recovery processes. In the second study, the authors report the empirical results on recovery rates from a foreign bank operating in the United States—Westpac Banking Corporation. The study focuses on small business loans and larger consumer loans, such as home loans and investment property loans.

Neto de Carvalho and Dermine (2003) analyse the determinants of loss given default rates using a portfolio of credits given by the largest private Portuguese bank, Banco Comercial Portugues. Their study is based on a sample of 371 defaulted loans to small and medium size companies, originally granted during the period June 1985—December 2000. The estimates of recovery rates are based on the discounted cash flows recovered after the default event. The authors report three main empirical results which are consistent with previous empirical evidence: (i) the frequency distribution of loan losses given default is bi-modal, with many cases presenting a 0% recovery and other cases presenting a 100% recovery; (ii) the size of the loan has a statistically significant negative impact on the recovery rate; (iii) while the type of collateral is statistically significant in determining the recovery, this is not the case for the age of the bank-company relationship.

10.2 More recent evidence

In Table 3.2, we present recent empirical evidence on bank loan recoveries (Keisman and Marshella Moody's 2009) and on corporate bonds by seniority (Altman and Karlin 2009) based on the average prices of these securities just after the date of default. Surprisingly, the highest mean recovery rates were on senior unsecured

Table 3.2 Recovery at Default[a] on Public Corporate Bonds (1978–2009–2Q) and Bank Loans (1988–2009–2Q)

Loan/bond seniority	Number of issues	Median	Mean	Standard deviation %
Senior secured loans	1,034	56.74	56.26	27.17
Senior unsecured loans	122	59.82	59.39	40.24
Senior secured bonds	360	59.08	59.96	18.30
Senior unsecured bonds	11,06	45.88	37.85	13.49
Senior subordinated bonds	443	32.79	31.03	14.23
Subordinated bonds	255	31.00	31.14	17.52
Discount bonds	157	19.00	25.83	20.84
Total sample bonds	**2,321**	**41.78**	**37.81**	**14.04**

[a]Based on prices just after default on bonds and 30 days after default on loans.
Source: Moody's (Keisman and Marshella Moody 2009) (Bank Loans) and Altman and Karlin 2009 (Bonds).

bonds (60%) and bank loans (59.4%) followed by senior secured loans (56.3%).[15] Although the data from Moody's and Altman were from different periods and samples, it is interesting to note that the recovery on senior unsecured bonds (45.9%) was significantly lower than senior unsecured bank loans (59.4%). The estimates of median recoveries on the senior-subordinated and subordinated bonds were very similar. Similar recoveries on defaulted bonds can be found in Varma, Cantor, and Hamilton (2003). Altman and Karlin's value weighted mean recovery rate on over 2,300 bond default issues was 37.8%.

Altman and Karlin (2009) further break down bond recoveries just after the default date by analysing recoveries based on the original rating (fallen angels vs. original rating non-investment grade ['junk'] bonds) of different seniorities. For example, in Table 3.3, we observe that senior-secured bonds, that were originally rated investment grade, recovered a median rate of 50.5% vs. just 39.0% for the same seniority bonds that were non-investment grade when issued. These are statistically significant differences for similar seniority securities. Since fallen angel defaults are much more prominent in some years in the United States (e.g. close to 50% in dollar amount of defaults in 2001 and 2002 were fallen angels prior to default), these statistics are quite meaningful. Note that for senior-subordinated and subordinated bonds, however, the rating at issuance is of little consequence, although the sample sizes for investment grade, low seniority bonds were very small. Varma et al. (2003) also conclude that the higher the rating prior to default, including the rating at issuance, the higher the average recovery rate at

[15] Interestingly, the comparable median for defaults through 2003 was about 4.5% lower (54.5%), showing the considerable increase in default recovery rates on bonds in the period 2004–9. This recovery rate was actually higher through 2008. Also, it is suprising that senior unsecured loans recovered more than senior secured loans, at least in terms of arithmetic average metrics. Ultimate recoveries, however (Table 3.4), demonstrate the expected hierarchy, with senior secured bank debt recovering far more than unsecured loans.

Table 3.3 Investment grade vs. non-investment grade (original rating) prices at default on public bonds (1978–2008)

Bond seniority	Number of Issues	Median Price (%)	Average Price (%)	Weighted Price (%)	Standard deviation (%)
Senior secured					
Investment grade	142	50.50	53.85	57.97	26.94
Non-investment grade	245	39.00	44.05	44.42	29.23
Senior unsecured					
Investment grade	374	43.50	44.84	38.75	24.92
Non-investment grade	519	32.50	36.04	34.79	23.31
Senior subordinated					
Investment grade	16	27.31	37.10	34.29	27.48
Non-investment grade	402	27.90	32.74	30.20	24.16
Subordinated					
Investment grade	18	4.00	24.27	6.38	29.52
Non-investment grade	204	28.92	32.54	29.64	22.68
Discount					
Investment grade	1	17.15	13.63	13.63	25.13
Non-investment grade	96	18.00	27.31	26.94	23.38

Source: NYU Salomon Center Default Database.

Table 3.4 Ultimate recovery rates on bank loan and bond defaults (discounted values, 1988–2Q 2009)

	Observations	Ultimate discounted recovery (%)	Standard deviation (%)	Ultimate nominal recovery (%)
All bank debt	1156	82.24%	29.53%	92.40%
Secured bank debt	1034	85.63%	27.17%	94.74%
Unsecured bank debt	122	56.34%	40.24%	66.05%
Senior secured bonds	320	62.00%	32.90%	76.03%
Senior unsecured bonds	863	43.80%	35.10%	59.29%
Senior subordinated bonds	489	30.50%	34.10%	38.41%
Subordinated bonds	399	28.80%	34.00%	34.81%

Source: D. Keisman (Moody's Ultimate LGD Database of defaulted loans and bond issues that defaulted between 1988–2009. Recoveries are discounted at each instruments' pre-default interest rate.

default. Apparently, the quality of assets and the structure of the defaulting company's balance sheets favour higher recoveries for higher-quality original issue bonds.

In Table 3.4, we again return to the data on ultimate recoveries and the results are from Moody's (2009) assessment of bank loan and bond recoveries. These results show the nominal and discounted (by the loan's pre-default interest rate) ultimate recovery at the end of the restructuring period for well over 3,000 defaulted loans and bonds over the period 1988–2009. Several items are of interest. First, the recovery on senior bank debt, which is mainly secured, was quite high at 87.3% and 77.2% for nominal and discounted values respectively. Senior secured and senior unsecured notes, which include loans and bonds, had lower recoveries and the more junior notes (almost all bonds) had, not surprisingly, the lowest recoveries. Note, the differential between the nominal and discounted recovery rates diminish somewhat at the lower seniority levels.

Standard & Poor's (Keisman 2004) also finds, not shown in any table, that during the 'extreme stress' default years of 1998 to 2002, the recovery rates on all seniorities declined compared to their longer 1988–2002 sample period. Since 1998 and 1999 were not really high default years, the results of S&P for 2000–2 are consistent with Altman, Resti, and Sironi's (2002) and Altman et al.'s (2003/2005) predictions of an inverse relationship between default and recovery rates. Indeed, recovery rates were a relatively low 25% in the corporate bond market for both 2001 and 2002 when default rates were in the double digits but increased to almost 70% in 2006 when default rates tumbled to well below average annual levels and then fell to about 22.5% in 2009 (2Q) as defaults surged (Altman and Karlin 2009).

Some recovery studies have concentrated on rates across different industries. Altman and Kishore (1996) and Verde (2003) report a fairly high variance across industrial sectors. For example, Verde (2003) reports that recovery rates in 2001 vs. 2002 varied dramatically from one year to the next (e.g. Gaming, Lodging and Restaurants recovered 16% in 2001 and 77% in 2002, Retail recovered 7% in 2001 and 48% in 2002, while Transportation recovered 31% in 2001 and 19% in 2002) but returned to more normal levels in 2003.

Another issue highlighted in some studies, especially those from S&P, (e.g. Van de Castle and Keisman 1999 and Keisman 2004) is that an important determinant of ultimate recovery rates is the amount that a given seniority has junior liabilities below its level; the greater the proportion of junior securities, the higher the recovery rate on the senior tranches. The theory being that the greater the 'equity cushion', the more likely there will be assets of value, which under absolute priority, go first in liquidation or reorganization to the more senior tranches.

11 CONCLUDING REMARKS

Table 3.5 summarizes the way RR and its relationship with PD are dealt with in the different credit models described in the previous sections of this chapter. While, in the original Merton (1974) framework, an inverse relationship between PD and RR exists, the credit risk models developed during the 1990s treat these two variables as independent. The currently available and most used credit pricing and credit VaR models are indeed based on this independence assumption and treat RR either as a constant parameter or as a stochastic variable independent from PD. In the latter case, RR volatility is assumed to represent an idiosyncratic risk which can be eliminated

Table 3.5 The Treatment of LGD and Default Rates within Different Credit Risk Models

	Main models & related empirical studies	Treatment of LGD	Relationship between RR and PD
First generation structural-form models	Merton (1974), Black and Cox (1976), Geske (1977), Vasicek (1984)	PD and RR are a function of the structural characteristics of the firm. RR is therefore an endogenous variable.	PD and RR are inversely related.
Second generation structural-form models	Kim, Ramaswamy, and Sundaresan (1993), Nielsen, Saà-Requejo, and Santa-Clara (1993), Hull and White (1995), Longstaff and Schwartz (1995).	RR is exogenous and independent from the firm's asset value.	RR is generally defined as a fixed ratio of the outstanding debt value and is therefore independent from PD.
Reduced-form models	Litterman and Iben (1991), Madan and Unal (1995), Jarrow and Turnbull (1995), Jarrow and Turnbull (1995), Lando (1998), Duffie and Singleton (1999), Duffie (1998), Duffie (1999).	Reduced-form models assume an exogenous RR that is either a constant or a stochastic variable independent from PD.	Reduced-form models introduce separate assumptions on the dynamic of PD and RR, which are modelled independently from the structural features of the firm.
Latest contributions on the PD–RR relationship	Frye (2000a and 2000b), Jarrow (2001), Carey and Gordy (2003), Altman, Resti, and Sironi (2002) (Altman et al. 2003/2005), Acharya, Bharath, and Srinivasan (2007), Miu and Ozdemir (2006).	Both PD and RR are stochastic variables which depend on a common systematic risk factor (the state of the economy).	PD and RR are negatively correlated. In the 'macroeconomic approach' this derives from the common dependence on one single systematic factor. In the 'microeconomic approach' it derives from the supply and demand of defaulted securities. Industry health is also a major factor. Downturn LGD studies.
Credit value at risk models			
CreditMetrics®	Gupton, Finger, and Bhatia (1997).	Stochastic variable (beta distr.)	RR independent from PD
CreditPortfolioView®	Wilson (1998).	Stochastic variable	RR independent from PD
CreditRisk+©	Credit Suisse Financial Products (1997).	Constant	RR independent from PD
PortfolioManager®	McQuown (1997), Crosbie (1999).	Stochastic variable	RR independent from PD

through adequate portfolio diversification. This assumption strongly contrasts with the growing empirical evidence—showing a negative correlation between default and recovery rates—that has been reported above in this chapter and in other empirical studies. This evidence indicates that recovery risk is a systematic risk component. As such, it should attract risk premia and should adequately be considered in credit risk management applications.

Empirical results, especially demonstrated by historical record high levels of recovery in the extreme benign credit environment of 2004–7 and then the opposite credit market turmoil and high-defaulted, low-recovery environment of 2009, show the potential cyclical impact as well as the supply and demand elements of defaults and recoveries on LGD. Finally, we feel that the microeconomic/financial attributes of an individual issuer of bonds or loans combined with the market's aggregate supply and demand conditions can best explain the recovery rate at default on a particular defaulting issue. An even greater challenge is to accurately estimate the ultimate recovery rate on individual issue as well as aggregate recoveries when the firm emerges from its restructuring.

References

Acharya, V., Bharath, S., and Srinivasan, A. (2007). 'Does industry-wide distress affect defaulted firms? Evidence from creditor recoveries'. *Journal of Financial Economics*, 85/3: 787–821.

Altman, E. I. (1989). 'Measuring corporate bond mortality and performance'. *Journal of Finance*, 44: 909–22.

——(2007). 'Global debt markets in 2007: new paradigm or great credit bubble'. *Journal of Applied Corporate Finance* (Summer), 17–31.

——and Eberhart, A. (1994). 'Do seniority provisions protect bondholders' investments?' *Journal of Portfolio Management* (Summer), 67–75.

——Haldeman, R., and Narayanan, P. (1977). 'ZETA analysis: a new model to identify bankruptcy risk of corporations'. *Journal of Banking & Finance*, 1/1: 29–54.

——and Karlin, B. (2009). 'Defaults and returns in the high-yield bond market and market outlook: 2009 first-half report'. NYU Salomon Center, Stern School of Business, Aug.

——————and Kishore, V. M. (1996). 'Almost everything you wanted to know about recoveries on defaulted bonds'. *Financial Analysts Journal*, (Nov./Dec.), 57–64.

——Resti, A., and Sironi, A. (2002). *Analyzing and Explaining Default Recovery Rates*. ISDA Research Report, London, Dec.

————(2006). 'Default recovery rates: a review of the literature and recent empirical evidence'. *Journal of Finance Literature* (Winter), 21–45.

——Brady, B., Resti, A., and Sironi, A. (2003/2005). 'The link between default and recovery rates: theory, empirical evidence and implications'. NYU Salomon Center Working Paper Series # S-03-4 (2003), and *Journal of Business* (Nov. 2005), 78/6: 2203–27.

Araten, M., Jacobs. M., and Varshny, P. (2004). 'Measuring LGD on commercial loans'. *The RMA Journal* (May).

Asarnow, E., and Edwards, D. (1995). 'Measuring loss on defaulted bank loans: a 24 year study'. *Journal of Commercial Bank Lending*, 77/1: 11–23.

Bakshi, G., Madan, D., and Zhang, F. (2001). 'Understanding the role of recovery in default risk models: empirical comparisons and implied recovery rates'. *Finance and Economics Discussion Series*, 2001-37, Federal Reserve Board of Governors, Washington, DC.

Basel Committee on Banking Supervision (2003). 'The new Basel Capital Accord'. Consultative Document, Bank for International Settlements, (Apr.).

Basel Commission on Bank Regulation (2004). 'International convergence on capital measurement and capital standards'. BIS (June).

—— (2005). 'Guidance on paragraph 468 of the Framework Document'. BIS (July).

Black, F., and Cox, J. C. (1976). 'Valuing corporate securities: some effects of bond indenture provisions'. *Journal of Finance*, 31: 351–67.

—— and Scholes, M (1973). 'The pricing of options and corporate liabilities'. *Journal of Political Economics*. (May), 637–59.

Carey, M., and Gordy, M. (2003). 'Systematic risk in recoveries on defaulted debt'. Mimeo, Federal Reserve Board, Washington, DC.

Chabane, A., Laurent, J.-P., and Salomon, J. (2004). 'Double impact: credit risk assessment and collateral value'. *Revue Finance*, 25: 157–78.

Credit Suisse Financial Products (1997). *CreditRisk+©. A Credit Risk Management Framework*. Technical document.

Crosbie, P. J. (1999). 'Modeling default risk', mimeo, KMV Corporation, San Francisco.

Crouhy, M., Galai, D., and Mark, R. (2000). 'A comparative analysis of current credit risk models'. *Journal of Banking & Finance*, 24: 59–117.

Das, S., and Hanonna, P. (2006). 'Implied recovery'. University of Santa Clara working paper (July).

Duffee, G. R. (1999). 'Estimating the price of default risk'. *Review of Financial Studies*, 12/1: 197–225.

Duffie, D. (1998). 'Defaultable term structure models with fractional recovery of par'. Graduate School of Business, Stanford University, CA.

—— and Lando, D. (2000). 'Term structure of credit spreads with incomplete accounting information'. *Econometrica*.

—— and Singleton, K. J. (1999). 'Modeling the term structures of defaultable bonds'. *Review of Financial Studies*, 12: 687–720.

Dullman, K., and Trapp, M. (2004). 'Systematic risk in recovery rates: an empirical analysis of U.S. corporate credit exposures'. EFWA Basel paper.

Eales, R., and Bosworth, E. (1998). 'Severity of loss in the event of default in small business and large consumer loans'. *Journal of Lending and Credit Risk management* (May), 58–65.

—— Cantor, R., and Avner, R. (2004). 'Recovery rates on North American syndicated bank loans, 1989–2003'. Moody's Investors Service (Mar.).

Emery, K. (2003). 'Moody's loan default database as of November 2003'. Moody's Investors Service, December.

Eom, Y. H., Helwege, J., and Huang, J. (2001). 'Structural models of corporate bond pricing: an empirical analysis'. Mimeo.

Finger, C. (1999). *Conditional Approaches for CreditMetrics® Portfolio Distributions*. CreditMetrics® Monitor (Apr.).

Franks, J., and Torous, W. (1994). 'A comparison of financial recontracting in distressed exchanges and Chapter 11 reorganizations'. *Journal of Financial Economics*, 35: 349–70.

Fridson, M. S., Garman, C. M., and Okashima, K. (2000). 'Recovery rates: the search for meaning'. Merrill Lynch & Co., High Yield Strategy.

Frye, J. (2000a). 'Collateral damage'. *Risk* (Apr.) 91–4.

——(2000b). 'Collateral Damage Detected', Federal Reserve Bank of Chicago, Working Paper, *Emerging Issues Series* (Oct.), 1–14.

——(2000c). 'Depressing recoveries'. *Risk* (Nov.).

Geske, R. (1977). 'The valuation of corporate liabilities as compound options'. *Journal of Financial and Quantitative Analysis*, 12: 541–52.

Gordy, M. (2000). 'A comparative anatomy of credit risk models'. *Journal of Banking and Finance* (Jan.), 119–49.

Gupton, G., Finger, C., and Bhatia, M. (1997). *CreditMetrics*[TM]*—Technical Document*. JPMorgan & Co., New York.

——Gates, D., and Carty, L. V. (2000). 'Bank loan loss given default'. Moody's Investors Service, Global Credit Research (Nov.).

——and Stein, R. M. (2002). 'LossCalc: Moody's model for predicting loss given default (LGD)', Moody's KMV, New York.

Hamilton, D. T., Gupton, G. M., and Berthault, A. (2001). 'Default and recovery rates of corporate bond issuers: 2000'. Moody's Investors Service, (Feb.).

Hu, Y.-T., and Perraudin, W (2002). 'The dependence of recovery rates and defaults'. Birk-Beck College, mimeo (Feb.) and CEPR Working Paper.

Hull, J. (1997). *Options, Futures and Other Derivative Securities*. Englewood Cliffs, NJ: Prentice-Hall.

——and White, A. (1995). 'The impact of default risk on the prices of options and other derivative securities'. *Journal of Banking and Finance*, 19: 299–322.

Jarrow, R. A. (2001).'Default parameter estimation using market prices'. *Financial Analysts Journal*, 57/5: 75–92.

——Lando, D., and Turnbull, S. M. (1997). 'A Markov model for the term structure of credit risk spreads'. *Review of Financial Studies*, 10: 481–523.

——and Turnbull, S. M. (1995). 'Pricing derivatives on financial securities subject to credit risk'. *Journal of Finance*, 50: 53–86.

Jones, E., Mason, S., and Rosenfeld, E. (1984). 'Contingent claims analysis of corporate capital structures: an empirical investigation'. *Journal of Finance*, 39: 611–27.

Jokivuolle, E., and Peura, S. (2003). 'A model for estimating recovery rates and collateral haircuts for bank loans'. *European Financial Management*.

Keisman, D. (2004). 'Ultimate recovery rates on bank loan and bond defaults'. S&P *Loss Stats*.

——and Marshella, T. (2009). 'Recoveries on defaulted debt in an era of black swans'. Moody's Global Corporate Finance, Moody's Investments Service (June).

Kim, I. J., Ramaswamy, K., and Sundaresan, S. (1993). 'Does default risk in coupons affect the valuation of corporate bonds? A contingent claims model'. *Financial Management*, 22/3: 117–31.

Lando, D. (1998). 'On Cox processes and credit risky securities'. *Review of Derivatives Research*, 2: 99–120.

Litterman, R., and Iben, T. (1991). 'Corporate bond valuation and the term structure of credit spreads'. *Financial Analysts Journal* (Spring), 52–64.

Liu, S., Lu, J. C., Kolpin, D. W., and Meeker, W. Q. (1997). 'Analysis of environmental data with censored observations'. *Environmental Science & Technology*, 31.

Longstaff, F. A., and Schwartz, E. S. (1995). 'A simple approach to valuing risky fixed and floating rate debt'. *Journal of Finance*, 50: 789–819.

Madan, D., and Unal, H. (1995). 'Pricing the risks of default'. *Review of Derivatives Research*, 2: 121–60.

Merton, R. C. (1974). 'On the pricing of corporate debt: the risk structure of interest rates'. *Journal of Finance*, 2: 449–71.

Miu, P., and Ozdemir, B. (2006). 'Basel requirements of downturn loss-given-default: modeling and estimating probability of default and LGD correlations'. *Journal of Credit Risk*, 2/2: 43–68.

Neto de Carvalho, C., and Dermine, J (2003). 'Bank loan losses-given-default: empirical evidence'.Working paper, INSEAD.

Nielsen, L. T., Saà-Requejo, J., and Pedro Santa-Clara, P. (1993). 'Default risk and interest rate risk: the term structure of default spreads'. Working paper, INSEAD.

Pan, J., and Singleton, K. (2005). 'Default and recovery implicit in the term structure of sovereign CDS spreads', Working paper, Stanford University, CA.

Pykhtin, M. (2003). 'Unexpected Recovery Risk', *Risk*, 16: 74–8.

Renault, O., and Scaillet, O. (2003). 'On the way to recovery: a nonparametric bias free estimation of recovery rate densities'. *Journal of Banking and Finance*.

Resti, A. (2002). *The New Basel Capital Accord: Structure, Possible Changes, Micro- and Macroeconomic Effects*. Brussels: Centre for European Policy Studies.

Saikat, N. (1998). 'Valuation models for default-risky securities: an overview'. Federal Reserve Bank of Atlanta, *Economic Review*, Fourth Quarter.

Schleifer, A., and Vishny, R. (1992). 'Liquidation values and debt capacity: a market equilibrium approach.' *Journal of Finance*, 47: 1343–66.

Schuermann, T. (2004). 'What do we know about loss given default?' Working paper, Federal Reserve Bank of New York, also in D. Shimko (ed.), *Credit Risk Models and Management*, 2nd edn., London, Risk Books (2006).

Van de Castle, K., and Keisman, D. (1999). 'Suddenly structure mattered: insights into recoveries of defaulted debt'. *S&P Corporate Ratings* (24 May).

Varma, P., Cantor, R., and Hamilton, D. (2003). 'Recovery rates on defaulted corporate bonds and preferred stocks', Moody's Investors Service, (Dec.).

Vasicek, O. A. (1984). *Credit Valuation*. KMV Corporation (Mar.).

Verde, M. (2003). 'Recovery rates return to historic norms'. FITCH ratings (Sept.).

Wilson, T. C. (1998). 'Portfolio credit risk'. Federal Reserve Board of New York, *Economic Policy Review* (Oct.), 71–82.

Zhou, C. (2001). 'The term structure of credit spreads with jump risk'. *Journal of Banking & Finance*, 25: 2015–40.

CHAPTER 4

A GUIDE TO MODELLING CREDIT TERM STRUCTURES

ARTHUR M. BERD

1 INTRODUCTION

Most of fixed income valuation and risk methodologies are centred on modelling yield and spread term structures. The main reason for this is that the vast majority of debt instruments exhibit very high correlation of price returns. Therefore the common pricing factors encoded in the yield curve have a high explanatory power. This is especially true for Treasury bonds, where the market is extremely efficient and any deviation of individual bond valuation from the common curve is quickly arbitraged away.

For corporate bonds the common yield curves are much less binding, since the market is substantially less liquid, even for investment grade benchmark issuers. The other driving factors of the valuation of credit-risky bonds are the credit quality of the name, the estimated recovery in case of default, geographic and industry as well as the issuer and security specifics.

The standard market practice in analysing investment grade credit bonds is to introduce the notion of spread to base (Treasury or swaps) curve. The sector or issuer spread curves are thought to reflect the additional specific information besides the underlying base yield curve. Among many definitions of spread measures used by practitioners who analyse credit bonds the most robust and consistent one is the

I would like to thank my collaborators Roy Mashal and Peili Wang with whom much of the presented methodology was implemented while the author was at Lehman Brothers, as well as Marco Naldi, Mark Howard, and many other colleagues at (formerly) Lehman Brothers Fixed Income Research department for numerous helpful discussions.

OAS (option-adjusted spread), also known as the Z-spread in case of bonds with no embedded options (in the sequel we use these terms interchangeably).

While the Z-spread term structures are commonly used to quote and analyse relative value among credit bonds, it is well known that these measures become inadequate for distressed credits for which the market convention reverts to quoting bond prices rather than spreads. This market convention reflects a fundamental flaw in the conventional credit valuation methodology, namely the assumption that a credit bond can be priced as a portfolio of cash flows discounted at a risky rate. The reason why this assumption is wrong is that the credit-risky bonds do not have fixed cash flows, and in fact their cash flows are variable and dependent on the future default risk even if contractually fixed. This methodological breakdown holds for any credits, whether investment grade, or distressed, with the errors being relatively small for investment grade bonds trading near par but growing rapidly with the rise in default risk expectations.

We develop an alternative valuation methodology and introduce new definitions of credit term structures that are consistent with the valuation of bonds for all credit risk levels. We propose an efficient and robust empirical estimation procedure for these new measures of credit risk and show examples of fitted credit term structures for both low and high default risk cases. The resulting relative value measures may differ from conventional ones not only quantitatively but also qualitatively—possibly even reversing the sign of rich/cheap signals and altering the composition of relative value trades.

The current methodology has been implemented within Lehman Brothers (now Barclays Capital) quantitative credit toolkit since 2003 (see Berd, Mashal, and Wang (2003, 2004b, 2004a)) and has been used by many investors focusing both on cash bonds and credit derivatives since then. It successfully stood the test of extreme stress during the recent credit crisis, while the conventional credit measures have become unusable. We hope that this experience will lead to the proposed methodology gaining in acceptance and that this review will help investors, traders, and researchers to become familiar with it and use it in daily practice.

2 THE CONVENTIONAL TERM STRUCTURE MEASURES

In this section we re-examine critically the standard lore of credit bond valuation methodologies in order to understand better their breakdown in case of distressed bonds which we mentioned in the Introduction. For a more detailed reference on the standard fixed income valuation methodology see Tuckman (2002).

2.1 The strippable cash flow valuation methodology

The main assumption of the strippable cash flow valuation methodology is that fixed-coupon debt instruments can be priced as a portfolio of N individual cash flows $CF(t_i)$ using the discount function $Z(t_i)$, which coincides with the present value of a zero coupon bond maturing at some future time t_i as observed today. This conclusion follows immediately from the assumption that the cash flows are completely fixed in all future states of the world, and therefore a portfolio of zero coupon bonds with maturities chosen to match the contractual cash flow payment dates and the notional chosen to equal the cash flow payment amounts will indeed provide a complete replication of the bond in all future states of the world, and therefore the present value of this portfolio should coincide with the present value of the bond:

$$PV_{bond} = PV\left\{\sum_{i=1}^{N} CF(t_i)\right\}$$

$$= \sum_{i=1}^{N} CF(t_i)\, PV\left\{1(t_i)\right\}$$

$$= \sum_{i=1}^{N} CF(t_i)\, Z(t_i) \tag{1}$$

Such an assumption is clearly valid for default risk-free instruments such as US Treasury bonds which can be contractually stripped, separating their coupon and notional cash flows. The Treasury strips trade in a liquid market and are often referenced for an estimation of the fair value discount term structure.

The strippable cash flow methodology is commonly extended to credit-risky bonds by assuming that they can be priced using a similarly defined 'risky discount function' $Z_{risky}(T)$. Since the pricing equation (1) is deterministic, one can express the risky discount function without loss of generality as a product of the risk-free base discount function and the risky excess discount function:

$$Z_{risky}(t) = Z_{base}(t)\, Z_{excess}(t) \tag{2}$$

Thus, in the conventional strippable cash flow methodology the fundamental pricing equation for a credit-risky bond reads as follows:

$$PV_{bond} = \sum_{i=1}^{N} CF(t_i)\, Z_{base}(t_i)\, Z_{excess}(t_i) \tag{3}$$

Let us express the same in plain language: *The present value of a contractually fixed cash flow security under a strippable cash flows valuation framework is equal to the sum of the present values of the individual cash flows.*

In other words, the conventional valuation methodology hinges on the ability to represent a fixed-income security as a portfolio of individual cash flows. Whether or not such a representation is possible for credit bonds, and what discount function applies if it is, depends on the realities of the market, and will be discussed in section 3.

2.2 The conventional bond yield and spread measures

In conventional approach the modelling of credit bonds centres on defining various spread measures to relevant base yield curves, which can be the Treasury curve or the swaps curve. We give only a cursory definition of the base curve for completeness of exposition, and refer the reader to Tuckman (2002) for details on the methodologies for defining and estimating base curve, and to O'Kane and Sen (2005) for conventional spread measures.

2.2.1 Risk-free bonds

Before proceeding to the case of credit-risky bonds, let us first define the term structure metrics used for pricing risk-free bonds. A convenient parameterization of the base discount function $Z(t)$ is given by the term structure of zero-coupon interest rates $r(t)$ in a continuous compounding convention:

$$Z(t) = e^{-r(t)t} \tag{4}$$

In this definition, the interest rates $r(t)$ correspond to pricing of zero-coupon risk-free bonds, as can be seen from equation (1), for which there is only a single unit cash flow at time t. One could express these rates in some fractional compounding frequency, such as annual or semi-annual, however given that there is no particular frequency tied to the coupon payments, it is more convenient to use the continuous compounding as in (4).

In a dynamic context, one can define a stochastic process for the short rate r_t, such that the expected discount function $Z(T)$ is the expected value of the unit amount payable at time T, with stochastic discount Z_t given by the compounded short-term rates along each possible future realization:

$$Z(t) = E_{t=0} \{Z_t\} = E_{t=0} \left\{ e^{-\int_0^t r_s \, ds} \right\} \tag{5}$$

Note the notational difference between $r(t)$ and $Z(t)$ which are deterministic functions of a finite maturity t measured at the initial time, and the stochastic processes r_t and Z_t denoting the value of the random variable at future time t. We will use the subscripts to denote the time dependence of stochastic processes, and function notation for deterministic variables of term to maturity.

A useful counterpart of the interest rate for finite maturity t is the forward rate which is defined as the breakeven future discounting rate between time t and $t + dt$.

$$\frac{Z(t + dt)}{Z(t)} = e^{-f(t) \, dt} \tag{6}$$

The relationships between the discount function, forward rate, and zero-coupon interest rate (in continuous compounding) can be summarized as follows:

$$f(t) = -\frac{\partial}{\partial t} \log Z(t) \tag{7}$$

$$r(t) = -\frac{1}{t} \int_0^t f(s)ds \tag{8}$$

One can follow the celebrated HJM (Heath, Jarrow, and Morton (1992)) approach to define the stochastic process for forward rates, and use the identity $r_t = f_t(t)$ to derive the expected discount function as in eq. (5). While this is certainly one of the mainstream approaches in modelling risk-free interest rates, it is less often used to model credit and we will not discuss it at length in this chapter.

Another often used metric is the yield to maturity $y(t)$. In a compounding convention with frequency q periods per annum, the standard pricing equation for a fixed-coupon bond is:

$$PV_{bond} = \sum_{i=1}^{N} \frac{C/q}{(1 + y/q)^{q\,t_i}} + \frac{1}{(1 + y/q)^{q\,t_N}} \tag{9}$$

Given a present value of a bond (including its accrued coupon), one can determine the yield to maturity from eq. (9). Of course, one must remember that unlike the term structure of interest rates $r(t)$, the yield to maturity $y(T)$ depends on the specific bond with its coupon and maturity. In particular, one cannot apply the yield to maturity obtained from a five-year bond with 4.5% coupon to value the fifth year cash flow of a ten-year bond with 5.5% coupon. In other words, the yield to maturity is not a metric that is consistent with a strippable discounted cash flow valuation methodology, because it forces one to treat all the coupons and the notional payment as inseparable under eq. (9).

In contrast, the zero-coupon interest rate $r(t)$ is well suited for fitting across all cash flows of all comparable risk-free bonds, Treasury strips, etc., with a result being a universal fair value term structure that can be used to price any appropriate cash flows. Therefore, we will primarily rely in this report on the definition (4) for the base discount function.

2.2.2 Bullet bonds: yield spread

The simplest credit-risky bonds have a 'bullet' structure, with a fixed coupon and the entire notional payable at maturity. Such bonds are free of amortizing notional payments, coupon resets, and embedded options, which could complicate the cash flow picture. Fortunately for the modellers, the bullet bonds represent the majority of investment grade credit bond market and therefore their modelling is not just an academic exercise.

The simplest (and naive) approach to valuing a credit bond is to apply the same yield-to-maturity methodology as for the risk-free bonds (9):

$$PV_{bond} = \sum_{i=1}^{N} \frac{C/q}{(1+Y/q)^{qt_i}} + \frac{1}{(1+Y/q)^{qt_N}} \tag{10}$$

The corresponding risky yield to maturity $Y(T)$ is then often compared with the yield to maturity of a benchmark reference Treasury bond $y(T)$ which is usually chosen to be close to the credit bond's maturity $T = t_N$. The associated spread measure is called the yield spread (to maturity):

$$S_Y(T) = Y(T) - y(T) \tag{11}$$

Since the benchmark Treasury bonds are often selected among the most liquid ones (recent issue 2, 5, 7, 10, or 30 year bonds), the maturity mismatch in defining the yield spread can be quite substantial. A slightly improved version of the yield spread is the so-called interpolated spread, or I-spread. Instead of using a single benchmark Treasury bond, it refers to a pair of bonds whose maturities bracket the maturity of the credit bond under consideration. Suppose the index 1 refers to the Treasury bond with a shorter maturity, and the index 2 refers to the one with longer maturity. The linearly interpolated I-spread is then defined as:

$$S_I(T) = Y(T) - \left(\frac{T_2 - T}{T_2 - T_1} y(T_1) + \frac{T - T_1}{T_2 - T_1} y(T_2) \right) \tag{12}$$

We emphasize that the yield spread (or the I-spread) measure for credit bonds calculated in such a manner is rather useless and can be very misleading. The reason is that it ignores a whole host of important aspects of bond pricing, such as the shape of the term structure of yields, the coupon and price level, the cash flow uncertainty of credit bonds, etc. We shall discuss these limitations in the latter parts of this chapter. For now, it suffices to say that even if one ignores the intricate details of credit risk, the yield spread is still not a good measure, and can be substantially improved upon.

2.2.3 Bullet bonds: Z-spread

As we noted in eq. (3), under the assumption of strippable cash flows, the pricing adjustment for a credit bond is contained within an excess discount function. This function can be expressed in terms of the Z-spread $S_Z(t)$:

$$Z_{excess}(t) = e^{-S_Z(t)t} \tag{13}$$

Note, that unlike the yield and spread to maturity, the Z-spread is tied only to the discount function, which in turn is assumed to be a universal measure for valuing all cash flows with similar maturity for the same credit, not just those of the particular bond under consideration. The corresponding risky discounting rate is consequently defined as:

$$R(t) = r(t) + S_Z(t) \tag{14}$$

such that the total risky discount function is related to the risky yield in the same manner as the risk-free discount function is to risk-free zero-coupon yield, and the strippable cash flow valuation framework (3) is assumed to hold:

$$Z_{risky}(t) = e^{-R(t)t} \tag{15}$$

As we shall argue in section 3, this assumption is, in fact, explicitly violated by actual credit market conventions and practices. However, Z-spread does remain moderately useful for high grade credit bonds which have very low projected default probability. Therefore, we encourage its use as a short-cut measure, but urge analysts to remember its limitations.

Similarly to the definition of the forward risk-free interest rates (7), one can define the forward risky rates $F(t)$ and forward Z-spreads $S_F(t)$:

$$F(t) = -\frac{\partial}{\partial t} \log Z_{risky}(t) \tag{16}$$

$$R(t) = -\frac{1}{t} \int_0^t F(s)ds \tag{17}$$

$$S_F(t) = -\frac{\partial}{\partial t} \log Z_{excess}(t) \tag{18}$$

$$S_Z(t) = -\frac{1}{t} \int_0^t S_F(s)ds \tag{19}$$

We will see from subsequent discussion that the forward Z-spread $S_F(t)$ has a particular meaning in reduced form models with so-called fractional recovery of market value, relating it to the hazard rate of the exogenous default process. This fundamental meaning is lost, however, under more realistic recovery assumptions.

2.2.4 Callable/puttable bonds: option-adjusted spread (OAS)

For bonds with embedded options, the most widely used valuation measure is the option-adjusted spread. The OAS can be precisely defined for risk-free callable/puttable bonds and allows one to disaggregate the value of an embedded option from the relative valuation of the bond's cash flows compared to the bullet bond case.

One way to define the OAS is to explicitly define the stochastic model for the short rates process r_t to value the embedded option, and to assume that the risk-free interest rate in this model is bumped up or down by a constant amount across all future times, such that after discounting the variable bond plus option cash flows CF_t with the total interest rate $r_t + OAS$ one gets the market observed present value of the bond.

$$PV_{bond} = E_{t=0}\left\{ \sum_{t=0}^{T} CF_t \, e^{-\sum_{u=0}^{t}(r_u + OAS)dt} \right\} \tag{20}$$

Note that this definition does not necessarily coincide with an alternative assumption where one adds a constant OAS to the initial term structure of interest rates.

Whether such initial constant will translate into a constant shift of future stochastic rates $r_0(t) + OAS \rightarrow r_t + OAS$, depends on the details of the short rate process. Generally speaking, only processes which are linear in r_t will preserve such a relationship, while frequently used lognormal or square-root processes will not.

The relationship between the OAS and Z-spread becomes clear if one assumes a zero volatility of interest rates in equation (20). In this case, the evolution of the short rate r_t becomes a deterministic function $r_t = f(t)$, and the random cash flows reduce to the deterministic cash flows 'to worst' $CF_w(t)$, as only one of the many embedded options (including maturity) will be the deepest in the money. Thus, under this assumption, the OAS coincides with the Z-spread calculated for the 'to worst' cash flow scenario— the 'Z' in Z-spread stands for *zero volatility*.

The discounted value of 'to worst' cash flows reflects the intrinsic value of the embedded option. Therefore, the difference between the full *OAS* calculated from (20) under stochastic interest rates and the Z-spread calculated under zero volatility assumption reflects the time value of the embedded option, plus any security-specific pricing premia, if any.

The base curve used for both OAS and Z-spread calculation is usually chosen to be the swaps curve, such that the base rate plus OAS resemble a realistic reinvestment rate for bond cash flows. While it is possible to use any other base discount curve, such as a Treasury zero-coupon rate term structure, the meaning of the OAS in those cases will be altered to include both security-specific and funding risks.

2.2.5 *Floating rate notes: discount margin*

The Floating Rate Notes (FRN) structure greatly mitigates market risk, insulating these securities from the market-wide interest rate fluctuations. The credit risk, however, still remains and the conventional methodology applies the additional discount spread to value the variable future cash flows. These variable cash flows are typically tied to the LIBOR-based index, such as three-month or twelve-month LIBOR rate, with a contractually specified additional *quoted margin*:

$$CF_i^{FRN} = L(t_i) + QM + 1_{\{t_i = t_N\}} \tag{21}$$

where $L(t_i)$ is the future LIBOR rate fixing valid for the period including the payment time t_i, and we have added an explicit term for the final principal payment.

In a conventional approach, instead of the unknown future rate $L(t_i)$ one takes the forward LIBOR rate $L(t_{i-1}, t_i)$ estimated for the reset time t_{i-1} and a forward tenor $\Delta_i = t_i - t_{i-1}$ until the next payment date, and thus reduces the valuation problem to a deterministic (zero volatility) one. Having projected these deterministic future cash flows, one can then proceed to value them with a discount curve whose rate is given by the same forward LIBOR rates with an added spread amount called *zero discount margin*.

$$PV_{bond} = \sum_{i=1}^{N} CF_i^{FRN} Z_{float}(t_i)$$

$$Z_{float}(t_i) = \prod_{i=1}^{N} \frac{1}{1 + \Delta_i \left(L(t_{i-1}, t_i) + DM \right)} \qquad (22)$$

The difference between the zero discount margin DM and the quoted margin QM reflects the potential non-par valuation of the credit-risky FRN which is due to changing default and recovery risks since the issuance. If the credit risk remained stable (and neglecting the possible term structure effects), the zero discount margin would be identical to the original issue quoted margin, and the FRN would be valued at par on the corresponding reset date. Unlike this, in case of a fixed coupon bond the price can differ from par even if the credit risk remains unchanged, solely due to interest rate changes or yield curve roll-down.

3 THE PHENOMENOLOGY OF CREDIT PRICING

3.1 Credit bond cash flows reconsidered

The root of the problem with the conventional strippable cash flow methodology as applied to credit-risky bonds is that credit bonds do not have fixed cash flows. Indeed, the main difference between a credit-risky bond and a credit risk-free one is precisely the possibility that the issuer might default and not honour the contractual cash flows of the bond. In this event, even if the contractual cash flows were fixed, the realized cash flows might be very different from the promised ones.

Once we realize this fundamental fact, it becomes clear that the validity of the representation of a credit bond as a portfolio of cash flows critically depends on our assumption of the cash flows in case of default. In reality, when an issuer defaults, it enters into often protracted bankruptcy proceedings during which various creditors including bondholders, bank lenders, and those with trading and other claims on the assets of the company settle with the trustees of the company and the bankruptcy court judge the priority of payments and manner in which those payments are to be obtained.

Of course, modelling such an idiosyncratic process is hopelessly beyond our reach. Fortunately, however, this is not necessary. Once an issuer defaults or declares bankruptcy its bonds trade in a fairly efficient distressed market and quickly settle at what the investors expect is the fair value of the possible recovery.

The efficiency of the distressed market and the accuracy and speed with which it zooms in on the recovery value is particularly high in the US, as evidenced by many studies (see Gupton and Stein (2002) and references therein). Assuming that the price of the bond immediately after default represents the fair value of the subsequent ultimate recovery cash flows, we can simply take that price as the single post-recovery cash flow which substitutes all remaining contractual cash flows of the bond.

The market practice is to use the price approximately one month after the credit event to allow for a period during which the investors find out the extent of the issuer's outstanding liabilities and remaining assets. This practice is also consistent with the conventions of the credit derivatives market, where the recovery value for purposes of cash settlement of CDS is obtained by a dealer poll within approximately one month after the credit event.

From a modelling perspective, using the recovery value after default as a replacement cash flow scenario is a well-established approach. However, the specific assumptions about the recovery value itself differ among both academics and practitioners. We will discuss these in detail in the next section as we develop a valuation framework for credit bonds. But first we would like to explore a few general aspects of credit bond valuation that will set the stage for an intuitive understanding of the formal methodology we present later in this chapter.

3.2 The implications of risky cash flows

The relevance of the uncertain cash flows of credit-risky bonds depends on the likelihood of the scenarios under which the fixed contractual cash flows may be altered. In other words, it depends on the level of default probability.[1] As we will find out shortly, what one has to consider here is not the real-world (forecasted) default probability, but the so-called implied (or break-even) default probability.

One of the most striking examples of the mis-characterization of credit bonds by the conventional spread measures is the often cited steeply inverted spread curve for distressed bonds. One frequently hears explanations for this phenomenon based on the belief that the near-term risks in distressed issuers are greater than the longer-term ones which is supposedly the reason why the near-term spreads are higher than the long maturity ones. However, upon closer examination one can see that the inverted spread curve is largely an 'optical' phenomenon due to a chosen definition of the spread measure such as the Z-spread rather than a reflection of the inherent risks and returns of the issuer's securities.

Indeed, the more important phenomenon in reality is that once the perceived credit risk of an issuer becomes high enough, the market begins to price the default scenario. In particular, investors recognize what is known in the distressed debt markets as the

---

[1] Strictly speaking, one must also consider the possibility of debt restructuring as another scenario where the contractually fixed cash flows will be altered. Assuming that such restructuring is done in a manner which does not change the present value of the debt (otherwise either the debtors or the company will prefer the bankruptcy option) one can argue that its effect on valuing credit bonds should be negligible. Of course, in practice the restructurings are often done in a situation where either the bondholders or the company is in a weak negotiating position, thereby leading to a non-trivial transfer of value in the process. We shall ignore this possibility in the present study.

acceleration of debt clause in case of default. The legal covenants on most traded bonds are such that, regardless of the initial maturity of the bond, if the issuer defaults on any of its debt obligations, all of the outstanding debt becomes due immediately. This is an important market practice designed to make sure that, in case of bankruptcy, investor interests can be pooled together by their seniority class for the purposes of the bankruptcy resolution process. As a result, both short and long maturity bonds begin trading at similar dollar prices—leading to a flat term structure of prices.

Let us now analyse how this translates into a term structure of Z-spreads. In the conventional spread-discount based methodology, one can explain an $80 price of a twenty-year bond with a spread of 500bp. However, to explain an $80 price for a five-year bond, one would need to raise the spread to very large levels in order to achieve the required discounting effect. The resulting term structure of spreads becomes downward sloping, or inverted. The inversion of the spread curve is due to the bonds trading on price, which is strongly dependent on the expected recovery, while the Z-spread methodology does not take recoveries into account at all!

In the survival-based methodology, which we describe in this chapter, the low prices of bonds are explained by high default rates, which need not have an inverted term structure. A flat or even an upward sloping term structure of default rates can lead to an inverted Z-spread term structure if the level of the default rates is high enough. This is not to say that the near-term perceived credit risks are never higher than the longer-term ones—just that one cannot make such a conclusion based on the inverted Z-spread term structure alone.

Consider for example the credit term structure of Ford Motor Co. as of 31 December 2002 shown in Figure 4.1. The default hazard rate is fitted using the survival-based methodology developed later in this chapter, and is upward sloping with a hump at fifteen-year range. However, the Z-spread curve fitted using the conventional methodology which does not take into account the potential variability of cash flows, is clearly inverted.

Figure 4.2 shows the Z-spread, Credit Default Swap (CDS), and the bond-implied CDS (BCDS, defined in section 6.5 below) term structures of Ford for the same date. From the figure it is clear that investors who looked at the Z-spread term structure and compared it to the cost of protection available via the CDS market, would have been misled to think that there was a small positive basis between the two, i.e. that the CDS traded wider by roughly 20 bp than bonds across most maturities, with the shape of the curve following closely the shape of the Z-spread curve with the exception of less than two-year maturities. In fact, if one had used the methodology presented in this chapter and derived the BCDS term structure and compared it with the market quotes, one would see a very different picture—the bond market traded more than 50 bp tighter than CDS at short maturities and more than 50 bp wider at maturities greater than five years, if measured on an apples-to-apples basis.

Both the bonds and the CDS of Ford Motor Credit are among the most liquid and widely traded instruments in the US credit market and these differences are clearly not a reflection of market inefficiency but rather of the difference between the

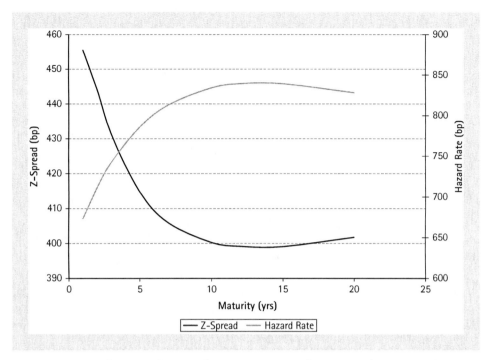

FIGURE 4.1 Optically inverted Z-spread term structure. Ford Motor Credit, 31 December 2002.

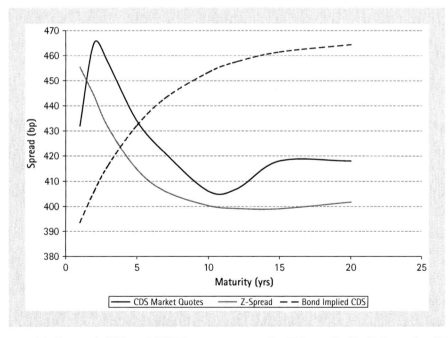

FIGURE 4.2 Z-spread, CDS, and BCDS term structures. Ford Motor Credit, 31 December 2002.

methodologies. Only for the very short-term exposures, where investors are forced to focus critically on the likelihood of the default scenarios and the fair value of the protection with a full account for cash flow outcomes do we see the CDS market diverging in shape from the cash market's optically distorted perception of the credit spreads.

4 THE SURVIVAL-BASED VALUATION OF CREDIT-RISKY SECURITIES

In this section we outline the credit valuation methodology which follows an assumption, known as the *reduced form framework*, that while the default risk is measurable and anticipated by the market, the timing of the actual event of the default is exogenous and unpredictable. This assumption critically differs from a more fundamental approach taken in *structural models* of credit risk (Merton 1974), and where not only the level of default risk but also its timing become gradually more predictable as the company nears the default barrier. Within this framework, we argue that only the so-called Fractional Recovery of Par (FRP) assumption is consistent with the market practices. We call this particular version of the reduced form framework combined with the FRP assumption the *survival-based valuation framework*.

4.1 The single-name credit market instruments

We will focus in our exposition on the single-name credit market (the multi-name structured credit market is discussed elsewhere in this book). The basic instruments of this market are:

Credit Bond (CB) is a security which entitles the investor to receive regular (typically semi-annual) coupon payments plus a return of the principal at the end of the maturity period. The security is purchased by making a cash payment upfront. Typically, the security is issued by a corporation or another entity borrowing the money, and represents a senior (compared to equity) claim against the assets of the borrower.

Credit Default Swap (CDS) is a contract between two counterparties, where the protection buyer makes regular (typically quarterly) premium payments until the earlier of the maturity or credit event, plus possibly a single up-front payment at the time of entering in the contract. In exchange for these, he expects to receive from the protection seller a single payment in case of credit event (default, bankruptcy or restructuring) prior to maturity, which is economically equivalent to making up the difference between the par value of the referenced credit bond(s) and their post-default market value, known as the recovery price.[2]

Digital Default Swap (DDS) is similar to the cash-settled CDS in most respects, except that the protection payment amount is contractually predefined and cited in terms of contractual recovery rate. For example, if the contractual recovery rate is set to zero, the protection payment would be equal to the contract notional.

Constant Maturity Default Swap (CMDS) is similar to conventional CDS, except that the periodic premium payment amount is not fixed but rather floating and is linked to some benchmark reference rate, such as the five-year par CDS rate of the same or related entity. CMDS reduces the mark-to-market risk of the CDS with respect to credit spread fluctuations in the same way as the floating rate notes reduce the mark-to-market risk of bullet bonds with respect to interest rate fluctuations.

Recovery Swap (RS) is a contract between two counterparties whereby they agree to exchange the realized recovery vs. the contractual recovery value (recovery swap rate) in case of default, with no other payments being made in any other scenario. The typical recovery swaps have no running or upfront payments of any kind. In keeping with the swaps nomenclature, the counterparties are denoted as the 'payer' and 'receiver' of the realized recovery rate, correspondingly (Berd 2005).

The conventional credit bonds and CDS still remain the linchpin of the credit market and continue to account for the majority of all traded volumes, according to the most recent statistics from the Bank of International Settlement (BIS 2009). But the existence of the expanded toolkit including the (niche markets for) CMDS, DDS, and RS implies certain connections and (partial) substitution ability between various credit derivatives instruments, which we will study in section 4.5.

The relationship between credit bonds and CDS is also non-trivial and leads to the existence of a pricing basis between the two liquid markets. While representing opportunities for relative value investment and even occasionally a true arbitrage, this basis remains driven by market segmentation and strong technical factors. We will discuss the CDS-Bond basis in detail and provide tools to analyse it in section 8.

4.2 The recovery assumptions in the reduced-form framework

The reduced-form framework for valuation of credit-risky bonds had a long history of development—see the pioneering works by Litterman and Iben (1991), Jarrow and Turnbull (1995), Jarrow, Lando and Turnbull (1997), and Duffie and Singleton (1999) as well as the textbooks by Duffie and Singleton (2003), Lando (2005), Schonbucher (2003), and O'Kane (2008) for detailed discussions and many more references. The

---

[2] Technical details include the definition of the deliverable basket of securities under the ISDA terms, netting of accrued payments, and the mechanism of settling the protection payment which can be via physical delivery or auction-driven cash settlement (O'Kane 2008).

key assumption in these models is what will be the market value of the bond just after the default. In other words, one must make an assumption on what is the expected recovery given default (or alternatively what is the loss given default). There are three main conventions regarding this assumption:

Fractional recovery of Treasury (FRT): In this approach, following Jarrow and Turnbull (1995), one assumes that upon default a bond is valued at a given fraction to the hypothetical present value of its remaining cash flows, discounted at the riskless rate.

Fractional recovery of market value (FRMV): Following Duffie and Singleton (1999), one assumes in this approach that upon default a bond loses a given fraction of its value just prior to default.

Fractional recovery of par (FRP): Under this assumption, a bond recovers a given fraction of its face value upon default, regardless of the remaining cash flows. A possible extension is that the bond additionally recovers a (possibly different) fraction of the current accrued interest.

Both FRMV and FRT assumptions lead to very convenient closed form solutions for pricing defaultable bonds as well as derivatives whose underlying securities are defaultable bonds. In both approaches one can find an equivalent 'risky' yield curve which can be used for discounting the promised cash flows of defaultable bonds and proceed with valuation in essentially the same fashion as if the bond was riskless—the only difference is the change in the discounting function. As a result, either of these approaches works quite well for credit-risky bonds that trade not too far from their par values (see Jarrow and Turnbull (2000) for a related discussion).

The main drawback of both of these approaches is that they do not correspond well to the market behaviour when bonds trade at substantial price discounts. Namely, the FRMV assumption fails to recognize the fact that the market begins to discount the future recovery when the bonds are very risky. In other words, the bonds are already *trading to recovery* just prior to default, therefore there is often relatively little additional market value loss when the actual event of default takes place.

The FRT assumption, on the other hand, does not recognize the acceleration of debt and we would argue is wholly unsuitable for the valuation of credit-risky instruments.

Of course, both FRMV and FRT approaches can be adjusted to conform to market behaviour by generalizing the expected recovery from a constant to a variable dependent on the current price of the bonds. However, such a generalization would invalidate the closed-form expressions for risky yields and negate the main advantage of these recovery assumptions. In fact, we think that what is normally considered to be an advantage of the FRMV and FRT recovery assumptions is actually a deficiency. Namely, the possibility of a strippable cash flow valuation under these assumptions with the present value of a credit bond being a simple sum of the present values of contractual cash flows is in contradiction with our understanding that all credit bonds, regardless of their contractual structure, have an embedded option to default and therefore they simply cannot be thought of as just a portfolio of coupon and principal cash flows—irrespective of whether the inherent option to default is exercised rationally by a limited liability issuer or is triggered by exogenous factors.

The only limiting case when the FRMV and FRT assumptions are in agreement with the acceleration of debt and equal priority recovery is when the expected recovery value is precisely equal to zero. We denote this as the zero recovery (ZR) assumption. As we will see in the subsequent sections, these three cases (FRMV, FRT, and ZR recovery assumptions) are the only cases when the valuation of a bond as a portfolio of individual contractual cash flows remains valid despite the possibility of a default scenario. This is simply due to the fact that under these assumptions one does not introduce any new cash flow values which were not already present in the bond's contractual description. Therefore, when calculating the present value of a credit bond, one can combine the riskless discount function, the survival probability, and the assumed recovery fraction into a *risky discount function* which can then be applied to the contractual cash flows (see Duffie, Schroder, and Skiadas (1996) for a discussion of conditions under which the valuation of defaultable securities can be performed by applying a risky stochastic discount process to their default-free payoff stream).

In contrast, the FRP assumption is fully consistent with the market dynamics, and can explain some of the salient features of the distressed credit pricing in a very intuitive manner as discussed in the previous section. During the recessions of 2001–2 and 2008–9 a large number of fallen angel issuer bonds of various maturities have been trading at deep discounts. The analysis of this large set of empirical data, whose results are partially reported in this review, confirms that the FRP recovery assumption indeed leads to a more robust modelling framework compared with the FRMV and FRT assumptions.

Despite the widespread use of alternative recovery assumptions by practitioners and academics, there are only a handful of studies which examine their importance for pricing of standard credit bonds and CDS. Finkelstein (1999) has pointed out the importance of the correct choice of the recovery assumption for the estimation of the term structure of default probabilities when fitted to observed CDS spreads, and the fact that the strippable valuation of credit bonds becomes impossible under the FRP assumption.

Duffie (1998) has explored the pricing of default-risky securities with fractional recovery of par. In particular, he derived a generic result relating the risk-neutral implied hazard rate to the short spread via the widely used credit triangle formula $h = S/(1 - R)$. The important question, however, is what is the meaning of the spread used in this relationship? Under the assumptions in Duffie (1998), this is the spread of a zero-coupon credit-risky principal strip—an asset that does not actually exist in the marketplace. In contrast, we develop an FRP-based pricing methodology with alternative definition of spreads that refers to either full coupon-bearing bonds or CDS.

Bakshi, Madan, and Zhang (2006) have specifically focused on the implications of the recovery assumptions for pricing of credit risk. Having developed a valuation framework for defaultable debt pricing under all three recovery assumptions (FRMV, FRT, and FRP), they have concluded from the comparison with time series of 25 liquid BBB-rated bullet bonds that the FRT assumption fits the bond prices best. While we agree with their methodology in general, we believe that in this case the *market is wrong* for a variety of legacy reasons discussed in the previous section, and one must insist on a better FRP model *despite* the empirical evidence from the investment grade bond prices. Our own estimates, based on fifteen years of monthly prices for more than 5,000 senior unsecured bonds across all rating categories, available for review via Barclays Capital Quantitative Credit Toolkit, suggest that the FRP assumption allows for a more robust fit across a larger sample.

Das and Hannona (2009) have extended the pricing framework by introducing a non-trivial implied recovery rate process. They have derived pricing formulae for credit bonds under various assumptions of the recovery rate dynamics. Their extended framework allows the incorporation of negative correlations of the recovery rate with the default process, achieving a closer agreement with the empirical observations (Altman et al. 2005). In our review, we will retain a simpler constant recovery rate assumption in order to derive intuitive relative value measures, most of which refer to a static set of bond and CDS prices at a given time and do not concern the dynamics of recovery rates.

Finally, in an important empirical study Guha (2003) examined the realized recoveries of US-based issuers and concluded that the FRP assumption is strongly favoured by the data in comparison with the FRMV or FRT assumptions. In particular, he has shown that the vast majority of defaulted bonds of the same issuer and seniority are valued equally or within one dollar, irrespective of their remaining time to maturity.

4.3 Pricing of credit bonds

Consider a credit-risky bond with maturity T that pays fixed cash flows with specified frequency (usually annual or semi-annual). According to the fractional recovery of par assumption, the present value of such a bond is given by the expected discounted future cash flows, including the scenarios when it defaults and recovers a fraction of the face value and possibly of the accrued interest, discounted at the risk-free (base) rates. By writing explicitly the scenarios of survival and default, we obtain the following pricing relationship at time t:

$$
PV(t) = \sum_{t_i > t}^{t_N} \left(CF_{pr}(t_i) + CF_{int}(t_i) \right) \, E_t \left\{ Z_{t_i} \, 1_{t_i < \tau} \right\}
$$

$$
+ \int_t^T E_t \left\{ R_{pr} \, F_{pr}(\tau) \, Z_\tau \, 1_{u < \tau \le u+du} \right\}
$$

$$
+ \int_t^T E_t \left\{ R_{int} \, A_{int}(\tau) \, Z_\tau \, 1_{u < \tau \le u+du} \right\}
\tag{23}
$$

The variable τ denotes the (random) default time, 1_X denotes an indicator function for a random event X, Z_t is the (random) base discount factor, and $E_t\{\cdot\}$ denotes the expectation under the risk-neutral measure at time t.

The first sum corresponds to scenarios in which the bond survives until the corresponding payment dates without default. The total cash flow at each date is defined as the sum of principal CF_{pr}, and interest CF_{int}, payments. The integral corresponds to the recovery cashflows that result from a default event occurring in a small time interval $u < \tau \le u + du$, with the bond recovering a fraction R_{pr} of the outstanding (amortized) principal face value $F_{pr}(\tau)$ plus a (possibly different) fraction R_{int} of the interest accrued $A_{int}(\tau)$.

Assuming the independence of default times, recovery rates and interest rates,[3] one can express the risk-neutral expectations in eq. (23) as products of separate factors encoding the term structures of (non-random) base discount function, survival probability, and conditional default probability, respectively:

$$Z_{base}(t, u) \;=\; E_t\{Z_u\} \tag{24}$$

$$Q(t, u) \;=\; E_t\{1_{u<\tau}\} \tag{25}$$

$$D(t, u) \;=\; \lim_{du \to 0} \frac{E_t\left\{1_{u<\tau\le u+du}\right\}}{du} = -\frac{d}{du}Q(t, u) \tag{26}$$

Many practitioners simply use a version of equation (23) assuming that the recovery cash flows occur on the next coupon day $\tau = t_i$, given a default at any time within the previous coupon payment period $[t_{i-1}, t_i]$. As a possible support for this assumption, one might argue that the inability to meet a company's obligations is more likely to be revealed on a payment date than at any time prior to that when no payments are due, regardless of when the insolvency becomes inevitable. Of course, this argument becomes much less effective if the company has other obligations besides the bond under consideration. Still, to simplify the implementation we will follow this approach in the empirical section of this chapter.

We assume that the unpaid accrued interest is added to the outstanding principal in case of default, as is the common practice in the US bankruptcy proceedings, and set $R_{int} = R_{pr} = R$. Any potential inaccuracy caused by these assumptions is subsumed by the large uncertainty about the level of the principal recovery, which is much more important.

For the case of fixed-coupon bullet bonds with coupon frequency q (e.g. semi-annual $q = 2$), the average timing of default is halfway through the coupon period, and the expected accrued interest amount is half of the next coupon payment. This gives a

---

[3] For alternative assumptions see Das and Hannona (2009), who considered the problem of credit pricing under correlated default and recovery rates, and Jarrow (2001); Jarrow and Yildirim (2002), who considered the correlated interest and hazard rates. Our simplified assumption of independence remains, however, among the more popular conventions used both in academia and among the practitioners.

simplified version of the pricing equation where we suppressed the time variable t (see also Appendix B for the continuous time approximation):

$$PV = Z_{base}(t_N) Q(t_N) + \frac{C}{q} \sum_{i=1}^{N} Z_{base}(t_i) Q(t_i)$$

$$+ R \left(1 + \frac{C}{2q}\right) \sum_{i}^{N} Z_{base}(t_i) \left(Q(t_{i-1}) - Q(t_i)\right) \tag{27}$$

Here, the probability $D(t_{i-1}, t_i)$ that the default will occur within the time interval $[t_{i-1}, t_i]$, conditional on surviving until the beginning of this interval, is expressed through the survival probability in a simple way:

$$D(t_{i-1}, t_i) = Q(t_{i-1}) - Q(t_i) \tag{28}$$

One can see quite clearly from this expression that under the FRP assumption the present value of the coupon-bearing credit bond does not reduce to a simple sum of contractual cash flow present values using any risky discount function. An obvious exception to this is the case of zero recovery assumption, under which the survival probability plays the role of a risky discount function.

4.4 Pricing of CDS

Unlike credit bonds, CDS have always been priced with FRP assumption, for the simple reason that the default scenario is central in the definition of this instrument. The credit default swap consists of two legs, the premium leg which corresponds to regular (typically quarterly) payments of the contractual premium amount by the buyer of protection, and the protection leg which corresponds to the contingent payment of the default payoff amount to the protection buyer in case of a qualified credit event.

The most generic case of a CDS which trades with an up-front payment UP amount and contractual premium payments $CF_{prem} = C_{CDS}/q$ is priced by requiring that the present value of the premium leg be equal to the present value of the protection leg, including the market standard convention for netting of the accrued premium A_{prem} and the principal protection payment $1 - R_{pr}$:

$$UP(t) + \frac{C_{CDS}}{q} \sum_{t_i > t}^{t_N} E_t \left\{ Z_{t_i} 1_{t_i < \tau} \right\} = \int_{t}^{T} E_t \left\{ (1 - R_{pr} - A_{prem,\tau}) Z_\tau 1_{u < \tau \le u + du} \right\} \tag{29}$$

Making a similar set of simplifications as in the case of credit bonds, we get (see also Appendix B for the continuous time approximation):

$$UP + \frac{C_{CDS}}{q} \sum_{i=1}^{N} Z(t_i) Q(t_i) = \left(1 - R - \frac{C_{CDS}}{2q}\right) \sum_{i=1}^{N} Z(t_i) \left(Q(t_{i-1}) - Q(t_i)\right) \tag{30}$$

If the up-front payment is equal to zero, the CDS is said to be trading at par, and its coupon then coincides with the par CDS spread, defined as follows:

$$S_{CDS} = 2q \, (1 - R) \, \frac{\sum_{i=1}^{N} Z(t_i) \, (Q(t_{i-1}) - Q(t_i))}{\sum_{i=1}^{N} Z(t_i) \, (Q(t_{i-1}) + Q(t_i))} \tag{31}$$

Equation (31) defines the par (or break-even) spread for CDS even if its contractual coupon is such that the upfront payment is non-zero. It is the best measure of relative value for comparing different CDS of the same maturity. One can express the amount of the up-front payment (which could also be interpreted as the mark-to-market value of CDS) through the difference between the par CDS spread S_{CDS} and the contractual premium C_{CDS}:

$$UP \;=\; (S_{CDS} - C_{CDS}) \, \pi \tag{32}$$

$$\pi \;=\; \frac{1}{2q} \sum_{i=1}^{N} Z(t_i) \, (Q(t_{i-1}) + Q(t_i)) \tag{33}$$

where π is known as the 'risky PV01', or the risky price of a basis point.

After the recent modifications of the CDS contract conventions, all single-name CDS trade with fixed coupons of either 100 bp or 500 bp plus appropriate up-front payment. As seen from eq. (32), in cases where the par spread is less than the contractual coupon, the upfront payment will actually be negative, i.e. the counterparty purchasing the protection will *receive* an up-front payment which will compensate it for greater-than-necessary premium payments in the future.

The critical question in these equations is, of course, the estimates of the survival probability $Q(t)$. The next section shows that it is directly related to CDS spread and recovery value via a so-called 'credit triangle' formula.

4.5 The credit triangle and default rate calibration

The phrase *credit triangle* refers to the relationship between the credit spread, default rate and recovery rate. It is often cited as follows:

$$\text{Credit Spread} = \text{Default Probability Rate} \times (1 - \text{Recovery Rate}) \tag{34}$$

The appealing simplicity of this formula masks some ambiguities associated with its interpretation. Within the reduced form model, the default probability rate is the hazard rate of the exogenous Poisson process of default event arrival, the recovery rate is a model parameter which can be considered constant or stochastic, and the credit spread is the combined measure of credit risk that remains open to interpretation depending on which particular assumption of recovery is assumed or which particular credit instrument is considered. Outside the model framework, the practitioners often (mis)use this formula by plugging into it the yield spread or the Z-spread of credit bonds, which are inconsistent measures of credit risk as explained in this chapter.

Table 4.1 Static replication of recovery swaps by CDS and DDS

	Notional		Cash Flows		
		Upfront	Premium	Default	Maturity
RS	$+1$	0	0	$R_{RS} - R$	0
DDS	$+H_{DDS}$	0	$-S_{DDS}$	$1 - R_{DDS}$	0
CDS	$-H_{CDS}$	0	$-S_{CDS}$	$1 - R$	0
Net		0	$-H_{DDS} S_{DDS}$ $+H_{CDS} S_{CDS}$	$R_{RS} - R$ $+H_{DDS}(1 - R_{DDS})$ $-H_{CDS}(1 - R)$	0

Rather than defining these metrics within a particular modelling framework, we propose to specify them in terms of observable quantities of tradeable instruments such as credit default swaps (CDS), digital default swaps (DDS), and recovery swaps (RS). The no-arbitrage relationship between the contractual rates of these instruments is the unambiguous alternative to the formula (34).

For example, the recovery swaps can be fully replicated by a combination of conventional and digital CDS. This replication, as usual, implies an arbitrage-free relationship between these three instruments which we will derive below.

Consider the replication trade depicted in Table 4.1: a unit notional payer recovery swap with the fixed swap rate R_{RS} is hedged with a long protection position in DDS with notional H_{DDS} and short protection in CDS with a notional $-H_{CDS}$. The cash flows columns indicate the cash flows per unit notional on each leg of the trade.

The net cash flows are identically zero for upfront payments. The hedge ratios H_{DDS} for the DDS and H_{CDS} for the CDS should be chosen so that the net cash flows are also zero for premium and default payments. Consider the case of default:

$$CF_{default} = R_{RS} - R + H_{DDS}(1 - R_{DDS}) - H_{CDS}(1 - R) \qquad (35)$$

In order to guarantee that these cash flows are equal to zero regardless of the realized recovery rate R, one must have:

$$H_{CDS} = 1 \qquad (36)$$

$$H_{DDS} = \frac{1 - R_{RS}}{1 - R_{DDS}} \qquad (37)$$

Consider now the net premium cash flows:

$$CF_{prem} = -H_{DDS} S_{DDS} + H_{CDS} S_{CDS} \qquad (38)$$

Because all other cash flows of the replication trade are identically zero, then plugging the hedge ratios (36) into (38) and requiring that the net premium cash flows be also equal to zero results in a no-arbitrage relationship between the matching maturity T recovery swaps, CDS and DDS rates:

$$S_{DDS}(T) = \frac{1 - R_{DDS}(T)}{1 - R_{RS}(T)} S_{CDS}(T) \tag{39}$$

Based on this relationship, it would be natural to use the recovery swap rates, rather than historical estimates or other forecasts of the realized recovery rate, for calibration of the implied hazard rates within the risk-neutral framework.

Indeed, imagine that we have observed the term structure of CDS spreads and recovery swap rates for a range of maturities $[0, T]$. According to (39) we can obtain without any further assumptions the term structure of DDS spreads with zero contractual recovery $R_{DDS} = 0$. The pricing of such DDS depends solely on the term structure of risk-neutral discount rates and survival probabilities and possibly on the correlation of the default process and the risk-free discount factor (compare with (29)):

$$S_{DDS}(T) \int_0^T du \, E\left\{Z_u \, 1_{u<\tau}\right\} = \int_0^T E\left\{Z_u \, 1_{u<\tau \leq u+du}\right\} \tag{40}$$

For convenience in notations, we have adopted an approximation of continuous DDS premium payments (this approximation is irrelevant for the subsequent discussion). Under the assumption of independence between the exogenous default process and the risk-free rates, we get:

$$\frac{S_{CDS}(T)}{1 - R_{RS}(T)} \int_0^T du \, Q(u) \, Z(u) = \int_0^T du \, h(u) \, Q(u) \, Z(u) \tag{41}$$

One can easily calibrate the term structure of implied hazard rates $h(s)$ to the market-observed CDS spreads and recovery swap rates from (41) without making any additional assumptions about the recovery and default process. For example, in the case of flat CDS spreads, recovery swap rates and hazard rates one immediately obtains the conventional 'credit triangle' (compare with (34)):

$$h = \frac{S_{CDS}}{1 - R_{RS}} \tag{42}$$

This confirms that the no-arbitrage relationship (39) is the unambiguous market-based generalization of the familiar credit triangle.

Note that in our derivation of the equations (41) and (42) we did not make an assumption about the existence of a liquid DDS market—it is sufficient to assume that the CDS and recovery swaps markets exist, and price the hypothetical DDS based on the known arbitrage-free relationship between the DDS and CDS spreads (39). Alternatively, if we assume the existence of CDS and DDS markets, the market triangle equation (39) directly defines the correct recovery swap rate, which should also be used in other instances wherever a risk-neutral 'implied recovery rate' is needed. In any case, only two out of three elements of the market triangle containing CDS, DDS, and RS need be observable.

Unfortunately, the state of the market is such that RS or DDS contracts are rarely traded, often only for distressed issuers where the default scenario is very likely. This leaves a lot of ambiguity for the choice of the recovery rate to be used in the calibration of the implied hazard rates.

The credit triangle formula states that the calibrated implied hazard rate is a growing function of assumed recovery rate, given a fixed level of observed CDS spreads S_{CDS}. This is in a stark contrast with the empirical evidence of a negative correlation between historical default rates and recovery rates Altman et al. (2005). Such difference in behaviour should not be puzzling since we are comparing the static dependence of implied hazard rates on implied recovery rates conditioned on constant CDS spread with dynamic historical rates that are not so conditioned. In fact, the calibration procedure for the implied hazard rates using the recovery swap rates is completely independent of assumptions regarding the correlation between the recovery rates and default events, since the realized recovery rate is simply absent from equation (40). The readers can refer to Bakshi, Madan, and Zhang (2006) and Das and Hannona (2009) for an expanded modelling framework including variable hazard rates and recovery rates, where the correlation between them is a tunable parameter and thus can match the observed negative correlation.

5 EMPIRICAL ESTIMATION OF SURVIVAL PROBABILITIES

Having derived the pricing relationship in the survival-based approach, we are now ready to estimate the implied survival probability term structure directly from the bond prices. The premise of our approach is that the survival probability is an exponentially decaying function of maturity, perhaps with a varying decay rate. This assumption is generally valid in Poisson models of exogenous default, where the default hazard rate is known but the exact timing of the default event is unpredictable. This is the same assumption made by all versions of reduced-form models regardless of the recovery assumptions discussed earlier. Notably, this assumption differs from the Merton-style structural models of credit risk (Merton 1974) where the timing of default becomes gradually more predictable as the assets of the firm fall towards the default threshold.

When it comes to the estimation of term structures based on a large number of off-the-run bonds across a wide range of maturities, most approaches based on yield or spread fitting are not adequate because they lead to a non-linear dependence of the objective function on the fit parameters. The most important aspect of this problem is the large number of securities to be fitted which makes a precise fit of all prices impractical (or not robust) and therefore creates a need for a clear estimate of the accuracy of the fit. After all one must know whether a given bond trading above or below the fitted curve represents a genuine rich/cheap signal or whether this mismatch is within the model's error range. Without such estimate relative value trading based on fitted curves would not be possible.

Vasicek and Fong (1982) (see also Shea 1985) suggested a solution to this dilemma, which has become a de facto industry standard for off-the-run Treasury and agency curve estimation. They noted that the above problem is best interpreted as a cross-sectional regression. As such, it would be best if the explanatory factors in this regression were linearly related to the observable prices, because this would lead to a (generalized) linear regression. Realizing further that the quantity which is linearly related to bond prices is the discount function, they proposed to estimate the term structure of risk-free discount function itself rather than the term structure of yields. Finally, they argued that the simplest discount function is exponentially decreasing with a constant rate, and concluded that one must use exponential splines, which are linear combinations of exponential functions, to best approximate the shape of realistic discount functions. We review the definition of exponential splines in Appendix A.

In the case of credit-risky bonds a similar logic also applies, except that one has to think about the survival probabilities rather than discount function, because it is the survival probabilities that appear linearly in the bond pricing equation (27). When the hazard rate is constant the survival probability term structure is exactly exponential. Therefore, it is indeed well suited for approximation by exponential splines (84):

$$Q(t) = \sum_{k=1}^{K} \beta_k \, \Phi_k \left(t \, | \eta \right) \tag{43}$$

where the spline factors $\Phi_k \left(t \, | \eta \right)$ depend on the tenor t and on the long-term decay factor η, which in this case has the meaning of the generic long-term default hazard rate $h(t \to \infty) = \eta$.

Assuming that we have already estimated the base discount function, and substituting the spline equation (43) into pricing equation (27) we obtain a cross-sectional regression setting for direct estimation of the survival probability term structure from observable bond prices:

$$V_j = \sum_{k=1}^{K} \beta_k \, U_{j,k} + \epsilon_n \tag{44}$$

which, assuming $k = 3$, in matrix notations looks like:

$$\begin{bmatrix} V_1 \\ \vdots \\ V_n \\ \vdots \end{bmatrix} = \begin{bmatrix} U_{1,1} & U_{1,2} & U_{1,3} \\ \vdots & \vdots & \vdots \\ U_{j,1} & U_{j,2} & U_{j,3} \\ \vdots & \vdots & \vdots \end{bmatrix} \cdot \begin{bmatrix} \beta_1 \\ \beta_2 \\ \beta_3 \end{bmatrix} + \begin{bmatrix} \epsilon_1 \\ \vdots \\ \epsilon_j \\ \vdots \end{bmatrix} \tag{45}$$

Here we introduced the explanatory variables $U_{j,k}$ for the j-th bond and k-th spline factor and the adjusted present value V_j for the j-th bond as:

$$U_{j,k} = \sum_{i=1}^{N} \Phi_k \left(t_{j,i} \,|\, \eta \right) \left(\frac{C_j}{q_j} Z(t_{j,i}) - R \left(1 + \frac{C_j}{2q_j} \right) \left(Z(t_{j,i}) - Z(t_{j,i+1}) \right) \right)$$

$$+ Z(t_{j,N}) \, \Phi_k \left(t_{j,N} \,|\, \eta \right) \left(\frac{C_j}{q_j} + 1 - R \left(1 + \frac{C_j}{2q_j} \right) \right) \tag{46}$$

$$V_j = P V_j - R \left(1 + \frac{C_j}{2q_j} \right) Z(t_{j,1}) \tag{47}$$

We have found empirically that it is often sufficient to retain only the first three factors for estimating the survival probability. Thus there are no knot-factors in our implementation of this approach. The first three coefficients of the spline expansion must satisfy an equality constraint, because the survival probability must be exactly equal to 1 when the time horizon is equal to zero.

$$\sum_{k=1}^{3} \beta_k = 1 \tag{48}$$

In addition to the equality constraint, we also impose inequality constraints at intermediate maturities T_c to make sure that the survival probability is strictly decreasing, and consequently the hazard rate is strictly positive. Their functional form is:

$$\sum_{k=1}^{3} \beta_k \, k \, e^{-k\eta T_c} > 0 \tag{49}$$

In addition, we impose a single constraint at the long end of the curve to make sure that the survival probability itself is positive.

$$\sum_{k=1}^{3} \beta_k \, e^{-k\eta T_c^{max}} > 0 \tag{50}$$

Together with the strictly decreasing shape of the survival probability term structure guaranteed by (49), this eliminates any possibility of inconsistency of default and survival probabilities in the exponential spline approximation.

It is worth noting that in most cases the inequality constraints (49), (50) will not be binding and therefore the regression estimates will coincide with the simple GLS formulas. The constraints will kick in precisely in those cases where the input data is not consistent with survival-based modelling, which can happen for variety of reasons including the imperfection of market pricing data, company-specific deviations of expected recovery rates, etc.

We use a two-tiered weighting scheme for the regression objective function with the first set of weights inversely proportional to the square of the bond's spread duration SD_j to make sure that the relative accuracy of the hazard rate estimates is roughly constant across maturities. The second set of weights is iteratively adjusted to reduce the influence of the outliers following the generalized M-estimator technique described in Wilcox (1997).

$$OF = \sum_{j=1}^{J_{bonds}} \frac{w_j^{outlier}}{SD_j^2} \, \epsilon_j^2 \qquad (51)$$

Equations (43)–(51) fully specify the estimation procedure for survival probability term structure. It satisfies the main goals that we have defined at the outset—the procedure is robust, it is consistent with market practices, and reflects the behaviour of distressed bonds, and is guaranteed to provide positive default probabilities and hazard rates.

Figure 4.3 demonstrates the results of the estimation procedure for the A-rated Industrials, performed monthly for ten years from July 1994 until June 2004, using the end-of-month prices of senior unsecured bonds in the Lehman Brothers credit database. We show the time series of the five-year annualized default probability versus the weighted average pricing error of the cross-sectional regression. The latter is defined as the square root of the objective function given by equation (51), with weights normalized to sum up to 1.

The regression quality has tracked the level of the implied default rates—higher implied default rates are associated with greater levels of idiosyncratic errors in the

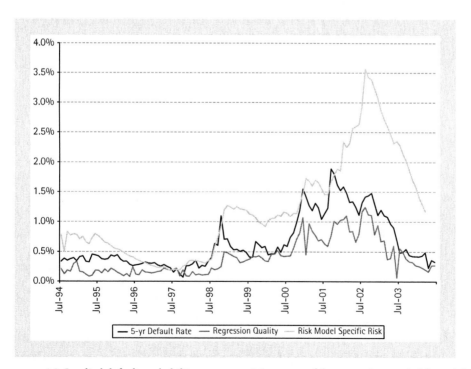

FIGURE 4.3 Implied default probability, average pricing error of the regression, and risk model specific risk, A-rated industrials.

cross-sectional regression. This pattern is consistent with the assessment of the issuer-specific excess return volatility during the same period given by the Lehman Brothers multi-factor risk model (see Naldi, Chu, and Chang 2002). We show for comparison the exponentially weighted specific risk estimates for the A-rated Basic Industries bucket.

As a final remark we would like to note that the choice of recovery rates used in our model is obviously very important. After all, the main impetus for this methodology was the recognition that recovery rates are a crucial determinant of the market behaviour for distressed bonds. Both the cross-sectional, i.e. industry and issuer dependence, and the time-series, i.e. business cycle dependence of the recovery rates is very significant (see Gupton and Stein 2002; Altman, Resti, and Sironi 2004; Altman et al. 2005). Nevertheless, it is often sufficient to use an average recovery rate, such as 40% which is close to the long-term historical average across all issuers, for the methodology to remain robust across the entire range of credit qualities.

In a more ambitious approach, the recovery rate can be estimated by a second-stage likelihood maximization after obtaining the best fit of the exponential spline coefficients given a recovery value as a parameter. This would yield best fit or 'market implied' recovery rates. Presumably, the industry dependence can also be handled by introducing different 'implied' recoveries for different industries, assuming the number of independently priced bonds is sufficiently large to maintain statistical significance of the obtained results. We have found, however, that the majority of investment grade bonds do not efficiently price the recovery and therefore this programme, while theoretically possible, is difficult to implement in practice.

6 ISSUER AND SECTOR CREDIT TERM STRUCTURES

Having estimated the term structure of survival probabilities, we can now define a set of valuation, risk, and relative value measures applicable to collections of bonds such as those belonging to a particular issuer or sector, as well as to individual securities. In practice, to preserve the consistency with market observed bond prices encoded in the survival probability, we define the issuer and sector credit term structures for the same set of bonds which were used in the exponential spline estimation procedures.

As discussed earlier, the conventional Z-spreads are not consistent with survival-based valuation of credit-risky bonds. The same can be said about the yield spreads, I-spreads, asset swap spreads, durations, convexities, and most other measures which investors currently use day to day. Ultimately, this inconsistency is the source of the breakdown of the conventional spread measures in distressed situations. The market participants know this very well and they stop using these measures for quoting or trading distressed bonds. This situation is commonly referred as *bonds trading on price*.

In this section we will define a host of measures which are consistent with the survival-based approach. We note, however, that the definitions presented in this section do not depend on the specific choice of the exponential splines methodology for fitting survival probability term structures. They can be used in conjunction with any term structure of survival probabilities which is consistent with reduced-form pricing methodology assuming fractional recovery of par—for example one calibrated to the CDS market.

6.1 Survival and default probability term structures

The survival probability term structure is a direct output from the empirical estimation process described in the previous section. Once we have estimated the spline coefficients β_k and the long-term decay parameter η, the survival probability is defined by equation (43).

Correspondingly, the cumulative default probability is defined as:

$$D(t) = 1 - Q(t) \tag{52}$$

which one can recognize as a special case of eq. (28). Figure 4.4 shows the shapes of the survival probabilities for credit sectors with varying risk levels, from BBB-rated to B-rated credit.

6.2 Hazard rate and ZZ-spread term structures

Credit investors and market practitioners have long used definitions of spread which correspond to the spread-discount-function methodology, outlined in section 2. The most commonly used measures, Z-spread and OAS, explicitly follow the discounting function approach. Others, such as yield spread or I-spread, implicitly depend on bond-equivalent yields which in turn follow from discounting function approach. Thus, all of these measures neglect the dependence of the bond price on the recovery value and the debt acceleration in case of default. Therefore, these measures become inadequate for distressed bonds.

In the survival-based approach, spreads are not a primary observed quantity. Only the prices of credit bonds have an unambiguous meaning. Spreads, however we define them, must be derived from the term structure of survival probabilities, fitted to the bond prices.

There is only one spread measure which is defined directly in terms of survival probabilities. It corresponds to the spread of a hypothetical credit instrument which pays $1 at a given maturity, pays no interest and pays nothing in case of default. The

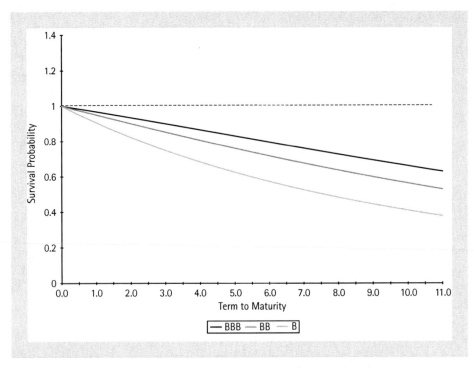

FIGURE 4.4 Survival probability term structures for different credit risk levels.

continuously compounded zero-recovery zero-coupon ZZ-yield for such a bond is
defined as:

$$e^{-Y_{ZZ} T} = Q(t) Z_{base}(T)$$

$$Y_{ZZ}(T) = -\frac{1}{T} \log(Q(t) Z_{base}(T)) \tag{53}$$

Recall that the corresponding continuously compounded risk-free zero-coupon rate
is defined as eq. (4).

$$y(T) = -\frac{1}{T} \log(Z_{base}(T)) \tag{54}$$

From these two definitions, we obtain the continuously compounded ZZ-spread as
the difference between the ZZ-yield and risk-free zero-coupon rate:

$$S_{ZZ}(T) = Y_{ZZ}(T) - y(T) = -\frac{1}{T} \log(Q(t)) \tag{55}$$

Substituting the definition of the survival probability, we see that the ZZ-spread is
equal to the average hazard rate for the maturity horizon of the hypothetical zero-
recovery zero-coupon credit bond.

$$S_{ZZ}(T) = \frac{1}{T} \int_0^T h(s)\, ds \tag{56}$$

Equivalently, we can say that the instantaneous forward ZZ-spread is identically equal to the hazard rate of the issuer. The hazard rate also has a meaning of instantaneous forward default probability, i.e. the probability intensity of default during a small time interval in the future provided that the issuer has survived until that time. Thus, the forward ZZ-spread is equal to the forward default intensity:

$$S_{ZZ}^{fwd}(t) = h(t) \tag{57}$$

This result coincides with the conclusions in Duffie (1998) regarding the hazard rate in reduced form models under the FRP recovery assumption. The novelty of our approach is that we do not estimate the hazard rate from spread curves, but conversely, derive the spread curves from hazard rates that are obtained directly from the bond prices via the fitted survival probability. Since the conventional spread estimates are not consistent with the survival-based approach, deriving the ZZ-spread or the hazard rates from such spread measures is fraught with inaccuracies and biases, especially for high hazard rates. Only if the recovery rate is equal to zero and for the case of zero coupon credit bonds the conventional Z-spread becomes equal to the forward ZZ-spread and becomes consistent with the survival-based valuation—in concordance with our earlier assertions.

Using the exponential spline representation of the survival probability term structure (43), we can derive the hazard rate term structure as follows:

$$h(t) = -\frac{d}{dt} \log Q(t) = \frac{\sum_{k=1}^{3} k\,\eta\,\beta_k\,e^{-k\eta t}}{\sum_{k=1}^{3} \beta_k\,e^{-k\eta t}} \tag{58}$$

where the constraint (49) guarantees the positivity of the hazard rates.

Figure 4.5 shows the result of estimation of the hazard rate (forward ZZ-spread) term structures for Ford and for the BBB Consumer Cyclicals sector.

Even though we classify the hazard rate primarily as a valuation measure, it can be used for relative value assessments. It is important to remember that the implied hazard rate does not correspond to an actual forecast. Like other market-implied parameters, it also incorporates in a complex way a host of risk premia which reflect both credit and non-credit factors such as recovery rate risk, liquidity, etc. Nevertheless, fitted hazard rate term structures may provide valuable clues beyond the conventional spread analysis.

For example, the Ford curve in Figure 4.5 is substantially wider than the sector curve, signalling the higher credit risk associated with Ford bonds. The Ford curve has a distinctive shape, with the maximum differential to sector curve in intermediate maturities, suggesting that these maturities offer the best opportunities for monetizing views on the relative risk and return between this issuer and the industry sector.

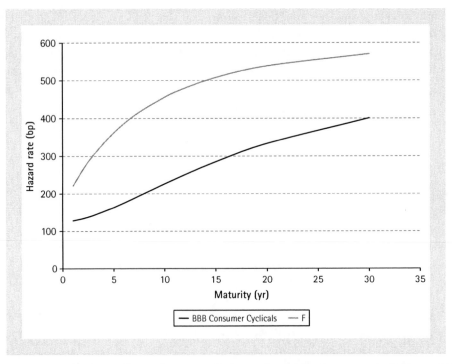

FIGURE 4.5 Hazard rates (forward ZZ-spreads) for Ford and BBB Consumer Cyclicals, as of 31 December 2003.

6.3 Par coupon and P-spread term structures

While the definition of the ZZ-spread presented in the previous subsection is quantitatively sound, it is not likely to be of much value for practitioners because the zero-coupon zero-recovery credit bonds do not actually exist in the marketplace. There exist pure discount (zero-coupon) securities, particularly in the short-term CP market, but all of them are subject to equal-priority recovery rules and therefore cannot be considered zero-recovery. On the other hand, there exist credit derivatives such as digital default swaps which can have a contractual zero recovery, but they do have premium payments and therefore cannot be considered as an equivalent of a zero-coupon bond. Therefore, the usefulness of the ZZ-spread as a relative value measure is limited—one can obtain from it some insight about the issuer or the sector but not about a particular security.

The vast majority of the credit market consists of interest-bearing instruments subject to equal-priority recovery in case of default. A practically useful relative value measure should refer to such instruments and should contrast them with credit risk-free instruments such as Treasury bonds or interest rate swaps which provide a funding rate benchmark. One such measure is the fitted par coupon—i.e. a coupon of a hypothetical bond of a given maturity which would trade at a par price if evaluated using the fitted issuer survival probability term structure. Correspondingly, the par spread is defined by subtracting the fitted par yield of risk-free bonds from the fitted par coupon of credit-risky bonds.

One must note that the par coupon and par spread measures do not correspond to a specific bond—these are derived measures based on the issuer survival curve and a specific price target equal to par, i.e. 100% of face value. The par price of the bond has a special significance, because for this price the expected price return of a risk-free bond to maturity is precisely zero. Therefore, the par yield of a risk-free bond reflects its expected (annualized) total return to maturity and the par spread of a credit-risky bond reflects its (risky) excess return to maturity. Thus, the par spread defined above can be considered a consistent (fair) relative value measure for a given issuer/sector for a given maturity horizon.

For example, if two different issuers wanted to buy back their outstanding bonds in the secondary market and instead issue new par bonds of the same maturity T then the fair level of the coupons which the market should settle at, assuming no material change in the issuers' credit quality, would be given by the respective fitted par coupons. Correspondingly, investors considering these new bonds can expect excess returns to maturity T equal to their respective fitted par spreads. If one of those spreads is greater than the other—this would represent a relative value which the investors should contrast with their views of the issuers' credit risks to the said maturity horizon. For bonds with coupon frequency q (usually annual $q = 1$, or semi-annual $q = 2$) with an integer number of payment periods until maturity $t_N = N/q$ we define the par coupon term structure by solving for the coupon level from the pricing equation (27).

$$C_P(t_N \,|q\,) = q \, \frac{1 - Z(t_N)\, Q(t_N) - R \, \sum_{i=1}^{N} Z(t_i)\, (Q(t_{i-1}) - Q(t_i))}{\sum_{i=1}^{N} Z(t_i)\, Q(t_i) + \frac{1}{2} R \, \sum_{i=1}^{N} Z(t_i)\, (Q(t_{i-1}) - Q(t_i))} \tag{59}$$

Contrast this definition with the one that would be consistent with spread discount function based approaches:

$$C_{disc}(t_N \,|q\,) = q \, \frac{1 - Z_{base}(t_N)\, Z_{spread}(t_N)}{\sum_{i=1}^{N} Z_{base}(t_i)\, Z_{spread}(t_i)} \tag{60}$$

We can see that the latter definition only coincides with the former if we assume that the recovery rate is zero and that the spread discount function is equal to the survival probability.

An example of the fitted par coupon term structure is shown in Figure 4.6 where we show our estimates for Ford and BBB Consumer Cyclicals sector as of 31 December 2003. Note that the shape of these fitted curves—very steep front end and flattish long maturities—is largely determined by the shape of the underlying risk-free curve (we used the swaps curve in this case), with the credit risk being a second-order modification for most issuers and sectors, except those that trade at very deep discounts.

Let us also define the par coupon of the risk-free bond in a similar fashion:

$$C_P^{base}(t_N \,|q\,) = q \, \frac{1 - Z_{base}(t_N)}{\sum_{i=1}^{N} Z_{base}(t_i)} \tag{61}$$

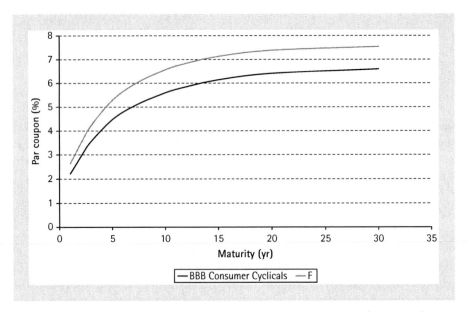

FIGURE 4.6 Fitted par coupon for Ford and BBB Consumer Cyclicals, as of 31 December 2003.

The par spread (P-spread) to the base curve (either Treasury or swaps) can then be derived by subtracting the par base yields from the par risky coupons of the same maturities:

$$S_P(T\,|q) = C_P(T\,|q) - C_P^{base}(T\,|q) \qquad (62)$$

Figure 4.7 demonstrates the fitted par Libor spread term structures using the same example of the Ford and BBB Consumer Cyclicals sectors.

6.4 Constant coupon price (CCP) term structure

Since we argued that the price-based estimation techniques are more consistent than those fitting yields or spreads, it is useful to define a set of credit term structures expressed in terms of bond prices. For any integer number of payment periods, we define the constant coupon price (CCP) term structure as the price level of the bond with a pre-set coupon (e.g. coupons of 6%, 8%, 10%).

$$P(t_N\,|C) = Z_{base}(t_N)\,Q(t_N) + \frac{C}{q}\sum_{i=1}^{N} Z_{base}(t_i)\,Q(t_i)$$

$$+ R\left(1 + \frac{C}{2q}\right)\sum_{i}^{N} Z_{base}(t_i)\,(Q(t_{i-1}) - Q(t_i)) \qquad (63)$$

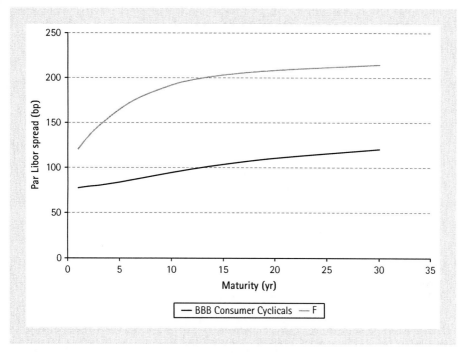

FIGURE 4.7 Fitted Libor P-spread for Ford and BBB Consumer Cyclicals, as of 31 December 2003.

Figure 4.8 shows estimated CCP term structures for Georgia Pacific as of 31 December 2003. The prices are calculated as fractions of a 100 face, i.e. par price 100% appears as 100. We observe that the 6%, 8%, and 10% Constant Coupon Price term structures neatly envelope the scatterplot of prices of individual bonds which have coupon levels ranging from 6.625% to 9.625%. Importantly, all three CCP term structures correspond to the same term structure of survival probability, and thus embody the same credit relative value. To the extent that a price of a bond with a particular fixed coupon is in line with the level suggested by the CCP term structures, this bond also reflects the same credit relative value. Thus, a graph like this can serve as a first crude indication of the relative value across bonds of a given issuer or sector—especially when there are securities whose prices are substantially different from the corresponding fitted price curve levels. In the next section we develop a more precise measure for assessing such relative value, which we call Default Adjusted Spread.

Note also how the CCP term structures tend to become flat at longer maturities—this is a reflection of the fact that Georgia Pacific was trading at elevated levels of the implied default risk, with the fitted hazard rate exceeding 1,000 bp at maturities longer than five years. At such levels of credit risk the implied survival probability to ten years or longer is only about 35%, and the recovery scenario at longer maturities becomes the dominant one. This, in turn, leads to a flat term structure of prices.

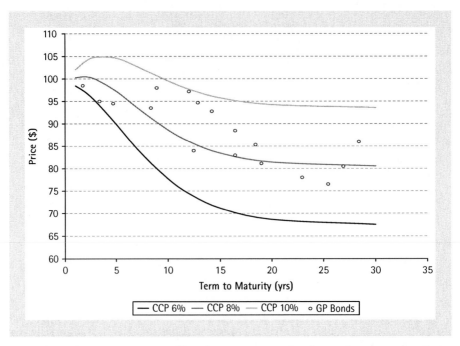

FIGURE 4.8 CCP term structures and bond prices, Georgia Pacific, as of 31 December 2003.

One might say that the reason for this is that the high probability of an early default scenario causes the bonds to trade with an effective life much shorter than their nominal maturity. We show in the next section that the properly defined duration measure for credit bonds that is consistent with the survival-based valuation will exhibit the same feature, with the duration becoming much shorter for bonds with higher levels of the implied credit risk.

6.5 Bond-implied CDS (BCDS) term structure

The survival-based valuation approach is well suited for the CDS market. In fact it has been the market practice since its inception. By deriving the bond-implied CDS spreads within the same framework we are aiming to give investors an apples-to-apples relative value measure across the bond and CDS markets. The pricing relationship for credit default swaps was defined in eq. (29). The only difference here is that rather than observing the CDS market and calibrating the survival probability to it, we derive the bond-implied CDS (BCDS) from the previously fitted values of the survival probability term structure.

$$S_{BCDS}(t_N) = 2q\,(1-R)\,\frac{\sum_{i=1}^{N} Z_{base}(t_i)\,(Q(t_{i-1}) - Q(t_i))}{\sum_{i=1}^{N} Z_{base}(t_i)\,(Q(t_{i-1}) + Q(t_i))} \tag{64}$$

Another difference of BCDS from bond-like spread measures such as P-spread, is that for BCDS we use the quarterly coupon frequency $q = 4$, rather than more common semi-annual $q = 2$ for bonds. The BCDS term structure gives yet another par-equivalent measure of spread for credit-risky issuers in addition to the P-spread. The base discounting function $Z_{base}(t_i)$ must be taken typically to be LIBOR or another funding-related function in order for the BCDS spread to have a meaning of excess return over cash. In section 8 we will show that there exists a complementarity between the BCDS term structure and the properly defined credit-risk-free benchmark security, proving that the BCDS spread is a clean measure of excess return, free of biases associated with non-par prices.

6.6 Forward spreads and forward trades

The BCDS spread definition is also the best starting point to define the forward credit spread measure consistent with survival-based methodology. Since most other measures rely on the comparison between the credit-risky and risk-free bonds, they would suffer from inherent biases if naively extrapolated to forward space. The forward prices are well defined only for zero-coupon riskless bonds, in which case the forward price is simply the price of final maturity bond expressed in units of bond maturing at the forward pricing date: $Z(t, T) = Z(T)/Z(t)$. However, a similar comparison is meaningless for coupon-bearing bonds, and especially if the bonds are credit risky. Therefore, the spread and yield measures defined for coupon-bearing bonds do not lend themselves well as a starting point for forward spread calculation.

In contrast, the BCDS spread is not defined with respect to any underlying bond—it is instead defined purely as a function of the survival probability and base discount function. Both of these quantities have a well-defined meaning in forward space:

$$Z_{base}^{fwd}(t, T) \; = \; E_0\left\{e^{-\int_t^T r_s\,ds}\right\} = e^{-\int_t^T f_s\,ds} \tag{65}$$

$$Q^{fwd}(t, T) \; = \; E_0\left\{1_{T<\tau}\,|t<\tau\right\} = e^{-\int_t^T h_s\,ds} \tag{66}$$

where the interpretation of the forward survival probability is as the conditional survival probability until time T, under the condition that the default has not occurred until time t.

Therefore, by simply replacing the current observed discount and survival functions in (64) with their forward counterparts estimated for the forward starting time t, one obtains the forward BCDS spread for time t and forward tenor $T = t_N$.

Let us now contrast this calculation with more market-driven notions of a forward CDS contract and a forward CDS trade (whether or not we are talking about the actual CDS or a hypothetical bond-implied CDS is not important at this point).

A forward CDS contract corresponds to buying or selling credit protection that is active for a period of time in the future at a premium whose level is pre-set today,

Table 4.2 Cash flows of forward CDS hedged by a CDS flattener

Cash flow time	$t = 0$	$[0 < t \leq T_1]$		$[T_1 < t \leq T_2]$		$t = T_2$
Cash flow type	Upfront	Premium	Default	Premium	Default	Maturity
Long FwdCDS $[T_1 \times T]$	0	0	0	$-S_{fwd}$	$1 - R$	0
Short CDS $[T_1]$	0	S_1	$-(1 - R)$	0	0	0
Long CDS $[T_2 = T_1 + T]$	0	$-S_2$	$1 - R$	$-S_2$	$1 - R$	0
Hedged Fwd	0	$S_2 - S_1$	0	$S_2 - S_{fwd}$	0	0

but payable only during that future period. For example, a five-year CDS two years forward, referred to as 2×5 forward CDS, provides protection which starts in year $T_1 = 2$ and continues for $T = 5$ years afterward, ending in year $T_2 = T_1 + T = 7$ from today, with premiums paid quarterly during that period. Importantly, the forward CDS knocks out and provides no protection if a credit event occurs prior to the forward start date.

While the market participants rarely trade such a contract, they often trade long-short pairs of spot CDS which are almost (but not exactly) identical to a forward CDS. These pair trades are known in the market as CDS steepeners and flatteners. For example, buying a 2×5 forward CDS protection is similar to a 2s-7s curve steepener trade whereby one sells protection to two-year maturity and buys equal notional protection to seven-year maturity. This trade would outperform if the spread curve steepens, hence the name *steepener*. The opposite trade, which would outperform if the spread curve flattens, is correspondingly known as a *flattener*.

In terms of protection payment leg such a trade is indeed equivalent to a forward CDS—if the credit event occurs before T_1 the long and the short protection payments will cancel each other, while if the credit event occurs between the year T_1 and T_2 only the long protection leg is active and it will provide the same protection payment as the forward CDS contract.

The premium legs are somewhat different between the forward CDS and the long-short pair trade. Table 4.2 demonstrates the premium cash flows for each of the trades. As we can see, the steepener pair trade potentially has non-zero premium payments during the first two years (unless the CDS term structure is flat), while the forward CDS does not. Correspondingly, the net premium paid on a steepener trade between T_1 and T_2 will also be different from the forward CDS premium in this example.

Since the forward CDS hedged by a long-short CDS pair provides no protection payment under any default scenario, the present value of the protection leg of such a trade is identically zero. Therefore, we must require that the net premium cash flows of a hedged forward CDS trade also have zero present value. The present value of each basis point paid from today until the earlier of a given maturity or the occurrence of the credit event is given by the risky PV01 $\pi(T)$ to corresponding maturity (33). Hence, this requirement can be written as:

$$(S_2 - S_1)\,\pi_1 + (S_2 - S_{fwd})\,(\pi_2 - \pi_1) = 0 \qquad (67)$$

Here, S_1 is the spot CDS spread for the starting date, S_2 is the spot CDS spread for the ending date, and S_{fwd} is the forward CDS spread for the given interval of maturities. π_1 and π_2 are the risky PV01s for the starting and ending dates, respectively. The first term represents the present value of the stream of cash flows between today and the starting date, and the second term corresponds to the present value of cash flows between the starting and ending dates.

From this condition we obtain the following simple relationship for forward CDS spreads:

$$S_{fwd} \;=\; \frac{S_2 - \kappa\,S_1}{1 - \kappa} = S_2 + \frac{\kappa}{1 - \kappa}(S_2 - S_1) \qquad (68)$$

$$\kappa \;=\; \frac{\pi_1}{\pi_2}$$

Thus, the forward CDS spread is equal to a weighted average of the spot CDS spreads to initial and final maturity, with the weights determined by the ratio of risky PV01s to each maturity (note that $0 < \kappa < 1$). If the CDS curve is upward sloping ($S_2 > S_1$), then the forward CDS spread is higher than the long maturity spot spread. If the CDS curve is inverted ($S_2 > S_1$), then the forward CDS spread is lower than the long maturity spot spread.

As a relative value measure, the forward spread of the issuer can be a powerful tool for investors seeking to choose the best exposure term for the given credit. Market segmentation plays an important role in driving the shapes of credit term structures, and it can lead at times to unusually rich or cheap segments of the term structure. Comparing the forward spreads across term structure segments is the most consistent way to zoom in on such relative value opportunities.

7 BOND-SPECIFIC VALUATION MEASURES

So far we have developed a set of term structures which encode our knowledge about the issuer (or sector) as a whole, rather than about the specific bond. In particular, our primary measure, the term structure of survival probability, clearly refers to the issuer and not to any particular bond issued by this issuer. It would make no sense to say that the XYZ 6.5% bond maturing in ten years has a term structure of survival probabilities, but it does make sense to say that the XYZ issuer has a term structure of survival probabilities which was fitted using the price of the above-mentioned bond, as well as other bonds of the same issuer, if available.

When it comes to a particular bond, investors are typically concerned with their fair value and relative value with respect to other bonds of the same issuer or sector. The estimate of the fair value for a given bond is a straightforward application of the issuer- or sector-specific fair value metrics to the particular maturity and coupon of the security under investigation. The answer to the second question lies in the comparison of the market-observed bond price with the estimated fair value price. The Default-Adjusted Spread (DAS) measure, introduced below, provides an unambiguous and consistent way to make such a comparison, free of biases associated with the term to maturity or level of coupon, which plague the conventional spread measures.

7.1 Fitted price and P-spread

The CCP measure introduced in the previous section determines the precise fit of the bond's price for a hypothetical bond with a pre-set coupon and maturity chosen so that there are integer number of payment periods and no accrued coupon amount as of pricing date.

We can easily extend this generic fitted price measure to any given bond by defining it as the clean price such a bond would have if it was priced precisely by the issuer- (or sector-) fitted survival probability term structure. Clearly, the notion of the fitted price depends on the context of the fit, i.e. whether we are talking about the fair value with respect to issuer or sector. A bond can be undervalued with respect to other bonds of the same issuer, but overvalued with respect to the majority of the bonds in the larger industry or rating sector.

Since the accrued interest $A_{int} = C\, t_{acc}$ is a known value depending on the coupon level and time accrued since issue or last coupon t_{acc}, the fitted price in our implementation is precisely equal to the market price less the regression residual from the cross-sectional estimation (44).

Outside of the regression context, one would calculate it using the term structure of the 'fair' survival probability for the issuer, such as the one calibrated from the benchmark CDS spread levels:

$$P^{fit} = Z_{base}(t_N)\, Q(t_N) + \frac{C}{q} \sum_{i=1}^{N} Z_{base}(t_i)\, Q(t_i)$$

$$+ R\left(1 + \frac{C}{2q}\right) \sum_{i}^{N} Z_{base}(t_i)\, (Q(t_{i-1}) - Q(t_i))$$

$$- C\, t_{acc} \tag{69}$$

The fitted par coupon of a given bond is defined as the coupon which would make this bond's clean price equal to par when evaluated using the suitably chosen fitted survival term structure. For a given maturity date, we must modify equation (59) for the par coupon to account for the effect of the non-current coupon and the non-zero accrued interest amount:

$$C_P^{fit} = q\, \frac{1 - Z_{base}(t_N)\, Q(t_N) - R \sum_{i=1}^{N} Z_{base}(t_i)\, (Q(t_{i-1}) - Q(t_i))}{\sum_{i=1}^{N} Z_{base}(t_i)\, Q(t_i) + \frac{1}{2} R \sum_{i=1}^{N} Z_{base}(t_i)\, (Q(t_{i-1}) - Q(t_i)) - q t_{acc}} \tag{70}$$

The difference between the fitted par coupon and the correspondingly defined fitted par base (LIBOR or Treasury) rate for the same maturity could be termed the fitted (or fair) P-spread.

$$S_P^{fit} = C_P^{fit} - C_P^{base} \tag{71}$$

This spread, however, does not correspond to the observed price of the bond. It is instead a P-spread that the bond would have if it was priced precisely, without any residual errors, by the corresponding issuer- or sector-specific fitted survival probability term structure. Next, we turn our attention to pricing errors and relative value measures.

7.2 Default-adjusted spread and excess spread

For a long time credit investors have been using spread measures such as nominal spread, I-spread, OAS, or Z-spread to assess the relative value across various bonds of the same issuer or sector (see O'Kane and Sen 2004 for a glossary of terms). In the previous sections we have demonstrated that these measures have inherent biases because all of them rely on the strippable cash flow valuation assumption which is inadequate for credit-risky bonds.

We argued that spread-like measures which can be interpreted in terms of risky excess return to maturity and are in agreement with the survival-based valuation, correspond to idealized par bonds or par-equivalent instruments such as CDS. However, bonds in the secondary market typically trade away from par. It is important to measure the degree by which the bond's price deviates from the 'fair' price corresponding to its coupon level and the term structure of the underlying interest rates. As explained in the previous subsection, the latter is the analogue of the constant coupon price term structure. For example, in terms of credit relative value a 6% bond trading at a price close to the 6% CCP curve is not any different from a 10% bond trading close to 10% CCP curve. On the other hand, if the first bond were trading above the 6% CCP price while the second was trading below the 10% CCP price, we would say that the first bond is rich and the second bond is cheap, even though the observed price of the first bond might be less than that of the second bond.

Fortunately, our estimation methodology for survival probability term structures lends itself naturally to a robust determination of the rich/cheap measures as described above. Indeed, we impose a fairly rigid structural constraint of the shape of the survival probability term structure by adopting the exponential splines approximation. The result was that the cross-sectional regression which gives the spline coefficients does not in general price any of the bonds precisely. Instead, we make a trade-off between the individual bond pricing precision and the robustness of the overall fit. The bond-specific pricing errors from the best fit of the survival probability term structure (i.e. cross-sectional regression residuals ϵ_{reg}) then become a natural candidate for the relative value across the bonds—if the residual is positive we say that the bond is rich, and if the residual is negative we say that it is cheap.

We can express the pricing error in terms of a constant DAS which acts as an additional discount (or premium) spread that replicates the bond's present value:

$$P^{mkt} = P^{fit} + \epsilon_{reg}$$

$$= Z_{base}(t_N)\, Q(t_N)\, e^{-DAS\, t_N} + \frac{C}{q} \sum_{i=1}^{N} Z_{base}(t_i)\, Q(t_i)\, e^{-DAS\, t_i}$$

$$+ R \left(1 + \frac{C}{2q}\right) \sum_{i}^{N} Z_{base}(t_i)\, (Q(t_{i-1}) - Q(t_i))\, e^{-DAS\, t_i}$$

$$- C\, t_{acc} \tag{72}$$

Here, P_{mkt} is the observed clean market price, and $A_{int} = C\, t_{acc}$ is the known accrued interest. Comparing this equation to (69) one can see that if $P_{mkt} = P_{fit}$ then $DAS = 0$. Default-Adjusted Spread should be interpreted as a bond-specific premium/discount which reflects both market inefficiencies such as liquidity premia and biases related to persistent market mispricing of credit bonds. We say that a positive DAS (negative regression residual ϵ_{reg}) signals cheapness and the negative DAS (positive residual ϵ_{reg}) signals richness across the bonds of the same issuer. This is in line with the usual meaning assigned to spreads. Moreover, we can say that the DAS differential for two bonds reflects the 'clean' relative value between them.

Having determined this last piece of the puzzle, we can now define the excess spread S_X of the credit bond as the previously derived fitted P-spread S_P plus the default-adjusted spread. Since both the fitted P-spread and DAS have a clear relative value interpretation, this measure of the total spread continues to have a meaning as a measure of excess return over the credit risk-free bonds or swaps curve, whichever is used as a base curve (hence the name *excess spread*).

$$S_X = S_P + DAS \tag{73}$$

It is clear from its definition that the excess spread measure should not be directly used in any discounting calculation, as it contains the P-spread measure that is not related to observed cash flows of the bond. This highlights one more time the fact that consistent relative value measures for credit bonds are not compatible with naive (strippable) discounted cash flow methodology.

Table 4.3 shows the calculated values for Calpine bonds as of 30 June 2003. Note the large differences between the Z-spread and P-spread measures of the bonds across all maturities, ranging from 250 to 400 bp. Note also that looking at Z-spreads alone it would be difficult to calculate the relative value between different bonds. By contrast, DAS provides a clean measure of such relative value. It appears that most high-coupon bonds are rich (have negative DAS), while the low-coupon bonds are cheap. Such

Table 4.3 Calpine bonds as of 6 June 2003

Description	Maturity (yrs)	Coupon	Z-spread	P-spread	DAS	Price	Fitted Price	price residual
CPN $8\frac{1}{4}$ 8/05	2.13	8.25	1649	1949	−68	82.00	81.02	0.98
CPN $7\frac{5}{8}$ 4/06	2.79	7.625	1690	2061	107	75.00	76.75	−1.75
CPN $10\frac{1}{2}$ 5/06	2.82	10.50	1594	1813	−97	83.30	81.30	1.71
CPN $8\frac{3}{4}$ 7/07	3.77	8.75	1568	1807	68	74.52	74.52	−1.34
CPN $7\frac{7}{8}$ 4/08	4.76	7.875	1376	1781	55	71.00	72.18	−1.18
CPN $7\frac{3}{4}$ 4/09	5.79	7.75	1210	1610	0	71.00	71.00	0.00
CPN $8\frac{5}{8}$ 8/10	7.13	8.625	1110	1457	−13	73.50	73.15	0.35
CPN $8\frac{1}{2}$ 2/11	7.63	8.50	1023	1353	−71	75.00	72.93	2.07

patterns of relative value driven by the coupon levels are quite often observed, and are a consequence of the market mispricing driven by the use of conventional spread measures.

Assuming an investor took a relative value trade in bonds maturing 4/06 and 5/06 as of the date in Table 4.3 in equal notional value (justified by closeness of maturities), such investor would have locked in $3.4 per $100 of notional value in such a trade, and would have realized at least that much in either bankruptcy (which actually occurred in December 2005) or maturity, since in both cases the bonds would have paid off the same final amount.

8 The CDS-Bond basis

Although CDS and cash bonds reflect the same underlying issuer credit risk, there are important fundamental and technical reasons why the CDS and bond markets can sometimes diverge from the economic parity (O'Kane 2008). Such divergences, commonly referred to as the CDS-Bond basis, are closely monitored by many credit investors. Trading the CDS-Bond basis is one of the widely used strategies for generation of excess returns using CDS.

There are a number of both fundamental and technical reasons that affect the pricing of bonds and CDS and lead to the presence of the CDS-Bond basis even after correcting for the inherent biases associated with the commonly used Z-spreads or asset swap spreads. We list some of them below.

Factors that drive CDS spreads wider than bonds:

- Delivery option: the standard CDS contract gives a protection buyer an option to choose a delivery instrument from a basket of deliverable securities in case of default.
- Risk of technical default and restructuring: the standard CDS contract may be triggered by events that do not constitute a full default or a bankruptcy of the obligor.
- Demand for protection: the difficulty of shorting credit risk in the bond market makes CDS a preferred alternative for hedgers and tends to push their spreads wider during the times of increasing credit risks.
- LIBOR-spread vs. Treasury spread: the CDS market implies trading relative to swaps curve, while most of the bond market trades relative to Treasury bond curve. Occasionally, the widening of the LIBOR spread that is driven by non-credit technical factors such as MBS hedging can make bonds appear *optically* tight to LIBOR.

Factors that drive CDS spreads tighter than bonds:

- Implicit LIBOR-flat funding: the CDS spreads imply a LIBOR-flat funding rate, which makes them cheap from the perspective of many protection sellers, such as hedge funds and lower credit quality counterparties, who normally fund at higher rates.
- Counterparty credit risk: the protection buyer is exposed to the counterparty risk of the protection seller and must be compensated by tighter CDS spreads.
- Differential accrued interest loss: in the CDS market, the accrued interest is netted with the protection payment in case of default. In the bond market, the accrued coupon amount is often lost or added to outstanding notional which recovers only a fraction in default.
- Differential liquidity: while the amount of the available liquidity in the top 50 or so bond issuers is greater in the cash market, the situation is often reverse for the rest of the credit market where writing protection can be easier than buying the bonds.

For all these reasons, the CDS-Bond basis can be and often is substantial. While the fundamental factors affect the proper value of the fair basis and are largely stable, the transient nature of the more powerful technical factors causes the basis to fluctuate around this fair value with a typical mean reversion time that ranges from a few weeks to a few months. This makes basis trading an attractive relative value investment strategy, albeit with its own inherent risks of liquidity-driven blow-ups, like any other such strategy. For example, during the market dislocation at the end of 2008 the CDS-Bond basis reached in some cases several hundred basis points.

Many investors have been actively trading such basis convergence strategies by relying on the conventional basis measure, the difference between the CDS spread and the bond's Z-spread. Since Z-spread itself is a biased measure of credit risk, therefore this conventional basis measure is also biased. In this section, we present the alternative measure, based on accurate replication of bonds with CDS.

8.1 The CDS-Bond complementarity

Assume that the underlying risk-free discount curve $r(t)$ (usually LIBOR) and the issuer's hazard rate term structure $h(t)$ are given. The forward base discount function and the forward survival probability are given by equations (65) and (66), respectively.

Consider a credit-risky bond with a given coupon C and final maturity T. The projected forward price of a fixed coupon bond depends on both riskless rate and hazard rate term structures as well as the level of the coupon in the following manner (for simplicity of exposition we use the continuous-time approximation and ignore the small corrections proportional to the coupon level—see Appendix B for detailed derivation):

$$P(t, T) = C \int_t^T du\, e^{-\int_t^u ds\,(f(s)+h(s))} + e^{-\int_t^T ds\,(f(s)+h(s))}$$

$$+ R \int_t^T du\, h(u)\, e^{-\int_t^u ds\,(f(s)+h(s))} \tag{74}$$

The first term reflects the present value of the coupon stream under the condition that the bond survived until some intermediate time u, the second term reflects the present value of the final principal payment under the condition that the bond survived until the final maturity T, the third term reflects the recovery of the fraction R of the face value if the issuer defaults at any time between the valuation time and the final maturity.

Let us define the *risk-free-equivalent coupon* stream $RFC(t, T)$ which would reproduce the same forward price term structure but only when discounted with the risk-free discount function, without any default probability. Such a coupon stream will not be constant in general and will have a non-trivial term structure, depending on both the underlying risk-free rates and, through the price of the risky bond, on the issuer hazard rates as well. The defining condition is:

$$P(t, T) = \int_t^T du\, RFC(t, u)\, e^{-\int_t^u ds\,(f(s)+h(s))} + e^{-\int_t^T ds\,(f(s)+h(s))} \tag{75}$$

The concept of a risk-free equivalent coupon stream is necessary for consistent definition of the difference between the default-risky and risk-free bonds when the underlying interest and hazard rates have non-trivial term structures and the bonds are expected to deviate from par pricing either currently or at any time in the future.

To find the relationship between the risk-free-equivalent coupon stream $RFC(t, T)$ and the forward price $P(t, T)$ of a credit-risky bond, let us take a derivative with respect to the valuation time t of both sides of equations (74) and (75).

$$\frac{\partial P(t, T)}{\partial t} = (r(t) + h(t))\, P(t, T) - C - R\, h(t) \tag{76}$$

$$\frac{\partial P(t, T)}{\partial t} = r(t)\, P(t, T) - RFC(t, T) \tag{77}$$

Since the left-hand sides are equal by construction, we can equate the right-hand sides and obtain the relationship between the risk-free-equivalent coupon stream and the forward price:

$$C - RFC(t, T) = h(t)(P(t, T) - R) \tag{78}$$

Consider now a forward CDS contract for the infinitesimal period $[t, t + dt]$. Since the hazard rate term structure can be ignored in such a short period, then the credit triangle formula (42) applies and the forward CDS spread is simply proportional to the hazard rate for that period:

$$S_{CDS}^{fwd}(t, t + dt) = (1 - R)h(t) \tag{79}$$

Substituting this definition into equation (78), we get a complementarity condition between the credit-risky coupon, risk-free-equivalent coupon stream, and the forward CDS spreads:

$$RFC(t, T) = C - S_{CDS}^{fwd}(t, t + dt) N_{CDS}^{fwd}(t, T) \tag{80}$$

$$N_{CDS}^{fwd}(t, T) = \frac{P(t, T) - R}{1 - R} \tag{81}$$

where we also introduced the forward CDS notional $N_{CDS}^{fwd}(t, T)$, which depends on the forward price of the credit bond.

8.2 Static hedging of credit bonds with CDS

This relationship suggests a consistent hedging strategy for non-par credit-risky bonds which consists of a stream of forward CDS with notionals $N_{CDS}^{fwd}(t, T)$ depending on the forward price of the bond. The residual cash-flows of the credit-risky bond after paying the required premiums coincide with the projected risk-free-equivalent coupon stream. Although there is still a timing risk associated with this hedging strategy, the notionals of the hedges are such that the recovered value will be equal to the correct forward price of the bond, and therefore the timing risk is unimportant when evaluating the present value of the hedged cash-flows to the initial time or to any future time before maturity.

Alternatively, one could replace the forward CDS in this hedging strategy with pairs of spot CDS of increasing maturities. If one chose a grid of maturities t_i for which the hedging is done, the corresponding notionals of the pairs of CDS for each interval $[t_i, t_{i+1}]$ would be given by:

$$N_{CDS}^{spot}(t_i, t_{i+1}, T) = \frac{P(t_i, T) - P(t_{i+1}, T)}{1 - R} \tag{82}$$

If we execute the hedging strategy with long-short pairs, the result becomes a staggered hedge which is nearly 100% notional for the final maturity, and which includes some additional relatively small long (or short) positions for shorter maturities depending on the forward prices of the credit bond being hedged. Each such position hedges the incremental digital price risk (with no recovery) corresponding to the next maturity interval on the hedging grid.

From the earlier discussions in this chapter, it is clear that both the coupon level of the credit bond and the term structure of the underlying interest rates and issuer's hazard rates may substantially affect the hedging strategy with forward CDS or long-short CDS pairs. Its dependence on the underlying bond is depicted in Figures 4.9, 4.10, and 4.11.

Figure 4.9 shows a case of a bond with a high coupon equal to 8% and a high current price of 116.69%. The forward price of the credit bond gradually declines toward maturity. The forward CDS hedge notional mirrors that behaviour, starting as high as 133% of the face value, and gradually decreases toward 100%. The spot CDS hedge contains the final notional hedge and relatively large additional hedges at earlier maturities. Despite the decrease in the forward hedge notional, the semi-annual cost of hedging grows gradually from 40bp to 44bp as a result of a relatively steep forward CDS curve term structure.

Figure 4.10 shows a case of a bond with a very low coupon equal to 3% and a current discount price equal to 94.33%. The forward price of the bond gradually grows towards maturity. The forward CDS hedge notional mirrors this, starting at 89% of the face

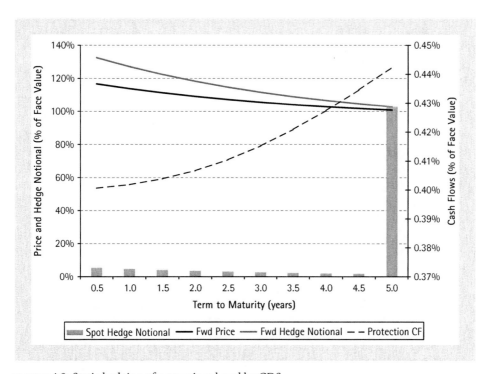

FIGURE 4.9 Static hedging of a premium bond by CDS.

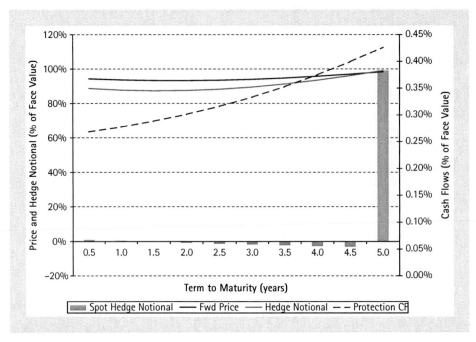

FIGURE 4.10 Static hedging of a discount bond by CDS.

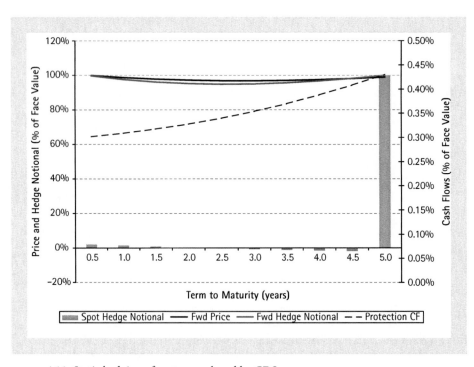

FIGURE 4.11 Static hedging of a near-par bond by CDS.

value, and gradually increases toward 100%. The spot CDS hedge contains the final notional hedge and additional hedges at intermediate maturities which actually change sign, with some offsetting short protection positions before the final maturity. The semi-annual cost of hedging grows more steeply from 27bp to 43bp as both forward CDS rates and hedge notionals grow.

Figure 4.11 shows a case of a bond with near-par coupon equal to 4.25% and a current price of 99.93%. Despite the fact that this is a par bond, the forward bond prices and forward CDS hedge notionals exhibit a non-trivial term structure, starting near 100%, then dropping to lower levels and only pulling back to par near final maturity. The spot CDS hedge also has non-trivial intermediate maturity hedges with changing sign. The semi-annual cost of hedging grows from 33bp to 43bp, which is somewhere between the high and low coupon cases.

The static hedging strategy using CDS addresses only the credit risk exposure. According to the complementarity principle proven in (80), the remainder of these hedging strategies is the risk-free-coupon stream (RFC) bond whose forward price profile matches precisely that of the credit bond. While this hypothetical RFC bond is no longer subject to credit loss risk, it is still subject to interest rate risk. In order to fully hedge the residual interest rate risk one would simply have to swap all the projected RFC cash flows into floating rate using a sequence of interest rate swaps of appropriate maturities.

This, however, does not fully eliminate the interest rate risk. Indeed, upon a default event the cash flows from the credit bond itself and all the CDS will terminate, while the interest rate swaps that have maturities longer than the date of default will still be outstanding. The expected net market value of these remaining swaps is equal to the expected variation of the interest rate hedge package from the forward price of the RFC bond. Hence, it is equal to zero by construction regardless of the default timing. In order to fully eliminate not only the expected risk exposure but also the residual risk in all states of the world both before and after the default event one would need to use the so-called *extinguishing asset swaps*, i.e. fixed-for-floating swaps which contractually terminate upon the default of the reference credit entity.

8.3 Consistent measures for CDS-Bond basis

If the bonds of a given issuer were perfectly priced according to our framework, and if the term structure of credit risk as well as the recovery value was in agreement between the bond and CDS markets, the bond prices would satisfy the survival-based fair value given by (27). The hazard rate in this equation would be identical to the one calibrated from the credit triangle relationship (41), and the BCDS term structure (64) would coincide with market observed CDS term structure. There would be no basis between the two markets, and the hedged cash bond would have zero expected excess return over the appropriately defined risk-free rate.

If, on the contrary, the market-observed CDS spreads were tighter than BCDS, one could hedge the credit bond by CDS at a lower cost than that implied by the model, thus locking in a positive expected excess return. Vice versa, if the market CDS spreads were wider than BCDS, the hedge would have a higher cost, and the expected excess return of the hedged position would be negative. Such non-zero expected excess return is what is supposed to be reflected by the consistent measure of the Bond-CDS basis.

When the two markets, bonds and CDS, show different levels of implied default probability, there is an ambiguity as to which of these is correct, if any. It is a common assumption that if there exists a liquid CDS market with full quoted term structure, then it is this market which is less biased as far as credit risk is concerned. We share this opinion since the CDS market is naturally focused on this particular source of risk, and since the metrics used (CDS spread, risky PV01, etc.) by most market participants are unbiased, unlike the case of cash bonds where most market participants use biased metrics like Z-spread.

In this case, the natural definition of the CDS-Bond basis would result from the comparison of the bond market price with its fair value in the survival-based framework where the hazard rate is taken from the CDS market. In the same way as the default-adjusted spread reflects the pricing basis of a given bond to best fit of the issuer or sector, the additional discount spread in this equation can be regarded as the pricing basis between this particular bond and the CDS market. Thus, the definition of the Basis Spread (BS) is:

$$
\begin{aligned}
P_{mkt} \; = \;\; & Z_{base}(t_N)\, Q_{CDS}(t_N)\, e^{-BS\, t_N} \\
+ \;\; & \frac{C}{q} \sum_{i=1}^{N} Z_{base}(t_i)\, Q_{CDS}(t_i)\, e^{-BS\, t_i} \\
+ \;\; & R\left(1 + \frac{C}{2q}\right) \sum_{i}^{N} Z_{base}(t_i)\, (Q_{CDS}(t_{i-1}) - Q_{CDS}(t_i))\, e^{-BS\, t_i} - C\, t_{acc} \quad (83)
\end{aligned}
$$

In the opposite case, if the CDS market is not very liquid beyond the benchmark five-year maturity while there are many cash bonds allowing one to derive a well-defined term structure of credit risk on the bond side, it would be natural to consider the latter as the unbiased measure of credit risk. Potentially, one can also take a compromise view and consider the bond market as the correct source for the shape of the credit risk term structure, but recalibrate the level of this risk by fitting the five-year CDS. One would then use this survival term structure in (83) for determining the basis for a particular bond.

8.4 The coarse-grained hedging and approximate basis

The static hedging strategy using a sequence of forward CDS is difficult to implement in practice. Although less precise, the staggered strategy using spot CDS is generally easier to put to work. However, even the staggered strategy, if implemented in short-term increments as presented in Figures 4.9–4.11, would lead to odd-lot hedge notionals for intermediate terms, and likely result in an unacceptable loss of liquidity.

As a compromise between accuracy and liquidity, we suggest a coarse-grained staggered hedge which can be constructed using a maturity grid with longer intervals. The forward price changes in these intervals will yield lumpier intermediate hedge notionals, according to (82). The optimal hedging grid will depend on the bond coupon level and the underlying interest rates. For bonds with modest premium or discount, just one or two additional hedges can result in sufficient accuracy.

Let us consider a single-CDS strategy first. Figure 4.12 shows an example of such strategy (the line with diamonds) contrasted with the theoretical precise strategy using forwards (the light solid line) in the case of a premium credit bond whose forward price (dashed line) gradually approaches par towards the five-year maturity. Such a simple hedging strategy would typically be underhedged (compared to the theoretical requirement) during the early years and overhedged during the later years of its projected existence. The optimal hedge notional will be such that the net present value of the outstanding risk exposures (positive for short terms and negative for long terms) become precisely zero.

Such a requirement also helps in explaining why the 'market hedge ratio' that is equal simply to the price premium of the underlying bond (which is quite popular

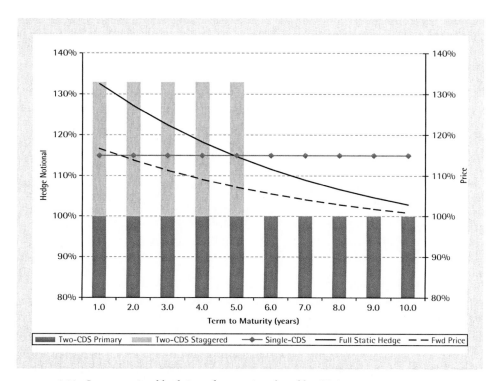

FIGURE 4.12 Coarse-grained hedging of a premium bond by CDS.

among the practitioners (see McAdie and O'Kane 2001), provides a good starting guess for the correct hedge amount. Indeed, had we approximated the theoretical hedge notional line by a straight line, and ignored the effect of interest rate discounting, the optimal notional would correspond to the mid-point between the final theoretical hedge ratio at maturity, i.e. 100%, and the initial theoretical hedge ratio at current time (79). If one used a recovery rate of $R = 50\%$ which is quite close to the long-term average recovery estimates, one would obtain the hedge notional equal to the current price of the bond.

We can see therefore, that the market practice is not too different from the correct single-CDS optimal hedge. One must ask, however, whether the single-CDS hedge itself is the optimal solution, or are we missing something important by limiting ourselves to only one hedging instrument?

Consider now the two-CDS hedging strategy depicted in Figure 4.12 by stacked bars. The strategy consists of a face value hedge to final maturity, plus an additional (staggered) hedge to a shorter maturity. We can arrange this strategy to be, for example, overhedged during the earlier years and underhedged during the later years of its projected existence. The same requirement of zero net present value of the outstanding risk exposures will define the optimal notional of the smaller staggered hedge, given its chosen maturity.

Note also, that by allowing the maturity of the add-on staggered hedge to be equal to the final maturity of the bond we would recover the case of a single-CDS strategy. Therefore, the two-CDS strategy will always be at least as good as the single-CDS one. When will it be better? It would be a better choice when the cost of hedging using two CDS turns out to be less than the cost of hedging using a single CDS. In the case of a premium bond, this will be the case if the CDS spread term structure is upward sloping, making the use of shorter-term CDS a preferable option.

The considerations above lead us to the following simple recipe for a practical and accurate hedging strategy of credit bonds with CDS:

- Set the primary hedge to the final maturity of the bond with a notional equal to par face value of the bond.
- Consider various intermediate maturities (including the bond's final maturity) for which a sufficiently liquid market in CDS exists, and determine the optimal staggered hedge amount for the second CDS position for each maturity.
- Select the lowest cost hedging strategy among all considered two-CDS combinations.

The corresponding approximate CDS-Bond basis for the bond under consideration will be determined by comparison of its theoretical full excess spread (73) where the P-spread is measured with respect to LIBOR base curve, and the rpv01-weighted aggregate CDS spread of the coarse-grained staggered hedging strategy. This means that, even in a simplified framework, the correct relative value measure for basis trading strongly depends on the bond's coupon level and price premium, and the term structures of both interest rates and CDS spreads.

9 CONCLUSIONS

In this chapter we have critically examined the conventional bond pricing methodology and have shown that it does not adequately reflect the nature of the credit risk faced by investors. In particular, we have demonstrated that the strippable discounted cash flows valuation assumption, which is normally taken for granted by most analysts, leads to biased estimates of relative value for credit bonds. Moreover, even the CDS market, which does not use this pricing methodology, is strongly influenced by its prevalence in the cash market because of the constant cross-benchmarking of cash bonds and CDS. The example of the 'optically distorted' term structures of Z-spreads and CDS spreads of such a highly liquid name as Ford Motor Credit shown in section 3 should convince investors that the conventional methodology can indeed be quite misleading.

We have introduced a consistent survival-based valuation methodology which is free of the biases mentioned above, albeit at a price of abandoning the strippable discounted cash flows valuation assumption. We also developed a robust estimation methodology for survival probability term structures using the exponential splines approximation, and implemented and tested this methodology in a wide variety of market conditions and across a large set of sectors and issuers, from the highest credit quality to highly distressed ones.

To remedy the loss of intuition due to the abandonment of OAS, Z-spreads, and other conventional spread measures, we have introduced a host of new definitions for credit term structures, ranging from valuation measures such as the hazard rate and P-spread to relative value measures such as the bond-specific Default Adjusted Spread.

In conclusion, we believe that the adoption of the survival-based methodologies advocated in this chapter by market participants will lead to an increase in the efficiency of the credit markets just as the adoption of better pre-payment models led to efficiency in the MBS (Mortgage-based securities) markets twenty years ago. Investors who will be at the forefront of this change will be in a position to benefit from the secular shift to a much more quantitative approach to credit portfolio management. We have witnessed many such turning points in recent years, including the widespread following attained by structural credit risk models pioneered by Merton and further developed by KMV (Kealhofer, McQuown, Varicek) and others, the explosive growth in the credit derivatives and structured credit market which proceeded alongside a dramatic progress in modelling complex risks of correlated defaults and losses, the adoption of new banking regulatory standards which place a much greater emphasis on quantitative measures of credit and counterparty risks, and finally the proliferation of credit hedge funds and relative value investors who stand ready to exploit any inefficiencies still present in the marketplace. It was long overdue that the most traditional of all credit instruments, the credit bonds, would also be considered in the light of this new knowledge.

APPENDICES

....

A Exponential splines

The exponential spline approximation is defined in a way which facilitates smooth fitting of functions which are exponentially decreasing with term to maturity but are not necessarily required to have a constant rate of decrease. The shape of the approximated function is given by a linear combination of spline factors:

$$F(t) = \sum_{k=1}^{K} \beta_k \, \Phi_k \left(t \, \middle| \, \eta \right) \tag{84}$$

where the spline coefficients β_k are constants derived from the best fit optimization procedure, such as minimization of the weighted average square of bond pricing errors in the case of fitting Treasury discount functions or credit survival probability term structures.

The exponential spline functions $\Phi_k \left(t \, \middle| \, \eta \right)$ have a fixed shape depending only on the remaining term to maturity, and on the decay parameter η.

The first three spline factors are known as no-knot factors because they are smooth in the entire range of maturities.

$$\Phi_k \left(t \, \middle| \, \eta \right) = e^{-k\,\eta\,t} \tag{85}$$

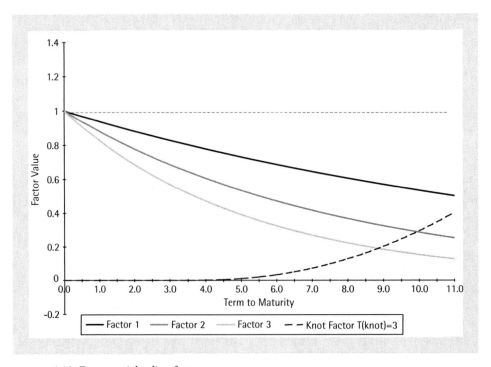

FIGURE 4.13 Exponential spline factors.

In fixed income applications, the shape of the yield curve often reflects market segmentation—the short, medium, and long maturities can have substantially different behaviour. To address this, one uses higher order spline factors (number 4 and above) which are exactly zero below certain maturity known as the *knot point* T_k^{knot}, have the familiar exponential shape above the knot point, and have a smooth value and first derivative at the knot point itself. These requirements determine the higher order spline factors uniquely as follows:

$$\Phi_k\left(t\,|\eta\right) = \Theta\left(t - T_k^{knot}\right)\left(\frac{1}{3} - e^{-\eta\left(t-T_k^{knot}\right)} + e^{-2\eta\left(t-T_k^{knot}\right)} - \frac{1}{3}e^{-3\eta\left(t-T_k^{knot}\right)}\right) \qquad (86)$$

The shapes of the spline factors are shown in Figure 4.13.

B Continuous time approximation for credit bond and CDS pricing

Continuous compounding is a convenient technique which may often simplify the analysis of relative value and forward pricing of credit bonds. It corresponds to coupon payments being made continuously. The present value for a hypothetical continuously compounded credit-risky bond can be calculated using the instantaneous forward interest rates (7) and hazard rates (58). The base discount function and the survival probability are given by (65) and (66), respectively:

Assuming uncorrelated interest, hazard and recovery rates, one can combine equations (65) and (66) to obtain a continuously compounded analogue of the bond pricing equation (27):

$$P(T) = C\int_0^T du\, e^{-\int_0^u ds\,(f(s)+h(s))} + e^{-\int_0^T ds\,(f(s)+h(s))} + R\int_0^T du\, h(u)\, e^{-\int_t^u ds\,(f(s)+h(s))}$$
$$(87)$$

This simple formula overestimates the present value of a credit bond for two distinct reasons:

- First, it neglects the expected accrued coupon loss and recovery in case of default.
- Second, it overestimates the present value of the regular coupon payments because it presumes that portions of the coupon were paid earlier and it discounts those portions with a correspondingly smaller discount factor (and higher survival probability).

The more accurate approximation which we derive here corrects for these two biases.

The correction for the coupon loss bias can be estimated by noting that the expected timing of the default event under a constant hazard rate assumption is roughly half-way through the payment period. Hence, the expected accrued interest equals to approximately half of the scheduled coupon payment, which in turn is equal to $1/q$ fraction of the coupon rate for a bond with frequency q. Consequently, to correct for this bias we should explicitly add the expected accrued interest at default to the principal amount, assuming that the coupon and principal recovery are the same $R_{int} = R_{pr} = R$.

The correction for the early discount bias can be estimated by noting that by distributing the coupon payments evenly between the two coupon dates we get the survival-weighted present value which is roughly half-way between the present value of a bullet coupon payment on the two ends of the coupon period. Thus, for each bullet coupon the continuous-time formula (87) corresponds to a present value bias equal to half of difference between the 'true' present value of the earlier coupon payment and the current coupon payment. When summing up all of these biases, the corrections for all intermediate coupon payments cancel each other, and the total present value bias is simply half of the difference between the present value of the first coupon payment and the last coupon payment. For the valuation date just prior to a coupon payment, this results in a simple estimate since the present value of that impending coupon payment is simply equal to its amount. For other valuation dates the situation is slightly more complicated but the approximation remains pretty close nevertheless.

We obtain the continuous-time approximation for the clean price of a q-frequency credit bond by subtracting these two bias estimates from the original 'naïve' formula. Finally, we should also include the Default-Adjusted Spread (DAS), an issue-specific discounting measure introduced above that allows us to use the issuer- or sector-specific hazard rate term structure while exactly fitting the observed price of individual bonds.

The final formula for the clean price of a fixed-coupon credit bond in the continuous-time approximation is:

$$
\begin{aligned}
P(T \mid q) \; = \; & C \int_0^T du\, e^{-\int_0^u ds\,(f(s)+h(s)+DAS)} + e^{-\int_0^T ds\,(f(s)+h(s)+DAS)} \\
& - \frac{C}{2q}\left(1 - e^{-\int_0^T ds\,(f(s)+h(s)+DAS)}\right) \\
& + R\left(1 + \frac{C}{2q}\right)\int_0^T du\, h(u)\, e^{-\int_t^u ds\,(f(s)+h(s)+DAS)} \qquad (88)
\end{aligned}
$$

This approximation is quite accurate across all values of coupons and for all shapes and levels of the underlying interest rate and hazard rate curves. Both correction terms can be quite important.

In a similar fashion, we can write the pricing equation for CDS in continuous compounding approximation as:

$$
UP(T) \; + \; C_{CDS}\int_0^T du\, e^{-\int_0^u ds\,(f(s)+h(s))} = (1-R)\int_0^T du\, h(u)\, e^{-\int_t^u ds\,(f(s)+h(s))} \qquad (89)
$$

After correcting for the biases associated with finite frequency (typically, $q = 4$) of premium payments, namely the discounting bias and the netting convention between unpaid accrued premium and the protection payment, we get:

$$
\begin{aligned}
UP(T \mid q) \; + \; & C_{CDS}\int_0^T du\, e^{-\int_0^u ds\,(f(s)+h(s))} \\
& - \frac{C_{CDS}}{2q}\left(1 - e^{-\int_0^T ds\,(f(s)+h(s))}\right) \\
& = \left(1 - R - \frac{C_{CDS}}{2q}\right)\int_0^T du\, h(u)\, e^{-\int_t^u ds\,(f(s)+h(s))} \qquad (90)
\end{aligned}
$$

Finally, the continuous-time approximation for the par CDS spread is given by solving for C_{CDS} in the above equation for the case $UP(T \mid q) = 0$:

$$
S_{CDS}(T \mid q) = (1-R)\frac{\int_0^T du\, h(u)\, e^{-\int_t^u ds\,(f(s)+h(s))}}{\int_0^T du\,\left(1 - \frac{f(u)}{2q}\right) e^{-\int_0^u ds\,(f(s)+h(s))}} \qquad (91)
$$

In particular, we get a simple correction to the credit triangle formula for the case of flat term structures of interest and hazard rates:

$$S_{CDS}(T \mid q) = \frac{1}{1 - \frac{f}{2q}} (1 - R) h \tag{92}$$

REFERENCES

Altman, E. I., Resti, A., and Sironi, A. (2004). 'Default recovery rates and LGD in credit risk modeling and practice: a review of the literature and empirical evidence'. *Economic Notes*, 33: 183–208.

Altman, E. I., Brooks, B., Resti, A., and Sironi, A. (2005). 'The link between default and recovery rates: theory, empirical evidence and implications'. *Journal of Business*, 78: 2203–27.

Bakshi, G., Madan, D., and Zhang, F. (2006). 'Understanding the role of recovery in default risk models: empirical comparisons and implied recovery rates'. CFR working paper, no. 06. FDIC.

Berd, A. M. (2005). 'Recovery swaps'. *Journal of Credit Risk*, 1/3: 61–70.

—— Mashal, R., and Wang, P. (2003). 'Estimating implied default probabilities from credit bond prices'. *Quantitative Credit Research Quarterly*, 2003-Q3. Lehman Brothers.

—— —— —— (2004a). 'Bond-implied CDS term structures and relative value measures for CDS-bond trading'. *Quantitative Credit Research Quarterly*, 2004-Q1. Lehman Brothers.

—— —— —— (2004b). 'Consistent risk measures for credit bonds'. *Quantitative Credit Research Quarterly*, 2004-Q3-Q4. Lehman Brothers.

BIS, (2009). *OTC Derivatives Market Activity in the First Half of 2009*. Technical report. Bank for International Settlements.

Das, S., and Hannona, P. (2009). 'Implied recovery'. *Journal of Economic Dynamics and Control*, 33/11: 1837–57.

Duffie, J. D. (1998). 'Defaultable term structure models with fractional recovery of Par'. Graduate School of Business working paper. Stanford University, CA.

—— and Singleton, K. (1999). 'Modeling term structures of defaultable bonds'. *Review of Financial Studies*, 12: 687.

—— —— (2003). *Credit Risk*. Princeton: Princeton University Press.

—— Schroder, M., and Skiadas, C. (1996). 'Recursive valuation of defaultable securities and the timing of resolution of uncertainty'. *Annals of Applied Probability*, 6/4: 1075.

Finkelstein, V. (1999). 'The Price of credit'. *Risk*, 12(Dec.): 68.

Guha, R. (2003). 'Recovery of Face Value at default: empirical evidence and implications for credit risk pricing'. Working paper. London Business School.

Gupton, G., and Stein, R. M. (2002). 'LossCalc: Moody's model for predicting loss given default'. Moody's Special Comment. Moody's.

Heath, D., Jarrow, R. A., and Morton, A. (1992). 'Bond pricing and the term structure of interest rates: a new methodology for contingent claims valuation'. *Econometrica*, 60/1: 77–105.

Jarrow, R. A. (2001). 'Default parameter estimation using market prices'. *Financial Analysts Journal*, 57/1: 75.

—— and Lando, D. (2000). 'The intersection of market and credit risk'. *Journal of Banking and Finance*, 24: 271.

Jarrow, R. A., and Yildirim, Y. (2002). 'Valuing default swaps under market and credit risk correlation'. *Journal of Fixed Income*, 11/4: 7.

—— and Turnbull, S. M. (1995). 'Pricing options on financial securities subject to default risk. *Journal of Finance*, 50: 53.

—— Lando, D., and Turnbull, S. M. (1997). 'A Markov model for the term structure of credit risk spreads'. *Review of Financial Studies*, 10: 481.

Lando, D. (2005). *Credit Models*. Princeton: Princeton University Press.

Litterman, R., and Iben, T. (1991). 'Corporate bond valuation and the term structure of credit spreads'. *Journal of Portfolio Management*, 17/3: 52.

McAdie, R., and O'Kane, D. (2001). 'Trading the default swap basis'. *Risk*, 14: (Oct.).

Merton, R. (1974). 'On the pricing of corporate debt: the risk structure of interest rates'. *Journal of Finance*, 29: 449.

Naldi, M., Chu, K., and Chang, G. (2002). 'The new Lehman Brothers credit risk model. *Quantitative Credit Research Quarterly*, 2002-Q2. Lehman Brothers.

O'Kane, D. (2008). *Modelling Single-Name and Multi-Name Credit Derivatives*. Chichester: John Wiley & Sons.

—— and Sen, S. (2005). 'Credit spreads explained'. *Journal of Credit Risk*, 1/2: 61.

Schonbucher, P. J. (2003). *Credit Derivatives Pricing Models*. Chichester: John Wiley & Sons.

Shea, G. S. (1985). Term structure estimation with exponential splines. *Journal of Finance*, 40: 319.

Tuckman, B. (2002). *Fixed Income Securities*, (2nd edn.) Chichester: John Wiley & Sons.

Vasicek, O., and Fong, G. (1982). 'Term structure modeling using exponential splines'. *Journal of Finance*, 37: 339.

Wilcox, R. (1997). *Introduction to Robust Estimation and Hypothesis Testing*. San Diego: Academic Press.

CHAPTER 5

....

STATISTICAL DATA MINING PROCEDURES IN GENERALIZED COX REGRESSIONS

....

ZHEN WEI

1 INTRODUCTION

....

SURVIVAL (default) data are frequently encountered in financial (especially credit risk), medical, educational, and other fields, where the 'default' can be regarded as the failure to fulfil debt payments of a specific company or the death of a patient in a medical study or the inability to pass some educational tests, etc.

Survival data usually consist of either cross-sectional data in the form of the triplet $(x_{ij}, z_{ij}, \delta_{ij})$ for $i = 1, \ldots, m$, and $j = 1, \ldots, J_i$ where

- m is the total number of groups and J_i is the number of subjects in the i-th group
- x_{ij} is a vector of covariates that is included to build the survival model. It can be random.
- z_{ij} is the observed failure time or censoring time, whichever comes first
- δ_{ij} is the default indicator for the j-th subject in the i-th group

or the survival data can consist of the time-series type data (x_{ijt}, δ_{ijt}), for $i = 1, \ldots, m$, $j = 1, \ldots, J_i$ and $t = t_{ij}, \ldots, T_{ij}$, where $m, J_i, x_{ijt}, \delta_{ijt}$ are similarly defined and the covariates x_{ijt} can be stochastic processes. Our goal is to make prediction on the survival probability of each subject (entity) and the survival correlation between a pool of them using the information from the covariates. Various models are proposed, built on the past data, and their predictive powers and accuracies are assessed. One important class of models prevailing in medical and biological practices is the Cox's (proportional) model, which also has potential applications in credit risk.

This chapter introduces the basic ideas of Cox's original proportional model for the hazard rates (Cox 1972) and extends the model within a general framework of statistical data mining procedures. Traditionally, these models are calibrated using the martingale approach, which is based on theories in counting processes, for example, see Anderson and Gill (1982). In contrast, this chapter presents a various pool of procedures that are based solely on maximum (partial) likelihoods without using the martingale properties. Moreover, the data mining procedures described in this chapter can also be employed to solve other regression/classification problems that are beyond the scope of survival analysis.

The rest of the chapter is divided into four sections. The first part (Section 2) introduces various statistical data mining procedures for (generalized) Cox regression with time-independent covariates (for cross-sectional type data). The second part (Section 3) deals with time-dependent covariates. It can be seen that the tools used in section 2 can also be applied to section 3 and vice versa. Although the described procedures are very efficient for model calibration and many of them have very profound theoretical backgrounds, we omit most of the theoretical proofs for the purpose of emphasizing the methods themselves. For example, there is a universal 'Oracle property' for many of the regularization methods, which states the asymptotic efficiency of the estimation and selection procedures. Whenever possible, we present the algorithm as a recipe in several iterative steps, so that the reader can easily implement the ideas. section 4 presents an example of using statistical factors to explain the default arrival intensities and to generate trading signals. The idea is quite general and can be extended to make other forms of factor models for credit derivatives. Concluding remarks are given in section 5.

2 GENERALIZED COX REGRESSION WITH TIME-INDEPENDENT COVARIATES

For a brief review of the definitions in classical survival analysis, I refer the reader to Appendix A. Under the settings in Appendix A, our goal is to predict the survival probability over time of a particular entity given the current status of covariates. Furthermore, by separating the elements of the covariate x into group of systematic and idiosyncratic factor components, one may further explore the correlation between the defaults of multiple names.

In this section, we only consider a single observation of default timing for each entity, which should be useful for cross-sectional data in default modelling or survival data for clinical (medical) experiments. Later, we will extend the model to time series data where the covarites could also have a stochastic feature.

2.1 Generalized Cox hazard models

2.1.1 *Proportional hazard model*

Let's first consider the model for hazard rate:

$$h(t) = h_0(t) \exp\left(x^T \beta\right) \tag{1}$$

for some baseline function $h_0(t)$. To estimate the survival probability of a given subject or correlation among the defaults, it suffices to estimate the parameter β (condition on current state of the covariates).

Given the observed data $\{(x_i, z_i, \delta_i) : i = 1, \ldots, n\}$, the likelihood function is given by (the defaults are independent given the covariates)

$$L = \prod_{\delta_i=1} f(z_i|x_i) \prod_{\delta_i=0} S(z_i|x_i) = \prod_{\delta_i=1} h(z_i) \prod_{i=1}^{n} S(z_i|x_i)$$

$$= \prod_{\delta_i=1} h_0(z_i) \exp\left(x_i^T \beta\right) \prod_{i=1}^{n} \exp\left(-H_0(z_i) \exp\left(x_i^T \beta\right)\right) \tag{2}$$

where

$$H_0(t) = \int_0^t h_0(u) \, du$$

is the cumulative baseline hazard function.

2.1.2 *Partial likelihood function*

Usually, it is not easy to directly maximize the criterion (2). Breslow (1974) assumes that H_0 is a step function that jumps only at censored observations:

$$H_0(t) = \sum_{\delta_j=1} h_j I\left(z_j \leq t\right)$$

where $I.$ is an indicator function.

Then, the logarithm of the likelihood function (2) is

$$\sum_{\delta_j=1} \left(\log(h_j) + x_j^T \beta\right) - \sum_{i=1}^{n} \left(\sum_{\delta_j=1} h_j I\left(z_j \leq z_i\right) \exp\left(x_i^T \beta\right)\right)$$

Taking the derivative with respect to h_j generates

$$\hat{h}_j = \left(\sum_{i=1}^{n} I\left(z_j \leq z_i\right) \exp\left(x_i^T \beta\right)\right)^{-1}$$

for $\delta_j = 1$. Plug $\hat{h}_j$ into (2) generates, up to a scalar product, the so-called partial likelihood function

$$\mathcal{L}(\beta) = \prod_{\delta_i=1} \frac{\exp\left(x_i^T \beta\right)}{\sum_{j=1}^{n} I\left(z_i \leq z_j\right) \exp\left(x_j^T \beta\right)} \tag{3}$$

We see that it is much easier to examine the properties of the partial likelihood function (3) than the likelihood function (2) itself.

2.1.3 *Generalized proportional models, parameter regularization and boosting*

It is natural to extend the proportional model (1) to the following form

$$h(t) = h_0(t) \exp\left(\eta(x)\right) \tag{4}$$

where $\eta(\cdot)$ can be a generic function. The linear form $x^T \beta$ can be regarded as the first order parameter expansion of η. It is also easy to see that the partial likelihood function for (4) is given by

$$\mathcal{L}(\eta(x)) = \prod_{\delta_i=1} \frac{\exp\left(\eta(x)\right)}{\sum_{j=1}^{n} I\left(z_i \leq z_j\right) \exp\left(\eta(x)\right)}.$$

Since in real situations, the dimensionality of the covariate is high and it is unrealistic (or less interpretable) to build a model by directly maximizing (3). For parametric model (1), we can usually use the idea of shrinkage (or regularization) to confine the parameters in a reasonable subspace. L1 regularization (LASSO) is one of the most popular methods, which, by controlling the absolute sum of the parameters, can often do the job of estimation and variable selection at the same time.

Now, let $\ell(\beta)$ be the log-partial likelihood function for the proportional hazard model (1)

$$\ell(\beta) = \log(\mathcal{L}(\beta)) = \sum_{i=1}^{n} \delta_i \left[x_i^T \beta - \log\left(\sum_{j=1}^{n} I\left(z_i \leq z_j\right) \exp\left(x_j^T \beta\right) \right) \right] \tag{5}$$

The LASSO estimate (Hastie, Tibshirani, and Friedman 2001) of β is given by

$$\hat{\beta} = \arg\max_{\beta} \ell(\beta), \text{ subject to } \sum |\beta_j| \leq s. \tag{6}$$

For non-parametric estimation of $h(t)$ by (4), we can use Friedman's general gradient boosting machine (Friedman 2001), with possible combination of basis expansion (spline) or kernel smoothing in the line search step.

The following sections will talk about the details of LASSO shrinkage and gradient boosting for parametric/non-parametric hazard models.

2.2 Regularized Cox regressions

2.2.1 LARS for L1 regularized partial likelihood

Let $\eta = (\eta_1, \ldots, \eta_n)$ with $\eta_i = x_i^T \beta$, then (5) can be written as

$$\ell(\eta) = \sum_{i=1}^n \delta_i \left[\eta_i - \log \left(\sum_{j=1}^n I\left(z_i \leq z_j\right) \exp\left(\eta_j\right) \right) \right] \tag{7}$$

Let $\mathbf{u} = (u_1, \ldots, u_n)$ with

$$u_i = \partial\ell/\partial\eta_i = \delta_i - e^{\eta_i} \sum_{k=1}^n \frac{\delta_k I\left(z_k \leq z_i\right)}{\sum_{l=1}^n I\left(z_k \leq z_l\right)\exp\left(\eta_l\right)}$$

and $\mathbf{A} = \left(a_{ij}\right)_{n \times n}$, where

$$a_{ii} = -\partial^2\ell/\partial\eta_i^2$$

$$= e^{\eta_i} \sum_{k=1}^n \frac{\delta_k I\left(z_k \leq z_i\right)}{\sum_{j=1}^n I\left(z_k \leq z_j\right)\exp\left(\eta_j\right)} - e^{2\eta_i} \sum_{k=1}^n \frac{\delta_k I\left(z_k \leq z_i\right)}{\left(\sum_{l=1}^n I\left(z_k \leq z_l\right)\exp\left(\eta_l\right)\right)^2}$$

and for $i \neq j$

$$a_{ij} = -\frac{\partial^2\ell}{\partial\eta_i\partial\eta_j} = e^{\eta_i+\eta_j} \sum_{k=1}^n \frac{\delta_k I\left(z_k \leq z_i\right) I\left(z_k \leq z_j\right)}{\left(\sum_{l=1}^n I\left(z_k \leq z_l\right)\exp\left(\eta_l\right)\right)^2}$$

The LASSO regularized partial likelihood is maximized by an iterative reweighted least square with L1 constraint procedure:

1. Fix s, and initialize $\hat\beta = 0$.
2. Compute η, $\mathbf{u}$, $\mathbf{A}$, and $\mathbf{z} = \eta + \mathbf{A}^-\mathbf{u}$ based on $\hat\beta$, where $\mathbf{A}^-$ is a generalized inverse of $\mathbf{A}$ satisfying $\mathbf{A}\mathbf{A}^-\mathbf{A} = \mathbf{A}$.
3. Minimize $(\mathbf{z} - \mathbf{X}\beta)^T \mathbf{A} (\mathbf{z} - \mathbf{X}\beta)$ subject to $\sum|\beta_i| \leq s$.
4. Repeat step 2 and 3 until $\hat\beta$ does not change.

In step 3 of each iteration, we need to solve a L1 regularized weighted least square problem. This task can be solved by the LARS (least angle regression) algorithm proposed by Efron et al. (2004), which takes only computing time of a least square fit and calculates the full LASSO path. Before applying LARS to the procedure, we should modify step 3 a little bit so that it can fit into the LARS procedure. Let the SVD (singular value decomposition) decomposition of $\mathbf{A}$ be $\mathbf{A} = \mathbf{V}\mathbf{D}\mathbf{V}^T$, and let $T = \mathbf{D}^{1/2}\mathbf{V}^T$, $\tilde{\mathbf{z}} = T\mathbf{z}$, and $\tilde{\mathbf{X}} = T\mathbf{X}$ then step 3 is equivalent to minimizing $(\tilde{\mathbf{z}} - \tilde{\mathbf{X}}\beta)^T (\tilde{\mathbf{z}} - \tilde{\mathbf{X}}\beta)$ subject to $\sum|\beta_i| \leq s$, which can be solved by the LARS algorithm taking $\tilde{\mathbf{z}}$ as the response variable and the columns of $\tilde{\mathbf{X}}$ as predictor variables.

The LARS algorithm for least square regression model works as follows. Consider we are doing a regression, where y is the response and $x_1, \ldots, x_p$ are the standardized predictors. The LARS algorithm works as follows:

1. Initialize $r = y$, $\hat{\beta}_1 = \hat{\beta}_2 = \cdots = \hat{\beta}_p = 0$.
2. Find predictor x_j most correlated with r.
3. Increase β_j in the direction of $\text{sign}(\text{corr}(r, x_j))$ until some other competitor x_k has as much correlation with current residual as does x_j.
4. Move $(\hat{\beta}_j, \hat{\beta}_k)$ in the joint least squares direction for (x_j, x_k) until some other competitor x_ℓ has as much correlation with current residual.
5. Continue until all predictors have been included. Stop when $\text{corr}(r, x_j) = 0$ for $\forall j$, and we get the ordinary least square solution.

It turns out that a slight modification of the above procedure can produce all the LASSO and forward stagewise regression paths.

2.2.2 L^d regularization and extensions

The idea of shrinkage can be extended fruitfully to other kinds of penalties. In a special tractable case, the L^2 regularized partial likelihood method replaces step 3 in last section by

$$\text{Minimize } (\mathbf{z} - \mathbf{X}\beta)^T \mathbf{A} (\mathbf{z} - \mathbf{X}\beta), \text{ subject to } \sum \beta_i^2 \leq s$$

for some s. This is a well-known weighted ridge regression, and the solution is given by

$$\hat{\beta} = \left(\mathbf{X}^T \mathbf{A}\mathbf{X} + \lambda\mathbf{I}\right)^{-1} \mathbf{X}^T \mathbf{A}\mathbf{z}$$

with λ depending on s. The optimization steps in this case can be solved by iterative re-weighted ridge regressions.

If we define a (generally convex) penalty function by $p(\cdot)$, then step 3 in the LASSO procedure can be changed to

$$\text{Minimize } (\mathbf{z} - \mathbf{X}\beta)^T \mathbf{A} (\mathbf{z} - \mathbf{X}\beta), \text{ subject to } p(\beta) \leq s$$

or

$$\text{Minimize } (\mathbf{z} - \mathbf{X}\beta)^T \mathbf{A} (\mathbf{z} - \mathbf{X}\beta) + \lambda \cdot p(\beta). \tag{8}$$

In the one-dimensional case of p, we see that, the LASSO (L1 regularization) is a special case when $p(x) = \sum |x_i|$, and the weighted L^d regularization corresponds to $p(x) = \sum \omega_i |x_i|^d$. Furthermore, the definition in the penalized log partial likelihood function in Huang and Harrington (2002) corresponds to $p(x) = x^T \Sigma x$ for some positive definite matrix Σ.

For a two-dimensional penalty example, let $\lambda = (\lambda_1, \lambda_2)^T$, $p(x) = \left(\sum |x_i|, \sum x_i^2\right)$, then problem (8) defines a naive elastic net (Hui and Hastie 2005). In this case, it is recommended that we use the elastic net estimate instead of the naïve one.

2.2.3 Regularized Cox regression with basis expansion

The idea from the previous sections can also be extended by using other data mining tools. The key lies in the functional expansion of $\eta(\cdot)$. If we replace the linear expansion by other basis functions, we will get other procedures for fitting the Cox regressions.

For example, if we expand η by natural cubic splines with K knots, or write

$$\eta(x) = \sum_{i=1}^{K} \beta_i N_i(x)$$

where for $0 \le k \le K - 2$

$$N_1(x) = 1, \; N_2(x) = x, \; N_{k+2}(x) = d_k(x) - d_{K-1}(x) \tag{9}$$

and

$$d_k(x) = \frac{(x - \xi_k)_+^3 - (x - \xi_K)_+^3}{\xi_K - \xi_k}$$

then step 3 of the iteration changes to

Minimize $(\mathbf{z} - \mathbf{N}\beta)^T \mathbf{A}(\mathbf{z} - \mathbf{N}\beta)$, subject to $p(\beta) \le s$

and the same method applies.

For another example, if we expand η by Gaussian Kernels with

$$\eta(x) = \sum_{i=1}^{K} \beta_i K_\alpha(x, x_i)$$

where

$$K_\alpha(x_i, x_j) = e^{-\alpha \|x_i - x_j\|^2} \tag{10}$$

for some $\alpha > 0$, then step 3 of the iteration changes to

Minimize $(\mathbf{z} - \mathbf{K}_\alpha\beta)^T \mathbf{A}(\mathbf{z} - \mathbf{K}_\alpha\beta)$, subject to $p(\beta) \le s$.

In the case of Kernel expansion, the penalty function p is often set to

$$p(\beta) = \beta^T \mathbf{K}_\alpha \beta$$

In the next subsection, we will introduce some of the details of elastic net.

2.2.4 Elastic net and flexible penalty

We are now considering a general setting of regression with elastic net penalty by Zou and Hastie (2005). The procedure can replace step 3 of the iterative updating algorithm for generalized Cox regression exactly, and it shows favourable properties over the LASSO and ridge regression.

Suppose we have already standardized the dataset, $(x_i, y_i)_{i=1}^n$

Definition 2.1 *The naive elastic net solution β^{naive} solves the following optimization problem*

$$\beta^{naive} = \arg\min_\beta L(\lambda_1, \lambda_2, \beta)$$

where

$$L\left(\lambda_1, \lambda_2, \beta\right) = |y - X\beta|^2 + \lambda_1 \sum_{i=1}^{p} |\beta_i| + \lambda_2 \sum_{i=1}^{p} \beta_i^2$$

Given the dataset $(x_i, y_i)_{i=1}^{n}$ and $\lambda = (\lambda_1, \lambda_2)^T$, then β^{naive} solves the LASSO problem

$$\beta^{\text{naive}} = \frac{1}{\sqrt{1 + \lambda_2}} \arg\min_\beta L\left(\gamma, \beta\right)$$

where

$$L\left(\gamma, \beta\right) = \left|\tilde{y} - \tilde{X}\beta\right|^2 + \gamma \sum_{i=1}^{p} |\beta_i|$$

$$\tilde{X} = (1 + \lambda_2)^{-1/2} \begin{pmatrix} X \\ \sqrt{\lambda_2} I_p \end{pmatrix}$$

$$\tilde{y} = \begin{pmatrix} y \\ 0 \end{pmatrix}$$

$$\gamma = \lambda_1 / \sqrt{1 + \lambda_2}.$$

From our former discussion, the entire path of naive elastic net can also be solved by the LARS algorithm with the computing time of least squares.

Empirical evidence shows that the naive elastic net does not perform satisfactorily, unless it is close to LASSO or ridge regression. This introduces our rescaled elastic net estimate:

Definition 2.2 *The elastic net solution β^{elastic} is defined by*

$$\beta^{\text{elastic}} = (1 + \lambda_2)\,\hat{\beta}$$

It is then natural to observe that

Theorem 2.3 *Given the dataset $(x_i, y_i)_{i=1}^{n}$ and $\lambda = (\lambda_1, \lambda_2)^T$, the elastic net estimate β^{elastic} is given by*

$$\beta^{\text{elastic}} = \arg\min_\beta \beta^T \left(\frac{X^T X + \lambda_2 I}{1 + \lambda_2}\right) \beta - 2y^T X\beta + \lambda_1 \sum_{i=1}^{p} |\beta_i|.$$

Comparing with the LASSO solution

$$\beta^{\text{LASSO}} = \arg\min_\beta \beta^T \left(X^T X\right) \beta - 2y^T X\beta + \lambda_1 \sum_{i=1}^{p} |\beta_i|$$

we can regard the elastic net estimate as a stablized version of LASSO. The two coincide when $\lambda_2 = 0$. The elastic net procedure is equivalent to shrinking the covariance matrix $\Sigma = X^T X$ towards the identity matrix I by $(1 - \gamma)\Sigma + \gamma I$. This observation also opens the possibility of other covariance matrix shrinkage procedures that will stablize the estimate of LASSO or Ridge regression.

2.2.5 Threshold gradient descent based forward stagewise selection

It has been pointed out by Hastie, Tibshirani, and Friedman (2001) and Efron et al. (2004) that the 'incremental' forward stagewise strategy is closely related to the LASSO (LARS) strategy. For example, if the paths of the coefficients are monotone, then the two strategies coincide exactly.

The threshold gradient descent method of Friedman and Popescu (2004) uses the above idea and provides a recipe for a more flexible way of variable selection and coefficient estimation. Specifically, under the Cox proportional model (1), the gradient of the negative log partial likelihood with respect to parameter β is given by

$$g = -\partial(-\ell)/\partial\beta = X\partial\ell/\partial\eta = X\mathbf{u}$$

where

$$u_i = \partial\ell/\partial\eta_i = \delta_i - e^{\eta_i}\sum_{k=1}^{n}\frac{\delta_k I(z_k \leq z_i)}{\sum_{l=1}^{n} I(z_k \leq z_l)\exp(\eta_l)}$$

and $\eta_i = x_i^T\beta$. Then if we fix a threshold value τ and a small Δ as increment size in the forward stagewise selection algorithm, the threshold gradient descent algorithm works as follows:

1. Initialize $\beta(0) = 0$, $s = 0$.
2. Calculate η, $\mathbf{u}$, g based on current value of β.
3. Calculate $f_i(s) = I\left\{|g_i(s)| \geq \tau\max_{0 \leq k \leq p}|g_k(s)|\right\}$
4. Update $\beta(s + \Delta) = \beta(s) + \Delta g(s) \cdot f(s)$, $s = s + \Delta$
5. Repeat 2–4 for M times for largest enough M. The optimal β is determined by the optimal tuning parameter s, the selection of which will be discussed later.

If we set $\tau = 0$, then the above algorithm produces the standard gradient descent based procedure that encourages equal coefficient changes in the direction of the path. On the other hand, if $\tau = 1$, then the algorithm only changes the coefficient of the predictor variable that has the largest absolute gradient value in the direction of its path in each step. The idea of this threshold gradient descent path finding algorithm is that, by choosing a suitable threshold parameter, we can have freedom in controlling the greediness of the algorithm in finding the optimal paths of the coefficients.

2.3 Cox regression with group frailty

It is frequently argued that the Cox regression is insufficient in capturing the correlation of defaults (survival) among subjects, since under the assumptions of Cox proportional model, conditional on the covariate values (which can be stochastic themselves), the survival time of subjects are independent. However, this is unrealistic for practical purposes.

In reality, it is reasonable to assume a 'group frailty' effect, i.e. a common stochastic factor within groups, which controls the in-group correlation effect. For example, it is reasonable to assume a frailty effect among patients of similar age and a similar likelihood to default among companies with a similar credit rating or industry. Under such an assumption, conditional on the covariate values, the default timing of the subjects are correlated through group frailty. To put it formally, let

$$h_{ij}(t) = h_0(t) u_i \exp\left(x_{ij}^T \beta\right)$$

for the j-th subject in the i-th group, $i = 1, \ldots, m$, $j = 1, \ldots, J_i$, where u_i is the frailty factor within the i-th group. It is usually assumed that u_i are i.i.d. and with mean 1 so that all the parameters in the model are estimable. Usually, we take a gamma frailty model with parameter a for mathematical tractability, i.e. the density for Z_i is given by

$$g(u) = \frac{a^a u^{a-1} e^{-au}}{\Gamma(a)}.$$

Then the likelihood condition on the frailty factor $\{u_i : i = 1, \ldots, m\}$ is given by

$$\mathcal{L}(\beta|x, \delta, z, u) = \prod_{i=1}^{m} \prod_{j=1}^{J_i} \left[\left(h\left(z_{ij}\right)\right)^{\delta_{ij}} S\left(z_{ij}\right)\right] \prod_{i=1}^{m} g(u_i)$$

$$= \exp\left(\beta^T \sum_{i=1}^{m} \sum_{j=1}^{J_i} \delta_{ij} x_{ij}\right) \prod_{i=1}^{m} \left[\left(\prod_{j=1}^{J_i} \left(h_0\left(z_{ij}\right)\right)^{\delta_{ij}}\right)\right.$$

$$\left. \times u_i^{A_i} e^{-\left(\sum_{j=1}^{J_i} H_0(z_{ij}) x_{ij}^T \beta\right) u_i} g(u_i)\right]$$

where

$$A_i = \sum_{j=1}^{J_i} \delta_{ij}.$$

By integrating with respect to $u_1, \ldots, u_m$, we get the likelihood function up to a multiplicative constant

$$\mathcal{L}(\beta|x, \delta, z) \propto \exp\left(\beta^T \sum_{i=1}^{m} \sum_{j=1}^{J_i} \delta_{ij} x_{ij}\right) \prod_{i=1}^{m} \frac{\prod_{j=1}^{J_i} \left(h_0\left(z_{ij}\right)\right)^{\delta_{ij}}}{\left(\sum_{j=1}^{J_i} H_0\left(z_{ij}\right) x_{ij}^T \beta + a\right)^{A_i + a}}.$$

Using the previous idea, the parameter estimation and variable selection can be done via the penalized log-likelihood (up to an additive constant):

$$\ell\left(\beta|x, \delta, z\right) = \sum_{i=1}^{m} \left\{ \sum_{j=1}^{J_i} \delta_{ij} \log h_0\left(z_{ij}\right) - \left(A_i + a\right) \log \left(\sum_{j=1}^{J_i} H_0\left(z_{ij}\right) x_{ij}^T \beta + a \right) \right\}$$

$$+ \beta^T \sum_{i=1}^{m} \sum_{j=1}^{J_i} \delta_{ij} x_{ij} + \lambda \cdot p\left(\beta\right) \tag{11}$$

for some penalty function p.

We use the least informative step function estimate for $H_0\left(\cdot\right)$ by Breslow (1974)

$$H_0\left(z\right) = \sum_{k=1}^{N} h_k I\left(z_k \leq z\right)$$

where $\{z_1, \ldots, z_N\}$ are pooled observed failure times, then differentiating (11) with respect to h_k gives

$$h_l^{-1} = \sum_{i=1}^{m} \frac{\left(A_i + a\right) \sum_{j=1}^{J_i} I\left(z_l \leq z_{ij}\right) \exp\left(x_{ij}^T \beta\right)}{\sum_{k=1}^{N} h_k \sum_{j=1}^{J_i} I\left(z_l \leq z_{ij}\right) \exp\left(x_{ij}^T \beta\right) + a}. \tag{12}$$

So, our estimation procedure can be done by an iterative procedure:

1. Initialize β, and $\{h_l\}$
2. Update $\{h_l\}$ by (12) using current values for β and $\{h_l\}$.
3. Update β by maximizing (11) for fixed tuning parameter λ using a Newton-Raphson procedure.
4. Repeat step 2 and 3 until the algorithm converges.

One can also extend the above algorithm to estimate the parameter a. The selection of the tuning parameter λ will be visited later. For frailty models with time dependent or hidden covariates, one may resort to the EM (expectation maximization) algorithm with possible combination of stochastic integration algorithms. For example, Gibbs sampling and the acceptance-rejection scheme may be employed to calculate the stochastic paths of the frailty factors.

2.4 Optimal choice of the parameter s or λ

Generally, the optimal tuning parameter s (or λ) is determined by (bootstrapped) cross validation, as in any model selection scenarios. Specifically, in our case of Cox regression, we have at least the following two choices:

- Generalized cross validation statistics (GCV)

Since the constraint in step 3 of our L^d regularization problem can be written as

$$\sum \beta_j^2 |\beta_j|^{d-2} \le s.$$

Hence, if we define

$$\mathbf{W} = \begin{cases} \left(\text{diag}\left\{\left|\hat{\beta}_j\right|\right\}\right)^{-} & \text{for } d = 1 \\ \text{diag}\left\{\left|\hat{\beta}_j\right|^{d-2}\right\} & \text{for } d \ge 2 \end{cases}$$

The effective number of parameters (degree of freedom) in our regularized fit $\hat{\beta}$ is given by

$$\text{df}(s) = \text{tr}\left(\mathbf{X}\left(\mathbf{X}^T \mathbf{A} \mathbf{X} + \lambda \mathbf{W}\right)^{-1} \mathbf{X}^T \mathbf{A}\right)$$

and the generalized cross validation statistic (Wahba 1980) is defined by

$$\text{GCV}(s) = \frac{-\ell(\hat{\beta})}{n\left(1 - \text{df}(s)/n\right)^2}.$$

The optimal s^* should minimize the criterion $\text{GCV}(s)$.

- Cross-validated partial likelihood (CVPL)

The cross-validated partial likelihood is defined by

$$\text{CVPL}(s) = -\frac{1}{n}\sum_{i=1}^{n}\left(\ell\left(\hat{\beta}_s^{(-i)}\right) - \ell^{(-i)}\left(\hat{\beta}_s^{(-i)}\right)\right).$$

where $\hat{\beta}_s^{(-i)}$ is the coefficient estimate without the i-th subject and using tuning parameter s and $\ell^{(-i)}$ is the log-partial likelihood function without the i-th subject.

Let β be the true value of coefficient if our model is right, then it can be shown that minimizing $\text{CVPL}(s)$ is asymptotically equivalent to minimizing

$$\text{CVPL}(0) + E\left[\left(\hat{\beta}_s - \beta\right)^T A \left(\hat{\beta}_s - \beta\right)\right]$$

2.5 Boosting generalized Cox regressions

2.5.1 *Friedman's gradient boosting machine*

Suppose we are under the general setting of estimating a function $F(\cdot)$ by the following expansion

$$F(x) = \sum_{m=0}^{M} \beta_m h(x; a_m)$$

where the base learner (or weak learner) $h(x; a_m)$ can be regarded as a basis function. It can be in the simple linear form $h(x; a_m) = x$, or be generated by more complicated machinery like spline, kernel expansion, neural net, CART (classification and regression trees), MARS (multiple adaptive regression splines), wavelets, SVM (support vector machine) etc.

For finite sample problems encountered in real world cases, we have sample $(x_i, y_i)_{i=1}^n$. Given a loss function L, our goal is to minimize over the functional space F the following criterion:

$$\hat{f}(x) = \min_F \sum_{i=1}^n L(y_i, F(x_i)). \tag{13}$$

Friedman (2001) proposed the influential idea of a general gradient boosting machine, which trains our estimate of F by the following steps:

1. Initialize $F_0(x) = \arg\min_\rho \sum_{i=1}^n L(y_i, \rho)$, or just initialize $F_0(x) = 0$.
2. For $m = 1$ to M do:
   (a) Compute the 'pseudo' responses $\tilde{y}_i = -\left[\frac{\partial L(y_i, F(x_i))}{\partial F(x_i)}\right]_{F(x)=F_{m-1}(x)}$ for $i = 1, \ldots, N$
   (b) Calculate the least square fit $a_m = \arg\min_{a_m, \beta} \sum_{i=1}^n [\tilde{y}_i - \beta h(x_i; a)]^2$
   (c) Line search:

$$\rho_m = \arg\min_\rho \sum_{i=1}^n L(y_i, F_{m-1}(x) + \rho h(x_i; a_m))$$

   (d) Update $F_m(x) = F_{m-1}(x) + \rho_m h(x; a_m)$
3. Boosted estimate: $\hat{f}(x) = F_M(x) = F_0(x) + \sum_{i=1}^M \rho_m h(x; a_m)$.

In particular, if $h(x; a_m)$ is a regression tree, the above steps describe the algorithm to construct a famous class of models: MART (multiple additive regression trees). See Hastie, Tibshirani, and Friedman (2001) for more details.

2.5.2 Boosted Cox regression using basis expansion

In the setting of Cox regression, our minimizing criterion (13) changes to

$$\hat{\eta}(x) = \min_{\eta \in F} l(\eta(x))$$

where

$$l(\eta(x)) = \sum_{i=1}^n \delta_i \left[\eta(x_i) - \log\left(\sum_{j=1}^n I(z_i \le z_j) \exp(\eta(x_i))\right)\right].$$

Then, in step 2a of the gradient machine (notice that the loss criterion is not additive),

$$\tilde{y}_i = -\frac{\partial l(\eta(x))}{\partial \eta(x_i)}$$

$$= \delta_i - \sum_{k=1}^n \frac{\delta_k I(z_k \le z_i) \exp(\eta(x_i))}{\sum_{j=1}^n I(z_k \le z_j) \exp(\eta(x_k))}.$$

We have flexibility in choosing the form of the basis $h(x; a)$ in step 2b. In the simplest case,

$$h(x; a) = a_0 + \sum_{i=1}^{p} a_i x_i$$

then, step 2b just fits a simple linear regression. As always, other choices of the form of $h(x; a)$ lead to other gradient boosting algorithms for the Cox regression.

For example, if $h(x; a)$ has the form

$$h(x; a) = \sum_{i=1}^{K} a_i N_i(x)$$

where N_i is the basis for natural cubic spline defined in (9), then step 2b will fit a unconstrained natural cubic spline with response $\tilde{y}$.

For another example, if $h(x; a)$ has the form

$$h(x; a) = \sum_{i=1}^{K} a_i K_a(x, x_i)$$

where K_a is the Gaussian Kernel defined in (10), then step 2b amounts to fit a kernel smoothed local regression.

Step 2c amounts to do a linear proportional hazard model to the responses $(z_i, \delta_i)_{i=1}^{n}$ with predictor $h(x; a_m)$, offset $\eta_{m-1}(x)$, and regression coefficient ρ.

2.6 Bagging and sub-sample aggregating

Bagging (or bootstrap aggregating) and sub-sample aggregating (also called subagging) are model averaging methods which are designed to stablized the fitting and predicting results. It turns out that they also increase the accuracy of parameter estimation or prediction as well.

The bootstrap is introduced by Efron (1979) and extended by many others. The original idea of bootstrap is to sample from the data using the same size and with replacement and to use the *bootstrap* sample to do estimation and inferences. For example, we can use the bootstrap procedure to estimate the standard deviation of any statistic. This is particularly useful for small datasets. For large datasets, we do not need to reuse the original data so many times and one can use the so-called sub-sampling procedure, which is to sample a subset of the data each time without replacement and use the resulting sub-samples to do estimation and inferences.

Now, we consider fitting a model to the dataset $\{x_i, y_i\}_{i=1}^{n}$, and make prediction $\hat{f}(x)$ at future inputs x. Bagging makes the prediction by averaging over a collection of bootstrap samples, and sub-sample aggregating makes the prediction by averaging over a collection of sub-samples. Similarly, sub-sample aggregating estimates the parameter by average over a collection of estimated parameters from bootstrap samples (sub-samples). This works for all the data mining procedures mentioned before.

Specifically, for each bootstrap sample $\{x_i^{*b}, y_i^{*b}\}_{i=1}^{n}$ for $b = 1, \ldots, B$, we fit our model and give the prediction $\hat{f}^{*b}(x)$, the bagging estimation is

$$\hat{f}_{\text{bag}}(x) = \frac{1}{B} \sum_{b=1}^{B} \hat{f}^{*b}(x)$$

A similar procedure works for subsample aggregating. Asymptotical results for bagging and sub-sample aggregating can be found in standard references. For example, see Peter Bühlmann (2002), who also proposes a more robust version of bagging.

3 GENERALIZED COX REGRESSION WITH TIME-DEPENDENT AND HIDDEN COVARIATES

3.1 Time-varying covariates

When our dataset has a time-series feature, instead of having only one survival time or censoring time for each subject, we have observations over time of the survival of a subject. For example, we may have the data consisting of the time series of multiple firms with a default indicator for each observation. In this case, the classical Cox proportional model (1) should be extended.

Now assume we have m entities, each with a time-series observation. Suppose the observation time for the i-th entity is $[t_i, T_i]$, and in time t we have the triplet $(x_{it}, \delta_{it}, t) : i = 1, \ldots, m$, where δ_{it} is the default (survival) indicator for the i-th entity at time t. Again, we model the hazard rate h_i for the i-th entity by the proportional model

$$h_i(t) = h_{0i}(t) \exp\left(x_{it}^T \beta\right)$$

Let's first suppose the covariates are deterministic. The complete likelihood for the data is given by

$$\mathcal{L}(\beta|x, z, \delta) = \prod_{i=1}^{m} \left(e^{-\sum_{t=t_i}^{T_i} h_i(t)\Delta t} \prod_{t=t_i}^{T_i} [\delta_{it} h_i(t) + (1 - \delta_{it})]\right)$$

and the log-likelihood function is given by

$$\ell(\beta|x, z, \delta) = \sum_{i=1}^{m} \sum_{t=t_i}^{T_i} \left(-h_i(t)\Delta t + \log(h_i(t))\delta_{it}\right)$$

$$= \sum_{i=1}^{m} \sum_{t=t_i}^{T_i} \left(-h_{0i}(t) \exp\left(x_{it}^T \beta\right) \Delta t + \log\left(h_{0i}(t) \exp\left(x_{it}^T \beta\right)\right) \delta_{it} \right) \quad (14)$$

where $\Delta t = t_{i+1} - t_i$ is the tenor for the i-th observation.

If we model $h_{0i}(t)$ by the least informative approach (piecewise constant), i.e. $h_{0i}(0) = 0$,

$$h_{0i}(t) = \lambda_{li} \text{ for } z_{l-1} < t \le z_l$$

or

$$h_{0i}(t) = \sum_{l=1}^{N} \lambda_{li} I\left(z_{l-1} < t \le z_l\right). \quad (15)$$

where $\{z_1, \ldots, z_N\}$ are pooled observed failure times and $z_0 = 0$ for positive constants $\lambda_{li}, l = 1, \ldots, N_i$ and $i = 1, \ldots, m$. Plugging in this estimate and taking the derivatives of (14) with respect to λ_{li} generates:

$$\lambda_{li} = \frac{\sum_{t=t_i}^{T_i} I\left(z_{l-1} < t \le z_l\right)}{\sum_{t=t_i}^{T_i} I\left(z_{l-1} < t \le z_l\right) \exp\left(x_{it}^T \beta\right) \Delta t}.$$

So basically, the problem can be solved by the following iterative scheme:

1. Initialize the values for β.
2. For current values of β, calculate the current values for λ_{li} for $l = 1, \ldots, N$, and $i = 1, \ldots, m$. Then, we have the current values for $h_{0i}(t)$ by (15).
3. Plug the current values for $h_{0i}(t)$ in (14) and solve for the following penalized (partial) log-likelihood problem:

$$\min_{\beta} \ell\left(\beta | x, z, \delta\right) + \lambda \cdot p\left(\beta\right)$$

   for some penalty function p, using Newton-Raphson's procedure.
4. Repeat step 2 and 3 until the algorithm converges.

Another treatment of $h_{0i}(z)$ is just simply set $h_{0i}(z) = 1$ for all i. Then the penalized log-likelihood reduces the following optimization problem,

$$\min_{\beta} \sum_{i=1}^{m} \sum_{t=t_i}^{T_i} \left(-\exp\left(x_{it}^T \beta\right) \Delta t + x_{it}^T \beta \delta_{it} \right) + \lambda \cdot p\left(\beta\right)$$

which is much simpler to solve.

3.2 Stochastic covariate processes

The model in the previous section simply assumes that the covariates are deterministic. However, we may encounter problems in survival (failure, default) analysis where the covariates themselves have the stochastic nature.

For example, to use macroeconomic variables like interest rates, money supply, GDP growth etc. or firm specific variables like return, debt, asset, etc. to model the defaults or default correlation of multiple firms, we may as well take in consideration that the covariates are also stochastically varying over time. For another, to predict the failure time in a medical experiment, the temperature as an external factor and the level of a certain chemical in the human body as an internal factor may both have some stochastic nature that is not captured by deterministic processes.

Now we suppose that the covariate X has a parametric form of stochastic process and its likelihood is given by $\mathcal{L}(\gamma|X)$. Under the doubly stochastic assumption (Duffie, Saita, and Wang 2007), condition on the paths of the covariate process, the default (survival) timing of the entities are independent, the full likelihood function is given by

$$\mathcal{L}(\beta, \gamma|x, z, \delta) = \mathcal{L}(\gamma|x)\,\mathcal{L}(\beta|x, z, \delta)$$

So, the maximum likelihood estimator $\left(\hat{\beta}, \hat{\gamma}\right)$ can be obtained by maximizing $\mathcal{L}(\gamma|x)$ and $\mathcal{L}(\beta|x, z, \delta)$ respectively.

For mathematical convenience, we usually model the covariate process by simple time series models, for instance, ARIMA (integrated autoregressive moving average) or its vector version (VARIMA). Here, I briefly review the vector autoregressive model with possible cointegration effect.

Suppose x_t is a $d \times 1$ vector for each t. A multivariate extension of AR(p) model for x (with 0 mean) is given by

$$x_t = A_1 x_{t-1} + A_2 x_{t-2} + \ldots + A_p x_{t-p} + \epsilon_t$$

and we say that $x \sim \text{VAR}(p)$

If the components of x are $I(1)$[1] and cointegrated, then it has the Granger's representation (VAR with co-integration)

$$\Delta x_t = \alpha \beta^T x_{t-1} + B_1 \Delta x_{t-1} + \ldots + B_{p-1} \Delta x_{t-p+1} + \epsilon_t$$

where β is the co-integration vector for x. The system is also called its *Error Correction form*.

Engle and Granger (1987) suggest the two-stage estimation method for

$$\Delta x_t = \alpha \beta^T x_{t-1} + B_1 \Delta x_{t-1} + \ldots + B_{p-1} \Delta x_{t-p+1} + \epsilon_t$$

(1) Estimate β by least square regression.
(2) Estimate α, B_j, $j = 1, \ldots, p-1$ by maximum likelihood.

It is proved that if we estimate the parameters in this way, then

(1) $\hat{\beta}$ is *super-consistent*: it converges to β at the rapid rate T^{-1}, where T is the sample size.
(2) $\hat{\alpha}$, $\hat{B}_j$, $j = 1, \ldots, p-1$ are consistent and asymptotically normal.

---

[1] $I(1)$ refers to non-stationary series with stationary first difference.

Another tractable type of model is affine process, which is discussed in section 4 in Wei (2006), and the estimation procedures are discussed in section 6.

3.3 Frailty factor for modelling dependence

The assumption that, conditional on the paths of the covariate processes, the default (survival) timing of the entities are independent may be violated in reality. For example, previous models generally cannot capture the 'contagion effect' of the defaults of multiple firms, which is essential to understanding the risks in the credit market. One remedy for this is to assume some subject-specific or time-dependent frailty factors that may have the effect of adding additional source of certainty in the default and default correlation among subjects.

Consider the following model

$$h_i(t) = h_{0i}(t) Y_t S_i \exp\left(x_{it}^T \beta\right) \tag{16}$$

where Y_t is a time-dependent frailty factor and S_i is a subject-specific frailty factor. Under the Gamma model, suppose S_i is i.i.d. with density

$$g(s) = \frac{a^a s^{a-1} \exp(-as)}{\Gamma(a)} \tag{17}$$

and Y_t is a positive process. For example, Y_t can be a Gamma process, Geometric Brownian Motion, or exponential of a Variance Gamma process; One can refer to the appendix for a review of Gamma and Variance Gamma processes, see also Madan and Seneta (1990).

A popular scheme of calibrating frailty related models is through MCMC EM (Markov Chain Monte Carlo Expectation Maximization) algorithm, which provides a general scheme for optimization involving stochastic (or hidden) factors. The following subsection gives a recipe for the MCMC EM optimization problem and we will narrow our focus in our Cox regression settings.

3.3.1 *The Expectation Maximization algorithm*

The Expectation Maximization (EM or Baum-Welch) algorithm is originally proposed for maximizing likelihoods in cases with latent (unobserved or missing) data. The latent data (frailty factor in the setting of Cox regression) can be introduced by model construction or by data augmentation in order to simplify the maximizing problem. Naturally, the EM algorithm can be used for minimizing any loss criterion with latent factor.

Suppose we are going to maximize a general function $\ell(\theta; X)$ of parameter θ and observed data X. For example, ℓ can be the (penalized) log-likelihood function or the negative value of any loss function. The augmented function $\ell_0(\theta; X, Z)$ also depends on the latent or missing data Z and usually we have $\ell(\theta; X) = E(\ell_0(\theta; X, Z)|X, \theta)$.

However, this relationship need not hold in general. The EM algorithm works as follows:

1. Initialize our guess for the parameters $\theta^{(0)}$.
2. (Expection Step) At the j-th step, compute the expectation

$$Q\left(\theta, \theta^{(j)}\right) = E\left(\ell_0\left(\theta; X, Z\right) | X, \theta^{(j)}\right)$$

as a function of θ.
3. (Maximization Step) Solve the maximization problem:

$$\theta^{(j+1)} = \arg\max_{\theta} Q\left(\theta, \theta^{(j)}\right). \tag{18}$$

4. Repeat step 2 and 3 until the algorithm converges.

At least two complications arise in the above EM algorithm. The first is that it is hard to compute the expectation in step 2 in general because the distribution of Z condition on X may not have an explicit solution. Even if the conditional density can be computed explicitly, the expectation involves (high-dimensional) numerical integration, which is usually not stable and reliable. One remedy for this is to use the Markov Chain Monte Carlo methods, specifically, the Gibbs sampler and the Metropolis (Metropolis-Hasting) algorithm for sampling the posterior distributions and use the sample average

$$\frac{1}{M} \sum_{n=N+1}^{N+M} \ell_0\left(\theta; X, Z^{(n)}\right)$$

to compute the expectation, where N is the 'burn-in' period in our sample generating procedure. We will introduce MCMC shortly.

The second problem is the maximization in step 3. The Newton-Raphson algorithm does not necessarily lead to nice solutions. Other optimization schemes like Simulated Annealing or the Genetic Algorithm may be employed to find the global maximum too. For computational reasons, it may be as well just to apply one step Gradient Descent to step 3 and hope the iterative procedure of step 2 and step 3 will lead to a sub-optimal solution. Our focus then will be the Markov Chain Monte Carlo calibration of the expectation in step 2.

3.3.2 The Markov Chain Monte Carlo methods

A particularly useful and the most simple Markov Chain simulation algorithm is called the *Gibbs sampler* or alternating conditional sampling. Following the notions of the previous section, suppose we want sample the distribution of $Z = (Z_1, \ldots, Z_K)$ condition on X, then the Gibbs sampler works as follows:

1. Initialize $Z_k^{(0)}$, $k = 1, \ldots, K$.
2. At the t-th step, sample $Z_k^{(t)}$ from the conditional distribution

$$Z_k^{(t)} | Z_1^{(t)}, \ldots, Z_{k-1}^{(t)}, Z_{k+1}^{(t-1)}, \ldots, Z_K^{(t-1)}, X$$

for $k = 1, \ldots, K$.

3. Repeat step 2, until the joint conditional distribution of $Z^{(t)}|X = Z_1^{(t)}, \ldots Z_K^{(t)}|X$ does not change or simply repeat a designated number of steps.

The Gibbs sampler works pretty well if we can easily generate the conditional sample in step 2. However, it may not be easy to generate such a sample directly, even if we have the explicit formula for the density. A more flexible sampling method is called the Metropolis algorithm, which can be seen as an adaptation of a random walk that uses an acceptance/rejection rule to converge to the target distribution. It only requires that we know the likelihood ratio of the target density.

Suppose we want to sample from a (conditional) density function $\mathcal{L}(\theta; Z, X)$ for Z. The Metropolis algorithm works as follows:

1. Initialize $Z_k^{(0)}$, $k = 1, \ldots, K$.
2. At the t-th step, sample a proposal Z^* from a *jumping distribution* (or *proposal distribution*) $J_t\left(Z^*|Z^{(t-1)}, X\right)$. The proposal distribution J_t should be symmetric, or $J_t(Z_1|Z_2, X) = J_t(Z_2|Z_1, X)$.
3. Calculate the likelihood ratio

$$r = \frac{\mathcal{L}(\theta; Z^*, X)}{\mathcal{L}\left(\theta; Z^{(t-1)}, X\right)}$$

where $\mathcal{L}$ is the (conditional) density function for Z.
4. Draw U uniformly from $[0, 1]$, and set

$$Z^{(t)} = \begin{cases} Z^* & \text{if } U < \min(r, 1) \\ Z^{(t-1)} & \text{otherwise.} \end{cases}$$

5. Repeat steps 2–4, until the conditional distribution $Z^{(t)}|X = Z_1^{(t)}, \ldots Z_K^{(t)}|X$ does not change or simply repeat a designated number of steps.

Usually, we set $J_t\left(Z^*|Z^{(t-1)}, X\right) = N\left(Z^{(t-1)}, \sigma I_K\right)$, where I_K is a K dimensional identity matrix. The Metropolis-Hastings algorithm slightly generalizes the above algorithm to asymmetric proposal distribution functions. If $J_t(Z_1|Z_2, X) = J_t(Z_2|Z_1, X)$ does not hold for any Z_1, Z_2, then in step 3, the formula for r changes to

$$r = \frac{\mathcal{L}(\theta; Z^*, X)/J_t\left(Z^*|Z^{(t-1)}, X\right)}{\mathcal{L}\left(\theta; Z^{(t-1)}, X\right)/J_t\left(Z^{(t-1)}|Z^*, X\right)}$$

It can be proved that in this way, the sampling distribution will converge to the stationary distribution of a Markov Chain, with the stationary distribution the same as our target distribution.

Steps 2–4 of the above algorithm can also consist of a series of K iterations, where we can perform acceptance-rejection updating procedure for each of the $Z_j^{(t)}$ for $j = 1, \ldots, K$ in each step. If we define the proposal distribution by

$$J_{j,t}^{\text{Gibbs}}\left(Z^*|Z^{(t-1)}, X\right) = \begin{cases} \mathcal{L}\left(\theta; Z_j^*, Z_{-j}^{(t-1)}, X\right) & \text{if } Z_{-j}^* = Z_{-j}^{(t-1)} \\ 0 & \text{otherwise} \end{cases}$$

then, we can prove that the Metropolis-Hastings algorithm produces a Gibbs sampler.

3.3.3 Calibrate the frailty model

Our basic scheme is to use the MCMC version of the EM algorithm to estimate the model parameters (and possibly to select the covariates by regularization). As mentioned before, we are most interested in step 2 of the EM algorithm. Since we can separate the estimation of the covariate processes and the hazard rate model, our likelihood function will only consist of the parameters in the hazard formulation.

Under the frailty model (16), the augmented likelihood function is given by

$$\mathcal{L}\left(\beta, \theta; x, Y, S, \delta\right) = \prod_{i=1}^{m} \left(e^{-\sum_{t=t_i}^{T_i} h_i(t)\Delta t} \prod_{t=t_i}^{T_i} [\delta_{it} h_i(t) + (1 - \delta_{it})] \right)$$

where

$$h_i(t) = Y_t S_i \exp\left(x_{it}^T \beta\right)$$

and θ is the parameter for the frailty factors Y_t, S_i, where S_i has the Gamma model (17). We set $h_{0i}(z) = 1$ for simplicity. Under a Markov model for $Y_t = g(W_t)$ (Geometrical Brownian Motion, Gamma process, exponential of a Variance Gamma process) where W is Markov and g is a deterministic function. We have the conditional density of W_t given $W_{(-t)} = (W_1, \ldots, W_{t-1}, W_{t+1}, \ldots, W_T)$ is

$$f\left(W_t|\beta, \theta, x, W_{(-t)}, S, \delta\right) \propto \mathcal{L}\left(\beta, \theta; x, Y, S, \delta\right) f\left(W_t|W_{t-1}, \theta\right) f\left(W_t|W_{t+1}, \theta\right)$$

The sampling procedure works as follows: for fixed parameters (β, θ)

1. Initialize $Y_t = 1$ and $S_i = 1$, $0 \le t \le T$ and $1 \le i \le m$.
2. Given the current values of Y_t, S_i in step j, use the Metropolis-Hastings algorithm to draw $Y_t^{(j+1)}$ [2] by the following scheme, where we can use a Gaussian proposal distribution in all cases:
   (a) If $Y_t = e^{bW_t}$ is a Geometric Brownian Motion, where W_t is a standard Brownian Motion. Then, the (conditional) likelihood ratio in step 3 of the Metropolis' algorithm is given by

$$r = \frac{f\left(W_t^*|\beta, \theta, x, W_{(-t)}, S, \delta\right)}{f\left(W_t|\beta, \theta, x, W_{(-t)}, S, \delta\right)}$$

$$= \frac{\mathcal{L}\left(\beta, \theta; x, Y_t^*, Y_{(-t)}, S, \delta\right) f\left(W_t^*|W_{t-1}, \theta\right) f\left(W_t^*|W_{t+1}, \theta\right)}{\mathcal{L}\left(\beta, \theta; x, Y, S, \delta\right) f\left(W_t|W_{t-1}, \theta\right) f\left(W_t|W_{t+1}, \theta\right)} \quad (19)$$

---

[2] The superscript $(j + 1)$ means we are in the $(j + 1)$-th step of our iteration procedure. We ignore this notation below when there is no confusion.

where $Y_t^* = e^{bW_t^*}$, and

$$f(W_t | W_{t-1}, \theta) = \frac{1}{\sqrt{2\pi}} e^{-(W_t - W_{t-1})^2/2}$$

$$f(W_t | W_{t+1}, \theta) = \frac{1}{\sqrt{2\pi}} e^{-(W_t - W_{t+1})^2/2}$$

(b) If Y_t is a Gamma process $\{G(t, u, v) : t \geq 0\}$, then $Y_t = W_t$,

$$f(W_t | W_{t-1}, \theta) = g_{u^2/v, v/u}(W_t - W_{t-1})$$
$$f(W_t | W_{t+1}, \theta) = g_{u^2/v, v/u}(W_{t+1} - W_t)$$

where $g_{a,\beta}(x)$ is a Gamma density

$$g_{a,\beta}(x) = \frac{1}{\beta^a \Gamma(a)} x^{a-1} e^{-x/\beta}$$

and the (conditional) likelihood ratio in step 3 of the Metropolis' algorithm is also given in (19).

(c) If Y_t is an exponential of a Variance Gamma process, then $Y_t = e^{bW_t}$, where W_t is a Variance Gamma process $\{VG(t, \theta, \sigma, v) : t \geq 0\}$. We have

$$f(W_t | W_{t-1}, \theta) = f_{VG(1, \theta, \sigma, v)}(W_t - W_{t-1})$$
$$f(W_t | W_{t+1}, \theta) = f_{VG(1, \theta, \sigma, v)}(W_{t+1} - W_t)$$

where $f_{VG(t,\theta,\sigma,v)}$ is the density function of a Variance-Gamma process with parameters (θ, σ, v) at time t. The formula for $f_{VG(t,\theta,\sigma,v)}$ is given in Appendix B, and since it is in the form of an integral, numerical approximation procedures should be employed. The (conditional) likelihood ratio in step 3 of the Metropolis algorithm is also given in (19).

3. Given $Y_t^{(j+1)}$ and $S_i^{(j)}$, we proceed to draw the conditional distributions of $S_i^{(j+1)}$ for $i = 1, \ldots, m$.

Under the i.i.d. Gamma model, since $S_i^{(j+1)}$ are conditionally independent, and each with density (assume $\Delta t = 1$)

$$f\left(s | Y^{(j+1)}, X, \delta, \beta, \theta\right) \propto g(s) \mathcal{L}\left(\beta, \theta; X, Y^{(j+1)}, s, \delta\right)$$

$$\propto s^{a-1} \exp(-as) e^{-\sum_{t=t_i}^{T_i} Y_t^{(j+1)} \exp(x_{it}^T \beta)s} \prod_{t=t_i}^{T_i} \left[\delta_{it} Y_t^{(j+1)} \exp\left(x_{it}^T \beta\right) s + (1 - \delta_{it})\right]$$

so, we can draw $S_i^{(j+1)}$ from the Gamma distribution $\Gamma(A_i, B_i)$ where

$$A_i = a + \sum_{t=t_i}^{T_i} Y_t^{(j+1)} \exp\left(x_{it}^T \beta\right)$$

$$B_i = a + \sum_{t=t_i}^{T_i} I\left(\delta_{it} = 1\right)$$

Particularly, if we ignore recovery from default, and regard entity i defaults only when $\delta_{i,T_i} = 1$, then

$$B_i = a + \delta_{i,T_i}$$

Our maximization step (18) may involve drawing the conditional samples for each set of parameter θ for a discretized grid in the parameter space. For computational considerations, we can make a very raw grid of the parameters in the initial steps and refine the grid in later steps for better results.

An extension of model (16) is given by

$$h_{ij}(t) = h_{0ij}(t) \, Y_t \, S_i \, O_j \exp\left(x_{ijt}^T \beta\right) \tag{20}$$

where Y_t is a time-dependent frailty factor, S_i is a subject-specific frailty factor, and O_j is a group-specific factor for $i = 1, \ldots, m$, $j = 1, \ldots, J_i$, and $t = t_i, \ldots, T_i$. For example, it is reasonable to assume a group frailty factor among companies in the same field, e.g. information technology, energy, material, retail etc. Calibration for model (20) is straightforward by our proposed MCMC EM method, where Metropolis-Hastings algorithm is used to draw samples from conditional distribution for Y_t. Under Gamma models for S_i and O_j, their conditional distributions in the iterative steps are Gamma distributions, making the sampling procedure easy to implement.

4 A SPLINE-BASED STRATEGY
FOR CREDIT INDICES

4.1 Index credit swap spread

We use a top-down approach to model the credit swap spread for an index. An index CDS is a basket of n individual CDS with common contract terms (notional, maturity etc). Let τ_i be the stopping time for the default of i-th name in the basket, the total defaults at time t is measured by

$$N_t = \sum_{i=1}^{n} 1\{\tau_i \leq t\}$$

If we assume common constant recovery R for all the names, the index loss at time t is: $L_t = (1 - R) N_t$.

The index credit swap spread is the quarterly premium paid on the remaining notional of an index (assume unit total notional)

$$I_t = 1 - \frac{N_t}{n}$$

to insure against the loss incurred by the defaults in the index basket.

We model N_t as a doubly stochastic process with intensity λ_t under measure Q. It follows that $N_t - \int_0^t \lambda_u du$ is a martingale and hence

$$E^Q(N_t) = \int_0^t E^Q(\lambda_u) du \qquad (21)$$

Let $s(T)$ be the fair index credit default swap spread for the protection from now $(t = 0)$ to $t = T$, it follows that

Present value of premium leg $= s(T) \, \text{IndexRiskyPV01}(0, T)$

$$\simeq \frac{s(T)}{4} E^Q \left[\sum_{i=1}^{4T} e^{-\int_0^{i/4} r_t dt} I_{i/4} \right]$$

$$\simeq s(T) \int_0^T e^{-\int_0^u r_t dt} \left[1 - \frac{E^Q(N_u)}{n} \right] du$$

and by change of integral

Present value of default leg $= (1-R) E^Q \left[\int_0^T e^{-\int_0^u r_t dt} d N_u \right]$

$$= (1-R) \left[e^{-\int_0^T r_u du} E^Q(N_T) + \int_0^T r_u e^{-\int_0^u r_t dt} E^Q(N_u) du \right]$$

Hence,

$$s(T) \simeq \frac{(1-R) \left[e^{-\int_0^T r_u du} E^Q(N_T) + \int_0^T r_u e^{-\int_0^u r_t dt} E^Q(N_u) du \right]}{\int_0^T e^{-\int_0^u r_t dt} \left[1 - \frac{E^Q(N_u)}{n} \right] du} \qquad (22)$$

4.2 A spline model for the default arrival intensity

The idea is to make cross-sectional constraint on the default intensity process to rule out arbitrage opportunities. Assume the intensity process λ for an index has the following functional basis expansion:

$$\lambda(t) = \lambda_t = \sum_{i=0}^{p} \beta_i B_i(t) + \varepsilon_t$$

where $B_1(\cdot), \ldots, B_p(\cdot)$ are the functional basis for a spline and $\varepsilon_t \sim N(0, \sigma^2)$.
It follows that

$$E^Q(N_t) = \sum_{i=0}^{p} \beta_i \int_0^t B_i(u) \, du$$

and by (21) and (22), we have a semi-explicit solution for $s(T)$.

The most liquid credit indices are with maturities 3Y, 5Y, and 10Y. Our trading strategy for the credit indices is based on the idea of 'butterfly' trade:

- Use the historical data to fit the about model for 3Y and 10Y maturities
- Compare the market quote for 5Y spread and model implied spread to generate long-short strategies

4.2.1 Piecewise constant spline

Assume

$$B_0(t) = 1\{t < 3\}$$
$$B_1(t) = 1\{3 \le t < 5\}$$
$$B_2(t) = 1\{t \ge 5\}$$

We can calulate that

$$s(3) = \frac{(1-R)\left[3\beta_0 e^{-\int_0^3 r_u du} + \beta_0 \int_0^3 r_u e^{-\int_0^u r_t dt} u \, du\right]}{\int_0^3 e^{-\int_0^u r_t dt}\left[1 - \frac{\beta_0 u}{n}\right] du}$$

$$s(5) = \frac{(1-R)\left[e^{-\int_0^5 r_u du}(3\beta_0 + 2\beta_1) + \beta_0 \int_0^3 r_u e^{-\int_0^u r_t dt} u \, du + \int_3^5 r_u e^{-\int_0^u r_t dt}(3\beta_0 + (u-3)\beta_1)\, du\right]}{\int_0^3 e^{-\int_0^u r_t dt}\left[1 - \frac{\beta_0 u}{n}\right] du + \int_3^5 e^{-\int_0^u r_t dt}\left[1 - \frac{3\beta_0 + (u-3)\beta_1}{n}\right] du}$$

and

$$s(10) = (1-R)\frac{a(10)}{b(10)}$$

where

$$a(10) = e^{-\int_0^{10} r_u du}(3\beta_0 + 2\beta_1 + 5\beta_2) + \beta_0 \int_0^3 r_u e^{-\int_0^u r_t dt} u \, du +$$

$$\int_3^5 r_u e^{-\int_0^u r_t dt}(3\beta_0 + (u-3)\beta_1)\, du +$$

$$\int_5^{10} r_u e^{-\int_0^u r_t dt}(3\beta_0 + 2\beta_1 + (u-5)\beta_2)\, du$$

and

$$b\,(10) = \int_0^3 e^{-\int_0^u r_t dt}\left[1 - \frac{\beta_0 u}{n}\right]du + \int_3^5 e^{-\int_0^u r_t dt}\left[1 - \frac{3\beta_0 + (u-3)\beta_1}{n}\right]du$$
$$+ \int_5^{10} e^{-\int_0^u r_t dt}\left[1 - \frac{3\beta_0 + 2\beta_1 + (u-5)\beta_2}{n}\right]du$$

To calculate the integral

$$\int_{T_1}^{T_2} g\,(u)\,e^{-\int_0^u r_t dt}\,du \simeq \sum_{i=4T_1+1}^{4T_2} g\,(i/4)\,D_{i/4}$$

where $g\,(\cdot)$ is a determinstic function and $D_{i/4}$ is the forward discount factor.

4.2.2 Cubic spline

Piecewise constant spline is discontinuous, quadratic spline is continuous but not smooth. Cubic spline is both continuous and smooth (continuously differentiable). Assume

$$B_0\,(t) = 1$$
$$B_1\,(t) = t$$
$$B_2\,(t) = t^2$$
$$B_3\,(t) = t^3$$
$$B_4\,(t) = (t-3)_+^3$$
$$B_5\,(t) = (t-5)_+^3$$

It follows that

$$f\,(t) = E^Q\,(N_t)$$
$$= \sum_{i=0}^P \beta_i \int_0^t B_i\,(u)\,du$$
$$= \begin{cases} \beta_0 t + \frac{\beta_1}{2}t^2 + \frac{\beta_2}{3}t^3 + \frac{\beta_3}{4}t^4 & t < 3 \\ \beta_0 t + \frac{\beta_1}{2}t^2 + \frac{\beta_2}{3}t^3 + \frac{\beta_3}{4}t^4 + \frac{\beta_4}{4}\left((t-3)^3 + 27\right) & 3 \le t < 5 \\ \beta_0 t + \frac{\beta_1}{2}t^2 + \frac{\beta_2}{3}t^3 + \frac{\beta_3}{4}t^4 + \frac{\beta_4}{4}\left((t-3)^3 + 27\right) + \frac{\beta_5}{4}\left((t-5)^3 + 125\right) & 5 \le t \le 10 \end{cases}$$

and hence

$$s\,(T) = \frac{(1-R)\left[e^{-\int_0^T r_u du} f\,(T) + \int_0^T r_u e^{-\int_0^u r_t dt} f\,(u)\,du\right]}{\int_0^T e^{-\int_0^u r_t dt}\left[1 - \frac{f(u)}{n}\right]du}$$

for $T = 3, 5,$ and 10.

4.3 Trading strategies for credit indices

4.3.1 *Estimating the parameters*

For the case of cubic spline, we assume the two degrees of freedom for the default intensity change overtime: parallel shift β_0 and proportional shift β_1, and other factors $\beta_2 - \beta_5$ do not change. The estimation goes as follows:

1. For fixed parameters $\sigma, \beta_2 - \beta_5$, calibrate $\hat{\beta}_{0i}, \hat{\beta}_{1i}$ to exactly match the market quote for 3Y and 10Y credit index spreads. From these parameters, we can get time series of $\lambda_i(0)$ for a sufficient period of time (more than 5 years)
2. Recalculate $\hat{\sigma}, \hat{\beta}_2 - \hat{\beta}_5$ by the regression

$$\lambda_t(0) - \hat{\beta}_{0t} - \hat{\beta}_{1t} = \beta_2 t^2 + \beta_3 t^3 + \beta_4 (t-3)^3 + \beta_5 (t-5)^3 + \varepsilon_t$$

3. Repeat 1–2 many times until convergence.

4.3.2 *Trading strategy*

Our model assumes that

$$s(t) = \beta_0 + \beta_1 t + \beta_2 t^2 + \beta_3 t^3 + \beta_4 (t-3)^3 + \beta_5 (t-5)^3 + \varepsilon_t$$

The parameters $\sigma, \beta_0 - \beta_1$ are estimated from historical data of credit index spreads for 3Y and 10Y maturities. Suppose at some time, $s(5)$ is above 95% upper confidence level of the model implied spread, we buy the 5Y index; if $s(5)$ is below 95% lower confidence level of the model implied spread, we sell the 5Y index; otherwise, do nothing.

Alternatively, we can define the trading signal as the

$$\gamma = \frac{\hat{s}(5) - s(5)}{\hat{\sigma}}$$

for the index. The above strategy longs the 5Y credit when γ is greater than the 95% standard normal quantile and shorts the credit when γ is less than the -95% standard normal quantile.

To make the strategy neutral to parallel and proportional move of the default intensity, we can construct a portfolio S by taking $a_1, 1, a_2$ positions in 3Y, 5Y and 10Y spreads. The strategy longs S if $s(5)$ is below 95% confidence level of the model implied spread; shorts S if $s(5)$ is below 95% confidence level of the model implied spread; otherwise, do nothing.

a_1 and a_2 are calculated via the following set of equations:

$$a_1 \frac{\partial s(3Y)}{\partial \beta_0} + \frac{\partial s(5Y)}{\partial \beta_0} + a_2 \frac{\partial s(10Y)}{\partial \beta_0} = 0$$

$$a_1 \frac{\partial s(3Y)}{\partial \beta_1} + \frac{\partial s(5Y)}{\partial \beta_1} + a_2 \frac{\partial s(10Y)}{\partial \beta_1} = 0$$

5 CONCLUDING REMARKS

This chapter introduces various statistical data mining procedures within the context of generalized Cox regressions. It is noteworthy that many iterative procedures described above can be embedded into others so that the practitioner really has a diversified pool of tools to build statistical models for survival probabilities and correlations. On the other hand, the practitioner should also be cautious when employing these data mining procedures. For example, it really makes no sense to bag a boosting procedure or vice versa in the hope of getting better results. Although both of them have the advantage of reducing prediction variance, the combination of the two will *not* produce more accurate results. On the contrary the computation is too *prohibitive* (especially for large datasets) to have any practical value.

Having constructed a parametric model for the hazard rate for the i-th subject, for example, in the time-dependent covariate case:

$$h_i(t) = \hat{h}_{i0}(t) \exp\left(x_{1t}^T \hat{\beta}_1 + x_{i2t}^T \hat{\beta}_2\right)$$

where x_1 is the systematic covariate and x_{i2} is the idiosyncratic covariate, then the joint survival function of the (i, j)-th subjects are specified by

$$P\left(\tau_i > T_1, \tau_j > T_2 | \mathcal{F}_t\right) = E\left(P\left(\tau_i > T_1, \tau_j > T_2 | \mathcal{F}_t, x_1, x_{i2}, x_{j2}\right) | \mathcal{F}_t\right)$$

$$= E_t\left(e^{-\int_t^{T_1} h_i(s)ds - \int_t^{T_2} h_j(s)ds}\right) \tag{23}$$

which can be calculated by Markov Chain Monte Carlo methods. The information filtration $\{\mathcal{F}_t : t \geq 0\}$ often reflects the econometrician or market investor's accumulation of knowledge in the setting of financial modelling. We ignore its construction just for the simplicity of illustration. Formula (23) also holds for frailty models, except that the conditional expectation will be calculated with respect to both the covariate processes and the frailty factors.

We also illustrate a working example of how to form factors from spline basis to model default arrival intensity for a credit index. The parameters can be calibrated from the market data for a specific on-the-run credit index, such as the North America Investment Grade Index or the High Grade iTraxx European index. Our model is actually sufficiently flexible to be extended to explain other types of default arrival intensities (such as those for a customized portfolio or for a single credit name) and to include other types of factors such as (Gaussian diffusion factors or pure Gamma jump factors).

APPENDICES

A Counting and intensity processes

Suppose a probability space $(\Omega, \mathcal{F}, P)$ with information filtration $(\mathcal{F}_t)_{t \geq 0}$ satisfying the *usual conditions*:

- (increasing) $\mathcal{F}_s \subseteq \mathcal{F}_t \subseteq \mathcal{F}$ for all $s < t$
- (right continuous) $\mathcal{F}_s = \cap_{t>s} \mathcal{F}_t$ for all s
- (complete) $A \subset B \in \mathcal{F}$, $P(B) = 0$ implies $A \in \mathcal{F}_0$

Definition   A.1 *(Counting   Process)   A   k-dimensional   counting   process $N = (N_1, \ldots, N_k)$ is a vector of k ($\mathcal{F}$-)adapted càdlàg processes, all zero at time zero, with piecewise constant and non-decreasing sample paths, having jumps of size 1 only and no two components jumping at the same time.*

For a classical survival analysis, we have a sample of n observations where $Z_i = \min\{T_i, C_i\}$ the minimum of the *survival time* T_i and *censoring time* C_i for the i-th observation. $\delta_i = I_{\{T_i \le C_i\}}$ is the corresponding *censoring indicator*.

For a complete description of the picture, we need further define:

- $R(t) = \{i : Z_i \ge t\}$ is the *risk set* just before time t.
- $Y(t) = \#R(t)$ is the *number at risk* just before time t.
- $S(t) = P(T_i > t)$ is the *survival function* for the default times.

Under the differentiability assumption of $S(t)$, we have the density function of the survival time to be: $f(t) = -\frac{dS(t)}{dt}$, and the hazard rate function $h(t) = f(t)/S(t)$. It can be verified that

$$S(t) = \exp\left(-\int_0^t h(s)\,ds\right) = \exp(-H(t)) \tag{24}$$

where $H(t) = \int_0^t h(s)\,ds$ is the *cumulative hazard function*.

Under the assumption of *independent censoring*, which means roughly[3] that the survival experience at any time t is independent of $\mathcal{F}_{t-}$, we have

$$P(Z_i \in [t, t+dt], \delta_i = 1 | \mathcal{F}_{t-}) = 1_{\{Z_i \ge t\}} h(t)\,dt. \tag{25}$$

Summing the above formula over i, we get

$$E\left(\#\{i : Z_i \in [t, t+dt], \delta_i = 1\} | \mathcal{F}_{t-}\right) = Y(t)h(t)\,dt. \tag{26}$$

On the other hand, if we define a process $N = (N(t))_{t \ge 0}$ counting the observed failures, where

$$N(t) = \#\{i : Z_i \le t, \delta_i = 1\}.$$

If we denote

$$dN(t) = N((t+dt)-) - N(t-)$$

to be the increment of observed failure over the small interval $[t, t+dt)$, then we can rewrite (26) as

$$E(dN(t) | \mathcal{F}_{t-}) = \lambda(t)\,dt \tag{27}$$

where $\lambda(t) = Y(t)h(t)$ is called the *intensity process* of the survival times.

---

[3] For a formal definition of independent censoring, refer to Andersen et al. (1993).

Proposition A.2 *Under above assumptions, $M(t) = N(t) - \Lambda(t)$ is a martingale ($t \geq 0$),* *where*

$$\Lambda(t) = \int_0^t \lambda(s)\,ds$$

is called the cumulative intensity process for the default times.

Since by definition $dN(t)$ can only be 0 or 1, (27) is equivalent to

$$P(dN(t) = 1|\mathcal{F}_{t-}) = \lambda(t)\,dt.$$

Hence, if we regard $N(t)$ to be the total number of observed defaults in a pool of names, then informally

$$P(\text{no default in } [t,s]\,|\mathcal{F}_{t-}) = \prod_{s \leq u \leq t} P(dN(u) = 0|\mathcal{F}_{u-})$$

$$= \prod_{s \leq u \leq t} (1 - \lambda(u)\,du)$$

$$= e^{-\int_t^s \lambda(u)du}.$$

In the case of constant hazard rate $h(t) \equiv h$, the intensity process λ is a piecewise constant and decreasing process.

Under the settings of credit risk, we can think of the censoring as caused by other types of exit except default of the entity of interest. So we can define the survival function for censoring to be

$$S^C(t) = P(C_i > t)$$

and the corresponding hazard rate function be $\beta(t)$. Then, similar to the previous arguments, we have

$$E\left(\#\{i : Z_i \in [t, t+dt), \delta_i = 0\}\,|\mathcal{F}_{t-}\right) = \omega(t)\,dt \tag{28}$$

where $\omega(t) = Y(t)\beta(t)$ is the intensity process of the censoring times and

$$\Omega(t) = \int_0^t \omega(s)\,ds$$

is the cumulative intensity process for the censoring times.

B Gamma and Variance Gamma processes

Before we go into the definition and properties of the Gamma and Variance Gamma processes, we first introduce a much larger class of processes: Lévy process and some familiar examples.

Definition B.1 *(Lévy process) A Lévy process is any continuous-time stochastic process that starts at 0, admits càdlàg modification and has 'stationary independent increments'.*

Example B.2 If X_t is a Lévy process and the increments $X_t - X_s$ have a Gaussian distribution with mean 0 and variance $(t - s)$ for $t \geq s$, then X_t is called a Standard Brownian Motion or Wiener process, often denoted by $X_t = B_t$ or W_t.

Example B.3 If X_t is a Lévy process and the increments $X_t - X_s$ have a Poisson distribution with parameter $\lambda(t - s)$ for $t \geq s$, or

$$P(X_t - X_s = k) = \frac{e^{-\lambda(t-s)}(\lambda(t-s))^k}{k!} \text{ for } k = 0, 1, \ldots$$

then X_t is called a Poisson process with intensity parameter (or rate) λ.

By the independent increment property of Lévy processes, it can be seen that

Corollary B.4 If X_t is a Lévy process, and $\phi(\theta) = E\left(e^{i\theta X_1}\right)$ be the characteristic function of X_1. Then the characteristic function of $X_{t+s} - X_s$ is $(\phi(\theta))^t$ for $t, s \geq 0$. Particularly, if $s = 0$, then X_t has characteristic function $(\phi(\theta))^t$.

Theorem B.5 *(Lévy-Khintchine representation) If X_t is a Lévy process, then its characteristic function satisfies the Lévy-Khintchine representation:*

$$E\left(e^{i\theta X_t}\right) = \exp\left(i\gamma\theta t - \frac{1}{2}\sigma^2\theta^2 t + t\int_{\mathbb{R}\backslash\{0\}}\left(e^{i\theta x} - 1 - i\theta x 1_{\{|x|<1\}}\right)\nu(dx)\right)$$

where $\gamma \in \mathbb{R}$, $\sigma \geq 0$ and ν is a measure defined on $\mathbb{R}\backslash\{0\}$ called the Lévy measure satisfying

$$\int_{\mathbb{R}\backslash\{0\}}\left(x^2 \wedge 1\right)\nu(dx) < \infty.$$

Thus a Lévy process can be seen as consisting of three components: a drift, a Brownian motion and a jump component.

From above Corollary and Theorem, we see that the *Lévy-Khintchine representation* is equivalent to

$$\psi(\theta) = \log(\phi(\theta)) = i\gamma\theta - \frac{1}{2}\sigma^2\theta^2 + \int_{\mathbb{R}\backslash\{0\}}\left(e^{i\theta x} - 1 - i\theta x 1_{\{|x|<1\}}\right)\nu(dx)$$

and $\psi(\theta)$ is called the *characteristic component* of X_t.

Before introducing the Gamma process, we first give a definition to the compound Poisson process:

Definition B.6 *(Compound Poisson process) A compound Poisson process Y_t with rate $\lambda > 0$ and jump size distribution G is a continuous stochastic process given by*

$$Y_t = \sum_{i=1}^{N(t)} D_i$$

where $N(t)$ is a Poisson process with rate λ, and D_i are i.i.d. with distribution G, which are also independent of $N(t)$.

It is easy to show that a Compound Poisson process is also a Lévy process by directly calculating its characteristic function. It turns out that we can construct a series of compound Poisson processes converging to a limit which is also a Lévy process. The limit process has independent increments with Gamma distribution, and thus has the name Gamma process. See, for example, David C. M. D. and Howard R. W. (1993) for the construction.

Let $\Gamma(\alpha, \beta)$ denote the Gamma distribution with density

$$f(x) = \frac{1}{\beta^\alpha \Gamma(\alpha)} x^{\alpha-1} e^{-x/\beta}, \ x > 0$$

Definition B.7 *A Lévy process X_t is a Gamma process with mean parameter $u > 0$ and variance parameter $v > 0$, if the increments $X_t - X_s$ has the Gamma distribution $\Gamma\left(u^2 (t - s)/v, v/u\right)$ for $t > s$.*

It can be shown by direct calculations that the characteristic function of a Gamma process X_t is given by

$$\phi(\theta) = E\left(e^{i\theta X_t}\right) = \left(\frac{1}{1 - i\theta \frac{v}{u}}\right)^{\frac{u^2 t}{v}}$$

and the Lévy measure for X_t is given by

$$v(dx) = \frac{u^2 \exp\left(-\frac{u}{v} x\right)}{vx} dx.$$

The Gamma process is always non-negative and increasing, which may restrict the practical applications of such processes. It turns out that by taking the difference of two independent Gamma processes with some specific parameters, we will get another Lévy process, which behaves somewhat like Brownian Motion, but has more preferable properties than Brownian Motion. Interestingly, this kind of process also has a construction closely related to Brownian Motion:

Definition B.8 *(Variance Gamma process or VG process) A VG process is obtained by evaluating Brownian Motion with drift at a random time given by a Gamma process. Specifically, let $b(t; \theta, \sigma) = \theta t + \sigma W_t$ where W_t is a standard Brownian Motion. The VG process X_t with parameter (θ, σ, v) is given by $X_t = b(Y_t; \theta, \sigma)$ where Y_t is a Gamma process with mean parameter 1 and variance parameter v. The process can also be seen as being generated by the independent increments:*

$$X_{t+s} - X_t = \theta(Y_{t+s} - Y_t) + \sigma(W(Y_{t+s}) - W(Y_t))$$

By Markov property, we see $X_{t+s} - X_t \sim b(Y_s; \theta, \sigma)$ for $t, s \geq 0$.

If X_t is a Variance Gamma process with parameter (θ, σ, v), then X_t has density function

$$f(x) = \int_0^\infty \frac{1}{\sigma\sqrt{2\pi s}} e^{-\frac{(x-\theta s)^2}{2\sigma^2 s}} \frac{s^{t/v-1} e^{-s/v}}{v^{t/v} \Gamma(t/v)} ds$$

and calculation shows it has the characteristic function

$$\phi(\theta) = E\left(e^{i\theta X_t}\right) = \left(\frac{1}{1 - i\theta v u + (\sigma^2 v/2) u^2}\right)^{t/v}$$

The Variance Gamma process X_t with parameter (θ, σ, v) can be expressed as the difference between two independent Gamma processes (see Madan et al. 1998): $X_t = Y_{1t} - Y_{2t}$ where Y_{1t}, Y_{2t} are Gamma processes with parameter (u_1, v_1) and (u_2, v_2) respectively and

$$u_1 = \frac{1}{2}\sqrt{\theta^2 + \frac{2\sigma^2}{v}} + \frac{\theta}{2}$$

$$u_1 = \frac{1}{2}\sqrt{\theta^2 + \frac{2\sigma^2}{v}} - \frac{\theta}{2}$$

$$v_1 = u_1^2 v$$

$$v_2 = u_2^2 v N$$

It can also be shown that the Lévy measure for X_t is given by

$$v(dx) = \begin{cases} \frac{u_1^2}{v_1 x} e^{-\frac{u_1}{v_1} x} dx & \text{for } x > 0 \\ -\frac{u_2^2}{v_2 x} e^{\frac{u_2}{v_2} x} dx & \text{for } x > 0 \end{cases}$$

$$= \frac{e^{\theta x/\sigma^2}}{v |x|} e^{-\frac{\sqrt{2/v + \theta^2/\sigma^2}}{\sigma} |x|} dx$$

which is symmetric if and only if $\theta = 0$.

References

Allen, D. (1971). 'Mean squared error of prediction as a criterion for selecting variables'. *Technometrics*, 13: 469–75.

Andersen, P. and Gill, R. (1982). 'Cox's regression model for counting processes: A large sample study'. *Annals of Statistics*, 10: 1100–20.

——Borgan, O., Gill, R. D., and Keiding, N. (1993). *Statistical Models Based on Counting Processes*. New York: Springer.

Bertoin, J. (1996). *Lévy Processes*. Cambridge Tracts in Mathematics 121, Cambridge: Cambridge, University Press.

Breslow, N. (1974). 'Covariance analysis of censored survival data'. *Biometrics*, 30: 89–99.

Bühlmann, P. (2002). 'Bagging, subagging, and bragging for improving some prediction algorithms'. Eidgenössische Technische Hochschule (ETH).

Cox, D. R. (1972). 'Regression models and life tables'. *Journal of the Royal Statistical Society*, B 34/2: 187–220.

David C. M. D. and Howard, R. W. (1993). 'Gamma process and finite time survival probabilities'. *Astin Bulletin*, 23/2: 259–72.

Davison, A., and Hinkley, D. (1997). *Bootstrap Methods and their Application*. Cambridge: Cambridge University Press.

Duffie, D., Saita, L. and Wang K. (2007). 'Multi-period corporate default prediction with stochastic covariates'. *Journal of Financial Economics*, 83: 635–65.

Efron, B. (1979). 'Bootstrap methods: another look at the jackknife'. *Annals of Statistics*, 7: 1–26.

——Hastie, T., Johnstone, I., and Tibshirani, R. (2004). 'Least angle regression'. *Annal of Statistics*, 32: 407–99.

Engle, R., and Granger, C. W. J. (1987). 'Co-integration and error correction: representation, estimation, and testing'. *Econometrica*, 55/2: 251–76.

Fan, J., and Li, R. (2002). 'Variable selection for Cox's proportional hazards model and frailty model'. *Annals of Statistics*, 30: 74–99.

Friedman, J. (2001). 'Greedy function approximation: a gradient boosting machine', Annals of Statistics, 29: 1189–1232.

Friedman, J., and Popescu, B. E. (2004). 'Gradient directed regularization for linear regression and classification'. Technical report, Stanford University, Department of Statistics.

Hastie, T., and Tibshirani, R. (1990). *Generalized Additive Models*. London: Chapman & Hall.

—————— and Friedman, J. H. (2001). *Elements of Statistical Learning*. New York: Springer-Verlag

Huang, J., and Harrington, D. (2002). Penalized partial likelihood Mgression for right-censored data with bootstrap selection of the penalty parameter'. Biometrics, 58: 781–91.

Li, H., and Gui, J. (2004). 'Partial Cox regression analysis for high-dimensional microarray gene expression data'. *Bioinformatics*, in press.

Lin, D. Y., and Ying, Z. (1995). 'Semiparametric analysis of general additive-multiplicative hazard models for counting processes'. *Annal of Statistics*, 23: 1712–34.

Madan, D. B., and Eugene Seneta, E. (1990). 'The variance gamma (V.G.) model for share market returns'. *Journal of Business*, 63/4: 511–24.

——Carr, Peter P., and Chang, E. C. (1998). 'The variance gamma process and option pricing'. *European Finance Review*, 2: 79–105.

Tibshirani, R. (1996) 'Regression shrinkage and selection via the lasso'. *Journal of the Royal Statistical Society*, B, 58: 267–88.

——(1997). 'The Lasso method for variable selection in the Cox model'. *Statistics in Medicine*, 16: 385–95.

Wei, L. J. (1984). 'Testing goodness of fit for proportional hazards model with censored observations'. *Journal of the Amercian Statistical Association*, 79: 649–52.

Wei, Z. (2006). 'Credit risk: modeling and application'. Working paper, Department of Statistics, Stanford University, CA.

Zou, H., and Hastie, T. (2005). 'Regularization and variable selection via the Elastic Net'. *Journal of the Royal Statistical Society*, B, 67/2: 301–20.

Wahba, E. (1980). 'Spline bases, regularization, and generalized cross validation for solving approximation problems with large quantities of noisy data'. In W. Cheney (ed.), *Approximation Theory III*. New York: Academic Press, 905–12.

PART III

SINGLE AND MULTI-NAME THEORY

....

CHAPTER 6

AN EXPOSITION OF CDS MARKET MODELS

....

LUTZ SCHLOEGL

1 INTRODUCTION

....

THE market model approach plays a key role in the modern literature on stochastic interest rate modelling. It was pioneered by Miltersen, Sandmann, and Sondermann (1997) and Brace, Gatarek, and Musiela (1997), and can be seen as a natural extension of the Heath, Jarrow, and Morton (1992) approach of describing the evolution of the whole term structure of interest rates in the sense that one tries to model directly observable rates, e.g. Libor forward rates.

For some time there has been a significant amount of effort devoted to developing a similar approach for credit spreads. While this work has to some extent been overshadowed by the immense amount of literature on the pricing of portfolio credit risk, it is nevertheless an important strand of the literature on credit modelling, in particular with regards to the modelling of actual credit spread dynamics, as opposed to describing the default dependence between multiple credits.

This chapter is expositional in nature. We hope to give an introduction into the mechanics and techniques used to develop market models for credit. We focus on the single credit case. This allows us to ignore the complicated issue of how to model default dependence between different credits, and also seems justified as at the time of this writing most practical applications for pricing models encompassing stochastic credit spreads seem to be in this area. As an exposition, this work is not a comprehensive literature survey, hence the bibliography is heavily slanted towards papers that we have found useful in thinking about this subject, and we have not made an exhaustive attempt to attribute every result or to determine matters of priority. Instead we have attempted to clarify some concepts and fill in details which may not be found elsewhere, but this work should not be construed as an original research article.

In the main, the literature on CDS market models goes back to Schönbucher (2000). This was the first to introduce the concept of survival contingent measures and derive arbitrage-free dynamics for discrete forward hazard rates as an expansion of a risk-free market model. It also provided a derivation of Black formulas for pricing default swaptions which are analogous to the caplet and swaption pricing formulas found in interest rate modelling.

In the Schönbucher (2000) set-up, survival measures are not equivalent martingale measures, but only absolutely continuous with respect to (default) risk-free forward measures. When working with this type of model, it is useful to be able to switch back and forth between measures at will. We therefore find it convenient to exploit the structure of the filtration and define background measures and price processes. This leads to equivalent martingale measures. The concept of a background filtration was introduced by Jeanblanc and Rutkowski (2000), and has been used by multiple authors since, e.g. Jamshidian (2004) and Brigo and Morini (2005). The theory is worked out in relative detail in section 2, where we have also formalized the concept of a background price process. We work in the conditional independence framework. While this is not the most general setting and rules out approaches to credit modelling along the lines of Giesecke and Azizpour (2008), for a single credit we believe this approach is perfectly satisfactory. In section 3 we show how this theory can be used to derive Black-type pricing formulas for default swaptions.

A full market model is developed in section 4, following Schönbucher (2000) and Brigo and Morini (2005). It turns out that, in the case where both credit spreads and interest rates are stochastic and dependent, the situation is not as clean as for interest rate market models. This is because default protection payoffs inherently contain a measure mismatch due to the timing of default and the payout. In the case where credit and interest rates are independent, the situation simplifies considerably. Under these simplifications, in section 5 we describe in detail the induction steps needed to construct a market model from scratch. We explicitly show how to close the loop to the actual definition of the default time, a detail which is usually neglected.

In section 6 we describe an alternative method of constructing CDS market models. Instead of using forward default intensities as model primitives, we directly describe the dynamics of certain survival probability ratios. This is analogous to the method of Zhao and Glasserman (2000). Its advantage is the fact that these probability ratios are martingales under the appropriate survival measures. This avoids the need for simulating stochastic differential equations (SDEs) with large drift terms, which can lead to problems when simulating the model e.g. using a Euler scheme. The model described in this section follows Samiri (2007).

Finally, the pricing of constant maturity CDS contracts is examined in section 7, following Brigo (2006).

2 MATHEMATICAL PRELIMINARIES

We now describe our mathematical framework, and discuss the two important concepts of a background filtration as well as that of survival measures.

2.1 General framework, the background filtration

We work on a measurable space $(\Omega, \mathcal{G})$. We think of the model construction as the extension of a default risk-free model to incorporate default risk of a single credit, accommodating both stochastic credit spread dynamics as well as dependence between credit spreads and the other financial variables of the model, in particular interest rates.

Our model will only exist up to a finite time horizon $T^* > 0$; this facilitates some change of measure arguments. We think of T^* as some arbitrarily large time horizon before which everything of interest to us takes place. We assume there is a filtration $\mathbb{F} = \{\mathcal{F}_t\}_{t \in [0, T^*]}$, which we will refer to as the background filtration. This concept was introduced by Jeanblanc and Rutkowski (2000). The background filtration contains all information available to market participants except for the explicit observation of the default event. All stochastic processes describing default risk-free financial variables will be adapted to $\mathbb{F}$. In particular, we assume there is a short rate process r, which also allows us to define the risk-free savings account process β with $\beta_t = e^{\int_0^t r_s ds}$. For each $T \in [0, T^*]$ and $t \in [0, T]$, we will denote by $B(t, T)$ the price at time t of a risk-free zero coupon bond maturing at T.

The default time itself is a random variable $\tau : \Omega \to \bar{\mathbb{R}}_+$. We denote the default indicator process by D, i.e. $D_t = \mathbf{1}_{\{\tau \leq t\}}$. The filtration generated by D is denoted by $\mathbb{D} = \{\mathcal{D}_t\}_{t \in [0, T^*]}$. It encapsulates the information a market participant obtains by observing at each point in time whether a default has occurred or not. Hence, the full information that market participants have is given by the filtration $\mathbb{G} := \mathbb{F} \vee \mathbb{D}$. So far we have not introduced any probability measure. We assume that there is a probability measure P on $(\Omega, \mathcal{G})$ which is a martingale measure for the risk-free savings account β. Note that we will not necessarily be pricing or modelling dynamics under P, however, it is useful to fix a spot martingale measure (i.e. one for the numeraire β) for reference. Other martingale measures will be derived from P by the change of numeraire technique, which is briefly reviewed in Appendix A.

We will now make the idea of a background filtration mathematically precise with two assumptions.

Assumption 2.1 *Based on the information available through* $\mathbb{F}$*, there is no certainty about whether default has occurred. In other words:*

$$\forall s, t \in [0, T^*] : P[\tau > t | \mathcal{F}_s] > 0 \quad P - a.s.$$

In general, derivative and asset prices must be computed by reference to the market filtration $\mathbb{G}$. If we have a $\mathcal{G}_T$-measurable claim X, then the price V_t of that claim at time $t \in [0, T]$ is given by

$$V_t = \beta_t \, E^P \left[\frac{X}{\beta_T} \middle| \mathcal{G}_t \right]. \tag{1}$$

The central idea of the background filtration is to reduce conditional expectations with respect to $\mathbb{G}$ to ones with respect to $\mathbb{F}$. For claims that are contingent on the survival of the credit, we will make extensive use of

Lemma 2.2 (Background Lemma) *Let $Y : \Omega \to \bar{\mathbb{R}}_+$ be $\mathcal{G}$-measurable, then for any $t \in [0, T^*]$ we have*

$$E^P[\mathbf{1}_{\{\tau>t\}}Y|\mathcal{G}_t] = \mathbf{1}_{\{\tau>t\}}\frac{E^P[\mathbf{1}_{\{\tau>t\}}Y|\mathcal{F}_t]}{P[\tau > t|\mathcal{F}_t]} \qquad P\text{-a.s.} \tag{2}$$

Proof. See Appendix B, also Jeanblanc and Rutkowski (2000). □

Note that the proof of Lemma 2.2 uses no assumptions about the probablity measure P, it is the special structure of the market filtration $\mathbb{G} = \mathbb{F} \vee \mathbb{H}$ which is exploited. If the claim X is of the form $X = \mathbf{1}_{\{\tau>T\}}\tilde{X}$ with an $\mathcal{F}_T$-measurable $\tilde{X}$, then the Background Lemma lets us see that

$$V_t = \mathbf{1}_{\{\tau>t\}}\beta_t \frac{E^P\left[\mathbf{1}_{\{\tau>T\}}\frac{\tilde{X}}{\beta_T}\middle|\mathcal{F}_t\right]}{P[\tau > t|\mathcal{F}_t]}.$$

We think of the credit risk part of the model as an extension of a default-free one. The pricing of a default-free claim should be handled purely within the context of $(\Omega, \mathcal{G}, \mathbb{F}, P)$, hence

Assumption 2.3 *There is no feedback from the default event to $\mathbb{F}$-adapted processes in the sense that every $(P, \mathbb{F})$-martingale is also a $(P, \mathbb{G})$-martingale.*

Assumption 2.3 is in some sense a conditional independence statement. In practice, models will be constructed in such a way that conditional default probabilities are generated via $\mathbb{F}$-adapted processes. In particular, these can induce dependence between credit spreads and interest rates. Once the conditional default probabilities have been computed, the actual default event is generated using a Poisson process which is independent of $\mathbb{F}$.

If X is $\mathcal{F}_T$-measurable, then Assumption 2.3 immediately implies that we can price this claim only with reference to the filtration $\mathbb{F}$:

$$V_t = \beta_t E^P\left[\frac{X}{\beta_T}\middle|\mathcal{F}_t\right].$$

So far we have formulated our assumptions in terms of the spot martingale measure P. We will often want to change numeraire though, e.g. making use of forward measures. As we have already stated above, the Background Lemma is also true for any other probability measure, as it only relies on the structure of the market filtration. The following Lemma shows that Assumption 2.3 also holds under any martingale measure deriving from an $\mathbb{F}$-adapted numeraire.

Lemma 2.4 *For $0 < T \leq T^*$, let $U = \{U_t\}_{t\in[0,T]}$ be an $\mathbb{F}$-adapted numeraire and let Q be the martingale measure for U derived from P via numeraire change. Every $(Q, \mathbb{F})$-martingale is then also a $(Q, \mathbb{G})$-martingale.*

Proof. For $t \in [0, T]$ we define $Z_t := \frac{U_t}{U_0 \beta_t}$, then $Q = Z_T P$ and $Z = (Z_t)_{t\in[0,T]}$ is a $(P, \mathbb{F})$-martingale. Let $X = (X_t)_{t\in[0,T]}$ be a $(Q, \mathbb{F})$-martingale. Using Bayes' Rule for conditional expectations we find that

$$X_t = E^Q[X_T|\mathcal{F}_t] = \frac{E^P[X_T Z_T|\mathcal{F}_t]}{E^P[Z_T|\mathcal{F}_t]},$$

and so

$$E^P[X_T Z_T|\mathcal{F}_t] = X_t Z_t.$$

In other words, $X Z$ is a $(P, \mathbb{F})$-martingale. Using Bayes' Rule once more and Assumption 2.3, we see that

$$E^Q[X_T|\mathcal{G}_t] = \frac{E^P[X_T Z_T|\mathcal{G}_t]}{E^P[Z_T|\mathcal{G}_t]} = \frac{X_t Z_t}{Z_t} = X_t.$$

$\square$

2.2 Pre-default and background processes, survival measures

An important focus in credit is the pricing of survival contingent claims. Let $T \in [0, T^*]$ and suppose that $X > 0$ is $\mathcal{F}_T$-measurable. We want to price the survival contingent claim $\mathbf{1}_{\{\tau>T\}} X$. A natural numeraire is the risk-free zero coupon bond maturing at T. If Q^T denotes the corresponding forward measure, then the price V_t at time $t \in [0, T]$ of this claim is

$$V_t = B(t, T) \, E^{Q^T} \left[\mathbf{1}_{\{\tau>T\}} X \big| \mathcal{G}_t \right]. \tag{3}$$

It is clear that $V_t = 0$ on the set $\{\tau \leq t\}$, we therefore want to remove this somewhat trivial dependency on the default time via the notion of a pre-default price process.

Proposition 2.5 *There is an $\mathbb{F}$-adapted process $\bar{V}$ such that $V_t = \mathbf{1}_{\{\tau>t\}} \bar{V}_t$, the so-called pre-default price process. It is given by*

$$\bar{V}_t = B(t, T) \, \frac{E^{Q^T} \left[\mathbf{1}_{\{\tau>T\}} X \big| \mathcal{F}_t \right]}{Q^T[\tau > t|\mathcal{F}_t]}. \tag{4}$$

Proof. Equation (4) follows immediately if we apply the Background Lemma under the measure Q^T to the conditional expectation in equation (3). $\square$

The introduction of a pre-default process lets us restrict ourselves to the filtration $\mathbb{F}$. However, $\bar{V}$ does not have the properties of an asset price process. In particular, $\frac{\bar{V}}{B(.,T)}$ is not a $(Q^T, \mathbb{F})$-martingale. For this we need the notion of a background process, which also lets us define the notion of a survival measure.

Definition 2.6 *The background process associated with V is defined as*

$$\hat{V}_t := B(t, T)\, E^{Q^T} \left[\mathbf{1}_{\{\tau > T\}} X \middle| \mathcal{F}_t \right]. \tag{5}$$

The price process can be recovered from the background process via

$$V_t = \mathbf{1}_{\{\tau > t\}} Q^T[\tau > t | \mathcal{F}_t] \hat{V}_t. \tag{6}$$

Furthermore, the process $\frac{\hat{V}}{B(.,T)}$ *is clearly a* $(Q^T, \mathbb{F})$*-martingale, so that* $\hat{V}$ *is an* $\mathbb{F}$*-adapted numeraire. In particular, we obtain an equivalent martingale measure* $\hat{Q}$ *by changing to the numeraire* $\hat{V}$. *We call this the survival measure associated with the claim X.*

A case of particular interest is that of a defaultable, zero recovery, zero coupon bond, where $X = 1$. We denote its price at time $t \in [0, T]$ by $B^d(t, T)$. Then

$$B^d(t, T) = B(t, T)\, Q^T[\tau > T | \mathcal{G}_t]. \tag{7}$$

In particular, we have

$$B^d(0, T) = B(0, T)\, Q^T[\tau > T]. \tag{8}$$

The pre-default process is (with a slight abuse of notation as we drop the d for defaultable)

$$\bar{B}(t, T) = B(t, T)\, \frac{Q^T[\tau > T | \mathcal{F}_t]}{Q^T[\tau > t | \mathcal{F}_t]}, \tag{9}$$

and the background process is

$$\hat{B}(t, T) = B(t, T)\, Q^T[\tau > T | \mathcal{F}_t]. \tag{10}$$

We denote the martingale measure associated with the numeraire $\hat{B}(., T)$ by $\hat{Q}^T$, this is the time T survival measure. Its usefulness follows from Proposition 2.9 below. Before we are in a position to prove Proposition 2.9 though, we need to resolve the arbitrariness of our choice of measure in defining the pre-default and the background price process.

Lemma 2.7 *Let* $T \in [0, T^*]$ *and let* $U = (U_t)_{t \in [0, T]}$ *be an* $\mathbb{F}$*-adapted numeraire, with corresponding martingale measure Q. For any* $t \in [0, T]$*, we then have*

$$Q[\tau > t | \mathcal{F}_t] = P[\tau > t | \mathcal{F}_t]. \tag{11}$$

Proof. 2.1 The density of Q with respect to P on $(\Omega, \mathcal{G})$ is given by $Z_T = \frac{U_T}{U_0 \beta_T}$. Define $Z_t := E^P[Z_T | \mathcal{F}_t]$, then $Z = (Z_t)_{t \in [0, T]}$ is of course a $(P, \mathbb{F})$-martingale. Using Bayes' Rule we see that

$$Z_t\, Q[\tau > t | \mathcal{F}_t] = E^P \left[\mathbf{1}_{\{\tau > t\}} Z_T \middle| \mathcal{F}_t \right].$$

Because of Assumption 2.3, we can write

$$E^P \left[\mathbf{1}_{\{\tau > t\}} Z_T \middle| \mathcal{F}_t \right] = E^P \left[E^P [\mathbf{1}_{\{\tau > t\}} Z_T | \mathcal{G}_t] \middle| \mathcal{F}_t \right] = E^P \left[\mathbf{1}_{\{\tau > t\}} Z_t \middle| \mathcal{F}_t \right] = Z_t P[\tau > t | \mathcal{F}_t].$$

$\square$

Proposition 2.8 *In the setting of Definition 2.6 and Proposition 2.5, let* $U = (U_t)_{t \in [0, T]}$ *be an $\mathbb{F}$-adapted numeraire and let Q denote the corresponding martingale measure. Then*

$$\hat{V}_t = U_t \, E^Q \left[\mathbf{1}_{\{\tau > T\}} \frac{X}{U_T} \middle| \mathcal{F}_t \right], \tag{12}$$

and

$$\bar{V}_t = \frac{U_t \, E^Q \left[\mathbf{1}_{\{\tau > T\}} \frac{X}{U_T} \middle| \mathcal{F}_t \right]}{Q[\tau > t \,|\, \mathcal{F}_t]}. \tag{13}$$

Proof. The density of Q with respect to Q^T is given by $Z_T := \frac{U_T B(0, T)}{U_0}$. More generally we define $Z_t := \frac{U_t B(0, T)}{B(t, T) U_0}$, then Z is a $(Q^T, \mathbb{F})$-martingale. Bayes' Rule once again lets us write

$$Z_t E^Q \left[\mathbf{1}_{\{\tau > T\}} \frac{X}{U_T} \middle| \mathcal{F}_t \right] = E^{Q^T} \left[\mathbf{1}_{\{\tau > T\}} \frac{X}{U_T} Z_T \middle| \mathcal{F}_t \right].$$

Inserting the definition of Z gives

$$U_t E^Q \left[\mathbf{1}_{\{\tau > T\}} \frac{X}{U_T} \middle| \mathcal{F}_t \right] = B(t, T) E^{Q^T} \left[\mathbf{1}_{\{\tau > T\}} X \middle| \mathcal{F}_t \right] = \hat{V}_t.$$

By definition we have $\bar{V}_t = \frac{\hat{V}_t}{Q^T[\tau > t | \mathcal{F}_t]}$. From Lemma 2.7 we know that $Q^T[\tau > t | \mathcal{F}_t] = Q[\tau > t | \mathcal{F}_t]$, hence the second claim about $\bar{V}_t$ immediately follows. $\qquad \square$

The content of Proposition 2.8 is that we could have used any $\mathbb{F}$-measurable numeraire to define the background and the pre-default process, we merely chose $B(t, T)$ for convenience. The next Proposition illustrates the practical use of the survival measure.

Proposition 2.9 *Let $T \in [0, T^*]$ and suppose that X is $\mathcal{F}_T$-measurable. For $t \in [0, T]$, the time t price V_t of the claim $\mathbf{1}_{\{\tau > T\}} X$ can be computed as*

$$V_t = B^d(t, T) \, E^{\hat{Q}^T} [X | \mathcal{F}_t]. \tag{14}$$

Proof. Because Assumption 2.3 holds, we can in fact use the numeraire $\hat{B}(., T)$ to compute the price V_t:

$$V_t = \hat{B}(t, T) \, E^{\hat{Q}^T} \left[\mathbf{1}_{\{\tau > T\}} \frac{X}{\hat{B}(T, T)} \middle| \mathcal{G}_t \right].$$

Using the Background Lemma, we see that

$$V_t = \mathbf{1}_{\{\tau > t\}} \hat{B}(t, T) \frac{E^{\hat{Q}^T} \left[\mathbf{1}_{\{\tau > T\}} \frac{X}{\hat{B}(T, T)} \middle| \mathcal{F}_t \right]}{\hat{Q}^T [\tau > t | \mathcal{F}_t]}.$$

Since $\hat{Q}^T[\tau > t | \mathcal{F}_t] = Q^T[\tau > t | \mathcal{F}_t]$, and recalling the definition of the background process $\hat{B}(t, T)$, we see that

$$V_t = B^d(t, T) \, E^{\hat{Q}^T} \left[\mathbf{1}_{\{\tau > T\}} \frac{X}{\hat{B}(T, T)} \middle| \mathcal{F}_t \right].$$

Now note that

$$\hat{B}(T, T) = Q^T[\tau > T | \mathcal{F}_T] = \hat{Q}^T[\tau > T | \mathcal{F}_T].$$

Thus we can use iterated conditional expectations to see that

$$E^{\hat{Q}^T} \left[\mathbf{1}_{\{\tau > T\}} \frac{X}{\hat{B}(T, T)} \middle| \mathcal{F}_t \right] = E^{\hat{Q}^T} [X | \mathcal{F}_t].$$

$\square$

With Proposition 2.9 we have achieved our aim of reducing the pricing of survival contingent claims to purely $\mathbb{F}$-measurable quantities. In other words, it is possible to price only with reference to the background filtration, without explicitly referencing the default time at all.

It should be emphasized that our definition of survival measures is somewhat different from that in Schönbucher (2000), instead following Brigo and Morini (2005). By focusing on the background filtration and formulating measure changes in terms of background price processes, it is possible to preserve the equivalence of martingale measures for different numeraires. This is convenient as one can change back and forth between measures at will. Survival contingent pricing is handled by Proposition 2.9.

3 DEFAULT SWAPTIONS

Using the theory developed in section 2, we can now turn to the pricing of default swaps and swaptions. We assume that the credit has a known deterministic recovery rate $R \in]0, 1[$. We fix a date grid $0 = T_0 < T_1 \ldots < T_n < T^*$ and let $\delta_k > 0$ denote the accrual factor for the period from T_k to T_{k+1}.

3.1 Forward default swap spreads

We consider a forward default swap running from T_i to T_j with $1 \leq i < j \leq n$. We will make some simplifying, but rather standard, assumptions about this contract in order to streamline notation and simplify the exposition. If the credit defaults before time T_i, then the contract simply knocks out. If, for $k \in \{i + 1, \ldots, j\}$, the credit defaults in $]T_{k-1}, T_k]$, then the protection buyer receives a payment of $1 - R$ at time T_k. For $t \in [0, T_i]$, the value of the protection leg is given by

$$\Pi_t^{i,j} = (1 - R) \sum_{k=i+1}^{j} B(t, T_k) E^{Q_k} \left[\mathbf{1}_{\{T_{k-1} < \tau \leq T_k\}} \middle| \mathcal{G}_t \right]. \tag{15}$$

We can also describe $\Pi^{i,j}$ using the spot martingale measure. For each $k \in \{1, \ldots, n\}$ define the stochastic discount factor $D(t, T_k) := \frac{\beta_t}{\beta_{T_k}}$ (note though that $D(t, T_k)$ is not

$\mathcal{F}_t$-measurable, we introduce this random variable purely for notational convenience). Then

$$\Pi_t^{i,j} = (1 - R) \sum_{k=i+1}^{j} E^P \left[D(t, T_k) \mathbf{1}_{\{T_{k-1} < \tau \leq T_k\}} \big| \mathcal{G}_t \right]. \tag{16}$$

With the help of the Background Lemma we see that this is equal to

$$\Pi_t^{i,j} = \mathbf{1}_{\{\tau > t\}} (1 - R) \sum_{k=i+1}^{j} \frac{E^P \left[D(t, T_k) \mathbf{1}_{\{T_{k-1} < \tau \leq T_k\}} \big| \mathcal{F}_t \right]}{P[\tau > t | \mathcal{F}_t]}. \tag{17}$$

Equation (17) lets us identify the background and the pre-default process of $\Pi^{i,j}$ as

$$\hat{\Pi}_t^{i,j} = (1 - R) \sum_{k=i+1}^{j} E^P \left[D(t, T_k) \mathbf{1}_{\{T_{k-1} < \tau \leq T_k\}} \big| \mathcal{F}_t \right], \tag{18}$$

$$\bar{\Pi}_t^{i,j} = \frac{\hat{\Pi}_t^{i,j}}{P[\tau > t | \mathcal{F}_t]}, \tag{19}$$

so that

$$\Pi_t^{i,j} = \mathbf{1}_{\{\tau > t\}} \bar{\Pi}_t^{i,j} = \mathbf{1}_{\{\tau > t\}} \frac{\hat{\Pi}_t^{i,j}}{P[\tau > t | \mathcal{F}_t]}. \tag{20}$$

The process $\hat{\Pi}^{i,j}$ is an $\mathbb{F}$-adapted numeraire, it is instructive to note that we can write $\hat{\Pi}^{i,j}$ with the help of forward measures as

$$\hat{\Pi}_t^{i,j} = (1 - R) \sum_{k=i+1}^{j} B(t, T_k) \left(Q^k[\tau > T_{k-1} | \mathcal{F}_t] - Q^k[\tau > T_k | \mathcal{F}_t] \right). \tag{21}$$

We now turn to the valuation of the fixed leg of the default swap, and assume that the protection buyer pays no accrued coupon. Therefore, the quantity of interest is the risky annuity given by

$$A_t^{i,j} = \sum_{k=i+1}^{j} \delta_{k-1} B^d(t, T_k). \tag{22}$$

In the same way as for the protection leg, one can show that the background and pre-default processes are given by

$$\hat{A}_t^{i,j} = \sum_{k=i+1}^{j} \delta_{k-1} \hat{B}(t, T_k), \tag{23}$$

$$\bar{A}_t^{i,j} = \frac{\hat{A}_t^{i,j}}{P[\tau > t | \mathcal{F}_t]}. \tag{24}$$

We are now in a position to define the forward default swap spread $s^{i,j}$. This is the breakeven spread which a buyer of protection should pay in the forward default swap contract. In other words, it must satisfy the following equation

$$s_t^{i,j} A_t^{i,j} = \Pi_t^{i,j}.$$

(25)

This is equivalent to

$$s_t^{i,j} \mathbf{1}_{\{\tau > t\}} \bar{A}_t^{i,j} = \mathbf{1}_{\{\tau > t\}} \bar{\Pi}_t^{i,j}.$$

(26)

We are therefore justified in making the following

Definition 3.1 *The forward default swap spread $s^{i,j}$ is defined as*

$$s_t^{i,j} = \frac{\bar{\Pi}_t^{i,j}}{\bar{A}_t^{i,j}}.$$

(27)

We can also write $s^{i,j}$ using the background processes as

$$s_t^{i,j} = \frac{\hat{\Pi}_t^{i,j}}{\hat{A}_t^{i,j}}.$$

In particular, the process $s^{i,j}$ is a martingale under the measure corresponding to the numeraire $\hat{A}^{i,j}$. It is useful to consider the one-period default swap running from T_i to T_{i+1}. We define $\hat{\Pi}^i := \hat{\Pi}^{i,i+1}$, $\hat{A}^i := \hat{A}^{i,i+1}$, and denote its spread by $s^i := s^{i,i+1}$. Using our previous results we have

$$\hat{\Pi}_t^i = (1 - R)B(t, T_{i+1})\left(Q^{i+1}[\tau > T_i|\mathcal{F}_t] - Q^{i+1}[\tau > T_{i+1}|\mathcal{F}_t]\right),$$

$$\hat{A}_t^i = \delta_i \hat{B}(t, T_{i+1}) = \delta_i B(t, T_{i+1})Q^{i+1}[\tau > T_{i+1}|\mathcal{F}_t],$$

so that

$$s_t^i = \frac{1 - R}{\delta_i}\left(\frac{Q^{i+1}[\tau > T_i|\mathcal{F}_t]}{Q^{i+1}[\tau > T_{i+1}|\mathcal{F}_t]} - 1\right),$$

(28)

and in particular we have the nice equation

$$1 + \frac{\delta_i}{1 - R}s_t^i = \frac{Q^{i+1}[\tau > T_i|\mathcal{F}_t]}{Q^{i+1}[\tau > T_{i+1}|\mathcal{F}_t]}.$$

(29)

Also, the default swap spread $s^{i,j}$ can be written as a weighted average of the one-period spreads.

Proposition 3.2 *Let $0 \leq i < j < n$, then on the set $\{\tau > t\}$*

$$s_t^{i,j} = \sum_{l=i}^{j-1}\left(\frac{\delta_l B^d(t, T_{l+1})}{\sum_{k=i}^{j-1}\delta_k B^d(t, T_{k+1})}\right)s_t^l.$$

(30)

Proof. It is easy to see that

$$\hat{\Pi}_t^{i,j} = \sum_{l=i}^{j-1}\hat{\Pi}_t^{l,l+1}.$$

Inserting the breakeven condition for the one-period default swap spreads gives

$$\hat{\Pi}_t^{i,j} = \sum_{l=i}^{j-1} \delta_l \hat{B}(t, T_{l+1}) s_t^l.$$

To obtain $s_t^{i,j}$, we need to divide by the background annuity $\hat{A}_t^{i,j}$, so that

$$s_t^{i,j} = \sum_{l=i}^{j-1} \left(\frac{\delta_l \hat{B}(t, T_{l+1})}{\sum_{k=i}^{j-1} \delta_k \hat{B}(t, T_{k+1})} \right) s_t^l. \tag{31}$$

Recall that $B^d(t, T) = \mathbf{1}_{\{\tau > t\}} \frac{\hat{B}(t,T)}{P[\tau > t | \mathcal{F}_t]}$. With this, it is clear that equations (30) and (31) coincide on the set $\{\tau > t\}$.   □

3.2 European default swaptions

We now consider the pricing of a European payer swaption, where the holder has the right to buy protection in a default swap from time T_i to T_j at a strike of K. The payer swaption payoff at time T_i is

$$PS_{T_i} = \mathbf{1}_{\{\tau > T_i\}} \left[\Pi_{T_i}^{i,j} - K A_{T_i}^{i,j} \right]^+. \tag{32}$$

So, for $t \leq T_i$ we have

$$PS_t = E^P \left[D(t, T_i) \mathbf{1}_{\{\tau > T_i\}} \left[\Pi_{T_i}^{i,j} - K A_{T_i}^{i,j} \right]^+ \Big| \mathcal{G}_t \right]. \tag{33}$$

Using the Background Lemma, this is equal to

$$PS_t = \mathbf{1}_{\{\tau > t\}} \frac{E^P \left[D(t, T_i) \mathbf{1}_{\{\tau > T_i\}} \left[\Pi_{T_i}^{i,j} - K A_{T_i}^{i,j} \right]^+ \Big| \mathcal{F}_t \right]}{P[\tau > t | \mathcal{F}_t]}. \tag{34}$$

We define

$$I := E^P \left[D(t, T_i) \mathbf{1}_{\{\tau > T_i\}} \left[\Pi_{T_i}^{i,j} - K A_{T_i}^{i,j} \right]^+ \Big| \mathcal{F}_t \right]. \tag{35}$$

Recall that $\Pi_{T_i}^{i,j} = \mathbf{1}_{\{\tau > T_i\}} \frac{\hat{\Pi}_{T_i}^{i,j}}{P[\tau > T_i | \mathcal{F}_{T_i}]}$ and similarly $A_{T_i}^{i,j} = \mathbf{1}_{\{\tau > T_i\}} \frac{\hat{A}_{T_i}^{i,j}}{P[\tau > T_i | \mathcal{F}_{T_i}]}$. Inserting this into equation (35), we find that

$$I = E^P \left[D(t, T_i) \frac{\mathbf{1}_{\{\tau > T_i\}}}{P[\tau > T_i | \mathcal{F}_{T_i}]} \left[\hat{\Pi}_{T_i}^{i,j} - K \hat{A}_{T_i}^{i,j} \right]^+ \Big| \mathcal{F}_t \right]. \tag{36}$$

Now, using iterated conditional expectations and first conditioning on $\mathcal{F}_{T_i}$, we see that this is equal to

$$I = E^P \left[D(t, T_i) \left[\hat{\Pi}_{T_i}^{i,j} - K \hat{A}_{T_i}^{i,j} \right]^+ \bigg| \mathcal{F}_t \right] = E^P \left[D(t, T_i) \hat{A}_{T_i}^{i,j} \left[s_{T_i}^{i,j} - K \right]^+ \bigg| \mathcal{F}_t \right]. \quad (37)$$

Let $Q^{i,j}$ denote the martingale measure corresponding to the numeraire $\hat{A}^{i,j}$. The density martingale Z of $Q^{i,j}$ with respect to P is given by $Z_t = \dfrac{\hat{A}_t^{i,j}}{\hat{A}_0^{i,j} \beta_t}$. Using Bayes' Rule for conditional expectations, we find that

$$I = \beta_t \, \hat{A}_0^{i,j} \, E^P \left[Z_{T_i} \left[s_{T_i}^{i,j} - K \right]^+ \bigg| \mathcal{F}_t \right] = \beta_t \, \hat{A}_0^{i,j} \, Z_t \, E^{Q^{i,j}} \left[\left[s_{T_i}^{i,j} - K \right]^+ \bigg| \mathcal{F}_t \right]$$

$$= \hat{A}_t^{i,j} \, E^{Q^{i,j}} \left[\left[s_{T_i}^{i,j} - K \right]^+ \bigg| \mathcal{F}_t \right]. \quad (38)$$

Plugging equation (38) into equation (34) and using the relationship between $\hat{A}^{i,j}$ and $A^{i,j}$, we see that

$$PS_t = A_t^{i,j} \, E^{Q^{i,j}} \left[\left[s_{T_i}^{i,j} - K \right]^+ \bigg| \mathcal{F}_t \right]. \quad (39)$$

As discussed before, the process $s^{i,j}$ is a martingale under the measure $Q^{i,j}$. If we assume that $s^{i,j}$ is a lognormal martingale, we recover the classic Black formula via the standard calculations.

Proposition 3.3 *Suppose that under the measure $Q^{i,j}$ the forward default swap spread $s^{i,j}$ has dynamics of the form*

$$ds_t^{i,j} = s_t^{i,j} \sigma dW_t \quad (40)$$

with a Brownian motion W, then the value of a payer default swaption with strike K and maturity T is given by

$$PS_0 = A_0^{i,j} \left(s_0^{i,j} \Phi(h_1) - K \Phi(h_2) \right) \quad (41)$$

where

$$h_{1/2} = \frac{1}{\sigma\sqrt{T}} \left(\log\left(\frac{s_0}{K} \right) \pm \frac{\sigma^2 T}{2} \right). \quad (42)$$

4 CDS MARKET MODEL SPECIFICATION

So far, we have seen how one can use the mathematical formalism of section 2 to derive pricing formulas for credit derivatives. This is however not the same as developing an arbitrage-free model from primitive modelling objects. As the title of Brigo and Morini (2005) aptly suggests, so far we have CDS market formulas, but not models. We now show how the dynamic relationships in an arbitrage-free CDS market model can be derived from modelling primitives.

4.1 Model specification

We use the same discrete tenor structure as in section 3. To lighten notation, for $k \in \{1, \ldots, n\}$ we define $B_k(t) := B(t, T_k)$, B_k^d and $\hat{B}_k$ are defined analogously. The processes B_k and $\hat{B}_k$ are defined on $[0, T_k]$. We also set $B_0(0) = \hat{B}_0(0) = 1$. We can now define for each $k \in \{0, 1, \ldots, n\}$

$$D_k := \frac{\hat{B}_k}{B_k} = Q^k[\tau > T_k | \mathcal{F}_t]. \tag{43}$$

The process D_k is a martingale under the risk-free forward measure Q_k, and up to a multiplicative constant it is the change of measure from Q_k to the survival measure $\hat{Q}_k$.

Because we want to construct our model as an extension of a non-defaultable Libor market model, it is clear that our modelling primitives for interest rates are the Libor forward rates L_k, $k \in \{0, 1, \ldots, n - 1\}$. Here L_k defines the forward rate resetting at T_k and paying at T_{k+1}, so that we have the following relationship between rates and bond prices

$$1 + \delta_k L_k(t) = \frac{B_k(t)}{B_{k+1}(t)}. \tag{44}$$

Clearly, L_k is a martingale under Q_{k+1}.

For the defaultable part of the model, the choice of modelling primitives is unfortunately not so clear. Ideally, we would like to use one-period forward default swap spreads as described in equation (29). However, there is a measure mismatch because the spread s^i references a payoff at time T_{i+1} which is dependent on the probability of surviving beyond T_i and T_{i+1}. This causes difficulties if interest rates are stochastic and not independent of credit spreads. Hence, following Schönbucher (2000) (albeit using the background filtration approach) we choose forward default intensities H_k, $k \in \{0, 1, \ldots, n - 1\}$ as modelling primitives, where H_k is defined via the equation

$$1 + \delta_k H_k = \frac{D_k}{D_{k+1}}. \tag{45}$$

The term forward default intensity is justified by the fact that from equation (43) we see that

$$1 + \delta_k H_k = \frac{Q^k[\tau > T_k | \mathcal{F}_t]}{Q^{k+1}[\tau > T_{k+1} | \mathcal{F}_t]}. \tag{46}$$

Note however that two different forward measures appear on the right of equation (46). It is also instructive to compare this with equation (29). The motivation for defining H_k in the way we have stems from the fact that H_k is closely related to the change of measure from $\hat{Q}_{k+1}$ to $\hat{Q}_k$. Up to a constant, this is given by $\frac{\hat{B}_k}{\hat{B}_{k+1}}$. Since

$$1 + \delta_k H_k = \frac{D_k}{D_{k+1}} = \frac{\hat{B}_k}{\hat{B}_{k+1}} \frac{B_{k+1}}{B_k},$$

it follows that

$$\frac{\hat{B}_k}{\hat{B}_{k+1}} = (1 + \delta_k H_k)(1 + \delta_k L_k). \tag{47}$$

We are now in a position to define our model as follows. Forward Libor rates and default intensities L_k and H_k, $k \in \{1, \ldots, n-1\}$ will be driven by an m-dimensional $\mathbb{F}$-Brownian motion. The $\mathbb{R}^m$-valued volatility processes are denoted by σ_k^L and σ_k^H respectively. Generically, we will denote the Brownian motion by W, using the Girsanov theorem to freely switch between measures. For each process L_k and H_k we will determine the drift via no-arbitrage arguments. We have mentioned before, and it is well known from the theory of non-defaultable Libor market models, that L_k is a martingale under Q_{k+1}. Our task is to determine the dynamics of Libor rates under survival measures and the appropriate drift for the processes H_k.

We now turn our attention back to the change of measure from Q_k to $\hat{Q}_k$, which, up to a constant, is given by D_k.

Definition 4.1 *For each $k \in \{1, \ldots, n\}$, we define the $\mathbb{R}^m$-valued process a_k^D on $[0, T_k]$ such that the martingale part of D_k is given by*

$$dD_k^M(t) = -D_k(t)\, a_k^D(t) dW_t. \tag{48}$$

We can derive a recursion for the different processes a_k^D.

Proposition 4.2 *Let $k \in \{1, \ldots, n-1\}$, then for $t \in [0, T_k]$ we have*

$$a_{k+1}^D(t) = a_k^D(t) + \frac{\delta_k H_k(t)}{1 + \delta_k H_k(t)} \sigma_k^H(t). \tag{49}$$

Proof. From the definition of H_k it follows that $D_{k+1} = \frac{D_k}{1+\delta_k H_k}$. Ito's Lemma shows that

$$dD_{k+1}^M = \frac{dD_k^M}{1 + \delta_k H_k} - \frac{\delta_k D_k dH_k^M}{(1 + \delta_k H_k)^2}. \tag{50}$$

Using equation (48) and the specification of dH_k^M gives

$$dD_{k+1}^M = -\frac{a_k^D D_k}{1 + \delta_k H_k} dW_t - \frac{\delta_k D_{k+1} H_k}{1 + \delta_k H_k} \sigma_k^H dW_t = -D_{k+1}\left(a_k^D + \frac{\delta_k H_k}{1 + \delta_k H_k}\sigma_k^H\right)dW_t. \tag{51}$$

$\square$

Equation (49) is not quite enough to fix the processes a_k^D completely. In addition, we also make the assumption that the volatility collapses on the final stub of process D_k. In other words, we augment Definition 4.1 by defining that for each $k \in \{1, \ldots, n\}$, we have

$$\forall t \in [T_{k-1}, T_k] : a_k^D(t) = 0. \tag{52}$$

With this, the processes D_k are completely defined in terms of primitives of our model. As we now know the change of measure from Q_{k+1} to $\hat{Q}_{k+1}$ for any $k \in \{1, \ldots, n-1\}$, we can compute the dynamics of L_k under $\hat{Q}_{k+1}$.

Proposition 4.3 *With a Brownian motion $\tilde{W}$ under $\hat{Q}_{k+1}$, the dynamics of L_k are given by*

$$dL_k(t) = L_k(t)\sigma_k^L(t)\left(d\tilde{W}_t - a_{k+1}^D(t)dt\right). \tag{53}$$

Proof. If W is a Brownian motion under Q_{k+1}, then using Girsanov's theorem (see also the results of Appendix A) we see that $\tilde{W}$ defined by

$$d\tilde{W}_t = dW_t - \frac{1}{D_{k+1}(t)}dD_{k+1}^M(t)dW_t = dW_t + a_{k+1}^D(t)dt \tag{54}$$

is a Brownian motion under $\hat{Q}_{k+1}$. Since L_k is a martingale under Q_{k+1} we have

$$dL_k(t) = L_k(t)\sigma_k^L(t)dW_t = L_k(t)\sigma_k^L(t)\left(d\tilde{W}_t - a_{k+1}^D(t)dt\right). \tag{55}$$

□

Lemma 4.4 *The process $(1 + \delta_k H_k)(1 + \delta_k L_k)$ is a martingale under $\hat{Q}_{k+1}$.*

Proof. 4.2 The assertion follows from the fact that

$$1 + \delta_k H_k = \frac{D_k}{D_{k+1}} = \frac{\hat{B}_k}{\hat{B}_{k+1}}\frac{B_{k+1}}{B_k},$$

and so

$$(1 + \delta H_k)(1 + \delta_k L_k) = \frac{\hat{B}_k}{\hat{B}_{k+1}}. \tag{56}$$

□

We can use Lemma 4.4 and the known dynamics of L_k to compute the dynamics of H_k under $\hat{Q}_{k+1}$.

Proposition 4.5 *With a Brownian motion W under $\hat{Q}_{k+1}$ the dynamics of H_k are given by*

$$dH_k = \frac{L_k\sigma_k^L\left[(1 + \delta_k H_k)a_{k+1}^D - \delta_k H_k\sigma_k^H\right]}{1 + \delta_k L_k}dt + H_k\sigma_k^H dW_t \tag{57}$$

Proof. We can write the dynamics of H_k under $\hat{Q}_{k+1}$ as

$$dH_k = H_k\left(\mu_k dt + \sigma_k^H dW_t\right)$$

with an as yet unkown drift process μ_k. Set $Z := (1 + \delta_k H_k)(1 + \delta_k L_k)$, then

$$dZ = \delta_k d H_k + \delta_k d L_k + \delta_k^2 d\,(H_k L_k).$$

Since Z is a martingale, using the dynamics of L_k it follows that

$$0 = H_k\mu_k - L_k\sigma_k^L a_{k+1}^D + \delta_k\left(-H_k L_k \sigma_k^L a_{k+1}^D + L_k H_k\mu_k + H_k L_k \sigma_k^L \sigma_k^H\right).$$

Collecting terms, we see that

$$\mu_k H_k = \frac{L_k \sigma_k^L \left[(1 + \delta_k H_k)\,a_{k+1}^D - \delta_k H_k \sigma_k^H\right]}{1 + \delta_k L_k},$$

equation (57) follows immediately. □

The result of Lemma 4.4 should not surprise us as the process $Z = (1 + \delta_k H_k)(1 + \delta_k L_k)$ is, up to a constant, the change of measure from $\hat{Q}_{k+1}$ to $\hat{Q}_k$. This is used again in the following

Proposition 4.6 *Suppose that W is an m-dimensional Brownian motion under $\hat{Q}_{k+1}$. Then the process $\tilde{W}$ defined via*

$$d\tilde{W}_t := dW_t - \left(\frac{\delta_k H_k \sigma_k^H}{1 + \delta_k H_k} + \frac{\delta_k L_k \sigma_k^L}{1 + \delta_k L_k}\right)dt \tag{58}$$

is a Brownian motion under $\hat{Q}_k$.

Proof. With the process $Z = (1 + \delta_k H_k)(1 + \delta_k L_k)$ we have

$$dZ^M = \delta_k \left\{(1 + \delta_k L_k)d H_k^M + (1 + \delta_k H_k)d L_k^M\right\}.$$

Hence

$$\frac{1}{Z}dZ^M = \left(\frac{\delta_k H_k \sigma_k^H}{1 + \delta_k H_k} + \frac{\delta_k L_k \sigma_k^L}{1 + \delta_k L_k}\right)dW_t.$$

Equation (58) now follows from Girsanov's Theorem. □

We now have a full dynamic description of the model in terms of the primitives H_k and L_k. We can switch between the forward measure Q_k and the survival measure $\hat{Q}_k$ thanks to Proposition 4.2. We fully know the dynamics of H_k and L_k under the survival measure $\hat{Q}_{k+1}$ thanks to Propositions 4.3 and 4.5. Finally, we can switch between any survival measures thanks to Proposition 4.6. So, we can choose any measure we like and consistently evolve all forward Libor rates and default intensities. A typical implementation would do this via Monte Carlo simulation, for example under the terminal survival measure.

However, one should note that we have not really provided an existence proof of such a model, which would consist of starting from modelling primitives, solving all the SDEs we have derived under a single measure and defining a default time which is consistent with the dynamics. In section 5 we carry out such a construction in detail for the case of independence between rates and credit.

To conclude our analysis of the general model, we examine how forward default swap spreads can be described via the model primitives L_k and H_k and how their dynamics can be approximated.

Proposition 4.7 *Let $1 \leq i < j \leq n$. For each $k \in \{i, \ldots, j-1\}$ define the weight $w_k(t)$ as*

$$w_k(t) := \frac{\delta_k \hat{B}_{k+1}(t)}{\sum_{l=i}^{j-1} \delta_l \hat{B}_{l+1}(t)}. \tag{59}$$

Then we have

$$s_t^{i,j} = (1-R) \sum_{k=i}^{j-1} w_k(t) E^{\hat{Q}_{k+1}} \left[H_k(T_k) \middle| \mathcal{F}_t \right]. \tag{60}$$

Proof. Recall from the definitions that $s_t^{i,j} = \frac{\hat{\Pi}_t^{i,j}}{\hat{A}_t^{i,j}}$ and that $\hat{A}_t^{i,j} = \sum_{k=i}^{j-1} \delta_k \hat{B}_{k+1}$. The protection leg can be written as

$$\hat{\Pi}_t^{i,j} = (1-R) \sum_{k=i}^{j-1} B(t, T_{k+1}) Q_{k+1}[T_k < \tau \leq T_{k+1}|\mathcal{F}_t]$$

$$= (1-R) \sum_{k=i}^{j-1} \left(B(t, T_{k+1}) Q_{k+1}[\tau > T_k|\mathcal{F}_t] - \hat{B}(t, T_{k+1}) \right).$$

We define $I_k := B(t, T_{k+1}) Q_{k+1}[\tau > T_k|\mathcal{F}_t]$. Since the payoff in this claim is known at time T_k, we can switch to the T_k-forward measure:

$$I_k = B(t, T_k) E^{Q_k} \left[\frac{Q^k[\tau > T_k|\mathcal{F}_{T_k}]}{1 + \delta_k L_k(T_k)} \middle| \mathcal{F}_t \right].$$

Note that $D_k(T_k) = Q^k[\tau > T_k|\mathcal{F}_{T_k}]$. By switching to the survival measure $\hat{Q}_k$ we see that

$$I_k = \hat{B}_k(t) E^{\hat{Q}_k} \left[\frac{1}{1 + \delta_k L_k(T_k)} \middle| \mathcal{F}_t \right].$$

Finally, we use the fact that $(1 + \delta_k H_k)(1 + \delta_k L_k) = \frac{\hat{B}_k}{\hat{B}_{k+1}}$ is (up to a constant) the change of measure from $\hat{Q}_{k+1}$ to $\hat{Q}_k$. By switching to $\hat{Q}_{k+1}$ we see that

$$I_k = \hat{B}_{k+1}(t) E^{\hat{Q}_{k+1}} [1 + \delta_k H_k(T_k)|\mathcal{F}_t],$$

and so

$$\hat{\Pi}_t^{i,j} = (1-R) \sum_{k=i}^{j-1} \delta_k \hat{B}_{k+1}(t) E^{\hat{Q}_{k+1}} [H_k(T_k)|\mathcal{F}_t].$$

$\square$

As we saw in Proposition 4.5, the process H_k is not a martingale under $\hat{Q}_{k+1}$ in the general setting. If we use the drift freezing technique, then we obtain the following approximation

Proposition 4.8 *If we freeze the drift coefficients in the dynamics for H_k, we have*

$$E^{\hat{Q}_{k+1}}[H_k(T_k)|\mathcal{F}_t] \approx H_k(t)\exp\left(\frac{L_k(0)(1+\delta_k H_k(0))}{H_k(0)(1+\delta_k L_k(0))}\sum_{l=1}^{k-1}\frac{\delta_l H_l(0)}{1+\delta_l H_l(0)}[T_l-t]^+\sigma_k^L\cdot\sigma_l^H\right).$$

$$(61)$$

Proof. Following Proposition 4.5, we can write the dynamics of H_k as

$$dH_k = H_k(\mu_k(t)dt + \sigma_k^H dW_t)$$

with

$$\mu_k = \frac{L_k\sigma_k^L\left[(1+\delta_k H_k)a_{k+1}^D - \delta_k H_k\sigma_k^H\right]}{H_k(1+\delta_k L_k)}.$$

$$(62)$$

Solving the SDE for H_k shows that

$$H_k(t) = H_k(0)e^{\int_0^t \mu_k(u)du}\mathcal{E}\left(\sigma_k^H\cdot W\right)_t.$$

By drift freezing we mean that we will freeze Libor rates and forward intensities at their time-zero values. Recall the recursion for a_k^D from Proposition 4.2, which states that

$$\forall t \in [0, T_k]; \; a_{k+1}^D(t) = a_k^D(t) + \frac{\delta_k H_k(t)}{1+\delta_k H_k(t)}\sigma_k^H,$$

and $a_{k+1}^D(t) = 0$ for $t \in]T_k, T_{k+1}]$. Under the drift freezing assumption we approximate a_{k+1}^D by $\tilde{a}_{k+1}^D$ where

$$\tilde{a}_{k+1}^D(t) = \sum_{l=1}^{k}\frac{\delta_l H_l(0)}{1+\delta_l H_l(0)}\sigma_l^H \mathbf{1}_{[0,T_l]}(t).$$

$$(63)$$

We denote by $\tilde{\mu}_k$ the expression we obtain by plugging equation (63) into (62) and using drift freezing there too. Then it is easy to see that

$$\int_t^{T_k}\tilde{\mu}_k(u)du = \frac{L_k(0)(1+\delta_k H_k(0))}{H_k(0)(1+\delta_k L_k(0))}\sum_{l=1}^{k-1}\frac{\delta_l H_l(0)}{1+\delta_l H_l(0)}[T_l-t]^+\sigma_k^L\cdot\sigma_l^H. \quad (64)$$

This result, in conjunction with the SDE for H_k, easily lets one obtain equation (61). $\square$

Propositions 4.7 and 4.8 allow us to represent the forward CDS spread as a weighted average of the forward default intensities. With further approximations, e.g. freezing the weights w_k, one can then derive swaption pricing formulas in this framework. We will not carry this out here but note

Corollary 4.9 *The initial forward CDS spread* $s_0^{i,j}$ *is approximately related to the forward default intensities as follows*

$$s_0^{i,j} \approx (1 - R) \sum_{k=i}^{j-1}$$

$$\times \left[\frac{\delta_k B^d(0, T_{k+1})}{\sum_{l=i}^{j-1} \delta_l B^d(0, T_{l+1})} \exp \left(\frac{L_k(0)(1 + \delta_k H_k(0))}{H_k(0)(1 + \delta_k L_k(0))} \sum_{l=1}^{k-1} \frac{\delta_l H_l(0)}{1 + \delta_l H_l(0)} T_l \, \sigma_k^L \cdot \sigma_l^H \right) \right] H_k(0).$$

$$(65)$$

Equation (65) is useful for the calibration of the model if rates and credit are not independent. It allows us to extract the initial forward hazard rates from spreads taking the dependence structure into account. Note that the exponential term is a convexity correction which disappears under independence.

4.2 Simplifications under Independence of Rates and Credit

We will now examine what simplifications of the general set-up we can make if the processes driving interest rates and credit spreads are independent. By this we mean the following: we assume we are in a set-up where the background filtration $\mathbb{F}$ is jointly generated by a credit driver and an interest rate driving process. For sake of concreteness, we assume that these are independent under the spot martingale measure. How exactly we will use this is best illustrated in the following

Lemma 4.10 *Suppose that interest rate and credit drivers are independent. Let* $S, T > 0$ *and suppose that* $t \in [0, S]$. *Then we have*

$$Q^S[\tau > T|\mathcal{F}_t] = P[\tau > T|\mathcal{F}_t]. \qquad (66)$$

In other words, conditional survival probabilities with respect to the background filtration do not change when changing between different risk-free forward measures.

Proof. Using Bayes' Rule for conditional expectations we have

$$Q^S[\tau > T|\mathcal{F}_t] = \frac{E^P \left[\mathbf{1}_{\{\tau > T\}} \frac{1}{\beta_S B(0,S)} \Big| \mathcal{F}_t \right]}{\frac{B(t,S)}{\beta_t B(0,S)}} = \frac{\beta_t}{B(t,S)} E^P \left[\mathbf{1}_{\{\tau > T\}} \frac{1}{\beta_S} \Big| \mathcal{F}_t \right]. \qquad (67)$$

The conditional expectation can be written as

$$E^P \left[\mathbf{1}_{\{\tau > T\}} \frac{1}{\beta_S} \Big| \mathcal{F}_t \right] = E^P \left[\frac{P[\tau > T|\mathcal{F}_S]}{\beta_S} \Big| \mathcal{F}_t \right], \qquad (68)$$

and using the independence assumption this becomes

$$E^P \left[\mathbf{1}_{\{\tau > T\}} \frac{1}{\beta_S} \Big| \mathcal{F}_t \right] = \frac{B(t,S)}{\beta_t} P[\tau > T|\mathcal{F}_t]. \qquad (69)$$

Inserting this into equation (67) proves our claim. $\qquad \square$

Under the independence assumption, we have the so-called credit triangle relationship between the discrete hazard rate H_k and the one-period default swap spread s^k, and the dynamics of L_k and H_k under the survival measure simplify.

Proposition 4.11 *If the interest rate and credit drivers are independent, then*

$$s_t^k = (1 - R)H_k(t). \tag{70}$$

Furthermore, both L_k and H_k are martingales under $\hat{Q}_{k+1}$

Proof. 1. Under the independence assumption we have $\hat{B}_k(t) = B_k(t)P[\tau > T_k|\mathcal{F}_t]$. The definition of H_k now implies that

$$1 + \delta_k H_k(t) = \frac{P[\tau > T_k|\mathcal{F}_t]}{P[\tau > T_{k+1}|\mathcal{F}_t]}.$$

The first claim now follows by comparing with equation (29) and using the previous Lemma.

2. Up to a constant, the change of measure from Q_{k+1} to $\hat{Q}_{k+1}$ is given by $D_{k+1} = \frac{\hat{B}_{k+1}}{B_{k+1}}$. The process L_k is a martingale under $\hat{Q}_{k+1}$ if and only if $L_k D_{k+1}$ is a martingale under Q_{k+1}. It actually suffices to show that $M := (1 + \delta_k L_k)D_{k+1}$ is a martingale under Q_{k+1}. We have

$$M_t = (1 + \delta_k L_k(t)) D_{k+1}(t) = \frac{B_k(t)}{B_{k+1}(t)} \frac{\hat{B}_{k+1}(t)}{\hat{B}_{k+1}(t)} = \frac{B_k(t)}{B_{k+1}(t)} Q_{k+1}[\tau > T_{k+1}|\mathcal{F}_t].$$

Under the independence assumption, M is the product of two independent Q_{k+1}-martingales, hence a Q_{k+1}-martingale itself.

3. To prove that H_k is a $\hat{Q}_{k+1}$-martingale, we show that $(1 + \delta_k H_k)D_{k+1}$ is a martingale under Q_{k+1}. Using the definitions of the various processes and equation (10), we see that

$$(1 + \delta_k H_k(t))D_{k+1}(t) = D_k(t) = \frac{\hat{B}_k(t)}{B_k(t)} = Q_k[\tau > T_k|\mathcal{F}_t].$$

From Lemma 4.10 we see that this is equal to $Q_{k+1}[\tau > T_k|\mathcal{F}_t]$, hence clearly a martingale under Q_{k+1}.   □

Note that the previous Proposition also implies that s^k is a martingale under $\hat{Q}_{k+1}$. In the following, for brevity we will use the notation $\tilde{\delta}_k := \frac{\delta_k}{1-R}$.

We will now study the change of measure between different survival measures. This will come in useful later, e.g. when pricing CMCDS. We will make the model setting specific in the sense that we assume there is an m-dimensional Brownian motion W under $\hat{Q}_{k+1}$ which is driving the model, and that for each $k \in \{1, \ldots, n-1\}$ we can write

$$ds_t^k = s_t^k \sigma_k^S(t)dW_t, \quad dL_k(t) = L_k(t)\sigma_k^L(t)dW_t.$$

The independence assumption manifests itself in the fact that $\sigma_k^S(t) \cdot \sigma_k^L(t) = 0$ for all $l, k \in \{1, \ldots, n-1\}$.

Proposition 4.12 *Let $1 \leq j \leq k \leq n-1$, then the process $\tilde{W}$ defined via*

$$d\tilde{W}_t = dW_t - \sum_{v=j+1}^{k} \left(\frac{\tilde{\delta}_v s_t^v}{1 + \tilde{\delta}_v s_t^v} \sigma_v^S(t) + \frac{\delta_v L_v(t)}{1 + \delta_v L_v(t)} \sigma_v^L(t) \right) dt \qquad (71)$$

is a Brownian motion under $\hat{Q}_{j+1}$. The dynamics of s^k under $\hat{Q}_{j+1}$ are given by

$$ds_t^k = s_t^k \sigma_k^S(t) \left(d\tilde{W}_t + \sum_{v=j+1}^{k} \frac{\tilde{\delta}_v s_t^v}{1 + \tilde{\delta}_v s_t^v} \sigma_v^S(t) dt \right). \qquad (72)$$

Proof. We compute the change of measure from $\hat{Q}_{k+1}$ to $\hat{Q}_k$. The density of $\hat{Q}_k$ with respect to $\hat{Q}_{k+1}$ is given by $\hat{Z} := \frac{\hat{B}_{k+1}(0)}{\hat{B}_k(0)} \frac{\hat{B}_k}{\hat{B}_{k+1}}$. We can ignore the multiplicative constant and concentrate on the process $Z := \frac{\hat{B}_k}{\hat{B}_{k+1}}$. Recall from equation (47) that

$$Z = \left(1 + \tilde{\delta}_k s^k\right)(1 + \delta_k L_k).$$

It follows that

$$dZ_t^M = \tilde{\delta}_k s_t^k (1 + \delta_k L_k(t)) \sigma_k^S(t) dW_t + \delta_k L_k(t) \left(1 + \tilde{\delta}_k s_t^k\right) \sigma_k^L(t) dW_t,$$

and so

$$\frac{1}{Z_t} dZ_t^M = \left(\frac{\tilde{\delta}_k s_t^k}{1 + \tilde{\delta}_k s_t^k} \sigma_k^S(t) + \frac{\delta_k L_k(t)}{1 + \delta_k L_k(t)} \sigma_k^L(t) \right) dW_t. \qquad (73)$$

With Girsanov's Theorem, equation (73) implies that the process $\bar{W}$ defined by

$$d\bar{W}_t = dW_t - \left(\frac{\tilde{\delta}_k s_t^k}{1 + \tilde{\delta}_k s_t^k} \sigma_k^S(t) + \frac{\delta_k L_k(t)}{1 + \delta_k L_k(t)} \sigma_k^L(t) \right) dt$$

is a Brownian motion under $\hat{Q}_k$. By iterating this procedure, we see that the process $\tilde{W}$ given by equation (71) is a Brownian motion under $\hat{Q}_{j+1}$. If we plug this into the dynamical equation for s^k and use the fact that $\sigma_k^S(t) \cdot \sigma_v^L(t) = 0$ for any $v \in \{j+1, \ldots, k\}$, we obtain equation (72). ☐

In Proposition 4.12 we go from a later to an earlier survival measure. In the same way, we can move forward in time to go from any particular survival measure to a later one. In particular, we can compute the dynamics of any one-period spread under the terminal survival measure $\hat{Q}_n$.

Proposition 4.13 *Let $1 \leq k \leq n - 1$, then there is a Brownian motion $\tilde{W}$ under $\hat{Q}_n$, such that the dynamics of s^k are given by*

$$ds_t^k = s_t^k \sigma_k^S(t) \left(d\tilde{W}_t - \sum_{v=k+1}^{m-1} \frac{\tilde{\delta} s_t^v}{1 + \tilde{\delta}_v s_t^v} \sigma_v^S(t) dt \right). \tag{74}$$

The proof of Proposition 4.13 is completely analogous to that of Proposition 4.12, so we omit it here.

5 DETAILED CONSTRUCTION OF A CDS MARKET MODEL

In the previous sections, we postulated the existence of an arbitrage-free CDS market model and analysed the relationships between its different components. Here we describe in detail the construction of such a model. Admittedly, this is a somewhat pedantic mathematical exercise, but it should be of some comfort to the theoretically inclined reader that all the dynamic assumptions can in fact be made fully consistent. Without such a construction, we would not be able to answer the simple practical question as to how to simulate the time of default in a CDS market model. Because we are limiting ourselves to the independence case, our fundamental modelling inputs are one-period spread volatility processes σ^j for $j \in \{1, \ldots, m - 1\}$, as well as the initial CDS and interest rate curves. With these inputs we want to construct forward CDS spread processes s^j and in particular a random time τ, such that we obtain a consistent CDS market model where we interpret τ as the default time of our credit.

Once again the fundamental timeline is $0 = T_0 < T_1 < \ldots < T_m$. We will assume that interest rates are deterministic for simplicity, though it is straightforward to apply this construction in the case where interest rates and credit are independent. On a filtered probability space $(\Omega, \mathcal{G}, \mathbb{F}, Q)$ with an $\mathbb{F}$-adapted d-dimensional Brownian motion W, we assume that we are also given $\mathbb{F}$-predictable, suitably integrable, $\mathbb{R}^d$-valued volatility processes $\sigma^0, \ldots, \sigma^{m-1}$. In particular, we assume that $\sigma_t^j = 0$ for $t > T_j$. To be able to construct the default time, we also assume the existence of a uniform random variable U which is independent of $\mathcal{F}_\infty$.

The measure Q will be the terminal survival contingent forward measure once our construction is finished. We define processes $s^0, \ldots, s^{m-1}$ by backward induction, i.e. we first define s^{m-1} and then work our way backwards to s^0, which is of course just a constant number. The SDE defining s^k is exactly equation (74), the initial condition can be read off the unconditional survival probabilities. At the moment, we cannot interpret s^k as a forward CDS spread, but of course this will turn out to be the case in the end. The fact that we force $\sigma_t^k = 0$ for $t > T_k$ ensures that the process s^k is stopped at T_k.

The clue to the correct definition of the default time is given by equation (29). This leads us to define the default time τ such that for each $i \in \{1, \ldots, m\}$ we have

$$\tau > T_i :\Longleftrightarrow U \leq \prod_{j=1}^{i} \frac{1}{1 + \tilde{\delta}_{j-1} s_{T_{j-1}}^{j-1}}. \tag{75}$$

However, to use this properly we must first identify the spot martingale measure, i.e. the martingale measure corresponding to the risk-free savings account β as numeraire. For each $k \in \{1, \ldots, m\}$, we define

$$N_t^k := \prod_{j=k}^{m}(1 + \tilde{\delta}_{j-1} s_t^{j-1}). \tag{76}$$

Lemma 5.1 *For each $k \in \{1, \ldots, m\}$ we have*

$$dN_t^k = \sum_{j=k}^{m} \tilde{\delta}_{j-1} s_t^{j-1} \left[\prod_{\substack{l=k \\ l \neq j}}^{m}(1 + \tilde{\delta}_{l-1} s_t^{l-1}) \right] \sigma_t^{j-1} dW_t. \tag{77}$$

In particular N^k is a martingale under Q.

Proof. The formula is clearly true for N^m. Suppose now that it is true for N^{k+1}. Then $N_t^k = (1 + \tilde{\delta}_{k-1} s_t^{k-1}) N_t^{k+1}$, hence

$$(1 + \tilde{\delta}_{k-1} s_t^{k-1}) dN_t^{k+1} = \sum_{j=k+1}^{m} \tilde{\delta}_{j-1} s_t^{j-1} \left[\prod_{\substack{l=k \\ l \neq j}}^{m}(1 + \tilde{\delta}_{l-1} s_t^{l-1}) \right] \sigma_t^{j-1} dW_t. \tag{78}$$

Furthermore

$$\tilde{\delta}_{k-1} dN_t^{k+1} ds_t^{k-1} = \tilde{\delta}_{k-1} s_t^{k-1} \sum_{j=k+1}^{m} \tilde{\delta}_{j-1} s_t^{j-1} \left[\prod_{\substack{l=k+1 \\ l \neq j}}^{m}(1 + \tilde{\delta}_{l-1} s_t^{l-1}) \right] \sigma_t^{j-1} \cdot \sigma_t^{k-1} dt. \tag{79}$$

We write $\tilde{\delta}_{k-1} ds_t^{k-1} = dM_t - dA_t$ with $dM_t = \tilde{\delta}_{k-1} s_t^{k-1} \sigma_t^{k-1} dW_t$ and

$$dA_t = \tilde{\delta}_{k-1} s_t^{k-1} \sum_{j=k+1}^{m} \frac{\tilde{\delta}_{j-1} s_t^{j-1} \sigma_t^{k-1} \cdot \sigma_t^{j-1}}{1 + \tilde{\delta}_{j-1} s_t^{j-1}} dt. \tag{80}$$

It follows that

$$N_t^{k+1} dM_t = \tilde{\delta}_{k-1} s_t^{k-1} \left[\prod_{\substack{l=k \\ l \neq k}}^{m}(1 + \tilde{\delta}_{l-1} s_t^{l-1}) \right] \sigma_t^{k-1} dW_t. \tag{81}$$

In other words

$$(1 + \tilde{\delta}_{k-1} d s_t^{k-1}) d N_t^{k+1} + N_t^{k+1} d M_t = \sum_{j=k}^{m} \tilde{\delta}_{j-1} s_t^{j-1} \left[\prod_{\substack{l=k \\ l \neq j}}^{m} (1 + \tilde{\delta}_{l-1} s_t^{l-1}) \right] \sigma_t^{j-1} d W_t.$$

(82)

Now compute

$$N_t^{k+1} d A_t = \tilde{\delta}_{k-1} s_t^{k-1} \sum_{j=k+1}^{m} \tilde{\delta}_{j-1} s_t^{j-1} \left[\prod_{\substack{l=k+1 \\ l \neq j}}^{m} (1 + \tilde{\delta}_{l-1} s_t^{l-1}) \right] \sigma_t^{k-1} \cdot \sigma_t^{j-1} dt.$$

(83)

From equation (83) we see that $N_t^{k+1} d A_t$ exactly offsets the covariation term in equation (79). Hence

$$d N_t^k = (1 + \tilde{\delta}_{k-1} s_t^{k-1}) d N_t^{k+1} + N_t^{k+1} d M_t.$$

(84)

In other words, equation (82) proves the formula.   □

We define the process Z via $Z_t := \frac{N_t^1}{N_0^1}$. According to the previous Lemma, this is a Q-martingale, we can define the measure P via $P := Z_{T_m} Q$. As will become clear very soon, if we postulate P as a spot martingale measure, then Q is indeed a terminal survival measure. We will now prove equation (29) in our set-up. For each $i \in \{1, \dots, m\}$ we define the process M^i via

$$M_t^i := \prod_{l=1}^{i} \frac{1}{1 + \tilde{\delta}_{l-1} s_t^{l-1}} = \frac{N_t^{i+1}}{N_t^1}.$$

(85)

Lemma 5.2 *Each process M^i is a P-martingale.*

Proof. 5.3 Let $s < t$ and $A \in \mathcal{F}_s$:

$$\int_A M_t^i dP = \int_A M_t^i Z_t dQ = \int_A \frac{N_t^{i+1}}{N_t^1} \frac{N_t^1}{N_0^1} dQ = \frac{1}{N_0^1} \int_A N_t^{i+1} dQ = \frac{1}{N_0^1} \int_A N_s^{i+1} dQ.$$

(86)

On the other hand, we have

$$\int_A M_s^i dP = \int_A \frac{N_s^{i+1}}{N_s^1} Z_s dQ = \int_A \frac{N_s^{i+1}}{N_0^1} dQ.$$

(87)

□

We can now identify the process M^i. Because each process s^{l-1} is stopped after T_{l-1}, we can rewrite equation (75) as

$$\tau > T_i \iff U \le \prod_{j=1}^{i} \frac{1}{1 + \tilde{\delta}_{j-1} s_{T_i}^{j-1}}. \tag{88}$$

Since U is independent of $\mathcal{F}_\infty$, it follows that

$$P[\tau > T_i | \mathcal{F}_{T_i}] = \prod_{l=1}^{i} \frac{1}{1 + \tilde{\delta}_{l-1} s_{T_i}^{l-1}} = M_{T_i}^i. \tag{89}$$

Because M^i is a P-martingale, we have for any $t \le T_i$:

$$P[\tau > T_i | \mathcal{F}_t] = M_t^i = \prod_{l=1}^{i} \frac{1}{1 + \tilde{\delta}_{l-1} s_t^{l-1}}. \tag{90}$$

From equation (90) we immediately see that equation (29) is also true. Now we define the processes $\hat{A}^i$ via

$$\hat{A}_t^i := \tilde{\delta}_{i-1} \frac{\beta_t}{\beta_{T_i}} \frac{N_t^{i+1}}{N_t^1}. \tag{91}$$

Postulating that P is the spot martingale measure, it is easy to see that $\hat{A}^i$ is the price process of a survival contingent one-period annuity, s^{i-1} is indeed the corresponding forward CDS spread and the measure Q is indeed a martingale measure for the numeraire $\hat{A}^m$.

Equation (88) tells us how to simulate the default time: we simulate the processes s^{i-1} and then check when the default occurs using a draw from the random variable U. Since this is independent of $\mathcal{F}_\infty$, it is also true that

$$Q[\tau > T_i | \mathcal{F}_{T_i}] = M_{T_i}^i = \prod_{l=1}^{i} \frac{1}{1 + \tilde{\delta}_{l-1} s_{T_i}^{l-1}}. \tag{92}$$

However, it is important to be aware that, because M^i is not a Q-martingale, for $t \le T_i$ we have

$$Q[\tau > T_i | \mathcal{F}_t] = E^Q[M_{T_i}^i | \mathcal{F}_t] \ne \prod_{l=1}^{i} \frac{1}{1 + \tilde{\delta}_{l-1} s_t^{l-1}}. \tag{93}$$

6 CONSTRUCTION OF A MARKET MODEL VIA PROBABILITY RATIOS

The set-up described in the previous section is quite satisfactory from a theoretical perspective. Starting from the volatility structure for CDS spreads we obtain a completely consistent model. However, the numerical implementation of the model can run into difficulties. CDS spread volatilities can be very high, causing difficulties when simulating the SDEs for the different spreads via a discretization scheme.

In this section, we describe an alternative specification of a CDS market model due to Samiri (2007). Based on Zhao and Glasserman (2000), the idea is to focus the modelling effort on quantities that are known to be martingales; this eliminates the need to discretize SDEs.

As in the previous section, we assume that interest rates are deterministic. Also, we take as given the initial survival probabilities of the credit under the spot martingale measure; we denote the probability of the credit surviving to time $t \geq 0$ by $S(t)$.

6.1 Preliminaries

Once again, we fix a timeline $0 = T_0 < T_1 < \ldots < T_m$. As in section 5, we work on a filtered probability space $(\Omega, \mathcal{G}, \mathbb{F}, Q)$, where Q will be the terminal survival contingent measure. We assume that we are given strictly positive $(Q, \mathbb{F})$-martingales M^i, $i \in \{1, \ldots, m-1\}$, with $M_0^i = 1$, and a uniform random variable U which is independent of $\mathcal{F}_\infty$. We want to construct the model by describing the dynamics of certain martingales $X^i = (X_t^i)_{t \in [0, T_m]}$, $i \in \{0, 1, \ldots, m-1\}$ under Q. As a part of this, we will also need to construct the spot martingale measure P, as well as the default time τ. We want to be able to interpret the processes X^i as

$$X_t^i = \frac{P[\tau > T_i | \mathcal{F}_t] - P[\tau > T_{i+1} | \mathcal{F}_t]}{P[\tau > T_m | \mathcal{F}_t]}. \tag{94}$$

Note that this should be a positive martingale under Q, because

$$X_t^i = \frac{\beta_{T_i} \hat{B}(t, T_i) - \beta_{T_{i+1}} \hat{B}(t, T_{i+1})}{\beta_{T_m} \hat{B}(t, T_m)}. \tag{95}$$

In particular

$$X_0^i = \frac{S(T_i) - S(T_{i+1})}{S(T_m)}. \tag{96}$$

We need to use some care though in choosing the dynamics of the X^i, because we want to ensure that

$$\forall i \in \{1, \ldots, m\} \forall t \geq T_{i-1} : P[\tau > T_i | \mathcal{F}_t] = P[\tau > T_i | \mathcal{F}_{T_{i-1}}]. \tag{97}$$

For each $i \in \{0, 1, \ldots, m\}$, the process D^i defined by

$$D^i_t := \frac{P[\tau > T_i | \mathcal{F}_t]}{P[\tau > T_m | \mathcal{F}_t]} = \frac{\beta_{T_i} \hat{B}(t, T_i)}{\beta_{T_m} \hat{B}(t, T_m)} \tag{98}$$

is a Q-martingale. Note that $D^m_t = 1$. Clearly, for $i \in \{0, 1, \ldots, m-1\}$ we have $X^i_t = D^i_t - D^{i+1}_t$. It is easy to show that for each $i \in \{0, 1, \ldots, m\}$ we have

$$D^i_t = 1 + \sum_{k=i}^{m-1} X^k_t. \tag{99}$$

Additionally, the following result will be useful in guiding our model construction:

Lemma 6.1 Let $j \in \{1, \ldots, m\}$ and $i \in \{0, 1, \ldots, j\}$, then

$$\forall t \in [T_{j-1}, T_j] : \quad D^i_t = D^i_{T_{j-1}} \frac{D^j_t}{D^j_{T_{j-1}}}. \tag{100}$$

Proof. Since $i < j$, we have $P[\tau > T_i | \mathcal{F}_t] = P[\tau > T_i | \mathcal{F}_{T_{j-1}}]$ almost surely for any $t \in [T_{j-1}, T_j]$. It follows that

$$D^i_t = \frac{P[\tau > T_i | \mathcal{F}_t]}{P[\tau > T_m | \mathcal{F}_t]} = \frac{P[\tau > T_i | \mathcal{F}_{T_{j-1}}]}{P[\tau > T_m | \mathcal{F}_{T_{j-1}}]} \frac{P[\tau > T_m | \mathcal{F}_{T_{j-1}}]}{P[\tau > T_m | \mathcal{F}_t]} = D^i_{T_{j-1}} \frac{P[\tau > T_m | \mathcal{F}_{T_{j-1}}]}{P[\tau > T_m | \mathcal{F}_t]}.$$

Also $P[\tau > T_j | \mathcal{F}_t] = P[\tau > T_j | \mathcal{F}_{T_{j-1}}]$, so

$$D^i_t = D^i_{T_{j-1}} \frac{P[\tau > T_m | \mathcal{F}_{T_{j-1}}]}{P[\tau > T_j | \mathcal{F}_{T_{j-1}}]} \frac{P[\tau > T_j | \mathcal{F}_{T_{j-1}}]}{P[\tau > T_m | \mathcal{F}_t]} = \frac{D^i_{T_{j-1}}}{D^j_{T_{j-1}}} \frac{P[\tau > T_j | \mathcal{F}_t]}{P[\tau > T_m | \mathcal{F}_t]} = D^i_{T_{j-1}} \frac{D^j_t}{D^j_{T_{j-1}}}.$$

$\square$

6.2 Probability ratio construction

We now construct the processes X^i for $i \in \{0, 1, \ldots, m-1\}$ on the interval $[0, T_m]$, we proceed by induction over the different time intervals $[T_{j-1}, T_j]$. Fix $j \in \{1, \ldots, m\}$, and suppose we have already constructed $X^0, \ldots, X^{m-1}$ on the interval $[0, T_{j-1}]$. In the case of $j = 1$, this follows from equation (96) because the initial values of the processes X^i are fixed by the initial survival probabilities. For $i \in \{j, \ldots, m-1\}$, we extend X^i via $X^i_t := X^i_0 M^i_t$. For $i < j$, we use Lemma 6.1 to see that the only possible definition for X_t^i is

$$X_t^i = D_t^i - D_t^{i+1} = \frac{D_t^j}{D_{T_{j-1}}^j}\left(D_{T_{j-1}}^i - D_{T_{j-1}}^{i+1}\right). \tag{101}$$

Using equation (99), we see that the correct definition of X_t^i for $t \in [T_{j-1}, T_j]$ is

$$X_t^i = \frac{1 + \sum_{k=j}^{m-1} X_t^k}{1 + \sum_{k=j}^{m-1} X_{T_{j-1}}^k} X_{T_{j-1}}^i. \tag{102}$$

To reiterate, the process X^0 is constant. For each $i \in \{1, \ldots, m-1\}$, the process X^i is defined such that

$$\forall t \in [0, T_i] : X_t^i = X_0^i M_t^i. \tag{103}$$

For $t \in [T_i, T_m]$, the dynamics of X^i are determined by pasting conditions such as those given in equation (102).

Proposition 6.2 *For each $i \in \{0, 1, \ldots, m-1\}$, the process X^i is a $(Q, \mathbb{F})$-martingale on $[0, T_m]$.*

Proof. We proceed by backwards induction. Clearly X^{m-1} is a martingale because

$$\forall t \in [0, T_{m-1}] : X_t^{m-1} = X_0^{m-1} M_t^{m-1}.$$

and $X_t^{m-1} = X_{T_{m-1}}^{m-1}$ for $t \in [T_{m-1}, T_m]$. Now suppose $i \in \{0, 1, \ldots, m-2\}$ and $X^{i+1}, \ldots, X^{m-1}$ are already known to be martingales. For $t \in [0, T_i]$, we have $X_t^i = X_0^i M_t^i$, hence X^i is a martingale on $[0, T_i]$. Let $T_i \leq s \leq t$. Without loss of generality we can assume there is a $j \in \{i+1, \ldots, m\}$ such that $T_{j-1} \leq s \leq t \leq T_j$. According to equation (102) we have

$$E[X_t^i|\mathcal{F}_s] = \frac{X_{T_{j-1}}^i}{1 + \sum_{k=j}^{m-1} X_{T_{j-1}}^k}\left(1 + \sum_{k=j}^{m-1} E[X_t^k|\mathcal{F}_s]\right). \tag{104}$$

For $k \in \{j, \ldots, m-1\}$ we know by induction that $E[X_t^k|\mathcal{F}_s] = X_s^k$. Inserting this into equation (104) and comparing with equation (102) shows that $E[X_t^i|\mathcal{F}_s] = X_s^i$. $\square$

We now turn to the question of what the conditional survival probabilities under the spot martingale measure must look like. For $i \in \{0, 1, \ldots, m\}$, we let $\tilde{P}^i$ denote our candidate process for the conditional survival probability beyond T_i under the spot martingale measure. From equations (98) and (99), we see that $\tilde{P}_t^i$ must be given by

$$\tilde{P}_t^i = \frac{1 + \sum_{k=i}^{m-1} X_t^k}{1 + \sum_{k=0}^{m-1} X_t^k} \tag{105}$$

Because the processes X^k are positive, it is clear that $\tilde{P}_t^i$ takes values in $[0, 1]$. Next, we verify that these processes indeed fulfil the condition of equation (97).

Proposition 6.3 *For each $i \in \{1, \ldots, m\}$ we have:*

$$\forall t \in [T_{i-1}, T_m] : \tilde{P}_t^i = \tilde{P}_{T_{i-1}}^i \tag{106}$$

Proof. Let $t \in [T_{i-1}, T_m]$, then there exists $j \in \{i, \ldots, m\}$ such that $T_{j-1} < t \le T_j$. We show that $\tilde{P}_t^i = \tilde{P}_{T_{j-1}}^i$, the general statement then easily follows by backward induction. For any $l \in \{0, 1, \ldots, j-1\}$, equation (102) tells us that

$$\sum_{\lambda=l}^{j-1} X_t^\lambda = \left(1 + \sum_{v=j}^{m-1} X_t^v\right) \sum_{\lambda=l}^{j-1} \frac{X_{T_{j-1}}^\lambda}{1 + \sum_{\mu=j}^{m-1} X_{T_{j-1}}^\mu}. \tag{107}$$

Consequently, for any $l \in \{0, 1, \ldots, j\}$, we have

$$1 + \sum_{\lambda=l}^{m-1} X_t^\lambda = \left(1 + \sum_{v=j}^{m-1} X_t^v\right)\left(1 + \sum_{\lambda=l}^{j-1} \frac{X_{T_{j-1}}^\lambda}{1 + \sum_{\mu=j}^{m-1} X_{T_{j-1}}^\mu}\right). \tag{108}$$

Comparing this with the numerator and denominator of equation (105), we immediately see that the dependence on t cancels out, hence $\tilde{P}_t^i = \tilde{P}_{T_{j-1}}^i$. $\square$

6.3 Spot martingale measure and default time

We now proceed to construct the spot martingale measure and the default time. Referring back to equations (90) and (76), we see that the density process of P with respect to Q must be given by

$$Z_t = \frac{\tilde{P}_0^m}{\tilde{P}_t^m} = \frac{1 + \sum_{k=0}^{m-1} X_t^k}{1 + \sum_{k=0}^{m-1} X_0^k}. \tag{109}$$

Because of Proposition 6.2, it is immediately clear that Z is a $(Q, \mathbb{F})$-martingale with $Z_0 = 1$. We define the probability measure P via $P := Z_{T_{m-1}} Q$.

Lemma 6.4 *For each $i \in \{0, 1, \ldots, m\}$, the process $\tilde{P}^i$ is a $(P, \mathbb{F})$-martingale.*

Proof. Let $s \le t \le T_m$. Following Bayes' Rule for conditional expectations, we find that

$$E^P\left[\tilde{P}_t^i \middle| \mathcal{F}_s\right] = \frac{E^Q\left[\tilde{P}_t^i Z_t \middle| \mathcal{F}_s\right]}{Z_s}. \tag{110}$$

Using the previous definitions, it follows that

$$\frac{E^Q\left[\tilde{P}_t^i Z_t \middle| \mathcal{F}_s\right]}{Z_s} = \frac{\tilde{P}_0^m\left(1 + \sum_{k=i}^{m-1} X_s^k\right)}{\tilde{P}_0^m\left(1 + \sum_{k=0}^{m-1} X_s^k\right)} = \tilde{P}_s^i.$$

$\square$

It is easy to see that U is still uniform and independent of $\mathcal{F}_\infty$ under Q. We now define the default time τ. We want to ensure that for each $i \in \{1, \ldots, m\}$ we have

$$\tau > T_i :\Leftrightarrow U \le \tilde{P}^i_{T_{i-1}}. \tag{111}$$

To this end, set

$$i_* := \inf\left\{i \in \{1, \ldots, m\} \mid U > \tilde{P}^i_{T_{i-1}}\right\} \tag{112}$$

with $\inf \emptyset = +\infty$. We set $T_\infty := +\infty$, and can finally define $\tau := T_{i_*}$. We see that equation (111) is indeed true with this definition.

Proposition 6.5 *For every $i \in \{1, \ldots, m\}$ and $t \in [0, T_m]$, we have*

$$P[\tau > T_i | \mathcal{F}_t] = \tilde{P}^i_t. \tag{113}$$

Proof. Equation (111) implies that

$$P[\tau > T_i | \mathcal{F}_t] = \tilde{P}^i_{T_{i-1}}.$$

for $t \ge T_{i-1}$. The general statement follows from Lemma 6.4, because $\tilde{P}^i$ is a $(P, \mathbb{F})$-martingale.   □

6.4 Default swaption pricing in the probability ratios model

We show how to price a European knock-out default swaption in the probability ratios model. We consider a payer swaption with strike spread k which matures at T_i and gives the holder the right to buy protection in a default swap from time T_i to T_j. The payoff of the payer swaption at maturity is

$$PS_{T_i} = \left[\Pi^{i,j}_{T_i} - k A^{i,j}_{T_i}\right]^+. \tag{114}$$

Note that the payoff is zero if $\tau \le T_i$. Given the formulation of the probability ratios model, it is convenient to price this payoff in the terminal survival contingent measure. Using Proposition 2.9, we see that

$$PS_t = B^d(t, T_m) E^Q\left[\frac{1}{\hat{B}(T_i, T_m)}\left[\hat{\Pi}^{i,j}_{T_i} - k\hat{A}^{i,j}_{T_i}\right]^+ \middle| \mathcal{F}_t\right]$$

$$= B^d(t, T_m) E^Q\left[\left[\frac{\hat{\Pi}^{i,j}_{T_i}}{\hat{B}(T_i, T_m)} - k\frac{\hat{A}^{i,j}_{T_i}}{\hat{B}(T_i, T_m)}\right]^+ \middle| \mathcal{F}_t\right]. \tag{115}$$

We need to express the two fractions occurring on the right-hand side of equation (115) using the probability ratio processes X^i. Recall that

$$\hat{\Pi}^{i,j}_{T_i} = (1 - R) \sum_{l=i+1}^{j} B(T_i, T_l) \left(P[\tau > T_{l-1} | \mathcal{F}_{T_i}] - P[\tau > T_l | \mathcal{F}_{T_i}]\right), \tag{116}$$

so that

$$\frac{\hat{\Pi}_{T_i}^{i,j}}{\hat{B}(T_i, T_m)} = (1 - R) \sum_{l=i}^{j-1} \frac{B(T_i, T_{l+1})}{B(T_i, T_m)} X_{T_i}^l. \tag{117}$$

Similarly:

$$\hat{A}_{T_i}^{i,j} = \sum_{l=i+1}^{j} a_l B(T_i, T_l) P[\tau > T_l | \mathcal{F}_{T_i}]. \tag{118}$$

With the definition from equation (98), we can write

$$\frac{\hat{A}_{T_i}^{i,j}}{\hat{B}(T_i, T_m)} = \sum_{l=i+1}^{j} a_l \frac{B(T_i, T_l)}{B(T_i, T_m)} D_{T_i}^l. \tag{119}$$

We also recall equation (99). Inserting this into the previous equation, we obtain

$$\frac{\hat{A}_{T_i}^{i,j}}{\hat{B}(T_i, T_m)} = \sum_{v=i+1}^{j} a_v \frac{B(T_i, T_v)}{B(T_i, T_m)} + \sum_{v=i+1}^{j} a_v \frac{B(T_i, T_v)}{B(T_i, T_m)} \sum_{\mu=k}^{m-1} X_{T_i}^\mu. \tag{120}$$

We want to organize the terms in equations (117) and (120) better. For $l \in \{i, \ldots, m-1\}$ we define the coefficient $C_l^{i,j}(k)$ as follows:

$$C_l^{i,j}(k) = \begin{cases} (1 - R)\frac{B(T_i, T_{i+1})}{B(T_i, T_m)}, & l = i \\ (1 - R)\frac{B(T_i, T_{i+1})}{B(T_i, T_m)} - k \sum_{v=i+1}^{l} a_v \frac{B(T_i, T_v)}{B(T_i, T_m)}, & l = i + 1, \ldots, j - 1 \\ -k \sum_{v=i+1}^{j} a_v \frac{B(T_i, T_v)}{B(T_i, T_m)}, & l = j, \ldots, m - 1 \end{cases} \tag{121}$$

Also, we define $D = \sum_{l=i+1}^{j} a_l \frac{B(T_i, T_l)}{B(T_i, T_m)}$. Then, the payer swaption price is given by

$$PS_t = B^d(t, T_m) E^Q \left[\left[\sum_{l=i}^{m-1} C_l^{i,j}(k) X_{T_i}^l - k D \right]^+ \middle| \mathcal{F}_t \right]. \tag{122}$$

To get a more explicit valuation formula than equation (122), we need to specify the dynamics of the martingales M^i which drive the processes X^i via $X_t^i = X_0^i M_t^i$. For example, the simplest model assumes that there is a Brownian motion W such that $M^i = \mathcal{E}(\sigma W)$. With $C^{i,j}(k) = \sum_{l=i}^{m-1} X_0^l C_l^{i,j}(k)$, we have

$$PS_t = B^d(t, T_m) E^Q \left[\left[C^{i,j}(k)\mathcal{E}(\sigma W)_{T_i} - k D \right]^+ \middle| \mathcal{F}_t \right]. \tag{123}$$

Since $C^{i,j}(k)$ and D are deterministic, it is now easy to derive a Black-Scholes type formula for the payer swaption price via the usual calculations.

7 PRICING OF CONSTANT MATURITY CDS

Constant maturity credit default swaps (CMCDS) are a very interesting application of the market model technology, though it should be said that at the time of this writing this is largely of theoretical interest, and there is no liquid market as such for these products. In a CMCDS, the protection seller insures the protection buyer against the loss on default of a reference credit in the same way as in a vanilla CDS. However, in return, the protection seller does not receive a fixed spread, but rather a certain multiple of the reference credit's CDS spread for a fixed tenor. In this, the CMCDS contract is somewhat analogous to a constant maturity interest rate swap.

The CMCDS contract has several features which make it interesting. While the protection seller is of course still assuming the default risk of the reference credit, he is somewhat immunized against spread risk: if the quality of the reference credit deteriorates, then of course the default protection that one has sold increases in value, causing negative P&L. However, this is offset by the fact that the premium leg of the swap also increases in value, as the CDS spread of the credit has widened and the protection seller can expect to receive larger coupon payments.

The valuation of the CMCDS contract is a function of the steepness of the credit curve. Recall from Proposition 3.2 that the forward CDS spread is the weighted average of one-period spreads. If the credit curve is upward sloping, then it can be advantageous to sell protection via a CMCDS rather than in plain vanilla form. Finally, a pair trade of a CMCDS versus a vanilla CDS isolates spread risk without any actual default contingent cash flows, allowing an investor to implement directional views on the spread of a credit in a controlled manner.

In this section, we present an approximate pricing formula for CMCDS contracts as an application of the market model technology, we closely follow Brigo (2006). We use the same timeline notation as in section 3. We fix i_1 and i_2, where $1 \leq i_1 \leq i_2 < n$. We focus on the premium leg of a contract running from T_{i_1} to T_{i_2+1}. The contract is linked to the c-period CDS spread, where $i_2 + c \leq n$. For each $j \in \{i_1, \ldots, i_2\}$ the coupon for the period from T_j to T_{j+1} is as follows: at time T_j we observe the c-period CDS spread $s_{T_j}^{j,j+c}$. A coupon linked to this spread is paid at time T_{j+1} if the credit survives until then. Following Proposition 2.9, we see that the value of this premium leg at time zero is given by

$$V_0 = \sum_{\nu=i_1}^{i_2} \delta_\nu B^d(0, T_{\nu+1}) E^{\hat{Q}_{\nu+1}} \left[s_{T_\nu}^{\nu,\nu+c} \right]. \tag{124}$$

Recall from Proposition 3.2 that $s_t^{\nu,\nu+c}$ can be written as a weighted sum of single-period CDS spreads. As our first approximation, we freeze these weights at their values for time zero, so that

$$s_t^{\nu,\nu+c} = \sum_{l=\nu}^{\nu+c-1} w_{\nu,l}(0) s_t^l$$

with

$$w_{v,l}(0) = \frac{\delta_l B^d(0, T_{l+1})}{\sum_{k=v}^{v+c-1} \delta_k B^d(0, T_{k+1})}.$$

This implies that

$$V_0 = \sum_{v=i_1}^{i_2} \delta_v B^d(0, T_{v+1}) \sum_{l=v}^{v+c-1} w_{v,l}(0) E^{\hat{Q}_{v+1}} \left[s_{T_v}^l \right]. \tag{125}$$

We will assume that rates and credit are independent. This streamlines the analysis. We also feel that this is somewhat justified, as CMCDS are primarily sensitive to the shape of the credit curve and the volatility of CDS spreads. From a technical point of view, we can make use of the results of section 4.2. We use the volatility specification from there and define $\sigma_l := \| \sigma_l^S \|$. The instantaneous correlation between the different one-period CDS spreads is denoted by $\sigma_l^S \cdot \sigma_\mu^S =: \sigma_l \sigma_\mu \rho_{l,\mu}$. We also assume that the volatilities are constant in time.

Proposition 7.1 *Let* $l \in \{v, \ldots, v+c-1\}$. *Under the drift freezing approximation we have*

$$E^{\hat{Q}_{v+1}} \left[s_{T_v}^l \right] = s_0^l \exp \left(\sigma_l T_v \sum_{\mu=v+1}^{l} \frac{\tilde{\delta}_\mu s_0^\mu}{1 + \tilde{\delta}_\mu s_0^\mu} \sigma_\mu \rho_{l,\mu} \right). \tag{126}$$

Proof. Recall from equation (72) that

$$ds_t^k = s_t^k \sigma_k^S(t) \left(d\tilde{W}_t + \sum_{v=j+1}^{k} \frac{\tilde{\delta}_v s_t^v}{1 + \tilde{\delta}_v s_t^v} \sigma_v^S(t) dt \right).$$

If we freeze the drift at its initial value, we can easily solve this SDE to obtain

$$s_{T_v}^l = s_0^l \mathcal{E} \left(\sigma_l^S \cdot W \right)_{T_v} \exp \left(T_v \sum_{\mu=v+1}^{l} \frac{\tilde{\delta}_\mu s_0^\mu}{1 + \tilde{\delta}_\mu s_0^\mu} \sigma_l^S \cdot \sigma_\mu^S \right). \tag{127}$$

Taking the expectation immediately gives equation (126). ☐

Using this result in equation (125) gives us

Corollary 7.2 *With the various weight and drift freezing approximations, the value of the premium leg of a CMCDS contract is given by*

$$V_0 = \sum_{v=i_1}^{i_2} \delta_v B^d(0, T_{v+1}) \sum_{l=v}^{v+c-1} w_{v,l}(0) s_0^l \exp \left(\sigma_l T_v \sum_{\mu=v+1}^{l} \frac{\tilde{\delta}_\mu s_0^\mu}{1 + \tilde{\delta}_\mu s_0^\mu} \sigma_\mu \rho_{l,\mu} \right). \tag{128}$$

The protection leg of the CMCDS is the same as that of a vanilla default swap, so that it is clear what the value of the CMCDS contract is. In general, it will not have zero value at inception, so usually only a certain participation rate κ of the c-period CDS spread is paid.

Corollary 7.3 *With a participation rate of κ, buying protection in CMCDS format has the approximate value*

$$V_0^{CMCDS} = \sum_{v=i_1}^{i_2} \delta_v B^d(0, T_{v+1}) \left[s_0^v - \kappa \sum_{l=v}^{v+c-1} w_{v,l}(0) s_0^l \exp\left(\sigma_l T_v \sum_{\mu=v+1}^{l} \frac{\tilde{\delta}_\mu s_0^\mu}{1 + \tilde{\delta}_\mu s_0^\mu} \sigma_\mu \rho_{l,\mu} \right) \right].$$

$$(129)$$

The participation rate is then set in such a way that the contract has zero value at inception. We see from equation (129) that value of the CMCDS is adjusted via a convexity correction, similar to the one for CMS using a Libor market model in the interest rate world. The magnitude of this correction depends on the volatilities and correlations of one-period CDS spreads. For more details and comparative statics, see Brigo (2006).

APPENDICES

A   Change of numeraire in a nutshell

In this appendix, we briefly review the calculus for changing numeraire. We are given a filtered probability space $(\Omega, \mathcal{F}, \mathbb{F}, P)$, and we denote the terminal horizon of interest by T. We also assume that $\mathcal{F}_0$ is trivial. Suppose that P is a martingale measure for the numeraire N, i.e. $N = (N_t)_{t \in [0,T]}$ is a strictly positive, $\mathbb{F}$-adapted process and for every asset price process A the process $\frac{A}{N}$ is a P-martingale. Now suppose that U is a another numeraire, i.e. a strictly positive process such that $\frac{U}{N}$ is a P-martingale. We define the density process $Z = (Z_t)_{t \in [0,T]}$ via

$$Z_t = \frac{N_0 \, U_t}{U_0 \, N_t}.$$

$$(130)$$

We immediately see that $Z_t = E^P[Z_T | \mathcal{F}_t]$. The process Z is a P-martingale with $E[Z_T] = E[Z_0] = 1$, hence we can define a probability measure Q via $Q = Z_T \, P$. We then have

Lemma A.1 *The measure Q is a martingale measure for the numeraire U.*

Proof. Let A be an asset price process. We must show that $\frac{A}{U}$ is a Q-martingale. Because A is an asset price process, $\frac{A}{N}$ is a P-martingale. First we show that $\frac{A_t}{U_t}$ is Q-integrable. We have

$$E^Q \left[\frac{|A_t|}{U_t} \right] = E^P \left[\frac{|A_t|}{U_t} Z_t \right] = \frac{N_0}{U_0} E^P \left[\frac{|A_t|}{N_t} \right] < +\infty$$

$$(131)$$

Now we show that $\frac{A}{U}$ is a Q-martingale. For $s < t$, using Bayes' Rule for conditional expectations and plugging in the definitions gives

$$E^Q \left[\frac{A_t}{U_t} \middle| \mathcal{F}_s \right] = E^P \left[\frac{A_t Z_t}{U_t} \middle| \mathcal{F}_s \right] = \frac{A_s}{U_s}. \tag{132}$$

$\square$

Suppose now that W is a d-dimensional Brownian motion under P. By Girsanov's theorem, the process $\tilde{W}$ given by

$$d\tilde{W}_t^j = dW_t^j - \frac{1}{Z_t} dZ_t dW_t^j \tag{133}$$

is a Brownian motion under Q. So, when changing measure, we need to compute $\frac{1}{Z_t} dZ_t^M$, and we are interested in doing this as efficiently as possible. From equation (130), we see that

$$\frac{1}{Z_t} dZ_t^M = \frac{N_t}{U_t} d\left(\frac{U}{N}\right)_t^M = \frac{N_t}{U_t} \left(\frac{1}{N_t} dU_t^M + U_t d\left(\frac{1}{N}\right)_t^M \right) = \frac{1}{U_t} dU_t^M - \frac{1}{N_t} dN_t^M \tag{134}$$

On the other hand, note that

$$d\left(\log\left(\frac{U}{N}\right)\right)_t^M = d\left(\log U - \log N\right)_t^M = \frac{1}{U_t} dU_t^M - \frac{1}{N_t} dN_t^M \tag{135}$$

The new process $\tilde{W}$ is given by

$$d\tilde{W}_t^j = dW_t^j - d\left(\log\left(\frac{U}{N}\right)\right)_t^M dW_t^j \tag{136}$$

So, in order to compute $\tilde{W}$, it is generally very useful to be able to calculate $d\left(\log\left(\frac{U}{N}\right)\right)^M$.

B Proof of the background lemma

In this appendix, we follow Jeanblanc and Rutkowski (2000) to give a proof of Lemma 2.2, which we refer to as the 'Background Lemma'. Mathematically, we are in the same set-up as in section 2. First, we need

Lemma B.1 Let $t \in \mathbb{R}_+$. For any $A \in \mathcal{G}_t$ there is a $B \in \mathcal{F}_t$ such that $A \cap \{\tau > t\} = B \cap \{\tau > t\}$.

Proof. 7.4 Define $\Sigma := \{A \in \mathcal{G} | \exists B \in \mathcal{F}_t : A \cap \{\tau > t\} = B \cap \{\tau > t\}\}$. We show that Σ is a σ-algebra. The only property which is not immediately clear is the fact that Σ is closed under complements. So, let $A \in \Sigma$ and $B \in \mathcal{F}_t$ with $A \cap \{\tau > t\} = B \cap \{\tau > t\}$. We have

$$A^c \cap \{\tau > t\} = \{\tau > t\} \setminus (A \cap \{\tau > t\}) = \{\tau > t\} \cap (B \cap \{\tau > t\})^c = \{\tau > t\} \cap B^c.$$

Consequently, we see that $A^c \in \Sigma$, so Σ is indeed a σ-algebra. Clearly $\mathcal{F}_t \subset \Sigma$ and $\mathcal{D}_t \subset \Sigma$, so that $\mathcal{G}_t \subset \Sigma$.

$\square$

Lemma B.2 *Suppose that* $f : \Omega \to \bar{\mathbb{R}}_+$ *is* $\mathcal{G}_t$*-measurable. Then, there exists an* $\mathcal{F}_t$*-measurable function* $\tilde{f} : \Omega \to \bar{\mathbb{R}}_+$ *such that* $f \mathbf{1}_{\{\tau > t\}} = \tilde{f} \mathbf{1}_{\{\tau > t\}}$.

Proof. 1. First, assume that f is a step function. Then there are $a_1, \ldots, a_n \in \mathbb{R}_+$ and $A_1, \ldots, A_n \in \mathcal{G}_t$ such that $f = \sum_{j=1}^{n} a_j \mathbf{1}_{A_j}$. For each $j \in \{1, \ldots, n\}$ we have a set $B_j \in \mathcal{F}_t$ such that $A_j \cap \{\tau > t\} = B_j \cap \{\tau > t\}$. Define $\tilde{f} := \sum_{j=1}^{n} a_j \mathbf{1}_{B_j}$, clearly $f \mathbf{1}_{\{\tau > t\}} = \tilde{f} \mathbf{1}_{\{\tau > t\}}$.

2. In the general case, there is a sequence (f_n) of step functions with $(f_n) \uparrow f$. For each $n \in \mathbb{N}$ there is an $\mathcal{F}_t$-measurable step function $\tilde{f}_n$ with $f_n \mathbf{1}_{\{\tau > t\}} = \tilde{f}_n \mathbf{1}_{\{\tau > t\}}$. It follows that:

$$f \mathbf{1}_{\{\tau > t\}} = \sup_{n \in \mathbb{N}} \left(f_n \mathbf{1}_{\{\tau > t\}} \right) = \mathbf{1}_{\{\tau > t\}} \sup_{n \in \mathbb{N}} \tilde{f}_n.$$

The function $\tilde{f} := \sup_{n \in \mathbb{N}} \tilde{f}_n$ is $\mathcal{F}_t$-measurable, hence it has all the required properties.

Proof. (*Proof of Lemma 2.2*) Let $Y : \Omega \to \bar{\mathbb{R}}_+$ be $\mathcal{G}$-measurable, and let Z_0 be a version of the conditional expectation $E[Y|\mathcal{G}_t]$. According to Lemma B.2, there is an $\mathcal{F}_t$-measurable function $Z : \Omega \to \bar{\mathbb{R}}_+$ with $\mathbf{1}_{\{\tau > t\}} Z_0 = \mathbf{1}_{\{\tau > t\}} Z$. It follows that

$$E\left[\mathbf{1}_{\{\tau > t\}} Y \mid \mathcal{G}_t\right] = \mathbf{1}_{\{\tau > t\}} E[Y|\mathcal{G}_t] = \mathbf{1}_{\{\tau > t\}} Z_0 = \mathbf{1}_{\{\tau > t\}} Z \quad P\text{-a.s.} \tag{137}$$

So, using the tower property of conditional expectations, it follows that

$$E\left[\mathbf{1}_{\{\tau > t\}} Y \mid \mathcal{F}_t\right] = E\left[\mathbf{1}_{\{\tau > t\}} Z \mid \mathcal{F}_t\right] = Z P[\tau > t | \mathcal{F}_t] \quad P\text{-a.s.} \tag{138}$$

This implies

$$Z = \frac{E\left[\mathbf{1}_{\{\tau > t\}} Y \mid \mathcal{F}_t\right]}{P[\tau > t | \mathcal{F}_t]} \quad P\text{-a.s.} \tag{139}$$

Inserting equation (139) back into (137) gives equation (2), proving the Background Lemma.

References

Brace, A., Gatarek, D., and Musiela, M. (1997). 'The market model of interest rate dynamics'. *Mathematical Finance*, 7: 127–154.

Brigo, D. (2006). 'CMCDS valuation with market models'. *Risk* 78–83.

——— Brigo, D., and Morini, M. (2005). 'CDS market formulas and models'. Working paper.

Giesecke, K., and Azizpour, S. (2008). 'Self-exciting corporate defaults: contagion vs frailty'. Working paper, Stanford University, CA.

Heath, D., Jarrow, R., and Morton, A. (1992), 'Bond pricing and the term structure of interest rates: a new methodology for contingent claim valuation'. *Econometrica*, 60: 77–105.

Jamshidian, F. (2004). 'Valuation of credit default swaps and swaptions'. *Finance and Stochastics*, **8/3**: 343–71.

Jeanblanc, M., and Rutkowski, M. (2000). 'Modelling of default risk: Mathematical tools'. Working paper.

Miltersen, K. R., Sandmann, K., and Sondermann, D. (1997). 'Closed form solutions for term structure derivatives with lognormal interest rates', *Journal of Finance*, 52: 409–430.

Samiri, I. (2007). 'Construction of CDS market models using probability ratios'. Private communication.

Schönbucher, P. J. (2000). 'A libor market model with default risk', Technical Report 15/2001. Bonn Econ Discussion Papers.

Zhao, X., and Glasserman, P. (2000). 'Arbitrage-free discretization of lognormal forward libor and swap rate models', *Finance and Stochastics*, 4/1: 35–68.

CHAPTER 7

SINGLE- AND MULTI-NAME CREDIT DERIVATIVES: THEORY AND PRACTICE

ALEXANDER LIPTON AND DAVID SHELTON

1 CREDIT DERIVATIVE CONTRACTS

Credit derivatives are contracts whose payouts reference credit events. Depending upon the precise terms of the contract, credit events may include not just the default of a company but also other events such as restructuring or conservatorship (for a detailed exposition of the most common credit events see O'Kane 2008). These subtle differences of definition make little difference in the benign stages of the credit cycle, but when credit events start occurring, they assume high importance. We summarize some of the most common credit derivative contracts below.

1.1 The single-name credit default swap

One of the simplest contracts in the world of corporate credit is the single-name credit default swap (CDS). This contract references a specific class of corporate debt issued by a company or *reference entity*. If a credit event occurs, for cash-settled deals, a recovery value R which represents the percentage of face value that dealers are prepared to pay for the debt is determined usually by dealer poll or auction. It may take many months to determine how much will in reality finally be recoverable by the creditors so a market mechanism is necessary to value the debt—in practice this may have more to do with dealers' hedging needs than the value that is eventually realized. Some deals are also physically settled, by delivering the impaired underlying bonds in exchange for the cash notional.

Table 7.1 Recoveries from some recent Credit Event Protocols

Issuer/seniority	Industry	Credit event determination date	Recovery (%)
Delphi	Automobile	8/10/2005	63.375
Northwest Airlines	Airline	14/9/2005	28.000
DANA	Automobile	7/03/2006	75.000
Kaupthing Senior	Financial	8/10/2008	6.625
Kaupthing Subordinated			2.375
Fannie Mae Senior	Financial	9/09/2008	91.510
Fannie Mae Subordinated			99.900
Freddie Mac Senior	Financial	9/09/2008	94.000
Freddie Mac Subordinated			98.000
Lehman Brothers	Financial	16/09/2008	8.625
Washington Mutual	Financial	29/09/2008	57.000

Source: CreditEx.

There have been extensive historical studies of the distribution of recovery (Emery et al. 2009). We present recovery values from some recent credit events in Table 7.1, which gives a sense of their wide variability. Because of the fact that the widely used pricing models are calibrated to on-market CDS prices, the value of a CDS typically has low sensitivity to recovery assumptions. In practice it is usual to assume that R has a deterministic and somewhat arbitrary value (often 40%). More complex contracts depend significantly on the assumed distribution of recoveries, as we will see later.

The CDS was originally conceived as a way of hedging a corporate bond against the risk of default. In exchange for a stream of premium payments paying an annualized coupon C at a series of coupon dates $\{T_j : j = 1, \ldots, m\}$, the protection buyer will upon a credit event be paid an amount $(1 - R) \times N$ where N is the contract notional, at which point the contract will terminate. If the protection buyer holds a notional N of the underlying debt, this payment will compensate them for the fact that in default the debt has diminished in value to $R \times N$. In mathematical terms, if we represent the time of the credit event by τ, the value of the CDS to the protection buyer at time t may be expressed as $V(t, C) = V_{CL}(t, C) + V_{DL}(t)$ where:

$$B_t^{-1} V_{CL}(t, C) = - \mathbb{E}_t \left[N \times C \sum_{j=1}^m \delta(T_{j-1}, T_j) B_{T_j}^{-1} \mathbb{1}_{\tau > T_j} \right]$$

$$- \mathbb{E}_t \left[N \times C \sum_{j=1}^m \delta(T_{j-1}, \tau) B_\tau^{-1} \mathbb{1}_{T_{j-1} < \tau \leq T_j} \right] \quad \text{-Coupon leg} \quad (1)$$

$$B_t^{-1} V_{DL}(t) = \mathbb{E}_t \left[\int_{T_0}^{T_m} B_u^{-1} dL_u \right] \quad \text{-Default leg} \quad (2)$$

where $L_u = N \times (1 - R)\mathbb{1}_{\tau \leq u}$ and we define $T_0 \geq t$ to be the start date of the trade, B_T to be the rolling money market account to time T and $\delta(T_{j-1}, T_j)$ to be the day count fraction from T_{j-1} to T_j. The first term in the coupon leg (1) corresponds to premium payments conditional on survival of the credit and the second to the payment of accrued premium in the case of default. In common with swap contracts in other asset classes, the contract is usually quoted on the basis of the *breakeven (par) coupon* C_{BE}: the value of C that sets the present value of the contract $V(t, C)$ to 0. However, in cases where the reference entity is distressed and the debt trades at a deep discount to its face value the running coupon C_{BE} quickly soars into the thousands and begins to lose its meaning. In cases such as this when $C_{BE} > 500\text{bp}$, dealers often agree on a fixed contractual coupon C_{fixed} such as 500bp, and start quoting instead the up-front payment $U = V(t, C_{fixed})/N$ a protection buyer would have to pay to enter the contract as a percentage of notional. Recently there have been some big changes in the way CDS contracts trade across the board ISDA 2009*a* 2009*b*, 2009*c*. This so-called 'big bang' introduced standardized coupons and changes in quotation style: ultimately there are proposals to trade these more fungible contracts via a central clearing house (Duffie and Zhu 2009). In common with other swap markets, the CDS market has quickly soared in volume to eclipse the size of the comparatively illiquid corporate bond market it references. We show some example time series of CDS spreads in Figure 7.1. This reveals clearly how spreads tightened prior to 2007, widened dramatically in the wake of the financial crisis, and then

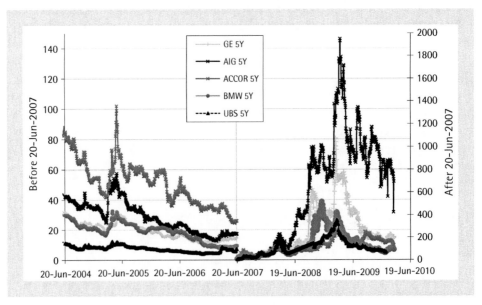

FIGURE 7.1 5y CDS spread in basis points of five well-known issuers. The spreads are plotted on a different scale before and after 20 June 2007.

Source: BofA Merrill Lynch Global Research.

tightened again, although not to pre-crisis levels. Options on CDS also trade, but in relatively small volume.

1.2 Reduced form modelling of single-name credit derivatives

The conventional approach to valuing CDS and most other credit derivatives contracts, at least for the purposes of exchanging price and quote information, is the so-called reduced form approach (Hull and White 2000; Jarrow and Turnbull 1995; Lando 1994, 1998; Bielecki and Rutkowski 2002). In this framework we assume default is driven by a Cox process, which is essentially a generalized Poisson process with a stochastic intensity $X(t)$. Denoting the number of events to time t by $n(t)$, in simple terms a Cox process is one in which conditional on a realization of the intensity process, the distribution of $n(t)$ is completely determined. We define the credit event time τ to be the first time at which $n(t) > 0$.

In order to completely represent the information contained in this process we define, following Lando (1994), the following augmented filtration:

$$\mathcal{F}_t = \mathcal{G}_t \vee \mathcal{H}_t \text{ where:} \tag{3}$$

$$\mathcal{G}_t = \sigma\{X(s) : 0 \le s \le t\} \tag{4}$$

$$\mathcal{H}_t = \sigma\{\xi(s) : 0 \le s \le t\} \tag{5}$$

where $\xi(s) = \mathbb{1}_{\tau \le s}$. The properties of the Cox process mean that the time t survival probability to time T conditioned on the filtration $\mathcal{G}_T$ containing information about the entire realisation of $(X(s))_{0 \le s \le T}$ can be expressed as follows:

$$\text{Prob}\left(\tau > T \big| (X(s))_{0 \le s \le T}, (\xi(s))_{0 \le s \le t}\right) = \mathbb{E}\left[\mathbb{1}_{\tau > T} \big| (X(s))_{0 \le s \le T}, (\xi(s))_{0 \le s \le t}\right]$$

$$= \mathbb{E}\left[\mathbb{1}_{\tau > T} | \mathcal{G}_T \vee \mathcal{H}_t\right]$$

$$= \mathbb{1}_{\tau > t}\exp\left(-\int_t^T X(s)ds\right) \tag{6}$$

The fact that we can express the conditional survival probability as a function of the diffusion process $X(s)$ alone means that in spite of the enlarged filtration $\mathcal{F}_t$, problems of contingent claims pricing may still be reduced to the solution of diffusion equations (Lando 1994) as for other asset classes (in this chapter we will sometimes represent the expectation $\mathbb{E}\left[\circ | \mathcal{F}_t\right]$ by $\mathbb{E}_t\left[\circ\right]$ for notational convenience). Specifically, considering the following three types of contingent claims:

1. A payment at a fixed date T of the form $\tilde{f}(X_T)\mathbb{1}_{\tau > T}$
2. A payment at a rate $\tilde{g}(X_s)\mathbb{1}_{\tau > s}$
3. A payment at the time of default of $\tilde{h}(X_\tau)$

and denoting the infinitesimal generator of the process X by $\mathcal{L}$, the value $U(t, X) = \mathbb{1}_{\tau>t} V(t, X)$ may be determined by solving the following partial differential equation (PDE) for $V(t)$ where $t \le T$:

$$V_t + \mathcal{L}V + (\tilde{g} + \tilde{h}X) - (r_t + X)V = 0$$

$$V(T, X) = \tilde{f}(X) \tag{7}$$

where r_t is the short-rate, assumed deterministic. We note as a general point that although this case is relatively simple, in credit derivatives it is generally necessary to treat questions of filtration carefully. Examples of cases where this needs to be handled with extra care are for example the pricing of credit options (Schönbucher 2003b) where a defaultable asset is used as numeraire. As we shall see later, copula models, since they are not based on an underlying process or dynamics but are really extensions of single time-horizon models, suffer from significant ambiguities in this respect. Precisely because it is not clear what we 'know' at different time-horizons, they cannot usually be used to price complex path-dependent payoffs.

To illustrate this approach, following Lipton (2010) we consider a particular and relatively tractable case where the intensity $X(t)$ is governed by a mean-reverting, non-negative jump-diffusion process:

$$dX(t) = f(t, X(t))\,dt + g(t, X(t))\,dW_t + J dN(t)$$

$$X(0) = X_0 \tag{8}$$

where W_t is a standard Wiener process, $N(t)$ is a Poisson process with intensity $\nu(t)$, and J is a positive jump distribution with jump values $J_m \ge 0, 1 \le m \le M$ occurring with probabilities $\pi_m \ge 0$: W, N, J are mutually independent. It is clear that we need to impose the following constraints:

$$f(t, 0) \ge 0, \quad f(t, \infty) < 0, \quad g(t, 0) = 0 \tag{9}$$

For analytical convenience it is customary to assume that X is governed by the square-root stochastic differential equation (SDE), which is a particular class of affine jump diffusion (AJD) process (Duffie, Pan, and Singleton 2000):

$$dX(t) = \kappa(\theta(t) - X(t))\,dt + \sigma\sqrt{X(t)}dW_t + J dN(t), \quad X(0) = X_0 \tag{10}$$

In this framework the survival probability conditional on $\mathcal{F}_t$ becomes, applying the law of iterated expectations to (6):

$$\begin{aligned}
S(t, T|X(t), Y(t)) &= \mathbb{E}\left[\mathbb{1}_{\tau>T}|\mathcal{G}_t \vee \mathcal{H}_t\right]\\
&= \mathbb{E}\left[\mathbb{E}\left[\mathbb{1}_{\tau>T}|\mathcal{G}_T \vee \mathcal{H}_t\right]|\mathcal{G}_t \vee \mathcal{H}_t\right]\\
&= \mathbb{1}_{\tau>t}\mathbb{E}\left[e^{-\int_t^T X(u)du}\middle| X(t), Y(t)\right]\\
&= e^{Y(t)}\mathbb{1}_{\tau>t}\mathbb{E}\left[e^{-Y(T)}\middle| X(t), Y(t)\right]
\end{aligned} \tag{11}$$

where we have defined $Y(T)$:

$$Y(T) = \int_0^T X(u)du \tag{12}$$

which is governed by the following degenerate SDE:

$$dY(t) = X(t)dt, \quad Y(0) = 0 \tag{13}$$

Although we could approach the pricing problem straightforwardly through the PDE (7), we take a different tack based on the expression (11) for the conditional survival probability. We make use of the fact that the expectation (11), and more generally expectations of the form $\mathbb{E}_t\left[e^{-\phi Y(T)}\big| X(t), Y(t)\right]$ can be computed by solving the following augmented PDE (Lipton 2001):

$$V_t + \mathcal{L}V(t, T, X, Y) + XV_Y(t, T, X, Y) = 0$$
$$V(T, T, X, Y) = e^{-\phi Y} \tag{14}$$

where

$$\mathcal{L}V \equiv \kappa(\theta(t) - X)V_X + \frac{1}{2}\sigma^2 X V_{XX} + \nu(t)\sum_m \pi_m (V(X + J_m) - V(X)) \tag{15}$$

Specifically, the following relation holds:

$$\mathbb{E}_t\left[e^{-\phi Y(T)}\big| X(t), Y(t)\right] = V(t, T, X(t), Y(t)) \tag{16}$$

The corresponding solution can be written in the so-called affine form

$$V(t, T, X, Y) = e^{a(t,T,\phi)+b(t,T,\phi)X - \phi Y} \tag{17}$$

where a and b are functions of time governed by the following system of ordinary differential equations (ODEs):

$$\frac{da(t, T, \phi)}{dt} = -\kappa\theta(t)b(t, T, \phi) - \nu\sum_m \pi_m \left(e^{J_m b(t,T,\phi)} - 1\right)$$

$$\frac{db(t, T, \phi)}{dt} = \phi + \kappa b(t, T, \phi) - \frac{1}{2}\sigma^2 b^2(t, T, \phi) \tag{18}$$

$$a(T, T, \phi) = 0, \quad b(T, T, \phi) = 0 \tag{19}$$

Although in the presence of discrete jumps this system cannot be solved analytically, it can easily be solved numerically via the standard Runge-Kutta method. The survival probability (11) can then be expressed as:

$$S(t, T\big| X(t), Y(t)) = \mathbb{1}_{\tau > t} e^{a(t,T,1)+b(t,T,1)X_t} \tag{20}$$

Now applying these results to the pricing of a T-expiry CDS, we consider the simple case where the short rate r_t is deterministic and the premium payments are made continuously. Then we can express the value U of a CDS paying an up-front amount

v at time t and a coupon s in exchange for receiving a deterministic amount $1 - R$ as follows:

$$U(t, X_t) = -v + V(t, X_t) \tag{21}$$

where $V(t, X)$ solves the pricing problem (7) with $\tilde{f} = 0, \tilde{g} = -s, \tilde{h} = (1 - R)$:

$$V_t + \mathcal{L}V - (r_t + X)V = s - (1 - R)X$$

$$V(T, X) = 0 \tag{22}$$

Using Duhamel's principle, we obtain the following expression for V:

$$V(t, X) = -s \int_t^T P(t, t') e^{a(t,t',1) + b(t,t',1)X} dt'$$

$$- (1 - R) \int_t^T P(t, t') d\left[e^{a(t,t',1) + b(t,t',1)X} \right] \tag{23}$$

where since we are assuming deterministic interest rates, the risk-free discount factor to time t' is given by:

$$P(t, t') = B_t B_{t'}^{-1} = e^{-\int_t^{t'} r(u)du} \tag{24}$$

Accordingly:

$$U(t, X_t) = -v - s \int_t^T P(t, t') S(t, t'|X_t) dt' - (1 - R) \int_t^T P(t, t') dS(t, t'|X_t) \tag{25}$$

The par or break-even spread $\hat{s}_t(T)$ is defined to be the spread that sets the value of the contract to zero, in the absence of any up-front payment:

$$\hat{s}_t(T) = \frac{-(1 - R) \int_t^T P(t, t') dS(t, t'|X_t)}{\int_t^T P(t, t') S(t, t'|X_t) dt'} \tag{26}$$

It is convenient to define the instantaneous forward hazard rate $\lambda(t, s)$:

$$S(t, T|X_t) = \mathbb{E}\left[\mathbb{1}_{\tau > T} | \mathcal{F}_t \right]$$

$$= \mathbb{1}_{\tau > t} \mathbb{E}\left[\exp\left(-\int_t^T X(s)ds \right) \Big| \mathcal{F}_t \right] \tag{27}$$

$$= \mathbb{1}_{\tau > t} \exp\left(-\int_t^T \lambda(t, s)ds \right) \tag{28}$$

By analogy with interest rates, the process $X(t)$ plays the role of the short rate, and $\lambda(t, s)$ is equivalent to the instantaneous forward rate.

Since the valuation of CDS contracts in the absence of optionality or counterparty risk only depends upon the process $X(t)$ via the instantaneous forward rates $\lambda(t, s)$ there is in this case no advantage in modelling the stochasticity of $X(t)$, and it is conventional (Hull and White 2000) to think of $\lambda(t, s)$ as being the hazard rate (intensity) at time s of an inhomogeneous Poisson process with survival probability $S(t, T) = \mathbb{1}_{\tau > t}\exp\left(-\int_t^T \lambda(t, s)ds\right)$. For simple CDS valuation, then, although the market convention of assuming deterministic hazard rates appears restrictive, in fact nothing would change if we assumed a much more complex Cox process, providing that it remained uncorrelated with interest rates .

In these terms the expectations (1), (2) reduce to the following closed form expressions (assuming deterministic recovery R):

$$V_{CL}(t, C) = -\mathbb{1}_{\tau > t} \times N \times C \sum_{j=1}^m \delta(T_{j-1}, T_j)P(t, T_j)S(t, T_j)$$

$$- \mathbb{1}_{\tau > t} \times N \times C \sum_{j=1}^m \int_{T_{j-1}}^{T_j} \delta(T_{j-1}, t')P(t, t')S(t, t')\lambda(t, t')dt' \quad \text{-Coupon leg}$$

$$(29)$$

$$V_{DL}(t) = \mathbb{1}_{\tau > t} \times N \times (1-R) \int_{T_0}^{T_m} P(t, t')S(t, t')\lambda(t, t')dt' \quad \text{-Default leg}$$

$$(30)$$

In practice, it is usual to assume that $\lambda(t, s)$ is piecewise constant in s, and bootstrap a survival curve term structure $S(t, T)$ such that we reprice a series of CDS contracts with successively longer maturities.

For more complex payouts such as options, or in the presence of a risky counterparty, the way we model $X(t)$ makes a great deal of difference. We will consider this case in more detail when we discuss the correlation of default.

1.3 The index default swap

The single name CDS contract also has an analogue referencing a portfolio of credits, the index default swap (IDS). These indices are based on a reference portfolio: in the case of CDX.IG and ITX.IG an equally weighted universe of 125 credits. On roll dates, which are usually every six months, a new series is defined in which the reference portfolio may change slightly to remove credits whose quality has deteriorated, or promote those which have improved. Old series continue to trade, although with reduced liquidity.

We define the loss on the portfolio of n credits at time T to be $L_T = \sum_{i=1}^n w_i \xi_T^i$ where τ_i denotes the time of the first credit event of the ith credit, $w_i = N_i(1 - R_i)$ and $\xi_T^i = \mathbb{1}_{\tau_i \le T}$ is a Bernoulli variable, the indicator function that credit i has experienced a credit event by time T. We also define the outstanding notional on the swap by $N_T = \sum_{i=1}^n N_i(1 - \xi_T^i)$. Then the value of the swap may be expressed as $U(t, C_{\text{fixed}}) = U_{CL}(t, C_{\text{fixed}}) + U_{DL}(t)$ where:

$$B_t^{-1} U_{CL}(t, C_{\text{fixed}}) = - \mathbb{E}_t \left[C_{\text{fixed}} \sum_{j=1}^{m} \delta(T_{j-1}, T_j) B_{T_j}^{-1} N_{T_j} \right]$$

$$+ \mathbb{E}_t \left[C_{\text{fixed}} \sum_{j=1}^{m} \int_{u=T_{j-1}}^{u=T_j} \delta(T_{j-1}, u) B_u^{-1} dN_u \right] \qquad \text{-Coupon leg} \qquad (31)$$

$$B_t^{-1} U_{DL}(t) = \mathbb{E}_t \left[\int_{T_0}^{T_m} B_u^{-1} dL_u \right] \qquad \text{-Default leg} \qquad (32)$$

where C_{fixed} is the fixed contractual coupon for the given series and maturity. The IDS legs (31), (32) may be decomposed into a linear combination of single name CDS legs (1), (2).

$$U_{CL}(t, C_{\text{fixed}}) = \sum_{i=1}^{n} V_{CL}^i(t, C_{\text{fixed}}) \qquad (33)$$

$$U_{DL}(t) = \sum_{i=1}^{n} V_{DL}^i(t) \qquad (34)$$

where V_{CL}^i and V_{DL}^i denote, respectively the single-name coupon and protection legs for a CDS referencing credit i. In theory, to value these contracts, we would need market quotes for all the underlying credits. This would introduce a great deal of ambiguity due to the uncertain levels of less liquid credits as well as a host of interpolation assumptions. In practice therefore, the market convention is to quote the IDS price based on the spread Q that when used to build a single name survival curve with a single-term point and value a single-name CDS with the formulas (29), (30) will give the correct up-front value for the IDS contract: $V(t, C_{\text{fixed}}; Q) = V_{CL} + V_{DL}$ (here V represents the single-name pricing formula evaluated using a survival curve built with a single quote Q). Some example historic time series for ITX and CDX investment grade are given in Figure 7.2. We note that this is just a medium for the exchange of price information. If we want a complete picture of the risk decomposed at the level of the underlying credits, we need to attempt to evaluate the decompositions (33), (34). However, in general, there is a basis between the intrinsic value $U(t, C_{\text{fixed}}; \{S\})$ and the price $V(t, C_{\text{fixed}}; Q)$ implied by the market quote Q ($\{S\}$ represents all the spread information used to build the single-name survival curves).

Since most of the classical literature on financial mathematics deals with the limit of zero transaction costs and unlimited liquidity, it is not possible either to explain the presence of such a basis or understand how to handle it mathematically in the standard framework. It is not necessarily small either; at the time of writing it could routinely be >30bp running for investment grade and in the hundreds of bp for high yield. We define the basis $B(\{S\}, Q) = Q - C_{\text{fixed}} \sum V_{DL}^i(S) / Q \sum V_{CL}^i(S)$ between the index quote and the weighted average of the single name quotes. In Figure 7.3. we plot the behaviour of this basis over time for the CDX IG showing how it has recently diverged significantly from zero.

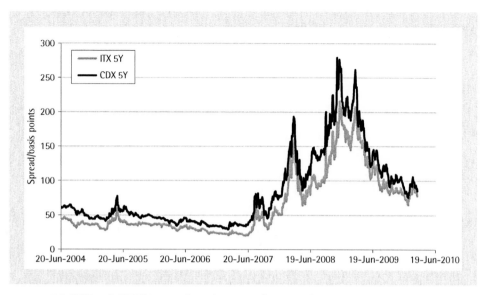

FIGURE 7.2 ITX and CDX historical on-the-run index spreads.

Source: BofA Merrill Lynch Global Research.

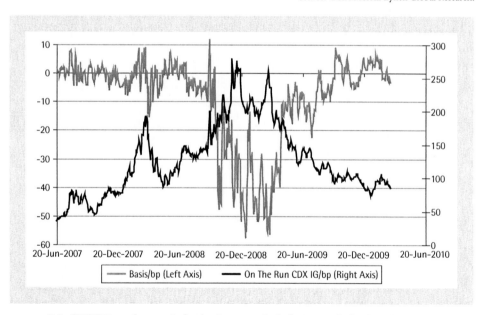

FIGURE 7.3 CDX IG on-the-run index basis versus 5y index quote in basis points.

Source: BofA Merrill Lynch Global Research.

The approach taken by practitioners has been based on the assumption that: (1) Since from a payoff point of view it is theoretically possible to replicate the IDS with a portfolio of CDS, the fair value of the basis in the long run must be 0, even if it fluctuates significantly. (2) For liquidity reasons the IDS quotes generally provide a more accurate reflection of the value of the index than the CDS quotes. As a result of these two assumptions, we need to ensure that IDS trades are marked consistently with index quotes. From the point of view of risk we need to be able to capture exposure to the underlying single names. Although we cannot necessarily hedge it, we also need to be able to measure our exposure to the basis between single names and index if we are trading a book containing both index and single-name exposures. These aims are commonly achieved by tweaking the single-name quotes from their observed values $\{S\}$ to a set of values $\{S'\}$ for which $U(t, C_{\text{fixed}}; \{S'\}) = V(t, C_{\text{fixed}}; Q)$. This is usually done by modifying the hazard rates by a proportional factor although clearly there is no unique prescription. Formally, the IDS value U can then be viewed as a function of the original spreads $\{S\}$ and the basis $B(\{S\}, Q)$ between the index quote and the weighted average of the single-name quotes.

Short-dated options on IDS are traded in reasonable volumes, and are usually modelled based on a generalization of the Black formula (Schönbucher 2003b; O'Kane 2008).

1.4 Correlation products: Nth to default baskets

We now turn to contracts with more complex payoffs which depend upon the correlation of defaults between different credits. The Nth to default contract (NTD) pays protection upon the Nth credit event in a basket of n credits (usually a relatively small basket of between 2 and 10 credits). By far the most common example is the first to default (FTD). Defining as before a portfolio of n credits with default times $\{\tau_i : i = 1, \ldots, n\}$, we define the first default time $\tau_{FTD} = \min(\tau_1, \ldots, \tau_n)$ (assuming no simultaneous defaults i.e. $\tau_i \neq \tau_j$ if $i \neq j$). Then the value of the coupon and protection legs can be expressed, respectively, as follows:

$$B_t^{-1} V_{CL}(t, C) = -\mathbb{E}_t \left[N \times C \sum_{j=1}^m \delta(T_{j-1}, T_j) B_{T_j}^{-1} \mathbb{1}_{\tau_{FTD} > T_j} \right]$$

$$- \mathbb{E}_t \left[N \times C \sum_{j=1}^m \delta(T_{j-1}, \tau_{FTD}) B_{\tau_{FTD}}^{-1} \mathbb{1}_{T_{j-1} < \tau_{FTD} \leq T_j} \right] \quad \text{-Coupon leg}$$

$$(35)$$

$$B_t^{-1} V_{DL}(t) = \mathbb{E}_t \left[N \times \sum_{i=1}^n (1 - R_i) \mathbb{1}_{\tau_{FTD} = \tau_i} B_{\tau_{FTD}}^{-1} \mathbb{1}_{T_0 \leq \tau_{FTD} \leq T_m} \right] \quad \text{-Protection leg}$$

$$(36)$$

In order to evaluate these expectations, we need to make some additional model assumptions about the correlations between defaults, which we will discuss later. Broadly, the protection has greater value if the credits are very uncorrelated, because it is then almost as valuable as owning individual CDS protection on each of the underlying names (because joint default events are rare). When the credits are highly correlated, on the other hand, the value is comparable to that of a single CDS on the riskiest name in the basket since this would usually default first with the others defaulting subsequently. Intermediate correlation assumptions result in valuations somewhere between these two boundary cases.

1.5 Correlation: CDS contracts with counterparty risk vs. Nth to default baskets

There are many similarities between valuing basket correlation products and CDS contracts with counterparty risk. In an earlier section on single-name CDS, we developed a reduced form approach to the valuation of these contracts for cases where there is no credit risk with respect to the counterparty. In reality, there are many cases where this assumption is not valid. We pause for a moment to indicate how the framework may be extended to simultaneously model the default of several reference entities, starting with the two-name case. Let us consider two reference entities A, B and assume for simplicity that their default intensities coincide:

$$X_A(t) = X_B(t) = X(t) \tag{37}$$

and that they share the same recovery $R_A = R_B = R$. For a given maturity T the default event correlation ρ_{AB} is defined as follows where τ_A, τ_B are their default times and $\xi_A(T) = \mathbb{1}_{\tau_A \leq T}, \xi_B(T) = \mathbb{1}_{\tau_B \leq T}$:

$$\rho_{AB}(0, T) = \frac{\text{cov}(\xi_A, \xi_B)}{\text{stdev}(\xi_A)\text{stdev}(\xi_B)}$$

$$= \frac{p_{AB}(0, T) - p_A(0, T)p_B(0, T)}{\sqrt{p_A(0, T)(1 - p_A(0, T))p_B(0, T)(1 - p_B(0, T))}} \tag{38}$$

where:

$$p_A(0, T) = \mathbb{E}_0\left[\xi_A(T)\right] \qquad\qquad = \text{Prob}\,(\tau_A \leq T)$$
$$p_B(0, T) = \mathbb{E}_0\left[\xi_B(T)\right] \qquad\qquad = \text{Prob}\,(\tau_B \leq T)$$
$$p_{AB}(0, T) = \mathbb{E}_0\left[\xi_A(T)\xi_B(T)\right] \qquad = \text{Prob}\,(\tau_A \leq T, \tau_B \leq T) \tag{39}$$

From (20) we have that:

$$p_A(0, T) = p_B(0, T) = 1 - e^{a(0,T,1)+b(0,T,1)X_0} \tag{40}$$

Applying (6) we derive:

$$p_{AB}(0, T) = \mathbb{E}_0\left[(1 - e^{-\int_0^T X_A(u)du})(1 - e^{-\int_0^T X_B(u)du})\right]$$

$$= \mathbb{E}_0\left[e^{-2\int_0^T X(u)du}\right] + p_A(0, T) + p_B(0, T) - 1 \tag{41}$$

Applying (17) with $\phi = 2$ we obtain:

$$\mathbb{E}_0\left[e^{-2\int_0^T X(u)du}\right] = e^{-a(0,T,2)+b(0,T,2)X_0} \tag{42}$$

Hence:

$$\rho_{AB}(0, T) = \frac{e^{a(0,T,2)+b(0,T,2)X_0} - (1 - p_A(0, T))(1 - p_B(0, T))}{\sqrt{p_A(1 - p_A)p_B(1 - p_B)}}$$

$$= \frac{e^{a(0,T,2)+b(0,T,2)X_0} - e^{2a(0,T,1)+2b(0,T,1)X_0}}{e^{a(0,T,1)+b(0,T,1)X_0}\left(1 - e^{a(0,T,1)+b(0,T,1)X_0}\right)} \tag{43}$$

It turns out that for simple diffusion processes without jumps, the corresponding event correlation is very low (Schönbucher 2003a). However, if large positive jumps are added (while overall survival probability is preserved), correlation can be increased all the way to one. Assuming $T = 5y$, $\kappa = 0.5$, $\sigma = 7\%$ and $J = 5.0$ we illustrate this observation in Figure 7.4.

The fact that large collective jumps in the intensity of default are necessary to get any significant degree of correlation between the defaults of different reference entities agrees with empirical studies such as Longstaff and Rajan (2006). In some asset classes, it may be possible to work with pure diffusion processes, but there is no getting away from the inherent 'jumpiness' of credit. The model described here could be said to express the very nature of the credit cycle in caricatured form, with periods of economic growth and very low default rate, followed by periods of contraction and much higher default rate.

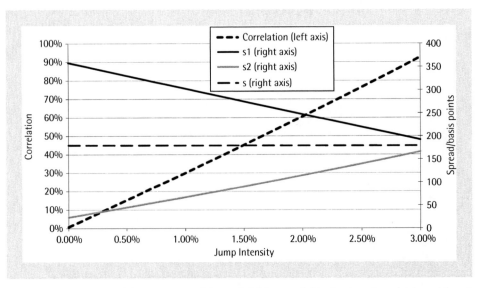

FIGURE 7.4 FTD spread $\hat{s}_1$, STD spread $\hat{s}_2$, and CDS spread $\hat{s}$ in basis points (right axis) and Default Correlation (left axis) as a function of Jump Intensity.

To return to the Nth to Default example, in a two-name portfolio we can define two types of CDS which depend upon the correlation: a first-to-default (FTD) and second-to-default (STD) swap. The corresponding par spreads (assuming continuous accrual of premium as before) are:

$$\hat{s}_t^1(T) = \frac{(1-R)\int_t^T P(t,t')d\left[1 - e^{a(t,t',2)+b(t,t',2)X_t}\right]}{\int_t^T P(t,t')e^{a(t,t',2)+b(t,t',2)X_t}dt'}$$

$$\hat{s}_t^2(T) = \frac{(1-R)\int_t^T P(t,t')d\left[1 + e^{a(t,t',2)+b(t,t',2)X_t} - 2e^{a(t,t',1)+b(t,t',1)X_t}\right]}{\int_t^T P(t,t')\left(2e^{a(t,t',1)+b(t,t',1)X_t} - e^{a(t,t',2)+b(t,t',2)X_t}\right)dt'} \quad (44)$$

It is clear from Figure 7.4. that the relative values of $\hat{s}_t^1$ and $\hat{s}_t^2$ depend strongly on the presence or otherwise of jumps in the model. The fact that these contracts trade at high values of implied default correlation would seem to demand a model with jumps if we wish to model default as a Cox process.

The most common model in use for trading these contracts is actually based on a very different approach, the Gaussian copula, of which more later, but since this model lacks the concept of a 'process' it has little explanatory power or relationship to financial observables like the dynamics of spread or hazard rate. For that reason it is valuable to approach the problem as we have here, in order to understand the types of dynamics that are consistent with the relatively high default correlations implied by the market.

An important application of the model considered here is to the effect of counterparty risk on fair CDS spreads. We consider a case where a risky counterparty A has sold CDS protection on reference name B. The value of this protection $\tilde{V}$ to a risk-free counterparty, in the absence of any collateral or margining agreements can be determined by solving the following pricing problem:

$$\tilde{V}_t + \mathcal{L}\tilde{V} - (r+2X)\tilde{V}(t,X) = s - (1-R)X - (RV_+(t,X) + V_-(t,X))X \quad (45)$$

where V is the value of a fully collateralized CDS on name B with spread s and $V_+ = \max(V,0)$, $V_- = \min(V,0)$. The discounting is increased from $r+X$ in equation (7) to $r+2X$ since there are two cases when the CDS can be terminated due to default: when the reference name B defaults or when the counterparty A defaults. The terms on the right represent the continuous stream of coupon payments, the amount received if B defaults before A, and the amount received (or paid) in the case where A defaults before B. Although (45) is no longer analytically solvable, it can be solved numerically by a generalization of the standard Crank-Nicholson method. In the presence of jumps, the value of the fair par spread decreases dramatically (Lipton and Sepp 2009).

If we consider the reverse situation, i.e. the risk-free counterparty has sold protection on name B to the risky counterparty A, we arrive at the following PDE for the value $\tilde{U}$:

$$\tilde{U}_t + \mathcal{L}\tilde{U} - (r+2X)\tilde{U}(t,X) = -s + (1-R)X + (RV_-(t,X) + V_+(t,X))X \quad (46)$$

It is clear that $\tilde{U} \neq -\tilde{V}$ so if two counterparties each view themselves as risk free and their counterparty as risky, they will disagree on the valuation of the CDS: the protection buyer will wish to pay a lower coupon to allow for the fact that the protection seller may default, reducing the value of the protection, and the protection seller will wish to charge a higher coupon, to allow for the fact that the protection buyer may default and cease paying coupons whilst still receiving the value of the protection. If both parties are prepared to compromise it is possible that they may be able to meet in the middle and execute a trade, but they will disagree on valuation.

Whilst some cases are as simple as this, for example when protection has been sold by a special purpose vehicle (SPV) with a very simple 'balance sheet', the question of counterparty risk generally becomes quite complicated when considered at the level of a firm or portfolio. Dealers usually have master agreements allowing them to net off-setting positions for the purposes of settlement in a default event, hence counterparty risk becomes a complicated function of the entire derivatives portfolio. As we have mentioned above, there is also the almost philosophical question of whether dealers should include their own probability of default in calculating bilateral counterparty risk (Gregory 2009). Arguably, if they do not, there is a danger that they will be unable to agree on prices and that counterparty exposure will be double-counted across the financial system.

Undeniably credit derivatives are more problematic than other asset classes from the point of view of counterparty risk because of the potentially high correlation between the counterparty and the underlying. Proposals to introduce a central clearing house purely for credit derivatives are intended to reduce this exposure across the financial system but some authors (Duffie and Zhu 2009) have suggested that this could actually *increase* total counterparty exposure, since dealers will forgo their ability to net credit derivatives contracts against other asset classes.

1.6 Correlation products: synthetic CDO tranches

By far the most important correlation product is the synthetic CDO tranche (CDO is short for 'collateralized debt obligation': synthetic because the payoff is 'synthesized' from underlying credit derivative contracts rather than an actual portfolio of cash bonds). This is defined on a much larger portfolio with n usually of order 100. As for the IDS we define the loss on the portfolio to be $L_T = \sum_{i=1}^{n} w_i \xi_T^i$ with $w_i = N_i(1 - R_i)$, and the total recovery on the portfolio to be $R_T = \sum_{i=1}^{n} N_i R_i \xi_T^i$ (such that $L_T + R_T + N_T = \sum_{i=1}^{n} N_i$). The loss $\hat{L}_T$ and outstanding notional $\hat{N}_T$ on a tranche with attachment point K_1 and detachment point K_2 is then defined to be:

$$\hat{L}_T(K_1, K_2) = \min(L_T, K_2) - \min(L_T, K_1) \tag{47}$$

$$\hat{N}_T = (K_2 - K_1) - \hat{L}_T - \hat{R}_T \text{ where:} \tag{48}$$

$$\hat{R}_T = \min\left(R_T, \sum_{i=1}^{n} N_i - K_1\right) - \min\left(R_T, \sum_{i=1}^{n} N_i - K_2\right) \tag{49}$$

This definition of the outstanding notional reflects the fact that the tranche notional can either be amortized from the bottom by the loss, or from the top by the recovered notional. This definition ensures that the total outstanding notional across all the tranches that compose the capital structure is consistent with the outstanding notional of the underlying portfolio. The value of the coupon and protection leg respectively can then be expressed (analogously to the index default swap) via the following expectations:

$$B_t^{-1} V_{CL}(t, C) = -\mathbb{E}_t \left[C \sum_{j=1}^{m} \delta(T_{j-1}, T_j) B_{T_j}^{-1} \hat{N}_{T_j} \right]$$

$$+ \mathbb{E}_t \left[C \sum_{j=1}^{m} \int_{u=T_{j-1}}^{u=T_j} \delta(T_{j-1}, u) B_u^{-1} d\hat{N}_u \right] \qquad \text{-Coupon leg} \qquad (50)$$

$$B_t^{-1} V_{DL}(t) = \mathbb{E}_t \left[\int_{T_0}^{T_m} B_u^{-1} d\hat{L}_u \right]$$

$$= \mathbb{E}_t \left[B_{T_m}^{-1} \hat{L}_{T_m} - B_{T_0}^{-1} \hat{L}_{T_0} - \int_{T_0}^{T_m} \hat{L}_u d B_u^{-1} \right] \qquad \text{-Protection leg} \qquad (51)$$

The idea of the CDO is to synthetically redistribute the portfolio default risk into more and less risky 'tranches', from the riskiest 'equity' tranche with $K_1 = 0$, to the least risky 'super-senior' tranches with very high attachment points where K_1 may equate to 20–30% of the portfolio notional. Originally, so-called cash-flow CDOs were constructed by tranching up the risk from an actual portfolio of bonds and finding buyers for all the different tranches. More recently, CDOs have generally been constructed 'synthetically' which simplifies the payoff and means that individual tranches can be synthesized and hedged in the CDS and index market without the need to construct an actual underlying portfolio or sell on all the other tranches making up the capital structure.

The way the risk is distributed into tranches of various seniorities can be thought of as analogous to the capital structure of a firm (with a lack of managerial discretion, except in managed structures). A key factor in the CDO market has been the role of the rating agencies, who saw an opportunity to expand their acknowledged expertise in rating corporate debt of various seniorities to develop rating models for these synthetic structures. Since the rating agency methodologies were based on historical analysis, not market observables, an industry grew up to exploit the 'ratings arbitrage' between risk-neutral market-based pricing and rating-based metrics of risk. Sophisticated optimizations were employed to find the tranche and portfolio that yielded the highest spread for a given rating criterion. Many of the underlying assumptions have been called into question subsequently, not least because of a perceived conflict of interest: the ratings agencies were paid by the dealers, not the investors who were in the end relying upon them (Jones, Tett, and Davies 2008).

Table 7.2 ITX Series 9 IG Tranche Prices, June 2009 (indicative)

Maturity:		20-Dec-12: Ref = 119		20-Dec-14: Ref = 115		20-Dec-17: Ref = 109	
Attach (%)	Detach (%)	UF	RC	UF	RC	UF	RC
0	3	44.250	500	51.000	500	55.375	500
3	6	5.750	500	11.000	500	15.500	500
6	9	−4.375	500	−3.250	500	−1.250	500
9	12	0	177	0	217	0	257
12	22	0	79	0	98.5	0	109

Source: BofA Merrill Lynch Global Research. UF is up-front in %, RC is Running Coupon in bp, Ref is the Reference Index Quote in bp.

As in the case of the NTD, the value of CDO tranches depends strongly on the correlation between defaults, or expressed differently, on the loss distribution on the portfolio. As dealers built up large portfolios of such trades, they ended up with large correlation exposures. In order to establish clearing prices for these correlation exposures, dealers initiated an index tranche market. As for index default swaps, these are based on a series of standard portfolios, maturities, attachment and detachment points. We show some example prices in Table 7.2, and a time series of historic ITX investment grade tranche spreads in Figure 7.5.

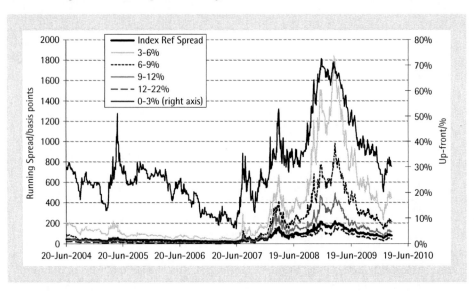

FIGURE 7.5 On-the-run ITX Tranche Quote History (0–3% maps to right axis and is % up-front. All other tranche prices are quoted as running spreads and map to the left axis. Since Q1 2009 the 3–6% and 6–9% have also been quoted as % up-front with 500bp running but for the purposes of this chart they have been converted to running spreads for the entire time series). Prior to Series 9 which was effective 21 Sept. 2007 and scheduled to roll on 20 Mar. 2008 the on-the-run index rolled every six months, subsequently, index tranche traders have continued to quote for Series 9.

Source: BofA Merrill Lynch Global Research.

2 THE GAUSSIAN COPULA MODEL

By far the most important problem in credit derivatives modelling, in terms both of mathematical complexity and the large size of the positions established by dealers, is modelling the correlation of defaults or equivalently, the loss distribution on a portfolio. Although various approaches have been tried, the de facto market standard remains the Gaussian copula in a form close to that formulated in Li (2000). We start from the assumption that for a given credit i with default time τ_i the survival probability $S_i(T)$ to time T is known at time t (by bootstrapping from single-name CDS quotes):

$$S_i(T) = \mathbb{E}_t \left[\mathbb{1}_{\tau_i > T} \right]$$

$$= \mathbb{1}_{\tau_i > t} \exp \left(- \int_t^T \lambda(t, s) ds \right) \tag{52}$$

Given a set of known *marginal* distributions, the copula function approach provides a general way of constructing a family of joint distributions consistent by construction with the marginals. A good review of the use of copulas in finance is given in Embrechts, Lindskog, and McNeil (2003), and Bouyé et al. (2000). The idea is based on Sklar's theorem, which we outline briefly here: Let $P(T_1, \ldots, T_n) = \mathrm{Prob}(\tau_1 > T_1, \ldots, \tau_n > T_n)$ be a multivariate cumulative distribution function with marginals $\{S_i\}$. Then there exists a copula function C such that:

$$P(T_1, \ldots, T_n) = C(S_1(T_1), \ldots, S_n(T_n)) \tag{53}$$

If the $\{S_i\}$ are continuous, C is unique. In the current context, we are more interested in the converse, which is that if C is an n-copula and the $\{S_i\}$ are distribution functions, then the function P defined in (53) is a cumulative distribution function with marginals $\{S_i\}$. The Gaussian copula is defined in this way via:

$$C_{GC}(U_1, \ldots, U_n) = \Phi^n \left(\Phi^{-1}(U_1), \ldots, \Phi^{-1}(U_n); \rho \right), \quad \{0 \le U_i \le 1\} \tag{54}$$

where Φ is the cumulative univariate standard normal and $\Phi^n(X_1, \ldots, X_n; \rho)$ is the cumulative multivariate standard normal with correlation matrix ρ. It is usual to assume a single uniform pairwise correlation ρ rather than any more complex correlation matrix, largely because there is no way of estimating a more complex matrix from the limited market data available (even if more visibility of individual pairwise correlations on specific portfolios were possible, the sheer combinatoric problem that there are exponentially large numbers of possible portfolio compositions given a specified universe of credits to choose from means there is a limit to how much this situation is likely to change).

An additional advantage of this simplified correlation assumption is that the model can then be formulated in a so-called central shock decomposition—conditional on a given univariate normal variate Y the defaults become independent, which results in far greater tractability. We decompose as follows:

$$Z^i = \sqrt{\rho}Y + \sqrt{1 - \rho}X^i$$
$$U_i = \Phi(Z^i) \tag{55}$$

where Y and the $\{X^i\}$ are independent N(0,1) variables. The simplest way of implementing this model via Monte Carlo would be to simulate a set of $\{U_i\}$ according to (55) and then generate the corresponding default times via $\{\tau_i = S_i^{-1}(U_i)\}$. In the early days of the industry this was probably the most common implementation although as we shall see later, there are much more efficient and accurate ways of calculating the loss distribution.

This, then, is the much-maligned market-standard 'recipe' for constructing a model of the loss distribution on a portfolio that is consistent with the individual single-name survival probabilities. Originally it was fêted to the extent that its creator appeared on the front page of the *Wall Street Journal* (Whitehouse 2005): at the time it was judged that the industry had successfully weathered the 'correlation crisis' of May 2005 which, traumatic though it was, seems in retrospect a pale foreshadowing of the carnage that was to follow two years later. The Gaussian copula has ended up being blamed by some for the subsequent financial crisis (Salmon 2009): its seductive simplicity, it is argued, concealing the underlying complexity and imponderability of pools of risky assets and promoting the illusion of certainty.

Although it is true that this approach, borrowed from the more sedate world of actuarial science (Bowers et al. 1997) where time series tend to exhibit more stability, does greatly simplify the problem and lacks financial justification, these limitations are generally well understood in the industry where it is treated as a formula like that of Black-Scholes (in single time-horizon, approximate form, its origins go back as far as 1987: to the large homogeneous pool approximation (Vasicek 1987). It is also worth pointing out that the asset class perceived to have been most egregiously misvalued, CDO of ABS, was generally not modelled in this way.

Probably some of the biggest concerns with this modelling approach are whether or not it makes sense from the point of view of risk, since the model formulation makes no reference to hedging. Criticisms that it is not 'dynamic' (in the sense that spreads or hazard rates follow a stochastic process) are not in our view the main issue, since the value of CDOs only depend upon terminal loss distributions which are inherently 'static' quantities, analogous to discount factors. Any dynamic model, no matter how esoteric, would still have to calibrate to roughly the same terminal loss distributions in order to match observed prices.

Although it is true that complex path-dependent structures may require a dynamic modelling approach, relatively few trades of this type have ever been done, with the notable exception of 'Leveraged Super-Senior' (LSS) trades: essentially leveraged CDO positions with unwind triggers contingent on loss, spread, or mark-to-market (O'Kane 2008). These trades, along with the constant proportion debt obligation

(CPDO) are no longer 'a disaster waiting to happen' (Heaton 2007); the unpleasant consequences of high leverage in a drastically spread-widening environment being all too clear in retrospect. Arguably this type of gap risk is hard to capture in a classic hedging-based derivatives pricing model.

Tranche options, in the form of cancellable CDO tranches, have also traded but as yet there is no liquid volatility market for these structures.

3 OTHER COPULA MODELS

A major concern with the Gaussian copula is its inability to calibrate to market prices. Researchers have developed a menagerie of different copula models in the hope that one or other will better fit the observed market prices. Simple variants of the standard elliptic and Archimedean copulas such as the t-copula (Mashal, Naldi, and Zeevi 2003) do not generally achieve results significantly different from the Gaussian copula. Although these copulas look superficially promising since some of the standard statistical measures of co-dependence (Kendall's Tau, Spearman's Rho, Tail Dependence (Embrechts, Lindskog, and McNeil 2003)) are higher than in the Gaussian copula, these measures do not seem to be good indicators of their capacity to fit the loss distribution. The generally upward sloping nature of the correlation skew expresses the fact that in less distressed states of the world (low attachment points) risk is predominantly idiosyncratic i.e. uncorrelated, and in more distressed states of the world it is predominantly systemic i.e. highly correlated. This is demonstrated graphically in Figure 7.7 where we show the loss distribution that is implied by ITX tranche quotes compared to those implied by the Gaussian copula with various flat correlation assumptions. The standard copula models generally cannot capture this behaviour due to their simple parametric form: those copulas that calibrate more successfully usually do so by, in one way or another, parameterizing these different states of the world.

One of the simplest and most intuitive approaches is the Composite Basket Model (Tavares, Nguyen, and Vaysburd 2004), in which the single-name conditional survival probability $S_i(T)$ is factorized into a term $S^{\text{syst}}(T)$ driven by a systemic (Poisson) shock that causes all credits to default with probability $1 - S^{\text{syst}}(T)$, a purely idiosyncratic part $S_i^{\text{idio}}(T)$, and a term correlated using the Gaussian copula $S_i^{GC}(T)$:

$$S_i(T) = S_i^{GC}(T) S_i^{\text{idio}}(T) S^{\text{syst}}(T)$$

$$S_i(T|Y) = S_i^{GC}(T|Y) S_i^{\text{idio}}(T) S^{\text{syst}}(T)$$

$$S_i^{GC}(T|Y) = N\left(\frac{N^{-1}\left(S_i^{GC}(T)\right) - \sqrt{\rho}Y}{\sqrt{1-\rho}} \right) \qquad (56)$$

This certainly accomplishes the goal of a loss distribution with an idiosyncratically uncorrelated lower part and a highly correlated upper part and is a relatively simple generalization of the Gaussian copula. Other variations on this theme include the double-t copula (Hull and White 2004) and various mixture models such as Burtschell, Gregory, and Laurent (2007), where eq. (55) is generalized so that the correlation ρ becomes a random variable $\tilde{\rho}_i$ independent of the Gaussian variables Y and X_i:

$$Z^i = \sqrt{\tilde{\rho}_i} Y + \sqrt{1 - \tilde{\rho}_i} X^i$$

$$\tilde{\rho}_i \in [0, 1] \tag{57}$$

The random factor loading model (RFL) (Andersen and Sidenius 2004) achieves the same thing by introducing a varying weighting on the central shock factor, so that eq. (55) is generalized to:

$$Z^i = a_i(Y)Y + v_i X^i + m_i \tag{58}$$

where Y and X_i are uncorrelated N(0,1) variables as before, and the coefficients m_i and v_i are used to ensure that Z^i has a mean of 0 and a variance of 1 for a given choice of function $a_i(Y)$.

The ultimate non-parametric development of this theme is the 'implied copula' (Hull and White 2006) (originally hubristically named the 'perfect copula') in which the central shock factor Y is assumed to have a discrete distribution with probabilities $\pi_i = \text{Prob}(Y = Y_i)$, and the single-name conditional survival probability $S_{ij}(T) = S_i(T|Y = Y_j)$ satisfies the following constraints:

$$\sum_j \pi_j S_{ij}(T) = S_i(T) \tag{59}$$

$$\sum_j \pi_j = 1 \tag{60}$$

where $\{0 \le S_{ij}(T) \le 1\}$ and $\{0 \le \pi_i \le 1\}$. All copula models of the central shock variety can be thought of abstractly in this way: either as a truly discrete model or as an integral quadrature of a continuous one. This totally non-parametric approach does not constrain $S_{ij}(T)$ to have an arbitrary functional form, which means that if this model cannot be calibrated to a set of market quotes it is unlikely that any more rigidly parameterized model can be. The difficulty with this extremely general formulation is that it has too many degrees of freedom: additional constraints need to be applied. These could include smoothness or relative entropy criteria, or formulating it in a more parametric way (Hull and White 2009).

The static limit of the factor model of Inglis and Lipton (Inglis and Lipton 2007; Inglis, Lipton, and Sepp 2009) can be viewed as a similar specification with a convenient parametric form. In this model we again adopt a central shock factor with discrete distribution $\pi_i = \text{Prob}(Y = Y_i)$ but we represent the conditional survival probability in terms of the logit function:

$$S_i(T|Y = Y_j) = \frac{1}{1 + e^{Y_j + \Theta_T^i}} \tag{61}$$

For a given set of $\{Y_j, \pi_j\}$ the function Θ_T^i must be calibrated to ensure that the survival probability of credit i is correctly reproduced:

$$\sum_j \pi_j \frac{1}{1 + e^{Y_j + \Theta_T^i}} = S_i(T) \tag{62}$$

The chosen functional form means that it is guaranteed that a solution Θ_T^i can be found. In the parameterization given in Inglis and Lipton (2007) it was assumed that there were only four states of the world $j = 0, 1, 2, 3$. They further impose that $Y_0 = 0$ and $Y_3 = \infty$ and the constraint that all the probabilities must sum to 1:

$$\sum_{j=0}^{j=3} \pi_j = 1 \tag{63}$$

This parsimonious specification leaves us with five free parameters: $Y_1, Y_2, \pi_0, \pi_1, \pi_2$ which is conveniently equal to the number of index tranche quotes at a single maturity. To calibrate the survival probabilities of individual names, we make the substitution $Z = e^{\Theta_T^i}$ in equation (62) at which point it becomes a simple cubic equation that can be solved via the Cardano formula.

In general, many of these central shock based approaches can do a pretty good job of calibrating to market prices at a single time horizon. However, on CDX and ITX several maturities now trade, with varying degrees of liquidity (typically 3y, 5y, 7y, and 10y): most of the few parameter copula models simply lack sufficient degrees of freedom to accurately calibrate to this term structure. Often only the implied copula and the static limit of Inglis and Lipton (2007) have sufficient parametric freedom to perfectly match prices. It could be argued that for the most non-parametric approaches this is only achieved at the cost of introducing more parameters than observables and hence the model is over-fitted, with limited explanatory power.

We briefly mention another important and fundamentally different approach: the Marshall-Olkin copula, defined based on the multivariate exponential distribution (Duffie and Pan 2001; Lindskog and McNeil 2003), in which defaults of credits in a portfolio are driven by various Poisson processes. Conditional on a given Poisson event each of the underlying credits has a certain probability of defaulting depending upon the value of an independent Bernoulli variable. In this model there can be Poisson processes driving the default of entire sectors, regions, or even the entire financial system, as well as idiosyncratic default. As a result high correlation may be achieved but there are a large number of parameters that cannot easily be constrained by financial observables.

Ultimately, the development of base correlations described in the next section extended the shelf life of the Gaussian copula by introducing a 'skew' and a heuristic mapping to bespoke portfolios, which meant that for a while at least, calibrating to market prices and pricing bespoke tranches was no longer a problem. The fact remains that pricing non-standard payoffs such as CDO-Squared and valuing bespokes in a theoretically consistent way does necessitate a new and improved modelling approach, but the industry has yet to reach consensus on what form this may take.

4 BASE CORRELATIONS

As we have mentioned, the Gaussian copula cannot simultaneously calibrate to all the tranche prices that are observed in the market with a single correlation parameter. Once again, a de facto market standard has developed, known as base correlations (McGinty et al. 2004). This is based on the fact that the loss on a tranche can be decomposed into a linear combination of the loss on two equity tranches:

$$\hat{L}_T(K_1, K_2) = \min(L_T, K_2) - \min(L_T, K_1) \tag{64}$$

$$= \hat{L}_T(0, K_2) - \hat{L}_T(0, K_1) \tag{65}$$

Denoting the expected loss on an equity tranche by $\hat{l}_T(0, K) = \mathbb{E}\left[\min(L_T, K)\right]$ we can derive the following relationship between the equity tranche expected loss and the loss distribution:

$$\frac{\partial}{\partial K}\hat{l}_T(0, K) = \frac{\partial}{\partial K}\int_0^\infty \varphi(L_T)\min(L_T, K)dL_T \tag{66}$$

$$= \int_K^\infty \varphi(L_T)dL_T = \mathrm{Prob}(L_T > K) \tag{67}$$

where $\varphi(L_T)$ is the loss density at time T. Hence the equity tranche expected loss can be represented as an integral of the cumulative loss probability:

$$\hat{l}_T(0, K) = \int_0^K \mathrm{Prob}(L_T > K')dK' \tag{68}$$

Thus parameterizing the expected loss on equity tranches can be viewed as a way of parameterizing the loss distribution on the portfolio. The base correlation methodology parameterizes the prices of equity tranches by introducing a correlation skew $\rho(T, K)$. If we view the expected loss on an equity tranche as a function of this correlation $\hat{l}_T(0, K; \rho(T, K))$, the expected loss on a mezzanine tranche with attachment point K_1 and detachment point K_2 is represented as a difference of two equity tranche expected losses evaluated with different correlations $\rho_1 = \rho(T, K_1)$ and $\rho_2 = \rho(T, K_2)$:

$$\hat{l}_T(K_1, K_2) = \hat{l}_T(0, K_2; \rho_2) - \hat{l}_T(0, K_1; \rho_1) \tag{69}$$

This is the equivalent of the well-known volatility smile extension of Black-Scholes, whose theoretical justification is also based on the relationship between option prices and the probability distribution. As in the case of options, there are a couple of conditions for the absence of arbitrage, the 'butterfly condition' (non-negative density), and the 'calendar spread' condition (probability that loss exceeds a given level is a non-decreasing function of time):

$$\frac{\partial}{\partial K}\text{Prob}(L_T > K) = \frac{\partial^2}{\partial K^2}\hat{l}_T(0, K; \rho(T, K)) \qquad \leq 0 \text{ - Butterfly} \qquad (70)$$

$$\frac{\partial}{\partial T}\text{Prob}(L_T > K) = \frac{\partial^2}{\partial K \partial T}\hat{l}_T(0, K; \rho(T, K)) \qquad \geq 0 \text{ - Calendar Spread} \qquad (71)$$

These do not translate in any very simple way to conditions on the form of $\rho(T, K)$ although it is straightforward to check after the fact whether or not a chosen interpolation leads to arbitrage-free prices. It is usual to interpolate ρ using a cubic or tension spline: since the loss density is related to the 2nd derivative of the expected loss, in order for the implied density to be 0th order continuous, the correlation must be 2nd order continuous in attachment point K. Although it is reasonable to question whether or not a given interpolation implies a theoretical arbitrage, this is usually only a significant practical concern for the pricing of very narrow tranches or 'tranchelets', which are by their nature very sensitive to the chosen interpolation of the correlation skew. For this reason although attempts were made by some dealers to develop a market in tranchelets (Muench and Sbityakov 2006; Davies 2006), because of the high degree of pricing uncertainty most dealers ultimately decided not to participate (although hedge funds were enthusiastic at yet another opportunity to pick off dealers who had not thought carefully enough about interpolation).

If one accepts this approach, since the value of a tranche involves integrals over the loss distributions to all maturities up to the maturity of the tranche, technically when valuing a tranche one should evaluate the loss distribution at each maturity with the correct interpolated correlation from a surface. This would ensure, for example that the first five years of a seven-year tranche were priced completely consistently with a five-year maturity tranche. This full term-structure approach was explored in Pain, Renault, and Shelton (2005). However, in practice the market standard approach is to do a completely independent calibration to each maturity. In Figure 7.6 we give an example base correlation calibration to the quotes given in Table 7.2.

Although the approach outlined here does make some theoretical sense, there are definitely concerns. It can be shown that introducing a time-dependent correlation in the Gaussian copula model of necessity implies arbitrage of the calendar-spread variety at some point in the capital structure (unlike the option analogy where introducing time-dependent volatility, providing it does not imply negative forward variances, does not cause any fundamental problem). Thus introducing a full term-structure surface of correlation could be said to represent tranche prices as differences of arbitrageable prices. The argument for sweeping this objection under the carpet would be that the risk in tranches is usually mostly in the maturity bucket, so some inconsistency across time may be liveable with. It is also true that skews are usually introduced on the grounds that they are relatively small corrections to a fundamentally reasonable financial model. But the correlation skew in the CDO market is so pronounced that it is a stretch to view it in this way. In Figure 7.7 we plot the cumulative probability

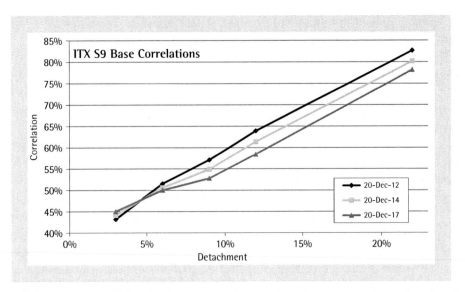

FIGURE 7.6 Base Correlation Calibration to ITX Tranches (June 2009, calibrated to data in Table 7.2).

Source: BofA Merrill Lynch Global Research.

distribution calculated from the correlation skew in Figure 7.6 using equation (67) and some interpolation assumptions (the loss distribution is not uniquely determined by the tranche quotes: there are infinitely many possible distributions corresponding to different interpolation assumptions). It reinforces the fact that the distribution we are trying to calibrate is not close to a Gaussian copula loss distribution for any flat value of the correlation. Finally, if we really question the financial basis of this approach, we

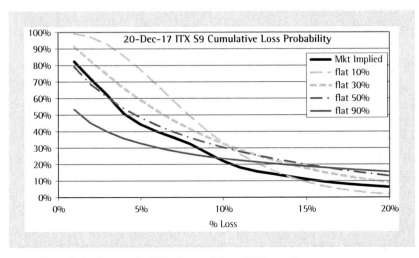

FIGURE 7.7 Cumulative loss probability implied from ITX tranche quotes.

Source: BofA Merrill Lynch Global Research.

are forced once more to admit that the correlation parameter has limited meaning, since it is not simply related to the correlation of any observables (again, in contrast to the case of options where volatility has a well-defined meaning in terms of market observables).

5 PRICING BESPOKE CDOS: CORRELATION 'MAPPING'

Overall, if this framework were only applied to the pricing and risk management of index tranches, it would probably be adequate for the purpose as long as it could calibrate all the standard market instruments, since flow traders generally run relatively flat books.

A major question though, is how to price 'bespoke' tranches with non-standard attachment points, maturities, and underlying portfolios. The desks that trade these 'structured products' have to manage extremely complex multi-dimensional and non-linear risk positions. Generally such desks are buyers of bespoke protection from investors, and must hedge this correlation exposure by selling index tranche protection. A number of different heuristic approaches to pricing bespokes have been developed. These define a 'mapping' between the correlation skew on an index and the correlation skew on a bespoke portfolio: by evaluating the first-order correlation risk of a given bespoke tranche with respect to the skew on the index according to this prescription, we can also determine hedge ratios of index tranches that will theoretically hedge the bespoke correlation exposure. Since such procedures make rather heroic assumptions about the relationship between index and bespoke tranches there are major questions as to the stability and appropriateness of these hedge ratios in practice.

We denote the correlation corresponding to attachment point $K_{\tilde{\pi}}$ on bespoke portfolio $\tilde{\pi}$ by $\tilde{\rho}(K_{\tilde{\pi}}; \tilde{\pi})$, and the correlation corresponding to attachment point K_{π} on the index portfolio π by $\rho(K_{\pi}; \pi)$. The simplest mapping prescription is given by the so-called portfolio expected loss mapping:

$$\tilde{\rho}(K_{\tilde{\pi}}; \tilde{\pi}) = \rho\left(K_{\tilde{\pi}}\frac{L_{\pi}}{L_{\tilde{\pi}}}; \pi\right) \tag{72}$$

where L_{π} and $L_{\tilde{\pi}}$ are the expected losses on the index and bespoke portfolios respectively to the maturity in question. The analogy that is appealed to here is the 'moneyness' of an option. Hence the 7% attachment point on a portfolio with high expected loss may end up mapping to the 3% attachment point on an index portfolio, because the 7% attachment on the bespoke portfolio is more 'equity-like' (likely to be hit) and hence more comparable to an equity tranche on the index.

Another widely used method is the tranche expected loss mapping method, in which we solve for K_π such that:

$$\frac{\hat{l}_{\tilde{\pi}}(0, K_{\tilde{\pi}}; \rho(K_\pi; \pi))}{L_{\tilde{\pi}}} = \frac{\hat{l}_\pi(0, K_\pi; \rho(K_\pi; \pi))}{L_\pi} \tag{73}$$

and then set $\tilde{\rho}(K_{\tilde{\pi}}; \tilde{\pi}) = \rho(K_\pi; \pi)$, where $\hat{l}_\pi(0, K; \rho)$ denotes the expected loss on an equity tranche on portfolio π with detachment point K evaluated with a correlation ρ. The intuition here is that we solve for the detachment point K_π on the index portfolio π for which the equity tranche expected loss as a percentage of portfolio expected loss is equal to the corresponding ratio on the bespoke portfolio—again a 'moneyness' argument (the financial institution that first promoted this method (Reyfman, Ushakova, and Kong 2004) no longer exists: we allow the reader to draw their own conclusions from this fact).

A related method is based on the probability $\mathrm{Prob}\,(L_\pi > K) = \partial \hat{l}_\pi(0, K; \rho)/\partial K$. Here we solve for K_π such that:

$$\frac{\partial \hat{l}_{\tilde{\pi}}(0, K_{\tilde{\pi}}; \rho(K_\pi; \pi))}{\partial K_{\tilde{\pi}}}\Big|_\rho = \frac{\partial \hat{l}_\pi(0, K_\pi; \rho(K_\pi; \pi))}{\partial K_\pi}\Big|_\rho \tag{74}$$

and once again set $\tilde{\rho}(K_{\tilde{\pi}}; \tilde{\pi}) = \rho(K_\pi; \pi)$. For the purposes of this method, when we evaluate the derivative with respect to K_π, we hold correlation fixed. Thus the probabilities referred to here are not the actual probabilities implied by the market correlation skew, which would include a term coming from the dependence of correlation on detachment point:

$$\frac{\partial \hat{l}_\pi(0, K_\pi; \rho(K_\pi; \pi))}{\partial K_\pi} = \frac{\partial \hat{l}_\pi(0, K_\pi; \rho(K_\pi; \pi))}{\partial K_\pi}\Big|_\rho + \frac{\partial \hat{l}_\pi(0, K_\pi; \rho(K_\pi; \pi))}{\partial \rho}\Big|_{K_\pi} \times \frac{\partial \rho}{\partial K_\pi} \tag{75}$$

We have glossed over the fact that there are a host of additional choices that need to be made, such as which index or indices a given bespoke portfolio should map to: given that it may contain both European and US credits, should it map to ITX, CDX, or a combination of both? Should this decision be based on regional composition or portfolio average spread, and how should correlations from more than one index be combined? How should we interpolate across time, and should the various losses be discounted or undiscounted? We have not elaborated on these points since to our knowledge, there is a lack of compelling financial argument for one approach over another.

All of these approaches are quasi-static rules, glorified interpolations, originally derived in a market when spreads were very low and inhomogeneities between different portfolios were minimal. In the current environment where large bases have opened up between riskier bespoke portfolios and the index, several difficulties have arisen. From a hedging point of view, the fact that a senior tranche of a bespoke portfolio may map to a much more junior tranche on the index has led some to question the correlation hedge ratios implied by these assumptions. The stability of these hedge ratios is also questionable: as the ratio of the expected loss on the bespoke to the index moves around, correlation hedges may flip from one detachment point bucket to another, hence if the strategy is followed religiously, high hedging costs will result. In general, the significant basis risk between index and bespoke portfolios is very difficult to risk manage.

In defence of these mapping approaches, qualitatively it makes sense that the correlation skew on bespoke portfolios should tend to flatten out as the portfolio becomes riskier. The argument is that the value of senior tranches like 30–100% should depend less on portfolio composition than junior tranches, because their value reflects systemic rather than idiosyncratic risk. If we were to assume that 30–100% tranches on all portfolios had the same price, this would immediately imply a lower 30% correlation on riskier portfolios than on the index. Parametrically, perhaps it would be better to try and parameterize this along the correlation axis rather than the strike axis so that senior tranches did not end up mapping to such junior tranches. Although this all makes qualitative sense, tranches are essentially call spreads on the loss, so their value is very sensitive to the quantitative details of how the correlation is interpolated: relatively small changes in the slope of the skew may translate into large pricing differences.

In view of the limitations of these approaches, dealers have considered various other initiatives. Markets in tranches on bespoke portfolios are intermittently offered in the broker market. Attempts were made to create a market in a standard set of tranches on a portfolio (STD1) closer to typical bespoke portfolios than the index. Another source of price information is the monthly Markit pricing exercise in which submissions from a range of dealers are combined anonymously to give a consensus view on bespoke CDO prices. In all these cases, it could be questioned whether the prices determined in this way represent true clearing prices, since the volumes are very limited.

Although it has received little attention in the academic literature, pricing and hedging bespoke tranches is one of the most important and difficult problems facing the industry. It has been proposed that models such as some of those discussed in a previous section (Hull and White 2009; Inglis and Lipton 2007) once successfully calibrated to index tranche prices can be used to extrapolate to bespokes. However, although this does have the virtue of theoretical consistency, relatively little has been published on the viability of this approach as a pricing methodology, and nothing on the hedging implications, i.e. how successfully a bespoke tranche may be dynamically correlation hedged with index tranches.

The market practice for risk managing bespoke tranches is to correlation hedge with index tranches and delta hedge the remaining spread risk to the underlying single-name CDS. In Figure 7.8 we show a scatter plot of single-name spread risk for ITX tranches against the spread of the underlying names (spread risk is here defined to be $\partial V/\partial S_i$ where S_i is the single-name spread for credit i). It shows how more senior tranches exhibit greater risk to tighter spread names and vice versa. In view of the non-linear nature of the payoff and its significant convexity and cross-convexity, dynamically hedging is a daunting prospect.

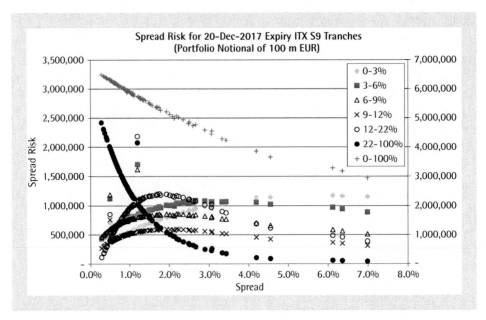

FIGURE 7.8 Scatter plot of single-name spread risk of ITX tranches against underlying single-name spreads (June 2009). For clarity, risk for tranches with a detachment point of 100% are plotted on the right hand axis, all other tranches correspond to the left-hand axis.

Source: BofA Merrill Lynch Global Research.

6 DEVELOPMENTS SINCE THE GAUSSIAN COPULA AND BASE CORRELATIONS

As we have discussed, the approach of employing the Gaussian copula with base correlations and various mapping methodologies is not totally satisfactory from a financial or theoretical point of view. However, it has proved very difficult to improve upon. Generally, in order to achieve widespread acceptance, models need to either be extremely simple, with well-understood limitations (such as Black-Scholes-Merton (Black and Scholes 1973)) or complex, but with such compelling financial underpinning that the implementational difficulty is worth overcoming (such as the Heath-Jarrow-Morton model for interest rates (Heath, Jarrow, and Morton 1992)). Unfortunately, most proposals for solving the current problem have been both highly complex and lacking in financial basis, i.e. not deriving from a convincing hedging argument.

Such failings are not surprising, however, in light of the complexity of the problem we are trying to solve. To make the analogy with options, it is like trying to derive a model for options on the S&P500 which incorporates sensitivities and a stochastic process for every single underlying stock. It is compounded by the fact that tranches are effectively tight call-spreads on the underlying, so just modelling the first few moments of the distribution (as commonly done for basket options and dispersion trades) does not necessarily approximate tranche prices accurately.

The approaches to solving this problem broadly fall into two categories: 'bottom-up' and 'top-down'. Bottom-up models propose an ambitious programme of modelling every single underlying credit in detail, and combining these to derive the overall behaviour of the portfolio. Here the problem is the sheer complexity and number of parameters, as well as implementational difficulties due to high dimensionality. Top-down models aim to be more tractable by proposing a simplified process for the loss on the portfolio. This reduces the dimensionality of the problem but unavoidably discards some granularity. Since in credit we generally care a great deal about the precise composition of a portfolio, there is a danger that this approach throws out the baby along with the bathwater (there is a big difference between a portfolio of 99 credits trading at 100bp and 1 at 10,000bp, and a portfolio of 100 credits all with a spread of 199bp even though both have the same average spread and hence the same instantaneous rate of expected loss).

6.1 Bottom-up models

The reduced form framework we discussed earlier in the context of single-name products can be expanded in various ways and used as a basis for several coherent intensity based models for credit baskets (Duffie and Garleanu 2001; Mortensen 2006; Chapovsky, Rennie, and Tavares 2001; Inglis and Lipton 2007; Inglis, Lipton, and Sepp 2009; Inglis et al. 2008).

To start we briefly summarize the affine jump-diffusion (AJD) model of Duffie-Garleanu (2001) and (2006). Consider a basket of N names with equal unit notionals and equal recoveries R. Let us assume that the corresponding default intensities can be decomposed as follows:

$$X_i(t) = \beta_i X_c(t) + \tilde{X}_i(t) \tag{76}$$

where, generalizing (10), X_c is the common intensity driven by the following SDE:

$$dX_c(t) = \kappa_c \left(\theta_c - X_c(t)\right) dt + \sigma_c \sqrt{X_c(t)} dW_c(t) + J_c dN_c(t)$$
$$X_c(0) = X_{c0} \tag{77}$$

while the $\left\{\tilde{X}_i(t)\right\}$ are idiosyncratic intensities driven by similar SDEs:

$$d\tilde{X}_i(t) = \kappa_i \left(\theta_i - \tilde{X}_i(t)\right) dt + \sigma_i \sqrt{\tilde{X}_i(t)} dW_i(t) + \tilde{J}_i dN_i(t)$$
$$\tilde{X}_i(0) = \tilde{X}_{i0} \tag{78}$$

where $1 \le i \le N$ and the processes $\left\{\tilde{X}_i(t)\right\}$, $X_c(t)$ are assumed to be independent. In this formulation the rôle of the β_i is similar to the β_i appearing in the capital asset pricing model (CAPM). We note that θ_c, θ_i are assumed to be constant. In the original Duffie-Garleanu formulation it was assumed that all $\beta_i = 1$. However, this assumption is very restrictive since it limits the magnitude of the common factor by the size of the lowest intensity X_i, so that high correlation cannot in general be achieved. It was lifted in the subsequent paper by Mortensen (Mortensen 2006). Of course to preserve analyticity, it is necessary to impose very rigid conditions on the coefficients of the corresponding SDEs, since in general, the sum of two affine processes is not an affine process. Specifically the following needs to hold:

$$\kappa_i = \kappa_c = \kappa, \quad \sigma_i = \sqrt{\beta_i}\sigma_c, \quad \nu_i = \nu, \quad J_{im} = \beta_i J_{cm} \tag{79}$$

Even when the above constraints are satisfied, there are too many free parameters in the model. A reduction in their number is achieved by imposing the following constraints:

$$\frac{\beta_i \theta_c}{\beta_i \theta_c + \theta_i} = \frac{\nu_c}{\nu_c + \nu} = \frac{X_c(0)}{X_c(0) + X_{\text{ave}}(0)} = \omega \tag{80}$$

where ω is a correlation-like parameter representing the systematic share of intensities, and X_{ave} is the average of the $X_i(0)$. When ω is low, the dynamics of intensities is predominantly idiosyncratic, and it is systemic when ω is close to 1. Provided that (79) is true, the affine ansatz (cf. (11),(20)) still holds so that survival probabilities of individual names can be written in the form:

$$S_i(t, T | X_i(t)) = \mathbb{1}_{\tau_i > t} \mathbb{E}_t \left[e^{-\int_t^T X_i(u)du} \Big| X_i(t) \right]$$

$$= \mathbb{1}_{\tau_i > t} \mathbb{E}_t \left[e^{-\beta_i(Y_c(T) - Y_c(t))} \Big| X_c(t) \right]$$

$$\times \mathbb{E}_t \left[e^{-(\tilde{Y}_i(T) - \tilde{Y}_i(t))} \Big| \tilde{X}_i(t) \right]$$

$$= \mathbb{1}_{\tau_i > t} e^{a_c(t, T, \beta_i) + b_c(t, T, \beta_i) X_c(t) + a_i(t, T, 1) + b_i(t, T, 1) \tilde{X}_i(t)} \tag{81}$$

where we have defined $Y_c(T) = \int_0^T X_c(s)ds$, $\tilde{Y}_i(T) = \int_0^T \tilde{X}_i(s)ds$ as in (12). Moreover, conditioning the dynamics of spreads on the common factor $Y_c(T)$ we can write the idiosyncratic survival probabilities as follows:

$$S_i\left(t, T \Big| \tilde{X}_i(t), Y_c(T)\right) = \mathbb{1}_{\tau_i > t} e^{-\beta_i(Y_c(T) - Y_c(t)) + a_i(t, T, 1) + b_i(t, T, 1) \tilde{X}_i(t)}$$

$$S_i\left(0, T \Big| \tilde{X}_{i0}, Y_c(T)\right) = \mathbb{1}_{\tau_i > 0} e^{-\beta_i Y_c(T) + a_i(0, T, 1) + b_i(0, T, 1) \tilde{X}_{i0}} \tag{82}$$

First we perform the $t = 0$ calibration of the model parameters to fit 1Y and 5Y CDS spreads for individual names. Once this calibration is performed, we can apply a variety of numerical techniques, including the recursion method described in a later section, and calculate the conditional probability of default of exactly n names, $0 \leq n \leq N$ in the corresponding portfolio, which we denote $p(0, T, n | Y_c)$. In order to find the unconditional expectation, we need to integrate the conditional expectation $p(0, T, n | Y_c)$ with respect to the distribution $f(Y_c)$ of $Y_c(T)$.

Two models without stochastic idiosyncratic components were independently proposed in the literature. The first (Chapovsky, Rennie, and Tavares 2001) assumes purely deterministic idiosyncratic components and represents S_i as follows:

$$S_i (0, T | Y_c(T)) = e^{-\beta_i Y_c(T) + \xi_i(T)} \tag{83}$$

where X_c, Y_c are driven by SDEs (8), (13) and $\xi(T)$ is calibrated to the survival probabilities of individual names. The second (Inglis and Lipton 2007) models conditional survival probabilities directly, and postulates that S_i can be represented in logit form:

$$S_i (0, T | Y_c(T)) = \psi (Y_c(T) + \chi_i(T)) \tag{84}$$

$$S_i (0, T) = \mathbb{E}_0 \left[\psi (Y_c(T) + \chi_i(T)) \right] \tag{85}$$

where $\psi(Y)$ is the logit function:

$$\psi(Y) = \frac{1}{1 + e^Y} \tag{86}$$

To calibrate this model to CDS spreads, we need to solve the following pricing problem:

$$V_t + \hat{\mathcal{L}}V + X V_Y(t, X, Y) = 0 \tag{87}$$

$$V(T, X, Y) = \frac{1}{1 + e^Y} \tag{88}$$

where similarly to (15):

$$\hat{\mathcal{L}}V \equiv f(t, X)V_X + \frac{1}{2}g^2(t, X)V_{XX} + \nu \sum_m \pi_m (V (X + J_m) - V (X)) \tag{89}$$

A convenient feature of this model is that since $\hat{\mathcal{L}}$ is invariant under the substitution $Y \to Y' = Y - \chi_i(T)$ the CDS spreads can be calibrated by solving the following algebraic equations for the $\chi_i(T)$ (rather than having to solve multiple PDEs repeatedly):

$$V(0, 0, \chi_i(T)) = S_i(0, T) \tag{90}$$

The reason that we chose the logit function for $\psi(Y)$ rather than another functional form such as e^{-Y} now becomes clear, since:

$$\lim_{\chi_i \to \infty} \psi (Y + \chi) = 0$$

$$\lim_{\chi_i \to -\infty} \psi (Y + \chi) = 1$$

$$0 \le \psi (Y + \chi) \le 1 \tag{91}$$

We can thus guarantee that it is always possible to find a solution to (90), and that the resulting conditional probabilities are always between 0 and 1 (this would clearly not be the case if an exponential function had been chosen).

The calibration of the survival probabilities can be achieved by a backward induction procedure, thus determining the time 0 value of V at all initial values of Y, and then repeatedly solving the algebraic equation (90). To calibrate the survival probability to n time horizons in this way necessitates performing n backward inductions. Alternatively, solving the forward version of (87) for the Arrow-Debreu security:

$$U(T, x, y|t, w, z) = \mathbb{E}\left[\delta(X_T - x)\delta(Y_T - y)\big| X_t = w, Y_t = z\right] \qquad (92)$$

$$-U_T + \hat{\mathcal{L}}^* U - XU_Y(T, X, Y) = 0 \qquad (93)$$

where:

$$\hat{\mathcal{L}}^* U \equiv -f(T, X)U_X + \frac{1}{2}\partial_{XX}\left((g^2(T, X)U)\right) + \nu\sum_m \pi_m\left(U(X - J_m) - U(X)\right) \quad (94)$$

and solving at each time horizon repeatedly for the $\chi_i(T)$ such that:

$$\int\left(\int U(T, x, y|0, 0, 0)\,dx\right)\psi(y + \chi_i(T))dy = S_i(0, T) \qquad (95)$$

we can perform a single forward induction procedure, but now have to solve the discretized integral equation (95) for each credit at each of the n time horizons. Which approach is more efficient may depend on the discretization used.

When it comes to evaluating the tranche expected loss for a given portfolio to time horizon T, the same forward induction procedure may be used to determine the distribution $\int U(T, x, y|0, 0, 0)\,dx$ of Y_T. Default events on the portfolio are independent conditional on Y_T, each credit's conditional survival probability is given by (84) and hence standard numerical techniques such as recursion, which will be covered in a later section, can be applied to determine the loss distribution.

Finally, we note that in this formalism we can also define conditional survival probabilities of individual names from t to T as follows:

$$S_i(t, T|X_t, Y_t) = \mathbb{1}_{\tau_i > t}\mathbb{E}\left[\frac{\psi(Y_T + \chi_i(T))}{\psi(Y_t + \chi_i(t))}\bigg| \mathcal{F}_t^{X,Y}\right] \qquad (96)$$

where $\mathcal{F}_t^{X,Y}$ denotes the filtration associated with the process X_t, Y_t.

Since the main motivation for introducing dynamic models of this type is to enable the valuation of contingent payoffs such as options, it is essential to be able to evaluate the survival probabilities conditional on $\mathcal{F}_t^{X,Y}$. There are still problems of dimensionality since the state of default of a portfolio of size n is represented by an n-dimensional vector and can attain 2^n values. It is for this reason that top-down models opt to simplify the problem further by projecting this complex default state into a single state variable representing the total loss on the portfolio, with an inevitable loss of information, as we will see in the next section.

As a final footnote, we briefly mention the fact that there have also been a number of attempts to model default correlation via Lévy intensity processes. Since the high observed default correlations seem to necessitate jumps, some authors have directly employed processes such as gamma or variance-gamma in both reduced form

(Joshi and Stacey 2005) and hybrid (Baxter 2007; Luciano and Schoutens 2006; Moos-brucker 2006) approaches to model this. Some success has been achieved at calibrating to the market prices of index tranches, albeit imperfectly, but there remain significant difficulties of implementation, and it is not clear that they can be applied to pricing contingent (volatility-dependent) payoffs in their current form.

6.2 Top-down models

Suppose that the state of loss on a portfolio of N_c credits can entirely be characterized by the number of defaults $0 \leq N_t \leq N_c$. In making this assumption we have discarded detailed information about the portfolio, such as which credits have defaulted and which still survive. We wish to model the evolution of the loss distribution to time T given the state at the current time t:

$$p_{n|m}(t, T) = \mathbb{E}_t \left[\mathbb{1}_{N_T=n} \middle| N_t = m \right] \tag{97}$$

Since N_T is an increasing process, we can assert the following identity:

$$\text{Prob} \left(N_t \leq N_T \leq N_{T+\Delta T} \right) = 1$$

$$\sum_{l=N_t}^{l=N_{T+\Delta T}} \mathbb{1}_{N_T=l} = 1 \tag{98}$$

Hence:

$$p_{n|m}(t, T + \Delta T) = \mathbb{E}_t \left[\mathbb{1}_{N_{T+\Delta T}=n} \middle| N_t = m \right]$$

$$= \mathbb{E}_t \left[\mathbb{1}_{N_{T+\Delta T}=n} \sum_{l=N_t}^{l=n} \mathbb{1}_{N_T=l} \middle| N_t = m \right]$$

$$= \sum_{l=N_t}^{l=n} q_{t,T} \left(n|l \right) p_{l|m}(t, T) \tag{99}$$

where:

$$q_{t,T} \left(n|l \right) = \frac{\mathbb{E}_t \left[\mathbb{1}_{N_{T+\Delta T}=n} \mathbb{1}_{N_T=l} \middle| N_t = m \right]}{\mathbb{E}_t \left[\mathbb{1}_{N_T=l} \middle| N_t = m \right]}$$

$$= \mathbb{E}_t \left[\mathbb{1}_{N_{T+\Delta T}=n} \middle| N_T = l, N_t = m \right]$$

$$= \text{Prob} \left(N_{T+\Delta T} = n | N_T = l, N_t = m \right) \tag{100}$$

We assume that the loss is a Markov process and hence there is no explicit dependence upon $N_t = m$ in the expression for $q_{t,T} \left(n|l \right)$, and that the rate of default is finite i.e. for $n \neq l$:

$$q_{t,T}(n|l) = \mathbb{1}_{l<n} a_{ln}(t, T)\Delta T + O(\Delta T^2) \tag{101}$$

where the a_{ln} are finite and non-negative. Note that even if the 'real' underlying process we are calibrating the model to is non-Markovian, or not top-down in nature, we should be still able to calibrate a model of this type if the loss distribution is arbitrage free (Cont and Minca 2008; Cont and Savescu 2008). This is because we only had to apply very limited no-arbitrage assumptions in order to arrive at (99), (101). By conservation of probability:

$$\sum_{l'\geq n} q_{t,T}(l'|n) = 1 \tag{102}$$

Therefore we must have the following expression for $q_{t,T}(n|n)$:

$$q_{t,T}(n|n) = 1 - \sum_{l'>n} q_{t,T}(l'|n)$$

$$= 1 - \sum_{l'>n} a_{nl'}\Delta T \tag{103}$$

Then, taking the limit $\Delta T \to 0$ we arrive at the following system of coupled ordinary differential (forward) Chapman-Kolmogorov equations for the continuous time Markov chain:

$$\frac{dp_{n|m}(t, T)}{dT} = \sum_{l<n} a_{ln}(t, T)p_{l|m}(t, T) - \sum_{l'>n} a_{nl'}(t, T)p_{n|m}(t, T) \tag{104}$$

Via similar arguments we can arrive at the corresponding backward equation:

$$-\frac{dp_{n|m}(t, T)}{dt} = \sum_{l>m} a_{ml}(t, t)p_{n|l}(t, T) - \sum_{l>m} a_{ml}(t, t)p_{n|m}(t, T) \tag{105}$$

Although the formal solution to these equations may be written down explicitly in some cases (Schönbucher 2005), in practice it is often more efficient to solve them numerically (using an implicit finite difference method in order to ensure unconditional stability).

Given this starting point, various different model specifications have been explored. Assuming no simultaneous defaults i.e.:

$$\lim_{\Delta T \to 0} \mathbb{E}_t\left[\mathbb{1}_{N_{T+\Delta T}-N_T>1}\right] \propto O\left(\Delta T^2\right)$$

$$a_{ln}(t, T) = \mathbb{1}_{l<N_c}\delta_{n,l+1}a_l(t, T) \tag{106}$$

we arrive at the approach of (Schönbucher 2005). He proposes a way of augmenting this simple Markov chain so that the transition rates $a_l(t, T)$ can be made stochastic and derives a formal expression for the necessary drift adjustments à la HJM (Heath, Jarrow, and Morton 1992).

The most general specification of this model is difficult to handle but calibration of a simple short-rate version of this model may be achieved by first calibrating the loss distribution to tranche prices using the forward equation (104). From this we determine a term structure of forward rates $a_l(t, T)$ (this is analogous to bootstrapping discount factors from the yield curve). Since the number of tranche prices is usually significantly less than the number of loss states, it is necessary to assume a parametric form or interpolation scheme for the a_l as a function of l. In practice, we find that the tranche data is frequently impossible to calibrate to without extending the specification (106) to include a rate of systemic default $b(t, T)$ such that:

$$a_{ln}(t, T) = \mathbb{1}_{l<N_c} \left(\delta_{n,l+1} a_l(t, T) + \delta_{n,N_c} b(t, T) \right) \tag{107}$$

We now assume that a single Brownian motion W_t drives all the short-rates $\{a_l(t, t)\}$, $b(t, t)$:

$$dX_t = \gamma dt + \sigma_t dW_t$$

$$a_l(t, t; X_t) = \exp(\mu_l(t) + X_t) \tag{108}$$

$$b(t, t; X_t) = \exp(\mu_b(t) + \beta X_t) \tag{109}$$

where β parameterizes how much the systemic risk changes as a function of market state. We define the Arrow-Debreu security:

$$A(n, y, T|m, x, t) = A(N_T = n, X_T = y|N_t = m, X_t = x)$$

$$= \mathbb{E}_t \left[\mathbb{1}_{N_T=n} \delta(X_T - y) | N_t = m, X_t = x \right] \tag{110}$$

The forward and backward Chapman-Kolmogorov equations (104), (105) then become respectively (omitting in each case the redundant arguments):

$$\frac{\partial A(n, y, T)}{\partial T} = \mathbb{1}_{n>0} a_{n-1}(T, T; y) A(n - 1, y, T)$$

$$- \mathbb{1}_{n<N_c} (a_n(T, T; y) + b(T, T; y)) A(n, y, T)$$

$$+ \mathbb{1}_{n=N_c} b(T, T; y) \sum_{l<N_c} A(l, y, T) + \hat{O} A(n, y, T) \tag{111}$$

with the boundary condition $A(n, y, t) = \delta_{n,m} \delta(x - y)$

and

$$-\frac{\partial A(m, x, t)}{\partial t} = \mathbb{1}_{m<N_c} a_m(t, t; x) A(m + 1, x, t)$$

$$- \mathbb{1}_{m<N_c} (a_m(t, t; x) + b(t, t; x)) A(m, x, t)$$

$$+ \mathbb{1}_{m<N_c} b(t, t; x) A(N_c, x, t) + \hat{O}' A(m, x, t) \tag{112}$$

with the boundary condition $A(m, x, T) = \delta_{n,m} \delta(x - y)$

where the generators of the diffusion are in this case given by:

$$\hat{O} A(n, y, T) = \frac{1}{2} \frac{\partial^2 \left(\sigma^2 A(n, y, T) \right)}{\partial y^2} - \frac{\partial \left(\gamma A(n, y, T) \right)}{\partial y} \tag{113}$$

$$\hat{O}' A(m, x, t) = \frac{\sigma^2}{2} \frac{\partial^2 \left(A(m, x, t) \right)}{\partial x^2} + \gamma \frac{\partial A(m, x, t)}{\partial x} \tag{114}$$

This may be generalized straightforwardly to incorporate jumps, mean reversion etc. in the state variable X_t if desired.

The calibration procedure consists in sequentially applying forward induction via a Crank-Nicholson discretization of (111) from $n = 0$ up to $n = N_c$, in each case using the solutions of the previous equations as source terms, to calibrate $\mu_n(t)$, μ_b such that at each timestep, we ensure we match the loss distribution:

$$\int \phi(y) A(n, y, T) dy = p_{n|m}(t, T) \tag{115}$$

Here $\phi(y)$ is the density of $y = X_T$ which can either be evaluated analytically for the simple diffusion we have chosen here, or numerically using a finite difference implementation if we have selected a more complex process. Essentially, this is the same as calibrating N_c coupled short-rate models, which is a relatively standard problem.

Pricing of contingent payoffs such as tranche options may be implemented via the backward equation (112) with the addition of source terms V_1 and V_2 to the diffusion operator (114) to account for protection and coupon payments respectively. Here we assume interest rates are independent of the loss process and all values are pre-discounted to time 0. For example, to price a tranche via the backward equation we would have terms of the form:

$$V_1 = a_1(t) \mathbb{1}_{m < N_c} \left(a_m(t, t; x) \left(P(m + 1) - P(m) \right) + b(t, t; x) \left(P(N_c) - P(m) \right) \right) \tag{116}$$

$$V_2 = a_2(t) \bar{P}(m) \tag{117}$$

where the payoff for the tranche with notional H is given by:

$$P(m) = H \times \frac{\left(\min(k_{\max}, m) - \min(k_{\min}, m) \right)}{k_{\max} - k_{\min}}$$

$$\bar{P}(m) = H - P(m) \tag{118}$$

Assuming continuous accrual of coupon and long protection, $a_1(t) = P(0, t)$ and $a_2(t) = -P(0, t) \times C$ where $P(0, t)$ is the risk-free discount factor to time t and C the coupon. In this case, the coupled system of equations must be solved from the highest loss state N_c downwards.

The attraction of this approach is that in general, providing that you can bootstrap a deterministic loss surface parameterized via the forward rate specification (107) (and this is usually fairly straightforward given a set of arbitrage free prices), there is a totally systematic forward induction procedure for calibrating the fully dynamic model that is essentially guaranteed to work: most other attempts to construct a fully dynamic model are extremely problematic to calibrate. There is also a simple finite difference based implementation of pricing via the backward equation. Ideas along these lines for the case of no systemic risk and generalized Cox-Ingersoll-Ross processes for the short rates were presented in Lopatin and Misirpashaev (2008).

In many ways, in this model the forward rates play the role of deterministic local volatility in option modelling (Derman and Kani 1994; Dupire 1994)—in the case of options, the deterministic local variance at a strike K is the expected local variance conditional on spot attaining a level K: $\sigma_t^2(T, K) = \mathbb{E}_t[\sigma_T^2 | S_T = K]$. Here the forward transition rates have a similar interpretation in terms of the expected short rate, conditional on the loss level (Cont and Savescu 2008). We recall that:

$$a_{ln}(t, T) = \frac{1}{\Delta T} \frac{\mathbb{E}_t\left[\mathbb{1}_{N_{T+\Delta T}=n}\mathbb{1}_{N_T=l} \middle| N_t = m\right]}{\mathbb{E}_t\left[\mathbb{1}_{N_T=l} \middle| N_t = m\right]} \tag{119}$$

Then, using the tower law and the Markov property of the $\{a_{ln}(T, T; X_T)\}$:

$$\mathbb{E}_t\left[\mathbb{1}_{N_{T+\Delta T}=n}\mathbb{1}_{N_T=l} \middle| N_t = m\right] = \mathbb{E}_t\left[\mathbb{E}_T\left[\mathbb{1}_{N_{T+\Delta T}=n}\mathbb{1}_{N_T=l} \middle| X_T\right] \middle| N_t = m\right]$$

$$= \Delta T \times \mathbb{E}_t\left[a_{ln}(T, T; X_T)\mathbb{1}_{N_T=l} \middle| N_t = m\right] \tag{120}$$

Hence by Bayes' law:

$$a_{ln}(t, T) = \mathbb{E}_t\left[a_{ln}(T, T; X_T) \middle| N_T = l, N_t = m\right] \tag{121}$$

The parameter β appearing in equation (109) may be used to vary the dynamics of the correlation skew, since systemic risk controls how much loss, relatively, appears in the senior tranches compared to the junior tranches. Without introducing some stochasticity in the systemic factor, the dynamics of the correlation skew are rather implausible—if b is deterministic, as junior tranches increase in riskiness, senior tranches hardly change in value. Interestingly, if we correlate the systemic risk with general market deterioration in this way, we end up with a large negative drift adjustment, which means that instantaneously, the probability of systemic default is low, but as the market factor X_t deteriorates, systemic risk can increase dramatically: this makes sense financially.

Since this model can be more or less perfectly calibrated to the market, combines volatility and default correlation and can be implemented efficiently on a lattice, it provides an interesting way of exploring the relationship between correlation and volatility products: calibrating to tranche prices severely constrains the possible implied volatilities of index default swaptions for example. Similar, although seemingly much less tractable, ideas are discussed in Sidenius Piterbarg, and Andersen (2008). Another approach (Bennani 2005), by directly modelling the loss process, essentially corresponds to the infinite portfolio limit of the Schönbucher model, in which the loss at each point can be replaced by its conditional expectation, as in the large homogeneous pool approximation (Vasicek 1987). This can cause calibration problems when it is applied to finite portfolios. Overall, a finite portfolio variant of the Schönbucher approach seems to be the most viable way of specifying models of this type. In its deterministic limit (104), (105) it can also provide a simple arbitrage-free way of interpolating tranche prices.

An approach that has more in common with the Marshall-Olkin copula (Lindskog and McNeil 2003) is known as the Generalized Poisson Loss Model (GPL) (Brigo, Pallavicini, and Torresetti 2006). Here the loss is assumed to be driven by a series of generalized Poisson processes with intensities $\{\lambda_j\}$ corresponding to jumps in loss of (integer) size $\{a_j\}$. In our notation:

$$a_{ln} = \mathbb{1}_{l < N_c} \sum_j \delta_{a_j, n-l} \lambda_j \tag{122}$$

Some care is required to ensure that the loss is capped at a maximum of N_c. Once more the intensities can be made stochastic. Although the calibration of the static version of the model can be quite accurate, it involves optimization and is hard to systematize. However, it is true that if a static calibration can be found, it is possible to implement forward induction similar to that described here in order to calibrate a dynamic version. One question with regard to this approach, though, is how realistic it is to model the loss on a portfolio such that there may be large numbers of simultaneous defaults, even in a non-distressed state of the market.

Other approaches worth mentioning include (Graziano and Rogers 2009) in which the unobservable variable X_t is a finite state Markov process. Another approach (Giesecke and Goldberg 2005) claims to solve the problem that top-down models inherently discard single-name level information when they restrict themselves to modelling the aggregate loss process N_t. It accomplishes this through a process known as 'random thinning' by retrospectively augmenting this reduced filtration. How viable this is in practice remains unclear: it is certainly not straightforward to implement and there is something counter-intuitive about an approach that simplifies the filtration, only to complicate it again. The inherent complexity of the problem is conserved no matter how it is reformulated: if the objective is to model single-name intensities, a top-down model does not seem the correct starting point.

7 THE PORTFOLIO LOSS DISTRIBUTION

As we have seen, to value synthetic CDO tranches it is sufficient to completely characterize the loss distribution at all time horizons to the maturity of the trade. We now review in much more detail some approaches to evaluating the loss distribution in a numerically efficient manner. Let us consider a CDO tranche on a portfolio of n credits, $i = 1 \ldots n$, where N_i and R_i are the notional and recovery respectively of credit i. Then the loss on the portfolio at time T can be written:

$$L_T = \sum_{i=1}^{n} w_i \xi_T^i \tag{123}$$

where τ_i denotes the default time of the ith credit, $w_i = N_i(1 - R_i)$ and $\xi_T^i = \mathbb{1}_{\tau_i \leq T}$ is a Bernoulli variable, the indicator function that credit i has defaulted by time T. In order to model the portfolio loss (123) we usually need to assume conditional independence of the $\{\xi_T^i\}$ (with the notable exception of the Marshall-Olkin copula (Lindskog and McNeil 2003). Generally it is hard to work out the distribution of sums of random variables unless they are independent. A great deal of research in credit derivatives has focused on the efficient calculation of the distribution of these sums and their sensitivities.

We assume that the variables $\{\xi_T^i\}$ are independent conditional on a common factor Y. The conditional survival probability for credit i to maturity T is denoted $S_i(T|Y) = 1 - P_i(T|Y)$ where $\mathbb{E}[\xi_T^i|Y] = P_i(T|Y)$. The model must be formulated in such a way that integrated over the common factor, the correct unconditional expectations are reproduced:

$$P_i(T) = \mathbb{E}[P_i(T|Y)] = \int \varphi(Y)P_i(T|Y)dY \tag{124}$$

where $\varphi(Y)$ is the probability density function of the common factor. In the special case of the single-factor Gaussian copula with correlation ρ:

$$\varphi(Y) = \frac{1}{\sqrt{2\pi}}e^{-\frac{1}{2}Y^2} \tag{125}$$

$$P_i(T|Y) = N\left(\frac{N^{-1}(P_i(T)) - \sqrt{\rho}Y}{\sqrt{1-\rho}}\right) \tag{126}$$

$$\text{where } N(X) = \int_{-\infty}^{X} \varphi(u)du \tag{127}$$

In general, most of the popular model frameworks can be expressed in this way.

For the simple case of equally weighted, i.i.d. variables for which $\{P_i(T|Y) = p, w_i = w\}$, the distribution of L_T conditional on Y reduces to the binomial distribution:

$$\Pr(L_T = j \times w|Y) = C_j^n p^j (1-p)^{n-j} \tag{128}$$

for $j = 0, \ldots, n$ where the binomial coefficient $C_j^n = \frac{n!}{(n-j)!j!}$. The unconditional distribution may then be obtained by numerically integrating (128) over Y.

$$\Pr(L_T = j \times w) = \int \varphi(Y)\Pr(L_T = j \times w|Y)dY \tag{129}$$

In credit derivatives we are usually dealing with inhomogeneous portfolios and hence there is no such explicit expression for the loss distribution. In subsequent sections we describe some of the approaches we can take to solve this problem. For the case of unequally weighted, non-i.i.d. variables the task of convoluting the individual loss distributions can be tackled in a number of ways.

7.1 FFT

Transform or characteristic function methods are one way of convoluting sums of random variables. We define the Fourier transform $\hat{p}(q)$ of a probability density function $p(x)$:

$$\hat{p}(q) = \int_{-\infty}^{+\infty} e^{iqx} p(x)dx = \mathbb{E}\left[e^{iqx}\right] \tag{130}$$

Subject to integrability conditions, the original density may be recovered from (130) via the inverse Fourier transform:

$$p(x) = \frac{1}{2\pi} \int_{-\infty}^{+\infty} e^{-iqx} \hat{p}(q)dq \tag{131}$$

The interesting feature of Fourier transforms for present purposes is the convolution theorem. Given two independent variables x and y, the Fourier transform of their sum is given by the product of their transforms:

$$\hat{p}_{x+y}(q) = \mathbb{E}\left[e^{iq(x+y)}\right] = \mathbb{E}\left[e^{iqx}\right]\mathbb{E}\left[e^{iqy}\right] \tag{132}$$

$$= \hat{p}_x(q)\hat{p}_y(q) \tag{133}$$

In transform space, convolution is therefore a very simple operation. In order to evaluate the Fourier transform of the conditional loss distribution on a portfolio we must calculate:

$$\hat{\Phi}(q|Y) = \mathbb{E}\left[e^{iqL_T}|Y\right] \tag{134}$$

$$= \mathbb{E}\left[e^{iq\sum_{j=1}^{n} w_j\xi_T^j}|Y\right] \tag{135}$$

$$= \prod_{j=1}^{n} \mathbb{E}\left[e^{iqw_j\xi_T^j}|Y\right] \tag{136}$$

where:

$$\mathbb{E}\left[e^{iqw_j\xi_T^j}|Y\right] = (1 - P_j(T|Y)) + P_j(T|Y)e^{iqw_j} \tag{137}$$

From (137) and (136) we can determine the Fourier transform of the conditional loss distribution. By integrating over the common factor we can find the Fourier transform of the unconditional distribution:

$$\hat{\Phi}(q) = \int \varphi(Y)\hat{\Phi}(q|Y)dY \tag{138}$$

This can then be inverted via (131) to give the loss distribution. In practice, the loss distribution is discrete, so a discrete Fourier transform (DFT) can be used. The simplest algorithm would have a computational cost of order N^2 where N is the number of loss units, but there are a number of Fast Fourier Transform (FFT) methods which have a cost of only $O(N\log N)$, the most famous of which is (Cooley and Tukey (1965), although it is said that the algorithm was known to Gauss in the early nineteenth century (Heideman, Johnson, and Burrus 1984). Contrary to popular belief, it is not essential for the number of nodes to be a power of two, so the constraints on choosing a loss unit are similar to the analogous problem for recursion algorithms, discussed in more detail later.

In practice, calculating the characteristic function has a computational cost of order $N \times n \times N_Y$, where n is the number of credits and N_Y the number of nodes used to discretize the integral over the common factor. This is typically higher than the cost of the FFT itself. As with most quant code, the dominant overhead is in calls to transcendental functions such as the exponential function, sine and cosine. The large number of calls of this type mean that FFT is usually significantly slower than recursion. This, combined with its greater implementational difficulty mean that although FFT experienced a heyday in the early days of the field (Debuysscher and Szego 2003; Merino and Nyfeler 2002; Mina and Stern 2003; Laurent and Gregory 2005), it has largely been superseded by recursion methods.

7.2 Recursion

One of the most widely used techniques for evaluating the loss distribution is recursion. The conditional distribution of the total loss on the portfolio (123) can be viewed as a convolution of the distributions of the individual loss variables:

$$L_T(n) = \sum_{i=1}^{n} L_T^i \xi_T^i \tag{139}$$

$$L_T^i = w_i \tag{140}$$

In general, computing high-order convolutions is very difficult. However, for the case where the $\{L_T^i\}$ and $\{\xi_T^i\}$ are independent and identically distributed (i.i.d.), a recursion relation can be derived which makes it computationally feasible. Formally, if we denote the density function of L_T^i by $f(x)$, $x > 0$, and the density of the random sum (139) by p^n, we are trying to calculate:

$$p^n(x) = \sum_{m=1}^{n} p_m f^{*m}(x) \tag{141}$$

where f^{*m} denotes the mth convolution of f, and $p_m = C_m^n p^m (1-p)^{n-m}$. It can be shown (Panjer 1981; Sundt and Jewell 1981) that for the restricted class of distributions of m for which $p_m = p_{m-1}(a + b/m)$ (including the binomial distribution as a special case for which $a = -p/(1-p)$, $b = (n+1)p/(1-p)$), p^n can be expressed via the following recursion relation:

$$p^n(0) = p_0 \tag{142}$$

$$p^n(x) = p_1 f(x) + \int_0^x \left(a + b\frac{y}{x} \right) f(y) p^n(x-y) dy, \quad x > 0 \tag{143}$$

If f is discrete and positive integer-valued rather than continuous, equations (141) and (143) become respectively:

$$p^n(i) = \sum_{m=0}^{i} p_m f_i^{*m}, \quad i = 0, 1, 2, 3, \ldots \tag{144}$$

$$p^n(i) = \sum_{j=1}^{i} \left(a + b\frac{j}{i} \right) f_j\, p^n(i-j), \quad i = 1, 2, 3, \ldots \tag{145}$$

where once more $p^n(0) = p_0$. Evaluating (144) involves of order i^2 computations, whereas (145) involves only i, which yields a big reduction in computational cost.

Up to this point we have considered the homogeneous case for which the $\{L_T^i\}$ are i.i.d., deterministic and equal to w, hence the solution of (145) is simply the binomial distribution. However, we can employ a similar approach (Andersen, Sidenius, Basu 2003 ; Brasch 2004) for the inhomogeneous case, where the $\{\xi_T^i\}$ are no longer i.i.d., and in general, neither are the $\{L_T^i\}$ (although they are assumed deterministic i.e. $w_i = N_i(1 - R_i)$). Let us assume initially that we can discretize the loss into a unit u which is the greatest common divisor (GCD) of the $\{w_i\}$, so that $p^m(i \times u)$ denotes the probability that the loss to time T on a portfolio of the first m credits equals $i \times u$, for $i = 0, \ldots, N$. Then we can derive the following series of recursion relationships:

$$p^0(i \times u) = \delta_{i,0} \tag{146}$$

$$p^{m+1}(i \times u) = p^m(i \times u)(1 - P_{m+1}) + p^m(i \times u - w_{m+1})P_{m+1} \mathbb{1}_{i \times u - w_{m+1} \geq 0} \tag{147}$$

where P_{m+1} is shorthand for $P_{m+1}(T|Y)$, the default probability of credit $m + 1$ conditional on the common factor. In the homogeneous case we could implement a single recursion relationship (145) for p^n and accomplish the convolution in a single step. Now, because the individual variables are no longer IID, we need to implement a series of recursions for progressively larger portfolios $m = 1, \ldots, n$ until we finally derive the loss distribution for the full portfolio of n credits. As a result, evaluating the loss distribution up to a loss level $i \times u$ has a cost proportional to $i \times n$, which for a large portfolio could be significantly greater than the cost of recursively evaluating (145) up to level i, which is only of order i^2. We note that for the case where u is a common divisor of all the $\{w_i\}$, although equation (147) defines a binomial tree, there is no approximation involved: the result is exact and for i.i.d. losses reduces to (128).

Care is required in the choice of loss unit u. Recovery values are generally marked at integral multiples of 1% and the notionals in the portfolio are usually mostly the same. In these cases it is possible to use the very efficient Euclidean algorithm Euclid (300BC) to derive the loss unit $u_{GCD} = \text{GCD}(\{w_i\})$ that is the GCD of the $\{w_i\}$. However, as the loss unit decreases, computational cost increases, so sometimes it may be necessary to adopt a compromise between having perfect accuracy and adequate performance. In such cases $u > u_{GCD}$ and it is necessary to modify the recursion relations (147) according to a prescription that will, as far as possible, minimize the resulting error, since now the recursion relations will no longer be exact.

We discretize on a lattice $\{x_i = i \times u : i = 0, \dots, N\}$ and denote $p^m(x_i) = p_i^m$. Defining the integer part of $x \geq 0$ by $\lfloor x \rfloor$, the simplest way of discretizing (147) is:

$$p_i^{m+1} = p_i^m (1 - P_{m+1}) + p_{i-\lfloor w_{m+1}/u \rfloor}^m P_{m+1} \tag{148}$$

In general, for $u > u_{\text{GCD}}$, this will introduce first order error in the loss distribution. One way of controlling this error is to choose the largest loss unit u such that the discretization error corresponding to the loss for credit j, given by $|w_j - \lfloor w_j/u \rfloor \times u|$ is less than a specified tolerance ϵ. An efficient algorithm for achieving this is given in (Andersen, Sidenius, Basu 2003).

A second solution to the problem (Hull and White 2004) is to discretize the loss distribution into K buckets, where the kth bucket is defined by $b_{k-1} \leq L_T < b_k$ and $b_0 = 0, b_K = \infty$. We then generalize the recursion to track not just the probability that the loss on the first m credits falls in the given bucket $p_k^m = \text{Prob}(b_{k-1} \leq L_T(m) < b_k)$ but also the expected loss Λ_k^m given that the loss falls in the bucket:

$$\Lambda_k^m = \mathbb{E}\left[L_T(m)\big| b_{k-1} \leq L_T(m) < b_k\right] \tag{149}$$

$$= \frac{\mathbb{E}\left[L_T(m)\mathbb{1}_{b_{k-1}\leq L_T(m)<b_k}\right]}{\mathbb{E}\left[\mathbb{1}_{b_{k-1}\leq L_T(m)<b_k}\right]} \tag{150}$$

We initialize the recursion with $\{p_k^0 = \delta_{k,0}, \Lambda_k^0 = 0\}$. In bucketed form, equation (147) is approximated by:

$$p_k^{m+1} = p_k^m (1 - P_{m+1}) + P_{m+1} \sum_{k'=1}^{k} p_{k'}^m \mathbb{1}_{b_{k-1}\leq \Lambda_{k'}^m + w_{m+1} < b_k} \tag{151}$$

$$\Lambda_k^{m+1} = \frac{1}{p_k^{m+1}} \left(p_k^m (1 - P_{m+1})\Lambda_k^m + P_{m+1} \sum_{k'=1}^{k} p_{k'}^m (\Lambda_{k'}^m + w_{m+1})\mathbb{1}_{b_{k-1}\leq \Lambda_{k'}^m + w_{m+1} < b_k} \right) \tag{152}$$

To derive these equations we needed to make the following approximations:

$$\mathbb{E}\left[\mathbb{1}_{b_{k-1}\leq L_T(m)+w_{m+1}<b_k}\big| b_{k'-1} \leq L_T(m) < b_{k'}\right]$$
$$\approx \mathbb{1}_{b_{k-1}\leq \Lambda_{k'}^m + w_{m+1} < b_k} \tag{153}$$

$$\mathbb{E}\left[(L_T(m) + w_{m+1})\mathbb{1}_{b_{k-1}\leq L_T(m)+w_{m+1}<b_k}\big| b_{k'-1} \leq L_T(m) < b_{k'}\right]$$
$$\approx (\Lambda_{k'}^m + w_{m+1})\mathbb{1}_{b_{k-1}\leq \Lambda_{k'}^m + w_{m+1} < b_k} \tag{154}$$

i.e. in these expectations we replace the random variable $L_T(m)$ conditioned on $b_{k'-1} \leq L_T(m) < b_{k'}$ by its expectation $\Lambda_{k'}^m = \mathbb{E}\left[L_T(m)\big| b_{k'-1} \leq L_T(m) < b_{k'}\right]$. Once again this will in general result in first-order error proportional to the size of the buckets, unless we are lucky with the discretization. An unfortunate feature of this approach is that in general, the results depend upon the order of insertion of the credits.

One final approach to the loss unit issue is to assume an interpolation prescription for the $p^m(x)$ (Parcell 2006). Once more we discretize on a lattice $\{x_i = i \times u\}$ and denote $p^m(x_i) = p_i^m$. Considering the case of linear interpolation, we express the last term in (147) as follows:

$$p^m(i \times u - w_{m+1}) = (1 - \lambda(w_{m+1}))\, p_{i-j}^m + \lambda(w_{m+1}) p_{i-j-1}^m \tag{155}$$

$$\lambda(w_{m+1}) = \frac{w_{m+1}}{u} - \left\lfloor \frac{w_{m+1}}{u} \right\rfloor \tag{156}$$

$$j(w_{m+1}) = \left\lfloor \frac{w_{m+1}}{u} \right\rfloor \tag{157}$$

Unlike the previous two approaches, it can be shown that the portfolio expected loss is now exactly reproduced, which is a significant improvement. The price that we pay for this is that in general the recursion relation (147) now relates the value at a given node in the $m + 1$-credit portfolio to three nodes in the m-credit portfolio, as opposed to two. This can make implementation more difficult especially for risk calculations where it becomes necessary to de-convolute the distributions.

On the whole, we believe that it is more common in the industry to implement a variant of either simple first-order recursion or the more complicated second-order accurate recursion described above than the bucketing approach.

One further aspect of recursion that has received a great deal of attention is the calculation of sensitivities. Synthetic CDOs usually have of order 100 underlying credits, and we are often interested in evaluating bucketed spread risk. Thus, it is necessary to recalculate the loss distribution hundreds of times as efficiently as possible. Rather than recalculating the entire series of recursions (147) from scratch many times, it is possible to remove credit k from the loss distribution p^n by inverting one step of the recursion, and then reinsert the credit with shifted market data. We initially consider the perfectly commensurate case $u = u_{\mathrm{GCD}}$. Then we can invert (147) to remove the kth credit as follows (since the results of the recursion are independent of the order of insertion of the credits, we can assume that the kth credit was the last to be inserted) starting from state 0 and working upwards:

$$p^{n-1}(i \times u) = \frac{1}{1 - P_k}\, p^n(i \times u)$$

$$\text{for } i = 0, \ldots, \frac{w_k}{u} - 1 \tag{158}$$

$$p^{n-1}(i \times u) = \frac{1}{1 - P_k}\, p^n(i \times u) - \left(\frac{P_k}{1 - P_k}\right) p^{n-1}(i \times u - w_k)$$

$$\text{for } i = \frac{w_k}{u}, \ldots, N \tag{159}$$

Alternatively we can start from the highest loss state N and work down, providing that we have evaluated the entire conditional loss distribution i.e. $N \times u = \sum_{i=1}^{n} w_i$:

$$p^{n-1}(i \times u) = 0$$

$$\text{for } i = N - \frac{w_k}{u} + 1, \ldots, N \tag{160}$$

$$p^{n-1}(i \times u) = \frac{1}{P_k} p^n(i \times u + w_k) - \left(\frac{1 - P_k}{P_k}\right) p^{n-1}(i \times u + w_k)$$

$$\text{for } i = N - \frac{w_k}{u}, \ldots, 0 \tag{161}$$

Care is required to ensure numerical stability. In the set of recursion relations (158), (159), the expansion parameter is $\lambda(k) = P_k/(1 - P_k)$. In (160), (161) the expansion parameter is $1/\lambda(k)$. Since we are dealing with n of order 100, if the expansion parameter is large in magnitude, small numerical errors can accumulate dramatically. In practice, a method that is guaranteed to be numerically stable is to use equations (158), (159) when $\lambda(k) \leq 1$ ($P_k < 1/2$) and equations (160), (161) when $\lambda(k) > 1$ ($P_k > 1/2$).

One difficulty with the more complex prescriptions for handling incommensurate loss units can be ensuring numerical stability for the operation of deconvolution. In general, unlike the commensurate case, it is not always possible to prove that the operation can be made numerically stable by construction. Practitioners have developed various ad hoc ways of controlling the numerical instability in such cases, adequate for applications but not entirely satisfactory from a mathematical point of view.

Once the recursion algorithm has been decided, major efficiency savings may also be obtained on the integration over the central shock factor. Suppose that we are evaluating the expected loss on an equity tranche with detachment K at a given time horizon T:

$$\mathbb{E}\left[\min\left(L_T, K\right)\right] = \int \varphi(Y) \mathbb{E}\left[\min\left(L_T, K\right)|Y\right] dY \tag{162}$$

(The conditional expected loss of a mezzanine tranche with attachment K_1 and detachment K_2 may be simply expressed as a difference of the expected losses on two equity tranches $\mathbb{E}\left[\min(L_T, K_2)\right] - \mathbb{E}\left[\min(L_T, K_1)\right]$). If the default probabilities $\{P_i(T|Y)\}$ are a monotonically increasing function of Y, the equity tranche expected losses will usually have the same property. Then we can find values of the central shock parameter $\{Y_{\min}, Y_{\max}\}$ such that:

$$\left|\mathbb{E}\left[\min\left(L_T, K\right)|Y_{\max}\right] - K\right| \leq \epsilon \tag{163}$$

$$\left|\mathbb{E}\left[\min\left(L_T, K\right)|Y_{\min}\right]\right| \leq \epsilon \tag{164}$$

where ϵ is a specified tolerance. Then the integral (162) can be decomposed as:

$$\mathbb{E}\left[\min\left(L_T, K\right)\right] \approx \int_{Y_{\min}}^{Y_{\max}} \varphi(Y) \mathbb{E}\left[\min\left(L_T, K\right)|Y\right] dY + K \int_{Y_{\max}}^{Y_\infty} \varphi(Y) dY \tag{165}$$

The parameters $\{Y_{\min}, Y_{\max}\}$ may be found efficiently by bisection. The integral can then be discretized over this reduced range, rather than the entire domain of the density $\varphi(Y)$. A simple numerical integration procedure, such as the trapezium rule, combined with this reduction of the domain of integration is typically better adapted to evaluating (162) efficiently than more sophisticated quadrature methods. Quadrature methods are well adapted to integrands that are close to polynomial whereas $\mathbb{E}[\min(L_T, K)|Y]$ is usually anything but.

7.3 Approximation of the loss distribution

There are a number of reasons why it may be useful to approximate the loss distribution. As well as being fairly involved to implement successfully, closed-form methods such as recursion and FFT may become computationally expensive when there are a large number of assets or their loss payouts are highly incommensurate. When it comes to higher-dimensional payoffs such as CDO-Squared, closed-form approaches are not applicable and the only viable alternative is Monte Carlo. Here approximating the loss distribution can be much more efficient, especially for the calculation of risks.

We once again write the loss on a portfolio of n credits $i = 1, \ldots, n$ at time T as:

$$L_T = \sum_{i=1}^{n} w_i \xi_T^i \tag{166}$$

where $\xi_T^i = \mathbb{1}_{\tau_i \leq T}$ is the indicator function of default of the ith credit.

An early attempt at approximating the loss distribution was the Large Homogeneous Pool approximation (LHP) (Vasicek 1987). Assuming all credits have identical default probability P, are equally weighted $w_i = w$, are correlated according to (55) and taking the limit of infinite portfolio size, the law of large numbers is used to derive a closed form expression for the loss distribution:

$$\lim_{n \to \infty} \text{Prob}(L_T < K) = \Phi\left(\frac{\sqrt{1-\rho}\Phi^{-1}\left(\frac{K}{W}\right) - \Phi^{-1}(P)}{\sqrt{\rho}}\right) \tag{167}$$

where $W = \sum w$ and we take the limit such that the percentage loss K/W remains finite. We plot this expression for various different correlation values in Figure 7.9. This important result is however of limited use in credit derivatives pricing and risk management because the portfolio size is usually not sufficiently large (typically of order 100 reference entities) or homogeneous. This is demonstrated graphically when we compare the density for a homogeneous 100-name portfolio to the LHP approximation in Figure 7.10: the infinite portfolio limit is much more sharply peaked as a result of the central limit theorem. It turns out that we can derive a more accurate approximation, valid for the case of the finite inhomogeneous portfolio.

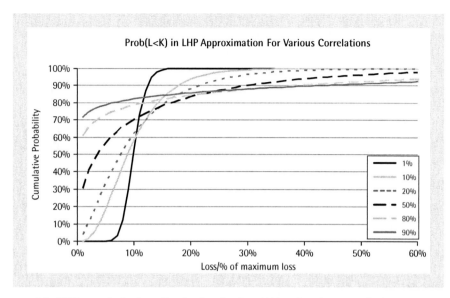

FIGURE 7.9 LHP cumulative loss distribution for $P = 10\%$ and various correlation assumptions.

Source: BofA Merrill Lynch Global Research.

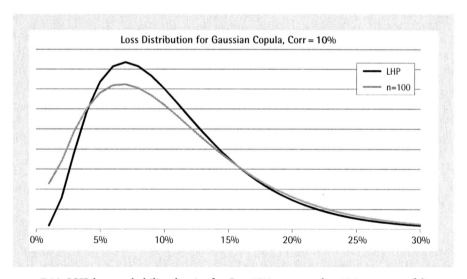

FIGURE 7.10 LHP loss probability density for $P = 10\%$ compared to 100 name portfolio.

Source: BofA Merrill Lynch Global Research.

In general, to value more complex payoffs such as CDO-Squared tranches, we need to track m loss variables $\{L_T^k : k = 1 \ldots m\}$ representing the loss on each of the m underlying portfolios.

$$L_T^k = \sum_{i=1}^{n} w_i^k \xi_T^i \qquad (168)$$

where $w_i^k = N_i^k \times (1 - R_i)$ represents the loss given default of credit i in portfolio k. A common approach to pricing derivatives involving baskets of many underlying assets is to reduce the dimensionality of the problem by approximating their distribution. A relatively accurate approximation may be obtained in this case by making use of the conditional independence property of copula models parameterized by a central shock factor. We consider a model in which the conditional survival probabilities are driven by an N-dimensional common factor Y. The conditional survival probability for credit i to maturity T is denoted $S_i(T|Y)$. Assuming conditional independence we find the following exact expressions for the first two moments of the loss variables $\{L_T^k\}$ conditional on the central shock factor:

$$\mu_T^k(Y) = \mathbb{E}\left[L_T^k \big| Y\right] = \sum_i w_i^k(1 - S_i(T|Y)) \tag{169}$$

$$c_T^{kk'}(Y) = \operatorname{cov}\left(L_T^k, L_T^{k'} \big| Y\right) = \sum_i w_i^k w_i^{k'} S_i(T|Y)(1 - S_i(T|Y)) \tag{170}$$

It can be shown (Shelton 2004) that for the purposes of CDO and CDO-Squared valuation, the m-dimensional normal distribution with first and second moments given by equations. (169), (170) provide a reasonably accurate approximation to the joint distribution of losses conditional on the common factor. This approximation is supported by the central limit theorem, which states that the sum of a set of finite variance independent random variables with arbitrary probability distribution converges to the normal distribution. In this case the random variables are the indicator functions of default. The two sources of error in this approximation are the fact that we are approximating a discrete distribution by a continuous one, and the fact that we are relying on the portfolio being sufficiently large for the distribution to have converged close to the normal limit.

For the case of a CDO, once we have made this approximation, we can obtain the following analytical expression for the conditional expected loss on an equity tranche with detachment point K:

$$\mathbb{E}\left[\min(L_T, K)\big| Y\right] = \mu_T - \sigma_T n\left(\frac{\mu_T - K}{\sigma_T}\right) - (\mu_T - K)N\left(\frac{\mu_T - K}{\sigma_T}\right) \tag{171}$$

where N denotes the cumulative normal, n the normal density, $\mu_T = \mu_T(Y)$ the conditional mean and $\sigma_T = \sigma_T(Y)$ the conditional standard deviation of the loss variable L_T. The conditional expected loss of a mezzanine tranche with attachment K_1 and detachment K_2 may be simply expressed as a difference of the expected losses on two equity tranches $\mathbb{E}\left[\min(L_T, K_2)\right] - \mathbb{E}\left[\min(L_T, K_1)\right]$. To determine the unconditional expected loss on a CDO it is then sufficient to numerically integrate the integrand (171) over all values of the central shock.

For the case of CDO-Squared trades the problem is still m-dimensional. Usually this number is larger than 3, so there is no simple closed-form expression for the conditional expected loss. However, one simple way to efficiently estimate this expectation is by using m-dimensional Monte Carlo integration over the correlated normal variables. This Monte Carlo is vastly lower in variance than the standard implementation based on simulated default times because it is much lower dimensional and the variables that are simulated are smooth loss variables, not indicators of default. In the standard approach, the indicators and hence the portfolio loss are inaccurately reproduced because only a small percentage of paths result in default events.

There are also some significant efficiency savings to be made when evaluating the Greeks. Conditional on the common factor, we assume that the loss variables on a given time horizon can be represented as a linear combination of Gaussian variables:

$$L^k = \mu^k + \sum_l M_{kl} X_l \tag{172}$$

where the $\{X_l\}$ are independent N(0,1) variables and M may be obtained from the Cholesky decomposition of eq. (170). We are interested in calculating expectations of a function F of the L^k conditional on Y:

$$f = \mathbb{E}\left[F(\{L^k\})|Y\right] \tag{173}$$

When we shift market data, the distributional parameters change. One can either directly calculate the Greeks by blipping all the underlying credit curves in turn, or alternatively evaluate the sensitivity of f with respect to distributional parameters and later calculate the Greeks with respect to the market data by using the chain rule. The advantage of the latter approach is that for a trade with many underlying credits, there are far fewer distributional parameters than market inputs and the computational cost of the calculation is much reduced. We define:

$$f_i = \mathbb{E}\left[\partial_{\mu^i} F(\{L^k\})|Y\right] \tag{174}$$

$$g_{ij} = \mathbb{E}\left[\partial_{M_{ij}} F(\{L^k\})|Y\right] = \mathbb{E}\left[X_j \partial_{\mu^i} F(\{L^k\})|Y\right] \tag{175}$$

In the last expression we have used the decomposition (172) to simplify the expectation. As a result, for each point in the integration we need to calculate $\{\partial_{\mu^i} F\}$ and $\{X_j \partial_{\mu^i} F\}$ by explicitly blipping the $\{\mu^i\}$. This only involves $m+1$ evaluations of the payoff function. When the integration is completed, we determine the shifts in the distributional parameters $\{\Delta\mu^i\}$ and $\{\Delta M_{ij}\}$ corresponding to each scenario and obtain the following first-order expression for the change in the expectation to first order:

$$\Delta f = \sum_i f_i \Delta\mu^i + \sum_{i,j} g_{ij}\Delta M_{ij} \tag{176}$$

Using this approach the cost of calculation of n risk numbers can be much less than n times the cost for a single PV (since usually $m \ll n$).

Although the analysis so far has made no assumptions about the choice of copula model other than the fact that it can be expressed in a conditional independence framework with central shock factor Y, there are a variety of ways in which the approximation can be generalized if we specialize to the commonly encountered Gaussian copula framework. We suppose that the n correlated N(0,1) variables $\{Z_i\}$ can be expressed in terms of the N components of the common factor $\{Y_i\}$ and n uncorrelated idiosyncratic factors $\{X_1 \ldots X_n\}$:

$$Z_i = \sum_{j=1}^{N} l_{ij} Y_j + \left(1 - \sum_{j=1}^{N} l_{ij}^2\right)^{1/2} X_i \tag{177}$$

$$\text{corr}(Z_i, Z_j) = \delta_{ij} + (1 - \delta_{ij})(ll^T)_{ij} \tag{178}$$

Even if we have projected the correlation matrix onto n factors, we can still choose to condition on only the first $m \leq n$ factors. If the first M factors account for most of the correlation, approximating the conditional joint distribution by a multivariate normal may still work reasonably well even though the defaults are no longer conditionally independent. In this case we find:

$$\mathbb{E}\left[L_T^k \middle| Y_1, \ldots, Y_M\right] = \sum_i w_i^k (1 - S_i^M(T)) \tag{179}$$

$$\text{cov}\left(L_T^k, L_T^{k'} \middle| Y_1, \ldots, Y_M\right) = \sum_i w_i^k w_i^{k'} S_i^M(T)(1 - S_i^M(T)) \tag{180}$$

$$+ \sum_{i,j} w_i^k w_j^{k'} \left(N_2(N^{-1}(S_i^M), N^{-1}(S_j^M); c_{ij}^M) - S_i^M S_j^M\right) \tag{181}$$

where $N_2(X, Y; \rho)$ is the bivariate cumulative normal distribution and:

$$S_i^M(T) = \mathbb{E}\left[\mathbb{1}_{\tau_i > T} \middle| Y_1, \ldots, Y_M\right] = N\left(\frac{N^{-1}(S_i(T)) - \sum_{j=1}^{M} l_{ij} Y_j}{\left(1 - \sum_{j=1}^{M} l_{ij}^2\right)^{1/2}}\right) \tag{182}$$

$$c_{ij}^M = \mathbb{1}_{i \neq j} \frac{\sum_{k>M}^{N} l_{ik} l_{jk}}{d_{Mi} d_{Mj}}, \quad d_{Mi} = \left(1 - \sum_{k=1}^{M} l_{ik}^2\right)^{1/2} \tag{183}$$

In this way we can handle more complex decompositions of the correlation matrix, for example by sector, whilst still retaining low dimensionality.

There have been several more recent efforts to improve on the approximation given here. One approach, the adjusted binomial approximation (O'Kane 2008), is based on the idea that the binomial distribution is a closer match to the actual conditional loss distribution than the normal distribution: as we have seen, in the homogeneous portfolio case, the binomial expression (128) is exact. In some cases, this approximation does give improved accuracy, whilst avoiding some of the obvious drawbacks of the normal distribution like finite probability of negative loss. However, it is not applicable to higher-dimensional problems such as CDO-squared pricing.

Another series of publications have investigated the saddle-point approach (Antonov, Mechkov, and Misirpashaev 2005; Veilex 2007). In this framework, the approximation given here is viewed as just one way of expanding the cumulant gen-erating function, which whilst it may be the simplest, may not always be the optimal one. A general description of the method is given by Richard Martin in this volume.

One final interesting application of directly approximating the loss distribution is pricing CDO-Squared trades in the presence of correlation skew. Since the base correlation skew is essentially a way of parameterizing the prices of CDOs, it can also be viewed as a way of parameterizing the loss distribution on a given portfolio. It tells us nothing, however, about the joint distributions of losses on different portfolios, which is necessary to price a CDO-Squared payoff. Since it is common to use the underlying CDOs as hedges, it is very important to ensure that the CDO-Squared and the underlying CDOs are marked consistently. In the absence of a universally accepted first principles based model for the correlation skew, one pragmatic approach to CDO-Squared pricing is to model the joint loss distribution directly.

Let us assume that we know the correlation skew $\rho_T^k(K)$ on portfolio k for all attachments K and maturities T. We express the loss of an equity tranche on this portfolio as $l_T^k(K, \rho_T^k(K)) = \mathbb{E}[\min(L_T^k, K)]$. From the expected loss we may derive the cumulative probability distribution by differentiation:

$$\Phi_T^k(K) = \Pr(L_T^k < K) = \mathbb{E}[\mathbb{1}_{L_T^k < K}] = 1 - \frac{dl_T^k(K, \rho_T^k(K))}{dK} \tag{184}$$

$$\frac{dl_T^k(K, \rho_T^k(K))}{dK} = \left.\frac{\partial l_T^k}{\partial K}\right|_{\rho_T^k} + \left.\frac{\partial l_T^k}{\partial \rho_T^k}\right|_K \frac{d\rho_T^k}{dK} \tag{185}$$

We can use a given central shock model to define a copula of conditional *loss* (rather than default times) that is consistent with the marginals (184) as follows. According to (169), (170), the conditional cumulative probability density in a given central shock model can be approximated as follows:

$$\Pr(L_T^1 < K_1, \ldots, L_T^m < K_m|Y) = N^{(m)}\left(\frac{K_1 - \mu_T^1}{\sigma_T^1}, \ldots, \frac{K_m - \mu_T^m}{\sigma_T^m}; \left\{\rho_T^{kk'}\right\}\right) \tag{186}$$

$$\Phi_T^{0,k}(K_k, Y) = \Pr(L_T^k < K_k|Y) = N\left(\frac{K_k - \mu_T^k}{\sigma_T^k}\right) \tag{187}$$

where we have defined $\sigma_T^k = \sqrt{c_T^{kk}}$ and the correlation matrix $\rho_T^{kk'} = c_T^{kk'}/(\sigma_k \sigma_{k'})$, and $N^{(m)}(X_1, \ldots, X_m; \rho)$ denotes the m-variate cumulative normal distribution with cor-relation matrix ρ. We use the equations (186), (187) to define the following Gaussian copula function, conditional on the central shock:

$$C(U_1, \ldots, U_m|Y) = N^{(m)}\left(N^{-1}(U_1), \ldots, N^{-1}(U_m); \left\{\rho_T^{kk'}(Y)\right\}\right) \tag{188}$$

Note the fact that we have arrived at a Gaussian copula for the conditional distrib-ution of *losses* has nothing to do with the copula model we originally assumed for *default times*: it derives from the conditional normal approximation for the joint loss distribution. Also note that once it is integrated over the central shock factor, the joint distribution of losses will in general be very far from a Gaussian copula. Although it does not have a simple analytical form we can numerically evaluate the *unconditional* marginal distribution by integrating over the common factor:

$$\Phi_T^{0,k}(K_k) = Pr(L_T^k < K_k) = \int \varphi(Y)\Phi_T^{0,k}(K_k, Y)dY \tag{189}$$

If we now define the transformed loss variables $\left\{ \hat{L}_T^k \right\}$ as follows:

$$\hat{L}_T^k = (\Phi_T^k)^{-1}(\Phi_T^{0,k}(L_T^k)) \tag{190}$$

where

$$\Phi_T^{0,k}(L_T^k, Y) = U_k \tag{191}$$

$$L_T^k = \mu_T^k + \sigma_T^k N^{-1}(U_k) \tag{192}$$

it can be seen that the transformed loss variables will have the desired marginal distributions (184), since:

$$\Pr(\hat{L}_T^k < K) = \mathbb{E}\left[\mathbb{1}_{\hat{L}_T^k < K}\right] \tag{193}$$

$$= \int \varphi(Y)dY\,\mathbb{E}\left[\mathbb{1}_{\hat{L}_T^k < K}\Big|Y\right] \tag{194}$$

$$= \int \varphi(Y)dY\,\mathbb{E}\left[\mathbb{1}_{L_T^k < (\Phi_T^{0,k})^{-1}(\Phi_T^k(K))}\Big|Y\right] \tag{195}$$

$$= \int \varphi(Y)dY\,\Phi_T^{0,k}\left((\Phi_T^{0,k})^{-1}(\Phi_T^k(K)), Y\right) \tag{196}$$

$$= \Phi_T^{0,k}\left((\Phi_T^{0,k})^{-1}(\Phi_T^k(K))\right) = \Phi_T^k(K) \tag{197}$$

By choosing the central shock model appropriately, the degree of correlation of the losses on different portfolios may be varied as desired, whilst ensuring that the marginal distributions are completely consistent with the base correlation skew. This approach also has the desirable feature that in the limit where the correlation skew reduces to the flat correlation copula model, the marginals $\Phi_T^k = \Phi_T^{0,k}$ and hence $\hat{L}_T^k = L_T^k$ and all expectations reduce to their usual values in the flat correlation copula. If the base correlation skew were viewed as a perturbation from a flat correlation world, this approach could be seen as an attempt to perturb the model in a minimal way which preserves the same dependence structure but modifies the marginal loss distributions.

The mapping (190) can be implemented efficiently using the normal approximation described above to evaluate it at a number of points, combined with a simple interpolation scheme. Valuing the CDO-Squared payoff itself can be implemented using Monte Carlo as before, with the additional mapping step (190).

8 STOCHASTIC RECOVERY

Fairly early on (Andersen and Sidenius 2004), an attempt was made to introduce non-deterministic recovery assumptions to the Gaussian copula model. The motivation at the time was to see to what extent stochastic recovery assumptions could better model observed features of the market such as the correlation skew. The conclusion was that it had very little effect. More recently, however, such models have been re-examined for a different reason. As correlations have drastically increased and senior tranches have become much riskier, situations have arisen, particularly in the CDX.IG index, where the deterministic recovery assumptions widely made for investment grade credits have become incompatible with observed tranche prices, and as a result it has become impossible to calibrate a base correlation skew.

More recent publications have therefore focused on how to modify the existing modelling framework in a simple way to enable the base correlation skew to be calibrated once more (Krekel 2008; Amraoui and Hitier 2008). A very simple change that would solve the calibration problem would simply be to mark the deterministic single-name recoveries to lower values. This would increase the maximum possible loss on the portfolio and thus make it easier to calibrate to the senior tranche quotes. However, in correlation modelling the single-name recoveries are generally taken as inputs, determined by market convention in the single-name market. As a result, the only way of increasing the probability of high losses is to make the recoveries stochastic, whilst ensuring that their conditional expected value is maintained at the level they are marked at in the single-name market (although if you are prepared to sacrifice agreement on the duration, the fact that CDS now largely trade on an up-front basis means that it is possible in principle to calibrate to the up-front prices of CDS with a different, lower, deterministic recovery assumption, whilst still reporting risk to the original quotes—the results of this approach can be qualitatively similar to introducing a stochastic recovery).

One naive approach is simply to assume that the recovery has a discrete distribution independent of default and time:

$$\text{Prob}\left(R_i = R_{ij}\right) = \pi_j$$

$$\sum_j \pi_j = 1, \quad \sum_j \pi_j R_{ij} = \bar{R}_i \tag{198}$$

where we have denoted the expected recovery given default for credit i by $\bar{R}_i$ (this is the recovery used to bootstrap the survival curve). A simple implementation that will usually enable calibration is to assume that the distribution is bimodal with one value lower than $\bar{R}_i$ and one that is higher. This changes the behaviour of the copula model significantly across the entire capital structure. A more targeted approach is to try and change the recovery distribution significantly only in states of the world where there are many defaults. This usually involves correlating the recovery with the factors that drive default.

In Andersen and Sidenius (2004) the researchers considered a general framework in which as usual $L_T = \sum_{i=1}^{n} w_i \xi_T^i$ but now the w_i are random variables:

$$w_i = N_i \left(1 - C_i(\mu_i + b_i \cdot Y + \zeta_i)\right) \tag{199}$$

where the $C_i : R \to [0, 1]$, $i = 1, \ldots, n$ are arbitrary mapping functions and the μ_i is a constant scalar, b_i a constant n-vector, Y the common factor and ζ_i an idiosyncratic random variable. In order to ensure consistency with the recovery assumptions used to bootstrap the survival probabilities, it is necessary to ensure that for all T:

$$\mathbb{E}\left[w_i | \tau_i \leq T\right] = \mathbb{E}\left[w_i \xi_T^i\right] / \mathbb{E}\left[\xi_T^i\right] \tag{200}$$

$$= N_i(1 - \bar{R}_i) \tag{201}$$

As noted in the original publication, if it is desired that $\bar{R}_i$ should be a time-independent constant, one or more of the parameters and the mapping function must in general be explicitly time dependent. Alternatively, if it is desired that the stochastic recovery parameters be time-independent, we will in general end up with a time dependent expected recovery $\bar{R}_i(t)$. In order to ensure consistency, we would then be obliged to modify the way single-name survival curves were bootstrapped to introduce a model-dependent term structure of recovery. This fact makes time-independent parameters an unpalatable choice.

If instead we allow the model parameters to be a function of maturity, we can adopt two different interpretations, either ensuring:

$$\mathbb{E}\left[w_i \xi_T^i\right] / \mathbb{E}\left[\xi_T^i\right] = N_i(1 - \bar{R}_i) \tag{202}$$

or

$$\mathbb{E}\left[\int_0^T w_i(t) d\xi_t^i\right] / \mathbb{E}\left[\xi_T^i\right] = N_i(1 - \bar{R}_i) \tag{203}$$

The first equation (202) adopts the criterion that the expectations at each time horizon must separately be correct but does not necessarily ensure consistency of the underlying process across multiple time horizons. The second equation (203) imposes theoretical consistency across all time horizons, but this is much more difficult to implement in practice. As a result the most popular models (Amraoui and Hitier 2008; Krekel 2008) ensure (202) but not (203), although recent attempts have been made (Bennani and Maetz 2009) to formulate a model that satisfies (203) whilst retaining tractability.

Suppose that the cumulative density of recovery conditional on default for a given credit i at a time horizon T is denoted $\Psi_i(R)$:

$$\Psi_i(R) = \text{Prob}(R_i < R | \tau_i \leq T)$$

$$\text{where } \bar{R}_i = \int_0^1 R_i d\Psi_i(R_i) \tag{204}$$

The overall idea behind most recent modelling approaches is to ensure that the recovery is anticorrelated to the central shock factor. This means that in scenarios where there are many defaults, the recovery is usually low, which gives us the best chance of calibrating when super-senior tranche spreads are high.

Let us first consider a model where we assume that R_i is a deterministic function of the central shock value Y. For definiteness, we specialize to the case of the Gaussian copula with decomposition (55). In order to ensure that (204) is satisfied, we find that R_i must have the following functional form:

$$R_i(Y) = \Psi_i^{-1}\left(\frac{\Phi_2\left(Y, \Phi^{-1}(q_i(T)); \sqrt{\rho}\right)}{q_i(T)}\right) \tag{205}$$

where $q_i(T) = 1 - S_i(T) = \mathbb{E}[\xi_T^i]$ is the unconditional default probability of credit i to maturity T. It can readily be confirmed that this expression satisfies (202) for any distribution Ψ_i satisfying (204). This provides a general way of setting up models of this type, but in practice by far the most popular specification is that suggested by Amraoui and Hitier (Amraoui and Hitier 2008):

$$R_i(Y) = 1 - \left(1 - \tilde{R}_i\right)\frac{g_\rho(\tilde{q}_i, Y)}{g_\rho(q_i, Y)} \tag{206}$$

where

$$\tilde{R}_i \le \bar{R}_i$$

$$g_\rho(q_i, Y) = \mathbb{E}\left[\xi_T^i \middle| Y\right] = \Phi\left(\frac{\Phi^{-1}(q_i) - \sqrt{\rho}Y}{\sqrt{1-\rho}}\right) \tag{207}$$

The single free parameter in this model is $\tilde{R}_i$ which specifies the minimum value that R_i may attain: it is found that in order to satisfy (202), we must impose:

$$\tilde{q}_i = \frac{1 - \bar{R}_i}{1 - \tilde{R}_i}q_i \tag{208}$$

Although there is no simple explicit expression for Ψ_i in this model, it has the advantage of a very simple functional form (206) for $R_i(Y)$ and a single free parameter. In Figure 7.11 we show how in this model with $\tilde{R}_i = 0$, the correlation skew for CDX moves down, and the 30% correlation, which was failing to calibrate the 15–30% tranche even at 100% correlation, is able to calibrate again.

Another popular approach, due to (Krekel 2008), assumes that R_i is a deterministic function of Z_i in (55). In order to ensure that (204) is satisfied we must have:

$$R_i(Z_i) = \mathbb{1}_{\Phi(Z_i) \le q_i}\Psi_i^{-1}\left(\frac{\Phi(Z_i)}{q_i}\right) \tag{209}$$

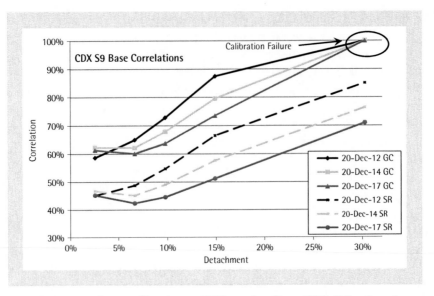

FIGURE 7.11 Base correlation calibration to CDX tranches (June 2009) GC = Gaussian copula, SR = Gaussian copula with stochastic recovery: showing that without SR, calibration of the 30% point fails even with an implied correlation of 100%.

Source: BofA Merrill Lynch Global Research.

With this choice, we find that the distribution of recovery conditional on the central shock is given by:

$$\Psi_i(R|Y) = \mathbb{E}\left[\mathbb{1}_{R_i(Z_i) \le R}\big|Y\right]$$

$$= \frac{\Phi\left(\frac{\Phi^{-1}(\Psi_i(R)q_i) - \sqrt{\rho}Y}{\sqrt{1-\rho}}\right)}{\Phi\left(\frac{\Phi^{-1}(q_i) - \sqrt{\rho}Y}{\sqrt{1-\rho}}\right)} \tag{210}$$

Krekel presented an example where $\Psi_i(R)$ was a non-parametric discrete distribution with four possible values of R_i although there is no reason why a parametric distribution with fewer parameters could not be used. A more serious objection is that conditional on the central shock, there is more than one possible value of R_i. This necessitates increasing the number of nodes if a recursion approach is used, which has a high performance cost.

9 CONCLUSIONS

We have presented a broad overview of the state of the modelling of single-and multi-name credit derivatives. It is clear that whilst much progress has been made, many challenges need to be overcome before the field matures. A lot of the modelling innovations described in this article were developed during a relatively benign period of the credit cycle, when spreads were tight, the volatility and tail risk implied by the market were low, and the focus of a lot of market practitioners was simply not on risk management.

Recent events have tested these modelling and hedging assumptions to destruction. It is to be hoped that researchers will learn from this experience and develop new, better, and more robust models in the future.

REFERENCES

Amraoui, S., and Hitier, S. (2008). 'Optimal stochastic recovery for base correlation'. Working paper.

Andersen, L., and Sidenius, J. (2004). 'Extensions of the gaussian copula: random recovery and random factor loadings'. *Journal of Credit Risk*, 1/1: 29–70.

——— and Basu, S. (2003). 'All your hedges in one basket', *Risk Magazine* (Nov.), 67–72.

Antonov, A., Mechkov, S., and Misirpashaev, T. (2005). 'Analytical techniques for synthetic cdos and credit default risk measures'. NumeriX working paper.

Baxter, M. (2007). 'Lévy simple structural models'. In A. Lipton and A. Rennie (eds.), *Credit Correlation: Life After Copulas*. Singapore: World Scientific.

Bennani, N. (2005). 'The forward loss model: a dynamic term structure approach for the pricing of portfolio credit derivatives'. Working paper.

——— and Maetz, J. (2009). 'A spot recovery rate extension of the gaussian copula'. Working paper.

Bielecki, T. R., and Rutkowski, M. (2002). *Credit Risk: Modeling, Valuation and Hedging*. Berlin: Springer Finance.

Black, F., and Scholes, M. (1973). 'The pricing of options and corporate liabilities'. *Journal of Political Economy* 81: 637–54.

Bouyé, E., Durrleman, V., Nikeghbali, A., Riboulet, G., and Roncalli, T. (2000). 'Copulas for finance: A reading guide and some applications'. Working paper: Groupe de Recherche Opérationelle, Credit Lyonnais.

Bowers, N. L., Gerber, H. U., Hickman, J. C., Jones, D. A., and Nesbitt, C. J. (1997). *Actuarial Mathematics*. Schanmberg, IL: Society of Actuaries.

Brasch, H.-J. (2004). 'A note on efficient pricing and risk calculation of credit basket products'. Working paper.

Brigo, D., Pallavicini, A., and Torresetti, R. (2006). 'Calibration of cdo tranches with the dynamical generalized-poisson loss model'. Working paper.

Burtschell, X., Gregory, J., and Laurent, J.-P. (2007). 'Beyond the gaussian copula: stochastic and local correlation'. *Journal of Credit Risk*, 3/1: 31–62.

Chapovsky, A., Rennie, A., and Tavares, P. (2001). 'Stochastic intensity modelling for structured credit exotics'. *International Journal of Theoretical and Applied Finance*, 10: 633–52.

Cont, R., and Minca, A. (2008). 'Recovering portfolio default intensities implied by cdo quotes'. Columbia University Center for Financial Engineering Financial Engineering Report No. 2008–01.

——— and Savescu, I. (2008). 'Forward equations for portfolio credit derivatives'. Columbia University Center for Financial Engineering Financial Engineering Report No. 2008–05.

Cooley, J. W., and Tukey, J. W. (1965). 'An algorithm for the machine calculation of complex fourier series'. *Mathematics of Computation*, 19: 297–301.

Davies, P. J. (2006). 'Bashful traders wait for a thinner slice'. *Financial Times*, 20 Feb.

Debuysscher, A., and Szego, M. (2003). 'The fourier transform method: overview'. Moody's Investors Service Structured Finance Special Report.

Derman, E., and Kani, I. (1994). 'The volatility smile and its implied tree'. Goldman Sachs Quantitative Strategies Research Notes.

Duffie, D., and Garleanu, N. (2001). 'Risk and valuation of collateralized debt obligations'. *Financial Analysis Journal*, 57: 41–59.

——Pan, J., and Singleton, K. (2000). 'Transform analysis and asset pricing for affine jump diffusions'. *Econometrica*, 68: 1343–76.

——and Zhu, H. (2009). 'Does a central clearing counterparty reduce counterparty risk?' Working paper.

Dupire, B. (1994). 'Pricing with a smile', *Risk*, 7/1: 18–20.

Embrechts, P., Lindskog, F., and McNeil, A. (2003). Modelling dependence with copulas and applications to risk management, in S. Rachev, (ed.), *Handbook of Heavy-Tailed Distributions in Finance*. Amsterdam: Elsevier/New-Holland.

Emery, K., Ou, S., Tennant, J., Matos, A., and Cantor, R. (2009). 'Corporate default and recovery rates 1920–2008'. *Moody's Global Credit Policy*.

Euclid (300 BC). *Elements*, Volume 7, Proposition 2.

Giesecke, K., and Goldberg, L. (2005). 'A top-down approach to multi-name credit'. Working paper.

Graziano, G. D., and Rogers, C. (2009). 'A dynamic approach to the modelling of correlation credit derivatives using markov chains'. *International Journal of Theoretical and Applied Finance*, 12/1: 45–62.

Gregory, J. (2009). 'Being two-faced over counterparty credit risk'. *Risk*, 22/2: 86–90.

Heath, D., Jarrow, R. A., and Morton, A. (1992). 'Bond pricing and the term structure of interest rates: a new methodology for contingent claims valuation'. *Econometrica*, 60/1: 77–105.

Heaton, C. S. (2007). 'Are cpdos a disaster waiting to happen?' MoneyWeek, 8 Oct.

Heideman, M., Johnson, D., and Burrus, C. (1984). 'Gauss and the history of the fast fourier transform'. *ASSP Magazine, IEEE*, 1/4: 14–21.

Hull, J., and White, A. (2000). 'Valuing credit default swaps i: no counterparty default risk'. *Journal of Derivatives*, 8/1: 29–40.

————(2004). 'Valuation of a cdo and an nth to default cds without monte carlo simulation'. *Journal of Derivatives*, 12/2: 8–23.

————(2006). 'Valuing credit derivatives using an implied copula approach'. *Journal of Derivatives*, 14/2: 8–28.

————(2009). 'An improved implied copula model and its application to the valuation of bespoke cdo tranches'. Preprint.

Inglis, S., and Lipton, A. (2007). 'Factor models for credit correlation'. *Risk*, 20: 110–115.

Inglis, S., Lipton, A., Savescu, I., and Sepp, A. (2008). 'Dynamic credit models'. *Statistics and its Interface*, 1: 211–227.

Inglis, S., Lipton, A., and Sepp, A. (2009). 'Factor models for credit correlation: brief communication'. *Risk*, 22(4).

ISDA (2009a). 'Isda standard cds converter specification', available from <http://cdsmodel.com>.

——(2009b). 'Standard european corporate cds contract specification', available from <http://cdsmodel.com>.

——(2009c). 'Standard north american corporate cds contract specification', available from <http://cdsmodel.com>.

Jarrow, R., and Turnbull, S. (1995). 'Pricing options on financial securities subject to credit risk'. *Journal of Finance*, 50: 53–85.

Jones, S., Tett, G., and Davies, P. J. (2008). 'Cpdos expose ratings flaw at moody's'. *Financial Times*, 21 May.

Joshi, M. S., and Stacey, A. M. (2005). 'Intensity gamma: a new approach to pricing portfolio credit derivatives'. Working paper.

Krekel, M. (2008). 'Pricing distressed cdos with base correlation and stochastic recovery'. Working paper.

Lando, D. (1994). 'Three essays on contingent claims pricing'. Ph.D. Thesis: Cornell University.

——(1998). 'On cox processes and credit risky securities'. *Review of Derivatives Research*, 2: 99–120.

Laurent, J.-P., and Gregory, J. (2005). 'Basket default swaps, cdos and factor copulas'. *Journal of Risk*, 7/4: 03–122.

Li, D. (2000). 'On default correlation: a copula approach'. *Journal of Fixed Income*, 9/4: 43–54.

Lindskog, F., and McNeil, A. (2003). 'Common poisson shock models: applications to insurance and credit risk modelling'. *ASTIN Bulletin*, 33/2: 209–38.

Lipton, A. (2001). *Mathematical Methods for Foreign Exchange*. Singapore: World Scientific.

——(2010). Multiname random intensity models. In R. Cont, (ed.), *Encyclopedia of Quantitative Finance*. Chichester: Wiley.

——and Sepp, A. (2009). 'Credit value adjustment for credit default swaps via the structural default model'. *Journal of Credit Risk*, 5/2: 1–25.

Longstaff, F. A., and Rajan, A. (2006). 'An empirical analysis of the pricing of collateralized debt obligations'. NBER Working Paper No. W12210.

Lopatin, A., and Misirpashaev, T. (2008). 'Two-dimensional markovian model for dynamics of aggregate credit loss'. In J.-P. Fouque, T. B. Fomby and K. Solna, (eds.), *Econometrics and Risk Management*, Vol. 22 of *Advances In Econometrics'*. Binglay: Emerald Group, 243–74.

Luciano, E., and Schoutens, W. (2006). 'A multivariate jump-driven financial asset model'. *Quantitative Finance*, 6/5: 385–402.

McGinty, L., Bernstein, E., Ahluwalia, R., and Watts, M. (2004). 'Introducing base correlations'. *JP Morgan Credit Derivatives Strategy*.

Mashal, R., Naldi, M., and Zeevi, A. (2003). 'Comparing the dependence structure of equity and asset returns'. *Lehman Brothers Quantitative Credit Research*.

Merino, S., and Nyfeler, M. (2002). 'Calculating portfolio loss'. *Risk* (Aug), 82–6.

Mina, J., and Stern, E. (2003). 'Examples and applications of closed-form cdo pricing'. *RiskMetrics Journal*, 4/1: 82–6.

Moosbrucker, T. (2006). 'Pricing cdos with correlated variance gamma distributions'. Working paper.

Mortensen, A. (2006). 'Semi-analytical valuation of basket credit derivatives in intensity-based models'. *Journal of Derivatives*, 13/4: 8–26.

Muench, D., and Sbityakov, A. (2006). 'An introduction to tranchelets'. *JP Morgan Global Credit Derivatives Research*.

O'Kane, D. (2008). *Modelling Single-Name and Multi-Name Credit Derivatives*. Chichester: Wiley Finance.

Pain, A., Renault, O., and Shelton, D. (2005). 'Base correlation: the term structure dimension'. *Citigroup Global Structured Credit Research*.

Panjer, H. (1981). 'Recursive evaluation of a family of compound distributions'. *ASTIN Bulletin*, 12: 22–6.

Parcell, E. (2006). 'Loss unit interpolation in the collateralized debt obligation model'. Preprint.

Reyfman, A., Ushakova, K., and Kong, W. (2004). 'How to value bespoke tranches consistently with standard ones'. *Bear Stearns Credit Derivatives Research*.

Salmon, F. (2009). 'Recipe for disaster: the formula that killed wall street'. *Wired Magazine*, 17.03.

Schönbucher, P. (2003a). *Credit Derivatives Pricing Models: Models Pricing and Implementation*. Chichester: Wiley Finance.

——(2003b). 'A note on survival measures and the pricing of options on credit default swaps'. Working paper, ETH, Zurich.

——(2005). 'Portfolio losses and the term structure of loss transition rates: a new methodology for the pricing of portfolio credit derivatives'. Working paper, ETH, Zurich.

Shelton, D. (2004). 'Back to normal. Proxy integration: a fast accurate method for cdo and cdo-squared pricing'. *Citigroup Global Structured Credit Research*.

Sidenius, J., Piterbarg, V., and Andersen, L. B. G. (2008). 'A new framework for dynamic credit portfolio loss modeling'. *International Journal of Theoretical and Applied Finance*, 11/2: 163–97.

Sundt, B., and Jewell, W. (1981). 'Further results on recursive evaluation of compound distributions'. *ASTIN Bulletin*, 12: 27–39.

Tavares, P., Nguyen, T.-U., and Vaysburd, I. (2004). 'Composite basket model'. *Merrill Lynch Credit Derivatives*.

Vasicek, O. (1987). 'Probability of loss on loan portfolio'. *KMV Corporation*.

Veilex, L. (2007). 'Higher order large deviation approximations applied to cdo pricing'. Preprint.

Whitehouse, M. (2005). 'Slices of risk: how a formula ignited market that burned some big investors'. *Wall Street Journal*, 12 Sept.

CHAPTER 8

....

MARSHALL-OLKIN
COPULA-BASED MODELS

....

YOUSSEF ELOUERKHAOUI

1 INTRODUCTION

....

THE problem of correlating multiple credits boils down to the specification of a copula function, which links the marginal default distributions. There is a growing literature that addresses this problem. The main approach that has emerged as the market standard is the Gaussian copula approach. The idea of using a Gaussian copula to model the default times' dependence in basket products goes back to Li (2000). It was also used implicitly in the CreditMetrics framework and the KMV (Kealhofer, McQuown, Vasicek) firm-value approach. The t-copula is an extension of the Gaussian copula with a higher tail dependence. It allows for a better modelling of extreme events' risk. A good reference on t-copulas and the pricing of small baskets can be found in Mashal and Naldi (2002a, 2002b).

In this chapter, we study another alternative: the Marshall-Olkin copula. This latter was first used in the context of basket credit derivatives pricing by Duffie (1998), then by Duffie and Garleanu (2001). The Marshall-Olkin copula was traditionally used in reliability theory to model the failure of multi-component systems. In this set-up, the failure of each component is assumed to be contingent on some independent Poisson shocks. This is also known as a multivariate Poisson model. A good description of these models can be found in Barlow and Proschan (1981). The Marshall-Olkin copula can also be viewed as the limiting distribution of a multivariate binary model (Wong 2000). One practical feature of the Marshall-Olkin approach is the simplicity of its Monte Carlo implementation. In addition, it has a number of useful analytical results for aggregate portfolio distributions (see Lindskog and McNeil 2003).

The purpose of this chapter is primarily to show that the Marshall-Olkin (MO) model can be a viable alternative to the standard Gaussian copula. This is achieved in three steps. First, we present the MO framework. Second, we propose a parameterization procedure of the model based on market intuition and observed market prices. And third, we compare the Marshall-Olkin copula with its elliptical counterparts: the Gaussian and the t-copula.

The rest of the chapter is structured as follows. In section 2, we introduce the Marshall-Olkin model. In section 3, we derive the copula function of default times. In section 4, we study the aggregate default distribution. In section 5, we discuss the model calibration. In section 6, we compare Marshall-Olkin with the Gaussian and t-copula. In section 7, we use the Marshall-Olkin copula to reproduce the correlation skew in the CDO market.

2 THE MODEL

We work on probability space $(\Omega, \mathcal{G}, P)$, on which is given a set of n non-negative random variables $(\tau_1, \dots, \tau_n)$ representing the default times of a basket of obligors.

We introduce, for each obligor i, the right-continuous process $D_t^i \triangleq \mathbf{1}_{\{\tau_i \le t\}}$ indicating whether the firm has defaulted or not.

We assume that there exists a set of m independent Poisson processes $\left(N_t^{c_j}\right)_{t \ge 0}$ with intensities $\lambda^{c_j} \in \mathbb{R}_+$, which can trigger simultaneous joint defaults.

Each Poisson process N^{c_j} can be equivalently represented by the sequence of event trigger times $\left\{\theta_r^{c_j}\right\}_{r \in \{1,2,\dots\}}$.

At the rth occurrence of an event of type c_j, we draw a set of independent $\{0, 1\}$-valued Bernoulli variables $\left(A_{\theta_r^{c_j}}^{1,j}, \dots, A_{\theta_r^{c_j}}^{n,j}\right)$ with probabilities $\left(p^{1,j}, \dots, p^{n,j}\right)$, $p^{i,j} \in [0, 1]$. The variable $A_{\theta_r^{c_j}}^{i,j}$ indicates whether a default of type i has occurred or not.

The process $\left(N_t^i\right)_{t \ge 0}$ defined as

$$N_t^i \triangleq \sum_{j=1}^{m} \sum_{\theta_r^{c_j} \le t} A_{\theta_r^{c_j}}^{i,j}, \tag{1}$$

is also a Poisson process with intensity

$$\lambda^i = \sum_{j=1}^{m} p^{i,j} \lambda^{c_j}. \tag{2}$$

It is obtained by superpositioning m independent (thinned) Poisson processes.

The default time τ_i is defined as the first jump time of the Poisson process $\left(N_t^i\right)_{t \ge 0}$:

$$\tau_i \triangleq \inf\left\{t : N_t^i > 0\right\}. \tag{3}$$

This common shock model can also be described formally by the following stochastic differential equation (SDE)

$$dD_t^i = \left(1 - D_{t-}^i\right) \sum_{j=1}^{m} A_t^{i,j} dN_t^{c_j}. \tag{4}$$

This description was used, for instance, in Duffie (1998).

3 THE COPULA FUNCTION

In this section, we derive the copula function of the shock model described above. To this end, we shall use the 'equivalent fatal shock model' of Lindskog and McNeil (2003).

3.1 Equivalent fatal shock model

Let $\Pi_{\mathbf{n}}$ be the set of all subsets of $\{1, \dots, n\}$, excluding the empty set $\emptyset$. For each $\pi \in \Pi_{\mathbf{n}}$, we introduce the point process N_t^{π}, which counts the number of shocks in $(0, t]$ resulting in joint defaults of the obligors in π only:

$$N_t^{\pi} \triangleq \sum_{j=1}^{m} \sum_{r=1}^{N_t^{c_j}} A_{\theta_r^{c_j}}^{\pi, j}, \tag{5}$$

where, for each trigger time $\theta_r^{c_j}$, $A_{\theta_r^{c_j}}^{\pi, j}$ is a Bernoulli variable, which is equal to 1 if all obligors $i \in \pi$ default and all the others, $i \notin \pi$, survive:

$$A_t^{\pi, j} \triangleq \prod_{i \in \pi} A_t^{i,j} \prod_{i \notin \pi} \left(1 - A_t^{i,j}\right). \tag{6}$$

At the occurrence of the rth common shock, of type c_j, at time $\theta_r^{c_j}$, the point process N_t^{π} gets incremented by $\Delta N_{\theta_r^{c_j}}^{\pi} = A_{\theta_r^{c_j}}^{\pi, j}$. For example, if $\pi = \{1, 2\}$, then the process $N_t^{\{1,2\}}$ counts the shocks, which trigger simultaneous defaults of obligors 1 and 2 but not the other obligors 3 to n.

We have the following fatal shock representation key result. We refer to Lindskog and McNeil (2003) for details (see Proposition 4).

Proposition 3.1 *(Fatal shock representation). The processes* $(N^{\pi})_{\pi \in \Pi_{\mathbf{n}}}$ *are independent Poisson processes with intensities*

$$\lambda^{\pi} = \sum_{j=1}^{m} p^{\pi, j} \lambda^{c_j},$$

where

$$p^{\pi,j} = \prod_{i \in \pi} p^{i,j} \prod_{i \notin \pi} \left(1 - p^{i,j}\right).$$

This provides a fatal shock representation of the original not-necessarily-fatal shock set-up. It will allow us to analyse the multivariate distribution of the default times.

For $\pi \in \Pi_{\mathbf{n}}$, let τ_π denote the first jump time of the Poisson process N^π:

$$\tau_\pi = \inf\left\{t : N_t^\pi > 0\right\}.$$

Each obligor i can be equivalently described using the fatal shock representation.

Lemma 3.2 *(Obligor description using the fatal shock representation).*

1. *The Poisson process N^i can be expressed as*

$$N_t^i = \sum_{\pi \in \Pi_{\mathbf{n}}} \mathbf{1}_{\{i \in \pi\}} N_t^\pi,$$

   and its intensity is given by

$$\lambda^i = \sum_{\pi \in \Pi_{\mathbf{n}}} \mathbf{1}_{\{i \in \pi\}} \lambda^\pi.$$

2. *The default time τ_i is given by*

$$\tau_i = \min\left\{\tau_\pi : i \in \pi, \pi \in \Pi_{\mathbf{n}}\right\}.$$

3.2 Multivariate exponential distribution

Since we have

$$\tau_i = \inf\left\{t : N_t^i > 0\right\} = \inf\left\{t : \sum_{\pi \in \Pi_{\mathbf{n}}} \mathbf{1}_{\{i \in \pi\}} N_t^\pi > 0\right\} = \min_{\pi : i \in \pi} \tau_\pi,$$

the multivariate distribution of $(\tau_1, \ldots, \tau_n) = \left(\min_{\pi : 1 \in \pi} \tau_\pi, \ldots, \min_{\pi : n \in \pi} \tau_\pi\right)$ can be computed as follows.

Proposition 3.3 *(Multivariate Exponential Distribution). The multivariate distribution of the default times $(\tau_1, \ldots, \tau_n)$ is*

$$\mathbb{P}\left(\tau_1 > T_1, \ldots, \tau_n > T_n\right) = \prod_{\pi \in \Pi_{\mathbf{n}}} \exp\left(-\Lambda^\pi_{\max_{i \in \pi} T_i}\right), \tag{7}$$

where $\Lambda^\pi_T \triangleq \int_0^T \lambda^\pi ds$.

This is the Multivariate Exponential Distribution developed by Marshall and Olkin (1967). We refer to Barlow and Proschan (1981), Joe (1997) or Nelsen (1999) for a detailed study of this distribution function:

$$\mathbb{P}\left(\tau_1 > T_1, \ldots, \tau_n > T_n\right) = \exp\left(-\sum_i \Lambda_{T_i}^{\{i\}} - \sum_{i,j} \Lambda_{\max(T_i, T_j)}^{\{i,j\}} - \cdots - \Lambda_{\max(T_1, \ldots, T_n)}^{\{1, \ldots, n\}}\right).$$

Proof. We proceed as follows:

$$\mathbb{P}\left(\tau_1 > T_1, \ldots, \tau_n > T_n\right) = \mathbb{P}\left(\min_{\pi:1\in\pi} \tau_\pi > T_1, \ldots, \min_{\pi:n\in\pi} \tau_\pi > T_n\right)$$

$$= \mathbb{P}\left(\bigcap_{\pi\in\Pi_n} \left\{\tau_\pi > \max_{i\in\pi} T_i\right\}\right)$$

$$= \mathbb{P}\left(\bigcap_{\pi\in\Pi_n} \left\{N_{\max_{i\in\pi} T_i}^\pi = 0\right\}\right)$$

$$= \prod_{\pi\in\Pi_n} \mathbb{P}\left(\left\{N_{\max_{i\in\pi} T_i}^\pi = 0\right\}\right)$$

$$= \prod_{\pi\in\Pi_n} \exp\left(-\Lambda_{\max_{i\in\pi} T_i}^\pi\right),$$

the third equality is from the definition of τ_π, the fourth equality is due to the independence of the Poisson processes $(N^\pi)_{\pi\in\Pi_n}$. □

The Multivariate Exponential distribution is 'memoryless', i.e. it has the property that

$$\mathbb{P}\left(\tau_1 > T_1, \ldots \tau_n > T_n \mid \tau_1 > t_1, \ldots \tau_n > t_n\right) = \mathbb{P}\left(\tau_1 > T_1 - t_1, \ldots \tau_n > T_n - t_n\right),$$

for all $T_1 > t_1, \ldots, T_n > t_n$. This is the multi-dimensional version of the well-known property for the exponential distribution.

Example. For $n = 2$, if we set $u_1 \triangleq \mathbb{P}(\tau_1 > t_1)$, $u_2 \triangleq \mathbb{P}(\tau_2 > t_2)$ and $a_1 \triangleq \frac{\lambda^{\{1,2\}}}{\lambda^{\{1\}}}$, $a_2 \triangleq \frac{\lambda^{\{1,2\}}}{\lambda^{\{2\}}}$, we get the bivariate Marshall-Olkin survival copula

$$\overline{C}(u_1, u_2) = u_1 u_2 \min\left(u_1^{-a_1}, u_2^{-a_2}\right) = \min\left(u_1^{1-a_1} u_2, u_1 u_2^{1-a_2}\right). \tag{8}$$

The copula function (8) has an absolutely continuous part on the upper and lower triangles: $\{u_1 < u_2\}$ and $\{u_2 < u_1\}$, and has a singular component on the diagonal $\{u_1 = u_2\}$.

4 THE AGGREGATE DEFAULT DISTRIBUTION

The central question in credit portfolio modelling is the study of the aggregate default distribution of a given portfolio. Let X_t denote the total number of defaults, for a fixed time horizon t:

$$X_t \triangleq \sum_{i=1}^{n} D_t^i. \tag{9}$$

The distribution of X_t is referred to as the aggregate default distribution at time t. In this section, we derive the aggregate default distribution in the Marshall-Olkin model.

4.1 Poisson approximation

In Lindskog and McNeil (2003), the default indicators D_t^i are approximated by their corresponding Poisson counters N_t^i. For low default probabilities this is a reasonable approximation. For $t \geq 0$, the total number of defaults X_t is then approximated by the random variable Z_t defined as

$$X_t \simeq Z_t \triangleq \sum_{i=1}^{n} N_t^i. \tag{10}$$

This is known in the actuarial literature as the approximation of the individual model with the collective model; for low individual default probabilities, the likelihood of multiple jumps in the Poisson process is small, and is neglected for the purposes of estimating the aggregate portfolio distribution.

The total number of losses $Z_t \triangleq \sum_{i=1}^{n} N_t^i$ is a compound Poisson process. It is the sum of m independent compound Poisson processes $Z_t^{c_j}$:

$$Z_t^{c_j} \triangleq \sum_{r=1}^{N_t^{c_j}} \sum_{i=1}^{n} A_{\theta_r^{c_j}}^{i,j}. \tag{11}$$

Next, we derive the distribution of Z_t, first, using its moment generating function, then using Panjer's algorithm.

4.2 Moment generating function (MGF)

The aggregate portfolio counter Z_t is a compound Poisson process, which is obtained as the sum of m independent compound Poisson processes:

$$Z_t = \sum_{j=1}^{m} Z_t^{c_j}. \tag{12}$$

The distribution of each compound Poisson $Z_t^{c_j}$ is not available in closed form, but one can compute its moment generating function $\mathcal{L}_{Z_t}(a) \triangleq \mathbb{E}\left[e^{-aZ_t}\right]$. Since the processes $Z_t^{c_j}$ are independent the MGF of Z_t is given by

$$\mathcal{L}_{Z_t}(a) = \prod_{j=1}^{M} \mathcal{L}_{Z_t^{c_j}}(a).$$

$Z_t^{c_j}$ is defined by the Poisson counter $N_t^{c_j}$ and its compounding distribution X^{c_j}, i.e.

$$Z_t^{c_j} \overset{d}{=} \sum_{r=1}^{N_t^{c_j}} X_r^{c_j}, \tag{13}$$

where $X_1^{c_j}, \dots, X_{N_t^{c_j}}^{c_j} \left(\overset{d}{=} X^{c_j}\right)$ are i.i.d. independent of $N_t^{c_j}$. When the jump sizes $X_r^{c_j}$ are discrete random variables taking values in $\{a_1, a_2, \dots\}$, one can write

$$Z_t^{c_j} = \sum_k a_k N_t^{a_k},$$

where $N_t^{a_k}$ are independent Poisson processes with intensities

$$\lambda^{a_k} = \lambda^{c_j} \mathbb{P}\left(X^{c_j} = a_k\right),$$

and the MGF of the compound Poisson process is obtained immediately as

$$\mathcal{L}_{Z_t^{c_j}}(a) = \mathbb{E}\left[e^{-aZ_t^{c_j}}\right] = \mathbb{E}\left[\exp\left(-a\sum_k a_k N_t^{a_k}\right)\right] = \exp\left(-t\sum_k \left(1 - e^{-aa_k}\right)\lambda^{a_k}\right).$$

Here, the jump sizes take values in $\{0, 1, \dots, n\}$ and the distribution of $X^{c_j} = \sum_{i=1}^{n} A^{i,j}$, where $A^{i,j}$ is a Bernoulli variable with probability $p^{i,j}$, can be computed by inverting its Fourier transform, which is given by the product

$$\mathcal{F}_{X^{c_j}}(a) = \mathbb{E}\left[e^{-iaX^{c_j}}\right] = \prod_{i=1}^{n} \left(p^{i,j} e^{-ia} + \left(1 - p^{i,j}\right)\right).$$

The moment generating function of Z_t is then given by

$$\mathcal{L}_{Z_t}(a) = \prod_{j=1}^{m} \exp\left(-t\sum_{k=0}^{n} \left(1 - e^{-ak}\right)\lambda^{c_j} \mathbb{P}\left(X^{c_j} = k\right)\right). \tag{14}$$

4.3 Panjer's recursion

As shown in Lindskog and McNeil (2003), the distribution of the compound Poisson Z_t can also be derived using Panjer's recursion. The total number of losses Z_t has the following representation (see Proposition 6 in Lindskog and McNeil 2003):

$$Z_t \overset{d}{=} \sum_{r=1}^{\widetilde{N}_t} \widetilde{X}_r, \tag{15}$$

where $\widetilde{N}_t$ is a Poisson process with intensity

$$\widetilde{\lambda} = \sum_{j=1}^{m} \lambda^{c_j} \left[1 - \prod_{i=1}^{n} \left(1 - p^{i,j} \right) \right].$$

It counts any loss-causing shock in $(0, t]$. $\widetilde{X}_1, \dots, \widetilde{X}_{N_t^{c_j}} \left(\overset{d}{=} \widetilde{X} \right)$ are Independent identically distributed (i.i.d.) and independent of $\widetilde{N}_t$. The distribution of $\widetilde{X}$ is given by

$$\mathbb{P} \left(\widetilde{X} = 0 \right) = 0,$$

$$\mathbb{P} \left(\widetilde{X} = k \right) = \frac{1}{\widetilde{\lambda}} \sum_{j=1}^{m} \lambda^{c_j} \mathbb{P} \left(X^{c_j} = k \right), \text{ for } k = 1, \dots, n,$$

$$\mathbb{P} \left(\widetilde{X} = k \right) = 0, \text{ for } k > n.$$

The distribution of Z_t can then be computed with Panjer's algorithm (see Panjer 1981):

$$\mathbb{P} \left(Z_t = 0 \right) = \exp \left(-\widetilde{\lambda} t \right),$$

$$\mathbb{P} \left(Z_t = l \right) = \frac{\widetilde{\lambda} t}{l} \sum_{k=1}^{l} k \mathbb{P} \left(\widetilde{X} = k \right) \mathbb{P} \left(Z_t = l - k \right), \text{ for } l > 0.$$

This recursive algorithm offers a more efficient method for computing the probabilities $\mathbb{P} \left(Z_t = l \right)$, than the inversion of the moment generating function.

4.4 Duffie's approximation

Duffie and Pan (2001) have suggested another approximation of the aggregate default distribution. They have neglected the probability of multiple jumps of the common market factor events and they have assumed that the solution of the SDE (4) can be approximated as

$$D_t^i \overset{d}{\simeq} \sum_{j=1}^{m} A^{i,j} N_t^{c_j}. \tag{16}$$

Using equation (16), we can easily compute the Laplace transform of $X_t \triangleq \sum_{i=1}^{n} D_t^i$ as a product of conditional market factor Laplace transforms:

$$\mathcal{L}_{X_t} (a) = \mathbb{E} \left[e^{-a X_t} \right]$$

$$\simeq \prod_{j=1}^{m} \left[\exp \left(-\Lambda_T^{c_j} \right) + \left(1 - \exp \left(-\Lambda_T^{c_j} \right) \right) \prod_{i=1}^{n} \left(p^{i,j} e^{-a} + \left(1 - p^{i,j} \right) \right) \right].$$

If $m > n$, so that we have n idiosyncratic factors and $m - n$ common market factors, i.e.,

$$D_t^i \simeq \sum_{j=1}^{m-n} A^{i,j} N_t^{c_j} + N_t^{0,i},$$

where $N_t^{0,i} \triangleq N_t^{c_{m-n+i}}$ is the idiosyncratic factor of obligor i. Then, the Laplace transform collapses to

$$\mathcal{F}_{X_t}(a) \simeq \varphi^0(a) \prod_{j=1}^{m} \left[\exp\left(-\Lambda_T^{c_j}\right) + \left(1 - \exp\left(-\Lambda_T^{c_j}\right)\right) \varphi_j^c(a) \right], \qquad (17)$$

where

$$\varphi^0(a) = \prod_{i=1}^{n} \left(\left(1 - \exp\left(-\Lambda_T^{0,i}\right)\right) e^{-\alpha} + \exp\left(-\Lambda_T^{0,i}\right) \right),$$

$$\varphi_j^c(a) = \prod_{i=1}^{n} \left(p^{i,j} e^{-\alpha} + \left(1 - p^{i,j}\right) \right).$$

A direct inversion of the Laplace transform (17) gives the aggregate default distribution.

4.5 Monte Carlo

The aggregate default distribution can also be estimated using a Monte Carlo method. A good reference on simulating Multivariate-Exponential Default Times can be found, for instance, in Duffie and Singleton (1999b).

We are interested in simulating the correlated default times $(\tau_1, \ldots, \tau_n)$ only if they occur before a fixed time horizon T. The basic algorithm proceeds as follows:

1. Simulate the jump times of the market factor Poisson processes $\left(N_T^{c_1}, \ldots, N_T^{c_m}\right)$: $\left\{\theta_r^{c_j}\right\}_{r \in \{1,2,\ldots\}}$, for $1 \leq j \leq m$,
   (a) Initialize $\theta_0^{c_j} = 0$,
   (b) While $\theta_r^{c_j} \leq T$, simulate a uniformly distributed variable U, find the inter-jump time S such that $1 - \exp\left(-\left(\Lambda_S^{c_j} - \Lambda_{\theta_{r-1}^{c_j}}^{c_j}\right)\right) = U$, set $\theta_r^{c_j} = \theta_{r-1}^{c_j} + S$;

2. For each market factor jump time $\theta_r^{c_j}$, simulate the individual default Bernoulli variables $\left(A_{\theta_r^{c_j}}^{1,j}, \ldots A_{\theta_r^{c_j}}^{n,j}\right)$:
   (a) Simulate a set of n independent uniformly distributed variables $(U_1, \ldots, U_n)$, set $A_{\theta_r^{c_j}}^{i,j} = \mathbf{1}_{\{U_i \leq p^{i,j}\}}$, for $1 \leq i \leq n$;

3. Set the individual default times:

$$\tau_i = \min\left(A_{\theta_r^{c_j}}^{i,j} \theta_r^{c_j} + \left(1 - A_{\theta_r^{c_j}}^{i,j}\right) T : 1 \leq j \leq m, \theta_r^{c_j} \leq T\right).$$

A variant of this simulation uses the fact that the process $N_t^c \triangleq N_t^{c_1} + \ldots + N_t^{c_m}$ is a Poisson process and its intensity is given by the sum of intensities $\lambda^c \triangleq \lambda^{c_1} + \ldots + \lambda^{c_m}$. The probability of having a market factor jump of type $\{c_j\}$ is given by the ratio $p_j^c = \frac{\lambda^{c_j}}{\lambda^c}$. Conditional on a market factor jump at θ_r^c, the identity of the market factor that triggered follows a multinomial distribution with parameters $\left(\frac{\lambda^{c_1}}{\lambda^c}, \ldots, \frac{\lambda^{c_m}}{\lambda^c}\right)$. We have the following algorithm:

1. Simulate the jump times of 'any type' of market factor events in the interval $(0, T]$: $\{\theta_r^c\}_{r \in \{1,2,\ldots\}}$,
   (a) Initialize $\theta_0^c = 0$,
   (b) While $\theta_r^c \leq T$, simulate a uniformly distributed variable U, find the inter-jump time S such that $1 - \exp\left(-\left(\Lambda_S^c - \Lambda_{\theta_{r-1}^c}^c\right)\right) = U$, set $\theta_r^c = \theta_{r-1}^c + S$;

2. For each jump time θ_r^c, simulate the identity of the market factor that has triggered J_r^c:
   (a) Simulate a uniformly distributed variable U, find the index J_r^c in $\{1, \ldots, m\}$ such that

$$\sum_{j=1}^{J_r^c - 1} p_j^c < U \leq \sum_{j=1}^{J_r^c} p_j^c;$$

3. For each pair $\left(\theta_r^c, J_r^c\right)$, simulate the individual Bernoulli variables $\left(A_r^{1,J_r^c}, \ldots A_r^{n,J_r^c}\right)$:
   (a) Simulate a set of n independent uniformly distributed variables $(U_1, \ldots, U_n)$, set $A_r^{i,J_r^c} = 1_{\{U_i \leq p^{i,J_r^c}\}}$, for $1 \leq i \leq n$;

4. Set the individual default times:

$$\tau_i = \min\left(A_r^{i,J_r^c} \theta_r^c + \left(1 - A_r^{i,J_r^c}\right) T : \theta_r^c \leq T\right).$$

The second algorithm is clearly more efficient than the first since we restrict the simulation to a single vector of market factor default times. The intensity of the 'any-type' market factor event is potentially m times larger than the individual market factor intensities, hence would produce more jump times. The conditional probabilities $\left(p_j^c\right)_{1 \leq j \leq m}$ provide a much better way to simulate the identity of the market event.

5 CALIBRATION

The Marshall-Olkin copula model offers a very rich correlation structure, which can be used to reproduce some observable measures of interdependence such as estimates of default correlations or basket credit derivative prices. In this section, we discuss the calibration of the model parameters.

In general, one needs to specify $m(n+1)$ parameters, corresponding to the vector of market factor intensities and the matrix of factor loadings. Market factor events can be classified in two categories: (a) 'common' market factors affecting a subset of credits, which share some common characteristics; (b) idiosyncratic factors specific to individual obligors. Suppose $m > n$, so that we have n idiosyncratic factors $N_t^{0,i}$, with intensities $\lambda^{0,i}$, and $m_c \triangleq m - n$ common factors. The decomposition (2) becomes

$$\lambda^i = \sum_{j=1}^{m_c} p^{i,j} \lambda^{c_j} + \lambda^{0,i}. \tag{18}$$

Each idiosyncratic factor $N^{0,i}$ triggers the default of obligor i only with probability 1. The number of unknown parameters is $m_c(n+1)$; the individual idiosyncratic terms are obtained directly by the residuals $\left[\lambda^i - \sum_{j=1}^{m_c} p^{i,j} \lambda^{c_j} \right]$.

The aim of the calibration procedure is threefold:

1. define the common market factor events that constitute the backbone of the correlation structure;
2. specify a parametric form of the market factor loadings;
3. calibrate the intensity levels of the pre-specified market factors in the model.

Next, we explore each point in turn.

5.1 Choice of common market factors

The first step consists in specifying the common market factors that explain joint default events. Clearly, this choice is market specific and depends on macro- and microeconomic factors, which prevail at a particular point in time. The set of economic drivers that explain the default correlation 'sentiment' for investment grade credits, for example, are different from the ones that affect emerging market or high-yield credits. On one hand, one would find that the behaviour of investment-grade credits is most likely to be explained by industry-sector events; on the other hand, in emerging markets the joint behaviour of credit entities is better explained by regional and country factors. Taking investment-grade credits as an example, one can highlight three distinct types of market behaviours:

- **Intra-sector segment:** it is commonly accepted that credit spreads of reference entities, belonging to the same industry-sector, have a tendency to move in tandem. This would seemingly imply the existence of a sector factor, which is generally stable in time and jumps occasionally. Sector factor shocks are observed through the joint co-movements of credit spreads in this particular sector. The sector factor itself cannot be observed but we can observe its effect.
- **Inter-sector segment:** historically, we observe that credit spreads in different industries have also a tendency to move together. The dependence between credits from different sectors is less important than the one observed intra-sector. This

would correspond to general economy-wide events such as economic cycles, recessions, etc. Using the equity market terminology, we refer to the inter-sector driver as the 'Beta' driver.

- **Super senior risk:** using the market-standard Gaussian copula model, one finds that the value attributed to a super senior CDO tranche is equal to zero. This is due to the 'zero-tail-dependence' property of the Gaussian copula. The credit CDO market, however, has a different view. Indeed, super senior tranches are priced and traded at a premium of the order of a few basis points. This suggests that the market is pricing the highly unlikely global Armageddon risk (a situation where everyone defaults), and attributes an insurance-like premium to this 'catastrophe' risk. Unlike the Gaussian copula, the Marshall-Olkin model is capable of capturing this effect. By assuming a low-probability global 'World' driver and letting every credit in our universe have a factor-loading equal to 1, we ensure that the premiums of super senior CDO tranches are floored at the world driver spread. We can view this as a background radiation effect: the world driver sits silently in the background, and would never be active (under the real probability measure), but if the event occurs, every credit entity would default almost surely.

Summary 4 *In this specification of the Marshall-Olkin model, we have the following decomposition:*

$$\lambda^i = \left[\lambda^W\right] + p^{i,B}\left[\lambda^B\right] + \sum_{j=1}^{m_c-2} p^{i,S_j}\left[\lambda^{S_j}\right] + \left[\lambda^{0,i}\right], \qquad (19)$$

where
λ^W *is the intensity of the 'World' driver;*
λ^B *is the intensity of the 'Beta' driver, and $p_{i,B}$ is the loading on that driver;*
λ^{S_j} *is the intensity of the 'Sector' driver S_j, and p_{i,S_j} is the loading on that sector[1];*
$\lambda^{0,i}$ *is the intensity of the idiosyncratic event.*

5.2 Parametric form of the factor loadings

The second step consists in fixing the matrix of factor loadings $\left[p^{i,j}\right]$. It is clear that given the large number of credits that one has to deal with, it is crucial to reduce the dimensionality of the parameters to be specified. A natural approach, as suggested in Lindskog and McNeil (2003) and Duffie and Pan (2001), is to assume that the contribution of each market factor component $\left(p^{i,j}\lambda^{c_j}\right)$, in equation (19), is a fixed percentage a_j of the total intensity λ^i, i.e. for all $1 \le i \le n$,

$$\frac{p^{i,j}\lambda^{c_j}}{\lambda^i} = a_j < 1.$$

---

[1] If $i \in S_j$ then $p_{i,S_j} > 0$ otherwise $p_{i,S_j} = 0$.

The market factor contributions $(a_1, \ldots, a_m)$ are chosen such that the residual idiosyncratic intensities are positive:

$$\lambda^i - \sum_{j=1}^{m_c} p^{i,j} \lambda^{c_j} \geq 0 \Leftrightarrow 1 \geq \sum_{j=1}^{m_c} a_j.$$

One consequence of this choice is that the loadings are completely specified by the individual intensities and the corresponding market factor intensities

$$p^{i,j} = a_j \frac{\lambda^i}{\lambda^{c_j}}.$$

Unfortunately, as the intensity λ^i increases, the loading $p^{i,j}$ increases and can breach the condition that it is a probability:

$$p^{i,j} \leq 1. \tag{20}$$

A suggested parameterization is to impose condition (20) by writing $p^{i,j}$ as a conditional probability function

$$p^{i,j} = 1 - \exp\left(-\gamma_{i,j}\right), \tag{21}$$

where the 'hazard' rate $\gamma_{i,j}$ is defined as

$$\gamma_{i,j} \overset{\triangle}{=} a_j \frac{\lambda^i}{\lambda^{c_j}}.$$

Expanding the exponential to first order, we find, for $a_j \frac{\lambda^i}{\lambda^{c_j}} \ll 1$,

$$p^{i,j} = 1 - \exp\left(-a_j \frac{\lambda^i}{\lambda^{c_j}}\right) \simeq a_j \frac{\lambda^i}{\lambda^{c_j}},$$

and as λ^i goes to $+\infty$, $p^{i,j}$ converges asymptotically to 1.

5.3 Calibration of the market factor intensities

Finally, given the parametric form (21), the only unknown parameters left are the common market factor intensities, which can be recovered from benchmark basket instruments such as first-to-default swaps, or CDO tranches. Another possibility for calibrating the driver intensities is to use empirical default correlations. For example, one can use the average inter-sector default correlation to fit the Beta driver, then for each sector driver use the average intra-sector default correlation.

Note that the calibration method presented in this section resembles the one used for an HJM (Heath-Jarrow-Morton) model of yield curve dynamics,

$$df(t, T) = (\ldots) dt + \sum_{i=1}^{n} \Sigma_i(t, T) dW_t^i,$$

which is also done in three steps:

1. define the number of drivers that explain the dynamics of the yield curve, e.g. $n = 3$;
2. specify a parameterization of the volatility curve for each driver:

$$\Sigma_i(t, T) = \sigma_i(t) F_i(T - t);$$

3. calibrate the instantaneous volatility levels $\sigma_i(t)$ on a set of benchmark swaption or cap instruments.

6 GAUSS VS. MARSHALL-OLKIN

In this section, we compare the Marshall-Olkin copula with the standard Gaussian and Student copulas.

6.1 Overview

The Gaussian copula is defined as

$$C(u_1, \ldots, u_n) = \Phi^n\left(\Phi^{-1}(u_1), \ldots, \Phi^{-1}(u_2)\right),$$

where $\Phi^n(.)$ is the joint distribution function of a normally distributed random vector with unit variances and zero means, and $\Phi^{-1}(.)$ is the inverse function of the univariate standard normal distribution. The Gaussian copula can be viewed as the copula function of a set of correlated Gaussian variables transposed back into 'uniform' space with the inverse normal function.

The t-copula is defined as

$$C(u_1, \ldots, u_n) = t_\nu^n\left(t_\nu^{-1}(u_1), \ldots, t_\nu^{-1}(u_2)\right),$$

where $t_\nu^n(.)$ is the joint distribution function of the multivariate student distribution and $t_\nu^{-1}(.)$ is the inverse function of the univariate student distribution. The t-copula is obtained from the multivariate dependence of a set of correlated student variables.

Some key differences between Marshall-Olkin, Gaussian, and t-copula are summarized below.

- Tail dependence: the upper tail dependence is defined as

$$\lambda_U = \lim_{u \nearrow 1} \mathbb{P}\left(X > F_X^{-1}(u) \mid Y > F_Y^{-1}(u)\right) \tag{22}$$

(see Embrechts, Lindskog, and McNeil, (2003). The expression of the tail dependence (22) for the three copula functions, Gaussian, t-copula, and MO, is given by:

$$\lambda_U^{Gaussian} = 0,$$

$$\lambda_U^{T-copula} = 2\left(1 - t_{\nu+1}\left(\sqrt{\nu+1}\frac{\sqrt{1-\rho}}{\sqrt{1+\rho}}\right)\right),$$

$$\lambda_U^{MO} = \min\left(\frac{\lambda^{\{1,2\}}}{\lambda^{\{1\}}}, \frac{\lambda^{\{1,2\}}}{\lambda^{\{2\}}}\right) \geq \left[\lambda^W\right]\min\left(\frac{1}{\lambda^{\{1\}}}, \frac{1}{\lambda^{\{2\}}}\right).$$

The tail dependence for a Gaussian copula is always equal to zero. The t-copula and the Marshall-Olkin copula can be parameterized to fit non-zero tail dependence and to capture more extreme tail events.

- Elliptical copulas do not allow for multiple defaults in the interval $[t, t + dt)$, i.e. $\mathbb{P}\left(\tau_i = \tau_j\right) = 0$, for $i \neq j$. In a Marshall-Olkin model, the probability of instantaneous joint defaults can be non-zero. In fact, the foundation of the correlation profile in MO is based on joint instantaneous defaults.

- The mixed partial derivatives of a copula function, $\frac{\partial^k C}{\partial u_1 \dots \partial u_k}$, exist for almost all $\mathbf{u} \in [0, 1]^n$. The copula function can then be decomposed into its absolutely continuous part $\mathbf{A}(u_1, \dots, u_n)$ and its singular part $\mathbf{S}(u_1, \dots, u_n)$:

$$\mathbf{C}(u_1, \dots, u_n) = \mathbf{A}(u_1, \dots, u_n) + \mathbf{S}(u_1, \dots, u_n),$$

$$\mathbf{A}(u_1, \dots, u_n) = \int_0^{u_1} \dots \int_0^{u_n} \frac{\partial^k C(x_1, \dots, x_n)}{\partial x_1 \dots \partial x_n} dx_1 \dots dx_n,$$

$$\mathbf{S}(u_1, \dots, u_n) = \mathbf{C}(u_1, \dots, u_n) - \mathbf{A}(u_1, \dots, u_n).$$

Elliptical copulas, by construction, are absolutely continuous. The Marshall-Olkin copula has a singular part and a continuous part (see, for example, Embrechts, Lindskog, and McNeil, 2003).

- Many analytical results are available for the Marshall-Olkin copula, and the pricing of credit derivatives such as first-to-default swaps can be implemented in closed form. In general, for the Gaussian and t-copula, one needs to use a Monte Carlo simulation, except in simplified one-factor models (as in Schonbucher 2000 or Frey and McNeil 2003), where semi-analytical results are available by using the conditional independence property and integrating over values of the conditioning latent variable.

6.2 Modes of the aggregate default distribution

Consider a portfolio of 100 obligors with 10 credits per sector. Set the intensities of the individual credits to $\lambda^i = 2\%$, the intensity of the World driver to $\lambda^W = 0.05\%$, the intensity of the Beta driver to $\lambda^B = 5\%$, and all the sector intensities to $\lambda^{S_j} = 2.5\%$. Attribute 60% of the credit intensity to the Beta factor, 20% to the sector factor, and the remaining 20% to the idiosyncratic factor. This implies the following values of the

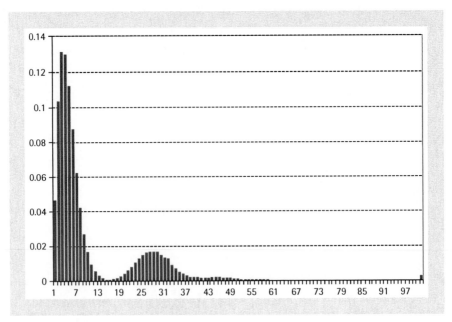

FIGURE 8.1 Default distribution for a portfolio of 100 credits: $\lambda^i = 2\%$, $\lambda^W = 0.05\%$, $\lambda^B = 5\%$, $\lambda^{S_j} = 2.5\%$, $p^{i,B} = 0.24$ and $p^{i,S_j} = 0.16$.

factor loadings: $p^{i,B} = 0.24$, and $p^{i,S_j} = 0.16$. The five-year default correlation in this model is 19.25% intra-sector, and 16.16% inter-sector.[2]

To begin with let us consider the aggregate default distribution at the five-year time horizon.

We plot the distribution of the portfolio specified here with $(p^{i,B} = 0.24; p^{i,S_j} = 0.16)$, and we compare it with the distribution of a portfolio with similar marginals but a different multivariate dependence $(p^{i,B} = 0; p^{i,S_j} = 0)$.

In Figure (8.1), we observe that the default distribution has four different modes: the first big hump corresponds to the idiosyncratic component, the second hump corresponds to the Beta contribution, the third hump is the sector contribution, and the last spike at the far end of the distribution is due to the world driver.

In the second model depicted in Figure (8.2), the Beta and sector factors are turned off. The joint dependence is built in via the world driver. Thus, the default distribution has only a single idiosyncratic mode and the world driver spike. Compared with Figure (8.1), the idiosyncratic mode has shifted to the right since the idiosyncratic default probabilities are higher in this case.

---

[2] The numerical values in this example are chosen arbitrarily to exhibit the shape of the distributions and compare the various copulas. For empirical studies of default correlation, we refer the reader to the article by Nagpal and Bahar (2001) and the paper by Servigny and Renault (2002).

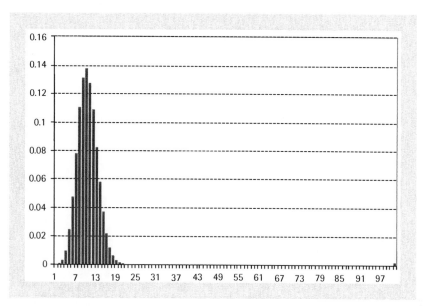

FIGURE 8.2 Default distribution for a portfolio of 100 credits: λ^i = 2%, λ^W = 0.05%, λ^B = 5%, λ^{S_j} = 2.5%, $p^{i,B}$ = 0 and p^{i,S_j} = 0.

Next, we compare the distribution in Figure (8.1) with the ones of a Gaussian copula and a t-copula. In order to do a meaningful comparison, we impose that the five-year default correlation is the same for the various models. Since the marginal distributions are unchanged, the mean of the aggregate default distribution is fixed independently from the copula function. The additional requirement to have the same pair-wise default correlations corresponds to keeping the variance fixed as well. In this example, the five-year default correlations of the Marshall-Olkin model are $\rho_{i,j}^D$ = 19.25% intra-sector, and $\rho_{i,j}^D$ = 16.16% inter-sector. A direct inversion of the default correlation formula, with a Gaussian copula dependence, gives the following values of the Gaussian asset correlation $\rho_{i,j}^A$ = 41.68% intra-sector, and $\rho_{i,j}^A$ = 36.39% inter-sector. Doing a similar calibration for a t-copula with a parameter ν = 9, we get $\rho_{i,j}^A$ = 35.92% intra-sector, and $\rho_{i,j}^A$ = 30.12% inter-sector. Note that to arrive at the same level of default correlation, the equivalent asset correlation in the t-copula is lower than the one in the Gaussian copula. This is natural since the t-copula has higher tail dependence. In fact, as pointed out in Mashal and Naldi (2002a), even with zero asset correlation, the implied default correlation with the t-copula is non-zero.

Figure (8.3) depicts the default distributions of the three calibrated copula models. Having matched the first two moments of the default distribution, the key difference between the Marshall-Olkin copula and the elliptical copulas is the shape of the distribution function. Marshall-Olkin implies a multi-modal distribution. Gaussian and Student copulas imply uni-modal distributions.

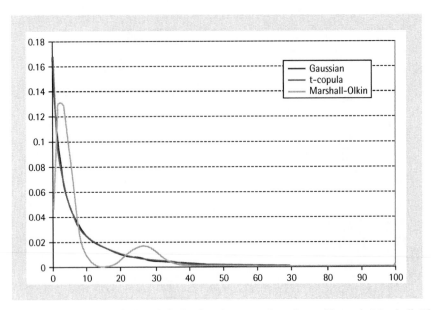

FIGURE 8.3 Comparison of the default distributions for the calibrated Marshall-Olkin, Gaussian and t-copula.

6.3 Tail of the distribution

The Marshall-Olkin and the Gaussian copulas have very different behaviours in the tail of the portfolio distribution. To highlight this difference, we plot the cumulative default distribution of the example portfolio in log-space. We introduce the re-scaled log variable h_k, for $k = 1, 2, \ldots, n$,

$$h_k \triangleq \frac{-\log\left[\mathbb{P}\left(X_T < k\right)\right]}{T}.$$

The re-scaled tail measure h_k can be interpreted as the 'hazard' rate of the kth-to-default time $\tau^{[k]}$,

$$\mathbb{P}\left(X_T < k\right) = \mathbb{P}\left(\tau^{[k]} > T\right) = \exp\left(-h_k T\right).$$

Figure (8.4) shows that, for the Gaussian and t-copula, h_k converges to zero as we move further into the tail of the distribution. In the Marshall-Olkin model, the values of h_k are floored at 0.05%. This is the effect of the World driver: it suffices to observe that

$$\mathbb{P}\left(X_T < k\right) \leq \mathbb{P}\left(X_T < n\right) = 1 - \mathbb{P}\left(X_T = n\right)$$

$$= 1 - \mathbb{P}\left(D_T^W = 1\right)$$

$$= \exp\left(-\lambda^W T\right).$$

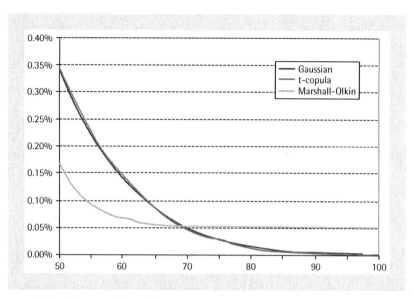

FIGURE 8.4 Tail of the portfolio default distribution for the Marshall-Olkin, Gaussian, and t-copula.

Here, we have used the property that all credits default if and only if the World driver triggers, i.e. $\{D_T^W = 1\}$. This part of the distribution is precisely the one that determines the value of the extreme events and catastrophe risk. The World driver plays a unique role since it can be used to match insurance premiums of super senior risk. This cannot be achieved with a Gaussian copula.

6.4 Time Invariance

Another major difference between Marshall-Olkin and the Gaussian copula is the 'time' behaviour. Consider an example with two obligors, and a one-factor MO model:

$$\lambda^i = p^{i,c}\lambda^c + \lambda^{0,i}.$$

Set the intensities to $\lambda^1 = \lambda^2 = \lambda^c = 1\%$, and the factor loadings to $p^{1,c} = p^{2,c} = 0.3915$. The five-year default correlation is equal to 15%. For the equivalent Gaussian copula, set the asset correlation to $\rho^A = 41.04\%$ in order to match the 15% default correlation at the five-year time horizon. With this specification, compute the default correlation at other time horizons between 0 and 5 years, and compare the implied term structures.

Figure (8.5) shows that the Marshall-Olkin default correlation is stable through time. This is not surprising, since, as mentioned before, the multivariate exponential distribution is memoryless, therefore the T-default correlation estimated at time t would be the same as the $(T - t)$-default correlation at time 0. The Gaussian copula, on the other hand, is highly time dependent. The upward sloping shape of

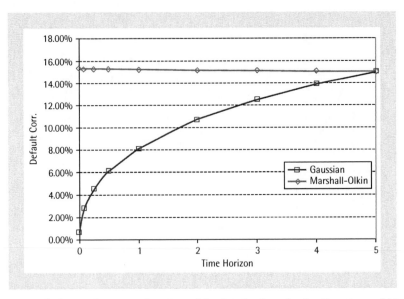

FIGURE 8.5 Default correlation as a function of the time horizon for the Gaussian and Marshall-Olkin copulas.

its default correlation term structure means that a first-to-default swap, for example, would become cheaper as time goes by, even if the underlying credit spreads remain unchanged. At time $t = 0$, the five-year FTD (first-to-default) basket would be priced at 15% default correlation. Then, after one year, the maturity of the FTD becomes four years, which corresponds to a default correlation of 13.8%. And at time $t = 4$ year, the same basket becomes a 1-year trade and would be marked at 8% default correlation. Rogge and Schonbucher (2003) point out the same deficiency of the Gaussian copula by analysing the size of the default contagion as a function of time.

7 CORRELATION SKEW

In this section, we discuss how the Marshall-Olkin copula can be used to match the correlation skew of the CDO market.

7.1 Overview

Over the last few years, we have seen an increased liquidity in CDO tranche trading, which resulted in an observable market of default correlation. Dealers are starting to quote a two-way market on a pre-specified set of tranches referenced to a given index portfolio. By inverting the Gaussian copula formula, one finds the implied level of correlation that would match the quoted tranche premiums. As with the Black-Scholes option model, there is not a single correlation number that would match all tranches at various attachment points. Supply and demand factors combined with the credit views and risk appetite of the market participants would explain the discrepancy of correlations across the capital structure. The example below gives the market bid/offer premiums of the European iTraxx index tranches.

0–3%	23.3	24.3
3–6%	134	137
6–9%	44	47
9–12%	28	32.3
12–22%	14.2	15.5

The index level is 37 bps. The (0–3%) tranche is quoted in points upfront for a tranche paying 500 bps running.

Next, we explain some concepts such as base correlation and compound correlation in a formal manner.

7.2 One-factor Gaussian copula

We give a formal definition of the one-factor Gaussian copula function.

Definition 7.1 *(One-factor Gaussian Copula). The one-factor Gaussian copula with parameter $\rho \in [0, 1)$ is defined as*

$$C(u_1, \ldots, u_n) \triangleq \int_{-\infty}^{+\infty} \left[\prod_{i=1}^{n} \Phi \left(\frac{\Phi^{-1}(u_i) - \sqrt{\rho}y}{\sqrt{1-\rho}} \right) \right] \phi(y) \, dy,$$

where $\Phi(.)$, $\Phi^{-1}(.)$ and $\phi(.)$ are the standard normal distribution function, its inverse and its density function respectively.

This formal definition can be understood by considering a simplified firm value model as in Schonbucher (2000) for example. The default of obligor i is triggered when the asset value of the firm, denoted V_i are below a given threshold. V_i is assumed to be normally distributed. The relationship between default and the asset value is given by

$$\{\tau_i \leq T\} \iff \{V_i \leq \Phi^{-1}(\mathbb{P}(\tau_i \leq T))\}.$$

The asset values of different obligors are correlated. Their joint dependence is defined via a common factor Y, which follows a standard normal distribution, and idiosyncratic standard normal noises $\epsilon_1, \ldots, \epsilon_n$:

$$V_i \triangleq \sqrt{\rho}Y + \sqrt{1-\rho}\epsilon_i,$$

where Y and $\epsilon_1, \ldots, \epsilon_n$ are i.i.d. standard normally distributed. The linear correlation between the asset values of two obligors is ρ. This coefficient, which is used to parameterize the family of one-factor Gaussian copulas, is sometimes called an asset correlation. Conditional on a given value of the systemic factor Y, the asset values are independent; hence, the default times are independent as well. This is the set-up of a conditionally independent defaults model.

One can write down the default times' copula function by conditioning on Y and using the law of iterated expectations:

$$\mathbb{P}(\tau_1 \leq T_1, \ldots, \tau_n \leq T_n)$$

$$= \int_{-\infty}^{+\infty} \mathbb{P}(\tau_1 \leq T_1, \ldots, \tau_n \leq T_n \mid Y = y) \, \phi(y) \, dy$$

$$= \int_{-\infty}^{+\infty} \mathbb{P}\left(V_1 \leq \Phi^{-1}\left(\mathbb{P}(\tau_1 \leq T_1)\right), \ldots, V_n \leq \Phi^{-1}\left(\mathbb{P}(\tau_n \leq T_n)\right) \mid Y = y\right) \phi(y) \, dy$$

$$= \int_{-\infty}^{+\infty} \mathbb{P}\left(\epsilon_1 \leq \frac{\Phi^{-1}\left(\mathbb{P}(\tau_1 \leq T_1)\right) - \sqrt{\rho}y}{\sqrt{1-\rho}}, \ldots, \epsilon_n \leq \frac{\Phi^{-1}\left(\mathbb{P}(\tau_n \leq T_n)\right) - \sqrt{\rho}y}{\sqrt{1-\rho}}\right) \phi(y) \, dy$$

$$= \int_{-\infty}^{+\infty} \left[\prod_{i=1}^{n} \Phi\left(\frac{\Phi^{-1}(u_i) - \sqrt{\rho}y}{\sqrt{1-\rho}}\right)\right] \phi(y) \, dy.$$

The one-factor Gaussian copula is the standard model used to quote CDO tranches in the market.

7.3 Pricing CDOs

Let us consider the pricing of a CDO tranche, which covers the losses of a given portfolio between two thresholds $0 \leq K_1 < K_2 \leq 1$.

Letting δ_i denote the recovery rate of obligor i, we define the portfolio loss process as

$$L_t \triangleq \frac{1}{n} \sum_{i=1}^{n} (1 - \delta_i) \, D_t^i.$$

The loss on the tranche (K_1, K_2) is defined as

$$M_t^{K_1, K_2} = \min\left(\max\left(L_t - K_1, 0\right), K_2 - K_1\right).$$

The processes L_t and $M_t^{K_1, K_2}$ are pure jump processes. The CDO payments correspond to the increments of $M_t^{K_1, K_2}$, i.e. there is a payment when the process $M_t^{K_1, K_2}$ jumps, which happens at every default time. The payoff of the protection leg of a CDO is therefore defined as the Stieljes integral

$$\text{protection\_leg} \triangleq \int_{]0,T]} \exp\left(-\int_0^t r_s ds\right) dM_t^{K_1, K_2}.$$

Letting $(T_0 = 0, T_1, \ldots, T_N)$ denote the cash flow dates, $\Delta T_i \triangleq T_i - T_{i-1}$, the payment fractions and S the tranche premium, the payoff of the premium leg is defined as:

$$\text{premium\_leg} \triangleq S \times \sum_{i=1}^{n} \exp\left(-\int_0^{T_i} r_s ds\right)\left[(K_2 - K_1) - M_{T_i}^{K_1, K_2}\right]\Delta T_i.$$

The value of the CDO tranche is given by the expected value of the discounted payoff under a risk neutral measure.

Assume deterministic interest rates and let $B(0, T) \triangleq \exp\left(-\int_0^T r_s ds\right)$ denote the discount factor maturing at time T. Using the integration by part formula and Fubini's theorem to interchange the order of integration, we can rewrite the protection integral as

$$\mathbb{E}\left[\int_{]0,T]} \exp\left(-\int_0^t r_s ds\right) dM_t^{K_1, K_2}\right] = B(0, t) \mathbb{E}\left[M_T^{K_1, K_2}\right] - \int_0^T \frac{\partial B(0, t)}{\partial t} \mathbb{E}\left[M_t^{K_1, K_2}\right] dt,$$

Similarly, to compute the value of the premium leg, we need to know the expected tranche losses at times T_i: $\mathbb{E}\left[M_{T_i}^{K_1, K_2}\right]$.

The pricing of CDO tranches boils down to computing the values of all 'tranchelets':

$$C_t(K_1, K_2) \triangleq \mathbb{E}\left[M_t^{K_1, K_2}\right], \text{ for } 0 \leq t \leq T. \tag{23}$$

For $t \geq 0$, if we know the density function $f_t(.)$ of the portfolio loss L_t:

$$f_t(x) \triangleq \mathbb{P}(L_t \in dx), \tag{24}$$

then, the expectation (23) is given by

$$\mathbb{E}\left[M_t^{K_1, K_2}\right] = \int_{K_1}^{K_2} (x - K_1) f_t(x) dx + (K_2 - K_1)(1 - F_t(x)), \tag{25}$$

where $F_t(x) = \int_{-\infty}^x f_t(z) dz$ is the cumulative probability function of L_t. With a given copula, such as the one-factor copula, it is easy to compute the density function $f_t(.)$ using techniques such as the FFT (see Gregory and Laurent 2002) or the convolution recursion (see Andersen, Sidenius, Basu, 2003).

7.4 Compound correlation

As mentioned earlier, the one-factor copula has been used by dealers to quote the standardized CDO tranches traded in the market. Since the prices of various tranches are driven by supply and demand, a single correlation parameter is not sufficient to reproduce market prices. Inverting the pricing formula of the one-factor Gaussian copula, one would find the implied correlation, which matches the market price of each tranche. This implied correlation is referred to as 'Compound Correlation'.

Definition 7.2 *(Compound Correlation). For a given CDO tranche with attachment points (K_1, K_2) and quoted premium S^{K_1, K_2}, let $G^{K_1, K_2}(S, \rho)$ denote the model price using the one-factor Gaussian copula with parameter ρ. We call compound correlation, the value of the parameter ρ such that*

$$G^{K_1, K_2}\left(S^{K_1, K_2}, \rho\right) = 0. \tag{26}$$

If a compound correlation exists, i.e. if the mapping (26) is invertible, then this offers a way to compare different tranches on a relative value basis. Unfortunately, it turns out that the model price is not a monotonic function of compound correlation. Therefore, it is not guaranteed that we can always find a solution. Moreover, in some instances, we can find more than one value of correlation, which satisfies (26). This usually happens with Mezzanine tranches, which are not correlation sensitive. This behaviour is well documented (see McGinty et al. 2004) and has motivated the base correlation approach that we describe next.

Solving for compound correlations in the previous example, we get the following results.

0–3%	20.08%	18.57%
3–6%	5.92%	6.17%
6–9%	13.56%	14.19%
9–12%	20.82%	22.42%
12–22%	29.54%	30.43%

7.5 Base correlation

One can view each CDO tranche with attachment points (K_1, K_2) as the difference between two equity tranches: $(0, K_2)$ and $(0, K_1)$. This can be checked easily from the definition of the payoff:

$$M_T^{K_1, K_2} = M_T^{0, K_2} - M_T^{0, K_1}, \text{ for all } T \geq 0.$$

Therefore, to price any CDO tranche it suffices to have the whole continuum of equity tranches $(0, K)$, for $K \in [0, 1]$. Each one of these equity tranches can be valued with a different one-factor Gaussian copula correlation $\rho(0, K)$. The function $\rho(0, K):$ $[0, 1] \to [0, 1]$ is called the 'Base Correlation' curve.

Definition 7.3 *(Base Correlation). The base correlation curve is a function $\rho(0, K):$ $[0, 1] \to [0, 1]$, which parameterizes the prices of all equity tranches $(0, K)$. In other words, the price of the $(0, K)$-tranche is given by the one-factor Gaussian copula model with parameter $\rho(0, K)$.*

Furthermore, the value of any tranche with attachment points (K_1, K_2) and quoted premium S^{K_1, K_2}, is given by

$$G^{0, K_2}\left(S^{K_1, K_2}, \rho(0, K_2)\right) - G^{0, K_1}\left(S^{K_1, K_2}, \rho(0, K_1)\right). \tag{27}$$

Using the standard tranches quoted in the market, one would proceed with a bootstrapping algorithm to find the base correlation curve, which reproduces the market quotes. The popularity of this method lies in the fact that the function

$$h(x) = G^{0,K}(S, x), \text{ for a given } K \in [0, 1] \text{ and } S \in \mathbb{R}_+,$$

is monotonic. Hence, we can always invert the relationship (27) for each attachment point.

Mathematically, base correlation is just another way of parameterizing the density function $f_T(.)$ of the portfolio loss L_T. Indeed, given a base correlation curve $(\rho(0, K))_{0 \le K \le 1}$, one can compute the value of all 'tranchelets' $(C_T(0, K))_{0 \le K \le 1}$:

$$C_T(0, K) \triangleq \mathbb{E}\left[M_T^{0,K}\right].$$

Assuming that, for $T \ge 0$, the function $K \to C_T(0, K)$ is $\mathcal{C}^2$, we can recover the density function as:

$$f_T(K) = -\frac{\partial^2 C_T(0, K)}{\partial K^2}. \tag{28}$$

This follows directly from equation (25). This is similar to the Breeden and Litzenberger (1978) formula in options theory where the implied density of the forward stock price is obtained from the continuum of call prices at different strikes.

Solving for base correlations in the previous example, we get the following results.

0–3%	20.08%	18.57%
0–6%	29.60%	27.43%
0–9%	37.10%	34.12%
0–12%	42.54%	38.50%
0–22%	56.04%	49.28%

7.6 Marshall-Olkin skew

As mentioned earlier, because of the multi-modality of the Marshall-Olkin loss distribution, it is possible to use each mode of the distribution to match various parts of the capital structure. Figure (8.1), for example, suggests that the idiosyncratic hump can be used to match the equity tranche (0–3%), the Beta hump can be used to match the mezzanine tranches (3–6%, 6–9%, and 9–12%), and the World driver can be used to match the senior tranche (12–22%). Additional tweaking of the calibration can also be done with sector drivers.

Figure (8.6) shows the results of the calibration using a MO model with one common Beta driver and the World driver.

Using the Beta driver, we can match accurately most of the equity and mezzanine tranches. The senior tranches are more sensitive to extreme events and require additional common factors to have a better market fit. Here our intent is solely to show that

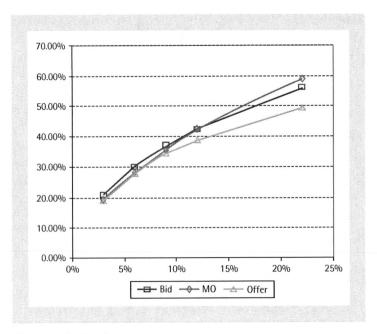

FIGURE 8.6 Base correlation skew.

the multi-modality feature of the MO copula generates a correlation skew curve, which mirrors the one observed in the market. A precise study of the market calibration is outside the scope of this chapter.

8 CONCLUSION

We have presented in this chapter the Marshall-Olkin copula in the context of default correlation modelling. We have proposed a calibration procedure to fit this rich correlation structure to an intuitively sound market dynamic. And we have shown that MO offers some desirable features that make it an eligible alternative to the Gaussian copula. The comparison between MO and the Gaussian copula is similar in many ways to the evolution from Black-Scholes to term-structure models in fixed income markets. Black-Scholes has been used as the model of choice by a lot of traders because of its simplicity. It converts one volatility number to a price. However, there is no guarantee that an exogenous BS swaption matrix is arbitrage free or at least self-consistent. On the other hand, a calibrated HJM model, which is built upon a defined set of yield curve deformations or drivers, is self-consistent by construction. The Gaussian copula can be viewed as the Black-Scholes of default correlation. The Marshall-Olkin approach corresponds to an HJM framework. Once the market factors are calibrated, all combinations of sub-baskets can be priced consistently in this calibrated term-structure of default inter-dependence.

REFERENCES

Andersen, L., Sidenius, J., and Basu, S. (2003). 'All your hedges in one basket'. *Risk* (Nov.) 67–70.

Barlow, R., and Proschan, F. (1981). *Statistical Theory of Reliability and Life Testing*. Silver Spring, MD.

Breeden, D. T., and Litzenberger, R. H. (1978). 'Prices of state-contingent claims implicit in options prices'. *Journal of Business*, 51/4.

Brémaud, P. (1980). *Point Processes and Queues: Martingale Dynamics*, New York: Springer-Verlag.

Duffie, D. (1998). 'First-to-default valuation'. Working paper, Graduate School of Business, Stanford University, CA.

—— and Garleanu, N. (2001). 'Risk and valuation of collateralized debt obligations'. *Financial Analysts Journal*, 57/1: 41–59.

—— and Pan, J. (2001). 'Analytical value-at-risk with jumps and credit risk'. *Finance and Stochastics*, 5: 155–80.

—— and Singleton, K. (1999a). 'Modeling term structures of defaultable bonds'. *Review of Financial Studies*, 12/4: 687–720.

—— —— (1999b). 'Simulating correlated defaults'. Working paper, Graduate School of Business, Stanford University, CA.

Elliott, R. J., Jeanblanc, M., and Yor, M. (2000). 'On models of default risk'. *Mathematical Finance*, 10/2: 179–95.

Embrechts, P., Lindskog, F., and McNeil, A. (2003). 'Modelling dependence with copulas and applications to risk management'. In S.T. Rechev (ed.), *Handbook of Heavy Tailed Distributions in Finance*. Amsterdam Elsevier/North-Holland,

Frey, R., and McNeil, A. (2003). 'Dependent defaults in models of portfolio credit risk'. *Journal of Risk*, 6/1: 59–92.

Gregory, J., and Laurent, J. P. (2002). 'Basket default swaps, CDO's and factor copulas'. Working paper, BNP Paribas and University of Lyon.

Joe, H. (1997). *Multivariate Models and Dependence Concepts*. London: Chapman & Hall.

Kevorkian, J., and Cole, J. D. (1996). *Multiple Scale and Singular Perturbation Methods*. New York: Springer-Verlag.

Lando, D. (1998). 'On Cox processes and credit risky securities'. *Review of Derivatives Research*, 2/2–3: 99–120.

Li, D. X. (2000). 'On default correlation: a copula function approach'. *Journal of Fixed Income*, 9: 43–54.

Lindskog, F., and McNeil, A. (2003). 'Common Poisson shock models: applications to insurance and credit risk modelling'. *ASTIN Bulletin*, 33/2: 209–38.

Marshall, A. W., and Olkin, I., (1967). 'A multivariate exponential distribution'. *Journal of the American Statistical Association*.

Mashal, R., and Naldi, M. (2002a). 'Pricing multiname credit derivatives: heavy tailed hybrid approach'. Working paper, Lehman Brothers.

—— —— (2002b). 'Extreme events and default baskets'. *Risk* (June), 119–22.

McGinty, L., Beinstein, E., Ahluwalia, R., and Watts, M. (2004). 'Introducing base correlations'. Credit Derivatives Strategy, JP Morgan.

Nagpal, K., and Bahar, R. (2001). 'Measuring default correlation'. *Risk* (Mar), 129–32.

Nelsen, R. (1999). *An Introduction to Copulas*, New York: Springer-Verlag.

Panjer, H., (1981). 'Recursive evaluation of a family of compound distributions'. *ASTIN Bulletin*, 12: 22–6.

Rogge, E., and Schonbucher, P. J. (2003). 'Modelling dynamic portfolio credit risk'. Working paper.

Schonbucher, P. J. (1998). 'The term structure of defaultable bond prices'. *Review of Derivatives Research*, 2/2–3: 161–92.

——(2000). 'Factor models for portfolio credit risk'. Working paper, Bonn University.

Servigny, A., and Renault, O. (2002). 'Default correlation: empirical evidence', Working paper, Standard & Poors.

Vasiceck, O. (1997). 'The loan loss distribution'. Working paper, KMV Corporation.

Wong, D. (2000). 'Copula from the Limit of a Multivariate Binary Model'. Working paper, Bank of America Corporation.

CHAPTER 9

CONTAGION MODELS
IN CREDIT RISK

MARK H. A. DAVIS

1 INTRODUCTION AND SUMMARY

THIS chapter aims to give an account of mathematical techniques for credit risk models where there is contagion between the obligors, i.e. default of one party either directly causes default of other parties or (more commonly) changes other parties' risk of default. While various approaches are possible, the treatment here concentrates on 'reduced-form' models based on Markov chains. We argue that such models provide a flexible and computationally efficient framework. Subsidiary but important themes of the chapter are the role of information (i.e. whether various factors influencing default risk are observable or 'latent'), and changes of measure, either from 'physical' to 'risk neutral' and vice versa or, in the context of econometric studies, computation of likelihood functions for parameter estimation.

We start in section 2 with a general discussion of joint distributions and copulas, mainly to point out that 'contagion' is in some sense already built into the copula concept. Section 3 gives a general formulation of the reduced-form model and a taxonomy of models distinguishing between factor, frailty, and contagion models. Section 4 gives some background information about Markov processes, Markov chains, and phase-type distributions as required for the subsequent sections. We then discuss, in section 5, four simple but effective Markov chain-based models with applications in counterparty risk and credit risk for inhomogeneous and homogeneous portfolios.[1] The following two sections, 6 and 7, develop the 'subsidiary themes' mentioned above, before we return in section 8 to further development of the Enhanced Risk homogeneous portfolio model, introduced in section 5.4, in the light of these these themes. Finally, following the concluding section 9, Appendix 9 summarizes information about

---

[1] This section is closely related to the chapter in this volume by Bielecki, Crépey, and Herbertsson.

Piecewise-Deterministic Markov Processes, which play an essential role in our discussion.

2 GENERAL DEPENDENCE CONCEPTS

Let $\tau \geq 0$ be a random variable with density $f(t)$. The *survivor function G* and *distribution function F* are

$$P[\tau > t] = G(t) = 1 - F(t) = \int_t^\infty f(u)du.$$

The *hazard rate* is

$$h(t)dt = \frac{f(t)}{G(t)}dt \approx P[\tau \in]t, t + dt]|\tau > t],$$

and there is a 1-1 relation between h and G in that

$$G(t) = e^{-\int_0^t h(u)du}.$$

Thus specifying h is equivalent to specifying f.

For random variables $\tau_1, \tau_2 \geq 0$ with joint density $f(t_1, t_2)$ the *marginal* and *joint* distributions are

$$F_1(t) = \int_0^t \int_0^\infty f(u, v)dv\, du$$

$$F_2(t) = \int_0^\infty \int_0^t f(u, v)dv\, du$$

$$F(t_1, t_2) = \int_0^{t_1} \int_0^{t_2} f(u, v)dv\, du,$$

while the survivor function is

$$G(t_1, t_2) = \int_{t_1}^\infty \int_{t_2}^\infty f(u, v)dv\, du$$

The marginal distribution functions F_1, F_2 are continuous and $U_i = F_i(\tau_i)$, $i = 1, 2$ are $U[0, 1]$ random variables[2]. If C denotes their joint distribution function then

$$F(t_1, t_2) = C(F_1(t_1), F_2(t_2)).$$

Thus

$$C(u_1, u_2) = F(F_1^{-1}(u_1), F_2^{-1}(u_2)). \tag{1}$$

[2] $U[0, 1]$ denotes the uniform distribution on the unit interval $[0, 1]$.

This is an example of a *copula*, which in general is a joint distribution function C : $[0, 1] \times [0, 1] \rightarrow [0, 1]$ such that the marginal distributions are uniform, i.e. $C(u, 1) = u$, $C(1, v) = v$.

Let us now consider the hazard rates for the two random variables $\tau_{\min} = \min(\tau_1, \tau_2)$, $\tau_{\max} = \max(\tau_1, \tau_2)$. Now

$$P[\tau_{\min} > t] = G(t, t),$$

so the initial hazard rate is (see Figure 9.1)

$$h_0(t) = \frac{1}{G(t, t)} \left(\int_t^\infty f(u, t)du + \int_t^\infty f(t, v)dv \right)$$

Suppose τ_1 occurs first. The conditional density of τ_2 is then

$$\frac{f(\tau_1, t)}{\int_{\tau_1}^\infty f(\tau_1, v)dv}$$

for $t \geq \tau_1$, so that the new hazard rate is

$$h_2(t) = \frac{f(\tau_1, t)}{\int_t^\infty f(\tau_1, v)dv},$$

while if τ_2 occurs first the hazard rate switches to

$$h_1(t) = \frac{f(t, \tau_2)}{\int_t^\infty f(u, \tau_2)du}.$$

The *hazard rate process* is therefore

$$h(t) = h_0(t)\mathbf{1}_{(t < \tau_{\min})} + \left(h_2(t)\mathbf{1}_{(\tau_{\min}=\tau_1)} + h_1(t)\mathbf{1}_{(\tau_{\min}=\tau_2)} \right) \mathbf{1}_{(\tau_{\min} \leq t < \tau_{\max})} \qquad (2)$$

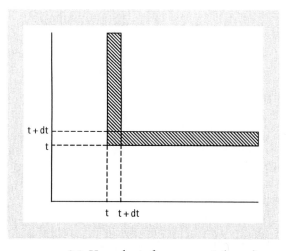

FIGURE 9.1 Hazard rate for $\tau_{\min} = \min(\tau_1, \tau_2)$.

Points to note here are (a) there is contagion: the hazard rate for obligor 2 is affected by default of obligor 1 (and conversely), and (b) the copula is essentially a *static* concept: there is no particular relationship between the copula of (τ_1, τ_2) and the copula of the conditional distribution of (τ_1, τ_2) given $\tau_{\min} > t > 0$.

2.1 Copulas for general joint distributions

Copulas are covered in detail by McNeil, Frey, and Embrechts (2005). The main general result is *Sklar's theorem* which states that for any distribution function F for τ_1, τ_2 with marginals F_1, F_2 there is a copula function C such that

$$F(t_1, t_2) = C(F_1(t_1), F_2(t_2)). \tag{3}$$

The proof is simple when F_1, F_2 are continuous because then, as in the preceding section, $F_1(\tau_1) \sim U[0, 1]$ and $F_1^{-1}(U) \sim F_1$ for $U \sim U[0, 1]$. When F_1 is not continuous then $F_1(\tau_1)$ is no longer uniform. There is a clean proof by Rüschendorf (2009) based on the 'distributional transform': for a random variable τ, let

$$\hat{F}(t, \lambda) = \mathbb{P}(\tau < t) + \lambda \mathbb{P}(\tau = t) = F(t) + \lambda(F(t^+) - F(t)).$$

We then have

- $U \sim U[0, 1] \Rightarrow F^{-1}(U) \sim F$; and
- If $\tau \sim F$ and $V \sim U[0, 1]$, independent of τ, then $\hat{F}(\tau, V) \sim U[0, 1]$.

In the present case we take $V \sim U[0, 1]$ independent of τ_1 and τ_2 and define (in obvious notation) $U_i = \hat{F}_i(\tau_i, V)$, $i = 1, 2$ and let C be the joint distribution of U_1, U_2. It is then not hard to show that (3) holds. Conversely, given marginal distributions F_1, F_2 and a copula C, formula (3) defines a bona fide joint distribution F.

C is called the 'gaussian copula' if C is defined by (1) with F the bivariate normal distribution with correlation parameter ρ. A commonly used alternative is the *t-copula*. The *t*-distribution with ν degrees of freedom is the distribution of $T = Z/\sqrt{V/\nu}$ where $Z \sim N(0, 1)$ and $V \sim \chi^2(\nu)$ (independent). For a bivariate t we take (T_1, T_2) where $T_i = Z_i/\sqrt{V/\nu}$, $\text{corr}(Z_1, Z_2) = \rho$. The *t*-distribution is often preferred because of its *tail-dependence* properties. For a bivariate random variable $X = (X_1, X_2)$ the coefficient of lower tail dependence is defined as

$$\lambda = \lim_{a \to 0} \mathbb{P}[X_2 < q_2(a) | X_1 < q_1(a)],$$

where $q_i(a)$ is the a'th quantile of X_i. Defined this way, λ depends only on the copula; indeed, if C is the copula of X, we have

$$\lambda = \lim_{u \to 0} \frac{C(u, u)}{u}.$$

The Gaussian copula has zero tail dependence $\lambda = 0$ whatever the correlation, so dependence somehow disappears at the lower tail of the distribution, while for the t_ν distribution

$$\lambda = 2\mathbf{t}_\nu\left(-\sqrt{\frac{(\nu + 1)(1 - \rho)}{1 + \rho}}\right),$$

where $\mathbf{t}_\nu$ denotes the scalar t_ν distribution function. Thus $\lambda > 0$ ('positive tail dependence') for any $\rho > -1$, meaning that the multivariate t distribution will give a more conservative estimate for the probabilities of joint extreme events. See McNeil, Frey, and Embrechts (2005) for more details.

2.2 Copula-based calibration

Let τ_1, τ_2, ... be the default times of issuers A_1, A_2, ... We express the joint distribution $F^{\theta,\xi}$ in terms of parametrized families $\{F_i^\theta : \theta \in \Theta\}$ of marginal distributions of τ_i and a parametrized family $\{C^\xi : \xi \in \Xi\}$ of copulas, so that

$$F^{\theta,\xi}(s_1, \ldots, s_n) = C^\xi(F_1^\theta(s_1), \ldots, F_n^\theta(s_n)). \tag{4}$$

Calibration to market data is a two-stage process: first one backs out the marginal default distributions $F_1^\theta(s)$, $F_2^\theta(s)$, ..., i.e. the value of the parameter vector θ, from market CDS rates on the individual obligors. Then the copula parameter ξ is chosen based on further market data as discussed below.

For the first step, recall that in a CDS contract written on A_j, the protection buyer pays a possible up-front premium π_j^0 and regular coupons at dates[3] $\{t_i\}$ and rates π_j^1 until $\min(\tau_j, T)$ where T is the contract expiry time and τ_j the default time of A_j. The protection seller pays $(1 - R_j)\mathbf{1}_{(\tau_j < T)}$ at next coupon date after τ_j, where R_j is the *recovery rate*.

If $G_j^\theta = 1 - F_j^\theta$ is the risk-neutral survivor function of τ_j, the 'fair' up-front and running premiums π_j^0, π_j^1 satisfy

$$\pi_0^j + \pi_j^1 \sum_{i=1}^n \eta_i\, p(t_0, t_i)G_j^\theta(t_i) = \sum_{i=1}^n (G_j^\theta(t_{i-1}) - G_j^\theta(t_i))(1 - R_j)p(t_0, t_i) \tag{5}$$

where η_i is the accrual factor for the ith coupon. The two conventional cases are (a) $\pi_j^0 = 0$, and then π_j^1 is the 'par spread', or (b) the running spread π_j^1 is fixed at some conventional level such as 100bp, and then (5) is used to determine π_j^0. In either case, if we have market data $(\pi_{j,k}^0, \pi_{j,k}^1)$ for maturities T_k, $k = 1, \ldots, m$ and a family of distributions parametrized by $\Theta = \mathbb{R}^m$ then we can determine the 'implied default distribution' $F_j^{\hat{\theta}}$. A standard procedure is to take

$$G_j^\theta(t) = \exp\left(-\int_0^t h(s)ds\right)$$

---

[3] Assumed the same for all contracts.

where

$$h(s) = \sum_{i=1}^{m} \theta_i \mathbf{1}_{]T_{i-1}, T_i]}(s) + \theta_m \mathbf{1}_{]T_m, \infty[}(s).$$

Then θ_i, θ_2, ... are determined recursively using $(\pi_{j,1}^0, \pi_{j,1}^1)$, $(\pi_{j,2}^0, \pi_{j,2}^1)$, ...

In (4) we are of course estimating the *risk-neutral* default distribution. To determine the copula parameter ξ we need correlation-sensitive market data, i.e. market prices of contracts that depend on joint default distributions. Unfortunately, there are very few such contracts, the primary ones being tranche contracts on the iTraxx and CDX indices. If our portfolio coincides with, say, the iTraxx portfolio then, having determined θ, we can search over the copula parameter space Ξ to find a parameter ξ such that current tranche prices are matched by our model. If there are no traded tranches of our portfolio then we have to resort to some proxy data, generally using techniques similar to those of CreditMetrics which ultimately involve estimating equity correlations. This is actually quite unsatisfactory since such procedures are estimating correlations in the real-world measure. In the Black-Scholes theory correlations are invariant under change of measure, but this is *not* generally true in credit risk models. How to get credible estimates of correlation is in fact the central problem of portfolio credit risk.

3 DYNAMIC DEFAULT MODELLING

While copula-based models are widely used, they are essentially restricted to a one-period setting and cannot form the basis for modelling credit-risky securities at the same level of generality as standard models for equities, foreign exchange, or interest rates. Even within a one-period setting copulas have some drawbacks: for example, as pointed out in section 2, the copula changes in a none-too-easily understood way as we move from an initial joint default distribution to a conditional distribution given survival up to some time. To get a dynamic theory of correlation, we need to posit some mechanism to describe the interaction between obligors, so that dynamic properties emerge in a natural way.

As is well known, dynamic models for credit risk divide into two general classes, *structural form* models and *reduced form* models. The former dates back to an early paper by Robert Merton (1974) which introduced the idea of corporate debt as a put option on the value of the firm. This spawned a large literature in which default times are modelled as barrier hitting times of some process, which may actually be a model for firm value or may be some abstract 'distance to default' factor process. In this chapter, however, we concentrate on reduced-form models, where the idea in general terms is to model the hazard rate corresponding to some default indicator process. As above, we consider n obligors with default times $\tau_1, \ldots, \tau_n$.

3.1 General formulation of reduced-form models

For a general multi-obligor reduced form model, we specify, on some filtered proba-bility space $(\Omega, (\mathcal{F}_t), \mathbb{P})$, an $\mathcal{F}_t$-adapted hazard rate process $h_i(t)$ for each obligor i, defined by the property that the process

$$M_i(t) = \mathbf{1}_{(t \geq \tau_i)} - \int_0^{t \wedge \tau_i} h_i(s)ds \qquad (6)$$

is a martingale. The interpretation here is that, on the set $\tau_i > t$,

$$\mathbb{P}[\tau_i \in (t, t+dt)|\mathcal{F}_t] \approx h_i(t)dt,$$

so that $h_i(t)dt$ is the incremental probability of default at time t. The second term on the right of (6) is often called the 'compensator' of the increasing process $\mathbf{1}_{(t \geq \tau_i)}$. The interpretation here is that $\mathcal{F}_t$ is the filtration of market-observable events, and default times τ_j of obligors are always $\mathcal{F}_t$-stopping times. We never consider 'background' filtrations. It may be that $\mathcal{F}_t$ is embedded in a larger filtration $\mathcal{G}_t$ generated by all modelled events and processes not all of which are market observed. Then we need to understand the relation between $\mathcal{F}_t$ and $\mathcal{G}_t$ compensators, which is provided by the notion of 'dual predictable projection', which we describe next.

3.2 Dual predictable projections

This topic is covered in section VI.1 of Rogers and Williams (2000). The very readable summary in lecture notes by Bass (1998) is also recommended.

If X is a bounded measurable process, there exists a unique $\mathcal{F}_t$-predictable process $^P X$, the *predictable projection* such that $\mathbb{E}[^P X_\tau \mathbf{1}_{\tau < \infty}] = \mathbb{E}[X_\tau \mathbf{1}_{\tau < \infty}]$ for all predictable stopping times τ. We have

$$^P X_\tau = \mathbb{E}[X_\tau|\mathcal{F}_{\tau-}], \quad \tau \text{ predictable.}$$

Let A_t be a right-continuous increasing process. For bounded measurable X define

$$\mu_A(X) = \mathbb{E} \int_0^T X_t dA_t$$

We can show there exists a unique predictable increasing process $\tilde{A}$ such that

$$\mu_A(^P X) = \mu_{\tilde{A}}(X) \quad \text{for all bounded measurable } X.$$

If A is adapted to $\mathcal{F}_t$ then $A_t - \tilde{A}_t$ is a martingale. $\tilde{A}$ is the *compensator* of A_t.

Suppose τ is an $\mathcal{G}_t$-stopping time representing a default time. Then τ is also an $\mathcal{F}_t$-stopping time if the events $\{\tau \leq t\}$ are $\mathcal{F}_t$-measurable. A *reduced form model* means, in general, the specification of a $\mathcal{G}_t$-compensator H_t of $N_t = \mathbf{1}_{t \geq \tau}$, i.e.

$$M_t = N_t - H_t$$

is a $\mathcal{G}_t$ martingale. The $\mathcal{F}_t$ compensator is then the dual predictable projection $\hat{H}_t$. Most often, $H_t = \int_0^t h(s)ds$ for some non-negative $\mathcal{G}_t$-adapted hazard rate process h. Then

$$\hat{H}_t = \int_0^t {}^P h(s)ds = \int_0^t \hat{h}(s)ds$$

is the $\mathcal{F}_t$-compensator, where $\hat{h}(s) = \mathbb{E}[h(s)|\mathcal{F}_{s-}]$. Computation of $\hat{h}$ is a problem of *non-linear filtering* about which we will say more below.

3.3 A taxonomy of modelling approaches

Having stated in general terms what a reduced-form model is, we now summarize the various ways in which it is conventionally instantiated, giving the background for the contagion models which are the main focus of this chapter. There are three main categories: factor models, frailty models, and contagion models. We give specific examples of each below. A *factor model* is one where the hazard rate takes the form $h_i(t) = h_i(X_t, t, \omega)$ for some (common) factor process X_t which may or may not be observable (i.e. $\mathcal{F}_t$-adapted). X_t will generally be multivariate and can be used to model the macroeconomy, sector-specific effects, etc. *Frailty models* are similar in form but the term is reserved for cases in which at least some of the factors are not directly observed, and these factors are 'latent variables' in that they are abstract statistical factors rather than specific economic variables. In a *contagion model* the hazard rate is $h_i(t)\mathbf{1}_{\tau_i > t} = h_i(S_t^i, t, \omega)$ where $S_t^i = \{\tau_j : \tau_j < t \wedge \tau_i\}$, so that the hazard rate for obligor i is directly affected by defaults of other obligors.

3.3.1 A factor model of rating transitions

This is the model introduced by Davis and Esparragoza Rodriguez (2007) and described as follows (see section 4.2 below for information about finite-state Markov chains).

- There is a finite-state Markov 'environment' process $X(t) \in \{1, 2, \ldots, K\}$ with generator matrix Q.
- There is a portfolio of n obligors, each obligor having one of m credit ratings. The m-vector process $q^n(t)$ has ith component $q_i^n(t)$, equal to the the number of obligors rated i at time t. The total portfolio size (=number of non-defaulted obligors) is therefore $\sum_{i=1}^m q_i^n(t)$.
- Obligors with the same credit rating are indistinguishable. All obligors are conditionally independent given $X(t)$.
- Conditioned on $X(t) = k$, the transition rate from rating i to rating j is $\mu_{ij}(k)$ and the default rate is $\lambda_i(k) \equiv \mu_{ii}(k)$. Thus the *portfolio* transition rates are $q_i^n(t)\mu_{ij}(X(t))$.

FIGURE 9.2 State transitions for portfolio of size 5.

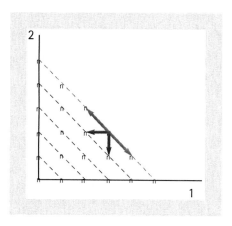

Figure 9.2 shows the possible transitions for a portfolio of size 5 with 2 rating categories. Diagonal moves are change of rating, while vertical and horizontal moves are default. From the description above, for $n > 0$ the process $q^n(t)$ can be expressed as the solution to the following integral equation

$$q^n(t) = q^n(0) + \sum_{i=1}^{m}\sum_{j=1}^{m} N_{ij}\left(\int_0^t \mu_{ij}(X_s)q_i^n(s)ds \right) v_{ij} \tag{7}$$

where for $i, j = 1, \ldots, m$, N_{ij} is a collection of independent Poisson processes, and v_{ij} is the set of vectors defined as

$$v_{ij} = \begin{cases} \mathbf{e}_j - \mathbf{e}_i & j \neq i \\ -\mathbf{e}_i & i = j \end{cases} \tag{8}$$

The joint process $(X(t), q^n(t))$ evolves on K 'layers' of $\mathbb{R}^m$ as shown in Figure 9.3. The generator matrix $A(x)$ associated with the process is defined as

$$A_{ij}(x) = \begin{cases} \mu_{ij}(x) & j \neq i \\ -\sum_l \mu_{il}(x) & j = i \end{cases}$$

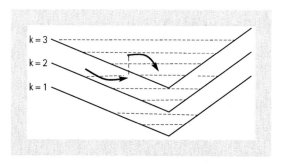

FIGURE 9.3 State space for rating transition model.

This is a classic factor model in that the factor process evolves autonomously and is not influenced by the history of default events and re-rating movements. The main interest of this model lies in its large-portfolio properties. By taking a law-of-large-numbers $1/n$ scaling we find that the Markov chain motion in each 'layer' converges as $n \to \infty$ to the solution of an ordinary differential equation, leaving the factor process $X(t)$ as the only stochastic variable. The model is in some sense a dynamic version of the well-known Vasicek large-portfolio model.

3.3.2 Frailty models

Frailty models originally arose in the statistical analysis of survival time data (see the book by Andersen et al. (1997) for an excellent treatment). In these applications we have survival times $\tau_1, \ldots, \tau_n$ where the hazard rate for τ_i is $H_i(t) = Y_i \lambda_i(t)$, where λ_i is often supposed to take the 'proportional hazards' form

$$\lambda_i(t) = h_0(t) \exp\left(\sum_{k=1}^{m} \beta_k x_{ik}\right).$$

$h_0(t)$ is a 'baseline hazard rate'. There are m known factors such as (in the default risk case) credit ratings, distance to default, industry sector, etc.; x_{ik} is the value of the kth factor for obligor i and the (initially unknown) coefficient β_k measures the influence of the kth factor on default. $Y = (Y_1, \ldots, Y_n)$ are 'frailty' factors—a vector of non-negative random variable with $\mathbb{E}[Y_i] = 1$. It is assumed that the τ_i are conditional independent given Y. Hence

$$\mathbb{P}[\cap_{i=1}^{n}(\tau_i > t_i)|Y] = \exp(-\Lambda(t_1, \ldots, t_n)Y)$$

where Λ is the row n-vector with ith component

$$\Lambda_i = \int_0^{t_i} \lambda_i(t)dt.$$

Hence the joint survivor function of the default times is

$$G(t_1, \ldots, t_n) = \mathbb{E}[\exp(-\Lambda(t_1, \ldots, t_n)Y)] = \phi_Y(\Lambda(t_1, \ldots, t_n)),$$

where ϕ_Y is the multivariate Laplace transform of the distribution function of Y, i.e.

$$\phi_Y(u) = \mathbb{E}[e^{-uY}], \quad u \in \mathbb{R}^n.$$

In some cases this is known in closed form, for example in the scalar case where $Y \sim \Gamma(\alpha, \beta)$ we have $\phi_Y(u) = (1 + \beta u)^{-\alpha}$. Then we have a well-defined likelihood function from which parameters may be estimated. We consider real-world-measure estimation of default models in section 26 below.

3.3.3 A contagion model: Infectious Defaults

Several dynamic contagion models will be discussed below, but we start with the single-period *Infectious Defaults* model introduced by Davis and Lo (2001a). Consider

n identical obligors and let Z_i be random variable such that $Z_i = 1$ if obligor i defaults and $Z_i = 0$ otherwise. For $i, j = 1, \ldots, n$ and $j \neq i$ let X_i, Y_{ij} be independent Bernoulli random variables with $\mathbb{P}[X_i = 1] = p$, $\mathbb{P}[Y_{ij} = 1] = q$. Then

$$Z_i = X_i + (1 - X_i)\left(1 - \prod_{j \neq i}(1 - X_j Y_{ji})\right).$$

The Z_i are exchangeable, and the distribution of $N = \sum_i Z_i$ is given by

$$\mathbb{P}[N = k] = F(n, k, p, q) = C_k^n a_{nk}^{pq}$$

and

$$\mathbb{E}[N] = n\left(1 - (1 - p)(1 - pq)^{n-1}\right)$$

where

$$a_{nk}^{pq} = p^k(1 - p)^{k(n-k)} + \sum_{i=1}^{k-1} C_i^k p^i(1 - p)^{n-i}(1 - (1 - q)^i)^{k-i}(1 - q)^{i(n-k)}.$$

The marginal probability $\mathbb{P}[Z_i = 1] = \mathbb{E}[Z_i] = \mathbb{E}[N]/n$ increases with q. To maintain fixed marginals, reduce p as q increases, keeping $\mathbb{E}[N]$ constant. The effect is to increase 'tail risk'. As can be seen in Figure 9.4, as q increases more weight is

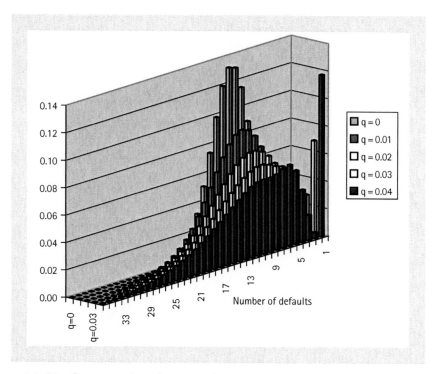

FIGURE 9.4 Distributions in the Infectious Defaults model.

Table 9.1 Calibration of the infectious defaults model

q	p	99% VaR	CVaR
0	0.1	17	17.83
0.01	0.0522	22	24.56
0.02	0.0351	25	27.05
0.03	0.0264	27	30.33
0.04	0.0212	29	32.62

shifted into the large-default end of the distribution. The whole point of the infection mechanism is to model this effect. A by-product is that, since the mean is constant, $\mathbb{P}[N = 0]$ also increases with q. In the extreme case $q = 1$ there are either no defaults (with probability 0.9) or 100% defaults.

4 MARKOV PROCESSES

This section summarizes information about Markov processes, which will be needed below. We formulate the theory using the martingale-based 'extended generator' concept. Originally introduced by Stroock and Varadhan (1969), this is now accepted as *the* way to treat the relationship between Markov processes and differential or integral operators.

All processes are defined on a probability space $(\Omega, (\mathcal{F}_t)_{0 \leq t \leq T}, \mathbb{P})$ where the filtration $\mathcal{F}_t$ represents the history of Market information. All processes X_t considered are adapted to $\mathcal{F}_t$.

A process X_t taking values in a *state space* E is a (homogeneous) *Markov process* if for all bounded measurable functions f and $\delta > 0$

$$\mathbb{E}[f(X_{t+\delta})|\mathcal{F}_t] = \mathbb{E}[f(X_{t+\delta})|X_t].$$

In principle, a Markov process is specified by its *transition measure* $p(A, t, x)$ such that

$$\mathbb{E}[f(X_{t+\delta})|X_t] = \int_E f(y)p(dy, \delta, x)\Big|_{x=X_t}.$$

For example, Brownian motion has transition measure

$$p(dy, t, x) = \frac{1}{\sqrt{2\pi t}}e^{-\frac{1}{2t}(y-x)^2}dy \quad \sim N(0, t).$$

For most processes this can't be computed and the process is specified by its *generator*.

4.1 Generators and backward equations

The generator (or 'extended generator') of a Markov process X_t is an operator $\mathcal{A}$ acting on functions $\mathcal{D}(\mathcal{A})$ such that

$$C_t^f = f(X_t) - f(x_0) - \int_0^t \mathcal{A}f(X_s)ds \tag{9}$$

is a martingale for $f \in \mathcal{D}(\mathcal{A})$, i.e. $\mathbb{E}[X_t|\mathcal{F}_s] = X_s$ for $s \leq t$. For example, if X_t satisfies the SDE

$$dX_t = m(X_t)dt + \sigma(X_t)dW_t$$

then the Ito formula states that for C^2 functions f

$$df(X_t) = (m(X_t)f'(X_t) + \frac{1}{2}\sigma^2(X_t)f''(X_t))dt + f'(X_t)\sigma(X_t)dW_t.$$

In this case $\mathcal{D}(\mathcal{A}) \subset C^2$ and

$$\mathcal{A}f(x) = m(x)f'(x) + \frac{1}{2}\sigma^2(x)f''(x).$$

Taking expectations in (9) gives the *Dynkin formula*

$$\mathbb{E}_x[f(X_t)] = f(x) + \int_0^t \mathbb{E}_x[\mathcal{A}f(X_s)ds].$$

The two-component process $\tilde{X}_t = (t, X_t)$ is a Markov process with generator $\tilde{\mathcal{A}}v(t, x) = \partial v/\partial t + \mathcal{A}v(t, x)$. The Dynkin formula for $\tilde{X}$ is then

$$\mathbb{E}_x[v(T, X_T)] = v(0, x) + \int_0^t \mathbb{E}_x\left[\frac{\partial v}{\partial s} + \mathcal{A}v(s, X_s)ds\right].$$

Thus if v satisfies the *backward equation*

$$\frac{\partial v(t, x)}{\partial s} + \mathcal{A}v(s, x) = 0 \tag{10}$$

$$v(T, x) = \Phi(x)$$

then

$$v(0, x) = \mathbb{E}_{0,x}\Phi(X_T)$$

and more generally

$$v(t, x) = \mathbb{E}_{t,x}\Phi(X_T) = \mathbb{E}[\Phi(X_T)|\mathcal{F}_t].$$

Note that (10) is a parabolic PDE when X_t is the stochastic differential equation as above.

A more general form of the backward equation is

$$\frac{\partial v}{\partial t} + \mathcal{A}v + g(t, x) - \beta v(t, x) = 0 \tag{11}$$

$$v(T, x) = \Phi(x)$$

The solution is now

$$v(t, x) = E_{t,x}\left[\int_t^T e^{-\int_t^s \beta(x_u)du} g(s, X_s)ds + e^{-\int_t^T \beta(x_u)du} h(x_T)\right]$$

This is the *Feynman-Kac formula* (as used to compute discounted expectations in Black-Scholes, for example).

4.2 Markov chains

A Markov chain is a Markov process X_t whose state space is a finite set $E = \{1, \ldots, N\}$. Note that a function $f : E \to \mathbb{R}$ can be identified with an N-vector $f = (f_1, \ldots, f_N)$ with $f_i = f(i)$. The generator is then identified with an $N \times N$ matrix, the so-called Q-matrix:

$$\mathcal{A}f(i) = (Qf)_i.$$

The off-diagonal elements q_{ij}, $i \neq j$ are non-negative, with the interpretation

$$\mathbb{E}[X_{t+\delta} = j | X_t = i] = q_{ij}\delta + o(\delta),$$

the 'rate of transition' from i to j, while

$$q_{ii} = -\sum_{j \neq i} q_{ij}.$$

Thus *the row sums of Q are zero* and $1 + q_{ii}\delta$ is the probability that the process stays at i over $[t, t + \delta]$. The backward equation (10) becomes the ordinary differential equation(ODE)

$$\frac{d}{dt}v(t) + Qv = 0, \quad v(T) = \Phi \tag{12}$$

for the function $v(t)$ with $v_i(t) = v(t, i)$. The solution is $v(t) = e^{Q(T-t)}\Phi$. The general backward equation is the ODE

$$\frac{d}{dt}v(t) + (Q - \beta I)v + g = 0, \quad v(T) = \Phi.$$

The solution is (with $Q_\beta = Q - \beta I$)

$$v(t) = e^{Q_\beta(T-t)}\Phi + \int_t^T e^{Q_\beta(s-t)}g(t)ds. \tag{13}$$

Let $\mu = (\mu_1, \ldots, \mu_N)$ be a *row* vector representing the distribution of X_0. Then the distribution of X_t is $p(t)$, the (row vector) solution of the *forward equation*

$$\frac{d}{dt}p(t) = p(t)Q, \quad p(0) = \mu, \tag{14}$$

i.e.

$$p(t) = \mu e^{Qt}. \tag{15}$$

The relation between the backward equation (12) and the forward equation (14) is determined as follows. Note from (13) and (15) that for arbitrary vector Φ, initial distribution μ and times $t < T$,

$$\mathbb{E}_\mu[\Phi \cdot X_T] = p(T)\Phi = \mu e^{QT}\Phi = \mu e^{Qt}e^{Q(T-t)}\Phi = p(t)v(t) = \mathbb{E}_\mu[\mathbb{E}_\mu[\Phi \cdot X_T|\mathcal{F}_t]].$$

Thus $p(t)v(t)$ is independent of t, so $\frac{d}{dt}(pv) = 0$, and this fact determines the forward equation given that we already have the backward equation.

4.2.1 *Phase-type distributions*

Phase-type distributions form a convenient class of univariate or multivariate distributions for non-negative random variables, widely used in applied probability. The reader can consult Asmussen (2003) for a full account of the theory and a variety of applications.

A distribution function F on $\mathbb{R}^+$ is a *phase-type distribution* if F is the distribution of a random variable τ taking the form

$$\tau = \inf\{t : X_t \in A\}$$

where X_t is a Markov chain in continuous time with finite state space E, $A \subset E$ and the initial distribution p is concentrated on $E \backslash A$. It is no loss of generality to suppose that $E = \{1, 2, \ldots, N\}$ and $A = \{k+1, \ldots, N\}$. The distribution of τ, the hitting time of A is preserved if we kill the chain at τ, forming a new process $\hat{X}_t$ on $\hat{E} = \{1, \ldots, k\} \cup \Delta$, where Δ is a 1-point 'cemetary' state, with Q-matrix $\tilde{Q}$ defined by

$$\tilde{Q} = \begin{bmatrix} q_{11} & q_{12} & \cdots & q_{1k} & \tilde{q}_{1(k+1)} \\ q_{21} & q_{22} & \cdots & q_{2k} & \tilde{q}_{2(k+1)} \\ \vdots & \vdots & \vdots & \vdots & \vdots \\ q_{k1} & q_{k2} & \cdots & q_{kk} & \tilde{q}_{k(k+1)} \\ 0 & 0 & 0 & 0 & 0 \end{bmatrix} = \begin{bmatrix} G & g \\ 0 & 0 \end{bmatrix},$$

where $\tilde{q}_{j(k+1)} = -\sum_{l=1}^{k} q_{jl}$ and G is the obvious $k \times k$ submatrix. Thus the vector g is determined by G. The main general result is

Proposition 4.1 *For the phase-type distribution described above*

(i) *The distribution function F is given by $F(t) = 1 - p\,e^{Gt}\mathbf{1}$.*

(ii) The Laplace transform $\hat{f}(s) = \int_0^\infty f(t)e^{-st}dt$ of the density function $f(t) = dF(t)/dt$ is a rational function given by $\hat{f}(s) = p(sI - G)^{-1}g$.

These results make the distribution functions and associated functionals of phase-type distributions exceptionally easy to compute, either by numerical linear algebra or transform methods. Note from (ii) that a phase-type distribution always has rational Laplace transform. A large class of distributions can be approximated by phase-type distributions (although not the whole class of distributions with rational spectral density; see Asmussen 2003).

5 MARKOV CHAIN MODELS

In this section we describe four dynamic credit models based on finite-state Markov chains: two versions of the so-called Diamond Default model, an inhomogeneous portfolio model due to Herbertsson (2007), and the homogeneous portfolio 'Enhanced Risk' model of Davis and Lo (2001b).

5.1 Diamond Default model I

This is a two-obligor infection model that can be thought of as a model for counterparty risk. Think of B as the underlying name in a CDS contract and A as the protection seller. The model is depicted in Figure 9.5. It is a four-state Markov chain X_t which starts at $X_0 = 0$ where neither obligor has defaulted and moves through the states with the hazard rates shown in the figure. The parameter a gives the infection effect: the initial hazard rate for A is h_1, while if B defaults first (i.e. we move to $X_t = 2$) then the hazard rate of A jumps to ah_1, so a quantifies the effect on A of a default by B. Note that an arbitrary joint density for the default times τ_A, τ_B could be achieved with

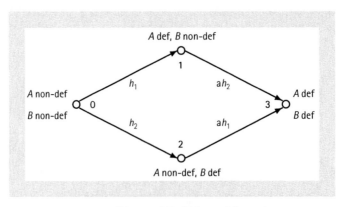

FIGURE 9.5 Diamond Default model, version 1.

this representation if we were to replace the hazard rates h_1, h_2, ah_1, ah_2 by arbitrary functions of time $h_i(t)$, $i = 1, \ldots, 4$.

The Q-matrix for the diamond model is

$$
\mathcal{A} = \begin{bmatrix}
-(h_A + h_B) & h_A & h_B & 0 \\
0 & -\beta h_B & 0 & \beta h_B \\
0 & 0 & -ah_A & ah_A \\
0 & 0 & 0 & 0
\end{bmatrix}.
$$

State 3 is absorbing. The marginal default-time distributions are

$$
F_A(t) = 1 - e^{-(h_1+h_2)t} - \frac{h_2 e^{-ah_1 t}}{h_1 + h_2 - ah_1}\left(1 - e^{-(h_1+h_2-ah_1)t}\right)
$$

$$
F_B(t) = 1 - e^{-(h_1+h_2)t} - \frac{h_1 e^{-ah_2 t}}{h_1 + h_2 - ah_2}\left(1 - e^{-(h_1+h_2-ah_2)t}\right).
$$

The double default distribution, i.e. the distribution of $\tau_{DD} = \max\{\tau_A, \tau_B\}$ is

$$
F_{DD}(t) = 1 - e^{-(h_1+h_2)t} - \frac{h_2 e^{-ah_1 t}}{h_1 + h_2 - ah_1}\left(1 - e^{-(h_1+h_2-ah_1)t}\right)
$$
$$
- \frac{h_1 e^{-ah_2 t}}{h_1 + h_2 - ah_2}\left(1 - e^{-(h_1+h_2-ah_2)t}\right).
$$

Calibration to market CDS rates for issuers A and B, for a given parameter a has to be done jointly—the model cannot be calibrated one issuer at a time as in the copula framework. However the computations required are simple. Note that time-dependent h_1, h_2 will be required if we have a term structure of CDS spreads. Calibration assumes recovery rates R_A, R_B.

The continuous-time CDS premium π_i on asset $i = A, B$, assuming no up-front premium, is determined by

$$
\pi_i \int_0^T e^{-rt}(1 - F_i(t))dt = (1 - R_i)\int_0^T e^{-rt} f_i(t)dt,
$$

where r is the riskless rate and $f_i(t) = dF_i(t)/dt$. From the model, we find

$$
\pi_A = (1 - R_A)\frac{I_2}{I_1}
$$

where, with $m(a, T) = \frac{1}{a}(1 - e^{-aT})$,

$$
I_1 = h_1(1 - a)m(r + h_1 + h_2, T) + h_2 m(r + ah_1, T),
$$

$$
I_2 = (h_1 + h_2)h_1(1 - a)m(r + h_1 + h_2, T) + ah_1 h_2 m(r + ah_1, T).
$$

There is a similar expression for π_B. The first default time $\tau_{\min} = \tau_A \wedge \tau_B$ is exponential with rate $(h_1 + h_2)$. Hence the FTD premium is

$$
\pi_{FTD} = (1 - R_A)h_1 + (1 - R_B)h_2.
$$

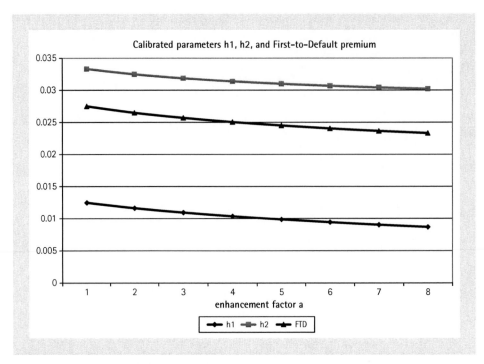

FIGURE 9.6 Calibrated parameters for Diamond Default model.

Figure 9.6 shows the calibrated h_1, h_2 as functions of the enhancement parameter a when the CDS rates are $\pi_1 = 75$bp, $\pi_2 = 200$bp, and $R_A = R_B = 40\%$.

The counterparty risk interpretation is as follows. Suppose A is the protection seller in a CDS contract with B as the underlying asset. Then protection payment $(1 - R_B)$ is made only if we reach state 2. We find that the CDS premium is $(1 - R_B)h_2$.

5.2 Diamond Default model II

This version of the Diamond Default model, shown in Figure 9.7 was introduced by Crépey, Jeanblanc, and Zargari (2009). It includes a positive probability of simultaneous default. The advantage is that, with a single CDS rate given for each obligor, the model can be calibrated to each obligor separately. Indeed, if we choose parameters satisfying

$$\lambda_1 + \lambda_3 = q_A \tag{16}$$

$$\lambda_2 + \lambda_3 = q_B, \tag{17}$$

then

$$\mathbb{P}[\tau_A > t] = e^{-q_A t}, \qquad \mathbb{P}[\tau_B > t] = e^{-q_B t}.$$

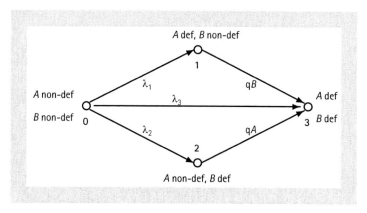

FIGURE 9.7 Diamond Default model, version II.

The condition (16) ensures that hazard rate for A is always $h_A(t) = q_A \mathbf{1}_{\tau_A > t}$. The extreme cases of this model are:

1. $\lambda_3 = 0$. Then $\lambda_1 = q_A$, $\lambda_2 = q_B$ and τ_A, τ_B are independent exponential times.
2. $\lambda_3 = q_B \leq q_A$. Then $\lambda_2 = 0$, $\lambda_1 = q_A - q_B$. In this case $\tau_A \leq \tau_B$ with probability 1.

5.3 An inhomogeneous contagion model for portfolio credit risk

This section is based on work by Herbertsson (2007) and Herbertsson and Rootzén (2008) and bears some similarity to a model discussed by Frey and Backhaus (2007). The reader can consult the chapter in this volume by Bielecki, Crepey and Hesbertsson for a more extended discussion. In the model, the hazard rate for each obligor is directly a function of default events of other obligors.

We have n obligors, denoted $1, 2, \ldots n$. Let $\mathcal{U}$, $\mathcal{O}$ denote the set of, respectively, unordered and ordered subsets of $N = \{1, \ldots, n\}$. Elements of these sets will be denoted $\{k_1, \ldots, k_j\}$ $[k_1, \ldots, k_j]$ respectively. $\mathcal{U}$, $\mathcal{O}$ have cardinality $c_{\mathcal{U}} = 2^n$ and $c_{\mathcal{O}} = 1 + n + n(n-1) + n(n-1)(n-2) + \cdots + n!$. For example, $c_{\mathcal{U}} = 1,024$ and $c_{\mathcal{O}} = 9,864,101$ when $n = 10$. For $i \in N$, we will denote by $\mathcal{U}_i$, $\mathcal{O}_i$ the set of subsets not including index i.

Let τ_i be the default time of obligor i. In an *ordered default times* model, we specify functions $\mu_i : \mathcal{O}_i \to \mathbb{R}^+$ and suppose that the hazard rate for τ_i at time t is $\lambda_i(t) = \mu_i([k_1, \ldots, k_j])$ when $\tau_{k_1} < \tau_{k_2} < \cdots < \tau_{k_j} < t$ and $\tau_l > t$ for $l \notin \{k_1, \ldots, k_j\}$. An *unordered model* is similar except that the hazard rate is defined by functions $\nu_i : \mathcal{U}_i \to \mathbb{R}^+$. In this case we can define $Y_i(t) = \mathbf{1}_{\tau_i \leq t}$ and identify elements of $\mathcal{U}$ with elements of $E = \{0, 1, \ldots, 2^n - 1\}$ where $y \in E$ expressed in binary notation identifies the defaulted obligors. The hazard rate then takes the form $\nu_i(Y(t))$ where $Y(t) = (Y_1(t), \ldots, Y_n(t))$. In Herbertsson's model

$$v_i(y) = a_i + b_i \cdot y, \quad a_i \in \mathbb{R}^+, b_i \in \mathbb{R}^n,$$

so that default of j permanently increases i's hazard rate by $b_{i,j}$, assuming that i has not already defaulted. An ordered or unordered model defines a Markov chain on a state space of cardinality c_O or c_U. By way of illustration, Figures 9.8 and 9.9 show the two cases for $n = 3$ (so $c_O = 16$, $c_U = 8$, though one could argue that the ordered cardinality is really 11 since there is no point in distinguishing between the permutations of 1,2,3 in the final column where everybody has defaulted.)

Of course, a 'model' is only specified when we say what the functions μ_i or v_i are. Ordered models have some intuitive appeal—for example, we can build in the idea that the most recent defaults are the ones having most effect on surviving obligors—but state space for these models is enormous: as pointed out above, there are close to 10 million states when $n = 10$. Unordered state spaces are much smaller but still large: $n = 23$ is the largest unordered portfolio with fewer than 10 million states ($2^{23} = 8,388,608$).

Every default time τ_i is the hitting time of some set and hence has a phase-type distribution. In Figures 9.8, 9.9 the default time of obligor 2 is the hitting time of the set whose elements are shown in the boxes. Essentially, this means that all computations reduce to computing $e^{\tilde{Q}t}v$ where $\tilde{Q}$ is Q, the $n \times n$ Q-matrix of the model, or some

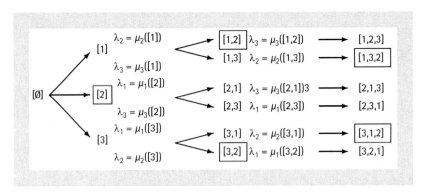

FIGURE 9.8 Inhomogeneous model: ordered states, $n = 3$.

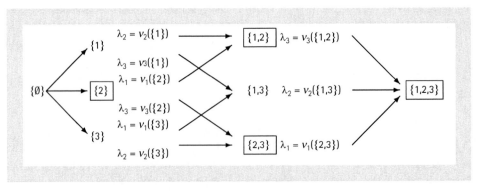

FIGURE 9.9 Inhomogeneous model: unordered states, $n = 3$.

sub-matrix. Q is a sparse matrix, and gets more sparse as n increases. Computing the matrix exponential has been the subject of decades of research (see the classic paper by Moler and Van Loan (2003)). In the author's view, this model is a 'proof of principle': it is not in its simplest form a serious contender for practical applications, but it does demonstrate that large models can be solved by harnessing the power of modern computational linear algebra, a technique that will certainly be more widely exploited in the future than it hitherto has been.

5.4 A homogeneous model: Enhanced Risk

This model, introduced by Davis and Lo (2001b) describes defaults in a portfolio of exchangeable[4] obligors.

The initial portfolio size is n, and the obligors are conditionally independent with hazard rate $h(t)$ given the risk state. Under 'normal risk' $h(t) = \lambda$, under 'enhanced risk' $h(t) = \kappa\lambda$ for $\kappa > 1$. The *portfolio* hazard rate is thus $j\lambda$ or $j\kappa\lambda$ where j is the number of non-defaulted obligors. The evolution of portfolio defaults is described by a continuous-time Markov chain X_t whose $(2n + 1)$-point state space and possible transitions are shown in Figure 9.10. Points in the state space are denoted $\{(j, k) : 0 \le j \le n, k = 0, 1\}$ (the point $(0, 0)$ is redundant). The left-hand column ($k = 0$) represents states of 'normal risk', while the right-hand column ($k = 1$) is 'enhanced risk'. The vertical level j is the number of undefaulted obligors. In the initial state $(n, 0)$ the hazard rate for transition to state $(n, 1)$ is ν and the hazard rate for transition to state $(n - 1, 1)$ is $n\lambda$ (there are n obligors, each with hazard rate λ). Thus the system may move 'spontaneously' from normal to enhanced risk, representing an exogenous shock, but *always* moves to enhanced risk (if not already there) on occurrence of a default. Transition back to normal risk takes place with constant hazard rate μ, so the periods spent in enhanced risk are exponential with mean $1/\mu$. As an example, the Q-matrix for X_t with $n = 3$ is as follows (the ordering of states is left-hand column, then right-hand column):

$$Q = \begin{bmatrix} -(\nu + 3\lambda) & 0 & 0 & \nu & 3\lambda & 0 & 0 \\ 0 & -(\nu + 2\lambda) & 0 & 0 & \nu & 2\lambda & 0 \\ 0 & 0 & -(\nu + \lambda) & 0 & 0 & \nu & \lambda \\ \mu & 0 & 0 & -(\mu + 3\kappa\lambda) & 3\kappa\lambda & 0 & 0 \\ 0 & \mu & 0 & 0 & -(\mu + 2\kappa\lambda) & 2\kappa\lambda & 0 \\ 0 & 0 & \mu & 0 & 0 & -(\mu + \kappa\lambda) & \kappa\lambda \\ 0 & 0 & 0 & 0 & 0 & 0 & 0 \end{bmatrix}$$

[4] i.e. all distributions are invariant under permutation of the portfolio members.

FIGURE 9.10 State space of enhanced risk model.

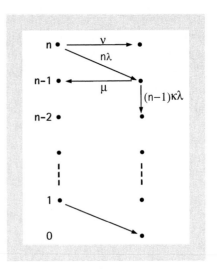

The expected number of defaults in $[0, T]$ is $\mathrm{ED}(\nu, \mu, \lambda, \kappa) = a'e^{QT}\beta$ where $a' = [1, 0, 0, 0, 0, 0, 0]$ and $\beta' = [0, 1, 2, 0, 1, 2, 3]$. Thus the individual default probability is

$$p = \frac{1}{n}\mathrm{ED}(\nu, \mu, \lambda, \kappa).$$

If p is known from a single CDS rate for maturity T (assumed the same for all of the homogeneous group of obligors) then we can calibrate λ for fixed ν, μ, κ. To calibrate to multiple CDS rates for maturities T_1, T_2, ... we need a time varying parameter $\lambda(t)$.

Let us now consider pricing of CDO tranches. For ease of exposition we will assume a constant continuously compounded rate r for discounting, and that the protection buyer pays premium in continuous time at at rate $c_\pi(X_t)$ where c_π is specified below in terms of the contracted premium-side rate π. We normalize the total portfolio notional to 1, so each obligor has notional $1/n$. The value of the premium leg is then

$$v_{\mathrm{prem}}(\pi) = \mathbb{E}^{\mathbb{Q}}_{0,x}\int_0^T e^{-rt}c(X_t)dt. \tag{18}$$

Suppose the CDO contract refers to the $[a\%, b\%]$ tranche and that the recovery rate is R. Then loss is incurred in the tranche when the number m of losses in the portfolio lies between m_1 and m_2, where m_1 is the smallest integer greater than $a^* = na/(1 - R)$ and m_2 is the largest integer less than $b^* = nb/(1 - R)$. Conventionally, premium is paid at a rate proportional to the remaining notional in the tranche and is normalized with respect to the tranche size $(b - a)$, so when there are m losses the premium is paid at rate

$$\tilde{c}(m) = \pi \times (b - a) \times \min\left(1, \frac{(b^* - m)^+}{b^* - a^*}\right)$$

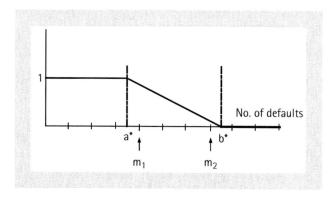

FIGURE 9.11 CDO premium reduction function for [a,b] tranche.

(see Figure 9.11), where π is the basic contract rate. Expressed in terms of the process X_t the rate is $c(X_t)$ where $c((j, k)) = \tilde{c}(n - j)$.

The protection seller pays an amount K_m at the mth default time, where $K_{m_1} = (m_1 - a^*)(1 - R)/n$, $K_m = (1 - R)/n$ for $m = m_1 + 1, \ldots, m_2$, $K_{m_2} = (b^* - m_2)(1 - R)/n$ and $K_m = 0$ otherwise. If N_t denotes the total number of defaults in the time interval $[0, t]$ then the value of the protection leg is

$$v_{\text{prot}} = \mathbb{E}^{\mathbb{Q}}_{0,x} \int_0^t e^{-rt} g(X_{t-})dN_t,$$

where $g((j, k)) = K_{n-j+1}$. Now N_t is a point process whose hazard rate is[5] $h(X_{t-})$ with

$$h((j, k)) = (n - m + 1)\lambda \mathbf{1}_{\{(j,k)=(m-n+1,0)\}} + (n - m + 1)\kappa\lambda \mathbf{1}_{\{(j,k)=(m-n+1,1)\}}.$$

Since $dN_t - h(X_{t-})dt$ is a martingale, we see that

$$v_{\text{prot}} = \mathbb{E}^{\mathbb{Q}}_{0,x} \int_0^t e^{-rt} g(X_t)h(X_t)dt. \qquad (19)$$

The tranche spread is simply the premium π such that $v_{\text{prem}}(\pi) = v_{\text{prot}}$. The basic calculation on both sides of this equation is to compute (18), for different functions c. In general $v(t, x) = \mathbb{E}_{t,x}[\int_t^T c(X_s)ds]$ solves the backward equation

$$\frac{\partial v}{\partial t} + \mathcal{A}v(t, x) + c(x) - rv(t, x) = 0, \quad v(T, x) = 0.$$

For an l-state Markov chain we identify functions $c(x)$ with l-vectors $c' = [c(1), c(2), \ldots, c(l)]$ and then the backward equation becomes the ODE

$$\frac{dv(t)}{dt} + (Q - rI)v(t) + c = 0, \quad v(T) = 0.$$

This is easily solved by Runge-Kutta integration. We can now calibrate the remaining parameters to market tranche spreads.

---

[5] or $h(X_t)$ since $X_t = X_{t-}$ almost everywhere with respect to Lebesgue measure.

If we wish to calibrate the model to market tranche spreads for the iTraxx or CDX indices, it may be found that this model as it stands cannot match the spread on the senior tranche. In the very similar model presented in Davis and Esparragoza Rodriguez (2007) we found—in common with similar studies elsewhere—that it is necessary to include a 'disaster scenario' in the model to achieve this. In the present context this is easily accomplished by adding a third column of states to the model with a second enhancement parameter $\kappa' >> \kappa$. The computations are the same but with a larger state space, but these computations are in any case trivially small compared to those of, say, the model of section 5.3 above.

6 CHANGES OF FILTRATION

It is of course well known that financial modelling often involves the consideration of several different probability measures: the 'historical', 'statistical', or 'real-world' measure, generally known as $\mathbb{P}$ and a variety of 'risk-neutral', 'pricing', or 'martingale' measures, generally known as $\mathbb{Q}$, corresponding to different choices of numéraire asset. $\mathbb{Q}$ is unique for a given numéraire only when the market is complete. The reader can refer to, for example, the elegant treatment in the recent textbook by Filipović (2009) for a discussion of these topics.

It is fair to say that the bulk of the literature on credit risk is concerned with pricing measure applications. In the credit context, markets are invariably incomplete, so there is no unique martingale measure or riskless hedge. The conventional approach is to write down a parametrized family of models with risk-neutral measures $\{\mathbb{Q}^\theta : \theta \in \Theta\}$ and calibrate the parameters to market prices, i.e. select parameters such that, for each market traded contract, its current price v_0 coincides with the model value

$$v_0^\theta = \mathbb{E}^\theta \left[\frac{V_T}{N_T} \right]. \tag{20}$$

Here, $\mathbb{E}^\theta$ denotes expectation with respect to $\mathbb{Q}^\theta$, $(N, \mathbb{Q}^\theta)$ is a numéraire pair and V_T is the random payoff of the contract at its maturity time T. In the present context the calibration data will consist of market prices of underlying assets (CDS quotes, yield curve ..) and derivatives (options, CDO tranche quotes ..). The purpose of the exercise is twofold: (a) to obtain market-consistent prices, using the valuation formula (20), for new or non-traded contracts, and (b) to determine hedging strategies.[6]

An issue of 'information' arises here, which goes back to the distinction we drew in section 3.3 between factor models and latent variable models, i.e. whether factor processes are observable data or abstract statistical factors. There is a very clear discussion of this in the recent paper by Frey and Schmidt (2009). Consider, for example, the Enhanced Risk model of section 5.4. Here the model is a Markov chain X_t taking

---

[6] This is of course not a clear-cut issue in incomplete markets where replicating strategies generally do not exist.

values (j, k) where j is the number of undefaulted obligors and $k \in \{0, 1\}$ is the 'risk state' (normal or enhanced). Thus j is observed directly but k is an abstract factor. However, this does not matter for the purposes of evaluating (20), which in this context is equivalent to computing v_{prot} and v_{prem} given by (18),(19). For this calculation we only need to know the initial state, which is $x = (n, k)$ where n is the initial portfolio size. But calibration is carried out on the assumption that $k = 0$, i.e. we start in 'normal risk', so this is the correct value of k for subsequent calculations.

The situation is different if we are interested in hedging strategies. Obviously, any strategy can only be a function of observed market data, while strategies derived from the model will naturally be 'state feedback' strategies of the form $\eta_t = \eta(t, X_t)$. Such strategies cannot be implemented because $X_t = (j_t, k_t)$ and we have no access to k_t. To get something usable we need a reduced model which *only* involves the evolution of j_t, i.e. a model with a *reduced filtration*. In general, obtaining such models is a problem of non-linear filtering, as we find for example in Frey and Schmidt (2009).[7] However, in the context of finite-state Markov chains, it turns out that reduced models can be obtained more simply as an application of the theory of Piecewise-Deterministic Markov Processes (PDP). For the reader's convenience the relevant PDP theory is summarized in the Appendix at the end of this chapter; a textbook account is given in Davis (1993). In the next section, section 6.1, we give a simple example which shows exactly how the reduction process works. The original Markov chain becomes a PDP on a more complicated state space.

In section 6.1 we also discuss questions of statistical parameter estimation for the example. This is a prelude to section 7 where we compute likelihood functions for '$\mathbb{P}$-measure' applications.

6.1 Incomplete observations: aggregated Markov chains

The simplest form of incomplete observation in a Markov chain model X_t is state aggregation: the state space E is partitioned into m disjoint subsets, $E = \bigcup_{i=1}^{m} G_i$ and we only know which of these subsets the process X_t lies in, i.e. we observe the process $Y_t = \sum_{k=1}^{m} k \mathbf{1}_{G_k}(X(t))$. Generally, Y_t is not a Markov process. However, Y_t can always be represented on an enlarged state space as a PDP. We illustrate this by considering a 4-state chain with $m = 2$. It will then be clear what the general case looks like.

Curiously, this same four-state example (but in discrete time) was considered by Blackwell and Koopmans (1957) in an early study of the identifiability problem for Markov chains. Some of the questions they posed are relevant here.

In the example, the state space $\{1, 2, 3, 4\}$ is partitioned, as shown in Figure 9.12, into the two sets $G_1 = \{1, 2\}$ and $G_2 = \{3, 4\}$, and Y_t is defined as above. With known parameters, Y_t together with a supplementary variable Z_t is a PDP, and this is enough information to do all calculations. If, however, one wishes to estimate the parameters

---

[7] For an up-to-date account of non-linear filtering theory, see Bain and Crisan (2008).

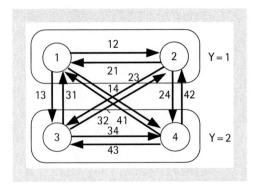

FIGURE 9.12 Aggregated four-state Markov chain.

from observations of Y_t, then we do not observe Z_t and the PDP representation is not the whole story. The theory of phase-type distributions is also relevant.

The PDP construction is as follows. Let X_t be a continuous-time Markov chain on the state space $G = \{1, 2, 3, 4\}$ with 4×4 Q-matrix $Q = [q_{ij}]$. Recall that, for $i \neq j$, q_{ij} is the rate of transition from i to j, and $q_{ii} = -\sum_{j \neq i} q_{ij}$, so $(1 + q_{ii})$ is the 'rate of non-transition' from state i. For simplicity we assume here that $q_{ij} > 0$ for all $i \neq j$. We observe the process

$$Y_t = 1 + \mathbf{1}_{G_2}(X_t),$$

so that $Y_t = k$ when $X_t \in G_k$, $k = 1, 2$.

Y_t is not a Markov process, but we can 'markovianize' it by adjoining a $[0, 1]$ valued process Z_t with the interpretation that

$$Z_t = \mathbb{P}[X_t = 2|\mathcal{F}_t]\mathbf{1}_{Y_t=1} + \mathbb{P}[X_t = 4|\mathcal{F}_t]\mathbf{1}_{Y_t=2}.$$

Proposition 6.1 *The process $W_t = (Y_t, Z_t)$ is a piecewise-deterministic Markov process on the state space $E = \{1, 2\} \times [0, 1]$, specified by its local characteristics as follows.*

(i) *The jump rate $\lambda(y, z)$ is*

$$\lambda(1, z) = z(q_{23} + q_{24}) + (1 - z)(q_{13} + q_{14})$$
$$\lambda(2, z) = z(q_{41} + q_{42}) + (1 - z)(q_{31} + q_{32}).$$

(ii) *The transition measure $Q(dw, w_-)$ giving the distribution of W_t as a function of $w_- = W_{t-}$ given that there is a jump at t, is*

$$Q(dw, (1, z)) = \delta_{(2, \chi_1(z))}(dw)$$
$$Q(dw, (2, z)) = \delta_{(1, \chi_2(z))}(dw)$$

where δ_w denotes the Dirac measure at w and

$$\chi_1(z) = z\frac{q_{24}}{q_{23} + q_{24}} + (1 - z)\frac{q_{14}}{q_{13} + q_{14}}, \quad \chi_2(z) = z\frac{q_{42}}{q_{41} + q_{42}} + (1 - z)\frac{q_{32}}{q_{31} + q_{32}}.$$

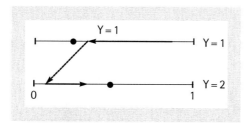

FIGURE 9.13 PDP representation of aggregated process.

(iii) *Between jumps, Z_t satisfies the ODEs*

$$\frac{d}{dt}Z_t = -(q_{12} - q_{22})Z_t + q_{12}, \qquad Y_t = 1 \tag{21}$$

$$\frac{d}{dt}Z_t = -(q_{34} - q_{44})Z_t + q_{34}, \qquad Y_t = 2. \tag{22}$$

The state space of the process (w_t), and a representative sample function, are shown in Figure 9.13. The formulas for λ and Q follow from the interpretation of the q_{ij} as jump rates and Z_t as a conditional probability within G_1 and G_2. Note that the process jumps from $(1, Z_{t-})$ to $(2, \chi_1(Z_{t-}))$ and from $(2, Z_{t-})$ to $(1, \chi_2(Z_{t-}))$.

The differential equation (21) arises from the idea that when $Y_t = 1$ then (roughly speaking)

$$\mathbb{P}[X_{t+dt} = 2] = \mathbb{P}[X_t = 2] \times \mathbb{P}[\text{no jump in } (t, t + dt)]$$
$$+ \mathbb{P}[X_t = 1] \times \mathbb{P}[X_t \text{ jumps from 1 to 2 in } (t, t + dt)],$$

giving

$$Z_{t+dt} = Z_t(1 + q_{22}dt) + (1 - Z_t)q_{12}dt$$

which is equivalent to (21). The other ODE (22) arises similarly. Note that the solutions converge to $q_{12}/(q_{12} - q_{22}) \in (0, 1)$ and $q_{34}/(q_{34} - q_{44}) \in (0, 1)$ respectively as $t \to \infty$.

The solution to the filtering problem of estimating the probabilities of hidden states given observations of Y_t is contained in (or, is equivalent to) the PDP representation.

6.1.1 *Estimation*

If we want to estimate the parameters of the chain from observations of a sample path $\{Y_t, t \in [0, T]\}$, then of course we do not have access to the supplementary variable Z_t. A sufficient statistic is the observed sequence of sojourn times of the Y_t process in the two states $\{1, 2\}$ and the likelihood function is the joint density function of these times. By definition these are phase-type distributions and we can make use of the theory described in section 4.2. Suppose $X_0 = 1, 2$ with probabilities $p, 1 - p$, so that $Y_0 = 1$, and let $\tau = \inf\{t : Y_t = 2\}$. As in section 4.2, we can represent τ as the killing time for a Markov chain with Q-matrix

$$Q = \begin{bmatrix} q_{11} & q_{12} & q_{13} + q_{14} \\ q_{21} & q_{22} & q_{23} + q_{24} \\ 0 & 0 & 0 \end{bmatrix} = \begin{bmatrix} G & g \\ 0 & 0 \end{bmatrix}.$$

From Proposition 4.1 we find

Proposition 6.2 *The exit time τ has density function f_1 given by*

$$f_1(t) = a_1\lambda_1 e^{-\lambda_1 t} + (1 - a_1)\lambda_2 e^{-\lambda_2 t}, \tag{23}$$

where

$$\lambda_1, \lambda_2 = -\frac{1}{2}\left(q_{11} + q_{22} \pm \sqrt{(q_{11} + q_{22})^2 - 4(q_{11}q_{22} - q_{12}q_{21})}\right),$$

$$a_1 = \frac{a(\beta - \lambda_1 g)}{\lambda_1(\lambda_2 - \lambda_1)},$$

and $a = [p, 1 - p]$, $\beta' = [-g_1 q_{22} + g_2 q_{12}, g_1 q_{21} - g_2 q_{11}]$.

We see that (23) is just a mixture of exponential distributions. There is an analogous result for f_2, the density function of the exit time from $\{3, 4\}$. The hazard rate corresponding to $f_1(\cdot)$ is

$$h(t) = \frac{a\lambda_1 e^{-\lambda_1 t} + (1 - a)\lambda_2 e^{-\lambda_2 t}}{ae^{-\lambda_1 t} + (1 - a)e^{-\lambda_2 t}}$$

so that $h_0 = a\lambda_1 + (1 - a)\lambda_2$ and $\lim_{t\to\infty} h(t) = \min\{\lambda_1, \lambda_2\}$.

Propositions 6.1 and 6.2 give us all the information we need to calculate the likelihood function $\Lambda(\theta, Y(\cdot))$ for estimating the model expressed in terms of the parameter vector θ which, assuming that the process starts at $Y_0 = 1$, is given—in obvious notation—by

$$\theta = [a_1, a_2, \lambda_{11}, \lambda_{12}, \lambda_{21}, \lambda_{22}, q_{12}, q_{12}, q_{34}, q_{44}].$$

We write $f_1^\theta(t, \tilde{p})$ for the density function (23) under parameter vector θ and $p = \tilde{p}$, and similarly for f_2^θ, where p is the prior probability that $X_0 = 2$ (for f_1) or 4 (for f_2). Given θ, we can compute the integral curves $\zeta_1(t, z)$, $\zeta_2(t, z)$ of the ODEs (21) and (27). Let $\bar{\tau} = (\tau_1, \tau_2, \ldots, \tau_n)$ be the observed sequence of jump times of the Y_t process (with n odd for ease of notation). τ_k is a jump from 1 to 2 when k is odd and from 2 to 1 when k is even. Define the sequence p_k by

$$p_1 = \chi_1 \circ \zeta_1(\tau_1, p),$$

$$p_k = \begin{cases} \chi_2 \circ \zeta_2(\tau_k - \tau_{k-1}, p_{k-1}), & k \text{ even}, \\ \chi_1 \circ \zeta_1(\tau_k - \tau_{k-1}, p_{k-1}), & k \text{ odd}. \end{cases}$$

Then the likelihood function is given by

$$\Lambda(\theta, \bar{\tau}) = f_1^{\theta}(\tau_1, p_1) \prod_{k=1}^{(n-1)/2} f_2^{\theta}(\tau_{2k} - \tau_{2k-1}, p_{2k}) f_1^{\theta}(\tau_{2k+1} - \tau_{2k}, p_{2k+1}).$$

The parameters p, θ can be estimated by maximum likelihood, but it is far from a trivial matter to relate these back to the Q-matrix parameters q_{ij}. The relations are highly non-linear, and there is obvious redundancy in that we can flip the identities of states 1 and 2 without affecting the distribution of τ. On the other hand there are 12 free parameters in Q while $\theta \in \mathbb{R}^{10}$. These are analogous to the 'identifiability problems' picked up by Blackwell and Koopmans (1957).

7 CHANGE OF MEASURE

As we pointed out earlier, much of the credit modelling literature relates to $\mathbb{Q}$-measure for pricing applications, but of course it is also necessary to undertake $\mathbb{P}$-measure modelling, for risk management purposes such as computation of value-at-risk, quantification of counterparty risk, or allocation of economic capital, as well as for prediction purposes in connection with trading strategies and for general economic studies. The primary data here is the history of actual defaults, possibly classified in various ways according to industry sector, rating category, geographical location, or other factors. The primary source for such data is the rating agencies. There is a large literature, but we just mention three recent studies, all of which use default data on US corporations over the past thirty years. The objective of Das et al. (2007) is to test the hypothesis that defaults are conditionally independent given the paths of observed factor processes (individual distances to default and stock returns, the S&P index, and the US three-month T-bill rate). The hypothesis is rejected, indicating that other elements such as latent variables or 'frailty' must be included in the models to enhance explanatory power. In Giampieri, Davis, and Crowder (2005) the authors assume conditional independence given a 'hidden Markov model'—using as latent variable a finite-state Markov process which determines default intensities. The model was estimated using the Baum-Welch algorithm, a variant on the EM algorithm widely used in signal processing applications. Even simple models turned out to have considerable explanatory power. Finally, Azizpour and Giesecke (2008) take a stochastic analysis-oriented approach, close to the methods of this chapter, in an empirical study designed to discover whether frailty or contagion is the dominant effect. Answer: contagion.

A key role both in pricing and risk management applications is played by Radon-Nikodým derivatives (RND) $d\mathbb{P}_2/d\mathbb{P}_1$ where $\mathbb{P}_1, \mathbb{P}_2$ are equivalent measures. In pricing, risk-neutral measures $\mathbb{Q}$ are by definition equivalent to the physical measure $\mathbb{P}$ and can be characterized by the RND $d\mathbb{Q}/d\mathbb{P}$. Getting the relationship between the two can be problematic when the measures themselves are obtained in such different ways. An interesting recent paper by Liu et al. (2007) addresses this question from the point of view of economic equilibrium theory. In the Arrow-Debreu theory of complete markets, $d\mathbb{Q}/d\mathbb{P}$ is the marginal utility of the representative investor at his optimal allocation (see for example Becherer and Davis 2010). Liu et al. (2007) parametrize $d\mathbb{Q}/d\mathbb{P}$ by the risk-aversion coefficient of the representative investor (in a HARA utility model) and then estimate this parameter from econometric data.

In econometric studies, families of RND $\Lambda(\theta) = d\mathbb{P}^{\theta}/d\mathbb{P}_0$ show up as likelihood functions, with $\mathbb{P}_0$ being some 'base' measure (not necessarily a probability measure) and θ a finite-dimensional parameter vector. The maximum-likelihood estimate is arg-max$_{\theta}\Lambda(\theta)$. Note that we cannot evaluate the likelihood function if it depends on unobserved data, i.e. the model contains latent variables. There are two ways around this, (a) use the EM algorithm (this was the approach taken in Giampieri, Davis, and Crowder 2005), or (b) obtain a 'projected' model adapted to the observable filtration. This is exactly what we did in the four-state Markov chain example in section 6.1 above. In that example we showed that if the original model is a Markov chain then the projected model is a PDP. It makes sense therefore to consider the general question of change of measure in PDP models, a question that was not addressed in the book (Davis 1993). This is the purpose of the present section. The main result is Theorem 7.4 which gives the general change-of-measure formula for PDPs. This is an application of the general 'Girsanov theorem' for semimartingales, the Doléans-Dade theorem, which we discuss first.

7.1 Changes of measure for semimartingales: the Doléans-Dade theorem

Readers will be familiar with the Girsanov theorem for Brownian motion, which shows that on Wiener space 'change of measure is change of drift' and gives an exponential formula for the Radon-Nikodým derivative. The analogous result for general semimartingales is known as the Doléans-Dade theorem. It is described in detail in section II.8 of Protter (2003). In particular, Theorem 37 of that section states the following. We are given a filtered probability space $(\Omega, \mathcal{F}, (\mathcal{F}_t), \mathbb{P})$.

Theorem 7.1 *Let M be an $\mathcal{F}_t$-semimartingale with $M_0 = 0$. Then there exists a unique semimartingale Z, denoted $Z = \mathcal{E}(M)$, satisfying the equation*

$$Z_t = 1 + \int_0^t Z_{s-} dM_t. \tag{24}$$

Z is given explicitly by

$$Z_t = e^{M_t - \frac{1}{2}[M,M]_t^c} \prod_{0 < s \le t} (1 + \Delta M_s) e^{-\Delta M_s}, \tag{25}$$

where the infinite product converges.

In (25), $[M, M]_t^c$ denotes the quadratic variation of the continuous martingale part M^c of M. *In this chapter, $M^c = 0$ and the product in (25) contains only a finite number of terms.*

When M is a local martingale, Z is a positive local martingale and hence a super-martingale, so that $\mathbb{E}[Z_T] \leq 1$. By standard arguments, it is a martingale on any finite time interval $[0, T]$ provided $\mathbb{E}[Z_T] = 1$. We may then define a measure $\mathbb{Q}$ on $\mathcal{F}_T$ by its Radon-Nikodym derivative

$$\frac{d\mathbb{Q}}{d\mathbb{P}} = \mathcal{E}(M)_T. \tag{26}$$

Theorem 7.2 *Let M, N be local martingales. Define $Z = \mathcal{E}(M)$, assume $\mathbb{E}[Z_T] = 1$ and define $\mathbb{Q}$ by (26). Let A be a predictable process and define $X_t = N_t - A_t$. Then X is a $\mathbb{Q}$-local martingale iff A is the predictable compensator of $[M, N]$. Here, $[M, N]$ is the cross-variation process defined by*

$$[M, N] = \frac{1}{4}([M + N, M + N] - [M - N, M - N]).$$

Proof. It is standard that X is a $\mathbb{Q}$-local martingale iff XZ is a $\mathbb{P}$-local martingale. By the Ito product formula

$$d(XZ) = X_- dZ + Z_- dN - Z_- dA + d[Z, N],$$

and from (24)

$$[Z, N] = [Z \cdot M, N] = Z \cdot [M, N].$$

Thus

$$d(XZ) = X_- dZ + Z_- dN + Z_-(d[M, N] - dA),$$

and XZ is a local martingale iff $[M, N] - A$ is a local martingale. $\qquad\square$

7.2 Application to point processes

As a first application, we consider absolutely continuous change of measure in point processes. The result here can be found in the book by Brémaud (1981).

Let N_t be a Poisson process with constant rate λ and let a_t be a predictable integrable process. We take

$$M_t = \int_0^t a_s(dN_s - \lambda ds).$$

Then $\Delta M_t = a_t$ and from (25) we have

$$\log \mathcal{E}(M)_t = M_t - \sum_{s \le t}(\Delta M_s + \log(1 + \Delta M_s))$$

$$= \int_0^t \log(1 + a_s)dN_s - \int_0^t a_s \lambda ds.$$

If we now define μ_t by $\mu_t = \lambda(1 + a_s)$ then

$$M_t = \int_0^t \frac{\mu_s - \lambda}{\lambda}(dN_s - \lambda ds)$$

and

$$\mathcal{E}(M)_t = \prod_{T_i \le t}\left(\frac{\mu_{T_i}}{\lambda}\right) e^{-\int_0^t (\mu_s - \lambda)ds}, \tag{27}$$

where (T_i) are the jump times of N_t. Since $\Delta M_t = (\mu_t - \lambda)/\lambda$ and $\Delta N_t = 1$, the predictable compensator of $[M, N]$ is $A_t = \int_0^t(\mu_s - \lambda)ds$ and we conclude that *under measure $\mathbb{Q}$ defined by (26), N_t is a point process with rate μ_t.*

Formula (27) provides us with the likelihood function needed to estimate the rate of the N_t under $\mathbb{Q}$ from observation of the sample path $\{N_t, 0 \le t \le T\}$. Suppose for example that (under our model) μ_t is constant: $\mu_t \equiv \mu$. Then the log likelihood function is

$$\log \mathcal{E}(M)_T = N_T \log(\mu/\lambda) - (\mu - \lambda)T$$

so—unsurprisingly—the maximum likelihood estimate of μ is just $\hat{\mu}_T = N_T/T$.

7.3 Change of measure for PDPs

We start by calculating the Doléans exponential when M is a local martingale in the natural filtration of a PDP.

Lemma 7.3 *For a PDP (X_t), let M^g be the stochastic integral defined by (39) for some $g \in L^1_{loc}(p)$. Then*

$$\mathcal{E}(M^g)_t = \left(\prod_{\substack{T_i \le t \\ X_{T_i^-} \notin \Gamma}} (1 + g(X_{T_i^-}, T_i)) \right)$$

$$\times \left(\prod_{\substack{T_i \le t \\ X_{T_i-} \in \Gamma}} (1 + g(X_{T_i}, T_i) - Rg(X_{T_i-}, T_i)) \right)$$

$$\times \exp\left(-\int_0^t Qg(X_s, s)\lambda(X_s)ds \right). \tag{28}$$

Proof. Writing $M^g = M$, we have from (25)

$$\mathcal{E}(M)_t = \exp\left(M_t - \sum_{s \le t} \Delta M_s \right) \prod_{s \le t} (1 + \Delta M_s).$$

Now

$$M_t = \sum_{\substack{T_i \le t \\ T_i \notin \Gamma}} g(X_{T_i}, T_i) + \sum_{\substack{T_i \le t \\ T_i \in \Gamma}} (g(X_{T_i}, T_i) - Rg(X_{T_i-}, T_i)) - \int_0^t Qg(X_s, s)\lambda(X_s)ds,$$

so

$$M_t - \sum_{s \le t} \Delta M_s = -\int_0^t Qg(X_s, s)\lambda(X_s)ds,$$

and

$$(1 + \Delta M_{T_i}) = 1 + g(X_{T_i}) \quad \text{if } X_{T_i-} \notin \Gamma,$$

$$(1 + \Delta M_{T_i}) = 1 + g(X_{T_i}, T_i) - Rg(X_{T_i-}, T_i) \quad \text{if } X_{T_i-} \in \Gamma.$$

The result follows. $\qquad \Box$

We now investigate what happens to the PDP when we replace the original measure $\mathbb{P}$ by a new measure $d\mathbb{Q} = \mathcal{E}(M^g)d\mathbb{P}$. In general, X_t will no longer be a PDP. However, we identify the class of integrands g for which X_t is a $\mathbb{Q}$-PDP and identify the new local characteristics. As a first observation, note that under any absolutely continuous change of measure the vector field $\mathcal{X}$ must remain the same. If we have a different vector field $\tilde{\mathcal{X}}$ then the sample paths are observably distinct and the measures are singular.

In the notation of Theorem 7.2, take $M = M^g$ and $N = M^{\mathcal{B}f}$, where $\mathcal{B}f$ is defined by (40). From the 'Ito formula' (41) we have

$$N_t = f(X_t) - f(X_0) - \int_0^t \mathcal{X}f(X_s)ds - \int_0^t (Qf(X_s) - f(X_s))\lambda(X_s)ds \tag{29}$$

$$- \int_0^t (f(X_{s-}) - Rf(X_{s-}))dp_s^*.$$

From (39) and (29) we see that when $t = T_i$ and $X_{T_i-} \notin \Gamma$ then $\Delta M_t = g(X_t, t)$ and $\Delta N_t = \Delta f_t = f(X_t) - f(X_{t-})$, while if $X_{T_i-} \notin \Gamma$ then $\Delta M_t = g(X_t, t) - Rg(X_{t-}, t)$ and $\Delta N_t = \Delta f_t = f(X_t) - Rf(X_{t-})$. Hence the predictable compensator of $[M, N]$ is

$$A_t = \int_0^t \int_E (f(y) - f(X_{s-})) g(y, t)) Q(dy, X_s) \lambda(X_s) ds \tag{30}$$

$$- \int_0^t \int_E (g(y) - Rg(X_{s-}))(f(y) - Rf(X_{s-})) R(dy, X_{s-}) dp_s^*.$$

From Theorem 7.2, $N - A$ is $\mathbb{Q}$-local martingale. From (29) and (30), the integrand of dp^* is (in compressed notation)

$$-f + Rf + R((g - Rg)(f - Rf)) = -f + R((1 + g - Rg)f).$$

Thus

$$N_t - A_t = f(X_t) - f(X_0) - \int_0^t \mathcal{X} f(X_s) ds \tag{31}$$

$$- \int_0^t \int_E (f(y) - f(X_{s-}))(1 + g(y, t)) Q(dy, X_s) \lambda(X_s) ds$$

$$- \int_0^t (f - R(1 + g - Rg)f)(X_{s-}) dp_s^*.$$

On the other hand X_t is a PDP under $\mathbb{Q}$ if and only if the last two terms above are given by

$$- \int_0^t (f(y) - f(X_{s-})) \tilde{Q}(dy, X_s) \tilde{\lambda}(X_s) ds - \int_0^t (f(X_{s-}) - \tilde{R} f(X_{s-})) dp_s^*. \tag{32}$$

where $(\mathcal{X}, \tilde{\lambda}, \tilde{Q}, \tilde{R})$ are the $\mathbb{Q}$-local characteristics of the process. We therefore have the following result.

Theorem 7.4 *PDPs with local characteristics $(\mathcal{X}, \lambda, Q)$ and $(\mathcal{X}, \tilde{\lambda}, \tilde{Q}, \tilde{R})$ have mutually absolutely continuous probability laws if and only if there is a strictly positive function $\beta : E \to \mathbb{R}^+$ and a measurable function $\gamma : E \times E \to \mathbb{R}^+$, satisfying $\int_E \gamma(y, x) Q(dy, x) = 1$ for all x, such that*

$$\tilde{\lambda}(x) = \beta(x) \lambda(x),$$

$$\tilde{Q}(A, x) = \int_A \gamma(y, x) Q(dy, x),$$

$$\tilde{R}(A, x) = \int_A \eta(y, x) R(dy, x).$$

The Radon-Nikodym derivative is

$$\frac{d\mathbb{Q}}{d\mathbb{P}}\bigg|_{\mathcal{F}_T} = \prod_{\substack{T_i \le T \\ X_{T_i-} \notin \Gamma}} \gamma(X_{T_i}, X_{T_i-}) \beta(X_{T_i-}) \prod_{\substack{T_i \le T \\ X_{T_i-} \in \Gamma}} \eta(X_{T_i}, X_{T_i-}) \tag{33}$$

$$\times \exp\left(- \int_0^T \int_E \gamma(y, X_s) Q(dy, X_s) \beta(X_s) \lambda(X_s) ds\right).$$

Proof. (Outline) Comparing the expressions in (31) and (32) we see that for X_t to be a PDP under $\mathbb{Q}$ with local characteristics $(\mathcal{X}, \tilde{\lambda}, \tilde{Q}, \tilde{R})$, the integrand g must be given in for $X_{t-} \in E$ by

$$g(y, t, \omega) = \gamma(y, X_{t-}(\omega))\beta(X_{t-}(\omega)) - 1$$

where γ, β have the stated properties.

Turning to the boundary term, the only way in which the dp^* integrand in (31) can be expressed in the form $f(x) - \tilde{R}f(x)$ is to suppose that

$$g(y, t, \omega) = \xi(y, X_{t-}(\omega)) \quad \text{for } X_{t-} \in \Gamma$$

for some function $\xi : E \times \Gamma \to \mathbb{R}$ such that

$$\int_E \eta(y, x)R(dy, x) = 0 \quad \forall x \in \Gamma.$$

Then taking $\eta(y, x) = 1 + \xi(y, x)$ we have $\int_\Gamma \eta(y, x)R(dy, x) \equiv 1$ and $\eta = d\tilde{R}/dR$.

8 ENHANCED RISK REVISITED

The enhanced risk model was described in section 5.4 above. In applications, we do not directly observe whether the process is in enhanced risk or not, but only the sequence of default events. The projected model on the observation filtration is a PDP with state space $E = \{0\} \cup_{j=1}^{n} I_j$ where $I_j = [0, 1]$; see Figure 9.14. The process is denoted $X_t = (J_t, Z_t)$ where J_t is the number of undefaulted obligors and $Z_t = \mathbb{P}[\text{ enhanced } |\mathcal{F}_t]$. The PDP characteristics are given by
(i) A vector field

$$\mathcal{X} = (v - (\mu + v)z)\frac{d}{dz},$$

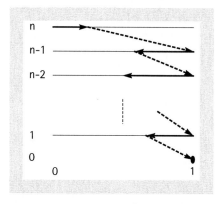

FIGURE 9.14 State space of projected model.

defining the deterministic motion Z_t by

$$\frac{d}{dt}Z_t = -(\mu + \nu)Z_t + \nu,$$

with $Z_\tau = 1$ at each default time τ, so that

$$Z_{\tau+t} = z^* + (1 - z^*)e^{-(\mu+\nu)t}, \quad z^* = \frac{\nu}{\mu + \nu}.$$

(ii) The hazard rate

$$h(x) = j\lambda(1 + (\kappa - 1)z), \quad x = (j, z).$$

(iii) The transition measure

$$Q(dy, x) = \delta_{(j-1,1)}(dy), \quad x = (j, z).$$

The PDP generator is

$$\mathcal{A}f(j, z) = \mathcal{X}f(x) + h(x)\int_E (f(y) - f(x))Q(dy, x)$$

$$= \mathcal{X}f(j, z) + h(j, z)(f(j - 1, 1) - f(j, z)).$$

To compute expected values we need to solve the backward equation for $v(t, x)$:

$$\frac{\partial v}{\partial t} + \mathcal{A}v + c(x) - rv = 0, \quad v(T, x) = 0.$$

On plane j we have, denoting $v_j(t, z) = v(t, (j, z))$

$$\frac{\partial v_j}{\partial t} + (\nu - (\mu + \nu)z)\frac{\partial v}{\partial z} + v_j(t, z) + h(j, z)(v_{j-1}(t, 1) - v_j(t, z)) = 0 \quad (34)$$

This is a triangular system of hyperbolic PDEs, coupled by the term $v_{j-1}(\cdot, 1)$ in (34). The equations can be solved by the method of characteristics: with $w_j(t) = v_j(t, z(t))$ we have

$$\frac{dw_j}{dt} = \frac{\partial v_j}{\partial t} + \frac{\partial v_j}{\partial z}\frac{dz}{dt},$$

so v_j satisfies an ODE along the integral curves of $\mathcal{X}$, provided we know $v_{j-1}(\cdot, 1)$. We have to use some interpolation to get all the required values, as described below. In summary, the algorithm is as follows.

1. Solve the ODE for $j = 1$ along a small number of integral curves (see Figure 9.15). We know $v_0(t, 1) = 0$.
2. (Induction) Suppose we have computed $\hat{v}_{j-1}(\cdot, 1)$ (an approximation to $v_{j-1}(\cdot, 1)$.
   • Solve ODE for v_j along a small number of integral curves, using $\hat{v}_{j-1}$.
   • Let $\hat{v}_j$ be the cubic spline interpolation of the computed points $v_j(t_l, 1)$
   • Repeat with $j := j + 1$.
3. Solve one further ODE to compute desired value $v(0, 0)$.

Methods similar to this have been successfully used in insurance applications, see Davis and Vellekoop (1995).

FIGURE 9.15 (X_t, t) state space.

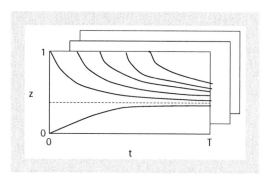

9 CONCLUDING REMARKS

As is commonly acknowledged, credit risk modelling is plagued by lack of data. In $\mathbb{Q}$-measure, just about the only market correlation data available is the set of tranche quotes on the iTraxx and CDX indices. This is good as far as it goes, but only relates to a small corner of the credit universe. It was already pointed out in section 2.2 that, in contrast to the Black-Scholes world, correlations in most credit models are not invariant under change of measure, so it is not generally valid to plug empirically estimated correlations into risk-neutral models. On the $\mathbb{P}$-measure side, realized defaults are (happily!) rare, leaving us with data sets stretching back over decades, of questionable relevance to the current situation.

Faced with these facts, the only sensible approach is to go for models that are as simple as possible consistent with capturing observed phenomena, and which model default interaction in intuitively credible ways. This chapter argues that Markov chain models provide an effective modelling framework, because of flexibility and computational efficiency. As we saw, for these models, with known parameters and including latent variables, filtering or projection process is equivalent to construction of a piecewise-deterministic process model. Within this class of models we can compute likelihood functions and do not need more computationally intensive methods such as the EM algorithm. The approach enables us to handle a variety of interaction mechanisms including, specifically, contagion.

Another very different approach to contagion, which unfortunately we cannot enlarge on here, is the network modelling approach in which each bank is linked to other banks by a network of mutual obligations. An early and influential paper in this direction is Eisenberg and Noe (2001) which studies the settlement process at a single date. The starting gun is fired and all banks in the network have to make the scheduled payments. The question is whether there is a settlement such that each bank pays in full if it can, and if not it makes payments in accordance with some pre-specified priority rule. The point is that one bank's asset is another bank's liability, so settlement is a *system-wide* question and in fact is a fixed point of some non-linear map.

Subsequent work in this area has diverged into two streams, the 'economic' stream and the 'statistical physics' stream. In the former, see for example Nier et al. (2007) and Shin (2008), a relatively detailed specification of each bank's balance sheet is made, and banks are able to value their inter-bank assets (in a one-period model) taking into account system-wide effects in a fairly small network. By contrast the statistical physics literature uses random graph theory to make statements about properties such as the probable sizes of clusters of defaults in a large network with only a rudimentary node description. This is done for example by Gai and Kapadia (2009), based on earlier work on cascades in random networks by Watts (2002). What is not available is any dynamic model addressing the same questions as those raised in this chapter but including network-wide interaction effects. It is a major challenge to produce one.

APPENDIX

A PIECEWISE-DETERMINISTIC MARKOV PROCESSES

A PDP (X_t) is a random motion in a state space $E \subset \mathbb{R}^d$ consisting of possibly disconnected components in $\mathbb{R}^d$. The process is specified by four 'local characteristics':

- A vector field $\mathcal{X}$ in E,
- A jump rate function $\lambda : E \to \mathbb{R}^+$,
- Transition measures $Q : E \to \mathcal{P}(E), \quad R : \Gamma \to \mathcal{P}(E)$

$\mathcal{P}(E)$ is the set of probability measures on E and Γ is a subset of the boundary ∂E, defined below.

A.1 PDP construction

Start with an open set $E^0 \subset \mathbb{R}^d$, let $\mathcal{X}$ be a C^1 vector field on E^0 and let $\zeta(t, x)$ be the integral curve of $\mathcal{X}$, i.e. $\zeta(t, x)$ is the solution of the ordinary differential equation

$$\frac{d}{dt} f(\zeta(t, x)) = \mathcal{X} f(\zeta(t, x)), \quad \zeta(0, x) = x, \quad f \in C^1(E^0).$$

FIGURE 9.16 PDP sample function.

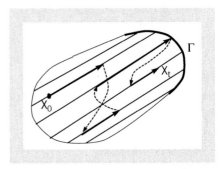

The 'active boundary' of E^0 is the set of points in ∂E^0 which are hit by some integral curve, i.e.

$$\Gamma = \{z \in \partial E^0 : z = \lim \zeta(t_n, x) \text{ for some } x, t \in E^0 \times \mathbb{R}^+ \text{ and sequence } t_n \uparrow t\}.$$

We now define $E = \overline{E^0}\backslash\Gamma$, and $t^*(x) = \inf\{t : \zeta(t, x) \in \Gamma\}$ (with $\inf \emptyset = +\infty$).

A.1.1 Construction

Starting at $x \in E$, $X_t = \zeta(t, x)$ for $t \in [0, T_1)$ where the first jump time T_1 is a random variable whose distribution function is

$$F(t, x) = \mathbb{P}(T_1 \leq t) = 1 - \mathbf{1}_{(t < t^*(x))} e^{-\int_0^t \lambda(\zeta(s,x))ds}.$$

Thus T_1 has hazard rate $\lambda(X_s)$ on $[0, t^*(x))$, with a mandatory jump at $t^*(x)$ if T_1 has not occurred by then.

The sample path is right-continuous, so $X_{T_1-} = \zeta(T_1, x)$.

If $X_{T_1-} \in E$ then $X_{T_1} \in E$ is a random variable whose conditional distribution given T_1 is given by the transition measure Q:

$$\mathbb{P}[X_{T_1} \in A|T_1] = Q(A, \zeta(T_1, x)), \quad A \in \mathcal{B}(E).$$

If $X_{T_1-} \in \Gamma$ then the recipe is the same, but using the transition measure R.

Having determined X_{T_1} we restart the process from $x' = X_{T_1}$, so that $X_t = \zeta(t - T_1, x')$ for $t \in [T_1, T_2)$, where the 'gap' $T_2 - T_1$ is determined by the same recipe as used above to determine T_1.

Continuing in this way we obtain an increasing sequence of random time T_n and, for any n, $X_t = \zeta(t - T_n, X_{T_n})$ for $t \in [T_n, T_{n+1})$. It is assumed that $\lim_n T_n = \infty$ a.s., a condition that is generally easily checked in applications.

A.2 The extended generator

The main general result of PDP theory is that the process just described is a homogeneous strong Markov process whose extended generator is the operator $(\mathcal{A}, \mathcal{D}(\mathcal{A}))$ given by

$$\mathcal{A}f(x) = \mathcal{X}f(x) + \lambda(x) \int_E (f(y) - f(x))Q(dy, x), \quad f \in \mathcal{D}(\mathcal{A}).$$

By definition, the extended generator has the property that for $f \in \mathcal{D}(\mathcal{A})$ the process

$$C_t^f = f(X_t) - f(x) - \int_0^t \mathcal{A}f(X_s)ds \tag{35}$$

is a local martingale. The domain $\mathcal{D}(\mathcal{A})$ can be precisely characterized. Sufficient conditions under which $f \in \mathcal{D}(\mathcal{A})$ are

$$\text{The function } t \mapsto f(\zeta(t, x)) \text{ is continuously differentiable} \tag{36}$$

$$\mathbb{E}_x \sum_i |f(X_{T_i \wedge t}) - f(X_{T_i \wedge t-})| < \infty \quad \text{for } (t, x) \in \mathbb{R}^+ \times E \tag{37}$$

$$f(x) = \int_E f(y)R(dy, x), \quad x \in \Gamma. \tag{38}$$

The key point here is that $f \in \mathcal{D}(\mathcal{A})$ only if the *boundary condition* (38) is satisfied for all $x \in \Gamma$.

A.2.1 Stochastic integrals

Let $(\mathcal{F}_t)_{t\in\mathbb{R}^+}$ be the natural filtration of a PDP, complete with all null sets of $\mathcal{F}_\infty$. For $A \in \mathcal{B}(E)$, define counting processes p, p^* as follows

$$p(t, A) = \sum_{j=1}^{\infty} \mathbf{1}_{(t\geq T_j)}\mathbf{1}_{(X_{T_j}\in A)},$$

$$p^*(t) = \sum_{j=1}^{\infty} \mathbf{1}_{(t\geq T_j)}\mathbf{1}_{(X_{T_j-}\in\Gamma)}$$

These count the number of times the process jumps into a given set A, and the number of times the boundary is hit, respectively. p^* is a predictable process (i.e. measurable with respect to the predictable σ-field in $\Omega \times \mathbb{R}^+$). Hence the process $\tilde{p}$ defined as follows is also predictable.

$$\tilde{p}(t, A) = \int_{(0,t]} Q(A, X_s)\lambda(X_s)ds + \int_{(0,t]} R(A, X_{s-})dp^*(s).$$

For each fixed A, $\tilde{p}$ is the *predictable compensator* of p, i.e. the process

$$q(t, A) = p(t, A) - \tilde{p}(t, A)$$

is a local martingale. In fact, these local martingales span the filtration $\mathcal{F}_t$, in that there is a 1-1 correspondence between $\mathcal{F}_t$-local martingales and stochastic integrals with respect to this family of fundamental local martingales. The appropriate class of integrands is the set $L^1_{loc}(p)$ of functions $g : E \times \mathbb{R}^+ \times \Omega \to \mathbb{R}$ such that

g is a measurable function on the product space;

for each $y \in E$, the function $(t, \omega) \mapsto g(y, t, \omega)$ is predictable

for $k = 1, 2 \ldots$ we have $\mathbb{E}\left[\sum_{j=1}^{k} |g(X_{T_j}, T_j, \omega)|\right] < \infty.$

For $g \in L^1_{loc}(p)$ and $t > 0$ we define the stochastic integral M^g pathwise by

$$M^g = \int_0^t g(y, t)q(dy, dt)$$

$$= \int_0^t g(y, t)p(dy, dt) - \int_0^t g(y, t)\tilde{p}(dy, dt)$$

$$= \sum_{T_i \leq t} g(X_{T_i}, T_i) - \int_0^t Qg(X_{s-}, s)\lambda(X_{s-})ds - \int_0^t Rg(X_{s-}, s)dp^*(s). \tag{39}$$

We use the notation $Qg(x, t, \omega) = \int_E g(y, t, \omega)Q(dy, x)$ and similarly for Rg.

With this definition, M^g is a local martingale for each $g \in L^1_{loc}(p)$.

Proposition A.2.1 *For the PDP (X_t) with extended generator $(\mathcal{A}, \mathcal{D}(\mathcal{A}))$ we have*

(i) For $f \in \mathcal{D}(\mathcal{A})$ the local martingale C^f of (35) is given by $C^f = M^{\mathcal{B}f}$, where

$$\mathcal{B}f(y, t, \omega) = f(y) - f(X_{t-}(\omega)). \tag{40}$$

(ii) (PDP 'Ito formula') If a function $f : E \to \mathbb{R}$ satisfies conditions (36) and (37) then

$$f(X_t) - f(X_0) = \int_0^t \mathcal{A}f(X_s)ds + \int_0^t \int_E \mathcal{B}f(y, X_{s-})q(dy, ds) + \int_0^t \mathcal{C}f(X_{s-})dp_s^*,$$

(41)

where $\mathcal{C}f(x) = Rf(x) - f(x)$.

(iii) (Martingale representation) If M is an $\mathcal{F}_t$-local martingale then $M = M^g$ for some $g \in L_{loc}^1(p)$.

Note: The multiplicity of $(\mathcal{F}_t)$ is determined by the support of $Q(\cdot, x)$ and $R(\cdot, x)$.

References

Andersen, P., Borgan, O., Gill, R., and Keiding, N. (1997). *Statistical Models Based on Counting Processes.* New York: Springer.

Asmussen, S. (2003). *Applied Probability and Queues,* 2nd edn. New York: Springer.

Azizpour, S., Giesecke, K. (2008). 'Self-exciting corporate defaults'. Working paper, Stanford University, CA, Aug.

Bain, A., and Crisan, D. (2008). *Fundamentals of Stochastic Filtering.* New York: Springer.

Bass, R. (1998). 'General theory of processes', lecture notes, available at <http://www.math.uconn.edu/ bass/gtp.pdf>.

Becherer, D., and Davis, M. (2010). 'Arrow-Debreu prices'. In *Wiley Encyclopaedia of Quantitative Finance.* Chichester: Wiley.

Blackwell, D., and Koopmans, L. (1957). 'On the identifiability problem for functions of finite Markov chains'. *Annals of Mathematical Statistics,* 28: 1011–15.

Brémaud, P. (1981). *Point Processes and Queues: Martingale Dynamics.* New York: Springer.

Crépey, S., Jeanblanc, M., and Zargari, B. (2009). 'Counterparty risk on a CDS in a Markov chain copula model with joint defaults'. Preprint, University of Evry.

Das, S., Duffie, D., Kapadia, N., and Saita, L. (2007). 'Common failings: how corporate defaults are correlated'. Journal of Finance, 62: 93–117.

Davis, M. (1993). *Markov Models and Optimization.* Monographs on Statistics and Applied Probability 49. London: Chapman & Hall.

——and Esparragoza Rodriguez, J. (2007). 'Large portfolio credit risk modelling'. *International Journal of Theoretical and Applied Finance* 10: 653–78.

——and Lo, V. (2001a). 'Infectious defaults'. *Quantitative Finance,* 1: 382–7.

—— —— (2001b). 'Modelling default correlation in bond portfolios'. In C. Alexander (ed.), *Mastering Risk,* Vol. 2: *Applications.* Upper Saddle River, NJ: Financial Times-Prentice Hall, 141–51.

——and Vellekoop, M. (1995). 'Permanent health insurance: a case study in piecewise-deterministic Markov modelling'. *Mitteilungen der Schweiz: Vereinigung der Versicherungsmathematiker,* 2: 177–212.

Eisenberg, L., and Noe, T. (2001). 'Systemic risk in financial systems'. *Management Science,* 47: 236–49.

Filipović, D. (2009). *Term Structure Models: A Graduate Course.* New York: Springer.

Frey, R., and Backhaus, J. (2007). 'Dynamic hedging of synthetic CDO tranches with spread risk and default contagion'. Preprint, University of Leipzig, Dec.

Frey, R., and Schmidt, T. (2009). 'Pricing and hedging of credit derivatives via the innovations approach to nonlinear filtering'. Preprint, University of Leipzig.

Gai, P., and Kapadia, S. (2009). 'Contagion in financial networks'. Working paper, Bank of England (to appear in Proceedings of the Royal Society London (A), July).

Giampieri, G., Davis, M., and Crowder, M. (2005). 'A hidden Markov model of default interaction'. *Quantitative Finance*, 5: 27–34.

Herbertsson, A. (2007). 'Modelling default contagion using multivariate phase-type distributions'. Preprint, Göteborg University (submitted to Review of Derivatives Research), App.

—— and Rootzén, H. (2008). 'Pricing kth-to-default swaps under default contagion'. *Journal of Computational Finance*, 12: 49–78.

Liu, X., Shackleton, M., Taylor, S., and Xu, X. (2007). 'Closed-form transformations from risk-neutral to real-world distributions'. *Journal of Banking and Finance*, 31: 1501–20.

McNeil, A., Frey, R., and Embrechts, P. (2005). *Quantitative Risk Management: Concepts, Techniques and Tools*. Princeton: Princeton University Press.

Merton, R. (1974). 'On the pricing of corporate debt: the risk structure of interest rates'. *Journal of Finance*, 29: 449–70.

Moler, C., and Van Loan, C. (2003). '19 dubious ways to compute the exponential of a matrix, twenty-five years later'. *SIAM Review*, 45: 3–48.

Nier, E., Yang, J., Yorulmazer, T., and Alentorn, A. (2007). 'Network models and financial stability'. *Journal of Economic Dynamics and Control*, 31: 2033–60.

Protter, P. (2003). *Stochastic Integration and Differential Equations*, 2nd edn. New York: Springer.

Rogers, L., and Williams, D. (2000). *Diffusions, Markov Processes and Martingales*. Vol. 2. Cambridge: Cambridge University Press.

Rüschendorf, L. (2009). 'On the distributional transform, Sklar's theorem, and the empirical copula process'. *Journal of Statistical Planning and Inference*, 139: 3921–7.

Shin, H. (2008). 'Risk and liquidity in a system context'. *Journal of Financial Intermediation*, 17: 315–29.

Stroock, D., and Varadhan, S. (1969). 'Diffusion processes with continuous coefficients i, ii'. Communications Pure and Applied Mathematics, 22: 345–400, 479–530.

Watts, D. (2002). 'A simple model of global cascades on random networks'. *Proceedings of National Academy of Sciences*, 99: 5766–71.

CHAPTER 10

MARKOV CHAIN MODELS OF PORTFOLIO CREDIT RISK

TOMASZ R. BIELECKI, STÉPHANE CRÉPEY
AND ALEXANDER HERBERTSSON

1 OUTLINE

THIS is a survey chapter in which we present a selection of methods and results regarding various applications of the theory of continuous time Markov chains to valuation of credit derivatives. We present both theoretical and numerical aspects of the Markovian methodology.

After a review of some basic notions and results from the theory of continuous-time Markov chains in section 2, sections 3 to 5 are devoted to the study of a few specific Markovian models of portfolio credit risk. This survey article is intended to illustrate the power and flexibility of the Markov chain approach to portfolio credit risk, yet it is by no means exhaustive and we refer the reader to, for instance, Frey and Backhaus (2004, 2008b, 2008a), Cont and Minca (2008), Albanese and Chen (2005), Halperin and Tomecek (2008), or Lopatin and Misirpashaev (2007), for other models, and more specifically to Frey and Backhaus (2004), Bielecki, Crépey, and Jeanblanc (2008), Bielecki, Vidozzi, and Vidozzi (2008) and Laurent, Cousin, and Fermanian (2008) regarding the issue of hedging, which we do not really discuss here due to space limitations.

The research of S. Crépey benefited from the support of the 'Chaire Risque de crédit', Fédération Bancaire Française, and of the Europlace Institute of Finance. Research of A. Herbertsson supported by the Jan Wallander and Tom Hedelius Foundation.

2 CONTINUOUS-TIME MARKOV CHAINS

The material presented in this section is, for the most part, taken from chapter 11 of Bielecki and Rutkowski (2002), to which we refer in particular for the proofs of all results. For a more exhaustive treatment of Markov chains, we refer to any of a large variety of available monographs on the theory of stochastic processes, to mention a few: Bhattacharya and Waymire (1990), Syski (1992), Last and Brandt (1995), and Rogers and Williams (2000).

Since most Markov chain models used in portfolio credit risk are time continuous, we shall focus on continuous-time Markov chains (except for the notion of discrete-time Markov Chain embedded to a continuous-time Markov chain which is dealt with in section 2.3). However it should be noted that completely analogous developments are in fact valid relatively to discrete time Markov chains (see chapter 11 of Bielecki and Rutkowski 2002), which is relevant to credit risk when it comes to model implementation, which often proceeds via time discretization (see, for instance, section 3.1.4).

After an introduction to time-inhomogeneous as well as time-homogeneous Markov chains, we examine conditional expectations, which in the financial interpretation is of course relevant for pricing purposes. We then consider some 'fundamental' martingales with respect to certain relevant filtrations, and we derive related martingale representation theorems. In the context of finance, such martingale representations are key to the issue of hedging (see, e.g., Frey and Backhaus 2008a; Bielecki, Vidozzi, and Vidozzi 2008, Bielecki, Crépey, and Jeanblanc 2008) or Laurent, Cousin, and Fermanian 2008. We also deal with various examples of random times associated with a Markov chain, such as the jump times and the absorption time, which in the context of credit risk are related to the issue of deriving univariate (see section 2.5) or multivariate (see section 4.1.2) default, survival, and conditional default and survival distributions. Finally, we study the behaviour of a time-homogeneous Markov chain under an equivalent change of a probability measure. In applications such equivalent changes of measure can be interpreted and used as a bridge between the statistical measure and a risk-neutral measure (see e.g. section 3.1.1 and Bielecki, Vidozzi, and Vidozzi 2008), or as a change of numeraire (see e.g. Bielecki et al. 2008, cf. section 3.1).

In what follows, we fix the underlying probability space $(\Omega, \mathcal{G}, \mathbb{Q})$, as well as a finite set $\mathcal{K} = \{1, \ldots, K\}$, which plays the role of the *state space* for a Markov chain of interest. Since the state space is finite, it is clear that any function $h : \mathcal{K} \to \mathbb{R}$ is bounded and measurable, provided that we endow the state space with the σ-field of all its subsets.

Let C_t, $t \in \mathbb{R}_+$, be a right-continuous stochastic process on $(\Omega, \mathcal{G}, \mathbb{Q})$ with values in the finite set $\mathcal{K}$, and let $\mathbb{F}^C$ be the filtration generated by this process. Also, let $\mathbb{G}$ be some filtration such that $\mathbb{F}^C \subseteq \mathbb{G}$.

Definition 2.1 A process C is a *continuous-time $\mathbb{G}$-Markov chain* if for an arbitrary function $h : \mathcal{K} \to \mathbb{R}$ and any $s, t \in \mathbb{N}$ we have

$$\mathbb{E}_{\mathbb{Q}}(h(C_{t+s}) \mid \mathcal{G}_t) = \mathbb{E}_{\mathbb{Q}}(h(C_{t+s}) \mid C_t).$$

A continuous-time $\mathbb{G}$-Markov chain C is said to be *time homogeneous* if, in addition, for any $s, t, u \in \mathbb{N}$ we have

$$\mathbb{E}_{\mathbb{Q}}(h(C_{t+s}) \mid C_t) = \mathbb{E}_{\mathbb{Q}}(h(C_{u+s}) \mid C_u).$$

Definition 2.2 A two-parameter family $\mathcal{P}(t, s)$, $t, s \in \mathbb{R}_+$, $t \le s$, of stochastic matrices is called the family of *transition probability matrices* for the $\mathbb{G}$-Markov chain C under $\mathbb{Q}$ if, for every $t, s \in \mathbb{R}_+$, $t \le s$,

$$\mathbb{Q}\{C_s = j \mid C_t = i\} = p_{ij}(t, s), \quad \forall i, j \in \mathcal{K}.$$

In particular, the equality $\mathcal{P}(t, t) = \mathrm{Id}$ is satisfied for every $t \in \mathbb{R}_+$.

2.1 Time-homogeneous chains

In case of a time-homogeneous Markov chain C, we introduce the following definition.

Definition 2.3 The one-parameter family $\mathcal{P}(t)$, $t \in \mathbb{R}_+$, of stochastic matrices is called the family of *transition probability matrices* for the time-homogeneous $\mathbb{G}$-Markov chain C under $\mathbb{Q}$ if, for every $t, s \in \mathbb{R}_+$,

$$\mathbb{Q}\{C_{s+t} = j \mid C_s = i\} = p_{ij}(t), \quad \forall i, j \in \mathcal{K}. \tag{1}$$

If $\mathcal{P}(t)$, $t \in \mathbb{R}_+$ is the family of transition matrices for C then for any subset $A \subseteq \mathcal{K}$ we have

$$\mathbb{Q}\{C_{t+s} \in A \mid C_t\} = \sum_{j \in A} p_{C_t, j}(s), \quad \forall s, t \in \mathbb{R}_+.$$

Moreover, the Chapman-Kolmogorov equation is satisfied, namely,

$$\mathcal{P}(t + s) = \mathcal{P}(t)\mathcal{P}(s) = \mathcal{P}(s)\mathcal{P}(t), \quad \forall s, t \in \mathbb{R}_+.$$

Equivalently, for every $s, t \in \mathbb{R}_+$ and $i, j \in \mathcal{K}$,

$$p_{ij}(t + s) = \sum_{k=1}^{K} p_{ik}(t) p_{kj}(s) = \sum_{k=1}^{K} p_{ik}(s) p_{kj}(t).$$

Let the K-dimensional (row) vector $\mu_0 = [\mu_0(i)]_{1 \le i \le K} = [\mathbb{Q}\{C_0 = i\}]_{1 \le i \le K}$ denote the initial probability distribution for the Markov chain C under $\mathbb{Q}$.

Likewise, let the (row) vector $\mu_t = [\mu_t(i)]_{1 \le i \le K} = [\mathbb{Q}\{C_t = i\}]_{1 \le i \le K}$ stand for the probability distribution of C at time $t \in \mathbb{R}_+$. It can be easily checked that

$$\mu_{t+s} = \mu_0 \mathcal{P}(t + s) = \mu_t \mathcal{P}(s) = \mu_s \mathcal{P}(t), \quad \forall s, t \in \mathbb{R}_+.$$

We now impose an important assumption on the family $\mathcal{P}(\cdot)$, specifically, that this family is right-continuous at time $t = 0$, that is, $\lim_{t \downarrow 0} \mathcal{P}(t) = \mathcal{P}(0)$. By virtue of the Chapman-Kolmogorov equation, this implies that

$$\lim_{s \to 0} \mathcal{P}(t + s) = \mathcal{P}(t), \quad \forall t > 0,$$

and thus

$$\lim_{s \to 0} \mathbb{Q}\{C_{t+s} = j \mid C_t = i\} = \delta_{ij}, \quad \forall i, j \in \mathcal{K}, \ t > 0.$$

It is a well-known fact (see, for instance, Theorem 8.1.2 in Rolski et al. 1998) that the right-hand side continuity at time $t = 0$ of the family $\mathcal{P}(\cdot)$ implies the right-hand side differentiability at $t = 0$ of this family. More specifically, the following finite limits exist, for every $i, j \in \mathcal{K}$,

$$\lambda_{ij} := \lim_{t \downarrow 0} \frac{p_{ij}(t) - p_{ij}(0)}{t} = \lim_{t \downarrow 0} \frac{p_{ij}(t) - \delta_{ij}}{t}. \tag{2}$$

Observe that for every $i \neq j$ we have $\lambda_{ij} \geq 0$, and $\lambda_{ii} = -\sum_{j=1, j \neq i}^{K} \lambda_{ij}$. The matrix $\Lambda := [\lambda_{ij}]_{1 \leq i, j \leq K}$ is called the *infinitesimal generator matrix* for a Markov chain associated with the family $\mathcal{P}(\cdot)$ via (1). Since each entry λ_{ij} of the matrix Λ can be shown to represent the intensity of transition from the state i to the state j, the infinitesimal generator matrix Λ is also commonly known as the *intensity matrix*.

Invoking the Chapman-Kolmogorov equation and equality (2), one may derive the *backward Kolmogorov equation*

$$\frac{d\mathcal{P}(t)}{dt} = \Lambda \mathcal{P}(t), \quad \mathcal{P}(0) = \text{Id}, \tag{3}$$

and the *forward Kolmogorov equation*

$$\frac{d\mathcal{P}(t)}{dt} = \mathcal{P}(t)\Lambda, \quad \mathcal{P}(0) = \text{Id}, \tag{4}$$

where, at time $t = 0$, we take the right-hand side derivatives. It is well known that both these equations have the same unique solution:

$$\mathcal{P}(t) = e^{t\Lambda} := \sum_{n=0}^{\infty} \frac{\Lambda^n t^n}{n!}, \quad \forall t \in \mathbb{R}_+. \tag{5}$$

We conclude that the generator matrix Λ uniquely determines all relevant probabilistic properties of a time-homogeneous Markov chain.

The following important result provides a martingale characterization of a time-homogeneous Markov chain C in terms of its infinitesimal generator. For the proof of Proposition 2.1, we refer to Last and Brandt (1995) or Rogers and Williams (2000). In the quoted references, the corresponding result is stated for an $\mathbb{F}^C$-Markov chain, rather than for a $\mathbb{G}$-Markov chain. However, the proof of this more general version is analogous. For any state $i \in \mathcal{K}$ and any function $h : \mathcal{K} \to \mathbb{R}$, we denote

$$(\Lambda h)(i) = \sum_{j=1}^{K} \lambda_{ij} h(j).$$

Proposition 2.1 *A process C is a time-homogeneous $\mathbb{G}$-Markov chain under $\mathbb{Q}$, with the initial distribution μ_0 and with the infinitesimal generator matrix Λ, if and only if the following conditions are satisfied:*

(i) $\mathbb{Q}\{C_0 = i\} = \mu_0(i)$ *for every $i \in \mathcal{K}$,*

(ii) *for any function $h : \mathcal{K} \to \mathbb{R}$ the process M^h, defined by the formula*

$$M_t^h = h(C_t) - \int_0^t (\Lambda h)(C_u)\, du, \quad \forall t \in \mathbb{R}_+,$$

follows a $\mathbb{G}$-martingale under $\mathbb{Q}$.

Example 2.4 Let C be a time-homogeneous $\mathbb{G}$-Markov chain with the infinitesimal generator matrix Λ. Applying Proposition 2.1 to the function $h(\cdot) = \mathbb{1}_{\{i\}}(\cdot)$, we conclude that the process

$$M_t^i = H_t^i - \int_0^t \lambda_{C_u i}\, du, \quad \forall t \in \mathbb{R}_+, \tag{6}$$

follows a $\mathbb{G}$-martingale (and an $\mathbb{F}^C$-martingale) under $\mathbb{Q}$. Conversely, if for every $i \in \mathcal{K}$ the process M^i follows a $\mathbb{G}$-martingale, then for any function $h : \mathcal{K} \to \mathbb{R}$ the process M^h is a $\mathbb{G}$-martingale under $\mathbb{Q}$.

2.2 Time-inhomogeneous chains

If a Markov chain is time inhomogeneous, the time-dependent transition intensities are introduced through the formula[1]

$$\lambda_{ij}(t) = \lim_{h \downarrow 0} \frac{p_{ij}(t, t+h) - \delta_{ij}}{h}.$$

It is obvious that $\lambda_{ij}(t) \geq 0$ for arbitrary $i \neq j$, and

$$\lambda_{ii}(t) = \lim_{h \downarrow 0} \frac{p_{ii}(t, t+h) - 1}{h} = -\lim_{h \downarrow 0} \frac{\sum_{j=1,\, j \neq i}^{K} p_{ij}(t, t+h)}{h} = -\sum_{j=1,\, j \neq i}^{K} \lambda_{ij}(t),$$

where

$$p_{ij}(t, t+h) = \mathbb{Q}\{C_{t+h} = j \mid C_t = i\}, \quad \forall i, j \in \mathcal{K}.$$

We shall write $\Lambda(t) = [\lambda_{ij}(t)]_{1 \leq i, j \leq K}$ to denote the infinitesimal generator matrix function associated with a time-inhomogeneous Markov chain C.

---

[1] Let us mention that mild regularity conditions need to be satisfied by the probabilities $p_{ij}(s, t)$ for the results of this subsection to be valid.

The two parameter family $\mathcal{P}(t, s) = [p_{ij}(t, s)]_{1 \leq i, j \leq K}$, $0 \leq t \leq s$, of transition matrices for C satisfies the Chapman-Kolmogorov equation:

$$\mathcal{P}(t, s) = \mathcal{P}(t, u)\mathcal{P}(u, s), \quad \forall\, t \leq u \leq s,$$

the forward Kolmogorov equation:

$$\frac{d\mathcal{P}(t, s)}{ds} = \mathcal{P}(t, s)\Lambda(s), \quad \mathcal{P}(t, t) = \mathrm{Id}, \tag{7}$$

and the backward Kolmogorov equation:

$$\frac{d\mathcal{P}(t, s)}{dt} = -\Lambda(t)\mathcal{P}(t, s), \quad \mathcal{P}(s, s) = \mathrm{Id}. \tag{8}$$

The next result is an immediate consequence of Kolmogorov's equations.

Corollary 2.2 *The family $\mathcal{P}(t, s)$, $0 \leq t \leq s$, satisfies the integral equations*

$$\mathcal{P}(t, s) = \mathrm{Id} + \int_t^s \mathcal{P}(t, u)\Lambda(u)\, du$$

and

$$\mathcal{P}(t, s) = \mathrm{Id} + \int_t^s \Lambda(u)\mathcal{P}(u, s)\, du.$$

The above equations can be used in order to derive some remarkable representations, which are important from the computational point of view, and which are counterparts of (5). For the proof of Corollary 2.3, the interested reader is referred to Rolski et al. (1998) (see Theorem 8.4.4 therein).

Corollary 2.3 *For every $0 \leq t \leq s$ we have*

$$\mathcal{P}(t, s) = \mathrm{Id} + \sum_{n=1}^{\infty} \int_t^s \int_{u_1}^s \cdots \int_{u_{n-1}}^s \Lambda(u_1) \ldots \Lambda(u_n)\, du_n \ldots du_1,$$

and

$$\mathcal{P}(t, s) = \mathrm{Id} + \sum_{n=1}^{\infty} \int_t^s \int_t^{u_1} \cdots \int_t^{u_{n-1}} \Lambda(u_1) \ldots \Lambda(u_n)\, du_n \ldots du_1.$$

Assume that the matrix function $\Lambda(t) = [\lambda_{ij}(t)]_{1 \leq i, j \leq K}$ satisfies the conditions, which characterize the infinitesimal generator of an inhomogeneous Markov chain, namely,

$$\lambda_{ij}(t) \geq 0, \quad i \neq j, \quad \lambda_{ii}(t) = -\sum_{j=1, j \neq i}^{K} \lambda_{ij}(t).$$

For any function $h : \mathcal{K} \to \mathbb{R}$, we introduce the mapping $\Lambda h : \mathcal{K} \times \mathbb{R}_+ \to \mathbb{R}$ by setting:

$$(\Lambda h)(i, t) = \sum_{j=1}^{K} \lambda_{ij}(t) h(j), \quad \forall i \in \mathcal{K}, \ t \in \mathbb{R}_+.$$

The following result is a natural extension of Proposition 2.1.

Proposition 2.4 *A process C is a $\mathbb{G}$-Markov chain under $\mathbb{Q}$, with the initial distribution μ_0 and with the infinitesimal generator matrix function $\Lambda(\cdot)$, if and only if:*

(i) $\mathbb{Q}\{C_0 = i\} = \mu_0(i)$ *for every $i \in \mathcal{K}$,*

(ii) *for any function $h : \mathcal{K} \to \mathbb{R}$ the process M^h, defined by the formula*

$$M_t^h = h(C_t) - \int_0^t (\Lambda h)(C_u, u) \, du, \quad t \in \mathbb{R}_+, \tag{9}$$

follows a $\mathbb{G}$-martingale under $\mathbb{Q}$.

Example 2.5 Let C be a time-inhomogeneous $\mathbb{G}$-Markov chain with the infinitesimal generator matrix function $\Lambda(\cdot)$. By applying Proposition 2.4 to the function $h(\cdot) = \mathbb{1}_{\{i\}}(\cdot)$, we find that the process

$$M_t^i = H_t^i - \int_0^t \lambda_{C_u i}(u) \, du, \quad \forall t \in \mathbb{R}_+, \tag{10}$$

follows a $\mathbb{G}$-martingale (and an $\mathbb{F}^C$-martingale) under $\mathbb{Q}$. Similarly as in the time-homogeneous case, if for every $i \in \mathcal{K}$ the process M^i is a $\mathbb{G}$-martingale, then for any function $h : \mathcal{K} \to \mathbb{R}$ the process M^h, given by formula (9), also follows a $\mathbb{G}$-martingale.

2.3 Embedded discrete-time Markov chain

Let C_t, $t \in \mathbb{R}_+$, stand for a continuous-time time-homogeneous $\mathbb{G}$-Markov chain (and thus a Markov chain w.r.t. its own filtration) under $\mathbb{Q}$ with the infinitesimal generator Λ. Let τ_n, $n \in \mathbb{N}$, denote the random sequence of successive jump times of C. More explicitly, for any $n \in \mathbb{N}$, the random variable τ_n defined as (by convention, $\tau_0 = 0$):

$$\tau_n = \inf\{t > \tau_{n-1} : C_t \neq C_{\tau_{n-1}}\}, \tag{11}$$

represents the time of the nth jump (or transition) for C. Let us recall few classic results related to the behaviour of a continuous-time Markov chain at its jump times.

First, it is well known that the following property holds, for any $n \in \mathbb{N}$ and every $t \in \mathbb{R}_+$,

$$\mathbb{Q}\{\tau_n - \tau_{n-1} > t \mid C_{\tau_{n-1}} = i\} = e^{\lambda_{ii} t}, \quad \forall i = 1, \ldots, K. \tag{12}$$

Equation (12) makes it clear that, conditionally on the position $C_{\tau_{n-1}} = i$ at the jump time τ_{n-1}, the random time that elapses until the next jump occurs has an exponential probability law with the parameter $-\lambda_{ii} > 0$.

Second, the conditional probabilities of transitions are known to satisfy:

$$\mathbb{Q}\{C_{\tau_n} = j \mid C_{\tau_{n-1}} = i\} = p_{ij} := -\frac{\lambda_{ij}}{\lambda_{ii}}, \quad \forall i, j \in \mathcal{K}, i \neq j. \tag{13}$$

Formula (13) specifies the conditional probability law of a continuous-time Markov chain C after its nth jump, given the position after the $(n-1)^{\text{th}}$ jump (it coincides, of course, with the position of C just before the nth jump).

Let us emphasize that since C is assumed to be a time-homogeneous Markov chain, both probability laws introduced above do not depend on the number of transitions in the past (that is, on n). They only depend on the value taken by C after the previous jump.

Define a random sequence $\widehat{C}_n = C_{\tau_n}$ for every $n \in \mathbb{N}$. It is well known that the sequence $\widehat{C}$ is a time-homogeneous Markov chain under $\mathbb{Q}$ with the one-step transition probability matrix $P = [p_{ij}]_{1 \leq i,j \leq K}$. The discrete-time Markov chain $\widehat{C}_n$, $n \in \mathbb{N}$, is called the *embedded Markov chain* corresponding to the continuous-time Markov chain C.

Remark 2.6 In the case of a *time-inhomogeneous* $\mathbb{G}$-Markov chain C, one may define likewise the embedded *Markov process in discrete time* $(\tau_n, C_{\tau_n}) n \in \mathbb{N}$, defined over the extended time-space state by the following analogues of (12), (13)

$$\mathbb{Q}\{\tau_n - \tau_{n-1} > t \mid C_{\tau_{n-1}} = i\} = e^{\int_{\tau_{n-1}}^{t+\tau_{n-1}} \lambda_{ii}(u)du}, \quad \forall i = 1, \ldots, K. \tag{14}$$

$$\mathbb{Q}\{C_{\tau_n} = j \mid C_{\tau_{n-1}} = i, \tau_n = t\} = p_{ij}(t) := -\frac{\lambda_{ij}(t)}{\lambda_{ii}(t)}, \quad \forall i, j \in \mathcal{K}, i \neq j. \tag{15}$$

The results of this subsection are important in practice regarding the issue, for instance, of numerical simulation (see e.g. section 3.1.4).

2.4 Conditional expectations

We say that a state $k \in \mathcal{K}$ is *absorbing* for a time-homogeneous $\mathbb{G}$-Markov chain C_t, $t \in \mathbb{R}_+$, if the following holds:

$$\mathbb{Q}\{C_s = k \mid C_t = k\} = 1, \quad \forall t, s \in \mathbb{R}_+, t \leq s.$$

In view of (2), it is clear that if a state $k \in \mathcal{K}$ is absorbing, then we have $\lambda_{kj} = 0$ for every $j = 1, \ldots, K$.

From now on, we shall postulate that the state K is absorbing. This implies that the infinitesimal generator of C under $\mathbb{Q}$ is given by the intensity matrix Λ of the following form:

$$\Lambda = \begin{pmatrix} \lambda_{1,1} & \cdots & \lambda_{1,K-1} & \lambda_{1,K} \\ \cdot & \cdots & \cdot & \cdot \\ \lambda_{K-1,1} & \cdots & \lambda_{K-1,K-1} & \lambda_{K-1,K} \\ 0 & \cdots & 0 & 0 \end{pmatrix}.$$

We assume that the initial state $C_0 = x \neq K$ is fixed, and we denote by τ the random time of absorption at K, i.e., $\tau = \inf\{t > 0 : C_t = K\}$. We assume that $\tau < \infty$, $\mathbb{Q}$-a.s.; this implies that the state K is the only recurrent state for C. As usual, we write $H_t^i = \mathbb{1}_{\{C_t=i\}}$ and $H_t = \mathbb{1}_{\{\tau \leq t\}} = \mathbb{1}_{\{C_t=K\}} = H_t^K$.

In the next few auxiliary results, we shall deal with the conditional expectations with respect to the filtrations $\mathbb{G}$ and $\mathbb{F}^C$. The absorption time τ is, of course, an $\mathbb{F}^C$-stopping time and a $\mathbb{G}$-stopping time. In what follows, Y will denote an integrable random variable, which is defined on the reference probability space $(\Omega, \mathcal{G}, \mathbb{Q})$.

Lemma 2.5 *We have*

$$\mathbb{1}_{\{\tau \leq t\}} \mathbb{E}_{\mathbb{Q}}(Y \mid \mathcal{G}_t) = \mathbb{E}_{\mathbb{Q}}(\mathbb{1}_{\{\tau \leq t\}} Y \mid \mathcal{G}_t \vee \sigma(\tau))$$

and

$$\mathbb{1}_{\{\tau \leq t\}} \mathbb{E}_{\mathbb{Q}}(Y \mid \mathcal{F}_t^C) = \mathbb{E}_{\mathbb{Q}}(\mathbb{1}_{\{\tau \leq t\}} Y \mid \mathcal{F}_t^C \vee \sigma(\tau)).$$

In the next lemma, we examine the case when the random variable Y has the form $h(C_{\tau-}, \tau)$ for some function $h : \mathcal{K} \times \mathbb{R}_+ \to \mathbb{R}$.

Lemma 2.6 *Let $Y = h(C_{\tau-}, \tau)$ for some function $h : \mathcal{K} \times \mathbb{R}_+ \to \mathbb{R}$. Then*

$$\mathbb{E}_{\mathbb{Q}}(\mathbb{1}_{\{\tau > t\}} Y \mid \mathcal{G}_t) = \sum_{i=1}^{K-1} H_t^i \, \mathbb{E}_{\mathbb{Q}}(\mathbb{1}_{\{\tau > t\}} Y \mid C_t = i).$$

The next two auxiliary results are simple corollaries to Lemma 2.6.

Corollary 2.7 *Let $Y = h(C_{\tau-}, \tau)$ for some function $h : \mathcal{K} \times \mathbb{R}_+ \to \mathbb{R}$. Then*

$$\mathbb{E}_{\mathbb{Q}}(Y \mid \mathcal{G}_t) = \mathbb{1}_{\{\tau \leq t\}} Y + \sum_{i=1}^{K-1} H_t^i \, \mathbb{E}_{\mathbb{Q}}(\mathbb{1}_{\{\tau > t\}} Y \mid C_t = i).$$

Corollary 2.8 *For any $s, t \in \mathbb{R}_+$, the following equalities are valid*

$$\mathbb{Q}\{\tau > s \mid \mathcal{G}_t\} = \mathbb{1}_{\{s \leq t\}} \mathbb{1}_{\{\tau > s\}} + \mathbb{1}_{\{s > t\}} \sum_{i=1}^{K-1} H_t^i \, \mathbb{Q}\{\tau > s \mid C_t = i\},$$

and

$$\mathbb{Q}\{\tau \geq s \mid \mathcal{G}_t\} = \mathbb{1}_{\{s \leq t\}} \mathbb{1}_{\{\tau \geq s\}} + \mathbb{1}_{\{s > t\}} \sum_{i=1}^{K-1} H_t^i \, \mathbb{Q}\{\tau \geq s \mid C_t = i\}.$$

2.5 Probability distribution of the absorption time

We maintain the assumptions of section 2.4. More explicit formulas for the conditional expectations with respect to the σ-field $\mathcal{G}_t$ can be obtained, if the knowledge of conditional laws of C is used. Notice that for every $0 \le t \le s$ we have

$$\mathbb{Q}\{\tau > s \mid C_t = i\} = 1 - \mathbb{Q}\{C_s = K \mid C_t = i\} = 1 - p_{iK}(s - t),$$

hence, the first formula of Corollary 2.8 can be rewritten as follows:

$$\mathbb{Q}\{\tau > s \mid \mathcal{G}_t\} = \mathbb{1}_{\{s \le t\}} \mathbb{1}_{\{\tau > s\}} + \mathbb{1}_{\{s > t\}} \sum_{i=1}^{K-1} H_t^i \left(1 - p_{iK}(s - t)\right). \tag{16}$$

To derive an alternative representation for the probability distribution of the absorption time, let us denote by $\widetilde{\Lambda}$ the matrix obtained from Λ by deleting the last row and the last column. Also, let $\widetilde{\mathcal{P}}(t) = [\widetilde{p}_{ij}(t)]_{i,j \in \widetilde{\mathcal{K}}}$ stand for the associated transition matrix, where $\widetilde{\mathcal{K}} = \{1, \dots, K - 1\}$.

Recall that the quantity $\mathbb{Q}\{\tau > s \mid C_t = i\}$ is of fundamental importance when studying the spread for a defaultable bond, see e.g. Jarrow, Lando, and Turnbull (1997: 496–7).

It is not difficult to check that the so-called *taboo probabilities* $\widetilde{p}_{ij}(t)$, $i, j \in \widetilde{\mathcal{K}}$ can be found by solving the following differential equation:

$$\frac{d}{dt}\widetilde{\mathcal{P}}(t) = \widetilde{\Lambda}\widetilde{\mathcal{P}}(t), \quad t > 0, \tag{17}$$

with the initial condition $\widetilde{\mathcal{P}}(0) = \mathrm{Id}$.

It is also clearly seen that (recall that we have assumed that $C_0 = i \in \widetilde{\mathcal{K}}$)

$$F(t) = 1 - \sum_{j=1}^{K-1} \widetilde{p}_{ij}(t) = 1 - \sum_{j=1}^{K-1} p_{ij}(t). \tag{18}$$

Since $F(t) < 1$ for every $t \in \mathbb{R}_+$, we may introduce the hazard function Γ of τ by setting $\Gamma(t) = -\ln(1 - F(t))$. Denoting by $f(t)$ the density of $F(t)$ with respect to the Lebesgue measure, and setting $\gamma(t) = f(t)(1 - F(t))^{-1}$, we obtain $\Gamma(t) = \int_0^t \gamma(u)\, du$. In view of (18), we have

$$f(t) = -\sum_{j=1}^{K-1} \frac{d\widetilde{p}_{ij}(t)}{dt} = -\sum_{j=1}^{K-1} \frac{dp_{ij}(t)}{dt}.$$

Corollary 2.9 *For every $t \in \mathbb{R}_+$ and any $i = 1, \dots, K - 1$, the conditional law of the absorption time τ is given by the formula*

$$\mathbb{Q}\{\tau \le t \mid C_0 = i\} = 1 - \sum_{j=1}^{K-1} p_{ij}(0, t).$$

Remark 2.7 (Phase-type distributions) Let α be the initial distribution of C on $E = \{1, \ldots, K - 1\}$, i.e. $\alpha = (\mathbb{Q}\{C_0 = j\})_{j=1}^{K-1}$ and assume that $\mathbb{Q}\{C_0 = K\} = 0$. Furthermore, note that we can rewrite the generator Λ as

$$\Lambda = \begin{pmatrix} T & t \\ 0 & 0 \end{pmatrix}$$

where t is a column vector with $K - 1$ rows. We assume that C_t is transient on $E = \{1, \ldots, K - 1\}$ so that T is invertible. Recall the definition of the time of absorbtion $\tau = \inf\{t > 0 : C_t = K\}$ and let $F(t) = \mathbb{Q}\{\tau \leq t\}$. We then say that $F(t)$, is a phase-type distribution (PH-distribution) with representation (E, α, T), or for short (α, T). Sometime we also say that τ is phase-type distributed with representation (α, T). The matrix T is called the *phase generator* and t the *exit vector*. The following proposition can be found in Asmussen (2003) and Rolski et al. (1998).

Proposition 2.10 *Let F be a PH-distribution with representation (E, α, T). Then*

$$F(t) = 1 - \alpha e^{Tt} 1$$

$$f(t) = \alpha e^{Tt} t$$

$$\mathbb{E}\left[\tau^n\right] = (-1)^n n! \alpha T^{-n} 1$$

$$\widehat{F}[s] = \int_0^\infty e^{-st} f(t) dt = \alpha \left(s I - T^{-1}\right) t$$

where $f(t)$ is the density of $F(t)$, $\widehat{F}[s]$ is the Laplace-transform of $f(t)$, $t = -T1$ and $1^T = (1, 1, \ldots, 1) \in \mathbb{R}^{K-1}$.

Note that the above quantities are computationally tractable given that we use mathematical software with a matrix-package. A short discussion of computing the matrix exponential is given in Appendix 5.4.

Phase-type distributions are dense (in a weak convergence sense) in the set of all probability distributions on $\mathbb{R}_+ = [0, \infty)$, see Asmussen (2003), Rolski et al. (1998). Hence, any random variable on $[0, \infty)$ can be approximated by a properly chosen PH-distribution. Furthermore, PH-distributions are closed under convolution and mixing.

All of the above properties have made phase-type distributions to be an important tool in queuing and reliability theory, but also in insurance, see e.g. Asmussen (2000, 2003), Neuts (1981, 1989) and Rolski et al. (1998). In sections 4.1 and 4.2 we will discuss the multivariate extensions of PH-distribution, so called multivariate phase type distributions (MPH) and their applications in portfolio credit risk.

2.6 Martingales associated with transitions

We shall now introduce some important examples of martingales associated with the absorption time τ and with the number of transitions. For any fixed $i \neq j$, let H_t^{ij} stand for the number of jumps of the process C from i to j in the interval $(0, t]$. Formally, for any $i \neq j$ we set

$$H_t^{ij} := \sum_{0 < u \leq t} H_{u-}^i H_u^j, \quad \forall t \in \mathbb{R}_+.$$

The following result is classic (see Brémaud 1981); Last and Brandt (1995) or (Rogers and Williams 2000).

Lemma 2.11 *For every $i, j \in \mathcal{K}, i \neq j$, the processes*

$$M_t^{ij} = H_t^{ij} - \int_0^t \lambda_{ij} H_u^i \, du = H_t^{ij} - \int_0^t \lambda_{C_u j} H_u^i \, du \tag{19}$$

and

$$M_t^K = H_t - \int_0^t \sum_{i=1}^{K-1} \lambda_{iK} H_u^i \, du = H_t - \int_0^t \lambda_{C_u K}(1 - H_u) \, du \tag{20}$$

follow $\mathbb{G}$-martingales (and $\mathbb{F}^C$-martingales).

2.7 Change of a probability measure

We shall now examine how the Markov property and the generator Λ of the time-homogeneous Markov chain C are affected by a change of the reference probability measure $\mathbb{Q}$ to an equivalent probability measure $\mathbb{Q}^*$ on $(\Omega, \mathcal{G}_{T^*})$ for some fixed $T^* > 0$. Let us emphasize that we do not need to assume here that the state K is absorbing.

Consider a family $\widetilde{\kappa}^{kl}$, $k, l \in \mathcal{K}$, $k \neq l$, of bounded, $\mathbb{F}^C$-predictable, real-valued processes, such that $\widetilde{\kappa}_t^{kl} > -1$. For the sake of notational convenience, we also introduce processes $\widetilde{\kappa}^{kk} \equiv 0$ for $k = 1, \ldots, K$. Let us define an auxiliary $\mathbb{G}$-martingale M (which is also an $\mathbb{F}^C$-martingale) by setting

$$M_t = \int_{]0,t]} \sum_{k,l=1}^K \widetilde{\kappa}_u^{kl} \, dM_u^{kl} = \int_{]0,t]} \sum_{k,l=1}^K \widetilde{\kappa}_u^{kl} \, dH_u^{kl} - M_t^c, \tag{21}$$

where M_t^c is the path-by-path continuous component of the process M, i.e.,

$$M_t^c = \int_0^t \sum_{k,l=1}^K \widetilde{\kappa}_u^{kl} \lambda_{kl} H_u^k \, du.$$

Remark 2.8 From Theorem 21.15 in Rogers and Williams (2000), we know that an arbitrary $\mathbb{F}^C$-local martingale M under $\mathbb{Q}$ admits the following representation

$$M_t = \sum_{0 < u \leq t} h_u(C_{u-}, C_u) - \int_0^t \sum_{j=1}^K \lambda_{C_{u-} j} \, h_u(C_{u-}, j) \, du,$$

where, for any states $i, j \in \mathcal{K}$, the process $h(i, j)$ is $\mathbb{F}^C$-predictable. In addition, we postulate that $h(j, j) \equiv 0$. Notice that the process M as in (21) can be obtained by setting:

$$h_t(i, j) = \sum_{k,l=1}^{K} \widetilde{\kappa}_t^{kl} \delta_{ik} \delta_{jl}.$$

Let us return to our problem. We fix a horizon date $T^* < \infty$, and we define an $\mathbb{G}$-martingale η_t, $t \in [0, T^*]$, by postulating that

$$\eta_t = 1 + \int_{]0,t]} \sum_{k,l=1}^{K} \eta_{u-} \widetilde{\kappa}_u^{kl} \, dM_u^{kl}. \tag{22}$$

It is known that the unique solution to the SDE (22) equals, for every $t \in [0, T^*]$,

$$\eta_t = e^{-M_t^c} \prod_{0 < u \leq t} (1 + \Delta M_u).$$

$$\eta_t = e^{-M_t^c} \prod_{0 < u \leq t} \left(1 + \sum_{k,l=1}^{K} \widetilde{\kappa}_u^{kl} (M_u^{kl} - M_{u-}^{kl})\right).$$

Observe that

$$1 + \sum_{k,l=1}^{K} \widetilde{\kappa}_u^{kl} (M_u^{kl} - M_{u-}^{kl}) = 1 + \sum_{k,l=1}^{K} \widetilde{\kappa}_u^{kl} (H_u^{kl} - H_{u-}^{kl}). \tag{23}$$

Since at most one of the differentials $H_u^{kl} - H_{u-}^{kl}$ is equal to one, and all those that are not equal to one are equal to zero, we see that the right-hand side of (23) is either equal to $1 + \widetilde{\kappa}_u^{ij}$ for some $i \neq j \in \mathcal{K}$, or it is equal to 1. Thus, in view of our assumption that $\widetilde{\kappa}_u^{kl} > -1$ for all $k \neq l$, we conclude that the product

$$\prod_{0 < u \leq t} \left(1 + \sum_{k,l=1}^{K} \widetilde{\kappa}_u^{kl} (M_u^{kl} - M_{u-}^{kl})\right)$$

is strictly positive. Consequently, the process η is strictly positive. Since, in addition, $\mathbb{E}_{\mathbb{Q}}(\eta_{T^*}) = 1$, we may define a probability measure $\mathbb{Q}^*$, equivalent to $\mathbb{Q}$ on $(\Omega, \mathcal{G}_{T^*})$, by setting

$$\left.\frac{d\mathbb{Q}^*}{d\mathbb{Q}}\right|_{\mathcal{G}_{T^*}} = \eta_{T^*}, \quad \mathbb{Q}\text{-a.s.} \tag{24}$$

It is clear that for any date $t \in [0, T^*]$ we have

$$\left.\frac{d\mathbb{Q}^*}{d\mathbb{Q}}\right|_{\mathcal{G}_t} = \eta_t, \quad \mathbb{Q}\text{-a.s.}$$

Before proceeding further, we need to impose an additional measurability condition on processes $\widetilde{\kappa}^{kl}$, namely, we postulate that, for any fixed $k, l \in \mathcal{K}$ and $t \in \mathbb{R}_+$, the random variable $\widetilde{\kappa}_t^{kl}$ is measurable with respect to the σ-field $\sigma(C_t)$. This implies that, for any fixed $k, l \in \mathcal{K}$ and $t \in \mathbb{R}_+$, there exists a function $g_t^{kl} : \mathcal{K} \to \mathbb{R}$ such that $\widetilde{\kappa}_t^{kl} = g_t^{kl}(C_t)$.

We assume that for any $i \in \mathcal{K}$ there exists a version of $g_t^{kl}(i)$, $t \in \mathbb{R}_+$ that is Borel measurable as a function of t, and we introduce a family of functions $\kappa_{kl} : \mathbb{R}_+ \to (-1, \infty)$ by setting $\kappa_{kl}(t) := g_t^{kl}(k)$ for every $k, l \in \mathcal{K}$ and $t \in \mathbb{R}_+$.

To further simplify the exposition, we shall only consider processes $\widetilde{\kappa}_t^{kl}$ of the special form: $\widetilde{\kappa}_t^{kl} = \kappa_{kl}(t)$, where for every $k, l \in \mathcal{K}$, $k \neq l$, the function $\kappa_{kl} : \mathbb{R}_+ \to (-1, \infty)$ is Borel measurable and bounded. We thus may and do assume that $\kappa_{kk} \equiv 0$ for every $k = 1, \dots, K$. Under this assumption, we have the following result that provides sufficient conditions for a $\mathbb{G}$-Markov chain C to remain a (time-inhomogeneous, in general) $\mathbb{G}$-Markov chain under $\mathbb{Q}^*$.

Proposition 2.12 *Let the probability measure $\mathbb{Q}^*$ by defined by (24) with the Radon-Nikodým density η_{T^*} given by (22). Then*

  (i) *the process C_t, $t \in [0, T^*]$, is a $\mathbb{G}$-Markov chain under $\mathbb{Q}^*$,*
  (ii) *the infinitesimal generator matrix function $\Lambda^*(t) = [\lambda_{ij}^*(t)]_{1 \leq i, j \leq K}$ for C under $\mathbb{Q}^*$ satisfies, for $i \neq j$,*

$$\lambda_{ij}^*(t) = (1 + \kappa_{ij}(t))\lambda_{ij}, \quad \forall t \in [0, T^*], \tag{25}$$

and

$$\lambda_{ii}^*(t) = - \sum_{j=1, j \neq i}^{K} \lambda_{ij}^*(t), \quad \forall t \in [0, T^*], \tag{26}$$

  (iii) *the two parameter family $\mathcal{P}^*(t, s)$, $0 \leq s \leq t \leq T^*$, of transition matrices for C relative to $\mathbb{Q}^*$ satisfies the forward Kolmogorov equation*

$$\frac{d\mathcal{P}^*(t, s)}{ds} = \mathcal{P}^*(t, s)\Lambda^*(s), \quad \mathcal{P}^*(t, t) = \mathrm{Id},$$

and the backward Kolmogorov equation

$$\frac{d\mathcal{P}^*(t, s)}{dt} = -\Lambda^*(t)\mathcal{P}^*(t, s), \quad \mathcal{P}^*(s, s) = \mathrm{Id}.$$

It is clear that $\Lambda^*(t) = \Lambda$ for every $t \in [0, T^*]$ if and only if $\kappa_{kl} \equiv 0$ for all $k \neq l$. Letting $\phi_{ij}(t) = 1 + \kappa_{ij}(t)$, we obtain $\lambda_{ij}^*(t) = \phi_{ij}(t)\lambda_{ij}$.

Example 2.9 Suppose that $\kappa_{kl}(t) = v_k(t)$, for every $k, l \in \mathcal{K}$, $l \neq k$, and $t \in [0, T^*]$. Then we obtain

$$\Lambda^*(t) = U(t)\Lambda, \quad \forall t \in [0, T^*],$$

where $U(t)$ is a diagonal K-dimensional matrix, specifically,

$$U(t) = \mathrm{diag}\,[1 + v_1(t), \dots, 1 + v_K(t)].$$

This type of relation between the pricing and real measure was to the best of our knowledge first used in Jarrow, Lando, and Turnbull (1997), see p. 495 therein.

3 MARKOVIAN MODELS OF PORTFOLIO CREDIT RISK

In the remainder of this chapter we shall review some Markovian models of portfolio credit risk. We shall be primarily concerned with models of dependent defaults, as well as models of the portfolio loss process. However, in subsection 3.1, we shall describe briefly a model of credit migrations; for a much more comprehensive study of Markovian models of credit migrations we refer to chapter 12 in Bielecki and Rutkowski (2002) and to references therein. The models of dependent defaults discussed in the following sections may, in principle, be considered as special cases of the model of subsection 3.1.

3.1 Market model

We begin with a brief description of the Markovian market model that was studied in Bielecki et al. (2008), Bielecki, Vidozzi, and Vidozzi (2008) with view at valuation and hedging of basket credit instruments. This framework allows one to incorporate information relative to the dynamic evolution of credit ratings in the pricing of basket instruments. We begin with some notation.

As before we denote the underlying probability space by $(\Omega, \mathcal{G}, \mathbb{Q})$, where $\mathbb{Q}$ is here and henceforth a risk-neutral measure inferred from the market. We endow this space with filtration $\mathbb{G} := \mathbb{H} \vee \mathbb{F}$, which contains all information available to market agents. Specifically, the filtration $\mathbb{H}$ carries information about the evolution of credit events, such as changes in credit ratings or defaults of respective credit names. The filtration $\mathbb{F}$ is a reference filtration containing information pertaining to the evolution of relevant macroeconomic variables.

We consider N obligors (or credit names) and we assume that the current credit quality of each reference entity can be classified into $\mathcal{K} := \{1, 2, \ldots, K\}$ rating categories. By convention, the category K corresponds to default. Let X^l, $l = 1, 2, \ldots, N$ be processes on $(\Omega, \mathcal{G}, \mathbb{Q})$ taking values in the finite state space $\mathcal{K}$. The process X^l represents the evolution of credit ratings of the lth reference entity. We define the *default time* τ_l of the lth reference entity by setting

$$\tau_l = \inf\{t > 0 : X^l_t = K\} \tag{27}$$

We assume that the default state K is absorbing, so that for each name the default event can only occur once.

We denote by $X = (X^1, X^2, \ldots, X^N)$ the joint credit rating process of the portfolio of N credit names. The state space of X is $\mathcal{X} := \mathcal{K}^N$ and the elements of $\mathcal{X}$ will be denoted by $x = \{x^1, \ldots, x^N\}$. We postulate that the filtration $\mathbb{H}$ is the natural filtration of the process X and that the filtration $\mathbb{F}$ is generated by a $\mathbb{R}^n$ valued factor process, Y, representing the evolution of relevant economic variables, like short rate or equity price processes.

We assume that the process $M = (X, Y)$ is jointly Markov under $\mathbb{Q}$, so that we have, for every $0 \le t \le s$, $x \in \mathcal{X}$, and any set $\mathcal{Y}$ from the state space of Y,

$$\mathbb{Q}(X_s = x, Y_s \in \mathcal{Y} \mid \mathcal{H}_t \vee \mathcal{F}_t^Y) = \mathbb{Q}(X_s = x, Y_s \in \mathcal{Y} \mid X_t, Y_t). \qquad (28)$$

The process M is constructed as a Markov chain modulated by a Lévy process. We shall refer to X (Y) as the *Markov chain* (*Lévy*) component of M. Given $X_t = x$ and $Y_t = y$, the intensity matrix of the Markov chain component is given by $\Lambda_t = [\lambda(x, x'; y)]_{x' \in \mathcal{X}}$. The Lévy component satisfies the SDE:

$$dY_t = b(X_t, Y_t)\, dt + \sigma(X_t, Y_t)\, dW_t + \int_{\mathbb{R}^n} g(X_{t-}, Y_{t-}, y')\, N(dy', dt),$$

where, for a fixed $y \in \mathbb{R}^n$, $N(dy', dt)$ is a counting process with Lévy measure $v(x, y, dy')$ and $\sigma(x, y)$ satisfies $\sigma(x, y)\sigma(x, y)^\mathsf{T} = a(x, y)$. We provide the following structure to the generator of the process M.

$$Af(x, y) = (1/2) \sum_{i,j=1}^{n} a_{ij}(x, y)\partial_i \partial_j f(x, y) + \sum_{i=1}^{n} b_i(x, y)\partial_i f(x, y)$$

$$+ \int_{\mathbb{R}^n} \big(f(x, y + g(x, y, y')) - f(x, y) \big) v(x, y; dy') \qquad (29)$$

$$+ \sum_{x' \in \mathcal{X} \setminus \{x\}} \lambda(x, x'; y) f(x', y).$$

We stress that, within the present set-up, the current credit rating of the credit name l directly impacts the intensity of transition of the rating of the credit name l', and vice versa. This property, known as *frailty*, may contribute to default contagion.

Remark 3.1 (Valuation of Basket Credit Derivatives) The model described above can be used to price various basket credit derivatives. In particular, computing the fair spreads of such products involves evaluating conditional expectations, under the risk-neutral measure $\mathbb{Q}$, of some quantities related to the cash flows associated to each instrument. For example, the fair spread at time 0 of the CDO equity tranche is (we refer for details to Bielecki, Vidozzi, and Vidozzi (2006), and to section 3.1.2 for implementation issues):

$$\kappa_0 = \frac{1}{C_0} \mathrm{E}_{\mathbb{Q}}^{x,y} \Big(\int_0^T \beta_t d M_t^0 - \sum_{j=0}^{J} \beta_{t_j} .05(C_0 - M_{t_j}^0) \Big), \qquad (30)$$

and the fair spread at time 0 of a CDS index is

$$\eta_0 = \frac{\mathbb{E}_{\mathbb{Q}}^{x,y} \sum_{i=1}^{L} \beta_{\tau_i} (1 - \delta) H_T^i}{\mathbb{E}_{\mathbb{Q}}^{x,y} \sum_{j=0}^{J} \beta_{t_j} \sum_{i=1}^{N} \left(1 - H_{t_j}^i (1 - \delta)\right)}. \tag{31}$$

3.1.1 Markovian changes of measure

For applications like performing changes of numeraire (which can be useful for simplifying the evaluation of quantities of the form (30) or (31), see Bielecki et al. (2008), or switching between the statistical and a risk-neutral measure. In a situation where the above model $M = (X, Y)$ would in fact be given under the statistical measure, which for pricing purposes would then need to be changed into a risk-neutral measure, see Bielecki, Vidozzi, and Vidozzi (2008), it is important to be able to apply changes of measure to the model M, whilst preserving Markovianity.

Towards this end we briefly state some facts concerning Markovian changes of measure. Let M_t (such as $M = (X, Y)$ above) be an E valued Markov process under $\mathbb{P}$ with extended generator A (see Palmowski and Rolski 2002). In addition define the process

$$M_t^f := \frac{f(M_t)}{f(M_0)} \exp\left(-\int_0^t \frac{Af(M_s)}{f(M_s)} ds\right). \tag{32}$$

Definition 3.2 We say that a strictly positive function $f \in \mathcal{D}(A)$ is a good function if M_t^f is a genuine martingale with $\mathbb{E}_{\mathbb{P}}(M_t^f) = 1$.

Let $f \in \mathcal{D}(A)$ and h be a good function in $C(E)$ or $\mathcal{M}_b(E)$ and define the operator

$$A^h f = h^{-1} A(fh) - f A(h). \tag{33}$$

In view of Definition 3.2, process M^h may play the rôle of the Radon-Nikodym density between measure $\mathbb{Q}$ and the resulting measure, say $\mathbb{Q}^h$. We have the following result (cf. Palmowski and Rolski 2002).

Theorem 3.1 Let $\mathbb{Q}^h$ be the probability measure associated to the density process M_t^h. Then M_t is a Markov process under $\mathbb{Q}^h$ with extended generator $(A^h, \mathcal{D}(A))$.

We now apply the above theorem to our model. The domain of $\mathcal{D}(A)$ contains all functions $f(x, y)$ with compact support that are twice continuously differentiable with respect to y. Let h be a good function. By application of Theorem 3.1, the generator of M under $\mathbb{P}^h$ is given as (see Bielecki, Vidozzi, and Vidozzi 2008)

$$A^h f(x, y) = (1/2) \sum_{i,j=1}^{n} a_{ij}(x, y) \partial_i \partial_j f(x, y) + \sum_{i=1}^{n} b_i^h(x, y) \partial_i f(x, y)$$

$$+ \int_{\mathbb{R}^n} \left(f(x, y + g(x, y, y')) - f(x, y)\right) v^h(x, y; dy') + \sum_{x' \in \mathcal{X}} \lambda^h(x, x'; y) f(x', y),$$

where

$$b_i^h(x, y) = b_i(x, y) + \frac{1}{h(x, y)} \sum_{i, j=1}^{n} a_{ij}(x, y) \partial_j h(x, y),$$

$$v^h(x, y; dy') = \frac{h(x, y + g(x, y, y'))}{h(x, y)} v(x, y; dy'), \tag{34}$$

$$\lambda^h(x, x'; y) = \lambda(x, x'; y) \frac{h(x', y)}{h(x, y)}, \quad x \neq x', \quad \lambda^h(x, x; y) = -\sum_{x' \neq x} \lambda^h(x, x'; y).$$

3.1.2 Model Implementation

Expectations such as the ones appearing in the fair spread valuation formulas (30) or (31) above, can in principle be computed by numerical resolution of the related Kolmogorov valuation systems of reaction-diffusions equations, or, in the special case of a time-homogeneous Markov chain model, by numerical exponentiation of the model generator (see sections 3.2–3.2.1). However all these analytical methods are limited in practice to low-dimensional models by the curse of dimensionality. In general simulation methods are then the only viable alternative. Implementation of the above Markovian model via simulation will now be described in the special case where the dynamics of the factor process Y do not depend on the credit migrations process X. The general case appears to be much harder.

3.1.3 Specification of credit ratings transition intensities

In order to alleviate the simulation of the model we specify the credit migrations intensity measure λ in (29) to be of the following form:

$$\sum_{x' \in \mathcal{X} \setminus \{x\}} \lambda(x, x'; y) f(x', y) = \sum_{l=1}^{N} \sum_{\xi \in \mathcal{K}} \lambda^l(x, x_l^\xi; y) f(x_l^\xi, y), \tag{35}$$

where we write $x_l^\xi = (x^1, x^2, \ldots, x^{l-1}, \xi, x^{l+1}, \ldots, x^N)$.

Note that the model specified by (35) does not allow for simultaneous jumps of the components X^l and $X^{l'}$ for $l \neq l'$. In other words, the ratings of different credit names may not change simultaneously. The advantage is that, for the purpose of simulation of paths of process X, rather than dealing with $\mathcal{X} \times \mathcal{X}$ intensity matrix $[\lambda(x, x'; y)]$, we shall deal with N intensity matrices $[\lambda^l(x, x_l^\xi; y)]$, each of dimension $\mathcal{K} \times \mathcal{K}$ (for any fixed y).

We now provide further structure to the generator of the Markov chain component of the joint process $M = (X, Y)$ and specify a general functional form for its transition intensities. We shall then briefly describe a recursive procedure for simulating the evolution of the process X.

Because we need to simulate the joint process (X, Y), it is important to specify its form in such a way to avoid unnecessary computational complexity. As noted earlier, the structure of the generator A that we postulate makes it so that simulation of the evolution of process X reduces to recursive simulation of the evolution of processes X^l, whose state spaces are only of size K each. In order to facilitate simulations even further, we also postulate that each migration process X^l behaves like a birth-and-death process with absorption at default, and with possible jumps to default from every intermediate state. In addition, we shall assume that the factor process, Y, is independent of X. Conditional upon $(X_t, Y_t) = (x, y)$, the infinitesimal generator governing the evolution of the credit ratings of the lth name is the sub-stochastic matrix:

$$
\begin{array}{cccccc}
 & 1 & 2 & 3 & \cdots & K-1 & K \\
1 & \begin{pmatrix} \lambda^l_{1,1} & \lambda^l_{1,2} & 0 & \cdots & 0 & \lambda^l_{1,K} \\
2 & \lambda^l_{2,1} & \lambda^l_{2,2} & \lambda^l_{2,3} & \cdots & 0 & \lambda^l_{2,K} \\
3 & 0 & \lambda^l_{3,2} & \lambda^l_{3,3} & \cdots & 0 & \lambda^l_{3,K} \\
 & \vdots & \vdots & \vdots & \ddots & \vdots & \vdots \\
K-1 & 0 & 0 & 0 & \cdots & \lambda^l_{K-1,K-1} & \lambda^l_{K-1,K} \\
K & 0 & 0 & 0 & \cdots & 0 & 0 \end{pmatrix}
\end{array},
$$

where, with a slight change of notation, $\lambda^l_{x^l,\xi} = \lambda^l_{x^l,\xi}(x, y) = \lambda^l(x, x^\xi_l; y)$. The functional form of the transition intensities should reflect the specific characteristics of the instruments we need to price and should be chosen to obtain the best possible fit in the calibration phase.

3.1.4 Simulation algorithm

In general, a simulation of the evolution of the process X entails high computational costs, as the the cardinality of the state space of X is equal to K^N. Thus, for example, in case of $K = 18$ rating categories, as in Moody's ratings, and in case of a portfolio of $N = 100$ credit ratings, the state space has 18^{100} elements. However, the specific assumptions on the structure of the generator allow to simulate the process in a recursive fashion, which has a relatively low computational complexity. We consider here simulations of sample paths over a generic time interval, $[t_1, t_2]$, where $0 \le t_1 < t_2$, and assume that the time t_1 state of the process (X, Y) is (x, y). Generating one sample path will, in general, involve the following steps:

Step 1: in step 1, a sample path of the process Y is simulated. Recall that the dynamics of the factor process are described by the SDE

$$
\begin{aligned}
dY_t &= b(Y_t)\, dt + \sigma(Y_t)\, dW_t + \int_{\mathbb{R}^n} g(Y_{t-}, y')\, N(dy', dt) \\
Y_{t_1} &= y
\end{aligned}
$$

Any standard procedure can be used to simulate a sample path of Y (the reader is referred, for example, to Cont and Tankov 2003). We denote by $\widehat{Y}$ the simulated sample path of Y.

Step 2: generate a sample path of X on the interval $[t_1, t_2]$.

Step 2.1: simulate the first jump time of the process X in the time interval $[t_1, t_2]$. Towards this end, draw from a unit exponential distribution. We denote by $\widehat{\eta}_1$ the value of the first draw. The simulated value of the first jump time, τ, is then given by:

$$\tau = \inf\left\{ t > t_1 : \int_{t_1}^{t} \lambda(x, \widehat{Y}_u)\, du \geq \widehat{\eta}_1 \right\},$$

where

$$\lambda(x, \widehat{Y}_t) := -\sum_{i=1}^{N} \lambda_{x^i, x^i}^{i}(x, \widehat{Y}_t)$$

and

$$\lambda_{x^l, x^l}^{l}(x, \widehat{Y}_t) = -\lambda_{x^l, x^l-1}^{l}(x, \widehat{Y}_t) - \lambda_{x^l, x^l+1}^{l}(x, \widehat{Y}_t) - \lambda_{x^l, K}^{l}(x, \widehat{Y}_t).$$

If $\tau > t_2$ return to step 1, otherwise go to step 2.2.

Step 2.2: simulate which component of the vector process X jumps at time τ, by drawing from the conditional distribution:

$$(X_\tau^l \neq X_{\tau-}^l) = -\frac{\lambda_{x^l, x^l}^{l}(x, \widehat{Y}_\tau)}{\lambda(x, \widehat{Y}_\tau)} \tag{36}$$

Recall that $\lambda_{x^l, x^l}^{l}(x, \widehat{Y}_t) = 0$ if $x^l = K$, since K is an absorbing state.

Step 2.3: assume the ith obligor jumps at τ. Simulate the direction of the jump by drawing from the conditional distribution

$$Q^i(X_\tau^i = \xi) = -\frac{\lambda_{x^i, \xi}^{i}(x, \widehat{Y}_\tau)}{\lambda_{x^i, x^i}^{i}(x, \widehat{Y}_\tau)} \tag{37}$$

where

$$\xi = \{x^i - 1; x^i + 1; K\}$$

Step 2.4: update the state of X and set $t_1 = \tau$. Repeat steps 2.1-2.3 on $[t_1, t_2]$ until $\tau > t_2$

Step 3: calculate the simulated value of a relevant functional. For instance, assume that Y represents the short rate process, and is used as a discount factor, i.e $\int_0^t Y_t = -\ln B_t$. In order to compute the protection leg of a CDS index, one would evaluate

$$\sum_{i=1}^{L} \frac{B_{\tau_i}}{B_t}(1 - \delta)(H_T^i - H_t^i)(\omega)$$

at each run ω, and obtain the Monte Carlo estimate by averaging over all sample paths.

Remark 3.3 An important issue in regard to simulation is *variance reduction*. Importance sampling is often regarded as the method of choice when it comes to variance reduction. Importance sampling and related particle methods for Markovian models of portfolio credit risk (in the Homogeneous Groups Model of section 3.2 particularly) are dealt with in Carmona and Crépey (2008).

3.2 Homogeneous groups model

We now describe in some detail a more specific version of the previous model, considered for different purposes by various authors in Bielecki, Crépey, and Jeanblanc (2008); Carmona and Crépey (2008); Frey and Backhaus (2008b); Herbertsson (2007a), among others. In this specification of the model, there is no factor process Y involved. We thus deal with a continuous-time Markov Chain denoted in this subsection by $\mathcal{N}$ (cf. X above), relative to the filtration and $\mathbb{F} = \mathbb{F}^{\mathcal{N}}$.

More precisely, a pool of n credit names is organized in d homogeneous groups of $(\nu - 1)$ obligors (so $n = (\nu - 1)d$, assuming $\frac{n}{d}$ integer), and N^l represents the number of defaulted obligors in the lth group (instead of X^l representing the credit rating of obligor l previously; so the interpretation of the Markov chain has changed, but the mathematical structure of the model is preserved). Moreover we assume that the N^l's can only jump one at a time *and by one*, so that we in fact deal with a d-variate Markov point process $\mathcal{N} = (N^1, \cdots, N^d)$. For each l, the ($\mathbb{F}$-)intensity of N^l is assumed to be of the form

$$\lambda^l(\mathcal{N}_t) = (\nu - 1 - N^l_t)\widetilde{\lambda}^l(\mathcal{N}_t), \tag{38}$$

for an *aggregated intensity function* $\lambda^l = \lambda^l(\iota)$, and *pre-default individual* intensity function $\widetilde{\lambda}^l(\iota)$, where $\iota = (i_1, \cdots, i_d) \in \mathcal{I} = \{0, 1, \cdots, \nu - 1\}^d$. We thus deal with a d-variate Markov point process $\mathcal{N} = (N^1, \cdots, N^d)$.

Since we assume that there are no common jumps between processes N^l, so the jump intensities λ^l are in one-to-one correspondence with the generator $\varLambda$ of $\mathcal{N}$, which consists of a $\nu^d \otimes \nu^d$ matrix $\varLambda$ (a very sparse matrix, since the components of $\mathcal{N}$ may only jump by one and only one at a time).

For $d = 1$, we recover the so called *Local Intensity Model* (birth-and-death process stopped at level n) used by Laurent, Cousin, and Fermanian (2008), Cont and Minca (2008) or Herbertsson (2007a) for modelling a credit portfolio cumulative default process N. This model, which will be intensively used in sections 4.1–4.2, can be considered as the analogue for credit derivatives of the local volatility model for equity and equity index derivatives (analogous in the sense that at any given time in any loss derivatives model, there exists a local intensity model with the same marginals for the portfolio loss process, see Cont and Minca (2008) and Gyöngy (1986).

At the other end of the spectrum, for $d = n$ (i.e. when each group has only a single element), we are in effect modeling the vector of default indicator processes $H = (H^i)_{1 \leq i \leq n}$ of the pool.

As d varies between 1 and n, we thus get a variety of models of credit risk, ranging from pure 'top-down' models for $d = 1$, to pure 'bottom-up' models for $d = n$ (see Bielecki, Crépey, and Jeanblanc (2008). Introducing parsimonious parameterizations of the intensities allows one to account for inhomogeneity between groups, and/or for defaults contagion.

Other examples related to intensities as in (38) can be found in section 2.3 and section 2.5 in Backhaus (2008), where a portfolio with 125 obligors is split in first three and then six subportfolios. Both examples use intensities similar to those in equation (38), with the aim to price CDO-tranches.

3.2.1 Pricing in the homogeneous groups model

Since $\mathcal{N}$ is a Markov process and the portfolio cumulative default process N is a function of $\mathcal{N}$, the model price process of a (stylized) loss derivative (protection leg of a CDO tranche, say) with payoff $\phi(N_T)$ writes, for $t \in [0, T]$:

$$\Pi_t = \mathbb{E}(\phi(N_T)|\mathcal{F}_t) = u(t, \mathcal{N}_t), \tag{39}$$

where $u(t, \iota)$ or $u_\iota(t)$ for $t \in [0, T]$ and $\iota \in \mathcal{I} = I^d$, is the *pricing function* (system of time-functionals u_ι), solution to the following *pricing equation* (system of ODEs) with generator Λ:

$$(\partial_t + \Lambda)u = 0 \text{ on } [0, T),$$

with terminal condition $u_\iota(T) = \phi(\iota)$, for $\iota \in \mathcal{I}$.

Likewise, the groups losses distribution at time t, that is, $q_\iota(t) = \mathbb{Q}(\mathcal{N}_t = \iota)$ for $t \in [0, T]$ and $\iota \in \mathcal{I}$, can be characterized in terms of the associated forward Kolmogorov equations (see e.g. Carmona and Crépey 2008).

These pricing and transition probability backward and forward Kolmogorov equations can then be solved by various means, like numerical matrix exponentiation (since the model is time homogeneous, see Appendix 5.4).

However, even if the matrix Λ is very sparse, its size is prohibitive in most cases as far as deterministic numerical methods are concerned. For instance, in the case of $d = 5$ groups of $\nu - 1 = 25$ names, one gets $\nu^{2d} = 26^{10}$. So for high values of d, Monte Carlo methods as of section 3.1.4 appear to be the only viable computational alternative. Appropriate variance reduction techniques may help in this regard (cf. Remark 3.3).

3.3 Markov copulas

Modelling of stochastic dependence between evolutions of credit migration processes (default processes, in particular) in a pool of credit names is of key importance of course. In the Markovian model presented in the previous section, the dependence was modelled in a way that did not, automatically, guarantee that desired marginal distributions (of credit migration processes of individual obligors) are preserved. In this section we shall present a methodology that, in the Markovian framework, allows for construction of a multivariate process with given univariate marginals.

For mathematical details pertaining to this section we refer to Bielecki, Jakubowski, Vidozzi, and Vidozzi (2008).

To simplify notation we shall only consider the case of bivariate Markov chains. The general multivariate case can be treated accordingly (it is even possible to treat the case of a general joint Markov process $M = (X, Y)$ as of section 3.1, see Bielecki et al. (2008)).

Given a bivariate processes $Z = (X, Y)$, which is a finite Markov chain with respect to to its natural filtration $\mathbb{F}^Z = \mathbb{F}^{X,Y}$, one is naturally confronted with the following two questions, which we shall address in this section:

(Q1): what are the sufficient and necessary conditions on the infinitesimal generator of Z so that the components X and Y are Markov chains with respect to their natural filtrations?

(Q2): how do we construct a bivariate Markov chain, whose components are themselves Markov chains w.r.t their natural filtration and have desired infinitesimal characteristics?

We denote by $\mathcal{S}$ and $\mathcal{O}$ two finite sets. Let $Z = (X, Y)$ denote a two-dimensional Markov chain on $\mathcal{Z} = \mathcal{S} \times \mathcal{O}$, with generator function $A^Z(t) = [\lambda_{jk}^{ih}(t)]_{i,j\in\mathcal{S},k,h\in\mathcal{O}}$. Consider the following condition
Condition (M)

$$\sum_{k\in\mathcal{O}} \lambda_{jk}^{ih}(t) = \sum_{k\in\mathcal{O}} \lambda_{jk}^{ih'}(t), \quad \forall h, h' \in \mathcal{O}, \forall i, j, \in \mathcal{S}, i \neq j,$$

and

$$\sum_{j\in\mathcal{S}} \lambda_{jk}^{ih}(t) = \sum_{j\in\mathcal{S}} \lambda_{jk}^{i'h}(t), \quad \forall i, i' \in \mathcal{S}, \forall k, h \in \mathcal{O} \; h \neq k.$$

The following proposition addresses the sufficiency part in question (Q1),

Proposition 3.2 *Suppose that condition (M) holds, and define*

$$f_j^i(t) := \sum_{k\in\mathcal{O}} \lambda_{jk}^{ih}(t), \quad i, j \in \mathcal{S}, i \neq j, \quad f_i^i(t) = - \sum_{j\in\mathcal{S}, j\neq i} f_j^i(t), \quad \forall i \in \mathcal{S},$$

and

$$g_k^h(t) := \sum_{j\in\mathcal{S}} \lambda_{jk}^{ih}(t), \quad k, h \in \mathcal{O}, h \neq k, \quad g_h^h(t) = - \sum_{k\in\mathcal{O}, k\neq h} g_k^h(t), \quad \forall h \in \mathcal{O}.$$

Then the components X and Y of the Markov chain Z are Markov chains with respect to their natural filtrations with generator functions $A^X(t) = [f_j^i(t)]_{i,j\in\mathcal{S}}$ and $A^Y(t) = [g_k^h(t)]_{k,h\in\mathcal{O}}$, respectively.

For the necessity part of question (Q1) we have

Proposition 3.3 *For the components X and Y of the Markov chain Z to be Markov chains with respect to their natural filtrations, with generator functions $A^X(t) = [f_j^i(t)]_{i,j\in\mathcal{S}}$ and $A^Y(t) = [g_k^h(t)]_{k,h\in\mathcal{O}}$, respectively, it is necessary that the following conditions hold for almost all $t \geq 0$, $\mathbb{Q} - a.s.$:*

$$\left({}^{o_x}\!\Lambda^{ij}\right)_t^{P_x} = \int_0^t \mathbb{1}_{\{X_{u-}=i\}} f_j^i(u)du, \tag{40}$$

$$\left({}^{o_y}\!\Gamma^{hk}\right)_t^{P_y} = \int_0^t \mathbb{1}_{\{Y_{u-}=i\}} g_k^h(u)du, \tag{41}$$

where ${}^{o_x}(\cdot)\ [(\cdot)^{P_x}]$ and ${}^{o_y}(\cdot)\ [(\cdot)^{P_y}]$ denote the optional [predictable] projection on $\mathbb{F}^X$ and $\mathbb{F}^Y$ respectively, and where

$$\Lambda_t^{ij} = \int_0^t \sum_{k\in\mathcal{O}}\sum_{h\in\mathcal{O}} \mathbb{1}_{\{X_{u-}=i,Y_{u-}=h\}}\lambda_{jk}^{ih}(u)du$$

and

$$\Gamma_t^{hk} = \int_0^t \sum_{j\in\mathcal{S}}\sum_{i\in\mathcal{S}} \mathbb{1}_{\{X_{u-}=i,Y_{u-}=h\}}\lambda_{jk}^{ih}(u)du.$$

The following corollary addresses question (Q2),

Corollary 3.4 *Consider two Markov chains X and Y, with respect to their own filtrations, and with values in $\mathcal{S}$ and $\mathcal{O}$, respectively. Suppose that their respective generators are $A^X(t) = [a_j^i(t)]_{i,j\in\mathcal{S}}$ and $A^Y(t) = [\beta_k^h(t)]_{h,k\in\mathcal{O}}$. Next, consider the system of equations in the unknowns $\lambda_{jk}^{ih}(t)$, where $i, j \in \mathcal{S}, h, k \in \mathcal{O}$ and $(i,h)\ne(j,k)$:*

$$\sum_{k\in\mathcal{O}}\lambda_{jk}^{ih}(t) = a_j^i(t),\ \forall h\in\mathcal{O},\ \forall i,j\in\mathcal{S},\ i\ne j \tag{42}$$

$$\sum_{j\in\mathcal{S}}\lambda_{jk}^{ih}(t) = \beta_k^h(t),\ \forall i\in\mathcal{S},\ \forall h,k\in\mathcal{O},\ h\ne k. \tag{43}$$

Suppose that the above system admits solution such that the matrix function $A(t) = [\lambda_{jk}^{ih}(t)]_{i,j\in\mathcal{S},k,h\in\mathcal{O}}$, with

$$\lambda_{ih}^{ih}(t) = -\sum_{(j,k)\in\mathcal{S}\times\mathcal{O},(j,k)\ne(i,h)}\lambda_{jk}^{ih}(t), \tag{44}$$

properly defines an infinitesimal generator function of a Markov chain with values in $\mathcal{S}\times\mathcal{O}$. Consider, a bivariate Markov chain $Z:=(Z_1, Z_2)$ on $\mathcal{S}\times\mathcal{O}$ with generator function $A^Z(t) = A(t)$. Then, the components Z_1 and Z_2 are Markov chains with respect to to their own filtrations, and their generators are $A^{Z_1}(t) = A^X(t)$ and $A^{Z_2}(t) = A^Y(t)$.

Note that, typically, system (42)–(43) contains many more unknowns than equations. In fact, given that cardinalities of $\mathcal{S}$ and $\mathcal{O}$ are $K_{\mathcal{S}}$ and $K_{\mathcal{O}}$, respectively, the system consists of $K_{\mathcal{S}}(K_{\mathcal{S}}-1)+K_{\mathcal{O}}(K_{\mathcal{O}}-1)$ equations in $K_{\mathcal{S}}K_{\mathcal{O}}(K_{\mathcal{S}}K_{\mathcal{O}}-1)$ unknowns.

Thus, in principle, one can create several bivariate Markov chains Z with the given margins X and Y. Thus, indeed, the system (42)–(43) essentially serves as a 'copula' between the Markovian margins X, Y and the bivariate Markov chain Z. This observation leads to the following definition,

Definition 3.4 A *Markov copula* between the Markov chains X and Y is any solution to system (42)–(43) such that the matrix function $A(t) = [\lambda_{jk}^{ih}(t)]_{i,j \in \mathcal{S}, k, h \in \mathcal{O}}$, with $\lambda_{ih}^{ih}(t)$ given in (44), properly defines an infinitesimal generator function of a Markov chain with values in $\mathcal{S} \times \mathcal{O}$.

Different Markov copulas will entail different dependence structure between the margins X and Y.

Markovian Changes of Measure

For pricing purposes the probability $\mathbb{P}$ above typically denotes the statistical probability, which needs to be changed to the EMM. Typically, the Radon-Nikodym density is chosen in such a way that the resulting (risk-neutral) default probabilities are consistent with the term structure of CDS spreads. In addition, we require that the process Z, which is Markovian under the statistical measure, is also Markovian under the pricing measure. As a consequence, such change of measure must be chosen with some care.

In the case of a finite state Markov chain, Theorem 3.1 yields the following corollary (cf. Palmowski and Rolski 2002).

Corollary 3.5 *Let Z_t be a finite state Markov chain on $\mathcal{K}$ with cardinality K and generator $A = a_{ij}$. In addition let $h = (h_1, \ldots, h_K)$ be a positive vector. Then Z_t is a Markov process under $\mathbb{Q}^h$ with generator $A^h = [a_{ij} h_j h_i^{-1}]$.*

Remark 3.5 We note that in case of Markov chains the formula for the Markovian change of measure presented in Proposition 2.12 (cf. formula (25)) appears to be more general than the change of measure resulting from the theory of Palmowski and Rolski presented in Palmowski and Rolski (2002), and leading to $A^h = [a_{ij} h_j h_i^{-1}]$. However, for the purpose of the following section about ratings triggered bonds, this less general result is sufficient.

3.3.1 *Application to ratings-triggered step-up bonds*

This application is taken from Bielecki, Vidozzi, and Vidozzi (2008), to which we refer the reader for more examples of application of the above theory to valuation and hedging of credit derivatives. Even though the ratings-triggered step-up bonds are not credit derivatives per se, we nevertheless give a brief account of their valuation, as the techniques exploited in this case may as well be used for valuation of credit derivatives whose cash flows may depend on history of credit ratings assigned to an obligor by various rating agencies.

Ratings-triggered step-up bonds were issued by some European telecom companies in the recent 6–7 years. As of now, to our knowledge, these products are not traded in baskets, however they are of interest because they offer protection against credit events other than defaults. In particular, ratings-triggered corporate step-up bonds (step-up bonds for short) are corporate coupon issues for which the coupon payment depends on the issuer's credit quality: in principle, the coupon payment increases when the credit quality of the issuer declines. In practice, for such bonds, credit quality is reflected in credit ratings assigned to the issuer by at least one credit ratings agency (Moody's-KMV or Standard & Poor's). The provisions linking the cash flows of the step-up bonds to the credit rating of the issuer have different step amounts and different rating event triggers. In some cases, a step-up of the coupon requires a downgrade to the trigger level by both rating agencies. In other cases, there are step-up triggers for actions of each rating agency. Here, a downgrade by one agency will trigger an increase in the coupon regardless of the rating from the other agency. Provisions also vary with respect to step-down features which, as the name suggests, trigger a lowering of the coupon if the company regains its original rating after a downgrade. In general, there is no step-down below the initial coupon for ratings exceeding the initial rating.

Let R_t stand for some indicator of credit quality at time t (note that in this case, the process R may be composed of two, or more, distinct rating processes). Assume that t_i, $i = 1, 2, \ldots, n$ are coupon payment dates. In this chapter we assume the convention that coupon paid at date t_n depends only on the rating history through date t_{n-1}, that is: $c_n = c(R_t, t \leq t_{n-1})$ are the coupon payments. In other words, we assume that no accrual convention is in force.

Assuming that the bond's notional amount is 1, the cumulative discounted cash flow of the step-up bond is (as usual we assume that the current time is 0):

$$(1 - H_T)\beta_T + \int_{(0,T]} (1 - H_u)\beta_u \, dC_u + \beta_\tau Z_\tau H_T, \tag{45}$$

where $C_t = \sum_{t_i \leq t} c_i$, τ is the bond's default time, $H_t = \mathbb{1}_{\tau \leq t}$, and where Z_t is a (predictable) recovery process.

Pricing ratings triggered step-up bonds via simulation

Here, using our results on Markov copulas, we shall apply a simulation approach to pricing ratings triggered step-up bonds.

Let us consider a ratings triggered step-up bond issued by an obligor XYZ. Recall that, typically, cashflows associated with a step-up bond depend on ratings assigned to XYZ by both Moody's Investors Service (Moody's in what follows) and Standard & Poor's (S&P in what follows). Thus, a straightforward way to model joint credit migrations would be to consider a credit migration process K such that $R_t = (M_t, SP_t)$, where M_t and SP_t denote the time t credit rating assigned to XYZ by Moody's and SP_t, respectively. We assume that process M is a time-homogeneous Markov chain w.r.t. its natural filtration, under the statistical probability $\mathbb{P}$, and that its state space is $\mathcal{K} = \{1, 2, \ldots, K\}$. Likewise, we assume that process SP is a time-homogeneous Markov chain w.r.t. its natural filtration, under the statistical probability $\mathbb{P}$, and that its state space is $\mathcal{K} = \{1, 2, \ldots, K\}$.

Typically, we are only provided with individual statistical characteristics of each of the processes M and SP. Thus, in a sense, we know the marginal distributions of the joint process R under the measure $\mathbb{P}$ (where M and SP are considered as the 'univariate' margins). The crucial issue is thus the appropriate modelling of dependence between processes M and SP. In particular, we want to model dependence, under $\mathbb{P}$, between M and SP so that the joint process R is a time-homogeneous Markov chain, and so that the components M and SP are time-homogeneous Markov chains with given $\mathbb{P}$-generators, say A^M and A^{SP}, respectively. Thus, essentially, we need to model a $\mathbb{P}$-generator matrix, say A^R, so that process R is a time-homogeneous Markov chain with $\mathbb{P}$-generator A^R and that processes M and SP are time-homogeneous Markov chains with $\mathbb{P}$-generators A^M and A^{SP}. We can of course deal with this problem using the theory of Markov copulas.

Towards this end, we fix an underlying probability space $(\Omega, \mathcal{F}, \mathbb{P})$. On this space we consider two univariate Markov chains M and SP, with given infinitesimal $\mathbb{P}$-generators $A^M = [a_{ij}^M]$ and $A^{SP} = [a_{hk}^{SP}]$, respectively. Next, we consider the system equations in variables

$$\sum_{k \in \mathcal{K}} a_{ih,jk}^R = a_{ij}^M, \ \forall i, j \in \mathcal{K}, i \neq j, \ \forall h \in \mathcal{K}, \tag{46}$$

$$\sum_{j \in \mathcal{K}_1} a_{ih,jk}^R = a_{hk}^{SP}, \ \forall h, k, \in \mathcal{K}, h \neq k, \ \forall i \in \mathcal{K}. \tag{47}$$

Now, provided that the system (46)–(47) has a positive solution, then it follows from Corollary 3.4 that resulting matrix[2] $A^R = [a_{ih,jk}^R]_{i,j \in \mathcal{K}_1, h,k \in \mathcal{K}_2}$ satisfies conditions for a $\mathbb{P}-$generator matrix of a bivariate time-homogenous Markov chain, say $R = (R^1, R^2)$ whose components take values in finite state spaces $\mathcal{K}_1$ and $\mathcal{K}_2$ with cardinalities K_1 and K_2, respectively, and, more importantly, they are Markov chains with the same distributions as M and SP under under $\mathbb{P}$. Thus, indeed, the system (46)–(47) essentially serves as a Markov copula between the Markovian margins M, SP and the bivariate Markov chain R.

Note that, typically, the system (46)–(47) contains many more variables than equations. Thus, one can create several bivariate Markov chains R with the given margins M and SP. In financial applications this feature leaves a lot of room for various modelling options and for calibration of the model. For example, as observed by Lando and Mortensen (2005) although the ratings assigned by S&P and Moody's to the same company do not necessarily coincide, split ratings are rare and are usually only observed in short time intervals. This feature can easily be modelled using the Markovian copula system (46)–(47) via imposing side constraints for the unknowns $a_{ih,jk}^R$'s. In order to model such observed behaviour of the joint rating process, we thus impose additional constraints on the variables in the system (46)–(47). Specifically, we postulate that

---

[2] System (46)–(47) does not include diagonal elements of A^R. These elements are obtained as $a_{ih,ih}^R = -\sum_{(j,k) \in \mathcal{K}} a_{ih,jk}^R$.

$$a_{ih,jk}^{R} = \begin{cases} 0, & \text{if } i \neq j \text{ and } h \neq k \text{ and } j \neq k, \\ \alpha \min(a_{ij}^{M}, a_{hk}^{SP}), & \text{if } i \neq j \text{ and } h \neq k \text{ and } j = k, \end{cases} \tag{48}$$

where $\alpha \in [0, 1]$ is a modelling parameter. Using constraint (48) we can easily solve system (46)–(47) (in this case the system actually becomes fully decoupled) and we can obtain the generator of the joint process. The interpretation of constraint (48) is the following: the components M and SP of the process R migrate according to their marginal laws, but they tend to join, that is, they tend to both take the same values. The strength of such tendency is measured by the parameter α. When $\alpha = 0$ then, in fact, the two components are independent processes; when $\alpha = 1$ the intensity of both components migrating simultaneously to the same rating category is maximum (given the specified functional form for the intensities of common jumps).

For pricing purposes the statistical probability measure is changed to the EMM. Typically, the Radon-Nikodym density is chosen in such a way that the resulting (risk-neutral) default probabilities are consistent with the term structure of CDS spreads. In addition, we require that the process R, which is Markovian under the statistical measure, is also Markovian under the pricing measure.

We recall that $A^R = [a_{ih,jk}^R]$ is the generator of R under the statistical measure $\mathbb{P}$. In view of Corollary 3.5, or, more generally, in view of formula (25) in Proposition 2.12, given a vector $h = [h_{11}, \cdots, h_{KK}] \in \mathbb{R}^{K^2}$, we can change statistical measure $\mathbb{P}$ to an equivalent 'risk-neutral' measure $\mathbb{Q}$ in such a way that process R is a time-homogeneous Markov chain under $\mathbb{Q}$, and its $\mathbb{Q}$-infinitesimal generator is given by

$$\widetilde{A}^R = [\widetilde{a}_{ih,jk}],$$

where $\widetilde{a}_{ih,jk} = a_{ih,jk}\frac{h_{jk}}{h_{ih}}$ for $ih \neq jk$ and $\widetilde{a}_{ih,jk} = -\sum_{jk\neq ih} a_{ih,jk}\frac{h_{jk}}{h_{ih}}$ for $ih = jk$.

Remark 3.6 Note that, although the change of measure preserves Markov property of the joint process R, its components may not be Markov (in their natural filtration) under the new probability measure. This however is not an issue for us, as all we need to conduct computations is the Markov property of the joint process R under the new measure.

An arbitrary choice of vector h may lead to a heavy parametrization of the pricing model. We suggest that the vector h_{ij} be chosen as follows:

$$h_{ij} = \exp(a_1 i + a_2 j), \quad \forall i, j \in \mathcal{K},$$

where a_1 and a_2 are parameters to be calibrated. It turns out, as the calibration results provided in Bielecki, Vidozzi, and Vidozzi (2008) indicate, that this is a good choice.

Remark 3.7 Note that the formalism of Markovian copulas can be exploited in a wide range of applications. See for instance Crépey Jeanblanc, and Zargari (2009) for a recent use in the modelling of *counterparty credit risk*.

4 MULTIVARIATE PHASE-TYPE DISTRIBUTIONS AND MATRIX-ANALYTICAL METHODS

In the remaining sections of this chapter we consider the intensity-based models for default contagion (with constant coefficients) which are studied in Herbertsson (2007a), Herbertsson and Rootzén (2008), Herbertsson (2008a, 2008b, 2007b). These intensity-based models are reinterpreted in terms of a time-homogeneous Markov jump process, a so-called multivariate phase-type distribution, introduced in Assaf et al. (1984). The translation makes it possible to use a matrix-analytic approach to derive practical formulas for all quantities that we want to study. To be more specific, we present convenient analytical formulas for multivariate default and survival distributions, conditional multivariate distributions, marginal default distributions, multivariate default densities, default correlations, and expected default times. Furthermore, computationally tractable closed-form expressions for credit derivatives such as synthetic CDO tranche spreads, index CDS spreads, k^{th}-to-default swap spreads, and single-name CDS spreads can also be obtained. However, these formulas are omitted in this article and we instead refer to the details in the literature.

Subsection 4.1 is devoted to inhomogeneous portfolios, whilst subsection 4.2 deals with homogeneous portfolios. Section 5 presents numerical results for some of the above quantities, in a homogeneous portfolio calibrated against CDO tranches from the iTraxx Europe series.

Note that multivariate phase-type distributions (MPH) can be viewed as a special case of the Markov models presented in section 2 and section 3. However, the practical formulas that can be derived in MPH settings, used particulary in reliability and queuing theory, has made MPH-distributions and matrix-analytical approaches grow into a subject of their own, see e.g. Asmussen (2000, 2003), Assaf et al. (1984), Neuts (1981, 1989), and (Rolski et al. 1998).

4.1 Inhomogeneous portfolios

In this subsection we study inhomogeneous credit portfolios. First, subsection 4.1.1 presents an intensity-based model with intuitive and explicit contagion effects. This model is then reformulated into a time-homogeneous Markov jump process which is used in subsections 4.1.2–4.1.4 in order to find practical formulas for multivariate default and survival distributions, conditional multivariate distributions, marginal default distributions, multivariate default densities, default correlations, and expected default times.

Subsection 4.1.6 shortly discuss the calibration of the parameters in our framework. Finally, subsection 4.1.7 outlines alternative parameterizations of the model presented in subsection 4.1.1

4.1.1 *Intensity based models reinterpreted as Markov jump processes*

For the default times $\tau_1, \tau_2 \ldots, \tau_m$, define the point process $N_{t,i} = 1_{\{\tau_i \leq t\}}$ and introduce the filtrations

$$\mathcal{F}_{t,i} = \sigma\left(N_{s,i}; s \leq t\right), \quad \mathcal{F}_t = \bigvee_{i=1}^{m} \mathcal{F}_{t,i}.$$

Let $\lambda_{t,i}$ be the $\mathcal{F}_t$-intensity of the point processes $N_{t,i}$. Below, we will for convenience often omit the filtration and just write intensity or 'default intensity'. With a further extension of language we will sometimes also write that the default times $\{\tau_i\}$ have intensities $\{\lambda_{t,i}\}$. The model studied in this section is specified by requiring that the default intensities have the following form,

$$\lambda_{t,i} = a_i + \sum_{j \neq i} b_{i,j} 1_{\{\tau_j \leq t\}}, \qquad t \leq \tau_i, \tag{49}$$

and $\lambda_{t,i} = 0$ for $t > \tau_i$. Further, $a_i \geq 0$ and $b_{i,j}$ are constants such that $\lambda_{t,i}$ is non-negative.

The financial interpretation of (49) is that the default intensities are constant, except at the times when defaults occur: then the default intensity for obligor i jumps by an amount $b_{i,j}$ if it is obligor j which has defaulted. Thus a positive $b_{i,j}$ means that obligor i is put at higher risk by the default of obligor j, while a negative $b_{i,j}$ means that obligor i in fact benefits from the default of j, and finally $b_{i,j} = 0$ if obligor i is unaffected by the default of j.

Equation (49) determines the default times through their intensities as well as their joint distribution. However, it is by no means obvious how to find these expressions. Here we will use the following observation, proved in Herbertsson and Rootzén (2008).

Proposition 4.1 *There exists a Markov jump process $(Y_t)_{t \geq 0}$ on a finite state space* **E** *and a family of sets $\{\Delta_i\}_{i=1}^{m}$ such that the stopping times*

$$\tau_i = \inf\{t > 0 : Y_t \in \Delta_i\}, \qquad i = 1, 2, \ldots, m, \tag{50}$$

have intensities (49). Hence, any distribution derived from the multivariate stochastic vector $(\tau_1, \tau_2, \ldots, \tau_m)$ can be obtained from $\{Y_t\}_{t \geq 0}$.

The joint distribution of $(\tau_1, \tau_2, \ldots, \tau_m)$ is sometimes called a multivariate phase-type distribution (MPH), and was first introduced in Assaf et al. (1984). Such constructions have largely been developed for queueing theory and reliability applications, see e.g. Asmussen (2000) and Assaf et al. (1984). In this section, Proposition 4.1 is throughout used for computing distributions. However, we still use equation (49) to describe the dependencies in a credit portfolio since it is more compact and intuitive.

Each state j in E is of the form $j = \{j_1, \ldots j_k\}$ which is a subsequence of $\{1, \ldots m\}$ consisting of k integers, where $1 \leq k \leq m$. The interpretation is that on $\{j_1, \ldots j_k\}$ the obligors in the set have defaulted. Furthermore, every permutation of $\{j_1, \ldots j_k\}$ is treated as the same state, that is, the order in which the obligors $j_1, \ldots j_k$ default is of no concern to us, which also is clear from equation (49). This implies that the cardinality of E will be 2^m, while keeping track of the ordering of $\{j_1, \ldots j_k\}$ implies that $|E| = \sum_{n=0}^{m} n! \binom{m}{n}$ which increases the number of states in E violently. For a more detailed discussion about ordered and unordered default contagion, see Herbertsson and Rootzén (2008).

Before we continue, further notation needed. In the sequel, we let Q and α denote the generator and initial distribution on E for the Markov jump process in Proposition 4.1. The generator Q is found by using the structure of E, the definition of the states j, and equation (49). To be more specific, for a state $j = \{j_1, j_2, \ldots, j_k\}$ a transition can only occur to a state $j' = (j, j_{k+1})$ where $j_{k+1} \neq j_i$ for $i = 1, 2, \ldots, k$. Further, the intensity for transitions from $j = \{j_1, j_2, \ldots, j_k\}$ to such a j' is

$$Q_{j,j'} = a_{j_{k+1}} + \sum_{i=1}^{k} b_{j_{k+1}, j_i} \tag{51}$$

where we remind the reader that every permutation of $\{j_1, \ldots j_k\}$ is treated as the same state. The diagonal elements of Q are determined by the requirement that the row sums of an intensity matrix is zero. The set Δ_i is defined as

$$\Delta_i = \{j \in E : j_n = i \text{ for some } j_n \in j\}$$

and since we define τ_i as $\tau_i = \inf\{t > 0 : Y_t \in \Delta_i\}$ for $i = 1, 2, \ldots, m$ is clear from the construction that $\tau_1, \ldots, \tau_m$ have the intensities (49), see e.g. Jacobsen (2006): Chapter 4. The construction is illustrated in Figure 10.1 for the case $m = 3$ (see also in e.g. Herbertsson and Rootzén (2008).

The states in E are ordered so that Q is upper triangular, see Herbertsson and Rootzén (2008). In particular, the final state $\{1, \ldots m\}$ is absorbing and $\{0\}$ is always the starting state. The latter implies that $\alpha = (1, 0, \ldots, 0)$. Furthermore, define the probability vector $p(t) = (\mathbb{P}[Y_t = j])_{j \in E}$. From Markov theory we know that

$$p(t) = \alpha e^{Qt}, \quad \text{and} \quad \mathbb{P}[Y_t = j] = \alpha e^{Qt} e_j, \tag{52}$$

where $e_j \in \mathbb{R}^{|E|}$ is a column vector where the entry at position j is 1 and the other entries are zero. Recall that e^{Qt} is the matrix exponential which has a closed form expression in terms of the eigenvalue decomposition of Q.

4.1.2 The multivariate default distributions

In this subsection we present some formulas for multivariate default and survival distributions, conditional multivariate default distributions, and multivariate default densities. Let G_i be $|E| \times |E|$ diagonal matrices, defined by

$$(G_i)_{j,j} = 1_{\{j \in \Delta_i^c\}} \quad \text{and} \quad (G_i)_{j,j'} = 0 \quad \text{if} \quad j \neq j'. \tag{53}$$

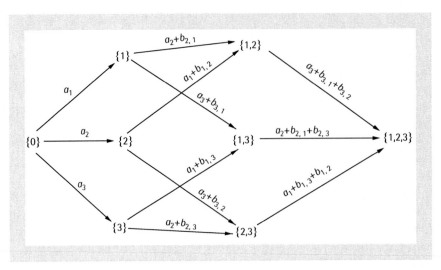

FIGURE 10.1 Illustration of construction for $m = 3$. Arrows indicate possible transitions, and the transition intensities are given on top of the arrows.

Further, for a vector $(t_1, t_2, \ldots, t_m)$ in $\mathbb{R}_+^m = [0, \infty)^m$, let the ordering of $(t_1, t_2, \ldots, t_m)$ be $t_{i_1} < t_{i_2} < \ldots < t_{i_m}$ where $(i_1, i_2, \ldots, i_m)$ is a permutation of $(1, 2, \ldots, m)$. The following proposition was stated in Assaf et al. (1984), but without a proof. A detailed proof is given in Herbertsson (2007b).

Proposition 4.2 *Consider m obligors with default intensities* (49). *Let* $(t_1, t_2, \ldots, t_m) \in \mathbb{R}_+^m$ *and let* $t_{i_1} < t_{i_2} < \ldots < t_{i_m}$ *be its ordering. Then,*

$$\mathbb{P}\left[\tau_1 > t_1, \ldots, \tau_m > t_m\right] = \alpha \left(\prod_{k=1}^{m} e^{\mathcal{Q}\left(t_{i_k} - t_{i_{k-1}}\right)} G_{i_k}\right) \mathbf{1} \tag{54}$$

where $t_{i_0} = 0$.

Let $(t_{i_1}, t_{i_2}, \ldots, t_{i_m})$ be the ordering of $(t_1, t_2, \ldots, t_m) \in \mathbb{R}_+^m$ and fix a p, $1 \leq p \leq m - 1$. We next consider conditional distributions of the types

$$\mathbb{P}\left[\tau_{i_{p+1}} > t_{i_{p+1}}, \ldots, \tau_{i_m} > t_{i_m} \mid \tau_{i_1} \leq t_{i_1}, \ldots, \tau_{i_p} \leq t_{i_p}\right].$$

These probabilities may of course be computed from (54) without any further use of the structure of the problem. However, using this structure leads to compact formulas. For this, further notation is needed. Define Δ as the final absorbing state for Y_t, i.e.

$$\Delta = \bigcap_{i=1}^{m} \Delta_i, \tag{55}$$

and let F_i and H_i be $|E| \times |E|$ diagonal matrices, defined by

$$(F_i)_{j,j} = 1_{\{j \in \Delta_i \setminus \Delta\}} \quad \text{and} \quad (F_i)_{j,j'} = 0 \quad \text{if} \quad j \neq j'. \tag{56}$$

$$(\boldsymbol{H}_i)_{j,j} = 1_{\{j \in \Delta_i\}} \quad \text{and} \quad (\boldsymbol{H}_i)_{j,j'} = 0 \quad \text{if} \quad j \neq j'. \tag{57}$$

Then we can state the following proposition, proved in Herbertsson (2007b).

Proposition 4.3 *Consider m obligors with default intensities (49). Let* $(t_1, t_2, \ldots, t_m) \in \mathbb{R}_+^m$ *and let* $t_{i_1} < t_{i_2} < \ldots < t_{i_m}$ *be its ordering. If* $1 \leq p \leq m - 1$ *then,*

$$\mathbb{P}\left[\tau_{i_1} \leq t_{i_1}, \ldots, \tau_{i_p} \leq t_{i_p}, \tau_{i_{p+1}} > t_{i_{p+1}}, \ldots, \tau_{i_m} > t_{i_m}\right]$$

$$= \boldsymbol{\alpha} \left(\prod_{k=1}^{p} e^{Q\left(t_{i_k} - t_{i_{k-1}}\right)} \boldsymbol{F}_{i_k}\right) \left(\prod_{k=p+1}^{m} e^{Q\left(t_{i_k} - t_{i_{k-1}}\right)} \boldsymbol{G}_{i_k}\right) \mathbf{1}. \tag{58}$$

and

$$\mathbb{P}\left[\tau_{i_{p+1}} > t_{i_{p+1}}, \ldots, \tau_{i_m} > t_{i_m} \mid \tau_{i_1} \leq t_{i_1}, \ldots, \tau_{i_p} \leq t_{i_p}\right]$$

$$= \frac{\boldsymbol{\alpha} \left(\prod_{k=1}^{p} e^{Q\left(t_{i_k} - t_{i_{k-1}}\right)} \boldsymbol{F}_{i_k}\right) \left(\prod_{k=p+1}^{m} e^{Q\left(t_{i_k} - t_{i_{k-1}}\right)} \boldsymbol{G}_{i_k}\right) \mathbf{1}}{\boldsymbol{\alpha} \left(\prod_{k=1}^{p} e^{Q\left(t_{i_k} - t_{i_{k-1}}\right)} \boldsymbol{H}_{i_k}\right) \mathbf{1}}. \tag{59}$$

where $t_{i_0} = 0$.

The following corollary is an immediate consequence of equation (58) in Proposition 4.3.

Corollary 4.4 *Consider m obligors with default intensities (49). Let* $\{i_1, \ldots, i_p\}$ *and* $\{j_1, \ldots, j_q\}$ *be two disjoint subsequences in* $\{1, \ldots, m\}$. *If* $t < s$ *then*

$$\mathbb{P}\left[\tau_{i_1} > t, \ldots, \tau_{i_p} > t, \tau_{j_1} < s, \ldots, \tau_{j_q} < s\right] = \boldsymbol{\alpha} e^{Qt} \left(\prod_{k=1}^{p} \boldsymbol{G}_{i_k}\right) e^{Q(s-t)} \left(\prod_{k=1}^{q} \boldsymbol{H}_{j_k}\right) \mathbf{1}$$

A similar expression can be found when $s < t$.

We can of course generalize, the above proposition for three time points $t < s < u$, four time points $t < s < u <$ etc. Using the notation of Corollary 4.4 we conclude that if $t < s$ then

$$\mathbb{P}\left[\tau_{j_1} < s, \ldots, \tau_{j_q} < s \mid \tau_{i_1} > t, \ldots, \tau_{i_p} > t\right] = \frac{\boldsymbol{\alpha} e^{Qt} \left(\prod_{k=1}^{p} \boldsymbol{G}_{i_k}\right) e^{Q(s-t)} \left(\prod_{k=1}^{q} \boldsymbol{H}_{j_k}\right) \mathbf{1}}{\boldsymbol{\alpha} e^{Qt} \left(\prod_{k=1}^{p} \boldsymbol{G}_{i_k}\right) \mathbf{1}}$$

and a similar expression can be found for $s < t$.

Let $f(t_1, \ldots, t_m)$ be the density of the multivariate random variable $(\tau_1, \ldots, \tau_m)$. For $(t_1, t_2, \ldots, t_m)$, let $(t_{i_1}, t_{i_2}, \ldots, t_{i_m})$ be its ordering where $(i_1, i_2, \ldots, i_m)$ is a permutation of $(1, 2, \ldots, m)$. We denote $(i_1, i_2, \ldots, i_m)$ by $\boldsymbol{i}$, that is, $\boldsymbol{i} = (i_1, i_2, \ldots, i_m)$. Furthermore, in view of the above notation, we let $f_{\boldsymbol{i}}(t_1, \ldots, t_m)$ denote the restriction of $f(t_1, \ldots, t_m)$ to the set $t_{i_1} < t_{i_2} < \ldots < t_{i_m}$. The following proposition was stated in Assaf et al. (1984), but without a proof. A detailed proof can be found in Herbertsson (2007b).

Proposition 4.5 *Consider m obligors with default intensities* (49). *Let* $(t_1, t_2, \ldots, t_m) \in \mathbb{R}_+^m$ *and let* $t_{i_1} < t_{i_2} < \ldots < t_{i_m}$ *be its ordering. Then, with notation as above*

$$f_i(t_1, \ldots, t_m) = (-1)^m \alpha \left(\prod_{k=1}^{m-1} e^{Q(t_{i_k} - t_{i_{k-1}})} \left(QG_{i_k} - G_{i_k} Q \right) \right) e^{Q(t_{i_m} - t_{i_{m-1}})} QG_{i_m} 1 \tag{60}$$

where $t_{i_0} = 0$.

4.1.3 *The marginal distributions*

In this subsection we state expressions for the marginal survival distributions $\mathbb{P}[\tau_i > t]$ and $\mathbb{P}[T_k > t]$, and for $\mathbb{P}[T_k > t, T_k = \tau_i]$ which is the probability that the k-th default is by obligor i and that it does not occur before t. The first ones are more or less standard, while the second one is less so. These marginal distributions are needed to compute single-name CDS spreads and k^{th}-to-default spreads, see e.g Herbertsson and Rootzén (2008). Note that CDSs are used as calibration instruments when pricing portfolio credit derivatives. The following lemma is trivial, and borrowed from Herbertsson and Rootzén (2008).

Lemma 4.6 *Consider m obligors with default intensities* (49). *Then,*

$$\mathbb{P}[\tau_i > t] = \alpha e^{Qt} g^{(i)} \quad and \quad \mathbb{P}[T_k > t] = \alpha e^{Qt} m^{(k)} \tag{61}$$

where the column vectors $g^{(i)}$, $m^{(k)}$ *of length* $|E|$ *are defined as*

$$g_j^{(i)} = 1_{\{j \in (\Delta_i)^C\}} \quad and \quad m_j^{(k)} = 1_{\{j \in \cup_{n=0}^{k-1} E_n\}}$$

and E_n *is set of states consisting of precisely n elements of* $\{1, \ldots m\}$ *where* $E_0 = \{0\}$.

The lemma immediately follows from the definition of τ_i in Proposition 4.1. The same holds for the distribution for T_k, where we also use that $m^{(k)}$ sums the probabilities of states where there has been less than k defaults. For more on this, see in Herbertsson and Rootzén (2008).

We next restate the following result, proved in Herbertsson and Rootzén (2008).

Proposition 4.7 *Consider m obligors with default intensities* (49). *Then,*

$$\mathbb{P}[T_k > t, T_k = \tau_i] = \alpha e^{Qt} \sum_{l=0}^{k-1} \left(\prod_{p=l}^{k-1} G^{i,p} P \right) h^{i,k}, \tag{62}$$

for $k = 1, \ldots m$, *where*

$$P_{j,j'} = \frac{Q_{j,j'}}{\sum_{k \neq j} Q_{j,k}}, \quad j, j' \in E,$$

and $h^{i,k}$ *is column vectors of length* $|E|$ *and* $G^{i,k}$ *is* $|E| \times |E|$ *diagonal matrices, defined by*

$$h_j^{i,k} = 1_{\{j \in \Delta_i \cap E_k\}} \quad and \quad G_{j,j}^{i,k} = 1_{\{j \in (\Delta_i)^C \cap E_k\}} \quad and \quad G_{j,j'}^{i,k} = 0 \quad if \quad j \neq j'.$$

Equipped with the above distributions, we can derive closed-form solutions for single-name CDS spreads and k^{th}-to-default swaps for a non-homogeneous portfolio, see Herbertsson and Rootzén (2008).

From equations (61) and (62) we see that all model parameters, including the jump parameters $\{b_{i,j}\}$ creating the default dependence, influence the marginal distributions $\{\mathbb{P}[\tau_i > t]\}$, $\{\mathbb{P}[T_k > t]\}$ and $\{\mathbb{P}[T_k > t, T_k = \tau_i]\}$. This has to be compared with copula models used in portfolio credit risk, where $\{\mathbb{P}[\tau_i > t]\}$ are modelled by idiosyncratic parameters unique for each obligor. Further, in a copula model, the joint dependence is introduced by the copula and its parameters, which are separated from the parameters describing each individual default distribution.

4.1.4 The default correlations and expected default times

In this subsection we derive expressions for pairwise default correlations, i.e. $\rho_{i,j}(t) = \mathrm{Corr}(1_{\{\tau_i \leq t\}}, 1_{\{\tau_j \leq t\}})$ between the obligors $i \neq j$ belonging to a portfolio of m obligors satisfying (49).

Lemma 4.8 Consider m obligors with default intensities (49). Then, for any pair of obligors $i \neq j$,

$$\rho_{i,j}(t) = \frac{\alpha e^{Qt} c^{(i,j)} - \alpha e^{Qt} h^{(i)} \alpha e^{Qt} h^{(j)}}{\sqrt{\alpha e^{Qt} h^{(i)} \alpha e^{Qt} h^{(j)} \left(1 - \alpha e^{Qt} h^{(i)}\right)\left(1 - \alpha e^{Qt} h^{(j)}\right)}} \tag{63}$$

where the column vectors $h^{(i)}$, $c^{(i,j)}$ of length $|E|$ are defined as

$$h_j^{(i)} = 1_{\{j \in \Delta_i\}} \quad and \quad c_j^{(i,j)} = 1_{\{j \in \Delta_i \cap \Delta_j\}} = h_j^{(i)} h_j^{(j)}. \tag{64}$$

The default correlations $\{\rho_{i,j}(T)\}$ can be used to calibrate the parameters in (49), as will be shortly discussed in subsection 4.1.6 (see also in Herbertsson (2007b)). In the standard copula model, $\rho_{i,j}(t)$ is assumed to be constant, and given by the correlation of some latent factor variables driving the individual defaults.

Next, let us consider the expected moments of $\{\tau_i\}$ and $\{T_k\}$. By construction (see Proposition 4.1), the intensity matrix Q for the Markov jump process Y_t on E has the form

$$Q = \begin{pmatrix} T & t \\ 0 & 0 \end{pmatrix}$$

where t is a column vector with $|E| - 1$ rows. The j-th element t_j is the intensity for Y_t to jump from the state j to the absorbing state $\Delta = \cap_{i=1}^m \Delta_i$. Furthermore, T is invertible since it is upper diagonal with strictly negative diagonal elements. Thus, we have the following lemma, proved in Herbertsson (2007b).

Lemma 4.9 Consider m obligors with default intensities (49). Then, with notation as above

$$\mathbb{E}[\tau_i^n] = (-1)^n n! \, \tilde{\alpha} T^{-n} \tilde{g}^{(i)} \quad and \quad \mathbb{E}[T_k^n] = (-1)^n n! \, \tilde{\alpha} T^{-n} \tilde{m}^{(k)}$$

for $n \in \mathbb{N}$ where $\tilde{\alpha}, \tilde{g}^{(i)}, \tilde{m}^{(k)}$ are the restrictions of $\alpha, g^{(i)}, m^{(k)}$ from E to $E \setminus \Delta$.

In the paper Herbertsson (2007b), the implied quantities $\mathbb{E}\,[\tau_i]$ are computed for two different calibrated portfolios.

4.1.5 *Pricing single-name credit default swaps and k^{th}-to-default swap spreads*

Given the marginal distributions $\{\mathbb{P}\,[\tau_i > t]\}$, $\{\mathbb{P}\,[T_k > t]\}$ and $\{\mathbb{P}\,[T_k > t, T_k = \tau_i]\}$ presented in Lemma 4.6 and Proposition 4.7 we can find compact, computationally tractable closed-form expression for single-name credit default swaps (CDSs) and k^{th}-to-default swap spreads. A detailed discussion derivation of these spreads can be found in Herbertsson and Rootzén (2008) and Herbertsson (2007b).

The CDS spreads are used as our main calibration tools when finding the parameters in the model (49). A short discussion of this topic is given in the next section.

4.1.6 *Calibrating the model via CDS spreads and correlation matrices*

The parameters in (49) can be obtained by calibrating the model against market CDS spreads and market CDS correlations. In Herbertsson and Rootzén (2008) and Herbertsson (2007b) the authors reparameterize the basic description (49) of the default intensities to the form

$$\lambda_{t,i} = a_i \left(1 + \sum_{j=1, j \neq i}^{m} \theta_{i,j} 1_{\{\tau_j \leq t\}} \right), \tag{65}$$

where the a_i-s are the base default intensities and the $\theta_{i,j}$ measure the 'relative dependence structure'. In Herbertsson and Rootzén (2008) the authors assumed that the matrix $\{\theta_{i,j}\}$ is exogenously given and then calibrated the a_i-s against the m market CDS spreads. In Herbertsson (2007b) the author determines the $\{\theta_{i,j}\}$ from market data on CDS correlations. To be more specific, if $\rho_{i,j}(T) = \mathrm{Corr}(1_{\{\tau_i \leq T\}}, 1_{\{\tau_j \leq T\}})$ denotes the default correlation matrix computed under the risk-neutral measure then Herbertsson (2007b) used $\beta\{\rho_{i,j}^{(\mathrm{CDS})}(T)\}$ as a proxy for $\{\rho_{i,j}(T)\}$. Here $\{\rho_{i,j}^{(\mathrm{CDS})}(T)\}$ is the observed correlation matrix for the T-years market CDS spreads, and β is a exogenously given parameter. The matrix $\{\rho_{i,j}(T)\}$ is a function of the parameters $\{\theta_{i,j}\}$, and Herbertsson (2007b) uses this fact in the calibration by matching $\rho_{i,j}(T)$ against $\beta\{\rho_{i,j}^{(\mathrm{CDS})}(T)\}$ together with the corresponding market spreads, in order to determine $\{\theta_{i,j}\}$, and the base default intensities a_i-s. However, in the calibration some restrictions have to be imposed on $\{\theta_{i,j}\}$ and we refer to Herbertsson (2007b) for more on this issue.

Furthermore, in the calibration as well as computation of the quantities presented in subsections 4.1.2–4.1.5, we need efficient methods to compute the matrix exponential e^{Qt}. For such discussions, we refer to appendix 5.4.

4.1.7 *Alternative parameterizations of the default intensities*

Finally we remark that MPH framework presented in this section also works for other parameterizations of the intensities than given by (49). To be more specific, in the inhomogeneous case, (49) can be replaced by

$$\lambda_{t,i} = f_i(N_{t,1}, \ldots, N_{t,i-1}, N_{t,i+1}, \ldots, N_{t,m}), \qquad t \le \tau_i, \tag{66}$$

and $\lambda_{t,i} = 0$ for $t > \tau_i$ where the function f_i can be arbitrarily chosen, as long as $\lambda_{t,i}$ is non-negative. Recall that $N_{t,j} = 1_{\{\tau_j \le t\}}$. One can for example choose a multiplicative parametrization of the default intensities, that is

$$\lambda_{t,i} = a_i \prod_{j=1, j \ne i}^{m} \left(1 + b_{i,j}\right)^{N_{t,j}}, \qquad t \le \tau_i, \tag{67}$$

and $\lambda_{t,i} = 0$ for $t > \tau_i$ where $a_i > 0$. This parametrization has the intuitive feature that $\Delta \lambda_{\tau_j,i} = b_{i,j} \lambda_{\tau_j-,i}$ for $\tau_i > \tau_j$ which implies that the jump in the default intensity is given by the pre-jump intensity times the constant $b_{i,j}$. Furthermore, the only constraints on $b_{i,j}$ is that $b_{i,j} > -1$ where the case $0 > b_{i,j} > -1$ implies negative default contagion (the intensities jump down at a default). Note that in calibrations with negative jumps, the multiplicative form (67) is much more practical (from an implementation point of view) than the additive framework (49), where we have to put constraints on the parameters to make sure we have non-negative intensities.

Similar multiplicative parameterizations can also be done for the homogeneous model to be presented in subsection 4.2.1.

4.2 Homogeneous portfolios

In the non-homogeneous portfolio presented in subsection 4.1.1, we have $|E| = 2^m$ which in practice will force us to work with portfolios of size m less or equal to 25, say (Herbertsson and Rootzén (2008) used $m = 15$). Standard synthetic CDO portfolios typically contains 125 obligors so we will therefore, in this subsection, consider a special case of (49) which leads to a symmetric portfolio where the state space E can be simplified to make $|E| = m + 1$. This allows us to practically work with the Markov set-up in Proposition 4.1 for large m, where $m \ge 125$ with no further complications.

First, subsection 4.2.1 gives a short introduction to the model. Then, subsections 4.2.3–4.2.5 discuss marginal and multivariate distributions and related quantites. Finally, subsection 4.2.6 gives a practical description how to calibrate the model against portfolio credit derivatives (which is performed in section 5).

4.2.1 The intensity specification for a homogeneous portfolio

We consider a special case of (49) where all obligors have the same default intensities $\lambda_{t,i} = \lambda_t$ specified by parameters a and $b_1, \ldots, b_m$, as

$$\lambda_t = a + \sum_{k=1}^{m-1} b_k 1_{\{T_k \le t\}} \tag{68}$$

where $\{T_k\}$ is the ordering of the default times $\{\tau_i\}$ and $\phi_1 = \ldots = \phi_m = \phi$ where ϕ is constant. In this model the obligors are exchangeable. The parameter a is the base intensity for each obligor i, and given that $\tau_i > T_k$, then b_k is how much the default intensity for each remaining obligor jumps at default number k in the portfolio. We start with the simpler version of Proposition 4.1. A detailed proof can be found in Herbertsson (2008a).

Corollary 4.10 *There exists a Markov jump process $(Y_t)_{t \geq 0}$ on a finite state space $\boldsymbol{E} = \{0, 1, 2, \ldots, m\}$, such that the stopping times*

$$T_k = \inf \{t > 0 : Y_t = k\}, \quad k = 1, \ldots, m$$

are the ordering of m exchangeable stopping times $\tau_1, \ldots, \tau_m$ with intensities (68). The generator $\boldsymbol{Q}$ to Y_t is given by

$$\boldsymbol{Q}_{k,k+1} = (m - k)\left(a + \sum_{j=1}^{k} b_j\right) \quad \text{and} \quad \boldsymbol{Q}_{k,k} = -\boldsymbol{Q}_{k,k+1} \; \text{for} \; k = 0, 1, \ldots, m-1$$

where the other entries in $\boldsymbol{Q}$ are zero. The Markov process always starts in $\{0\}$.

By Corollary 4.10, the states in $\boldsymbol{E}$ can be interpreted as the number of defaulted obligors in the portfolio. In the sequel, we let $\boldsymbol{\alpha} = (1, 0, \ldots, 0)$ denote the initial distribution on $\boldsymbol{E}$. Further, if k belongs to $\boldsymbol{E}$ then $\boldsymbol{e}_k$ denotes a column vector in $\mathbb{R}^{m+1}$ where the entry at position k is 1 and the other entries are zero. From Markov theory we know that $\mathbb{P}[Y_t = k] = \boldsymbol{\alpha} e^{\boldsymbol{Q}t} \boldsymbol{e}_k$ where $e^{\boldsymbol{Q}t}$ is the matrix exponential which has a closed form expression in terms of the eigenvalue decomposition of $\boldsymbol{Q}$.

We remark that the framework (68) is equivalent to the local intensity model which was the starting point in the papers by Arnsdorf and Halperin (2008), Lopatin and Misirpashaev (2007), Schönbucher (2005) and Sidenius Piterbarg, and Andersen (2008).

4.2.2 *Pricing CDOs and index CDSs in a homogeneous portfolio*

By using Corollary 4.10 we can derive practical formulas for CDO tranche spreads and index CDS spreads. The derivations and other issues regarding the computations, can be found in Herbertsson (2008a, 2008b).

The formulas for CDO tranches are used to calibrate the parameters in a homogeneous model specified by (68), under the risk-neutral measure. We will discuss this in subsection 4.2.6 and section 5.

4.2.3 *The multivariate distributions*

In this subsection we present formulas for multivariate default and survival distributions both for ordered as well as unordered default times. We start with the latter. Let $\boldsymbol{M}_k$ be $(m + 1) \times (m + 1)$ diagonal matrices, defined by $(\boldsymbol{M}_k)_{j,j} = 1_{\{j < k\}}$ and $(\boldsymbol{M}_k)_{j,j'} = 0$ if $j \neq j'$. The following proposition is similar to Proposition 4.2.

Proposition 4.11 *Consider m obligors with default intensities (68) and let $k_1 < \ldots < k_q$ be an increasing subsequence in $\{1, \ldots, m\}$ where $1 \leq q \leq m$. Furthermore, let $t_1 < t_2 < \ldots < t_q$. Then,*

$$\mathbb{P}\left[T_{k_1} > t_1, \ldots, T_{k_q} > t_q\right] = \boldsymbol{\alpha} \left(\prod_{i=1}^{q} e^{Q(t_i - t_{i-1})} \boldsymbol{M}_{k_i}\right) \boldsymbol{1} \tag{69}$$

where $t_{i_0} = 0$.

A similar expression can also be found for $\mathbb{P}\left[T_{k_1} \leq t_1, \ldots, T_{k_q} \leq t_q\right]$, see in Herbertsson (2008b). An explicit proof of Proposition 4.11 is given in Herbertsson (2008b).

Finding joint distributions for $\{\tau_i\}$ in a homogeneous model with default intensities (68) is a more complicated task than in an inhomogeneous model. For $1 \leq q \leq m$, fix a vector $t_1, \ldots, t_q \in \mathbb{R}_+^q$. For a set of q distinct obligors $i_1, i_2, \ldots, i_q$, the probability $\mathbb{P}\left[\tau_{i_1} \leq t_1, \ldots, \tau_{i_q} \leq t_q\right]$ is by exchangeability the same for any such distinct sequence of q obligors. Therefore we will in this subsection without loss of generality only consider $\mathbb{P}\left[\tau_1 \leq t_1, \ldots, \tau_q \leq t_q\right]$ where $t_1 \leq \ldots \leq t_q$ and similarly for $\mathbb{P}\left[\tau_{i_1} > t_1, \ldots, \tau_{i_q} > t_q\right]$. To exemplify, we state the following proposition proved in Herbertsson (2008b), where we let $q = 2$ and $t_1 < t_2$.

Proposition 4.12 *Consider m obligors with default intensities* (68) *and let* $t_1 < t_2$. *Then,*

$$\mathbb{P}\left[\tau_1 \leq t_1, \tau_2 \leq t_2\right] = \frac{(m-2)!}{m!} \boldsymbol{\alpha} e^{Q t_1} \boldsymbol{n} + \frac{(m-2)!}{m!} \sum_{k_1=1}^{m} \sum_{k_2=k_1+1}^{m} \boldsymbol{\alpha} e^{Q t_1} \boldsymbol{N}_{k_1} e^{Q(t_2 - t_1)} \boldsymbol{N}_{k_2} \boldsymbol{1}.$$
$$\tag{70}$$

where $\boldsymbol{n}$ *is a column vector in* $\mathbb{R}^{m+1}$ *such that* $\boldsymbol{n}_j = \frac{j(j-1)}{2}$.

A similar expression can also be found for $\mathbb{P}\left[\tau_1 > t_1, \tau_2 > t_2\right]$, see in Herbertsson (2008b).

It is possible to generalize Proposition 4.12 to more that two default times. These expressions do not seem to be easily simplified. However, if $t_1 = \ldots = t_q = t$ we can find compact formulas.

Proposition 4.13 *Consider m obligors with default intensities* (2.1) *and let* q *be a integer where* $1 \leq q \leq m$. *Then,*

$$\mathbb{P}\left[\tau_1 \leq t, \ldots, \tau_q \leq t\right] = \boldsymbol{\alpha} e^{Q t} \boldsymbol{d}^{(q)} \quad and \quad \mathbb{P}\left[\tau_1 > t, \ldots, \tau_q > t\right] = \boldsymbol{\alpha} e^{Q t} \boldsymbol{s}^{(q)} \tag{71}$$

where $\boldsymbol{d}^{(q)}$ *and* $\boldsymbol{s}^{(q)}$ *are column vectors in* $\mathbb{R}^{m+1}$ *defined by*

$$d_j^{(q)} = \frac{\binom{j}{q}}{\binom{m}{q}} \boldsymbol{1}_{\{j \geq q\}} \quad and \quad s_j^{(q)} = \frac{\binom{m-j}{q}}{\binom{m}{q}} \boldsymbol{1}_{\{j \leq m-q\}}. \tag{72}$$

A proof of Proposition 4.13 can be found in Herbertsson (2008b).

4.2.4 The marginal distributions

By Proposition 4.13 with $q = 1$ we get $\mathbb{P}\left[\tau_i > t\right] = \boldsymbol{\alpha} e^{Q t} \boldsymbol{s}^{(1)}$ where $s_j^{(1)} = (m - j)/m = 1 - j/m$. Furthermore, letting $\boldsymbol{m}^{(k)}$ denote $\boldsymbol{m}^{(k)} = \boldsymbol{M}_k \boldsymbol{1}$, then Proposition 4.11 with $q = 1$ for any $1 \leq k \leq m$, renders that $\mathbb{P}\left[T_k > t\right] = \boldsymbol{\alpha} e^{Q t} \boldsymbol{m}^{(k)}$ where $m_j^{(k)} = \boldsymbol{1}_{\{j < k\}}$.

Recall that $\mathbb{P}[\tau_i > t]$ is used to find formulas for the CDS spread in the model specified by (68).

4.2.5 *The default correlations and expected default times*

In this subsection we use Proposition 4.13 to state expressions for pairwise default correlations between two different obligors belonging to a homogeneous portfolio of m obligors satisfying (68). By exchangeability, $\mathrm{Corr}(1_{\{\tau_i \le t\}}, 1_{\{\tau_j \le t\}})$ is the same for all pairs $i \ne j$ so we let $\rho(t)$ denote $\mathrm{Corr}(1_{\{\tau_i \le t\}}, 1_{\{\tau_j \le t\}})$.

Lemma 4.14 *Consider m obligors with default intensities (68). Then, with notation as in subsection 4.2.3*

$$\rho(t) = \frac{\alpha e^{Qt} d^{(2)} - \left(\alpha e^{Qt} d^{(1)}\right)^2}{\alpha e^{Qt} d^{(1)} \left(1 - \alpha e^{Qt} d^{(1)}\right)}. \tag{73}$$

In section 5 we shall calibrate CDO portfolio for against market data on CDOs and then use Proposition 4.14 to plot the implied default correlation $\rho(t)$ as function of time t.

Next, let us consider the expected moments of $\{T_k\}$ in a homogeneous portfolio. By construction, the intensity matrix Q for the Markov jump process (see Proposition 4.10) has the form

$$Q = \begin{pmatrix} T & t \\ 0 & 0 \end{pmatrix}$$

where t is a column vector such that t_{m-1} is non-zero and $t_k = 0$ for $k = 0, 1, \ldots, m - 2$, because the k-th element t_k, $k \le m - 1$ is the intensity for the Markov jump process Y_t to jump from the state k to the absorbing state $\{m\}$. Furthermore, T is invertible since it is upper diagonal with strictly negative diagonal elements. The following lemma is proved as in Lemma 4.8.

Lemma 4.15 *Consider m obligors with default intensities (68). Then,*

$$\mathbb{E}\left[\tau_i^n\right] = (-1)^n n! \tilde{\alpha} T^{-n} \tilde{s}^{(1)} \quad and \quad \mathbb{E}\left[T_k^n\right] = (-1)^n n! \tilde{\alpha} T^{-n} \tilde{m}^{(k)}$$

for $n \in \mathbb{N}$ where $\tilde{\alpha}, \tilde{s}^{(1)}, \tilde{m}^{(k)}$ are the restrictions of $\alpha, s^{(1)}, m^{(k)}$ from E to $E \setminus \{m\}$.

In section 5 we shall study the implied expected default times $\mathbb{E}[T_k]$ as function of the number of defaults k. This is done for three different calibrated CDO portfolios.

4.2.6 *Calibrating the homogeneous portfolio using CDO tranchs and index CDSs*

In this subsection we discuss how to calibrate the model (68) against portfolio credit derivatives.

Let $a = (a, b_1, b_2, \ldots, b_{m-1})$ denote the m parameters in (68). Furthermore, let $\{C_j(T; a)\}$ be the $\kappa + 2$ model spreads which are: the CDS spread, the index CDS

Table 10.1 The integers $1, \mu_1, \mu_2, \ldots, \mu_c$ define a partition of $\{1, 2, \ldots, m\}$ used in the models that generate the spreads in Table 10.2

partition	μ_1	μ_2	μ_3	μ_4	μ_5	μ_6
	7	13	19	25	46	125

spread, and the κ different CDO tranche spreads. We let $\{C_{j,M}(T)\}$ denote the corresponding market spreads. In $C_j(T; a)$ we have emphasized that the model spreads are functions of $a = (a, b_1, b_2, \ldots, b_{m-1})$ but suppressed the dependence of interest rate, payment frequency, etc. The vector a is then obtained as

$$a = \operatorname*{argmin}_{\hat{a}} \sum_{j=1}^{\eta} \left(C_j(T; \hat{a}) - C_{j,M}(T) \right)^2 \tag{74}$$

with the constraint that all elements in a are non-negative. For a fixed maturity T, we use $\kappa = 5$ tranche spreads. This gives us 7 market observations, while the model can contain up to $m = 125$ parameters. In order to reduce the number of unknown parameters to as many as the market observations, we make following assumption on the parameters b_k for $1 \leq k \leq m - 1$

$$b_k = \begin{cases} b^{(1)} & \text{if } 1 \leq k < \mu_1 \\ b^{(2)} & \text{if } \mu_1 \leq k < \mu_2 \\ \vdots \\ b^{(c)} & \text{if } \mu_5 \leq k < \mu_6 = m \end{cases} \tag{75}$$

where $1, \mu_1, \mu_2, \ldots, \mu_6$ is an partition of $\{1, 2, \ldots, m\}$. This means that all jumps in the intensity at the defaults $1, 2, \ldots, \mu_1 - 1$ are the same and given by $b^{(1)}$, all jumps in the intensity at the defaults $\mu_1, \ldots, \mu_2 - 1$ are the same and given by $b^{(2)}$, and so on. Hence, in (74) we now minimize over the unknown vector $a = (a, b^{(1)}, \ldots, b^{(6)})$. Furthermore, if we for example want to calibrate our model against CDO tranches from the iTraxx-series, we can use a recovery of $\phi = 40\%$ with $m = 125$ and let $\mu_1, \mu_2, \ldots, \mu_6$ be given as in Table 10.1. In this way we assign one parameter for each tranche $[0, 3]$, $[3, 6]$, $[6, 9]$, $[6, 12]$ $[12, 22]$ and also one parameter for the loss interval $[22, 60]$.

5 NUMERICAL STUDIES

This section presents a few illustrative numerical results on CDO tranches and related quantities. We consider the simple case of a time-homogeneous and exchangeable model of portfolio credit risk. We will therefore use the results of subsection 4.2. First, subsection 5.1 discusses the datasets used in the calibration, as well as the obtained parameters and related quantities. In subsection 5.2 we present and study the implied loss distribution. The topic of subsection 5.3 is the implied expected ordered default times. Finally, subsection 5.4 studies the implied default correlations which possess some interesting features.

5.1 Model calibration

We first calibrate the model (68) against credit derivatives on the iTraxx Europe series with maturity of five years. We do this for three different datasets, sampled on 2004-08-04, 2006-11-28, and 2008-03-07. The spreads in these series differ substantially, where the last set was collected during the sub-prime crises. Each dataset contain five different CDO tranche spreads with tranches [0, 3], [3, 6], [6, 9], [9, 12], and [12, 22], the index CDS spreads and the average CDS spread. We use the same parametrization of the jumps $\{b_k\}_{k=1}^{m}$ as described in subsection 4.2.6. We choose the partition $\mu_1, \mu_2, \ldots, \mu_6$ so that it roughly coincides with the number of defaults needed to reach the upper attachment point for each tranche, see Table 10.1. In all three calibrations the interest rate was set to 3%, the payment frequency was quarterly, and the recovery rate was 40%.

In all three datasets we obtain perfect fits, although in the 2008 portfolio the accumulated calibration error is around nine times higher than it is in the 2006 portfolio. The relative calibration error is, however, very good. Furthermore, due to the sub-prime crises some of the corresponding spreads in the 2008 data have increased by a factor of 50 compared with the 2006 portfolio, see Table 10.2.

The calibrated parameters, displayed in Table 10.3 are obtained by using a stiff-ODE solver, as discussed in Appendix 5.4. For more details on different numerical methods used in the calibration, see in Herbertsson (2008a). In Figure 10.2 we have displayed the next-to-default intensities, that is $Q_{k,k+1}$, for the three calibrated portfolios with parameters given by Table 10.3. The next-to-default intensities have similar shapes for the three portfolios, but differ in magnitude, especially when k is bigger than 25 defaults.

Having calibrated the portfolio, we can compute implied quantities that are relevant to credit portfolio management, for example the implied loss distribution (and the loss surface), the implied default correlations and the implied expected ordered default times. To do this we use the calibrated parameters in Table 10.3 and the closed formulas presented in subsections 4.2.3–4.2.5. All computations of the matrix-exponential are performed with either a stiff ODE-solver, or the Padé-method, both discussed in Appendix 5.4.

Besides the above quantities, we can also compute more exotic credit derivatives that are not liquidly quoted on the market, such as tranchlets and basket default swaps on subportfolios in the CDO portfolio. The latter quantities are not treated in this chapter, and we refer to Herbertsson (2008a) for such studies.

Table 10.2 iTraxx Europe Series 3, 6 and 8 collected at 4 August 2004, 28 November 2006 and 7 March 2008. The market and model spreads and the corresponding absolute errors, both in bp and in percent of the market spread. The [0,3] spread is quoted in %. All maturities are for five years

2004-08-04	Market	Model	error (bp)	error (%)
[0, 3]	27.6	27.6	3.851e-005	1.4e-006
[3, 6]	168	168	0.000316	0.0001881
[6, 9]	70	70	0.000498	0.0007115
[9, 12]	43	43	0.0005563	0.001294
[12, 22]	20	20	0.0004006	0.002003
index	42	42.02	0.01853	0.04413
avg CDS	42	41.98	0.01884	0.04486
Σ abs.cal.err			0.03918 bp	

2006-11-28	Market	Model	error (bp)	error (%)
[0, 3]	14.5	14.5	0.008273	0.0005705
[3, 6]	62.5	62.48	0.02224	0.03558
[6, 9]	18	18.07	0.07275	0.4042
[9, 12]	7	6.872	0.1282	1.831
[12, 22]	3	3.417	0.4169	13.9
index	26	26.15	0.1464	0.5632
avg CDS	26.87	26.13	0.7396	2.752
Σ abs.cal.err			1.534 bp	

2008-03-07	Market	Model	error (bp)	error (%)
[0, 3]	46.5	46.5	0.0505	0.001086
[3, 6]	567.5	568	0.4742	0.08356
[6, 9]	370	370	0.04852	0.01311
[9, 12]	235	234	1.035	0.4404
[12, 22]	145	149.9	4.911	3.387
index	150.3	144.3	5.977	3.978
avg CDS	145.1	143.8	1.296	0.8933
Σ abs.cal.err			13.79 bp	

Table 10.3 The calibrated parameters that give the model spreads in Table 10.2

	a	$b^{(1)}$	$b^{(2)}$	$b^{(3)}$	$b^{(4)}$	$b^{(5)}$	$b^{(6)}$
2004/08/04	33.07	16.3	86.24	126.2	200.3	0	1379×10^{-4}
2006/11/28	24.9	13.93	73.36	62.9	0.2604	2261	5904×10^{-4}
2008/03/07	44.2	22.66	159.8	0	6e-008	1107	779700×10^{-4}

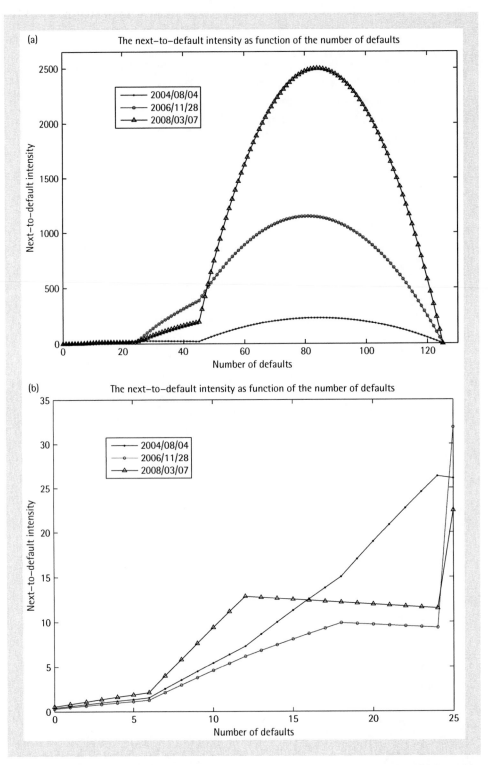

FIGURE 10.2 The next-to-default intensities, i.e. $Q_{k,k+1}$, in the three calibrated portfolios with parameters given by Table 10.3. The upper plot is for $0 \leq k \leq 125$, while the lower displays $Q_{k,k+1}$ when $0 \leq k \leq 26$.

5.2 Loss distributions

The implied loss distribution on the interval $0 \leq x \leq 22\%$ for $t = 5$ is displayed in Figure 10.3 and the distribution for the whole loss-interval $0 \leq x \leq 60\%$ is shown in the first subfigure of Figure 10.4. Furthermore, Table 10.4 displays the probabilities $\mathbb{P}[L_5 \geq x\%]$ for $x = 3, 6, 9, 12, 22$ and $x = 60$. With 40% recovery, $\mathbb{P}[L_5 \geq 60\%] = \mathbb{P}[L_5 = 60\%] = \mathbb{P}[Y_5 = 125]$ is the so called five-year 'Armageddon probability', i.e. the probability that all obligors in the portfolio have defaulted within five years from the date the portfolio was calibrated. The five-year 'Armageddon probabilities' are negligible for the 2004 and 2006 portfolios (0.08 % and 0.127 respectively), but very big for the 2008 dataset, where $\mathbb{P}[L_5 = 60\%] = 7.11\%$. Thus, there is 7% probability (under

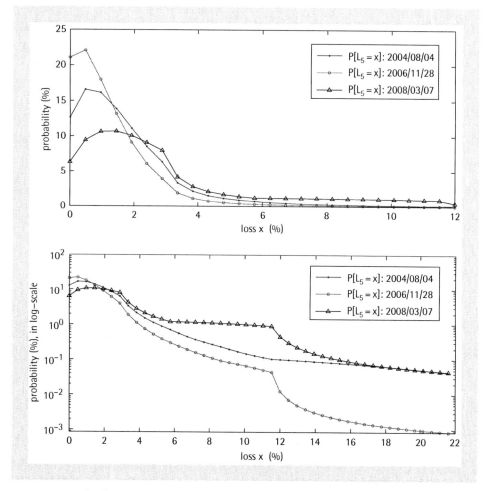

FIGURE 10.3 The five year implied loss distributions $\mathbb{P}[L_5 = x\%]$ (in %) for the 2004-08-04, 2006-11-28 and 2008-03-07 portfolios, where $0 \leq x \leq 12$ (upper) and $0 \leq x < 22$ (lower). The lower graph is in log-scale.

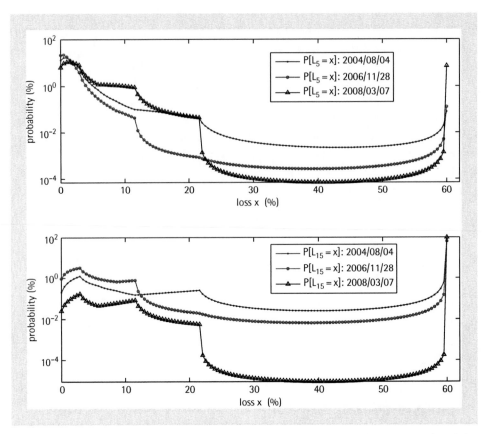

FIGURE 10.4 The five-year (upper) and fifteen-year (lower) implied loss distributions (in %) for the 2004-08-04, 2006-11-28, and 2008-03-07 portfolios, where $0 \leq x \leq 60$. Both graphs are in log-scale.

Table 10.4 The probabilities $\mathbb{P}[L_5 \geq x\%]$ (in %) where x = 3, 6, 9, 12, 22 and x = 60, for the 2004-08-04, 2006-11-28 and 2008-03-07 portfolios

$\mathbb{P}[L_5 \geq x\%]$	x = 3	x = 6	x = 9	x = 12	x = 22	x = 60
2004/08/04	14.7	4.976	2.793	1.938	0.4485	0.07997
2006/11/28	6.466	1.509	0.5935	0.2212	0.1674	0.1265
2008/03/07	35.67	22.26	15.44	9.552	7.122	7.108

the risk-neutral measure) that all 125 obligors in the portfolio have defaulted within five years from March 2008. The huge differences in the 'Armageddon probabilities' between the 2006 and 2008 portfolios are due to the sub-prime crises that emerged 2007 and continued into 2008.

We also study the dynamics of the implied loss model over time, Figure 10.5 displays the loss distribution at the time points $t = 1, 5, 10$ and $t = 15$ (time measured in years) and where the loss x ranges between 0% to 24%. The two sub-pictures in Figure 10.4 clearly depict the shift of probability mass due to contagion, as time progresses. For example in the 2006 portfolio it holds that $\mathbb{P}\,[L_5 = 60\%] = \mathbb{P}\,[Y_5 = 125] = 0.127\%$ while $\mathbb{P}\,[L_{15} = 60\%] = 64.5\%$. Figure 10.6 shows the implied loss surface, i.e. the loss probabilities as function of time and loss, for the calibrated 2006 portfolio.

Further, for the 2006-11-28 and 2008-03-07 portfolios, we clearly see the effect of default contagion on the upper tranche losses, making them lie close to each other, see Figure 10.8. From Figure 10.7 we conclude that our model, with a constant recovery rate of 40%, calibrated to market spreads on the five-year iTraxx Europe Series in Table

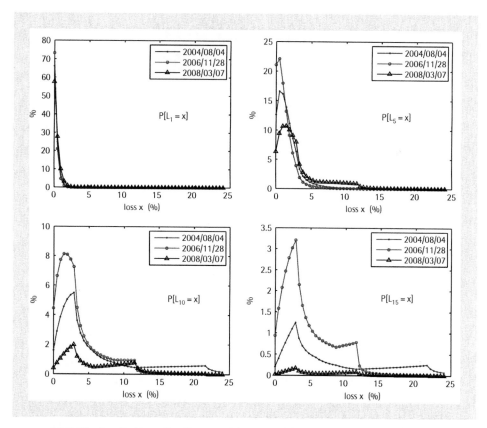

FIGURE 10.5 The implied loss distributions $\mathbb{P}\,[L_t = x\%]$ (in %) for the 2004-08-04, 2006-11-28, and 2008-03-07 portfolios at the time points $t = 1, 5, 10, 15$ and where the loss x ranges from 0% to 24%.

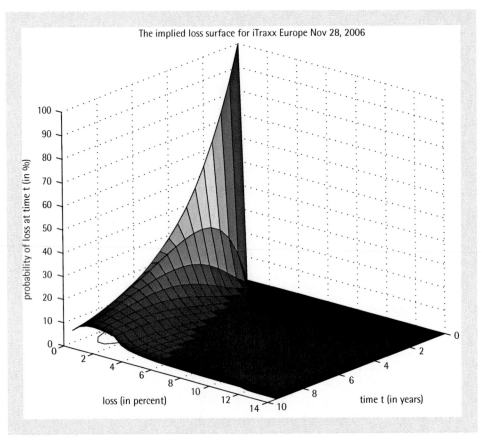

FIGURE 10.6 The implied loss surface for iTraxx Europe 28 November 2006, where 0% < x < 14% and 0 ≤ t < 10.

10.2, implies that the whole portfolio has defaulted within approximately thirty years, under the risk-neutral measure (for all three datasets). In reality, this will likely not happen, since risk-neutral (implied) default probabilities are substantially larger than the 'real', so-called actuarial, default probabilities.

5.3 Expected ordered default times

Next, let us study the implied expected ordered default times $\mathbb{E}[T_k]$. In Figure 10.9, left, we note that the implied expected ordered default times take values roughly between 3.5 years and 14 years. A striking feature in the 2006-11-28 portfolio is that after the 25th default, the $\mathbb{E}[T_k]$ cluster around 14 years. This is a consequence of the explosion in the jump intensities for $k \geq 25$, see Table 10.3. Under the risk-neutral measure, implied by the market data in Table 10.2, this clustering of $\mathbb{E}[T_k]$ means that we expect extreme losses in year 13 and 14 for the 2006-11-28 portfolio. The clustering

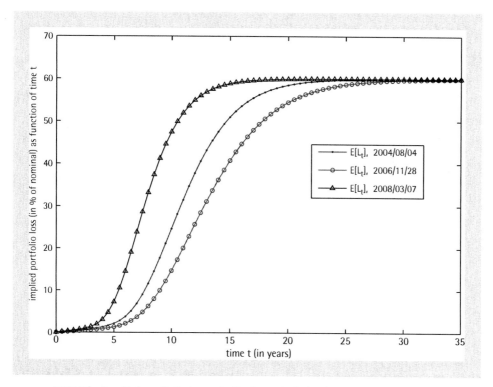

FIGURE 10.7 The implied portfolio losses in % of nominal, for the 2004-08-04, 2006-11-28, and 2008-03-07 portfolios.

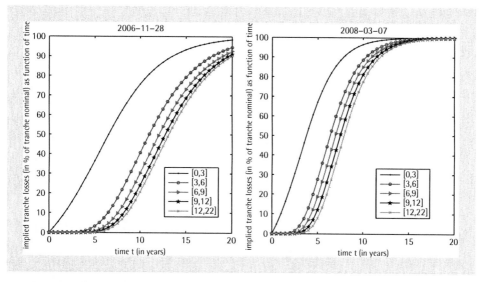

FIGURE 10.8 The implied tranche losses in % of tranche nominal for the 2006-11-28 (left) and 2008-03-07 (right) portfolios.

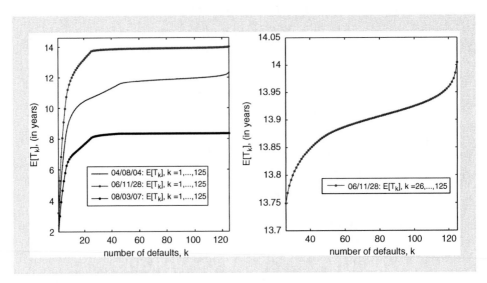

FIGURE 10.9 The implied expected ordered default times $\mathbb{E}\,[T_k]$ for the 2004-08-04, 2006-11-28, and 2008-03-07 portfolios where $k = 1, \ldots, 125$ (left) and $k = 26, \ldots, 125$ (right, for 2006-11-28).

effect is also present in the 2008 dataset, which indicates that the whole portfolio is expected to be wiped out within nine years. Again, recall that all computations are under the risk-neutral measure, and should not be confused with real default probabilities and their expectations. These are likely to be substantially smaller for the loss probability and much bigger for the expected ordered default times.

5.4 Default correlations

Finally, we study the implied pairwise default correlation $\rho(t) = \mathrm{Corr}(1_{\{\tau_i \leq t\}}, 1_{\{\tau_j \leq t\}})$ for two distinct obligors i, j, as function of time t, see Figure 10.10. In e.g. the 2006-11-28 portfolio, we see that $\rho(t)$ is less than 2% when $t \leq 4$, but then starts to increase rapidly, first to 4% for $t = 4.5$, then to 77% for $t = 10$ and reaches 88% at $t = 15$. After this drastic development, the implied default correlation flattens out and converges to 91% as time increases against 30 years. The explosive increase of $\rho(t)$ from 2% to 88% in the time interval [4.5, 15] is due to the default contagion and is also consistent with the clustering of $\{T_k\}$ around $t = 14$. We also note that the implied default correlation for the 2004-08-04 portfolio follows an almost identical trend up to 8 years. This is consistent with the jump-to-default parameters for the first 13 defaults, which are in the same order as in 2006-11-28 case, see also Figure 10.9. Even though there is a big difference between the corresponding contagious parameters for $k > 13$ in the 2004 and 2006 portfolio, the implied default correlations never differ more than $10 - 12\%$ during the first 30 years between these portfolios. The default correlation for 2008 portfolio has similar shape as the 2004 and 2006 portfolios, but the steep increase in

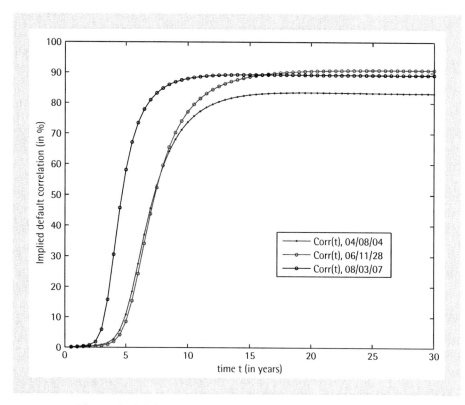

FIGURE 10.10 The implied default correlation $\rho(t) = \mathrm{Corr}(1_{\{\tau_i \le t\}}, 1_{\{\tau_j \le t\}})$, $i \ne j$ as function of time for the 2004-08-04, 2006-11-28, and 2008-03-07 portfolios.

the correlation curve (due to contagion) starts earlier in the 2008 portfolio. Given the huge spreads in the 2008 set compared with the 2004 and 2006 portfolios, this does not come as a surprise.

For more numerical studies of the model (68) we refer to the papers by Herbertsson (2008a, 2008b).

APPENDIX

EFFICIENT COMPUTATIONS OF MATRIX EXPONENTIALS ARISING IN PORTFOLIO CREDIT RISK MODELS

The main challenge when pricing portfolio credit products in a time-homogeneous Markovian model, is to compute the matrix exponential e^{Qt} where Q is the generator. This subsection briefly discusses some techniques for computing matrix exponentials when pricing portfolio credit derivatives in models such as those presented in subsection 4.1 and subsection

4.2. A more extensive discussion of the material below can be found in Herbertsson (2007a), Herbertsson and Rootzén (2008), Herbertsson (2008a, 2008b, 2007b).

There are many different methods to compute the matrix exponential (Moeler and Loan 1978, 2003). However, most of the standard methods are not adapted to very large, but sparse, matrices and don't seem possible when the state space is larger than a few hundred (see Sidje and Stewart, 1999, Gross and Miller 1984). In contagion models Q is often upper diagonal (see e.g. subsection 4.1.1) , so the eigenvalues are given by the diagonal of Q. It is therefore tempting to try eigenvalue decomposition. In Herbertsson and Rootzén (2008), the authors showed that this method for credit derivatives may fail already for relatively small matrices (500×500), since the eigenvector matrices turned out to be ill-conditioned, which introduced large numerical errors in the computations. Furthermore, Herbertsson and Rootzén (2008) experimented with two different numerical methods for large sparse matrices arising in contagion models; direct series expansion of the matrix exponential and the uniformization method (which sometimes also is called the randomization method, (Gross and Miller 1984). Both methods were fast and robust for pricing basket default swaps, but uniformization method was consequently faster than the Taylor method. The series expansion method also lacks lower bounds on possible worst case scenarios (see Moeler and Loan 1978), while the uniformization method provides analytical expressions for the residual error as will be seen below, see also e.g. Herbertsson (2007b). Furthermore, previous studies indicate that uniformization method can handle large sparse matrices with remarkable robustness, see e.g. Sidje and Stewart (1999), Gross and Miller (1984) or Appendix C.2.2 in Lando (2004). A probabilistic interpretation of this method can be found in Gross and Miller (1984), and Herbertsson (2007b) and pure matrix arguments which motivate the method are given in Sidje and Stewart (1999) and Appendix C.2.2 in Lando (2004). The uniformization method works as follows. Let $\Lambda = \max\left\{|Q_{j,j}| : j \in E\right\}$ and set $\widetilde{P} = Q/\Lambda + I$. Then, $e^{\widetilde{P}\Lambda t} = e^{Qt}e^{\Lambda t}$ since I commutes with all matrices, and using the definition of the matrix exponential renders

$$e^{Qt} = \sum_{n=0}^{\infty} \widetilde{P}^n e^{-\Lambda t} \frac{(\Lambda t)^n}{n!}. \tag{76}$$

Recall that $p(t) = \alpha e^{Qt}$ and define $\widetilde{p}(t, N) = \alpha \sum_{n=0}^{N} \widetilde{P}^n e^{-\Lambda t} \frac{(\Lambda t)^n}{n!}$. Furthermore, for a vector $x = (x_1, \ldots, x_n) \in \mathbb{R}^n$, let $||x||_1$ denote the L_1 norm, that is $||x||_1 = \sum_{i=1}^{n} |x_i|$. Given Q, the uniformization method allows us to find the L_1 approximation error for $\widetilde{p}(t, N)$ apriori, as shown in the following lemma, proved in Herbertsson (2007b) (the lemma is also stated in Gross and Miller (1984) and Sidje and Stewart (1999), but without a proof).

Lemma D.1 *Let $\varepsilon > 0$ and pick $N(\varepsilon)$ so that $1 - \sum_{n=0}^{N(\varepsilon)} e^{-\Lambda t} \frac{(\Lambda t)^n}{n!} < \varepsilon$. Then,*

$$||p(t) - \widetilde{p}(t, N(\varepsilon))||_1 < \varepsilon. \tag{77}$$

The above result implies that given Q we can for any $\varepsilon > 0$ find an integer $N(\varepsilon)$ so that $\widetilde{p}(t, N(\varepsilon))$ approximates $p(t)$ with an accumulated absolute error which is less than ε. The sharp error estimation in Lemma $D.1$ relies on a probabilistic argument, see Lemma 6.1 in Herbertsson (2007b). Another benefit with the uniformization method is that all entries in $\widetilde{p}(t, N(\varepsilon))$ are positive so there are no cancelation effects and the approximation error decreases monotonically with increasing N.

A further point is that the matrices Q constructed in subsection 4.1.1, in general are very large, for example if $m = 10$ then the generator has $2^{10} = 1,024$ rows and thus contain $2^{20} \approx 1$

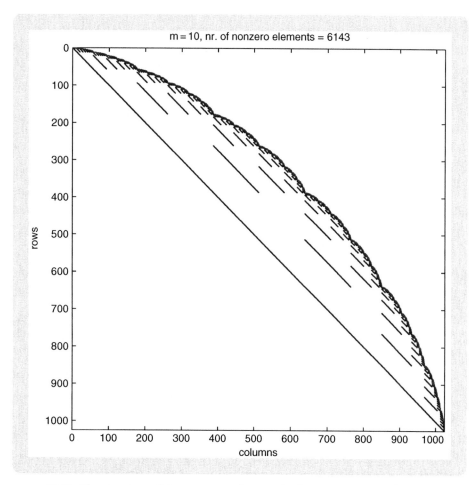

FIGURE 10.11 The structure of the non-zero elements in the sparse matrix Q constructed in subsection 4.1.1 (see Equation (51)) with $m = 10$.

millon entries. However, at the same time they are extremely sparse, see Figure 10.11. For $m = 10$ there are only 0.59% non-zero entries in Q, and hence only about 6100 elements have to be stored, which roughly is the same as storing a full quadratic matrix with 78 rows. For $m = 15$ the generator has $2^{15} = 32768$ rows and thus contain $2^{30} \approx 1$ billion entries but there are only 0.025% nonzero entries in Q, and hence only about 280.000 elements have to be stored, see in Herbertsson and Rootzén (2008).

A final point regarding very large sparse matrices Q arising in portfolio credit models as in subsection 4.1.1, is that we are not interested in finding the matrix exponential e^{Qt} itself, but only the probability vector $p(t) = e^{Qt}$, or a subvector of $p(t)$. This is important, since computing e^{Qt} is very time and memory consuming compared with computing αe^{Qt}, see e.g. Herbertsson and Rootzén (2008) or Herbertsson (2007b).

For smaller generators, of size 126×126, arising in e.g. contagion models for symmetric CDO portfolios, such as in Herbertsson (2008a) and Herbertsson (2008b) (see Subsection 4.2), or in local intensity top-down models (i.e. no spread risk, just default risk) such as

Schönbucher (2005), Sidenius Piterbarg, and Andersen (2008), Cont and Minca (2008) and Lopatin and Misirpashaev (2007), the Taylor-series method and the uniformitarian method are inappropriate due to slow convergence of the matrix-sum. Fortunately, there are other much more effective methods. In Herbertsson (2008a) the author investigated three different methods. The first was Padé-approximation with scaling and squaring, (see Moeler and Loan 1978), the second was a standard Runge-Kutta ODE solver, and the third approach was a numerical ODE-solver adapted for stiff ODE system. An ODE-system is called stiff if the absolute values of the eigenvalues of the Jacobian to the system greatly differ in value, that is $\Lambda_{min} << \Lambda_{max}$ where $\Lambda_{min} = \min\{|\Lambda_i|\}$ and $\Lambda_{max} = \max\{|\Lambda_i|\}$ and $\{\Lambda_i\}$ are the corresponding eigenvalues (see also Section 5). In Herbertsson (2008a) the Markov chain was time-homogeneous so the Jacobian was the generator Q, and the eigenvalues $\{\Lambda_i\}$ where given by the diagonal elements in Q, because the next-to-default intensity was a pure death-process. Herbertsson (2008a) showed that for a fixed accuracy of the solution, the Runge-Kutta method (or any ODE routine not adapted for stiff ODE solvers) was outperformed by the Padé approximation on levels such as computational time, accuracy of the solution and analytical error-control. Herbertsson (2008a) also concluded that a numerical ODE solver adapted for stiff ODE system, based on backward differentiation formulas with multistep properties, outperformed the Padé approximation with respect to computational time. However, this could only be done when the stiff ODE solver used the fact that the Jacobian of the ODE is given by the constant generator Q. Without this observation, the Padé method was much more accurate than the stiff ODE solver.

References

Albanese, C., and Chen, O. (2005). 'Discrete credit barrier models'. *Quantitative Finance*, 5/3: 247–56.

Arnsdorf, M., and Halperin, I. (2007). 'BSLP: Markovian bivariate spread-loss model for portfolio credit derivatives'. *Journal of Computational Finance*, 12/2.

Asmussen, S. (2000). 'Matrix-analytic models and their analysis'. *Scandinavian Journal of Statistics* 27: 193–226.

——(2003). *Applied Probability and Queues*. 2nd edn., London: Springer.

Assaf, D., Langbert, N. A., Savis, T. H., and Shaked, M. (1984). 'Multivariate phase-type distributions'. *Operations Research*, 32: 688–701.

Backhaus, J. (2008). 'Pricing and hedging of credit derivatives in a model with interacting default intensities: a Markovian approach'. Ph.D. Thesis, University of Leipzig.

Bhattacharya, R. N., and Waymire, E. C. (1990). *Stochastic Processes with Applications*. Chichester: J. Wiley.

Bielecki, T. R., Crépey, S., and Jeanblanc, M. (2008). 'Up and down credit risk'. *Quantitative Finance*, forthcoming.

——and Rutkowski, M. (2002). *Credit Risk: Modeling, Valuation and Hedging*. Berlin: Springer-Verlag.

——Vidozzi, A., and Vidozzi, L. (2008). 'A Markov copulae approach to pricing and hedging of credit index derivatives and ratings triggered step-up bonds'. *Journal of Credit Risk*, 4/1.

————(2006). 'An efficient approach to valuation of credit basket products and ratings triggered step-up bonds'. Working Paper.

——Crépey, S., Jeanblanc, M., and Rutkowski, M. (2008). 'Valuation of basket credit derivatives in the credit migrations environment', In J. Birge and V. Linetsky (eds)., *Handbook of Financial Engineering*, Amsterdam: Elsevier.

——Jakubowski, J., Vidozzi, A. and Vidozzi, L. (2008). 'Study of dependence for some classes of stochastic processes'. *Stochastic Analysis and Applications*, 26/4: 903–24.

Brémaud, P. (1981). *Point Processes and Queues, Martingale Dynamics*. New York: Springer-Verlag.

Carmona, R., and Crépey, S. (2008). 'Particle methods for the estimation of Markovian credit portfolios loss distribution'. Forthcoming in *International Journal of Theoretical and Applied Finance*.

Cont, R., and Minca, A. (2008). 'Recovering portfolio default intensities implied by CDO quotes'. Working paper.

——and Tankov, P. (2003). *Financial Modeling with Jump Processes*. Chapman & Hall/CRC, Boca Raton.

Crépey, S., Jeanblanc, M. and Zargari, B. (2009). 'CDS with counterparty risk in a Markov chain copula model with joint defaults'. Working paper.

Frey, R. and Backhaus, J. (2004). 'Portfolio credit risk models with interacting default intensities: a Markovian approach'. Working paper.

————(2008a), 'Dynamic hedging of synthetic CDO-tranches with spread- and contagion risk'. Forthcoming in *Journal of Economic Dynamics and Control*.

————(2008b). 'Pricing and hedging of portfolio credit derivatives with interacting default intensities'. *International Journal of Theoretical and Applied Finance*, 11/6: 611–34.

Gross, D., and Miller, D. R. (1984). 'The randomization technique as a modelling tool and solution procedure for transient markov processes'. *Operations Research*, 32/2: 343–61.

Gyöngy, I. (1986). 'Mimicking the one dimensional distributions of processes having an Ito differential'. *Probability theory and related fields*, 71/4: 501–16.

Halperin, I., and Tomecek, P. (2008). 'Climbing down from the top: single name dynamics in credit top down models'. Working paper.

Herbertsson, A. (2007a). 'Pricing portfolio credit derivatives'. Ph.D. Thesis, University of Gothenburg.

——(2007b). 'Modelling default contagion using Multivariate Phase-Type distributions'. Forthcoming in *Review of Derivatives Research*.

——(2008a). 'Pricing synthetic CDO tranches in a model with default contagion using the matrix-analytic approach'. *Journal of Credit Risk* 4/4: 3–35.

——(2008b). Handbook of Global Perspectives, Innovations, and Market Drivers 'Default contagion in large homogeneous portfolios', in G. N. Gregoriou and Ali P.U. (eds), *The Credit Derivatives*, New York: McGraw-Hill.

——and Rootzén, H. (2008). 'Pricing kth-to-default swaps under default contagion: the matrix-analytic approach'. *Journal of Computational Finance*, 12/1: 49–78.

Jacobsen, M. (2006). *Point Process Theory and Applications, Marked Point and Piecewise Deterministic Processes*. Boston: Birkhäuser.

Jarrow, R., Lando, D., and Turnbull, S. (1997). 'A Markov Model for the term structure of credit risk spreads'. *Review of Financial Studies*, 10/2: 481–523.

Lando, D. (2004). *Credit Risk Modeling: Theory and Applications*. Princeton: Princeton University Press.

——and Mortensen, A. (2005). 'On the pricing of step-up bonds in the European telecom sector'. *Journal of Credit Risk*, 1/1: 71–110.

Last, G., and Brandt, A. (1995). *Marked Point Processes on the Real Line: The Dynamical Approach*, New York: Springer.

Laurent, J. P., Cousin, A., and Fermanian, J. D. (2008). 'Hedging default risks of CDOs in Markovian contagion models'. Forthcoming in *Quantitative Finance*.

Lopatin, A., and Misirpashaev, T. (2007). 'Two-dimensional Markovian model for dynamics of adequate credit loss'. Working paper.

Moeler, C., and Loan, C. V. (1978). 'Nineteen dubious ways to compute the exponential of a matrix'. *SIAM Review*, 20/4: 801–836.

——— (2003). 'Nineteen dubious ways to compute the exponential of a matrix, twenty-five years later'. *SIAM Review*, 45/1: 3–49.

Neuts, M. F. (1981). *Matrix-Geometric Solutions in Stochastic Models: An Algorithmic Approach*. Baltimore: Johns Hopkins University Press.

—— (1989). *Structured Stochastic Matrices of M/g/1 Type and Their Applications*. New York: Dekker.

Palmowski, Z., and Rolski, T. (2002). 'A technique for exponential change of measure for Markov processes'. *Bernoulli*, 8/6: 767–85.

Rogers, L. C. G., and Williams, D. (2000). *Diffusions, Markov Processes and Martingales*, 2nd edn., Cambridge: Cambridge University Press.

Rolski, T., Schmidli, H., Schmidt, V., and Teuggels, J. (1998). *Stochastic Processes for Insurance and Finance*. Chichester: J. Wiley.

Schönbucher, P. J. (2005). 'Portfolio losses and the term structure of loss transition rates: a new methodology for the pricing of portfolio credit derivatives'. Working paper, Department of Mathematics, ETH Zürich.

Sidenius, J., Piterbarg, V., and Andersen, L. (2008). 'A new framework for dynamic credit portfolio loss modelling'. *International Journal of Theoretical and Applied Finance*, 11/2: 163–97.

Sidje, R. B., and Stewart, W. J. (1999). 'A numerical study of large sparse matrix exponentials arising in Markov chains', *Computational Statistics and Data Analysis*, 29/3: 345–68.

Syski, R. (1992). *Passage Times for Markov Chains*. Amsterdam: IOS Press.

CHAPTER 11

COUNTERPARTY RISK IN CREDIT DERIVATIVE CONTRACTS

JON GREGORY

1 INTRODUCTION

COUNTERPARTY credit risk is the risk that a counterparty in a financial contract will default prior to the expiration of the contract and fail to make future payments. Counterparty risk is taken by each party in an over-the-counter (OTC) derivative and is therefore present in all asset classes, including interest rates, foreign exchange, equity derivatives, commodities, and credit derivatives. Given the recent credit crisis and the high-profile failures such as Lehman Brothers, the topic of counterparty risk management has become critically important for many financial institutions and derivatives users. Credit derivatives counterparty risk has been shown to be particularly important and a key driver of some of the financial problems underlying the credit crisis.

CVA (credit value adjustment) is a traditionally applied adjustment to adjust the value of derivative contracts for counterparty risk. CVA accounts for potential future losses due to an institution's counterparties defaulting. The quantification of CVA is therefore an important component in pricing and managing counterparty risk on derivative instruments. Historically, CVA charges have often been incorporated into transactions in favour of the stronger credit quality counterparty. For example, banks trading with corporate counterparties have for many years charged CVAs linked to the credit quality of the corporate and the exposure in question. Recent accountancy rules have also given importance to CVA as a key element in the reporting of accurate earnings information. Accounting standards require an appropriate mark-to-market of derivatives positions including the possibility of future defaults. For example, FASB 157 and IAS39 define fair value and require banks to adjust the risk-free value of derivatives positions for the CVA (expected loss) associated with future counterparty defaults.

The credit derivatives market has grown dramatically over the last decade, fuelled by the need to transfer credit risk efficiently and develop products that are ever more sophisticated for investors. In the early years of the credit derivative market, counterparty risk concerns were in the back of most people's minds. This, in retrospect, is surprising since the very nature of credit derivative products generates so-called 'wrong-way' counterparty risk, a phenomenon arising from an unfavourable relationship between the exposure of a contract and the underlying counterparty default probability. The use of collateral agreements and the perceived creditworthiness of the large credit derivative dealers were two key reasons why counterparty risk (and indeed wrong-way counterparty risk) was not considered a problem. However, in 2007, the beginnings of the credit crisis crushed such notions and market participants realized the severe nature of counterparty risks in single-name CDS products and portfolio credit derivatives. A successful future for the credit derivative market is very much linked on the ability to control the inherent counterparty risks.

2 Credit value adjustment (CVA)

Credit value adjustment is the key component for defining counterparty risk and allows one to express the risky value of a transaction with a given counterparty via:

$$\text{Risky MtM} = \text{Risk free MtM} - \text{CVA}. \tag{1}$$

We should note that CVA is not additive with respect to individual transactions across a 'netting set'. A netting set defines a group of transactions whose values may be legally netted in the event a counterparty defaults. Netting is a way to mitigate counterparty risk and one or more netting sets may exist for a given counterparty. CVA terms must therefore be computed for each netting set and the risky value of a given transaction cannot be calculated individually as it is defined with respect to other transactions within the same netting set. In this chapter, we will focus on individual transactions and not describe netting effects, which are discussed in more detail by Gregory (2009b).

There have been many models proposed for pricing counterparty risk via CVA, which mostly cover the 'classic' instrument types. For example, Sorenson and Bollier (1994), Jarrow and Turnbull (1992, 1995, 1997), Duffie and Huang (1996) and Brigo and Masetti (2006) describe reduced form models for counterparty risk and focus mainly on interest rate and foreign exchange products. Whilst there is a now a reasonably rich literature on pricing counterparty risk, the discussion of wrong-way CVA such as seen in credit derivative products has also been given only limited coverage. In this chapter, we will explain the nature of counterparty risk in credit derivative products and present quantitative results showing some of the key features.

3 COUNTERPARTY RISK IN CDS

A credit default swap (CDS) is the basic building block of the credit derivative market. CDS, whilst reasonable simple products, have potentially extreme counterparty risks as a direct consequence of their structure. We will start with a discussion and quantification of counterparty risk in the basic CDS product before moving on to consider the more complicated portfolio credit derivative structures.

3.1 CDS valuation with no counterparty risk

With no counterparty risk, a CDS can be rather easily defined by the value of the two payment legs corresponding to the premium payments and contingent default payments (more details can be found in O'Kane 2008). The present value of the premium leg of a CDS contract is given by:—

$$V_{premium}(t, T) = \sum_{i=1}^{n} S(t, t_i) B(t, t_i) \varDelta_{i-1,i} X_{CDS},\tag{2}$$

where n represents the number of remaining premium payments on the CDS, $S(t, t_i)$ represents the risk-neutral survival probability of the reference entity in the period $[t, t_i]$,[1] $B(t, t_i)$ represents the risk-free discount factor for time t_i as seen from time t, $\varDelta_{i-1,i}$ is the coverage, and X_{CDS} is the contractual CDS premium paid on the contract. The default payment made in a CDS contract will occur when the reference entity has suffered a credit event which can occur at any point during the life of the contract. Denoting the reference entity default time by τ and the recovery rate by δ, the contingent default payment leg is written as:

$$V_{default}(t, T) = -E^Q\left[(1 - \delta) B(t, \tau) I(\tau < T)\right].\tag{3}$$

Assuming a fixed recovery value[2] of δ, this can be expressed in terms of the survival probability of the reference entity and calculated by discretization of the resulting integral:

$$V_{default}(t, T) = (1 - \bar{\delta}) \int_t^T B(t, u) dS(u) \approx (1 - \bar{\delta}) \sum_{i=1}^{m} B(t, t_i) \left[S(t, t_{i-1}) - S(t, t_i)\right].$$

$$\tag{4}$$

---

[1] This is the probability of the reference entity not defaulting before time t_i conditional upon not being in default at the current time t.

[2] Or equivalently taking the expected recovery value and assuming independence between recovery value and both the default time and risk-free interest rate.

3.2 CDS payoff under counterparty default

A protection buyer in a CDS contract has a payoff with respect to a reference entity's default but is at risk in case the counterparty to the contract suffers a similar fate. The CDS product therefore has a highly asymmetric payoff profile due to being essentially an insurance contract as illustrated in Figure 11.1.

In addition to the asymmetry described above, default correlation is also an important component in defining CDS counterparty risk. Buying CDS protection represents a very definite form of wrong-way risk that increases as the correlation between the credit quality of the reference entity and the counterparty increases. There are four possible cases of relevance when buying protection in a single-name CDS transaction as illustrated in Figure 11.2:

- *Case 1—Reference entity defaults followed by counterparty.* Here, there is no loss since the reference entity defaults first.
- *Case 2—Counterparty defaults followed by reference entity.* Here, there is a significant loss since the counterparty defaults before the reference entity defaults and hence the default payment will not be made.
- *Case 3—Reference entity defaults first.* Here there will be no counterparty risk since the counterparty has not defaulted and the reference entity default will be settled as required.

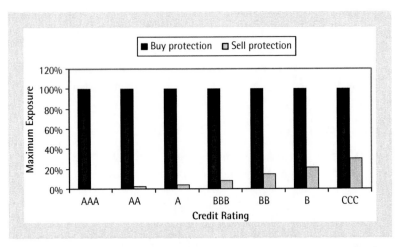

FIGURE 11.1 Illustration of the asymmetry of counterparty risk for a CDS. When buying protection, the maximum loss is 100% (reference entity default with zero recovery) but when selling protection it is smaller since it is related only to a tightening of the reference entity CDS premium. We have used ratings as a proxy for credit quality changes and have assumed a 5-year maturity and CDS premiums of 25, 50, 100, 200, 400, 600, and 1000 bp for AAA, AA, A, BBB, BB, B, and CCC respectively.

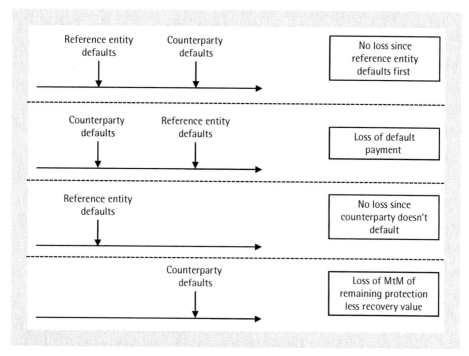

FIGURE 11.2 Illustration of counterparty risk scenarios for a CDS contract.

- *Case 4—Counterparty defaults but reference entity does not.* This is the most complex case. The counterparty defaults and, although the reference entity does not default, any potential positive MtM of the contract will be lost, less some recovery value. If the counterparty default implies a significantly positive MtM on the CDS protection (since the correlated reference entity is expected to have a worsening credit quality), then this loss would be expected to be significant—this is the manifestation of wrong-way risk.

3.3 Quantifying CVA for a CDS

When calculating the CVA adjustment for CDS, one must account for the default of both the counterparty and the reference entity and, more specifically, the order in which they occur. The pricing requires valuing the two legs of a CDS contingent to the counterparty surviving (since once the counterparty has defaulted an institution would neither make premium payments nor receive default payments) and adding a final term depending on the MtM of the CDS contract at the default time.

We denote by $S^1(t, T)$ the risk-neutral survival probability of both the counterparty and reference entity in the CDS contract. The time t premium payments made in a CDS contract of final maturity T represent an annuity stream with cash flows contingent on joint survival, which can be written as:

$$\tilde{V}_{premium}(t, T) = \sum_{i=1}^{n} S^1(t, t_i)B(t, t_i)\varDelta_{i-1,i}X_{CDS},$$ (5)

where the other components are as defined for equation (2). The default payment made in a CDS contract will be made when the reference entity has defaulted but only if the counterparty has not previously defaulted. Denoting the counterparty default time as τ_C and the 'first-to-default' time by $\tau^1 = \min(\tau_C, \tau)$, the contingent default payment leg is written as:

$$\tilde{V}_{default}(t, T) = -E^Q\left[(1 - \delta)B(t, \tau)I(\tau^1 < T)I(\tau_C > \tau)\right],$$ (6)

where δ is a percentage recovery value for the underlying reference entity, $E^Q[.]$ represents an expectation under the risk-neutral measure and $I(.)$ is an indicator function, which takes the value one if the statement is true and zero otherwise. As for equation (4) and again assuming a fixed recovery rate, equation (6) can be computed via a simple discretisation procedure:

$$\tilde{V}_{default}(t, T) \approx (1 - \bar{\delta}) \sum_{i=1}^{m} B(t, t_i)Q(\tau \in [t_{i-1}, t_i], \tau_C > \tau),$$ (7)

where $Q(\tau \in [t_{i-1}, t_i], \tau_C > \tau)$ gives the marginal default probability of the reference entity conditional on survival of the counterparty. This assumes that simultaneous default of counterparty and reference entity is not possible.

Finally, we must add on the payment made at the counterparty default time (case 4 defined previously and illustrated in Figure 11.2). Denote by $V_{CDS}(\tau, T)$ the (no counterparty risk) MtM or replacement cost of the CDS at some future default date τ including discounting. If this value is positive then the protection buyer will receive only a fraction $\bar{\delta}V_{CDS}(\tau, T)$ of the amount whilst if it is negative then the MtM must be paid to the defaulted counterparty. Hence the payoff in default is $\bar{\delta}V_{CDS}(\tau, T)^+ + V_{CDS}(\tau, T)^-$. Finally, we can write the total value of the CDS with counterparty risk as being:

$$\tilde{V}_{CDS}(t, T) = \tilde{V}_{premium}(t, T) + \tilde{V}_{default}(t, T) + E^Q\left[\left(\bar{\delta}_C V_{CDS}(\tau, T)^+ + V_{CDS}(\tau, T)^-\right)\right],$$ (8)

where δ_C is the counterparty recovery (as opposed to the reference entity recovery). Equation (8) represents the situation from the protection provider's point of view, the protection buyer's position is given simply by reversing the signs on the terms $V_{CDS}(\tau, T)$, $\tilde{V}_{premium}(t, T)$ and $\tilde{V}_{default}(t, T)$.

3.4 Modelling approach

We define the random default time of the reference entity via a Gaussian copula as $\tau = S^{-1}(\Phi(Z))$ where $S(t, T)$ represents the survival probability of the reference entity and $\Phi(.)$ denotes the cumulative Gaussian distribution function with Z a standard

Gaussian random variable. Then the default time of the counterparty is defined to be correlated and given by $\tau_C = S_C^{-1}(\Phi(Y))$ where $S_C(t, T)$ represents the survival probability of the counterparty. The correlation is introduced by defining $Y = \rho Z + \sqrt{1 - \rho^2}\varepsilon$ with ε being an additional independent standard Gaussian random variable with ρ identified as the correlation parameter. The correlation between the reference entity and counterparty default times can also be represented via a bivariate Gaussian distribution. This would mean that the joint survival probability would be given by:

$$S^1(t, T) = \Phi_{2d}\left[\Phi^{-1}(S(t, T)), \Phi^{-1}(S_C(t, T); \rho)\right], \qquad (9)$$

where $\Phi^{-1}(.)$ is the inverse of a cumulative Gaussian distribution function and $\Phi_{2d}(.)$ represents a cumulative bivariate Gaussian distribution function with correlation parameter ρ. The marginal default probability term can be approximated by:

$$
\begin{aligned}
Q(\tau \in [t_{i-1}, t_i], \tau_C > \tau) &\approx Q(\tau > t_{i-1}, \tau_C > t_i) - Q(\tau > t_i, \tau_C > t_i)\\
&= \Phi_{2d}\left[\Phi^{-1}(S(t, t_{i-1})), \Phi^{-1}(S_C(t, t_i)); \rho\right] - \Phi_{2d}\left[\Phi^{-1}(S(t, t_i)), \Phi^{-1}(S_C(t, t_i)); \rho\right],
\end{aligned}
$$
$$(10)$$

which will be accurate for small time intervals where the probability of both reference entity and counterparty defaulting within the interval is negligible. The contingent premium and default terms, $\tilde{V}_{premium}(t, T)$ and $\tilde{V}_{default}(t, T)$, can then be computed analytically from equations (6) and (7) using the expressions in equation (9) and (10). The number of points used in equation (7) needs to be reasonably large (at least 20 per year), especially when correlation is high.

The computation of the last term in equation (8) is more complicated since it involves the replacement cost corresponding to the risk-free value of the CDS at some future date τ_C. Furthermore, the option like payoff of this term means that not only the expected value of the CDS is required but also the distribution of future CDS value at the counterparty default time. Whilst the expected value of the CDS at the default time can be calculated in the static copula approach, the optionality inherent in the counterparty risk calculation requires the use of a dynamic credit model. Furthermore, the computation of this replacement cost involves a classic American Monte Carlo problem. More complex models are described, for example, by Brigo and Capponi (2009) and Lipton and Sepp (2009). We will take a more simple pricing approach based on the fact that, as pointed out by Mashal and Naldi (2005), upper and lower bounds for the final term in equation (8) can be defined by:

$$\bar{\delta}.\mathrm{E}^Q\left[V_{CDS}(\tau_C, T)\right]^+ + \mathrm{E}^Q\left[V_{CDS}(\tau_C, T)\right]^-, \qquad \text{(upper bound)} \qquad (11a)$$

$$\mathrm{E}^Q\left[(\delta C_{CDS}(\tau_C, T)^+ + C_{CDS}(\tau_C, T)^-)\right], \qquad \text{(lower bound)} \qquad (11b)$$

where $C_{CDS}(\tau_C, T)$ represents the value of the cash flows in the CDS contract at time τ_C in a given scenario, discounted back to today. The upper and lower bounds defined by the above equation can be computed by Monte Carlo simulation directly as discussed also by Turnbull (2006). It is possible to compute the upper bound analytically since we can use the results of Laurent and Gregory (2005) to calculate the survival probability of the reference entity conditional upon the counterparty default:

$$Q(\tau \geq t_2 | \tau_C = t_1) = \frac{\int\limits_{-\infty}^{\infty} \Phi\left(\frac{\sqrt{\rho(1-\rho)}u - \rho\Phi^{-1}(S_C(t_1)) + \Phi^{-1}(S(t_1))}{\sqrt{1-\rho}}\right)\varphi(u)du}{\int\limits_{-\infty}^{\infty} \Phi\left(\frac{\sqrt{\rho(1-\rho)}u - \rho\Phi^{-1}(S_C(t_1)) + \Phi^{-1}(S(t_2))}{\sqrt{1-\rho}}\right)\varphi(u)du}. \tag{12}$$

The above term is rather conveniently calculated via standard quadrature methods. The conditional survival function above allows us to calculate the expected value of the CDS contract at the counterparty default time as required by the term $E^Q\left[V_{CDS}(\tau_C, T)\right]$ in equation (9).

We will use both the Monte Carlo and analytical approaches to calculate the fair CDS premium in the presence of counterparty risk. We note a final complexity, which is that, since the term $V_{CDS}(\tau_C, T)$ depends on the premium itself, we need to solve recursively for this premium. In practice, due to the relative linearity in the region of the solution, the convergence is almost immediate.

We note that the above expressions describe the risky MtM of a CDS without explicit reference to a CVA term. Given the wrong-way risk inherent in the product, this is more rigorous and easier to understand. The CVA could be computed simply by comparison to the risk-free MtM value as indicated by equation (1).

We will also ignore the impact of any collateral in the following analysis. This will be conservative since the use of collateral may be considered to reduce significantly CDS counterparty risk. However, due to the highly contagious and systemic nature of CDS risks, the impact of collateral may be hard to assess and indeed may be quite limited, especially in cases of high correlation. We note also that many protection sellers in the CDS market (such as monolines) have not traditionally entered into collateral arrangements anyway.

3.5 Parameters

In order to compute the risky value of buying CDS protection as a function of correlation between the reference entity and counterparty (the counterparty is selling protection in the base case). We assume the following base case parameters:

$h = 2\%$ Hazard rate of reference entity.
$h_C = 4\%$ Hazard rate of counterparty.
$\bar{\delta} = 40\%$ Recovery rate for reference entity.
$\bar{\delta}_C = 40\%$ Recovery rate for counterparty.
$T = 5$ Maturity of CDS contract.

The survival probabilities of reference entity and counterparty are defined by the hazard rates according to $S(t, u) = \exp\left[-h(u - t)\right]$ and $S_C(t, u) = \exp\left[-h_C(u - t)\right]$. We can calculate the approximate CDS premiums for reference entity and counterparty from $X_{CDS} \approx h(1 - \bar{\delta})$ which gives 240 and 120 basis points per annum.[3]

---

[3] The calculations used hazard rates to give precisely these CDS premiums.

This assumes approximately equal CDS premiums for all maturities. It is possible to lift this assumption and calibrate $S(.)$ and $S_C(.)$ to a term structure of default probability without significant additional complexity.

3.6 CDS replacement cost

We begin by calculating the long protection CDS replacement cost at the counterparty default time that defines the final term in equation (8). If positive, this term will relate to a recovery amount of the CDS MtM at the counterparty default time. If negative then it corresponds to an amount owed to the defaulted counterparty. For the example concerned, the CDS replacement cost is shown in Figure 11.3 for a correlation parameter of 50%. It is interesting to quantify the expected MtM of the CDS at the counterparty default time. With positive correlation, counterparty default represents 'bad news' for the reference entity credit quality and hence the long protection CDS is expected to have a positive value. The sooner the counterparty default time, the more significant this impact.[4]

In Figure 11.4, we show the expected CDS MtM at the counterparty default time as a function of correlation. Higher correlation has a more significant impact on the expected value of the long protection CDS contract since the reference entity credit quality is expected to be significantly worse at the counterparty default time. This suggests that at high correlation the upper bound may be close to the actual result since there is little chance that the long protection position can have negative value, meaning that the first term in equation (11a) will dominate and hence the last term in equation (8) will be well approximated by ignoring the negative contribution. Put differently, the option payoff with respect to the replacement CDS is very in-the-money and hence the impact of volatility should be small.

3.7 Buying CDS protection

We start by considering the fair premium (i.e. reduced in order to account for counterparty risk) that one should pay in order to buy protection, which is shown in Figure 11.5. Firstly, we see that the upper and lower bounds are quite close, making a more costly computation of the exact result less important. Furthermore, the upper and lower bounds converge at high correlation which can be understood by the previous impact of correlation on CDS replacement value in Figure 11.4. We can also observe the very strong impact of correlation: one should be willing only to pay 100bp at 60% correlation to buy protection compared with paying 120bp with a 'risk-free'

---

[4] At some point, the counterparty default becomes no longer 'bad news' as the default is expected. In this example, the expected counterparty default time is 25 years (the inverse of the hazard rate) and hence within 5 years is rather unexpected and has a significant impact on the expected value of the CDS contract.

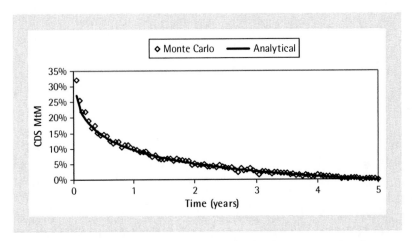

FIGURE 11.3 Expected long protection CDS MtM value (replacement cost) at the counterparty default time computed using analytical and Monte Carlo approaches for an assumed correlation of 50% between the counterparty and reference entity. The Monte Carlo results use 1,000,000 simulations with the calculations bucketed with a width of 0.05 years.

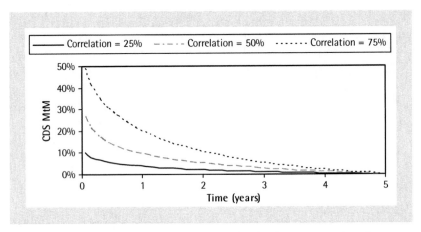

FIGURE 11.4 Expected long protection CDS MtM value (replacement cost) at the counterparty default time as a function of correlation computed analytically.

counterparty. The CVA in this case is effectively 20bp or one-sixth of the risk-free CDS premium. At extremely high correlations, the impact is even more severe and the CVA adjustment can be seen to be huge. At a maximum correlation of 100%, the CDS premium is just above 48bp, which relates entirely to the recovery value.[5] A long protection CDS contract has an increasing CVA as correlation increases due to wrong-way risk.

---

[5] The premium based only on recovery value, i.e. the protection buyer will always receive the recovery fraction times the MtM of the contract at the counterparty default time and there is no chance of receiving any default payment, is $120 \times 40\% = 48$bp.

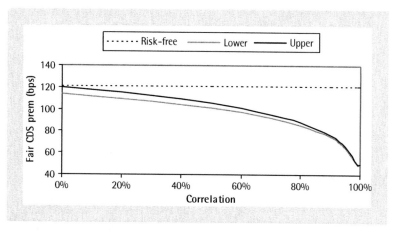

FIGURE 11.5 Upper and lower bounds for the fair CDS premium when buying protection subject to counterparty risk compared to the standard (risk-free) premium.

In Figure 11.6, we show the same example but with the hazard rates of the reference entity and counterparty exchanged. We can notice that the contract does not contain as much counterparty risk since the protection seller has a better credit quality than the reference entity. We also observe that the counterparty risk vanishes as the correlation goes to 100%. This is due to the fact that, with perfect correlation, the more risky reference entity will always default first. This facet might be considered slightly unnatural. An obvious way to correct for it would be to have some concept of joint default of the reference entity and counterparty or build in a settlement period to the analysis. These points are discussed respectively by Gregory (2009a) and Turnbull (2005).

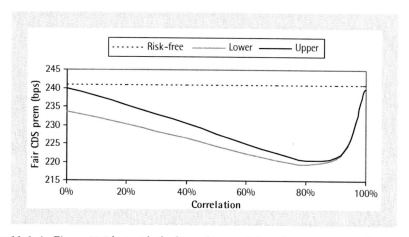

FIGURE 11.6 As Figure 11.5 but with the hazard rates of the reference entity and counterparty swapped.

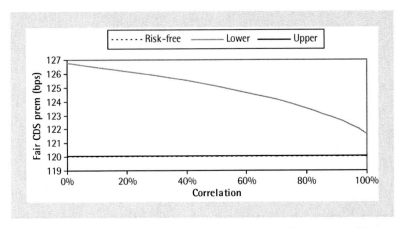

FIGURE 11.7 Upper and lower bounds for the fair CDS premium when selling protection subject to counterparty risk compared to the standard (risk-free) premium.

3.8 Selling CDS protection

We now consider the impact of selling CDS protection to a risky counterparty and use the same base case parameters as in the previous section. In Figure 11.7 and Figure 11.8, we show the fair CDS premiums (increased to account for counterparty risk). We ignore the impact of negative correlations, which are highly unlikely in practice due to the correlation inherent in credit markets. The use of upper and lower bounds is not as useful as in the long protection case. For zero or low correlation values, the lower bound is more relevant since the protection seller may possibly suffer losses due to the counterparty defaulting when the CDS has a positive MtM (requiring a

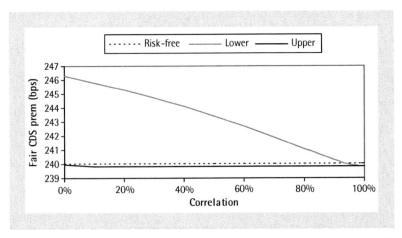

FIGURE 11.8 As previous figure but with the hazard rates of the reference entity and counterparty swapped.

somewhat unlikely tightening of the reference entity credit spread). However, for high correlation values, the upper bound is more relevant since the short CDS replacement cost is very likely to be negative, meaning that there is no recovery value according to equation (11a) and virtually no counterparty risk. A short protection CDS contract has a decreasing CVA as correlation increases due to right-way risk.

3.9 Bilateral CDS counterparty risk

A trend that has become increasingly relevant and popular recently has been to consider the bilateral nature of counterparty risk meaning that an institution would evaluate CVA under the assumption that they, as well as their counterparty, may default. This is done on the basis that a defaulting institution 'gains' on any outstanding liabilities that need not (cannot) be paid in full. This component is often named DVA (debt value adjustment). DVA is becoming commonly accepted by market participants and indeed is allowed under accountancy regulations. Many institutions regard bilateral considerations as important in order to agree on new transactions, unwinds, and minimizing P&L volatility.

In the last few years, many institutions have included their own default probability when quantifying counterparty risk. The use of DVA is somewhat controversial (e.g. see Gregory 2009a). However, when considering wrong-way risk products such as credit derivatives, bilateral counterparty risk is less of an issue. The two terms (CVA and DVA) will likely be linked to either wrong or right-way risk. Wrong-way risk will have the impact of increasing either CVA (DVA)[6] whilst right-way risk will correspondingly decrease DVA (CVA). This then removes some of the complexity of bilateral counterparty risk and creates a situation closer to the unilateral treatment. To evaluate CDS counterparty risk, the protection seller's default probability is the main component to consider, with the protection buyer's default having only secondary importance. In terms of agreeing on transaction counterparty risk charges, a protection seller would probably have to agree to the pricing of a long CDS position as shown in section 3.6.

It is possible to do the above calculations under the assumption that both counterparties may default as described by Turnbull (2005). However, this has a limited impact on the calculations since the counterparty risk all resides with the protection buyer in the contract. Hence, the DVA component from the protection buyer's point of view will simply be reduced by a small amount due to the possibility that they may default first. Other than that, the conclusions are similar.

---

[6] Assuming there is not a substantial difference between the impact of the counterparty and institution defaults on the exposure distribution.

4 COUNTERPARTY RISK IN STRUCTURED CREDIT PRODUCTS

Whilst CDS counterparty risk represents a challenge to quantify due to the wrong-way risk and uncertainty of the correlation between reference entity and protection seller (or buyer), structured credit has given rise to even more complex counterparty risk in the form of tranches. There exist many kinds of so-called CDO (collateralized debt obligation) structures, which are all broadly characterized by their exposure to a certain range of losses on a portfolio. The counterparty risk problem now becomes more complex since one needs to assess where the counterparty might default compared to all the reference names underlying the portfolio. Our discussion will consider index tranches, the most commonly traded portfolio credit derivatives. However, the general conclusions will hold for all CDO products.

4.1 Index tranches

Credit indices represent the most liquid forms of traded credit risk. A credit index can be thought of as an equally weighted combination of single-name CDS and the fair premium on the index will be close to the average CDS premium within that index.[7] The two most common credit indices are:

- DJ iTraxx Europe. This contains 125 European corporate investment grade reference entities, which are equally weighted.
- DJ CDX NA IG. This contains 125 North American (NA) corporate investment grade reference entities that are also equally weighted.

Other indices exist for different underlying reference entities and regions but they are less liquid. Buying CDS protection on $125m of the DJ CDX NA IG index (for example) is almost[8] equivalent to buying $1m of CDS protection on each of the underlying reference entities within the index. Whilst a credit index references all losses on the underlying names, a tranche will only reference a certain portion of those losses. So, for example, an [X, Y%] tranche will reference losses between X% and Y% on the underlying index. The 'subordination' of the tranche is X% whilst Y% is referred to as the 'detachment point'. The size of the tranche is (Y − X)%. The standard index tranches for the DJ iTraxx Europe and DJ CDX NA indices are illustrated in Figure 11.9. The [0–3%] equity tranches are the most risky instruments since they are

---

[7] This is not quite true for two reasons. Firstly, a theoretical adjustment must be made to the average CDS premium to account for the heterogeneity of the constituents. Secondly, the index will typically trade at a basis to the average CDS premiums (bid-offer costs will prevent arbitrage of this difference).

[8] Aside from the theoretical adjustment due to a premium mismatch and the fact that there will be different contractual payments.

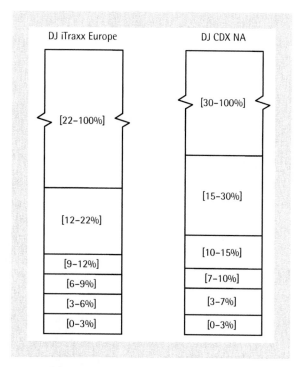

FIGURE 11.9 Illustration of the index tranches corresponding to the DJ iTraxx Europe and DJ CDX North American credit indices. All tranches are shown to scale except the [22–100%] and [30–100%].

completely exposed to the first few defaults on the portfolio. As one moves up through the 'capital structure', the tranches becomes less risky.

Equity tranches ([0–3%]) have always traded with an up-front premium and fixed running spread of 500bp to avoid the annuity risk that exists for such a relatively high-risk tranche. For iTraxx, more recently the [3–6%] and [6–9%] have changed to trade in the same way. The remaining tranches trade on a running basis. CDX tranches (which used to trade in a similar way to iTraxx) currently trade at 500 basis points running for [0–3%], [3–7%] and [7–10%] and 100bp running for [10–15%], [15–30%], and [30–100%]. Example tranche quotes for iTraxx and CDX are shown in Table 11.1.

Irrespective of trading convention, the important aspect of an index tranche is that it covers only a certain range of the losses on the portfolio. Index tranches vary substantially in the risk they constitute: equity tranches carry a large amount of risk and pay attractive returns whilst tranches that are more senior have far less risk but pay only moderate returns. At the far end, super senior tranches ([22–100%] and [30–100%]) might be considered to have no risk whatsoever (in terms of experiencing losses). Tranching creates a leverage effect since the more junior tranches carry more risk than the index whilst the most senior tranches[9] have less risk. For ease of comparison,

[9] Due to its size, usually only the super senior may have a leverage of less than one and all other tranches may be more highly leveraged than the index.

Table 11.1 Example tranche quotes for iTraxx and CDX investment grade tranches at 5, 7, and 10-year maturities for 28 August 2009

DJ iTraxx Europe Tranches

	5Y	7Y	10Y
[0–3%]	38.00%	45.00%	50.75%
[3–6%]	2.000%	7.000%	12.750%
[6–9%]	−7.625%	−6.000%	−2.875%
[9–12%]	160	200	246
[12–22%]	66.5	92.0	101.5
[22–100%]	28.75	34.00	38.25

DJ CDX NA

	5Y%	7Y%	10Y%
[0–3%]	70.125	76.250	77.875
[3–7%]	24.500	32.375	36.875
[7–10%]	1.125	6.000	10.750
[10–15%]	4.500	9.438	13.625
[15–30%]	−1.280	−1.150	1.030
[30–100%]	−2.300	−3.400	−4.800

Note: The first three tranches in each case trade with a fixed 500bp running coupon with the quote reflecting the up-front payment required. The final three iTraxx tranches trade with a variable coupon (shown in bps) only whilst the final three CDX tranches trade at a fixed running coupon of 100bp with the quote reflecting the up-front payment required. Up-front payments are negative when the fixed coupon is higher than the fair coupon.

the results below will assume that all tranches trade on a fully running basis to ease the comparison across the capital structure. Whilst tranches have different trading conventions, as noted above, this does not influence the results substantially as shown by Gregory (2009b).

The goal is to understand the impact of counterparty risk for index tranches or CDO products traded in unfunded form. It is possible to extend the analysis of the previous section to calculate the upper and lower bounds on the value of a tranche product in the presence of counterparty risk. More details on this can be found in Turnbull (2005) and Pugachevsky (2005). Our calculations follow these authors, although we will again calculate the fair premiums for risky tranche instruments, which are probably the easiest numbers to illustrate the impact of counterparty risk.

The following parameters will be used in the examples:

$n = 125$ Number of reference entities within the portfolio (consistent with iTraxx).

$\bar{h} = 2\%$ Average hazard rate of a name in the portfolio.[10]

---

[10] All of the following results have been computed with both homogeneous and heterogeneous hazard rates. There were no significant qualitative differences in the results and so for ease of replication of results we show the former results. We also note that the precise hazard rate was chosen to give a fair price for the index of 120bp.

$h_C = 4\%$ Hazard rate of counterparty.
$\bar{\delta} = 40\%$ Recovery rate of reference entity.
$\bar{\delta}_C = 40\%$ Recovery rate of counterparty.
$T = 5$ Maturity of CDS contract.

4.2 Credit indices and counterparty risk

We first compute the fair CDS premium when buying protection on a CDS index. In Figure 11.10, we show the fair CDS premium upper and lower bounds compared to the risk-free value. We see almost exactly the same result as seen previously for a single name CDS with equivalent parameters in Figure 11.5. Hence we can conclude that a credit index behaves in a very similar way to a similar single-name CDS in terms of counterparty risk.

4.3 Index tranches and counterparty risk

For tranches of a portfolio, it is important to understand how the impact of counterparty risk can change across the capital structure. As mentioned previously, we choose tranches according to the standard iTraxx Europe portfolio that are defined by the attachment and detachment points [0%, 3%, 6%, 9%, 12%, 22%, 100%]. Since we are interested only in understanding the qualitative impact of counterparty risk for different tranches, we choose the market standard Gaussian copula model (see Li 2000) with a fixed correlation parameter of 50%.[11] Due to constraints on the correlation matrix, this means we consider the correlation between the counterparty default and the other names in the portfolio in the range [0, 70%].[12]

We first show the fair premium for buying [0–3%] protection (Figure 11.11) and can see that the counterparty risk impact is actually quite small, even at high correlation values. At the 40% recovery rate assumed, the equity tranche covers the first 6.25 defaults[13] in the portfolio. Even though the counterparty is more risky, the chance that it defaults at some point before the equity tranche has completely defaulted is relatively small.[14] The impact of correlation (between counterparty default and the reference names in the portfolio) is quite subtle. As correlation increases, the counterparty risk at first increases also (decreasing fair premium) due to the more risky counterparty

---

[11] This does not produce prices close to the market but the standard approach of 'base correlation' used to reproduce market prices does not have an obvious associated way in which to price correctly counterparty risk. We have checked that the qualitative conclusions of these results hold at different correlations levels.

[12] The upper limit for this correlation due to constraints of positive semi-definitiveness on the correlation matrix is approximately $\sqrt{50\%} = 70.7\%$.

[13] $3\% \times 125 / (1-40\%)$.

[14] The counterparty must be one of the first seven defaults for there to be any counterparty risk since after this point the tranche is completely wiped out.

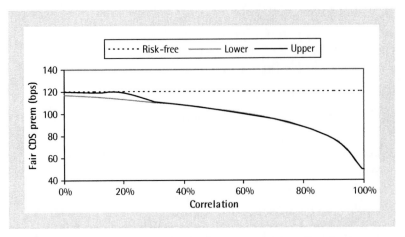

FIGURE 11.10 Upper and lower bounds for the fair CDS premium when buying protection on a CDS index subject to counterparty risk compared to the standard (risk-free) premium.

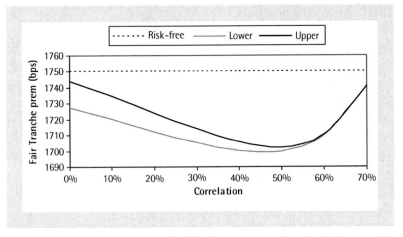

FIGURE 11.11 Upper and lower bounds for the fair premium when buying protection on the [0–3%] equity tranche (assuming the premium is paid on a running basis) as a function of correlation with the parameters given in the text.

being more likely to default earlier. However, for very high correlations, we see the effect reversing which is due to approaching the maximum correlation allowed which makes the counterparty default time increasingly certain vis à vis the other defaults.[15]

We now look at a significantly more senior part of the capital structure with the [6–9%] tranche in Figure 11.12. We can see that the counterparty risk is much more significant, and increases substantially with the correlation between the counterparty

---

[15] This is a subtle point relating to the order of default times at high correlation. Due to the relative riskiness of the counterparty with respect to the other names and the correlation structure, the counterparty default is expected to be early but unlikely to be within the first seven defaults and hence the equity tranche has little counterparty risk.

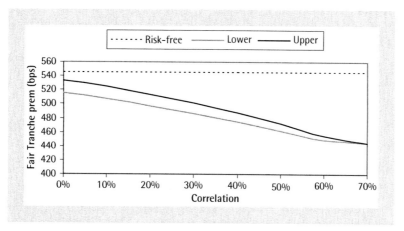

FIGURE 11.12 Upper and lower bounds for the fair premium when buying protection on the [6–9%] tranche as a function of correlation with the parameters given in the text.

and reference entities in the portfolio. At high correlation, the fair risky premium is decreased by around 100bp compared to the risk-free premium. The impact of increasing correlation can again be understood by increasing the likelihood that the more risky counterparty will default sooner rather than later. Since the [6–9%] tranche is only hit after 12.5 defaults, there is more chance that the counterparty will have defaulted prior (or during) the tranche taking losses.

4.4 Super senior risk

Super senior tranches have created a big headache for the credit market in terms of their counterparty risk. Let us start by asking ourselves how many defaults would cause a loss on a super senior tranche of DJ iTraxx Europe. We can represent the number of defaults a given tranche can withstand as:

$$\text{Num Defaults} = n\frac{X}{(1 - \delta_{wa})}, \tag{13}$$

where X represents the attachment point of the tranche in per cent, n is the number of names in the index, and δ_{wa} is the (weighted[16]) average recovery rate for the defaults that occur.

Super senior tranches clearly have very little default risk. Even assuming (conservatively) zero recovery, default rates over several years would have to be many multiples[17] of historical averages to wipe out the subordination on the super senior

---

[16] Since the default that actually hits the tranche may have only a fractional impact as in the previous example.

[17] For example, Gregory (2009b) estimates default rates of 4 to 6 times for a 5-year [22–100%] tranche and 8 to 11 times for a 10-year tranche.

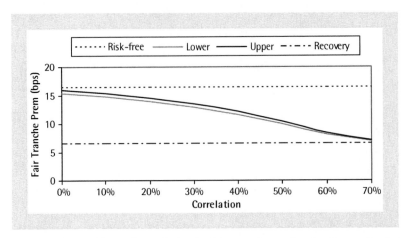

FIGURE 11.13 Upper and lower bounds for the fair premium when buying protection on the [22–100%] super senior tranche as a function of correlation with the parameters given in the text. The fair premium based on a recovery only assumption is shown—this assumes the counterparty will never settle any losses before defaulting.

tranches. This default remoteness has led to terms such as 'super triple-A' or 'quadruple A' being used to describe the risk on super senior tranche since they constitute what we might call 'end of the world' risk.

Finally, we consider the most senior tranche in the capital structure, the super senior [22–100%] in Figure 11.13. Assuming 40% recovery, there need to be 45.8 defaults[18] before this tranche takes any loss and so the chance that the counterparty is still around to honour these payments is expected to be much smaller than for other tranches. Not surprisingly, the counterparty risk impact is now dramatic with the fair premium tending towards just a recovery value at high correlation (40% of the risk-free premium). In such a case there is virtually no chance to settle losses on the protection before the counterparty has defaulted. We could argue that a more appropriate recovery rate would be close to zero (since an institution selling protection on super senior positions is likely to be highly leveraged as in the case of monolines). The monolines that have suffered credit events to date had rather low recovery values. This would of course mean that the protection could have little or no value at high correlation.

4.5 Counterparty risk distribution across capital structure

We summarize the above results by showing the impact of counterparty risk across the entire capital structure in Figure 11.14. In order to compare all tranches on the same scale, we plot the ratio of fair risky premium (as an average of the upper and lower bounds) to the risk-free premium: this value will have a maximum at unity

[18] $22\% \times 125/(1 - 40\%)$

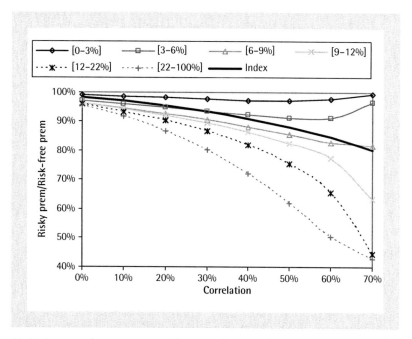

FIGURE 11.14 Impact of counterparty risk across the capital structure. Fair risky tranche premium divided by the risk-free premium for all tranches in the capital structure and compared to the index ([0–100%] tranche).

and decrease towards the recovery (of the counterparty) as counterparty risk becomes more significant. Whereas the equity tranche has less risk than the index, all other more senior tranches have more risk (except the [3–6%] tranche at most correlation levels). Indeed, from a counterparty risk perspective, we can view tranching as segregating the counterparty risk—the more senior a tranche, the more counterparty risk it contains on a relative basis.

The above analysis concerned a situation where the counterparty is more risky than the average of the portfolio. We briefly summarize results for a less risky counterparty with a hazard rate of $h_C = 1.5\%$ in Figure 11.15. Whilst the overall impact is, as expected, not so significant we still see that there is still considerable counterparty risk, especially for the most senior tranches.

The fact that counterparty risk increases with the seniority of the tranche is an important aspect of portfolio credit products. We can also note from the above figure that the extreme counterparty risk of the [22–100%] tranche is not significantly decreased from trading with the counterparty that is two and a half times less risky. Very importantly, we see that the seniority of a tranche can dominate over even the credit quality of the counterparty. This was an important lesson in some of the problems banks had in buying super senior protection from monoline insurers (see Gregory 2008b).

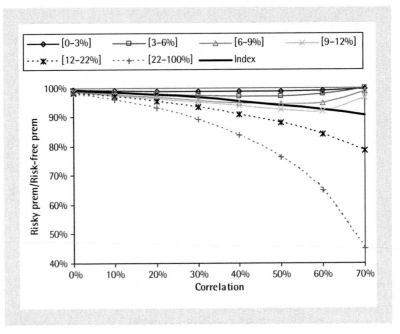

FIGURE 11.15 As Figure 11.14 but for a less risky counterparty with $h_C = 1.5\%$.

5 SUMMARY

In this chapter, we have described the counterparty risk of credit derivative instruments. We have discussed the so-called 'wrong-way risk' in credit derivatives products and how this has been a significant issue for controlling their counterparty risk. We have quantified counterparty risk on single-name credit default swaps, showing that a high correlation between the reference entity and counterparty can create significant counterparty risks for a buyer of protection. This analysis has been extended to value the counterparty risk in tranches of credit portfolios, showing a strong increase for more senior tranches. Indeed, we have shown that the counterparty risk in so-called super senior tranches is massive.

REFERENCES

Brigo, D., and Masetti, M. (2005). 'Risk neutral pricing of counterparty risk'. In M. Pykhtin (ed.), *Counterparty Credit Risk Modelling*. London: Risk Books.

Brigo, D., and Capponi, A. (2009). 'Bilateral counterparty risk valuation with stochastic dynamical models and application to Credit Default Swaps'. Working paper available on <www.defaultrisk.com>.

Canabarro, E., and Duffie, D. (2003). 'Measuring and marking counterparty risk'. In L. Tilman (ed.), Asset/Liability Management for Financial Institutions. London: Euromoney Institutional Investor Books.

Duffie, D., and Huang, M. (1996). 'Swap rates and credit quality'. Journal of Finance, 51: 921–50.

Gregory J. (2008a). 'A trick of the credit tail'. Risk (Mar.), 88–92.

—— (2008b). 'A free lunch and the credit crunch'. Risk (Aug.), 74–7.

—— (2009a). 'Being two faced over counterparty credit risk'. Risk 22/12: 86–90.

—— (2009b). Counterparty Credit Risk: The New Challenge for Global Financial Markets. Chichester: John Wiley & Sons.

—— and Laurent, J-P. (2003). 'I will survive'. Risk (June), 103–07.

Hille, C. T., Ring, J., and Shimanmoto, H. (2005). 'Modelling Counterparty Credit Exposure for Credit Default Swaps'. In M. Pykhtin (ed.), 'Counterparty Credit Risk Modelling'. London: Risk Books.

Jarrow, R. A., and Turnbull, S. M. (1992). 'Drawing the analogy'. Risk, 5/10: 63–70.

—— —— (1995). 'Pricing options on financial securities subject to default risk'. Journal of Finance, 50: 53–86.

—— —— (1997). 'When swaps are dropped'. Risk, 10/5: 70–5.

Laurent, J-P., and Gregory, J. (2005). 'Basket default swaps, CDOs and factor copulas'. Journal of Risk, 7/4: 103–122.

Li, D. X. (2000). 'On default correlation: a copula function approach'. Journal of Fixed Income, 9/4: 43–54.

Lipton, A., and Sepp, A. (2009). 'Credit value adjustment for credit default swaps via the structural default model'. Journal of Credit Risk, 5/2: 123–46.

Mashal, R., and Naldi, M. (2005). 'Pricing multiname default swaps with counterparty risk'. Journal of Fixed Income, 14/4: 3–16.

O'Kane, D. (2008). 'Pricing single-name and portfolio credit derivatives'. Chichester: Wiley Finance.

Pugachevsky, D. (2005). 'Pricing counterparty risk in unfunded synthetic CDO tranches'. In M. Pykhtin (ed.) 'Counterparty Credit Risk Modelling'. London: Risk Books.

Sorenson, E. H., and Bollier, T. F. (1994). 'Pricing swap default risk'. Financial Analyst's Journal, 50/3: 23–33.

Turnbull, S. (2005). 'The pricing implications of counterparty risk for non-linear credit products'. In M. Pykhtin, (ed.), 'Counterparty Credit Risk Modelling'. London: Risk Books.

CHAPTER 12

··

CREDIT VALUE
ADJUSTMENT IN THE
EXTENDED STRUCTURAL
DEFAULT MODEL

··

ALEXANDER LIPTON AND ARTUR SEPP

1 INTRODUCTION

··

1.1 Motivation

IN view of the recent turbulence in the credit markets and given a huge outstanding notional amount of credit derivatives, counterparty risk has become a critical issue for the financial industry as a whole. According to the most recent survey conveyed by the International Swap Dealers Association (see <www.isda.org>), the outstanding notional amount of credit default swaps was $38.6 trillion as of 31 December 2008 (it has decreased from $62.2 trillion as of 31, December 2007). By way of comparison, the outstanding notional amount of interest rate derivatives was $403.1 trillion, while the outstanding notional amount of equity derivatives was $8.7 trillion. The biggest bankruptcy in US history filed by one of the major derivatives dealers, Lehman Brothers Holdings Inc., in September of 2008 makes counterparty risk estimation and management vital to the financial system at large and all the participating financial institutions.

The key objective of this chapter is to develop a methodology for valuing the counterparty credit risk inherent in credit default swaps (CDSs). For the protection buyer (PB), a CDS contract provides protection against a possible default of the reference name (RN) in exchange for periodic payments to the protection seller (PS) whose magnitude is determined by the so-called CDS spread. When a PB buys a CDS from a risky PS they have to cope with two types of risk: (a) market risk which comes directly from changes in the mark-to-market (MTM) value of the CDS due to credit spread and interest rate changes; (b) credit risk which comes from the fact that PS may be unable to honour their obligation to cover losses stemming from the default of the corresponding RN. During the life of a CDS contract, a realized loss due to the counterparty exposure arises when PS defaults before RN and, provided that MTM of the CDS is positive, the counterparty pays only a fraction of the MTM value of the existing CDS contract (if MTM of the CDS is negative to PB, this CDS can be unwound at its market price).

Since PB realizes positive MTM gains when the credit quality of RN deteriorates (since the probability of receiving protection increases), their realized loss due to PS default is especially big if the credit quality of RN and PS deteriorate simultaneously but PS defaults first. We define the credit value adjustment (CVA), or the counterparty charge (CC), as the maximal expected loss on a short position (protection bought) in a CDS contract.

In order to describe CVA in quantitative rather than qualitative terms, in this chapter we build a multi-dimensional structural default model. Below we concentrate on its two-dimensional (2D) version and show that the evaluation of CVA is equivalent to pricing a 2D down-and-in digital option with the down barrier being triggered when the value of the PS's assets crosses their default barrier and the option rebate being determined by the value of the RN's assets at the barrier crossing time. We also briefly discuss the complementary problem of determining CVA for a long position (protection sold) in a CDS contract.

Traditionally, the par CDS spread at inception is set in such a way that the MTM value of the contract is zero.[1] Thus, the option underlying CVA is at-the-money, so that its value is highly sensitive to the volatility of the RN's CDS spread, while the barrier triggering event is highly sensitive to the volatility of the PS's asset value. In addition to that, the option value is sensitive to the correlation between RN and PS. This observation indicates that for dealing with counterparty risk we need to model the correlation between default times of RN and PS as well as CDS spread volatilities for both of them. It turns out that our structural model is very well suited to accomplish this highly non-trivial task.

1.2 Literature overview

Merton developed the original version of the so-called structural default model (Merton 1974). He postulated that the firm's value V is driven by a lognormal diffusion and that the firm, which borrowed a zero-coupon bond with face value N and maturity T, defaults at time T if the value of the firm V is less than the bond's face value N.

---

[1] Subsequent to the so-called 'big bang' which occurred in 2009, CDS contracts frequently trade on an up-front basis with fixed coupon.

Following this pioneering insight, many authors proposed various extensions of the basic model (Black and Cox 1976; Kim, Ramaswamy, and Sundaresan 1993; Nielsen, Saa-Requejo, and Santa-Clara 1993; Leland 1994; Longstaff and Schwartz 1995; Leland and Toft 1996; Albanese and Chen 2005) among others. They considered more complicated forms of debt and assumed that the default event may be triggered continuously up to the debt maturity. More recent research has been concentrated on extending the model in order to be able to generate the high short-term CDS spreads typically observed in the market. It has been shown that the latter task can be achieved either by making default barriers curvilinear (Hyer et al. 1998; Hull and White 2001; Avellaneda and Zhou 2001), or by making default barriers stochastic (Finger et al. 2002), or by incorporating jumps into the firm's value dynamics (Zhou 2001a; Hilberink and Rogers 2002; Lipton 2002b; Lipton, Song, and Lee 2007; Sepp 2004, 2006; Cariboni and Schoutens 2007; Feng and Linetsky 2008).

Multi-dimensional extensions of the structural model have been studied by several researchers (Zhou 2001b; Hull and White 2001; Haworth 2006; Haworth, Reisinger and Shaw 2006; Valužis 2008), who considered bivariate correlated log-normal dynamics for two firms and derived analytical formulas for their joint survival probability; Li (2000), who introduced the Gaussian copula description of correlated default times in multi-dimensional structural models; Kiesel and Scherer (2007), who studied a multi-dimensional structural model and proposed a mixture of semi-analytical and Monte Carlo (MC) methods for model calibration and pricing.

While we build a general multi-dimensional structural model, our specific efforts are aimed at a quantitative estimation of the counterparty risk. Relevant work on the counterparty risk includes, among others, Jarrow and Turnbull (1995), who developed the so called reduced-form default model and analysed the counterparty risk in this framework; Hull and White (2001), Blanchet-Scalliet and Patras (2008), who modelled the correlation between RN and the counterparty by considering their bivariate correlated lognormal dynamics; Turnbull (2005), Pugachevsky (2005), who derived model-free upper and lower bounds for the counterparty exposure; Jarrow and Yu (2001), Leung and Kwok (2005) who studied counterparty risk in the reduced-form setting; Pykhtin and Zhu (2005), Misirpashaev (2008), who applied the Gaussian copula formalism to study counterparty effects; Brigo and Chourdakis (2008), who considered correlated dynamics of the credit spreads, etc.

Our approach requires the solution of partial integro-differential equations (PIDE) with a non-local integral term. The analysis of solution methods based on the Fast Fourier Transform (FFT) can be found in Broadie and Yamamoto (2003), Jackson, Jaimungal, and Surkov (2007), Boyarchenko and Levendorski (2008), Fang and Oosterlee (2008), Feng and Linetsky (2008), and Lord et al. (2008). The treatment via finite-difference (FD) methods can be found in Andersen and Andreasen (2000), Lipton (2003), d'Halluin, Forsyth, and Vetzal (2005), Cont and Voltchkova (2005), Carr and Mayo (2007), Lipton, Song, and Lee (2007), Toivanen (2008), and Clift and Forsyth (2008).

1.3 Contribution

In this chapter, we develop a novel variant of the one-dimensional (1D), two-dimensional (2D), and multi-dimensional structural default model based on the assumption that firms' values are driven by correlated additive processes. (Recall that an additive process is a jump-diffusion process with time-inhomogeneous increments.) In order to calibrate the 1D version of our structural model to the CDS spread curve observed in the market, we introduce jumps with piecewise constant intensity. We correlate jumps of different firms via a Marshall-Olkin inspired mechanism (Marshall and Olkin 1967). This model was presented for the first time by Lipton and Sepp (2009).

In this chapter, we develop robust FFT- and FD-based methods for model calibration via forward induction and pricing via backward induction in one and two dimensions. While the FFT-based solution methods are easy to implement, they require uniform grids and a large number of discretization steps. At the same time, FD-based methods, while computationally more challenging, tend to provide greater flexibility and stability. As part of our FD scheme development, we obtain new explicit recursion formulas for the evaluation of the 2D convolution term for discrete and exponential jumps. In addition, we present a closed-form formula for the joint survival probability of two firms driven by correlated lognormal bivariate diffusion processes by using the method of images, thus complementing results obtained by He, Keirstead, and Rebholz, (1998), Lipton (2001), and Zhou (2001b) via the classical eigenfunction expansion method. As always, the method of images works well for shorter times, while the method of eigenfunction expansion works well for longer times.

We use the above results to develop an innovative approach to the estimation of CVA for CDSs. Our approach is dynamic in nature and takes into account both the correlation between RN and PS (or PB) and the CDS spread volatilities. The approaches proposed by Leung and Kwok (2005), Pykhtin and Zhu (2005), and Misirpashaev (2008) do not account for spread volatility and, as a result, may underestimate CVA. Blanchet-Scalliet and Patras (2008) consider a conceptually similar approach; however, their analytical implementation is restricted to lognormal bivariate dynamics with constant volatilities, which makes it impossible to fit the term structure of the CDS spreads and CDS option volatilities implied by the market. Accordingly, the corresponding CVA valuation is biased. In contrast, our model can be fitted to an arbitrary term structure of CDS spreads and market prices of CDS and equity options. The approach by Hull and White (2001) uses MC simulations of the correlated lognormal bivariate diffusions. In contrast, our approach assumes jump-diffusion dynamics, potentially more realistic for default modelling, and uses robust semi-analytical and numerical methods for model calibration and CVA valuation.

This chapter is organized as follows. In section 2 we introduce the structural default model in one, two, and multi-dimensions. In section 3 we formulate the generic pricing problem in one, two and multi-dimensions. In section 4 we consider the pricing problem for CDSs, CDS options (CDSOs), first-to-default swaps (FTDSs), and the valuation problem for CVA. In section 5 we develop analytical, asymptotic, and numerical methods for solving the 1D pricing problem. In particular, we describe MC, FFT, and FD methods for solving the calibration problem via forward induction and the pricing problem via backward induction. In section 6 we present analytical and numerical methods for solving the 2D pricing problem, including FFT and FD methods. In section 7 we provide an illustration of our findings by showing how to calculate CVA for a CDS on Morgan Stanley (MS) sold by JP Morgan (JPM) and a CDS on JPM sold by MS. We formulate brief conclusions in section 8.

2 STRUCTURAL MODEL AND DEFAULT EVENT

In this section we describe our structural default model in one, two, and multi-dimensions.

2.1 Notation

Throughout the chapter, we model uncertainty by constructing a probability space $(\Omega, \mathcal{F}, \mathbb{F}, \mathbb{Q})$ with the filtration $\mathbb{F} = \{\mathcal{F}(t), t \geq 0\}$ and a martingale measure $\mathbb{Q}$. We assume that $\mathbb{Q}$ is specified by market prices of liquid credit products. The operation of expectation under $\mathbb{Q}$ given information set $\mathcal{F}(t)$ at time t is denoted by $\mathbb{E}_t^{\mathbb{Q}}[\cdot]$. The imaginary unit is denoted by $\mathbf{i}$, $\mathbf{i} = \sqrt{-1}$.

The instantaneous risk-free interest rate $r(t)$ is assumed to be deterministic; the corresponding discount factor, $D(t, T)$ is given by:

$$D(t, T) = \exp\left\{-\int_t^T r(t')dt'\right\} \tag{1}$$

It is applied at valuation time t for cash flows generated at time T, $0 \leq t \leq T < \infty$.

The indicator function of an event ϕ is denoted by $\mathbf{1}_\phi$:

$$\mathbf{1}_\phi = \begin{cases} 1 & \text{if } \phi \text{ is true} \\ 0 & \text{if } \phi \text{ is false} \end{cases} \tag{2}$$

The Heaviside step function is denoted by $\mathbf{H}(x)$,

$$\mathbf{H}(x) = \mathbf{1}_{\{x \geq 0\}} \tag{3}$$

the Dirac delta function is denoted by $\delta(x)$; the Kronecker delta function is denoted by δ_{n,n_0}. We also use the following notation

$$\{x\}_+ = \max\{x, 0\} \tag{4}$$

We denote the normal probability density function (PDF) by $\mathbf{n}(x)$; and the cumulative normal probability function by $\mathbf{N}(x)$; besides, we frequently use the function $\mathbf{P}(a, b)$ defined as follows:

$$\mathbf{P}(a, b) = \exp\left\{ab + b^2/2\right\} \mathbf{N}(a + b) \tag{5}$$

2.2 One-dimensional case

2.2.1 Asset value dynamics

We denote the firm's asset value by $a(t)$. We assume that $a(t)$ is driven by a 1D jump-diffusion under $\mathbb{Q}$:

$$da(t) = (r(t) - \zeta(t) - \lambda(t)\kappa)a(t)dt + \sigma(t)a(t)dW(t) + (e^j - 1)a(t)dN(t) \tag{6}$$

where $\zeta(t)$ is the deterministic dividend rate on the firm's assets, $W(t)$ is a standard Brownian motion, $\sigma(t)$ is the deterministic volatility, $N(t)$ is a Poisson process independent of $W(t)$, $\lambda(t)$ is its intensity, j is the jump amplitude, which is a random variable with PDF $\varpi(j)$; and κ is the jump compensator:

$$\kappa = \int_{-\infty}^0 e^j \varpi(j)dj - 1 \tag{7}$$

To reduce the number of free parameters, we concentrate on one-parametric PDFs with negative jumps which may result in random crossings of the default barrier. We consider either discrete negative jumps (DNJs) of size $-\nu, \nu > 0$, with

$$\varpi(j) = \delta(j + \nu), \ \kappa = e^{-\nu} - 1 \tag{8}$$

or exponential negative jumps (ENJs) with mean size $\frac{1}{\nu}, \nu > 0$, with:

$$\varpi(j) = \nu e^{\nu j}, \ j < 0, \ \kappa = \frac{\nu}{\nu + 1} - 1 = -\frac{1}{\nu + 1} \tag{9}$$

In our experience, for 1D marginal dynamics the choice of the jump size distribution has no impact on the model calibration to CDS spreads and CDS option volatilities, however, for the joint correlated dynamics this choice becomes very important, as we will demonstrate shortly.

2.2.2 Default boundary

The cornerstone assumption of a structural default model is that the firm defaults when its value crosses a deterministic or, more generally, random default boundary. The default boundary can be specified either endogenously or exogenously.

The endogenous approach was originated by Black and Cox (1976) who used it to study the optimal capital structure of a firm. Under a fairly strict assumption that the firm's liabilities can only be financed by issuing new equity, the equity holders have the right to push the firm into default by stopping issuing new equity to cover the interest payments to bondholders and, instead, turning the firm over to the bondholders. Black and Cox (1976) found the critical level for the firm's value, below which it is not optimal for equity holders to sell any more equity. Equity holders should determine the critical value or the default barrier by maximizing the value of the equity and, respectively, minimizing the value of outstanding bonds. Thus, the optimal debt-to-equity ratio and the endogenous default barrier are decision variables in this approach. A nice review of the Black-Cox approach and its extensions is given by Bielecki and Rutkowski (2002), and Uhrig-Homburg (2002). However, in our view, the endogenous approach is not realistic given the complicated equity-liability structure of large firms and the actual relationships between the firm's management and its equity and debtholders. For example, in July 2009 the bail-out of a commercial lender CIT was carried out by debtholders, who proposed debt restructuring, rather than by equity holders, who had no negotiating power.

In the exogenous approach, the default boundary is one of the model parameters. The default barrier is typically specified as a fraction of the debt per share estimated by the recovery ratio of firms with similar characteristics. While still not very realistic, this approach is more intuitive and practical (see, for instance, Kim, Ramaswamy, and Sundaresan 1993; Nielsen, Saa-Requejo, and Santa-Clara 1993; Longstaff and Schwartz 1995; etc.).

In our approach, similarly to Lipton (2002b) and Stamicar and Finger (2005), we assume that the default barrier of the firm is a deterministic function of time given by

$$l(t) = E(t)l(0) \tag{10}$$

where $E(t)$ is the deterministic growth factor:

$$E(t) = \exp \left\{ \int_0^t (r(t') - \zeta(t'))dt' \right\} \tag{11}$$

and $l(0)$ is defined by $l(0) = RL(0)$, where R is an average recovery of the firm's liabilities and $L(0)$ is its total debt per share. We find $L(0)$ from the balance sheet as the ratio of the firm's total liability to the total number of common shares outstanding; R is found from CDS quotes, typically, it is assumed that $R = 0.4$.

2.2.3 Default triggering event

The key variable of the model is the random default time which we denote by τ. We assume that τ is an $\mathbb{F}$-adapted stopping time, $\tau \in (0, \infty]$. In general, the default event can be triggered in three ways.

First, when the firm's value is monitored only at the debt's maturity time T, then the default time is defined by:

$$\tau = \begin{cases} T, & a(T) \leq l(T) \\ \infty, & a(T) > l(T) \end{cases} \tag{12}$$

This is the case of terminal default monitoring (TDM) which we do not use below.

Second, if the firm's value is monitored at fixed points in time, $\{t_m^d\}_{m=1,\dots,M}$, $0 < t_1^d < \dots < t_M^d \leq T$, then the default event can only occur at some time t_m^d. The corresponding default time is specified by:

$$\tau = \min\{t_m^d : a(t_m^d) \le l(t_m^d)\}, \ \min\{\varnothing\} = \infty \tag{13}$$

This is the case of discrete default monitoring (DDM).

Third, if the firm's value is monitored at all times $0 < t \le T$, then the default event can occur at any time between the current time t and the maturity time T. The corresponding default time is specified by:

$$\tau = \inf\{t, 0 \le t \le T : a(t) \le l(t)\}, \ \inf\{\varnothing\} = \infty \tag{14}$$

This is the case of continuous default monitoring (CDM).

The TDM assumption is hard to justify and apply for realistic debt structures.

The DDM assumption is reasonably realistic. Under this assumption, efficient quasi-analytical methods can be applied in one and two dimensions under the log-normal dynamics (Hull and White 2001) and in one dimension under jump-diffusion dynamics (Lipton 2003; Lipton, Song, and Lee 2007; Feng and Linetsky 2008). Numerical PIDE methods for the problem with DDM tend to have slower convergence rates than those for the problem with CDM, because the solution is not smooth at default monitoring times in the vicinity of the default barrier. However, MC-based methods can be applied in the case of DDM in a robust way, because the firm's asset values need to be simulated only at default monitoring dates. Importantly, there is no conceptual difficulty in applying MC simulations for the multi-dimensional model.

In the case of CDM closed-form solutions are available for the survival probability in one dimension (see e.g. Leland 1994; Leland and Toft 1996) and two dimensions (Zhou 2001b) for lognormal diffusions; and in one dimension for jump-diffusions with negative jumps (see e.g. Hilberink and Rogers 2002; Lipton 2002b; Sepp 2004, 2006). In the case of CDM, numerical FD methods in one and two dimensions tend to have a better rate of convergence in space and time than in the case of DDM. However, a serious disadvantage of the CDM assumption is that the corresponding MC implementation is challenging and slow because continuous barriers are difficult to deal with, especially in the multi-dimensional case.

Accordingly, CDM is useful for small-scale problems which can be solved without MC methods, while DDM is better suited for large-scale problems, such that semi-analytical FFT or PIDE-based methods can be used to calibrate the model to marginal dynamics of individual firms and MC techniques can be used to solve the pricing problem for several firms. In our experience, we have not observed noticeable differences between DDM and CDM settings, provided that the model is calibrated appropriately. We note in passing that, as reported by Davidson (2008), the industry practice is to use about 100 time steps with at least 60 steps in the first year in MC simulations of derivatives positions to estimate the counterparty exposure. This implies weekly default monitoring frequency in the first year and quarterly monitoring in the following years.

2.2.4 Asset value, equity, and equity options

We introduce the log coordinate $x(t)$:

$$x(t) = \ln\left(\frac{a(t)}{l(t)}\right) \tag{15}$$

and represent the asset value as follows:

$$a(t) = E(t)l(0)e^{x(t)} = l(t)e^{x(t)} \tag{16}$$

where $x(t)$ is driven by the following dynamics under $\mathbb{Q}$:

$$dx(t) = \mu(t)dt + \sigma(t)dW(t) + jdN(t) \tag{17}$$

$$x(0) = \ln\left(\frac{a(0)}{l(0)}\right) \equiv \xi, \quad \xi > 0$$

$$\mu(t) = -\frac{1}{2}\sigma^2(t) - \lambda(t)\kappa$$

We observe that, under this formulation of the firm value process, the default time is specified by:

$$\tau = \min\{t : x(t) \leq 0\} \tag{18}$$

triggered either discretely or continuously. Accordingly, the default event is determined only by the dynamics of the stochastic driver $x(t)$.

We note that the shifted process $y(t) = x(t) - \xi$ is an additive process with respect to the filtration $\mathbb{F}$ which is characterized by the following conditions: $y(t)$ is adapted to $\mathcal{F}(t)$, increments of $y(t)$ are independent of $\mathcal{F}(t)$, $y(t)$ is continuous in probability, and $y(t)$ starts from the origin, Sato (1999). The main difference between an additive process and a Levy process is that the distribution of increments in the former process is time dependent.

Without loss of generality, we assume that volatility $\sigma(t)$ and jump intensity $\lambda(t)$ are piecewise constant functions of time changing at times $\{t_k^c\}$, $k = 1, \ldots, \bar{k}$:

$$\sigma(t) = \sum_{k=1}^{\bar{k}} \sigma^{(k)}\mathbf{1}_{\{t_{k-1}^c < t \leq t_k^c\}} + \sigma^{(\bar{k})}\mathbf{1}_{\{t > t_{\bar{k}}^c\}} \tag{19}$$

$$\lambda(t) = \sum_{k=1}^{\bar{k}} \lambda^{(k)}\mathbf{1}_{\{t_{k-1}^c < t \leq t_k^c\}} + \lambda^{(\bar{k})}\mathbf{1}_{\{t > t_{\bar{k}}^c\}}$$

where $\sigma^{(k)}$ defines the volatility and $\lambda^{(k)}$ defines the intensity at time periods $(t_{k-1}^c, t_k^c]$ with $t_0^c = 0$, $k = 1, \ldots, \bar{k}$. In the case of DDM we assume that $\{t_k^c\}$ is a subset of $\{t_m^d\}$, so that parameters do not jump between observation dates.

We consider the firm's equity share price, which is denoted by $s(t)$, and, following Stamicar and Finger (2006), assume that the value of $s(t)$ is given by:

$$s(t) = \begin{cases} a(t) - l(t) = E(t)l(0)\left(e^{x(t)} - 1\right) = l(t)\left(e^{x(t)} - 1\right), & \{t < \tau\} \\ 0, & \{t \geq \tau\} \end{cases} \tag{20}$$

At time $t = 0$, $s(0)$ is specified by the market price of the equity share. Accordingly, the initial value of the firm's assets is given by:

$$a(0) = s(0) + l(0) \tag{21}$$

It is important to note that $\sigma(t)$ is the volatility of the firm's assets. The volatility of the equity, $\sigma^{eq}(t)$, is approximately related to $\sigma(t)$ by:

$$\sigma^{eq}(t) = \left(1 + \frac{l(t)}{s(t)}\right)\sigma(t) \tag{22}$$

As a result, for fixed $\sigma(t)$ the equity volatility increases as the spot price $s(t)$ decreases creating the leverage effect typically observed in the equity market. The model with equity volatility of the type (22) is also known as the displaced diffusion model (Rubinstein 1983).

2.3 Two-dimensional case

To deal with the counterparty risk problem, we need to model the correlated dynamics of two or more credit entities. We consider two firms and assume that their asset values are driven by the following stochascic differential equations (SDEs):

$$da_i(t) = (r(t) - \zeta_i(t) - \kappa_i \lambda_i(t))a_i(t)\,dt + \sigma_i(t)\,a_i(t)\,dW_i(t) + \left(e^{j_i} - 1\right)a_i(t)\,dN_i(t) \tag{23}$$

where

$$\kappa_i = \int_{-\infty}^{0} e^{j_i}\varpi_i(j_i)dj_i - 1 \tag{24}$$

jump amplitudes j_i has the same PDF $\varpi_i(j_i)$ as in the marginal dynamics, jump intensities $\lambda_i(t)$ are equal to the marginal intensities calibrated to single-name CDSs, volatility parameters $\sigma_i(t)$ are equal to those in the marginal dynamics, $i = 1, 2$. The corresponding default boundaries have the form:

$$l_i(t) = E_i(t)l_i(0) \tag{25}$$

where

$$E_i(t) = \exp\left\{\int_0^t (r(t') - \zeta_i(t'))dt'\right\} \tag{26}$$

In log coordinates with

$$x_i(t) = \ln\left(\frac{a_i(t)}{l_i(t)}\right) \tag{27}$$

we obtain:

$$dx_i(t) = \mu_i(t)dt + \sigma_i(t)\,dW_i(t) + j_i dN_i(t) \tag{28}$$

$$x_i(0) = \ln\left(\frac{a_i(0)}{l_i(0)}\right) \equiv \xi_i, \quad \xi_i > 0$$

$$\mu_i(t) = -\frac{1}{2}\sigma_i^2(t) - \kappa_i \lambda_i(t)$$

The default time of the i-th firm, τ_i, is defined by

$$\tau_i = \min\{t : x_i(t) \leq 0\} \tag{29}$$

Correlation between the firms is introduced in two ways. First, standard Brownian motions $W_1(t)$ and $W_2(t)$ are correlated with correlation ρ. Second, Poisson processes $N_1(t)$, $N_2(t)$ are represented as follows:

$$N_i(t) = N_{\{i\}}(t) + N_{\{1,2\}}(t) \tag{30}$$

where $N_{\{1,2\}}(t)$ is the systemic process with the intensity:

$$\lambda_{\{1,2\}}(t) = \max\{\rho, 0\} \min\{\lambda_1(t), \lambda_2(t)\} \tag{31}$$

while $N_{\{i\}}(t)$ are idiosyncratic processes with the intensities $\lambda_{\{i\}}(t)$, specified by:

$$\lambda_{\{1\}}(t) = \lambda_1(t) - \lambda_{\{1,2\}}(t), \quad \lambda_{\{2\}}(t) = \lambda_2(t) - \lambda_{\{1,2\}}(t) \tag{32}$$

This choice, which is Marshall-Olkin (1967) inspired, guarantees that marginal distributions are preserved, while sufficiently strong correlations are introduced naturally.

Expressing the correlation structure in terms of one parameter ρ has an advantage for model calibration. After the calibration to marginal dynamics is completed for each firm, and the set of firm's volatilities, jump sizes, and intensities is obtained, we estimate the parameter ρ by fitting the model spread of a FTDS to a given market quote.

It is clear that the default time correlations are closely connected to the instantaneous correlations of the firms' values. For the bivariate dynamics in question, we calculate the instantaneous correlations between the drivers $x_1(t)$ and $x_2(t)$ as follows:

$$\rho_{12}^{DNJ} = \frac{\rho\sigma_1\sigma_2 + \lambda_{\{1,2\}}\nu_1\nu_2}{\sqrt{\sigma_1^2 + \lambda_1\nu_1^2}\sqrt{\sigma_2^2 + \lambda_2\nu_2^2}}, \quad \rho_{12}^{ENJ} = \frac{\rho\sigma_1\sigma_2 + \lambda_{\{1,2\}}/(\nu_1\nu_2)}{\sqrt{\sigma_1^2 + 2\lambda_1/\nu_1^2}\sqrt{\sigma_2^2 + 2\lambda_2/\nu_2^2}} \tag{33}$$

where we suppress the time variable. Here ρ_{12}^{DNJ} and ρ_{12}^{ENJ} are correlations for DNJs and ENJs, respectively.

For large systemic intensities $\lambda_{\{1,2\}}$, we see that $\rho_{12}^{DNJ} \sim 1$, while $\rho_{12}^{ENJ} \sim \frac{1}{2}$. Thus, for ENJs correlations tend to be smaller than for DNJs. In our experiments with different firms, we have computed implied Gaussian copula correlations from model spreads of FTDS referencing different credit entities and found that, typically, the maximal implied Gaussian correlation that can be achieved is about 90% for DNJs and about 50% for ENJs (in both cases model parameters were calibrated to match the term structure of CDS spreads and CDS option volatilities). Thus, the ENJs assumption is not appropriate for modelling the joint dynamics of strongly correlated firms belonging to one industry, such as, for example, financial companies.

2.4 Multi-dimensional case

Now we consider N firms and assume that their asset values are driven by the same equations as before, but with the index i running from 1 to N, $i = 1, \ldots, N$.

We correlate diffusions in the usual way and assume that:

$$dW_i(t)dW_j(t) = \rho_{ij}(t)dt \tag{34}$$

We correlate jumps following the Marshall-Olkin (1967) idea. Let $\Pi^{(N)}$ be the set of all subsets of N names except for the empty subset $\{\varnothing\}$, and π be its typical member. With every π we associate a Poisson process $N_\pi(t)$ with intensity $\lambda_\pi(t)$, and represent $N_i(t)$ as follows:

$$N_i(t) = \sum_{\pi \in \Pi^{(N)}} \mathbf{1}_{\{i \in \pi\}} N_\pi(t) \tag{35}$$

$$\lambda_i(t) = \sum_{\pi \in \Pi^{(N)}} \mathbf{1}_{\{i \in \pi\}} \lambda_\pi(t)$$

Thus, we assume that there are both systemic and idiosyncratic jump sources. By analogy, we can introduce systemic and idiosyncratic factors for the Brownian motion dynamics.

3 GENERAL PRICING PROBLEM

In this section we formulate the generic pricing problem in 1D, 2D, and multi-dimensions.

3.1 One-dimensional problem

For DDM, the value function $V(t, x)$ solves the following problem on the entire axis $x \in \mathbb{R}^1$:

$$V_t(t, x) + \mathcal{L}^{(x)} V(t, x) - r(t) V(t, x) = 0 \tag{36}$$

supplied with the natural far-field boundary conditions

$$V(t, x) \underset{x \to \pm\infty}{\to} v_{\pm\infty}(t, x) \tag{37}$$

Here $t_{m-1}^d < t < t_m^d$. At $t = t_m^d$, the value function undergoes a transformation

$$V_{m-}(x) = \Pi\{V_{m+}(x)\} \tag{38}$$

where $\Pi\{.\}$ is the transformation operator, which depends on the specifics of the contract under consideration, and $V_{m\pm}(x) = V(t_{m\pm}^d, x)$. Here $t_{m\pm}^d = t_m^d \pm \varepsilon$. Finally, at $t = T$

$$V(T, x) = v(x) \tag{39}$$

the terminal payoff function $v(x)$ is contract specific. Here $\mathcal{L}^{(x)}$ is the infinitesimal operator of process $x(t)$ under dynamics (17):

$$\mathcal{L}^{(x)} = \mathcal{D}^{(x)} + \lambda(t)\mathcal{J}^{(x)} \tag{40}$$

$\mathcal{D}^{(x)}$ is a differential operator:

$$\mathcal{D}^{(x)}V(x) = \frac{1}{2}\sigma^2(t)V_{xx}(x) + \mu(t)V_x(x) - \lambda(t)V(x) \tag{41}$$

and $\mathcal{J}^{(x)}$ is a jump operator:

$$\mathcal{J}^{(x)}V(x) = \int_{-\infty}^{0} V(x+j)\varpi(j)dj \tag{42}$$

For CDM, we assume that the value of the contract is determined by the terminal payoff function $v(x)$, the cash flow function $c(t, x)$, the rebate function $z(t, x)$ specifying the payoff following the default event (we note that the rebate function may depend on the residual value of the firm), and the far-field boundary condition. The backward equation for the value function $V(t, x)$ is formulated differently on the positive semi-axis $x \in \mathbb{R}^1_+$ and negative semi-axis $\mathbb{R}^1_-$:

$$\begin{aligned} V_t(t, x) + \mathcal{L}^{(x)}V(t, x) - r(t)V(t, x) &= c(t, x), \quad x \in \mathbb{R}^1_+ \\ V(t, x) &= z(t, x), \qquad\qquad x \in \mathbb{R}^1_- \end{aligned} \tag{43}$$

This equation is supplied with the usual terminal condition on $\mathbb{R}^1$:

$$V(T, x) = v(x) \tag{44}$$

where $\mathcal{J}^{(x)}$ is a jump operator which is defined as follows:

$$\mathcal{J}^{(x)}V(x) = \int_{-\infty}^{0} V(x+j)\varpi(j)dj \tag{45}$$

$$= \int_{-x}^{0} V(x+j)\varpi(j)dj + \int_{-\infty}^{-x} z(x+j)\varpi(j)dj$$

In particular,

$$\mathcal{J}^{(x)}V(x) = \begin{cases} V(x-v)\,1_{\{v\le x\}} + z(x-v)\,1_{\{v>x\}}, & \text{DNJs} \\ v\int_{-x}^{0} V(x+j)\,e^{vj}dj + v\int_{-\infty}^{-x} z(x+j)\,e^{vj}dj, & \text{ENJs} \end{cases} \tag{46}$$

For ENJs $\mathcal{J}^{(x)}V(x)$ also can be written as

$$\mathcal{J}^{(x)}V(x) = v\int_{0}^{x} V(y)\,e^{v(y-x)}dy + v\int_{-\infty}^{0} z(y)\,e^{v(y-x)}dy \tag{47}$$

In principle, for both DDM and CDM, the computational domain for x is $\mathbb{R}^1$. However, for CDM, we can restrict ourselves to the positive semi-axis $\mathbb{R}^1_+$. We can represent the integral term in problem eq. (46) as follows:

$$\mathcal{J}^{(x)}V(x) \equiv \widehat{\mathcal{J}}^{(x)}V(x) + Z^{(x)}(x) \tag{48}$$

where $\widehat{\mathcal{J}}^{(x)}$, $Z^{(x)}(x)$ are defined by:

$$\widehat{\mathcal{J}}^{(x)}V(x) = \int_{-x}^{0} V(x + j)\varpi(j)dj \tag{49}$$

$$Z^{(x)}(x) = \int_{-\infty}^{-x} z(x + j)\varpi(j)dj \tag{50}$$

so that $Z^{(x)}(x)$ is the deterministic function depending on the contract rebate function $z(x)$. As a result, by subtracting $Z(x)$ from rhs of eq. (43), we can formulate the pricing equation on the positive semi-axis $\mathbb{R}_+^1$ as follows:

$$V_t(t, x) + \widehat{\mathcal{L}}^{(x)}V(t, x) - r(t)V(t, x) = \hat{c}(t, x) \tag{51}$$

It is supplied with the boundary conditions at $x = 0$, $x \to \infty$:

$$V(t, 0) = z(t, 0), \quad V(t, x) \underset{x \to \infty}{\to} v_\infty(t, x) \tag{52}$$

and the terminal condition for $x \in \mathbb{R}_+^1$:

$$V(T, x) = v(x) \tag{53}$$

Here

$$\widehat{\mathcal{L}}^{(x)} = \mathcal{D}^{(x)} + \lambda(t)\widehat{\mathcal{J}}^{(x)} \tag{54}$$

$$\hat{c}(t, x) = c(t, x) - \lambda(t)Z^{(x)}(t, x) \tag{55}$$

We introduce the Green's function denoted by $G(t, x, T, X)$, representing the probability density of $x(T) = X$ given $x(t) = x$ and conditional on no default between t and T. For DDM the valuation problem for G can be formulated as follows:

$$G_T(t, x, T, X) - \mathcal{L}^{(X)\dagger}G(t, x, T, X) = 0 \tag{56}$$

$$G(t, x, T, X) \underset{X \to \pm\infty}{\to} 0 \tag{57}$$

$$G(t, x, t_{m+}, X) = G(t, x, t_{m-}, X)\mathbf{1}_{\{X > 0\}} \tag{58}$$

$$G(t, x, t, X) = \delta(X - x) \tag{59}$$

where $\mathcal{L}^{(x)\dagger}$ being the infinitesimal operator adjoint to $\mathcal{L}^{(x)}$:

$$\mathcal{L}^{(x)\dagger} = \mathcal{D}^{(x)\dagger} + \lambda(t)\mathcal{J}^{(x)\dagger} \tag{60}$$

$\mathcal{D}^{(x)\dagger}$ is the differential operator:

$$\mathcal{D}^{(x)\dagger}g(x) = \frac{1}{2}\sigma^2(t)g_{xx}(x) - \mu(t)g_x(x) - \lambda(t)g(x) \tag{61}$$

and $\mathcal{J}^{(x)\dagger}$ is the jump operator:

$$\mathcal{J}^{(x)\dagger} g(x) = \int_{-\infty}^{0} g(x - j)\varpi(j)dj \tag{62}$$

For CDM, the PIDE for G is defined on $\mathbb{R}_+^1$ and the boundary conditions are applied continuously:

$$G_T(t, x, T, X) - \mathcal{L}^{(X)\dagger} G(t, x, T, X) = 0 \tag{63}$$

$$G(t, x, T, 0) = 0, \quad G(t, x, T, X) \xrightarrow[X\to\infty]{} 0 \tag{64}$$

$$G(t, x, t, X) = \delta(X - x) \tag{65}$$

3.2 Two-dimensional problem

We assume that the specifics of the contract are encapsulated by the terminal payoff function $v(x_1, x_2)$, the cash flow function $c(t, x_1, x_2)$, the rebate functions $z_a(t, x_1, x_2)$, $a = (-, +), (-, -), (+, -)$, the default-boundary functions $v_{0,i}(t, x_{3-i})$, $i = 1, 2$, and the far-field functions $v_{\pm\infty,i}(t, x_1, x_2)$ specifying the conditions for large values of x_i. We denote the value function of this contract by $V(t, x_1, x_2)$.

For DDM, the pricing equation defined in the entire plane $\mathbb{R}^2$ can be written as follows:

$$V_t(t, x_1, x_2) + \mathcal{L}^{(x)} V(t, x_1, x_2) - r(t) V(t, x_1, x_2) = 0 \tag{66}$$

As before, it is supplied with the far-field conditions

$$V(t, x_1, x_2) \xrightarrow[x_i \to \pm\infty]{} v_{\pm\infty,i}(t, x_1, x_2), \quad i = 1, 2 \tag{67}$$

At times t_m^d the value function is transformed according to the rule

$$V_{m-}(x_1, x_2) = \Pi\{V_{m+}(x_1, x_2)\} \tag{68}$$

The terminal condition is

$$V(T, x_1, x_2) = v(x_1, x_2) \tag{69}$$

Here $\mathcal{L}^{(x_1,x_2)}$ is the infinitesimal backward operator corresponding to the bivariate dynamics (28):

$$\mathcal{L}^{(x_1,x_2)} = \mathcal{D}^{(x_1)} + \mathcal{D}^{(x_2)} + \mathcal{C}^{(x_1,x_2)} \tag{70}$$

$$+\lambda_{\{1\}}(t)\mathcal{J}^{(x_1)} + \lambda_{\{2\}}(t)\mathcal{J}^{(x_2)} + \lambda_{\{1,2\}}(t)\mathcal{J}^{(x_1,x_2)}$$

Here, $\mathcal{D}^{(x_1)}$ and $\mathcal{D}^{(x_2)}$ are the differential operators in x_1 and x_2 directions defined by eq. (41) with $\lambda(t) = \lambda_{\{i\}}(t)$; $\mathcal{J}^{(x_1)}$ and $\mathcal{J}^{(x_2)}$ are the 1D orthogonal integral operators in x_1 and x_2 directions defined by eq. (45) with appropriate model parameters; $\mathcal{C}^{(x_1,x_2)}$ is the correlation operator:

$$C^{(x_1,x_2)}V(x_1,x_2) \equiv \rho\sigma_1(t)\sigma_2(t)V_{x_1 x_2}(x_1,x_2) - \lambda_{\{1,2\}}(t)\,V\,(x_1,x_2) \qquad (71)$$

and $\mathcal{J}^{(x_1,x_2)}$ is the cross integral operator defined as follows:

$$\mathcal{J}^{(x_1,x_2)}V(x_1,x_2) \equiv \int_{-\infty}^{0}\int_{-\infty}^{0} V(x_1+j_1,x_2+j_2)\varpi_1(j_1)\varpi_2(j_2)dj_1 dj_2 \qquad (72)$$

For CDM, $V(t,x_1,x_2)$ solves the following problem in the positive quadrant $\mathbb{R}^2_{+,+}$:

$$V_t(t,x_1,x_2) + \widehat{\mathcal{L}}^{(x_1,x_2)}V(t,x_1,x_2) - r\,(t)\,V(t,x_1,x_2) = \hat{c}(t,x_1,x_2) \qquad (73)$$

$$V(t,0,x_2) = v_{0,1}(t,x_2), \quad V(t,x_1,x_2) \underset{x_1\to\infty}{\to} v_{\infty,1}(t,x_1,x_2) \qquad (74)$$

$$V(t,x_1,0) = v_{0,2}(t,x_1), \quad V(t,x_1,x_2) \underset{x_2\to\infty}{\to} v_{\infty,2}(t,x_1,x_2)$$

$$V(T,x_1,x_2) = v(x_1,x_2) \qquad (75)$$

where $\widehat{\mathcal{L}}^{(x_1,x_2)}$ is the infinitesimal backward operator defined by:

$$\widehat{\mathcal{L}}^{(x_1,x_2)} = \mathcal{D}^{(x_1)} + \mathcal{D}^{(x_2)} + \mathcal{C}^{(x_1,x_2)} \qquad (76)$$

$$+\lambda_{\{1\}}(t)\widehat{\mathcal{J}}^{(x_1)} + \lambda_{\{2\}}(t)\widehat{\mathcal{J}}^{(x_2)} + \lambda_{\{1,2\}}(t)\widehat{\mathcal{J}}^{(x_1,x_2)}$$

with

$$\widehat{\mathcal{J}}^{(x_1,x_2)}V(x_1,x_2) \equiv \int_{-x_1}^{0}\int_{-x_2}^{0} V(x_1+j_1,x_2+j_2)\varpi_1(j_1)\varpi_2(j_2)dj_1 dj_2 \qquad (77)$$

The 'equivalent' cash flows can be represented as follows:

$$\hat{c}(t,x_1,x_2) = c(t,x_1,x_2) - \lambda_{\{1\}}(t)\,Z^{(x_1)}(t,x_1,x_2) - \lambda_{\{2\}}(t)\,Z^{(x_2)}(t,x_1,x_2) \qquad (78)$$

$$-\lambda_{\{1,2\}}\left(Z^{(x_1,x_2)}_{-,+}(t,x_1,x_2) + Z^{(x_1,x_2)}_{-,-}(t,x_1,x_2) + Z^{(x_1,x_2)}_{+,-}(t,x_1,x_2)\right)$$

where

$$Z^{(x_1)}(t,x_1,x_2) = \int_{-\infty}^{-x_1} z_{-,+}(x_1+j_1,x_2)\varpi_1(j_1)dj_1 \qquad (79)$$

$$Z^{(x_2)}(t,x_1,x_2) = \int_{-\infty}^{-x_2} z_{+,-}(x_1,x_2+j_2)\varpi_2(j_2)dj_2$$

$$Z^{(x_1,x_2)}_{-,+}(x_1,x_2) = \int_{-\infty}^{-x_1}\int_{-x_2}^{0} z_{-,+}(x_1+j_1,x_2+j_2)\varpi_1(j_1)\varpi_2(j_2)dj_1 dj_2$$

$$Z^{(x_1,x_2)}_{-,-}(x_1,x_2) = \int_{-\infty}^{-x_1}\int_{-\infty}^{-x_2} z_{-,-}(x_1+j_1,x_2+j_2)\varpi_1(j_1)\varpi_2(j_2)dj_1 dj_2$$

$$Z^{(x_1,x_2)}_{+,-}(x_1,x_2) = \int_{-x_1}^{0}\int_{-\infty}^{-x_2} z_{+,-}(x_1+j_1,x_2+j_2)\varpi_1(j_1)\varpi_2(j_2)dj_1 dj_2$$

For DDM, the corresponding Green's function $G(t, x_1, x_2, T, X_1, X_2)$, satisfies the following problem in the whole plane $\mathbb{R}^2$:

$$G_T(t, x_1, x_2, T, X_1, X_2) - \mathcal{L}^{(X_1, X_2)\dagger} G(t, x_1, x_2, T, X_1, X_2) = 0 \tag{80}$$

$$G(t, x_1, x_2, T, X_1, X_2) \underset{X_i \to \pm\infty}{\to} 0 \tag{81}$$

$$G(t, x_1, x_2, t_{m+}, X_1, X_2) = G(t, x_1, x_2, t_{m-}, X_1, X_2) \mathbf{1}_{\{X_1 > 0, X_2 > 0\}} \tag{82}$$

$$G(t, x_1, x_2, t, X_1, X_2) = \delta(X_1 - x_1)\delta(X_2 - x_2) \tag{83}$$

where $\mathcal{L}^{(x_1, x_2)\dagger}$ is the operator adjoint to $\mathcal{L}^{(x_1, x_2)}$:

$$\mathcal{L}^{(x_1, x_2)\dagger} = \mathcal{D}^{(x_1)\dagger} + \mathcal{D}^{(x_2)\dagger} + \mathcal{C}^{(x_1, x_2)} \tag{84}$$

$$+\lambda_{\{1\}}(t)\mathcal{J}^{(x_1)\dagger} + \lambda_{\{2\}}(t)\mathcal{J}^{(x_2)\dagger} + \lambda_{\{1,2\}}(t)\mathcal{J}^{(x_1, x_2)\dagger}$$

and

$$\mathcal{J}^{(x_1, x_2)\dagger} g(x_1, x_2) = \int_{-\infty}^0 \int_{-\infty}^0 g(x_1 - j_1, x_2 - j_2)\varpi_1(j_1)\varpi_2(j_2)dj_1 dj_2 \tag{85}$$

For CDM, the corresponding Green's function satisfies the following problem in the positive quadrant $\mathbb{R}^2_{+,+}$:

$$G_T(t, x_1, x_2, T, X_1, X_2) - \mathcal{L}^{(X_1, X_2)\dagger} G(t, x_1, x_2, T, X_1, X_2) = 0 \tag{86}$$

$$G(t, x_1, x_2, T, 0, X_2) = 0, \quad G(t, x_1, x_2, T, X_1, 0) = 0 \tag{87}$$

$$G(t, x_1, x_2, T, X_1, X_2) \underset{X_i \to \infty}{\to} 0$$

$$G(t, x_1, x_2, t, X_1, X_2) = \delta(X_1 - x_1)\delta(X_2 - x_2) \tag{88}$$

3.3 Multi-dimensional problem

For brevity, we restrict ourselves to CDM. As before, we can formulate a typical pricing problem for the value function $V(t, \vec{x})$ in the positive cone $\mathbb{R}^N_+$ as follows:

$$V_t(t, \vec{x}) + \widehat{\mathcal{L}}^{(\vec{x})} V(t, \vec{x}) - r(t) V(t, \vec{x}) = \hat{c}(t, \vec{x}) \tag{89}$$

$$V(t, \vec{x}_{0,k}) = v_{0,k}(t, \vec{y}_k), \quad V(t, \vec{x}) \underset{x_k \to \infty}{\to} v_{\infty,k}(t, \vec{x}) \tag{90}$$

$$V(T, \vec{x}) = v(\vec{x}) \tag{91}$$

where $\vec{x}, \vec{x}_{0,k}, \vec{y}_k$ are N and $N-1$ dimensional vectors, respectively,

$$\vec{x} = (x_1, \ldots, x_k, \ldots x_N)$$
$$\vec{x}_{0,k} = \left(x_1, \ldots, \underset{k}{0}, \ldots x_N\right) \tag{92}$$
$$\vec{y}_k = (x_1, \ldots x_{k-1}, x_{k+1}, \ldots x_N)$$

Here $\hat{c}(t, \vec{x})$, $v_{0,k}(t, \vec{y})$, $v_{\infty,k}(t, \vec{x})$, $v(\vec{x})$ are known functions which are contract specific. The function $\hat{c}(t, \vec{x})$ incorporates the terms arising from rebates. The corresponding operator $\widehat{\mathcal{L}}^{(\vec{x})}$ can be written in the form

$$\widehat{\mathcal{L}}^{(\vec{x})} f(\vec{x}) = \frac{1}{2} \sum_i \sigma_i^2 \partial_i^2 f(\vec{x}) + \sum_{i,j,j>i} \rho_{ij} \sigma_i \sigma_j \partial_i \partial_j f(\vec{x}) \tag{93}$$

$$+ \sum_i \mu_i \partial_i f(\vec{x}) + \sum_{\pi \in \Pi^{(N)}} \lambda_\pi \left(\prod_{i \in \pi} \widehat{\mathcal{J}}^{(x_i)} f(\vec{x}) - f(\vec{x}) \right)$$

where

$$\widehat{\mathcal{J}}^{(x_i)} f(\vec{x}) = \begin{cases} f(x_1, \ldots, x_i - v_i, \ldots x_N), & x_i > v_i \\ 0 & x_i \le v_i \\ v_i \int_{-x_i}^0 f(x_1, \ldots, x_i + j_i, \ldots x_N) e^{v_i j_i} dj_i, & \text{ENJs} \end{cases} \quad \begin{matrix} \text{DNJs} \\ \\ \end{matrix} \tag{94}$$

3.4 Green's formula

Now we can formulate Green's formula adapted to the problem under consideration. To this end we introduce the Green's function $G\left(t, \vec{x}, T, \vec{X}\right)$, such that

$$G_T\left(t, \vec{x}, T, \vec{X}\right) - \mathcal{L}^{(\vec{X})\dagger} G\left(t, \vec{x}, T, \vec{X}\right) = 0 \tag{95}$$

$$G\left(t, \vec{x}, T, \vec{X}_{0k}\right) = 0, \quad G\left(t, \vec{x}, T, \vec{X}\right) \underset{X_k \to \infty}{\longrightarrow} 0 \tag{96}$$

$$G\left(t, \vec{x}, t, \vec{X}\right) = \delta\left(\vec{X} - \vec{x}\right) \tag{97}$$

Here $\mathcal{L}^{(\vec{x})\dagger}$ is the corresponding adjoint operator

$$\mathcal{L}^{(\vec{x})\dagger} g(\vec{x}) = \frac{1}{2} \sum_i \sigma_i^2 \partial_i^2 g(\vec{x}) + \sum_{i,j,j>i} \rho_{ij} \sigma_i \sigma_j \partial_i \partial_j g(\vec{x}) \tag{98}$$

$$- \sum_i \mu_i \partial_i g(\vec{x}) + \sum_{\pi \in \Pi^{(N)}} \lambda_\pi \left(\prod_{i \in \pi} \mathcal{J}^{(x_i)\dagger} g(\vec{x}) - g(\vec{x}) \right)$$

where

$$\mathcal{J}^{(x_i)\dagger} g(\vec{x}) = \begin{cases} g(x_1, \ldots, x_i + v_i, \ldots x_N), & \text{DNJs} \\ v_i \int_{-\infty}^0 g(x_1, \ldots, x_i - j_i, \ldots x_N) e^{v_i j_i} dj_i, & \text{ENJs} \end{cases} \tag{99}$$

It is easy to check that for both DNJs and ENJs the following identity holds:

$$\int_{\mathbb{R}^N_+} \left[\widehat{\mathcal{J}}^{(x_i)} f(\vec{x}) g(\vec{x}) - f(\vec{x}) \mathcal{J}^{(x_i)\dagger} g(\vec{x}) \right] d\vec{x} = 0 \tag{100}$$

Accordingly, integration by parts yields

$$V(t, \vec{x}) = - \int_t^T \int_{\mathbb{R}_+^N} \hat{c}(t', \vec{x}') D(t, t') G(t, \vec{x}, t', \vec{x}') d\vec{x}' dt' \tag{101}$$

$$+ \sum_k \int_t^T \int_{\mathbb{R}_+^{N-1}} v_{0,k}(t', \vec{y}_k') D(t, t') g_k(t, \vec{x}, t', \vec{y}_k') d\vec{y}_k' dt'$$

$$+ D(t, T) \int_{\mathbb{R}_+^N} v(\vec{x}') G(t, \vec{x}, T, \vec{x}') d\vec{x}'$$

where

$$g_k(t, \vec{x}, T, \vec{Y}_k) = \frac{1}{2} \sigma_k^2 \partial_k G(t, \vec{x}, T, \vec{X}) \Big|_{X_k=0} \tag{102}$$

$$\vec{Y}_k = (X_1, \ldots, X_{k-1}, X_{k+1}, \ldots, X_N)$$

represents the hitting time density for the corresponding point of the boundary. In particular, the initial value of a claim has the form

$$V(0, \vec{\xi}) = - \int_0^T \int_{\mathbb{R}_+^N} \hat{c}(t', \vec{x}') D(0, t') G(0, \vec{\xi}, t', \vec{x}') d\vec{x}' dt' \tag{103}$$

$$+ \sum_k \int_0^T \int_{\mathbb{R}_+^{N-1}} v_{0,k}(t', \vec{y}_k') D(0, t') g_k(0, \vec{\xi}, t', \vec{y}_k') d\vec{y}_k' dt'$$

$$+ D(0, T) \int_{\mathbb{R}_+^N} v(\vec{x}') G(0, \vec{\xi}, T, \vec{x}') d\vec{x}'$$

This extremely useful formula shows that instead of solving the backward pricing problem with inhomogeneous right hand side and boundary conditions, we can solve the forward propagation problem for the Green's function with homogeneous rhs and boundary conditions and perform the integration as needed.

4 PRICING PROBLEM FOR CREDIT DERIVATIVES

In this section we formulate the computational problem for several important credit products. We also formulate the CVA problem for CDSs.

4.1 Survival probability

The single-name survival probability function, $Q^{(x)}(t, x, T)$, is defined as follows:

$$Q^{(x)}(t, x, T) \equiv \mathbf{1}_{\{\tau > t\}} \mathbb{E}_t^{\mathbb{Q}}[\mathbf{1}_{\{\tau > T\}}] \tag{104}$$

Using the default event definition (13), one can show that for DDM, $Q^{(x)}(t, x, T)$ solves the following backward problem on $\mathbb{R}^1$:

$$Q_t^{(x)}(t, x, T) + \mathcal{L}^{(x)} Q^{(x)}(t, x, T) = 0 \tag{105}$$

$$Q^{(x)}(t, x, T) \xrightarrow[x \to -\infty]{} 0, \quad Q^{(x)}(t, x, T) \xrightarrow[x \to \infty]{} 1 \tag{106}$$

$$Q_{m-}^{(x)}(x, T) = Q_{m+}^{(x)}(x, T)\mathbf{1}_{\{x > 0\}} \tag{107}$$

$$Q^{(x)}(T, x, T) = \mathbf{1}_{\{x > 0\}} \tag{108}$$

with the infinitesimal operator $\mathcal{L}^{(x)}$ defined by eq. (40).

Likewise, using the default event definition (14), one can show that for CDM, $Q^{(x)}(t, x, T)$ solves the following backward problem on the positive semi-axis $\mathbb{R}_+^1$:

$$Q_t^{(x)}(t, x, T) + \widehat{\mathcal{L}}^{(x)} Q^{(x)}(t, x, T) = 0 \tag{109}$$

$$Q^{(x)}(t, 0, T) = 0, \quad Q^{(x)}(t, x, T) \xrightarrow[x \to \infty]{} 1 \tag{110}$$

$$Q^{(x)}(T, x, T) = 1 \tag{111}$$

Here the far field condition for $x \to \infty$ expresses the fact that for large values of x survival becomes certain. Green's formula (101) yields

$$Q^{(x)}(t, x, T) = \int_0^\infty G(t, x, T, X)\, dX \tag{112}$$

We define the joint survival probability, $Q^{(x_1, x_2)}(t, x_1, x_2, T)$, as follows:

$$Q^{(x_1, x_2)}(t, x_1, x_2, T) \equiv \mathbf{1}_{\{\tau_1 > t, \tau_2 > t\}} \mathbb{E}_t^{\mathbb{Q}}[\mathbf{1}_{\{\tau_1 > T, \tau_2 > T\}}] \tag{113}$$

For DDM, the joint survival probability function $Q^{(x_1, x_2)}(t, x_1, x_2, T)$ solves the following problem:

$$Q_t^{(x_1, x_2)}(t, x_1, x_2, T) + \mathcal{L}^{(x_1, x_2)} Q^{(x_1, x_2)}(t, x_1, x_2, T) = 0 \tag{114}$$

$$Q^{(x_1, x_2)}(t, x_1, x_2, T) \xrightarrow[x_i \to -\infty]{} 0 \tag{115}$$

$$Q^{(x_1, x_2)}(t, x_1, x_2, T) \xrightarrow[x_i \to \infty]{} Q^{(x_{3-i})}(t, x_{3-i}, T)$$

$$Q_{m-}^{(x_1, x_2)}(t, x_1, x_2, T) = Q_{m+}^{(x_1, x_2)}(t, x_1, x_2, T)\mathbf{1}_{\{x_1 > 0, x_2 > 0\}} \tag{116}$$

$$Q^{(x_1, x_2)}(T, x_1, x_2, T) = \mathbf{1}_{\{x_1 > 0, x_2 > 0\}} \tag{117}$$

where the infinitesimal operator $\mathcal{L}^{(x_1, x_2)}$ is defined by eq. (70). Here $Q^{(x_i)}(t, x_i, T)$, $i = 1, 2$, are the marginal survival probabilities obtained by solving eq. (105).

For CDM, $Q^{(x_1,x_2)}(t, x_1, x_2, T)$ solves the following problem in $\mathbb{R}^2_{+,+}$:

$$Q_t^{(x_1,x_2)}(t, x_1, x_2, T) + \widehat{\mathcal{L}}^{(x_1,x_2)} Q^{(x_1,x_2)}(t, x_1, x_2, T) = 0 \tag{118}$$

$$Q^{(x_1,x_2)}(t, x_1, 0, T) = 0, \quad Q^{(x_1,x_2)}(t, 0, x_2, T) = 0 \tag{119}$$

$$Q^{(x_1,x_2)}(t, x_1, x_2, T) \underset{x_i \to \infty}{\longrightarrow} Q^{(x_{3-i})}(t, x_{3-i}, T)$$

$$Q^{(x_1,x_2)}(T, x_1, x_2, T) = 1 \tag{120}$$

where the infinitesimal operator $\widehat{\mathcal{L}}^{(x_1,x_2)}$ is defined by eq. (76). As before

$$Q^{(x_1,x_2)}(t, x_1, x_2, T) = \int_0^\infty \int_0^\infty G(t, x_1, x_2, T, X_1, X_2) \, dX_1 dX_2 \tag{121}$$

4.2 Credit default swap

A CDS is a contract designed to exchange the credit risk of RN between PB and PS. PB makes periodic coupon payments to PS, conditional on no default of RN up to the nearest payment date, in exchange for receiving loss given RN's default from PS. For standardized CDS contracts, coupon payments occur quarterly on the 20th of March, June, September, and December. We denote the annualized payment schedule by $\{t_m\}$, $m = 1, \ldots, M$. The most liquid CDSs have maturities of $5y$, $7y$, and $10y$.

We consider a CDS with the unit notional providing protection from the current time t up to the maturity time T. Assuming that RN has not defaulted yet, $\tau > t$, we compute the expected present value of the annuity leg, $A(t, T)$, as:

$$A(t, T) = \int_t^T D(t, t') \, Q(t, t') dt' \tag{122}$$

where $Q(t, t')$ is the corresponding survival probability, and the expected present value of the protection leg, $P(t, T)$, as:

$$P(t, T) = -(1 - R) \int_t^T D(t, t') \, dQ(t, t') \tag{123}$$

$$= (1 - R) \left(1 - D(t, T) Q(t, T) - \int_t^T r(t') D(t, t') Q(t, t') dt'\right)$$

where R is the expected debt recovery rate which is assumed to be given for valuation purposes (typically, R is fixed at 40%).

For PB the present value of the CDS contract with coupon (or spread) c, is given by:

$$V^{CDS}(t, T) = P(t, T) - cA(t, T) \tag{124}$$

The par coupon $c(0, T)$ is defined in such a way that the time $t = 0$ and the value of the CDS contract is zero:

$$c(0, T) = \frac{P(0, T)}{A(0, T)} \tag{125}$$

The market-standard computation of the value of a CDS relies on the reduced-form approach (see, for example, Jarrow and Turnbull 1995; Duffie and Singleton 1997; Lando 1998; Hull and White 2000). Typically, a piecewise constant hazard rate is used to parametrize the risk-neutral survival probability of RN. Hazard rates are inferred from the term structure of CDS spreads via bootstrapping.

One of the drawbacks of the reduced-form approach is that it assumes that CDS spreads are static and evolve deterministically along with hazard rates. Importantly, this approach does not tell us how CDS spreads change when the RN's value changes. In contrast, the structural approach does explain changes in the term structure of CDS spreads caused by changes in the firm's value. Thus, the structural model can be used for valuing credit contracts depending on the volatility of credit spreads.

For DDM, the value function for PB of a CDS contract, $V^{CDS}(t, x, T)$, solves eq. (36), supplied with the following conditions:

$$V^{CDS}(t, x, T) \underset{x \to -\infty}{\to} 1 - Re^x, \quad V^{CDS}(t, x, T) \underset{x \to \infty}{\to} -c \sum_{m'=m+1}^{M} \delta t_{m'} D(t, t_{m'}) \tag{126}$$

$$V_{m-}^{CDS}(x, T) = (V_{m+}^{CDS}(x, T) - \delta t_m c)\mathbf{1}_{\{x>0\}} + (1 - Re^x)\mathbf{1}_{\{x\leq 0\}} \tag{127}$$

$$V^{CDS}(T, x, T) = -\delta t_M c \mathbf{1}_{\{x>0\}} + (1 - Re^x)\mathbf{1}_{\{x\leq 0\}} \tag{128}$$

where $\delta t_m = t_m - t_{m-1}$.

For CDM, $V^{CDS}(t, x, T)$ solves eq. (51) with

$$\hat{c}(t, x) = c - \lambda(t) Z^{(x)}(x) \tag{129}$$

$$Z^{(x)}(x) = \begin{cases} H(v - x)(1 - Re^{x-v}), & \text{DNJs} \\ (1 - R\frac{v}{1+v})e^{-vx}, & \text{ENJs} \end{cases} \tag{130}$$

Here we assume that the floating recovery rate, Re^x, represents the residual value of the firm's assets after the default. The corresponding boundary and terminal conditions are

$$V^{CDS}(t, 0, T) = (1 - R), \quad V^{CDS}(t, x, T) \underset{x \to \infty}{\to} -c \int_t^T D(t, t')dt' \tag{131}$$

$$V^{CDS}(T, x, T) = 0 \tag{132}$$

The boundary condition for $x \to \infty$ expresses the fact that for large positive x the present value of CDS becomes a risk-free annuity.

4.3 Credit default swap option

A CDSO contract serves as a tool for locking in the realized volatility of CDS rate up to the option's maturity. By using CDSOs quotes we can calibrate the model to this volatility. The payer CDSO with maturity T_e and tenor T_t gives its holder the right to enter in a CDS contract providing the protection starting at time T_e up to time $T_e + T_t$ with a given coupon K. The option knocks out if RN defaults before time T_e. Thus, the payout of the payer CDSO is given by:

$$V^{CDS}(T_e, T_e + T_t; K) = \mathbf{1}_{\{\tau > T_e\}} \{P(T_e, T_e + T_t) - K A(T_e, T_e + T_t)\}_+ \qquad (133)$$

For DDM, the value function for the buyer of CDSO, $V^{CDSO}(t, x, T_e)$, solves eq. (36) with $c = 0$, and the following conditions:

$$V^{CDSO}(t, x, T_e) \underset{x \to \pm\infty}{\to} 0 \qquad (134)$$

$$V_{m-}^{CDSO}(x, T_e) = V_{m+}^{CDSO}(x, T_e) \mathbf{1}_{\{x>0\}} \qquad (135)$$

$$V^{CDSO}(T_e, x, T_e) = \left\{V^{CDS}(T_e, x, T_e + T_t; K)\right\}_+ \mathbf{1}_{\{x>0\}} \qquad (136)$$

For CDM, $V^{CDSO}(t, x, T_e)$ is governed by eq. (51) with $\hat{c} = 0$, supplied with the following conditions:

$$V^{CDSO}(t, 0, T_e) = 0, \quad V^{CDSO}(t, x, T_e) \underset{x \to \infty}{\to} 0 \qquad (137)$$

$$V^{CDSO}(T_e, x, T_e) = \left\{V^{CDS}(T_e, x, T_e + T_t; K)\right\}_+ \qquad (138)$$

4.4 Equity put option

In our model, we can value European style options on the firm's equity defined by eq. (20). In the context of studying credit products, the value of the equity put option is the most relevant one, since such options provide protection against the depreciation of the stock price and can be used for hedging against the default event.

For DDM, the value function of $V^P(t, x, T)$ solves eq. (36) with $c = 0$, supplied with the following conditions:

$$V^P(t, x, T) \underset{x \to -\infty}{\to} D(t, T)K, \quad V^P(t, x, T) \underset{x \to \infty}{\to} 0 \qquad (139)$$

$$V_{m-}^P(x, T) = V_{m+}^P(x, T) \mathbf{1}_{\{x>0\}} + D(t_m, T) K \mathbf{1}_{\{x \leq 0\}} \qquad (140)$$

$$V^P(T, x, T) = \left\{K - l(T)(e^x - 1)\right\}_+ \mathbf{1}_{\{x>0\}} + K \mathbf{1}_{\{x \leq 0\}} \qquad (141)$$

For CDM, $V^P(t, x, T)$ solves eq. (51) with

$$\hat{c}(t, x) = -\lambda(t) Z^{(x)}(t, x) \qquad (142)$$

$$Z^{(x)}(t, x, T) = \begin{cases} D(t, T) K \mathbf{H}(v - x), & \text{DNJs} \\ D(t, T) K e^{-vx} & \text{ENJs} \end{cases} \qquad (143)$$

and the following conditions:

$$V^P(t, 0, T) = D(t, T)K, \quad V^P(t, x) \underset{x \to \infty}{\to} 0 \qquad (144)$$

$$V^P(T, x, T) = \left\{ K - l(T)(e^x - 1) \right\}_+ \qquad (145)$$

We note that, in this model, put-call parity for European options should be expressed in terms of defaultable forward contracts.

Since, in general, we have to solve the pricing problem numerically, American style options can be handled along similar lines with little additional effort.

4.5 First-to-default swap

An FTDS references a basket of RNs. Similarly to a regular CDS, PB of an FTDS pays PS a periodic coupon up to the first default event of any of RNs, or the swap's maturity, whichever comes first; in return, PS compensates PB for the loss caused by the first default in the basket. The market of FTDSs is relatively liquid with a typical basket size of five underlying names.

In this chapter we consider FTDSs referencing just two underlying names. The premium leg and the default leg of a FTDS are structured by analogy to the single-name CDS. For brevity we consider only CDM. To compute the present value $V^{FTDS}(t, x_1, x_2, T)$ for PB of a FTDS, we have to solve eq. (73) with $\hat{c}(t, x_1, x_2)$ of the form:

$$\hat{c}(t, x_1, x_2) = c - \lambda_{\{1\}}(t) Z^{(x_1)}(x_1) - \lambda_{\{2\}}(t) Z^{(x_2)}(x_2) \qquad (146)$$

$$-\lambda_{\{1,2\}}(t) \left(Z_{-,+}^{(x_1,x_2)}(x_1, x_2) + Z_{-,-}^{(x_1,x_2)}(x_1, x_2) + Z_{+,-}^{(x_1,x_2)}(x_1, x_2) \right)$$

$$Z_{-,+}^{(x_1,x_2)}(x_1, x_2) = Z^{(x_1)}(x_1) \qquad (147)$$

$$Z_{-,-}^{(x_1,x_2)}(x_1, x_2) = \frac{1}{2} \left[Z^{(x_1)}(x_1) + Z^{(x_2)}(x_2) \right]$$

$$Z_{+,-}^{(x_1,x_2)}(x_1, x_2) = Z^{(x_2)}(x_2)$$

where $Z^{(x_i)}(x_i)$ are given by eq. (130). Here we assume that in case of simultaneous default of both RNs, PB receives the notional minus their average recovery. The corresponding boundary and terminal conditions are

$$V^{FTDS}(t, 0, x_2, T) = 1 - R_1, \quad V^{FTDS}(t, x_1, 0, T) = 1 - R_2 \qquad (148)$$

$$V^{FTDS}(t, x_1, x_2, T) \underset{x_i \to \infty}{\to} V^{CDS}(t, x_{3-i}, T) \qquad (149)$$

$$V^{FTDS}(T, x_1, x_2, T) = 0 \qquad (150)$$

The market practice is to quote the spread on a FTDS by using the Gaussian copula with specified pair-wise correlation, ρ, between default times of RNs (see, for example, Li 2000 and Hull, Nelkin, and White 2004). Thus, we can calibrate the model correlation parameter to FTDS spreads observed in the market.

4.6 Credit default swap with counterparty risk

4.6.1 *Credit value adjustment*

First, we consider a CDS contract sold by a risky PS to a non-risky PB. We denote by τ_1 the default time of RN and by τ_2 the default time of PS. We assume that this CDS provides protection up to time T and its coupon is c. We also assume that the recovery rate of RN is R_1 and of PS is R_2.

We denote by $\tilde{V}^{CDS}(t', T)$ the value of the CDS contract with coupon c maturing at time T conditional on PS defaulting at time t'. We make the following assumptions about the recovery value of the CDS given PS default at time $t' = \tau_2$: if $\tilde{V}^{CDS}(t', T) < 0$, PB pays the full amount of $-\tilde{V}^{CDS}(t', T)$ to PS; if $\tilde{V}^{CDS}(t', T) > 0$, PB receives only a fraction R_2 of $\tilde{V}^{CDS}(t', T)$.

Thus, CVA for PB, $V_{PB}^{CVA}(t, T)$, is defined as the expected maximal potential loss due to the PS default:

$$V_{PB}^{CVA}(t, T) = 1_{\{\tau_1, t, \tau_2, t\}} \mathbb{E}_t^Q \left[\int_t^T D(t, t')(1 - R_2) \left\{ \tilde{V}^{CDS}(t', T) \right\}_+ dt' \right] \quad (151)$$

Accordingly, to value CVA we need to know the survival probability $Q(t', t'')$ for RN conditional on PS default at time t'. In this context, Pykhtin and Zhu (2005) and Misirpashaev (2008) applied the Gaussian copula model, while Blanchet-Scalliet and Patras (2008) applied a bivariate lognormal structural model to calculate the relevant quantity.

Similarly, for a CDS contract sold by a non-risky PS to a risky PB we have the following expression for CVA for PS:

$$V_{PS}^{CVA}(t, T) = 1_{\{\tau_1, t, \tau_2, t\}} \mathbb{E}_t^Q \left[\int_t^T D(t, t')(1 - R_3) \left\{ -\tilde{V}^{CDS}(t', T) \right\}_+ dt' \right] \quad (152)$$

where R_3 is the recovery rate for PB.

How to calculate CVA when both PS and PB are risky is not completely clear as of this writing.

4.6.2 *Credit value adjustment in the structural framework*

We start with the risky PS case and denote by x_1 the driver for the RN's value and by x_2 the driver for the PS's value.

In the context of the structural default model, the 2D plane is divided into four quadrants as follows: (A) $\mathbb{R}^2_{+,+}$, where both RN and PS survive; (B) $\mathbb{R}^2_{-,+}$, where RN defaults and PS survives; (C) $\mathbb{R}^2_{-,-}$, where both the reference name and the counterparty default; (D) $\mathbb{R}^2_{+,-}$, where the reference name survives while the counterparty defaults. In $\mathbb{R}^2_{-,+}$ CVA is set zero, because PS is able to pay the required amount to PB. In $\mathbb{R}^2_{-,-}$ CVA is set to the fraction of the payout which is lost due to the counterparty default, $(1 - R_1 e^{x_1})(1 - R_2 e^{x_2})$. In $\mathbb{R}^2_{+,-}$ CVA is set to $(1 - R_2 e^{x_2}) \left\{ V^{CDS}(t, x_1, T) \right\}_+$, where $V^{CDS}(t, x_1, T)$ is the value of the CDS on RN at time t and state x_1, because the CDS protection is lost following PS default. The value of CVA is computed as the solution to a 2D problem with given rebates in regions $\mathbb{R}^2_{-,+}$, $\mathbb{R}^2_{-,-}$, and $\mathbb{R}^2_{+,-}$.

For DDM, the value of CVA, $V_{PB}^{CVA}(t, x_1, x_2, T)$, satisfies eq. (66) and the following conditions

$$V_{PB}^{CVA}(t, x_1, x_2, T) \underset{x_1 \to -\infty}{\to} (1 - R_1 e^{x_1})(1 - R_2 e^{x_2}) \mathbf{1}_{\{x_2 \leq 0\}} \tag{153}$$

$$V_{PB}^{CVA}(t, x_1, x_2, T) \underset{x_1 \to \infty}{\to} 0$$

$$V_{PB}^{CVA}(t, x_1, x_2, T) \underset{x_2 \to -\infty}{\to} (1 - R_2 e^{x_2}) \left\{ V^{CDS}(t, x_1, T) \right\}_+$$

$$V_{PB}^{CVA}(t, x_1, x_2, T) \underset{x_2 \to \infty}{\to} 0$$

$$V_{PB,m-}^{CVA}(x_1, x_2, T) = V_{PB,m+}^{CVA}(x_1, x_2, T) \mathbf{1}_{\{x_1 > 0, x_2 > 0\}} \tag{154}$$

$$+ (1 - R_1 e^{x_1})(1 - R_2 e^{x_2}) \mathbf{1}_{\{x_1 \leq 0, x_2 \leq 0\}}$$

$$+ (1 - R_2 e^{x_2}) \left\{ V^{CDS}(t, x_1, T) \right\}_+ \mathbf{1}_{\{x_1 > 0, x_2 \leq 0\}}$$

$$V_{PB}^{CVA}(T, x_1, x_2, T) = 0 \tag{155}$$

where $V^{CDS}(t, x_1, T)$ is the value of the non-risky CDS computed by solving the corresponding 1D problem.

For CDM, we have to solve eq. (73) with $\hat{c}(t, x_1, x_2)$ of the form:

$$\hat{c}(t, x_1, x_2) = -\lambda_{\{2\}}(t) Z^{(x_2)}(t, x_1, x_2) \tag{156}$$

$$- \lambda_{\{1,2\}}(t) \left(Z_{-,-}^{(x_1, x_2)}(t, x_1, x_2) + Z_{+,-}^{(x_1, x_2)}(t, x_1, x_2) \right)$$

where

$$Z^{(x_2)}(t, x_1, x_2) = \left\{ V^{CDS}(t, x_1, T) \right\}_+ Z^{(x_2)}(x_2) \tag{157}$$

$$Z_{-,-}^{(x_1, x_2)}(t, x_1, x_2) = Z^{(x_1)}(x_1) Z^{(x_2)}(x_2)$$

$$Z_{+,-}^{(x_1, x_2)}(t, x_1, x_2) = \varkappa(t, x_1) Z^{(x_2)}(x_2)$$

$Z^{(x_i)}(x_i)$ are given by eq. (130), and

$$\varkappa(t, x_1) = \begin{cases} H(x_1 - \nu_1) \left\{ V^{CDS}(t, x_1 - \nu_1, T) \right\}_+ & \text{DNJs} \\ \nu_1 \int_{-x_1}^{0} \left\{ V^{CDS}(t, x_1 + j_1, T) \right\}_+ e^{\nu_1 j_1} dj_1 & \text{ENJs} \end{cases} \tag{158}$$

The corresponding boundary and final conditions are

$$V_{PB}^{CVA}(t, 0, x_2, T) = 0, \quad V_{PB}^{CVA}(t, x_1, x_2, T) \underset{x_1 \to \infty}{\to} 0 \tag{159}$$

$$V_{PB}^{CVA}(t, x_1, 0, T) = (1 - R_2)\left\{V^{CDS}(t, x_1, T)\right\}_+$$

$$V_{PB}^{CVA}(t, x_1, x_2, T) \underset{x_2 \to \infty}{\to} 0$$

$$V_{PB}^{CVA}(T, x_1, x_2, T) = 0 \tag{160}$$

For risky PB, the formulation is similar and we leave it to the reader.

5 ONE-DIMENSIONAL PROBLEM

5.1 Analytical solution

In this section we derive some analytic solutions for jump-diffusion dynamics with ENJs. Unfortunately, similar solutions for DNJs are not readily available. Results presented in this section rely on certain exceptional features of the exponential distribution and do not extend to other jump distributions. In this section, we assume constant model parameters, CDM, and restrict ourselves to ENJs. In more general cases, we need to solve the corresponding problems directly. Analytical results can serve as a useful tool for testing the accuracy of numerical calculations needed for less restrictive cases.

5.1.1 Green's function

Due to the time-homogeneity of the problem under consideration, the Green's function $G(t, x, T, X)$ depends on $\tau = T - t$ rather than on t, T separately, so that we can represent it as follows:

$$G(t, x, T, X) = \Gamma(\tau, x, X) \tag{161}$$

where $\Gamma(\tau, x, X)$ solves the following problem:

$$\Gamma_\tau(\tau, x, X) - \mathcal{L}^{(X)\dagger}\Gamma(\tau, x, X) = 0 \tag{162}$$

$$\Gamma(\tau, x, 0) = 0, \quad \Gamma(\tau, x, X) \underset{X \to \infty}{\to} 0 \tag{163}$$

$$\Gamma(0, x, X) = \delta(X - x) \tag{164}$$

The Laplace transform of $\Gamma(\tau, x, X)$ with respect to τ

$$\Gamma(\tau, x, X) \to \hat{\Gamma}(p, x, X) \tag{165}$$

solves the following problem:

$$p\hat{\Gamma}(p, x, X) - \mathcal{L}^{(X)\dagger}\hat{\Gamma}(p, x, X) = \delta(X - x) \tag{166}$$

$$\hat{\Gamma}(p, x, 0) = 0, \quad \hat{\Gamma}(p, x, X) \underset{X \to \infty}{\to} 0 \tag{167}$$

The corresponding forward characteristic equation is given by:

$$\frac{1}{2}\sigma^2\psi^2 - \mu\psi - (\lambda + p) + \frac{\lambda\nu}{-\psi + \nu} = 0 \tag{168}$$

This equation has three roots, which, to facilitate comparison with earlier work, we denote by $-\psi_j$, $j = 1, 2, 3$. It is easy to show that these roots can be ordered in such a way that $\psi_1 < -\nu < \psi_2 < 0 < \psi_3$. Hence, the overall solution has the form:

$$\hat{\Gamma}(p, x, X) = \begin{cases} C_3 e^{-\psi_3(X-x)}, & X \geq x \\ \sum_{j=1}^{3} D_j e^{-\psi_j(X-x)}, & 0 < X \leq x \end{cases} \tag{169}$$

where

$$D_i = -\frac{2}{\sigma^2}\frac{(\nu + \psi_i)}{(\psi_i - \psi_{3-i})(\psi_i - \psi_3)}, \quad i = 1, 2 \tag{170}$$

$$D_3 = -e^{(\psi_1 - \psi_3)x}D_1 - e^{(\psi_2 - \psi_3)x}D_2, \quad C_3 = D_1 + D_2 + D_3$$

The inverse Laplace transform of $\hat{\Gamma}(p, x, X)$ yields $\Gamma(\tau, x, X)$ (Lipton 2002b). A review of relevant algorithms can be found in Abate, Choudhury, and Whitt (1999).

Without jumps, all the above formulas can be calculated explicitly. Specifically, method of images yields:

$$\Gamma(\tau, x, X) = \frac{e^{-\vartheta/8 - (X-x)/2}}{\sqrt{\vartheta}}\left(\mathbf{n}\left(\frac{X - x}{\sqrt{\vartheta}}\right) - \mathbf{n}\left(\frac{X + x}{\sqrt{\vartheta}}\right)\right) \tag{171}$$

where $\vartheta = \sigma^2\tau$.

5.1.2 Survival probability

By using eqs. (112), (169) we compute the Laplace-transformed survival probability as follows:

$$Q^{(x)}(\tau, x) \to \hat{Q}^{(x)}(p, x) \tag{172}$$

$$\hat{Q}^{(x)}(p, x) = \int_0^\infty \hat{\Gamma}(p, x, X)\,dX \tag{173}$$

$$= \int_x^\infty C_3 e^{-\psi_3(X-x)}dX + \sum_{j=1}^{3}\int_0^x D_j e^{-\psi_j(X-x)}dX = \sum_{j=0}^{2} E_j e^{\psi_j x}$$

where

$$\psi_0 = 0, \quad E_0 = \frac{1}{p}, \quad E_1 = \frac{(\psi_1 + v)\psi_2}{(\psi_1 - \psi_2)vp}, \quad E_2 = \frac{(\psi_2 + v)\psi_1}{(\psi_2 - \psi_1)vp} \tag{174}$$

This result was first obtained by Lipton (2002b).

The default time density can be defined as follows:

$$q(\tau, x) = -\frac{\partial Q^{(x)}(\tau, x)}{\partial \tau} \tag{175}$$

Using eq. (112) we obtain:

$$q(\tau, x) = -\int_0^\infty \frac{\partial \Gamma(\tau, x, X)}{\partial \tau} dX = g(\tau, x) + f(\tau, x) \tag{176}$$

where $g(\tau, x)$ is the probability density of hitting the barrier:

$$g(\tau, x) = \frac{\sigma^2}{2} \left.\frac{\partial \Gamma(\tau, x, X)}{\partial X}\right|_{X=0} \tag{177}$$

and $f(\tau, x)$ is the probability of the overshoot:

$$f(\tau, x) = \lambda \int_0^\infty \left(\int_{-\infty}^{-X} \varpi(j)dj\right) \Gamma(\tau, x, X)dX \tag{178}$$

Formula (178) is generic and can be used for arbitrary jump size distributions. For ENJs, we obtain:

$$f(\tau, x) = \lambda \int_0^\infty e^{-vX} \Gamma(\tau, x, X)dX \tag{179}$$

Using eq. (169), the Laplace-transformed default time density can be represented as:

$$\hat{q}(p, x) = \hat{g}(p, x) + \hat{f}(p, x) \tag{180}$$

where

$$\hat{g}(p, x) = \frac{(v + \psi_2)e^{\psi_2 x} - (v + \psi_1)e^{\psi_1 x}}{\psi_2 - \psi_1} \tag{181}$$

and

$$\hat{f}(p, x) = \frac{2\lambda(e^{\psi_2 x} - e^{\psi_1 x})}{\sigma^2(\psi_2 - \psi_1)(v + \psi_3)} \tag{182}$$

Alternatively, by taking the Laplace transform of eq. (175) and using eq. (173), we obtain:

$$\hat{q}(p, x) = \frac{(\psi_1 + v)\psi_2 e^{\psi_1 x}}{(\psi_2 - \psi_1)v} + \frac{(\psi_2 + v)\psi_1 e^{\psi_2 x}}{(\psi_1 - \psi_2)v} \tag{183}$$

Straightforward but tedious algebra shows that expressions (180)–(182) and (183) are in agreement.

Without jumps, straightforward calculation yields

$$Q^{(x)}(\tau, x) = \mathbf{N}\left(\frac{x}{\sqrt{\vartheta}} - \frac{\sqrt{\vartheta}}{2}\right) - e^x \mathbf{N}\left(-\frac{x}{\sqrt{\vartheta}} - \frac{\sqrt{\vartheta}}{2}\right) \tag{184}$$

$$= e^{-\vartheta/8 + x/2}\left(\mathbf{P}\left(\frac{x}{\sqrt{\vartheta}}, -\frac{\sqrt{\vartheta}}{2}\right) - \mathbf{P}\left(-\frac{x}{\sqrt{\vartheta}}, -\frac{\sqrt{\vartheta}}{2}\right)\right)$$

and,

$$q(\tau, x) = g(\tau, x) = \frac{x}{\tau\sqrt{\vartheta}}\mathbf{n}\left(\frac{x}{\sqrt{\vartheta}} - \frac{\sqrt{\vartheta}}{2}\right), \quad f(\tau, x) = 0 \tag{185}$$

5.1.3 Credit default swap

We use the general formula (124) together with eq. (176), and express the present value $V^{CDS}(\tau, x)$ of a CDS contract with coupon c as:

$$V^{CDS}(\tau, x) = -c \int_0^\tau e^{-r\tau'} Q^{(x)}(\tau', x)d\tau' \tag{186}$$

$$+(1 - R)\int_0^\tau e^{-r\tau'} g(\tau', x)d\tau' + \left(1 - R\frac{\nu}{1+\nu}\right)\int_0^\tau e^{-r\tau'} f(\tau', x)d\tau'$$

By using eqs. (173), (181), (182), we can compute the value of the CDS via the inverse Laplace transform.

Without jumps $V^{CDS}(\tau, x)$ can be found explicitly. The annuity leg can be represented in the form

$$A(\tau, x) = \frac{1}{r}\left(1 - e^{-r\tau}\left(Q^{(x)}(\tau, x) + e^{-\vartheta/8 + x/2}\left(\mathbf{P}\left(-\frac{x}{\sqrt{\vartheta}}, \frac{\gamma\sqrt{\vartheta}}{2}\right) + \mathbf{P}\left(-\frac{x}{\sqrt{\vartheta}}, -\frac{\gamma\sqrt{\vartheta}}{2}\right)\right)\right)\right) \tag{187}$$

where $\gamma = \sqrt{8r/\sigma^2 + 1}$, while the protection leg can be represented as follows

$$P(\tau, x) = (1 - R)\left(1 - e^{-r\tau}Q^{(x)}(\tau, x) - rA(\tau, x)\right) \tag{188}$$

Accordingly,

$$V^{CDS}(\tau, x) = (1 - R)\left(1 - e^{-r\tau}Q^{(x)}(\tau, x)\right) - ((1 - R)r + c)A(\tau, x) \tag{189}$$

5.1.4 Credit default swap option

In the time-homogeneous setting of the present section, we can represent the price of a CDSO as follows

$$V^{CDSO}(\tau_e, x) = e^{-r\tau_e}\int_0^{X^*} \Gamma(\tau_e, x, X) V^{CDS}(\tau_t, X)dX \tag{190}$$

where X^* is chosen in such a way that $V^{CDS}(\tau_t, X^*) = 0$. We can use our previous results to evaluate this expression via the Laplace transform.

As before, without jumps V^{CDSO} can be evaluated explicitly.

5.1.5 *Equity put option*

We use eq. (139) and represent the value of the put option with strike K and maturity T as follows:

$$V^P(\tau, \xi, T) = e^{-r\tau}\left[V_0^P(\tau, \xi, T) + K\left(1 - Q^{(x)}(\tau, \xi)\right)\right] \tag{191}$$

The Laplace transform of $V_0^P(\tau, \xi, T)$ is given by

$$\hat{V}_0^P(p, \xi, T) = \int_0^\infty \left\{K - l(T)\left(e^X - 1\right)\right\}_+ \hat{\Gamma}(p, \xi, X)\, dX \tag{192}$$

Straightforward calculation yields:

$$\hat{V}_0^P(p, \xi, T) = l(T)\sum_{j=1}^3 D_j e^{\psi_j\xi}\left(\frac{e^{k(T)} - e^{(1-\psi_j)k(T)}}{\psi_j} + \frac{1 - e^{(1-\psi_j)k(T)}}{1 - \psi_j}\right) \tag{193}$$

for out-of-the-money puts with $\xi \geq k(T)$, and

$$\hat{V}_0^P(p, \xi, T) = l(T)\left\{\sum_{j=1}^3 D_j e^{\psi_j\xi}\left(\frac{e^{k(T)} - e^{k(T)-\psi_j\xi}}{\psi_j} + \frac{1 - e^{(1-\psi_j)\xi}}{1 - \psi_j}\right)\right.$$

$$\left. +C_3 e^{\psi_3\xi}\left(\frac{e^{k(T)-\psi_3\xi} - e^{(1-\psi_3)k(T)}}{\psi_3} + \frac{e^{(1-\psi_3)\xi} - e^{(1-\psi_3)k(T)}}{1 - \psi_3}\right)\right\} \tag{194}$$

for in-the-money puts with $\xi < k(T)$. Here $k(T) = \ln\left((K + l(T))/l(T)\right)$.

Without jumps, we can find $V_0^P(\tau, \xi, T)$, and hence the price of a put option, explicitly:

$$V_0^P(\tau, \xi, T) = l(T)e^{-\vartheta/8+\xi/2}\left\{e^{k(T)/2}\left[\mathbf{P}\left(\frac{k(T)-\xi}{\sqrt{\vartheta}}, \frac{\sqrt{\vartheta}}{2}\right) - \mathbf{P}\left(\frac{k(T)+\xi}{\sqrt{\vartheta}}, \frac{\sqrt{\vartheta}}{2}\right)\right.\right. \tag{195}$$

$$\left. -\mathbf{P}\left(\frac{k(T)-\xi}{\sqrt{\vartheta}}, -\frac{\sqrt{\vartheta}}{2}\right) + \mathbf{P}\left(\frac{k(T)+\xi}{\sqrt{\vartheta}}, -\frac{\sqrt{\vartheta}}{2}\right)\right]$$

$$-e^{k(T)}\left[\mathbf{P}\left(-\frac{\xi}{\sqrt{\vartheta}}, \frac{\sqrt{\vartheta}}{2}\right) - \mathbf{P}\left(\frac{\xi}{\sqrt{\vartheta}}, \frac{\sqrt{\vartheta}}{2}\right)\right]$$

$$\left. +\mathbf{P}\left(-\frac{\xi}{\sqrt{\vartheta}}, -\frac{\sqrt{\vartheta}}{2}\right) - \mathbf{P}\left(\frac{\xi}{\sqrt{\vartheta}}, -\frac{\sqrt{\vartheta}}{2}\right)\right\}$$

5.1.6 *Example*

In Figure 12.1 we illustrate our findings. We use the following set of parameters: $a(0) = 200, l(0) = 160, s(0) = 40, \xi = 0.22, r = \zeta = 0, \sigma = 0.05, \lambda = 0.03, \nu = 1/\xi$. We compare results obtained for the jump-diffusion model with the ones obtained for the diffusion model the 'equivalent' diffusion volatility σ^{diff} specified by $\sigma^{\text{diff}} = \sqrt{\sigma^2 + 2\lambda/\nu^2}$,

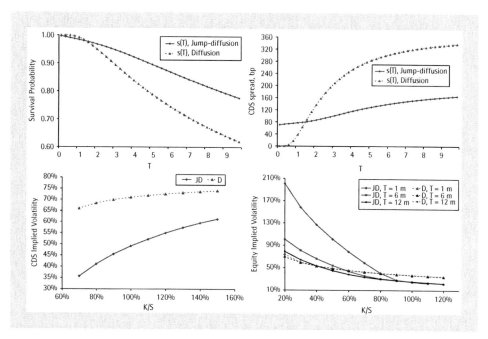

FIGURE 12.1 The model implied survival probabilities for $1y \leq T \leq 10y$ (top lhs); CDS spreads for $1y \leq T \leq 10y$ (top rhs); volatility skew for CDSO (bottom lhs); volatility skew for put options with $T = 1m, 6m, 12m$ (bottom rhs).

$\sigma^{\text{diff}} = 0.074$ for the chosen model parameters. First, we show the term structure of the implied spread generated by the jump-diffusion and diffusion models. We see that, unlike the diffusion model, the jump-diffusion model implies a non-zero probability of default in the short term, so that its implied spread is consistent with the one observed in the market. If needed, we can produce different shapes of the CDS curve by using the term structure of the model intensity parameter λ. Second, we show the model implied volatility surface for put options with maturity of $0.5y$. We see that the jump-diffusion model generates the implied volatility skew that is steeper that the diffusion model, so that, in general, it can fit the market implied skew more easily. An interesting discussion of the equity volatility skew in the structural framework can be found in Hull, Nelkin, and White (2004/05).

5.2 Asymptotic solution

In this section, we derive an asymptotic expansion for the Green's function solving problem (63) assuming that the jump-intensity parameter λ is small. More details of the derivation (which is far from trivial) and its extensions will be given elsewhere.

We introduce a new function $\tilde{\Gamma}(\tau, x, X)$ such that:

$$\Gamma(\tau, x, X) = \exp\left\{-\left(\frac{\mu^2}{2\sigma^2} + \lambda\right)\tau + \frac{\mu}{\sigma^2}(X - x)\right\} \tilde{\Gamma}(\tau, x, X) \qquad (196)$$

The modified Green's function solves the following propagation problem on the positive semi-axis:

$$\tilde{\Gamma}_\tau(\tau, x, X) - \tilde{\mathcal{L}}^{(X)\dagger} \tilde{\Gamma}(\tau, x, X) = 0 \tag{197}$$

$$\tilde{\Gamma}(\tau, x, 0) = 0, \quad \tilde{\Gamma}(\tau, x, X) \underset{X\to\infty}{\to} 0 \tag{198}$$

$$\tilde{\Gamma}(0, x, X) = \delta(X - x) \tag{199}$$

where

$$\tilde{\mathcal{L}}^{(x)\dagger} g(x) = \frac{1}{2}\sigma^2 g_{xx}(x) + \lambda v \int_{-\infty}^0 g(x - j)e^{\bar{v}j} dj \tag{200}$$

and $\bar{v} = v - \mu/\sigma^2$.

We assume that $\lambda \ll 1$ and represent $\tilde{\Gamma}(\tau, x, X)$ as follows:

$$\tilde{\Gamma}(\tau, x, X) = \tilde{\Gamma}^{(0)}(\tau, x, X) + \lambda \tilde{\Gamma}^{(1)}(\tau, x, X) + \dots \tag{201}$$

The zero-order term $\tilde{\Gamma}^{(0)}(\tau, x, X)$ solves the following problem:

$$\tilde{\Gamma}_\tau^{(0)}(\tau, x, X) - \frac{1}{2}\sigma^2 \tilde{\Gamma}_{XX}^{(0)}(\tau, x, X) = 0 \tag{202}$$

$$\tilde{\Gamma}^{(0)}(\tau, x, 0) = 0, \quad \tilde{\Gamma}^{(0)}(\tau, x, X) \underset{X\to\infty}{\to} 0 \tag{203}$$

$$\tilde{\Gamma}^{(0)}(0, x, X) = \delta(X - x) \tag{204}$$

It is well-known that it can be written as follows:

$$\tilde{\Gamma}^{(0)}(\tau, x, X) = \frac{1}{\sqrt{\vartheta}}\left(\mathbf{n}\left(\frac{X - x}{\sqrt{\vartheta}}\right) - \mathbf{n}\left(\frac{X + x}{\sqrt{\vartheta}}\right)\right) \tag{205}$$

The first-order term $\tilde{\Gamma}^{(1)}(\tau, x, X)$ solves the following problem:

$$\tilde{\Gamma}_\tau^{(1)}(\tau, x, X) - \frac{1}{2}\sigma^2 \tilde{\Gamma}_{XX}^{(1)}(\tau, x, X) = \Delta(\tau, x, X) \tag{206}$$

$$\tilde{\Gamma}^{(1)}(\tau, x, 0) = 0, \quad \tilde{\Gamma}^{(1)}(\tau, x, X) \underset{X\to\infty}{\to} 0 \tag{207}$$

$$\tilde{\Gamma}^{(1)}(0, x, X) = 0 \tag{208}$$

where

$$\Delta(\tau, x, X) = v \int_{-\infty}^0 \tilde{\Gamma}^{(0)}(\tau, x, X - j)e^{\bar{v}j} dj \tag{209}$$

$$= v\mathbf{P}\left(-\frac{X - x}{\sqrt{\vartheta}}, -\bar{v}\sqrt{\vartheta}\right) - v\mathbf{P}\left(-\frac{X + x}{\sqrt{\vartheta}}, -\bar{v}\sqrt{\vartheta}\right)$$

and $\mathbf{P}(a, b)$ is defined by eq. (5). We use Duhamel's principle and represent $\Gamma^{(1)}(\tau, x, X)$ as follows:

$$\tilde{\varGamma}^{(1)}(\tau, x, X) = \int_0^\tau \int_0^\infty \tilde{\varGamma}^{(0)}(\tau - \tau', x, X - X')\varDelta(\tau', x, X')dX'd\tau' \tag{210}$$

Fairly involved algebra yields:

$$\tilde{\varGamma}^{(1)}(\tau, x, X) = \frac{\nu}{\bar{\nu}\sigma^2}\left(\bar{\nu}\vartheta\mathbf{P}\left(-\frac{X-x}{\sqrt{\vartheta}}, -\bar{\nu}\sqrt{\vartheta}\right)\right. \tag{211}$$

$$+X\mathbf{P}\left(-\frac{X+x}{\sqrt{\vartheta}}, -\bar{\nu}\sqrt{\vartheta}\right) - (X - \bar{\nu}\vartheta)\mathbf{P}\left(-\frac{X+x}{\sqrt{\vartheta}}, \bar{\nu}\sqrt{\vartheta}\right)$$

$$\left. -(X + \bar{\nu}\vartheta)e^{-\bar{\nu}x}\mathbf{P}\left(-\frac{X}{\sqrt{\vartheta}}, -\bar{\nu}\sqrt{\vartheta}\right) + (X - \bar{\nu}\vartheta)e^{-\bar{\nu}x}\mathbf{P}\left(-\frac{X}{\sqrt{\vartheta}}, \bar{\nu}\sqrt{\vartheta}\right)\right)$$

For DNJs we can derive a similar expression:

$$\tilde{\varGamma}^{(1)}(\tau, x, X) = \frac{e^{\mu\nu/\sigma^2}}{\sigma^2}\begin{cases} X\left(\mathbf{N}\left(-\frac{X-x+\nu}{\sqrt{\vartheta}}\right) - \mathbf{N}\left(-\frac{X+x+\nu}{\sqrt{\vartheta}}\right)\right) & x < \nu \\ X\left(\mathbf{N}\left(-\frac{X+x-\nu}{\sqrt{\vartheta}}\right) - \mathbf{N}\left(-\frac{X+x+\nu}{\sqrt{\vartheta}}\right)\right) & \\ +\sqrt{\vartheta}\left(\mathbf{n}\left(\frac{X-x+\nu}{\sqrt{\vartheta}}\right) - \mathbf{n}\left(\frac{X+x-\nu}{\sqrt{\vartheta}}\right)\right) & x \geq \nu \end{cases} \tag{212}$$

5.3 Numerical solution

In this section we describe several complementary numerical methods for solving the calibration and pricing problems in 1D. Specifically, we present the MC, FFT, and FD-based methods. The MC method, due to its generic nature, is easily applicable to the problem at hand, particularly for DDM. However, it comes with the usual drawbacks and is to be avoided whenever possible. The FFT method is well suited to solving problems with DDM, however it has several well-known disadvantages including the need for uniform grids with a large number of steps, and complicated treatment of aliasing effects. In our opinion, the FD method is the most powerful of the three. It can be used for both DDM and CDM. The key difficulty in applying the FD method for jump-diffusions is the treatment of the integral term. The direct integration method (see, for example, Cont and Tankov 2004; Cont and Voltchkova 2005) has a complexity of $O(N^2)$ operations per time step, where N is the spatial grid size. To obviate this difficulty we can use the FFT method to compute the convolution term with a complexity of $O(N \log N)$, see (Andersen and Andreasen 2000; d'Halluin, Forsyth, and Vetzal 2005 among others), however, this approach shares the disadvantages of the conventional FFT method. It turns out that for DNJs and ENJs one can compute the integral term explicitly with a complexity of $O(N)$ (Lipton 2003; Carr and Mayo 2007; Lipton, Song, and Lee 2007; Toivanen 2008)

Let us briefly compare the FFT and FD-based methods. In 1D, the complexity of the FFT method is $O(N \log N)$ per each time step, so that the overall complexity with M default monitoring is $O(MN \log N)$. The complexity of the FD method with explicit treatment of the integral term and L time steps is $O(LN)$ (we note that if the set of monitoring times is sparse, we would need to add extra time steps to improve accuracy of the FD method). Thus, the overall competitiveness of the methods depends on the number of time steps needed to achieve the desired accuracy. In the case of DDM, the value function is not continuous at the barrier, so that both the FFT and FD-based methods are expected to be only first-order accurate in space, which is indeed confirmed by our numerical experiments. In the case of CDM, the FD-based method is expected to have second-order accuracy in space; while the FFT-based method cannot easily be applied in this case.

5.3.1 Monte Carlo method

We assume DDM and describe the corresponding MC simulations. There are two methods for the simulation of the 1D dynamics. The first method is based on the direct integration of dynamics (17):

$$\Delta x_m \equiv x(t_m) - x(t_{m-1}) = \overline{\mu}_m + \overline{\sigma}_m \epsilon_m + \sum_{k=1}^{n_m} j_k \qquad (213)$$

where ϵ_m are standard independent normals, j_k are independent variables with PDF $\varpi(j)$, $n_m = N(t_m) - N(t_{m-1})$ is the Poisson random variable with intensity $\overline{\lambda}_m$, and $x(t_0) = \xi$. Here

$$\overline{\mu}_m = \int_{t_{m-1}}^{t_m} \mu(t')dt', \; \overline{\sigma}_m = \sqrt{\int_{t_{m-1}}^{t_m} \sigma^2(t')dt'}, \; \overline{\lambda}_m = \int_{t_{m-1}}^{t_m} \lambda(t')dt' \qquad (214)$$

The second method is based on the simulation of the increment Δx_m by the inversion of the PDF corresponding to the exact Green's function. We note that in the presence of jumps the Green's function can be represented as follows:

$$G(\Delta t_m, \Delta x_m) = \sum_{k=0}^{\infty} w_k \Phi_k(\theta) \qquad (215)$$

where $\Delta t_m = t_m - t_{m-1}$ and w_k is the probability of exactly k jumps for the Poisson distribution with intensity $\overline{\lambda}_m$:

$$w_k = \frac{e^{-\overline{\lambda}_m}(\overline{\lambda}_m)^k}{k!}, \quad k = 0, 1, \ldots$$

$$\Phi_0(\theta) = \frac{1}{\overline{\sigma}_m}\mathbf{n}(\theta)$$

$$\Phi_1(\theta) = \frac{1}{\overline{\sigma}_m}\mathbf{n}\left(\theta + \frac{\nu}{\overline{\sigma}_m}\right) \quad \text{DNJs} \qquad (216)$$

$$\Phi_k(\theta) = \frac{1}{\overline{\sigma}_m}\mathbf{n}\left(\theta + \frac{k\nu}{\overline{\sigma}_m}\right)$$

$$\Phi_0(\theta) = \frac{1}{\bar{\sigma}_m}\mathbf{n}(\theta)$$

$$\Phi_1(\theta) = v\mathbf{P}(-\theta, -\sigma_-) \qquad \text{ENJs}$$

$$\Phi_k(\theta) = \frac{\sigma_-(-(\theta+\sigma_-)\Phi_{k-1}(\theta)+\sigma_-\Phi_{k-2}(\theta))}{k-1}$$

where $\theta = (\Delta x_m - \bar{\mu}_m)/\bar{\sigma}_m$, $\sigma_- = v\bar{\sigma}_m$. Typically, we can restrict ourselves to the combination of the first two terms.

Once the evolution of the driver x is described, the valuation can be performed in the standard fashion.

5.3.2 Fast Fourier Transform method

In this section we show how to use the FFT method for valuing credit products in 1D. As we mentioned earlier, this method is not well suited to the case of CDM, so we only apply it in the case of DDM. The advantage of this method is that its implementation is relatively easy and it can be applied for relatively wide class of jump-size distributions. Its disadvantages are the need for a dense uniform grid, which has to be wide enough in order to avoid aliasing effects becoming important.

The Green's function

To start with, we consider the unbounded Green's function governed by eqs. (56), (57), (59). We emphasize that the coefficients of the infinitesimal generator are spatially independent, so that the Green's function depends on $X - x$ rather than X and x separately:

$$G(t, x, T, X) \equiv Y(t, T, Y) \tag{217}$$

where $Y = X - x$. Due to this fact, the Fourier transform of Y can be found explicitly:

$$\hat{Y}(t, T, k) = \int_{-\infty}^{\infty} e^{ikY} Y(t, T, Y) dY = e^{-\int_t^T \psi(t', k) dt'} \tag{218}$$

where k is the transform variable, and $\psi(t, k)$ is the characteristic exponent:

$$\psi(t, k) = \frac{1}{2}\sigma^2(t)k^2 - i\mu(t)k - \lambda(t)(\hat{\varpi}(k) - 1) \tag{219}$$

with the function $\hat{\varpi}(k)$ given by:

$$\hat{\varpi}(k) = \int_{-\infty}^{0} e^{ikj}\varpi(j)dj = \begin{cases} e^{-ik\nu}, & \text{DNJs} \\ \frac{\nu}{\nu+ik}, & \text{ENJs} \end{cases} \tag{220}$$

Given $\hat{Y}$ we can compute the Green's function Y via the inverse Fourier transform as follows:

$$Y(t, T, Y) = \frac{1}{2\pi} \int_{-\infty}^{\infty} e^{-ikY} \hat{Y}(t, T, k) dk \tag{221}$$

When parameters are time independent we have

$$\hat{Y}(t, T, k) = e^{-\tau\psi(k)} \tag{222}$$

$$\psi(k) = \frac{1}{2}\sigma^2 k^2 - i\mu k - \lambda(\hat{\varpi}(k) - 1)$$

where $\tau = T - t$. This formula can be trivially generalized to the case of piecewise constant parameters but we don't present the corresponding expression here since we are only interested in time intervals between observation times where parameters are constant by construction.

Backward problem

We start by considering the backward problem (36), (37) for the value function $V(t, x)$ on the time interval (t_{m-1}, t_m). The value function $V_{(m-1)+}(x)$ can be represented as follows:

$$V_{(m-1)+}(x) = D(t_{m-1}, t_m) \int_{-\infty}^{\infty} V_{m-}(X) Y(t_{m-1}, t_m, X - x) dX \tag{223}$$

For convenience, we introduce the inverse Fourier transform of $V_{m-}(x)$:

$$\hat{V}_{m-}(k) = \frac{1}{2\pi} \int_{-\infty}^{\infty} e^{-ikx} V_{m-}(x) dx \tag{224}$$

Here we assume that V_{m-} is regularized as appropriate, so that the above integral converges. By applying the Fourier transformed density function (218) and exchanging the integration order, we obtain:

$$V(t_{(m-1)+}, x) \tag{225}$$

$$= D(t_{m-1}, t_m) \int_{-\infty}^{\infty} V_{m-}(X) \left\{ \frac{1}{2\pi} \int_{-\infty}^{\infty} e^{-ik(X-x)} \hat{Y}(t_{m-1}, t_m, k)dk \right\} dX$$

$$= D(t_{m-1}, t_m) \int_{-\infty}^{\infty} e^{ikx} \left\{ \frac{1}{2\pi} \int_{-\infty}^{\infty} e^{-ikX} V_{m-}(X) dX \right\} \hat{Y}(t_{m-1}, t_m, k)dk$$

$$= D(t_{m-1}, t_m) \int_{-\infty}^{\infty} e^{ikx} \hat{V}_{m-}(k) \hat{Y}(t_{m-1}, t_m, k)dk$$

Variants of formula (225) for option pricing in 1D case were proposed and analysed by Carr and Madan (1999); Lewis (2001); Lipton (2001, 2002a), among others.

We can apply the above formula repeatedly for DDM at times $\{t_m^d\}_{m=1,...,M}$. Let today's time be $t_0 = 0$. We represent the following backward induction algorithm based on the recurrent application of eq. (225): (a) Set $m = M$ and apply the terminal condition by $v_M(x) = v(x)$; (b) Compute the auxiliary function $V_{(m-1)+}(x)$ by virtue of eq. (225); (c) Evaluate $V_{(m-1)-}$ by applying the projection operator $\Pi\{V(x)\}$ as needed

$$V_{(m-1)-}(x) = \Pi\left\{V_{(m-1)+}(x)\right\} \tag{226}$$

(d) Repeat steps (b), (c) until $m = 1$, when $V(0, \xi)$ is calculated and the recursion is stopped. For financial instruments of interest, explicit expressions for v, $\Pi\{.\}$ are given in section 4. To calculate the survival probability, we run the above scheme without discounting.

To apply the above algorithm in practice, we restrict the value function $V(t, x)$ and the payoff function $v(x)$ to the uniform spatial grid $\{x_0, \ldots, x_N\}$ with the uniform step Δx, where x_0 is a large negative number and x_N is a large positive number, and $N = 2^n - 1$, which is required for the standard FFT algorithm to be efficient (but is not necessary in general). For the sake of computational efficiency, the spatial grid is defined in such a way that $x_{n_0} = 0$, and $\xi = x_{n_\xi}$, for some n_0, n_ξ, respectively. The transformed density function $\hat{Y}(t, T, k)$ is defined on the discrete Fourier grid $\{k_0, \ldots, k_N\}$ with uniform step Δk, such that $\Delta x \Delta k = 2\pi/2^n$, and

$$k_n = \frac{2\pi(n - N/2)}{N\Delta x} \tag{227}$$

The discretized version of eq. (225) can be written as

$$V_{(m-1)+}(x) = D\,(t_{m-1}, t_m)\,\text{fft}\left(\text{ifft}(V_{m-}(x)) \odot \hat{Y}(t_{m-1}, t_m, k)\right) \tag{228}$$

where $\odot$ denotes element-wise multiplication

Forward problem

Similarly, we consider the forward problem for the Green's function $G(T, X)$ governed by eqs. (56), (57) on the time interval (t_{m-1}, t_m). This function can be written as follows:

$$G_{m-}(X) = \int_{-\infty}^{\infty} G_{(m-1)+}(x) Y(t_{m-1}, t_m, X - x) dx \tag{229}$$

By analogy with eq. (225), we obtain:

$$G_{m-}(X) = \int_{-\infty}^{\infty} G_{(m-1)+}(x) \left\{\frac{1}{2\pi} \int_{-\infty}^{\infty} e^{-ik(X-x)} \hat{Y}(t_{m-1}, t_m, k) dk\right\} dx \tag{230}$$

$$= \frac{1}{2\pi} \int_{-\infty}^{\infty} e^{-ikX} \left\{\int_{-\infty}^{\infty} e^{ikx} G_{(m-1)+}(x) dx\right\} \hat{Y}(t_{m-1}, t_m, k) dk$$

$$= \frac{1}{2\pi} \int_{-\infty}^{\infty} e^{-ikX} \hat{G}_{(m-1)+}(k) \hat{Y}(t_{m-1}, t_m, k) dk$$

We note that the expression in the curly brackets can be viewed as the direct Fourier transform of the initial value function $G_{(m-1)+}(x)$. Thus, the discrete version of eq. (230) can be represented by analogy to eq. (228):

$$G_{m-}(X) = \text{ifft}\left(\text{fft}(G_{(m-1)+}(X)) \odot \hat{Y}(t_{m-1}, t_m, k)\right) \tag{231}$$

For calibration purposes it is important to solve the problem for the survival probability $Q^{(x)}(t, x, T)$ via forward induction. For this purpose we present forward induction with time stepping based on the recursive application of eq. (231) as follows:
(a) Set $m = 1$ and specify the initial condition for G as a Kronecker's delta function

centred at n_0:

$$G(t_0, X) = g(X_n) = \delta_{n,n_\xi} \tag{232}$$

(b) Given the value of G at time $t_{(m-1)+}$, $G_{(m-1)+}(X)$, apply the forward convolution (231); (c) Set to zero the value function $G_{m+}(X)$ outside the barrier region:

$$G_{m+}(X) = G_{m-}(X)\mathbf{1}_{\{X>0\}} \tag{233}$$

(d) Evaluate the current value of the survival probability $Q^{(x)}(0, \xi, t_m)$ by computing the sum over the discrete spatial grid:

$$Q^{(x)}(0, \xi, t_m) = \sum_{n=n_0}^{N} G_{m+}(x_n) \tag{234}$$

(e) Repeat steps (b), (c) until $m = M$, then stop the recursion.

Implementation details

When implementing the FFT method with time stepping we need to consider the following important aspects: periodicity, finiteness, and convergence.

The applicability of FFT is based on the assumption that the relevant functions are periodic. If it is not the case, so-called aliasing effects tend to spoil the solution near the end points of the computational domain. We first notice that, provided the spatial grid is large enough, the periodicity is not an issue for the computation of the Green's function since asymptotically it approaches zero. For the backward recursion, we can deal with aliasing effects by modifying the solution near the edges of the grid. We note that near the edges of the grid the second derivative of the value function should gradually approach zero (from above for convex payoffs, from below for concave ones). However, aliasing effects destroy the convexity/concavity of the corresponding solution. To rectify this fact, we alter the value function by detecting remote areas where its convexity/concavity is violated, and linearly extrapolating the function there, thus achieving zero convexity/concavity in these regions.

Formulas (225) and (230) are based on the requirement that the Fourier transform of the payoff function exists. This requirement can be satisfied by applying a damping factor as needed. For the FFT method, this requirement is not too restrictive since the calculations are performed in a finite domain. In our experiments, we have found no advantage in using damping.

The convergence of the integral formulas (225) and (230) is affected by the rate of decay of the transformed Green's function (218) for large k. Asymptotically, using eq. (219) we obtain the following result:

$$\lim_{|k| \to \pm\infty} \Re\left[\hat{Y}(t_{m-1}, t_m, k)\right] = e^{-\frac{1}{2}\tau_m \sigma^2 k^2} \tag{235}$$

where $\tau_m = t_m - t_{m-1}$. Typically, the volatility is small, $\sigma \approx 0.01$, and $\tau_m \approx 0.25y$, so that the upper bound for k, $k_N = \pi/2\Delta x$ needs to be large enough ($k_N \sim 1000$). In our experiments, we have found that for typical model parameters it is safe to choose $N = 2^{12} - 1$, $\Delta x \sim 10^{-4}$.

5.3.3 Finite difference method

Backward equation

We start with the backward problem for the value function $V(t, x)$. For DDM, this function is solving problem (43) on $\mathbb{R}^1$, while for CDM this function is solving a similar problem on $\mathbb{R}^1_+$. For brevity, we consider only the latter case.

We introduce a discrete spatial grid of size $N + 1$, $\{x_0, x_1, \ldots, x_{N-1}, x_N\}$, where $x_0 = 0$; and x_N is a large positive number, and a discrete time grid of size L, $\{t_0, t_1, \ldots, t_L\}$, where $t_0 = 0$ and $t_L = T$, in such a way that the set of times when parameters jump, and other special times, if any, belong to the grid. The values $V(t_l, x_n)$ are denoted by $V_{l,n}$, and similarly for other relevant quantities. For fixed l we use the notation $\vec{V}_l$, and think of $\vec{V}_l$ as an $(N + 1)$-component vector. We discretize the evolution operator (54) at time t_l:

$$\widehat{\mathcal{L}}^{(x)}(t_l) \Longrightarrow \widehat{\mathfrak{L}}^{(x)}_l \tag{236}$$

$$\mathcal{D}^{(x)}(t_l) + \widehat{\mathcal{J}}^{(x)}(t_l) \Longrightarrow \mathfrak{D}^{(x)}_l + \widehat{\mathfrak{J}}^{(x)}_l$$

where $\widehat{\mathfrak{L}}^{(x)}_l$, $\mathfrak{D}^{(x)}_l$, $\widehat{\mathfrak{J}}^{(x)}_l$ are $(N + 1) \times (N + 1)$ matrices with elements $\widehat{\mathfrak{L}}^{(x)}_{l,n,n'}$, $\mathfrak{D}^{(x)}_{l,n,n'}$, $\widehat{\mathfrak{J}}^{(x)}_{l,n,n'}$.

As usual, $\mathfrak{D}^{(x)}_l$ is a tridiagonal matrix. Typically the diffusion term is small compared to the advection and jump terms, so that an appropriate discretization of the first derivative is necessary for the stability of the numerical scheme, see, for example, d'Halluin, Forsyth, and Vetzal (2005).

In general, the matrix $\widehat{\mathfrak{J}}^{(x)}_l$ is not tridiagonal. However, as we shall demonstrate presently, for DNJs and ENJs, the product $\widehat{\mathfrak{J}}^{(x)}_l \vec{V}_l$ can be evaluated in a way which requires only $O(N)$ operations. To this end, we introduce an auxiliary function

$$\varphi_l(x) \equiv \widehat{\mathcal{J}}^{(x)} V(t_l, x) \tag{237}$$

which we intend to treat fully explicitly.

For DNJs, we can approximate φ_l on the grid via the linear interpolation to second order accuracy:

$$\phi_{l,n} = \begin{cases} \omega_{\bar{n}} V_{l,\bar{n}-1} + (1 - \omega_{\bar{n}}) V_{l,\bar{n}}, & x_n \geq \nu \\ 0, & x_n < \nu \end{cases} \tag{238}$$

where

$$\bar{n} = \min\{j : x_{j-1} \leq x_n - \nu < x_j\}, \quad \omega_{\bar{n}} = \frac{x_{\bar{n}} - (x_n - \nu)}{x_{\bar{n}} - x_{\bar{n}-1}} \tag{239}$$

For ENJs, we choose a small step h, $h > 0$, and write:

$$\varphi_l(x + h) = v \int_{-x-h}^{0} e^{vj} V(t_l, x + h + j)dj \tag{240}$$

$$= ve^{-vh}\left(\int_{-x}^{0} e^{vz} V(t_l, x + z)dz + \int_{0}^{h} e^{vz}V(t_l, x + z)dz \right)$$

$$= e^{-vh}\varphi_l(x) + w_0(v, h)V(t_l, x) + w_1(v, h)V(t_l, x + h) + O(h^3)$$

where $z = h + j$, and

$$w_0(v, h) = \frac{1 - (1 + vh)e^{-vh}}{vh}, \quad w_1(v, h) = \frac{-1 + vh + e^{-vh}}{vh} \tag{241}$$

Accordingly, we obtain a recursive scheme for computing $\varphi(x)$ to second-order accuracy:

$$\varphi_l(x + h) = e^{-vh}\varphi_l(x) + w_0(v, h)V(t_l, x) + w_1(v, h)V(t_l, x + h) \tag{242}$$

On the grid, we choose $h_n = x_n - x_{n-1}$, and represent eq. (242) as follows:

$$\varphi_{l,n+1} = e^{-vh_{n+1}}\varphi_{l,n} + w_0(v, h_{n+1})V_{l,n} + w_1(v, h_{n+1})V_{l,n+1} \tag{243}$$

with the initial condition specified by $\varphi_{l,0} = 0$. Thus, by introducing an auxiliary vector $\vec{\varphi}_l = \{\varphi_{l,n}\}$ we can calculate the matrix product $\mathcal{K}_l \vec{V}_l$ with $O(N)$ operations in both cases.

To compute the value $\vec{V}_{l-1}$ given the value $\vec{V}_l$, $l = 1, \ldots, L$, we introduce auxiliary vectors $\vec{\varphi}_l$, $\vec{V}^*$, $\vec{V}^{**}$, and apply the following scheme:

$$\vec{V}^* = \vec{V}_l + \frac{1}{2}\delta t_l \left(\vec{c}_{l-1} + \vec{c}_l \right) + \delta t_l \lambda(t_l)\vec{\varphi}_l \tag{244}$$

$$\left(\mathcal{I} - \delta t_l \mathfrak{D}_l^{(x)} \right) \vec{V}^{**} = \vec{V}^*$$

$$\vec{V}_{l-1} = D(t_{l-1}, t_l) \vec{V}^{**}$$

where $\delta t_l = t_l - t_{l-1}$, $l = 1, \ldots, L$, and $\mathcal{I}$ is the identity matrix. Thus, we use an explicit scheme to approximate the integral step and compute $\vec{V}^*$ given $\vec{V}_l$; then we use an implicit scheme to approximate the diffusive step and compute $\vec{V}^{**}$ given $\vec{V}^*$, finally, we apply the deterministic discounting. Boundary values V_0^{**} and V_N^{**} are determined by the boundary conditions. The second implicit step leads to a system of tridiagonal equations which can be solved via $O(N)$ operations. The time-stepping numerical scheme is straightforward. The terminal condition is given by:

$$\vec{V}_L = \vec{v} \tag{245}$$

The implicit diffusion step in scheme (244) is first-order accurate in time, but it tends to be more stable than the Crank-Nicolson scheme which is typically second-order accurate in time (without the jump part). The explicit treatment of the jump operator is also first-order accurate in time. With an appropriate spatial discretization, the scheme is second-order accurate in the spatial variable. As usual, see, for example, d'Halluin, Forsyth, and Vetzal (2005), predictor-corrector iteration improves the scheme convergence in both time and space. At each step in time, the scheme with fixed point iterations is applied as follows. We set

$$\vec{U}^0 = \vec{V}_l + \frac{1}{2}\delta t_l \left(\hat{c}_{l-1} + \hat{c}_l\right) \tag{246}$$

and, for $p = 1, 2, \ldots, \overline{p}$ (typically, it is enough to use two iterations, $\overline{p} = 2$) apply the following scheme:

$$\vec{U}^* = \vec{U}^0 + \delta t_l \lambda(t_l)\vec{\varphi}_l^{p-1} \tag{247}$$

$$\left(\mathcal{I} - \delta t_l \mathfrak{D}_l^{(x)}\right)\vec{U}^p = \vec{U}^*$$

where $\vec{\varphi}_l^{p-1} = \widehat{\mathfrak{J}}_l^{(x)}\vec{U}^{p-1}$. Provided that the difference $||U^{\overline{p}} - U^{\overline{p}-1}||$ is small in an appropriate norm, we stop and apply the discounting:

$$V_{l-1} = D(t_{l-1}, t_l)U^p \tag{248}$$

Forward equation

For calibration purposes we have to calculate the survival probability forward in time by finding the Green's function, $G(t, x, T, X)$, defined by eq. (63).

By analogy with the backward equation, we use a time-stepping scheme with fixed-point iterations in order to calculate $\vec{G}_l = \{G_{l,n}\} = \{G(t_l, x_n)\}$. We introduce

$$\psi_l(x) \equiv \mathcal{J}^{(x)\dagger}G(t_l, x) \tag{249}$$

For DNJs, we approximate this function on the grid to second-order accuracy:

$$\psi_{l,n} = \begin{cases} \omega_{\tilde{n}}G_{l,\tilde{n}-1} + (1 - \omega_{\tilde{n}})G_{l,\tilde{n}}, & x_n + \nu \leq x_N \\ G_{l,N}, & x_n + \nu > x_N \end{cases} \tag{250}$$

where

$$\tilde{n} = \min\{j : x_{j-1} \leq x_n + \nu < x_j\}, \quad \omega_{\tilde{n}} = \frac{x_{\tilde{n}} - (x_n + \nu)}{x_{\tilde{n}} - x_{\tilde{n}-1}} \tag{251}$$

For ENJs, by analogy with eq. (242), we use the following scheme which is second-order accurate:

$$\psi_{l,n-1} = e^{-\nu h_n}\psi_{l,n} + w_0(\nu, h_n)G_{l,n} + w_1(\nu, h_n)G_{l,n-1} \tag{252}$$

where w_0 and w_1 are defined by eq. (241).

The time-stepping numerical scheme is straightforward. The initial condition is given by:

$$G_{0,n} = 2\delta_{n,n_\xi}/\left(x_{n_\xi+1} - x_{n_\xi-1}\right) \tag{253}$$

where the spatial grid in chosen in such a way that $x_0 = 0$ and $x_{n_\xi} = \xi$. To compute the value $\vec{G}_l$ given the value $\vec{G}_{l-1}, l = 1, \ldots, L$, we introduce auxiliary vectors $\vec{\psi}, \vec{G}^*$, and apply the following scheme:

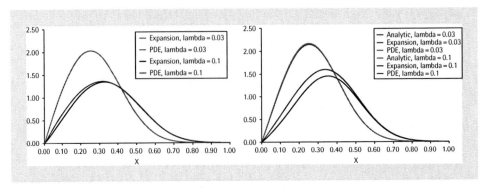

FIGURE 12.2 Asymptotic and numerical Green's functions for DNJs (lhs), and analytical, asymptotic and numerical Green's functions for ENJs (rhs). The relevant parameters are the same as in Figure 1, $T = 10y$.

$$\vec{G}^* = \vec{G}_{l-1} + \delta t_l \lambda(t_l) \vec{\psi}_{l-1} \tag{254}$$

$$\left(\mathcal{I} - \delta t_l \mathfrak{D}_l^{(x)\dagger}\right) \vec{G}_l = \vec{G}^*$$

As before, we use predictor-corrector iterations to improve the rate of convergence. It is extremely useful to construct schemes (244), (254) is such a way that they are exactly (rather than approximately) adjoint (without discounting).

Given the Green's function at time t_l, we can compute the survival probability via a simple summation rule:

$$Q^{(x)}(t_0, \xi, t_l) = \sum_{n=1}^{N} (x_n - x_{n-1}) G_{l,n} \tag{255}$$

5.3.4 *Useful comparisons*

In Figure 12.2 we compare analytical, asymptotic, and numerical solutions for ENJs, and asymptotic and numerical solutions for DNJs. This figure shows that analytical and numerical solutions agree perfectly (when both are known), while an asymptotic solution is respectable if not perfect.

6 TWO-DIMENSIONAL PROBLEM

6.1 Analytical solution

In this section we study the 2D CVA problem semi-analytically under bivariate dynamics without jumps assuming CDM.

We start by constructing the 2D Green's function semi-analytically. We assume constant volatility parameters and consider the Green's function for the corresponding diffusion advection which solves the following problem in $\mathbb{R}^2_{+,+}$:

$$\Gamma_\tau - \frac{1}{2}\left(\sigma_1^2\left(\Gamma_{X_1X_1} + \Gamma_{X_1}\right) + 2\rho\sigma_1\sigma_2\Gamma_{X_1X_2} + \sigma_2^2\left(\Gamma_{X_2X_2} + \Gamma_{X_2}\right)\right) = 0 \tag{256}$$

$$\Gamma(\tau, X_1, 0) = 0, \quad \Gamma(\tau, 0, X_2) = 0 \tag{257}$$

$$\Gamma(0, X_1, X_2) = \delta(X_1 - \xi_1)\,\delta(X_2 - \xi_2) \tag{258}$$

To simplify the problem, we introduce new independent and dependent variables $r, \phi, \mathcal{G}$ such that

$$r = \sqrt{\left(\frac{\sigma_2 X_1 - \sigma_1\rho X_2}{\bar{\rho}\sigma_1\sigma_2}\right)^2 + \left(\frac{X_2}{\sigma_2}\right)^2}, \quad \phi = \operatorname{atan}\left(\frac{\bar{\rho}\sigma_1 X_2}{\sigma_2 X_1 - \sigma_1\rho X_2}\right) \tag{259}$$

$$\mathcal{G} = \bar{\rho}\sigma_1\sigma_2 \exp\left(\frac{1}{8}\left(\sigma_1^2 + \sigma_2^2\right)\tau + \frac{1}{2}(X_1 - \xi_1) + \frac{1}{2}(X_2 - \xi_2)\right)\Gamma$$

where $\bar{\rho} = \sqrt{1 - \rho^2}$. In these variables the pricing problem becomes:

$$\mathcal{G}_\tau - \frac{1}{2}\left(\mathcal{G}_{rr} + \frac{1}{r}\mathcal{G}_r + \frac{1}{r^2}\mathcal{G}_{\phi\phi}\right) = 0 \tag{260}$$

$$\mathcal{G}(\tau, r, 0) = 0, \quad \mathcal{G}(\tau, r, a) = 0 \tag{261}$$

$$\mathcal{G}(0, r, \phi) = \frac{1}{r'}\delta(r - r')\,\delta(\phi - \phi') \tag{262}$$

where

$$r' = \sqrt{\left(\frac{\sigma_2\xi_1 - \sigma_1\rho\xi_2}{\bar{\rho}\sigma_1\sigma_2}\right)^2 + \left(\frac{\xi_2}{\sigma_2}\right)^2}, \quad \phi' = \operatorname{atan}\left(\frac{\bar{\rho}\sigma_1\xi_2}{\sigma_2\xi_1 - \sigma_1\rho\xi_2}\right) \tag{263}$$

Thus, we have reduced the original problem to the standard heat problem in an angle. This angle is formed by the horizontal axis $\phi = 0$ and the sloping line $\phi = a$ where $a = \operatorname{atan}(-\bar{\rho}/\rho)$; for convenience, we think of atan(.) as defined on the interval $[0, \pi)$. This angle is acute when $\rho < 0$ and obtuse otherwise.

Problem (260)–(262) can be solved in two complementary ways: (a) via the eigenfunction expansion method; (b) via the method of images. Solution of this problem via the eigenfunction expansion method is classical; it has been introduced in mathematical finance independently by (He, Keirstead, and Rebholz 1998; Lipton 2001; and Zhou 2001b). In this method the Green's function is presented in the form:

$$\mathcal{G}_a(\tau, r', \phi', r, \phi) = \frac{2e^{-(r^2+r'^2)/2\tau}}{a\tau} \sum_{n=1}^{\infty} I_{\frac{n\pi}{a}}\left(\frac{rr'}{\tau}\right) \sin\left(\frac{n\pi\phi'}{a}\right) \sin\left(\frac{n\pi\phi}{a}\right) \tag{264}$$

where $I_\nu(x)$ is the modified Bessel function with index ν.

It turns out that the Green's function in an angle also can be constructed via the method of images by using the non-periodic Green's function defined in the half-plane $0 < r < \infty, -\infty < \phi < \infty$. The latter Green's function is given by:

$$G(\tau, r', r, \chi) = G_1(\tau, r', r, \chi) - G_2(\tau, r', r, \chi) \tag{265}$$

where

$$G_1\left(\tau, r', r, \chi\right) = \frac{e^{-(r^2+r'^2)/2\tau}}{2\pi\tau} \frac{(s_+ + s_-)}{2} e^{(rr'/\tau)\cos\chi} \tag{266}$$

$$G_2\left(\tau, r', r, \chi\right) = \frac{e^{-(r^2+r'^2)/2\tau}}{2\pi^2\tau} \int_0^\infty \frac{s_+ e^{-(rr'/\tau)\cosh((\pi+\chi)\zeta)} + s_- e^{-(rr'/\tau)\cosh((\pi-\chi)\zeta)}}{\zeta^2 + 1} d\zeta$$

and $\chi = \phi - \phi'$, $s_\pm = \text{sign}(\pi \pm \chi)$. This formula seems to be new; it was presented by Lipton (2008), its detailed derivation will be given elsewhere. To solve the problem in an angle $0 \le \phi \le a$, we use the method of images and represent the fundamental solution in the form

$$\mathcal{G}_a\left(\tau, r', \phi', r, \phi\right) = \sum_{n=-\infty}^\infty \left[G\left(\tau, r', r, \phi - \phi' + 2na\right) - G\left(\tau, r', r, -\phi - \phi' + 2na\right)\right]$$

$$\tag{267}$$

This series converges since simple balancing of terms shows that

$$G_2\left(\tau, r', r, \chi\right) = O\left(|\chi|^{-2}\right) \tag{268}$$

As always, the eigenfunction expansion method works well when τ is large, while the method of images works well when τ is small.

For the survival probability, we obtain the following expression:

$$Q^{(x_1,x_2)}\left(\tau, \xi_1, \xi_2\right) = e^{-\left(\sigma_1^2+\sigma_2^2\right)\tau/8+(\xi_1+\xi_2)/2} \tag{269}$$

$$\times \int_0^\infty \int_0^a e^{-\sigma_{12}r\cos(\phi-\beta)/2}\mathcal{G}_a\left(\tau, r', \phi', r, \phi\right) r\,dr\,d\phi$$

where $\sigma_{12} = \sqrt{\sigma_1^2 + 2\rho\sigma_1\sigma_2 + \sigma_2^2}$, $\beta = \text{atan}((\sigma_1\rho + \sigma_2)/\sigma_1\bar{\rho})$. We combine formula (260) with the well-known identity

$$e^{-z\cos\theta} = I_0\left(z\right) + 2\sum_{k=1}^\infty (-1)^k I_k\left(z\right)\cos\left(k\theta\right) \tag{270}$$

and obtain

$$Q^{(x_1,x_2)}\left(\tau, \xi_1, \xi_2\right) = \frac{4e^{-\left(\sigma_1^2+\sigma_2^2\right)\tau/8+(\xi_1+\xi_2)/2-r'^2/2\tau}}{a\tau} \tag{271}$$

$$\times \sum_{n=1}^\infty \sum_{k=1}^\infty c_{n,k} \int_0^\infty e^{-r^2/2\tau} I_{\frac{n\pi}{a}}\left(\frac{rr'}{\tau}\right) I_k\left(\frac{\sigma_{12}r}{2}\right) r\,dr$$

where

$$c_{n,k} = \frac{(-1)^k\left(n\pi/a\right)\sin\left(n\pi\phi'/a\right)\left(\cos\left(k\beta\right) - (-1)^n\cos\left(k\left(a - \beta\right)\right)\right)}{\left(n\pi/a\right)^2 - k^2} \tag{272}$$

The corresponding integrals are easy to evaluate numerically. If necessary, one can use appropriate classical formulas for the product of modified Bessel function to simplify them further.

The probability of hitting the boundary $X_i = 0$, $i = 1, 2$, which is needed in order to calculate the value of FTDS and CVA, can be computed by using definition (102). Tedious algebra yields:

$$g_i(\tau, \xi_1, \xi_2, X_{3-i}) = \frac{\sigma_i^2}{2}\, \Gamma_{X_i}(\tau, \xi_1, \xi_2, X_1, X_2)\big|_{X_i=0} \tag{273}$$

$$= \frac{\pi e^{-(\sigma_1^2+\sigma_2^2)\tau/8+(\xi_1+\xi_2)/2-r'^2/2\tau-X_{3-i}/2-X_{3-i}^2/2\bar{\rho}^2\sigma_{3-i}^2\tau}}{a^2\tau X_{3-i}} \sum_{n=1}^{\infty} I_{\frac{n\pi}{a}}\left(\frac{X_{3-i}r'}{\bar{\rho}\sigma_{3-i}\tau}\right) \sin\left(\frac{n\pi\phi'}{a}\right)$$

By using formula (101), we can represent $V^{FTDS}(\tau, \xi_1, \xi_2)$, and $V_{PB}^{CVA}(\tau, \xi_1, \xi_2)$ as follows

$$V^{FTDS}(\tau, \xi_1, \xi_2) = -c \int_0^\tau e^{-r\tau'} Q^{(x_1,x_2)}(\tau', \xi_1, \xi_2) d\tau' \tag{274}$$

$$+ \sum_{i=1,2}(1 - R_i) \int_0^\tau \int_0^\infty e^{-r\tau'} g_i(\tau', \xi_1, \xi_2, X_{3-i}) dX_{3-i} d\tau'$$

$$V_{PB}^{CVA}(\tau, \xi_1, \xi_2) = (1 - R_2) \int_0^\tau \int_0^\infty e^{-r\tau'} \left\{V^{CDS}(\tau - \tau', X_1)\right\}_+ g_2(\tau', \xi_1, \xi_2, X_1) dX_1 d\tau' \tag{275}$$

where $V^{CDS}(\tau, X_1)$ is given by eq. (189). Here r is the interest rate (not to be confused with the radial independent variable).

6.2 Numerical solution

In this section we develop robust numerical methods for model calibration and pricing in 2D. As before, we describe the MC, FFT, and FD methods.

To our knowledge, only Clift and Forsyth (2008) develop an FD method for solving the 2D pricing problem with jumps by computing the 2D convolution term using the FFT method with a complexity of $O(N_1 N_2 \log(N_1 N_2))$, where N_1 and N_2 are the number of points in each dimension. As we have noticed, the application of the FFT method is not straightforward due to its inherent features. In contrast, we apply an explicit second-order accurate method for the computation of the jump term with a complexity of $O(N_1 N_2)$.

In two dimensions, the complexity of the FFT method is $O(L N_1 N_2 \log(N_1 N_2))$ and the complexity of the FD method with explicit treatment of the integral term is $O(L N_1 N_2)$. Accordingly the FFT method is attractive provided that N_2 is not too large, say $N_2 < 100$, otherwise the FD method is more competitive.

6.2.1 *Monte Carlo method*

The MC simulation of the multi-dimensional dynamics (28) is performed by analogy with eq. (213). As before, we restrict ourselves to the case of DDM. The simulation of the multi-dimensional trajectories is based on direct integration:

$$\Delta x_{i,m} = \bar{\mu}_{i,m} + \bar{\sigma}_{i,m}\epsilon_{i,m} + \sum_{k=1}^{n_{i,m}} j_{i,k} \tag{276}$$

where $\epsilon_{i,m}$ and $\epsilon_{j,m}$ are standard normals with correlation $\rho_{i,j}$, $j_{i,k}$ are independent variables with PDF $\varpi_i(j)$,

$$n_{i,m} = \sum_{\pi \in \Pi(N)} 1_{\{i \in \pi\}} n_{\pi,m} \tag{277}$$

where $n_{\pi,m}$ are Poisson random variables with intensities $\bar{\lambda}_{\pi,m}$, and $x_i(t_0) = \xi_i$. Here

$$\bar{\mu}_{i,m} = \int_{t_{m-1}}^{t_m} \mu_i(t')dt', \quad \bar{\sigma}_{i,m} = \sqrt{\int_{t_{m-1}}^{t_m} \sigma_i^2(t')dt'}, \quad \bar{\lambda}_{\pi,m} = \int_{t_{m-1}}^{t_m} \lambda_\pi(t')dt' \tag{278}$$

As soon as sample trajectories of the drivers are determined, the relevant instruments can be priced in the standard fashion.

6.2.2 *Fast Fourier Transform method*

We consider the 2D version of the FFT method for the case of DDM. As in the 1D case, we consider the Green's function in $\mathbb{R}^2$, which we denote by $Y(t, T, Y_1, Y_2)$, where $Y_i = X_i - x_i$. As before, without loss of efficiency, we can assume that the coefficients are time independent. The Fourier transform of $Y(t, T, Y_1, Y_2)$ can be written as follows:

$$\hat{Y}(t, T, k_1, k_2) = \int_{-\infty}^{\infty} \int_{-\infty}^{\infty} e^{ik_1 Y_1 + ik_2 Y_2} Y(t, T, Y_1, Y_2)dY_1 dY_2 \tag{279}$$

$$= e^{-\tau\psi(k_1,k_2)}$$

where $(k_1, k_2) \in \mathbb{R}^2$ are the transform variables, and $\psi(k_1, k_2)$ is the characteristic exponent:

$$\psi(k_1, k_2) = \frac{1}{2}\sigma_1^2 k_1^2 + \rho\sigma_1\sigma_1 k_1 k_2 + \frac{1}{2}\sigma_2^2 k_2^2 - i\mu_1 k_1 - i\mu_2 k_2 \tag{280}$$

$$-\lambda_{\{1,2\}}(\hat{\varpi}_1(k_1)\hat{\varpi}_2(k_2) - 1) - \lambda_{\{1\}}(\hat{\varpi}_1(k_1) - 1) - \lambda_{\{2\}}(\hat{\varpi}_2(k_2) - 1)$$

with

$$\hat{\varpi}_i(k_i) = \int_{-\infty}^{0} e^{ik_i j_i} \varpi_i(j_i)dj_i, \quad i = 1, 2 \tag{281}$$

Given $\hat{Y}(t, T, k_1, k_2)$ we can compute the Green's function via the inverse Fourier transform as follows:

$$Y(t, T, Y_1, Y_2) = \frac{1}{(2\pi)^2} \int_{-\infty}^{\infty} \int_{-\infty}^{\infty} e^{-ik_1 Y_1 - ik_2 Y_2} \hat{Y}(t, T, k_1, k_2) dk_1 dk_2 \qquad (282)$$

Once $\hat{Y}(t, T, k_1, k_2)$ is obtained, we can generalize formulas (225), (230) in an obvious way. As before, we apply the backward recursion scheme with time stepping and control functions specified in section 4. The forward recursion is performed by the same token.

6.2.3 Finite Difference method

Now we develop an FD method for solving the 2D backward problem (73) for the value function $V(t, x_1, x_2)$. For brevity, we consider only the backward problem with CDM, a numerical scheme for the 2D forward equation can be developed by analogy.

We introduce a 2D discrete spatial grid $\{(x_{1,n_1}, x_{2,n_2})\}$, and a time grid $\{t_0, \ldots, t_L\}$ which includes all the special times. As before $V\left(t_l, x_{1,n_1}, x_{2,n_2}\right)$ is denoted by V_{l,n_1,n_2}, and similarly for other relevant quantities.

We denote the discretized 1D operators by $\mathfrak{D}_l^{(x_i)}$, $\hat{\mathfrak{J}}_l^{(x_i)}$, $i = 1, 2$. The correlation operator, $\mathcal{C}^{(x_1,x_2)}(t_l)$ is discretized via the standard four-stencil scheme:

$$\mathcal{C}^{(x_1,x_2)}(t_l) \Rightarrow \mathfrak{C}_l^{(x_1,x_2)} \qquad (283)$$

In order to discretize the cross-integral operator $\hat{\mathcal{J}}^{(x_1,x_2)}$ efficiently, we introduce an auxiliary function $\phi(x_1, x_2)$, such that

$$\varphi_l(x_1, x_2) \equiv \hat{\mathcal{J}}^{(x_1,x_2)} V(t_l, x_1, x_2) \qquad (284)$$

as well as an auxiliary function

$$\chi_l(x_1, x_2) \equiv \hat{\mathcal{J}}^{(x_1)} V(t_l, x_1, x_2) \qquad (285)$$

It is clear that

$$\varphi_l(x_1, x_2) = \hat{\mathcal{J}}^{(x_2)} \chi_l(x_1, x_2) \qquad (286)$$

so that we can perform calculations by alternating the axis of integration.

We consider DNJs and ENJs separately. For DNJs, we approximate $\varphi_l(x_1, x_2)$ on the grid in two steps via the linear interpolation:

$$\chi_{l,n_1,n_2} = \begin{cases} \omega_{\bar{n}_1} V_{l,\bar{n}_1-1,n_2} + (1 - \omega_{\bar{n}_1}) V_{l,\bar{n}_1,n_2}, & x_{n_1} \geq v_1 \\ 0, & x_{n_1} < v_1 \end{cases} \qquad (287)$$

$$\varphi_{l,n_1,n_2} = \begin{cases} \omega_{\bar{n}_2} \chi_{l,n_1,\bar{n}_2-1} + \left(1 - \omega_{\bar{n}_2}\right) \chi_{l,n_1,\bar{n}_2}, & x_{n_2} \geq v_2 \\ 0, & x_{n_2} < v_2 \end{cases}$$

where

$$\bar{n}_i = \min\{j : x_{i,j-1} \leq x_{i,n_i} - v_i < x_{i,j}\}, \quad \omega_{\bar{n}_i} = \frac{x_{i,\bar{n}_i} - (x_{i,n_i} - v_i)}{x_{i,\bar{n}} - x_{i,\bar{n}-1}}, \quad i = 1, 2 \quad (288)$$

For ENJs jumps with jump sizes ν_1 and ν_2 we write:

$$\chi_{l,n_1+1,n_2} = e^{-\nu_1 h_{1,n_1+1}} \chi_{l,n_1,n_2} + w_0(\nu_1, h_{1,n_1+1}) V_{l,n_1,n_2} + w_1(\nu_1, h_{1,n_1+1}) V_{l,n_1+1,n_2} \quad (289)$$

$$\varphi_{l,n_1,n_2+1} = e^{-\nu_2 h_{2,n_2+1}} \varphi_{l,n_1,n_2} + w_0(\nu_2, h_{2,n_2+1}) \chi_{l,n_1,n_2} + w_1(\nu_2, h_{2,n_2+1}) \chi_{l,n_1,n_2+1} \quad (290)$$

where $h_{i,n_i} = x_{i,n_i} - x_{i,n_i-1}$. The initial conditions are set by

$$\chi_{l,0,n_2} = 0, \quad n_2 = 0, \ldots, N_2, \quad \varphi_{l,n_1,0} = 0, \quad n_1 = 0, \ldots, N_1 \quad (291)$$

Thus, in both cases, φ_{l,n_1,n_2} can be evaluated via $O(N_1 N_2)$ operations to second-order accuracy.

For DDM, we can proceed along similar lines.

We develop a modified Craig and Sneyd (1988) discretization scheme using explicit time stepping for jump and correlation operators and implicit time stepping for diffusion operators to compute the solution at time t_{l-1}, V_{l-1,n_1,n_2}, given the solution at time t_l, V_{l,n_1,n_2}, $l = 1, \ldots, L$, as follows:

$$(\mathcal{I} - \delta t_l \mathfrak{D}_l^{(x_1)}) \vec{V}^* = \left(\mathcal{I} + \delta t_l \left(\mathfrak{D}_l^{(x_2)} + \mathfrak{C}_l^{(x_1,x_2)} \right) \right) \vec{V}_l + \delta t_l \frac{1}{2} \left(\hat{c}_{l-1} + \hat{c}_{l-1} \right) \quad (292)$$

$$+ \delta t_l \left(\lambda_{\{1\}} (t_l) \vec{\varphi}_{\{1\}} + \lambda_{\{2\}} (t_l) \vec{\varphi}_{\{2\}} + \lambda_{\{1,2\}} (t_l) \vec{\varphi}_{\{1,2\}} \right)$$

$$(\mathcal{I} - \delta t_l \mathfrak{D}_l^{(x_2)}) \vec{V}^{**} = \vec{V}^* - \delta t_l \mathfrak{D}_l^{(x_2)} \vec{V}_l$$

$$\vec{V}_{l-1} = D(t_{l-1}, t_l) \vec{V}^{**}$$

When solving the first equation, we keep the second index n_2 fixed, apply the diffusion operator in the x_2 direction, the correlation operator, the coupon payments (if any), and the jump operators explicitly, and then solve the tridiagonal system of equations to get the auxiliary solution $V_{\cdot,n_2}^*$. When solving the second equation, we keep n_1 fixed, and solve the system of tridiagonal equations to obtain the solution $V_{n_1,\cdot}^{**}$. The overall complexity of this method is $O(N_1 N_2)$ operations per time step. The terminal condition is given by:

$$\vec{V}_L = \vec{v} \quad (293)$$

Similarly to the 1D case, we apply fixed point iterations at each step in time, in order to improve convergence.

7 EVALUATION OF THE CREDIT VALUE ADJUSTMENT IN PRACTICE

In this section we discuss forward model calibration and backward credit value adjustment valuation.

We start with the calibration of the marginal dynamics to CDS spreads, CDSO prices, and equity option prices. First, we find the initial value for each firm and its default barrier from the balance sheet as discussed in section 2.2. Second we calibrate the model parameters as follows. We specify the time horizon T and determine the term structure of CDS spreads with maturities $\{t_k^c\}$, $t_K^c \leq T$, $k = 1, \ldots, K$ referencing the i-th firm. We assume that the model parameters change at times $\{t_k^c\}$, but otherwise stay constant. Then, we make an initial guess regarding the term structure of the firm's volatility $\{\sigma_k\}$ and the magnitude of the parameter ν. Specifically, we choose $\sigma^{(k)}$ in the form

$$\left(\sigma^{(k)}\right)^2 = \sigma_\infty^2 + \left(\sigma_0^2 - \sigma_\infty^2\right) e^{-\varpi t_k^c} \tag{294}$$

Starting with this guess, a fast bootstrapping is implemented for the jump intensity $\{\lambda_k\}$ by means of forward induction with time stepping, resulting in matching the term structure of CDS spreads of the i-th name. Bootstrapping is done by first fitting λ_1 to the nearest CDS quote (via 1D numerical root searching) and inductive fitting of $\lambda_{k'+1}$, given $\{\lambda_k\}$, $k = 1, \ldots, k'$, to the CDS quote with maturity time $t_{k'+1}^c$ (via numerical root searching). Finally, given the parameter set thus obtained, we compute model prices of a set of CDSO and equity options. If differences between model and market prices are small, we stop; otherwise we adjust σ_0, σ_∞, ϖ and ν and recompute $\{\lambda_k\}$. Typically, the market data for CDSO and equity options with maturities longer than one year are scarce, so that a parametric choice of σ_k is necessary.

For the purposes of illustration, we use market data for two financial institutions: JP Morgan (JPM) and Morgan Stanley (MS). In Table 12.1 we provide market data, as of 2 November 2009, which we use to calculate the initial firm's value $a(0)$ and its default barrier $l(0)$ for both firms. In Table 12.2, we provide the term structure of spreads for CDSs on JPM and MS, their survival probabilities implied from these spreads using the hazard rate model, and the corresponding default and annuity legs. It is clear that, compared to MS, JPM is a riskier credit, since it has more debt per equity.

We use jump-diffusion models with DNJs and ENJs. We set the jump amplitude ν to the initial log-value of the firm, $\nu = \xi$ in the model with DNJs, and $\nu = 1/\xi$ in the model with ENJs. The volatility of the firm's value σ is chosen using eq. (22), so that the 1y at-the-money implied volatility of equity options is close to the one observed in the market for both DNJs and ENJs.

The computations are done via the FD method with weekly DDM. For both choices of jump distributions, the model is calibrated to the term structure of CDS spreads given in Table 12.2 via forward induction.

Table 12.1 Market data, as of 2 October 2009, for JPM and MS

	s(0)	L(0)	R	a(0)	l(0)	ξ	ν^{DNJ}	ν^{ENJ}	σ_0	σ_∞	ϖ
JPM	41.77	508	40%	245	203	0.1869	0.1869	5.35	53%	2%	4
MS	32.12	534	40%	246	214	0.1401	0.1401	7.14	42%	2%	4

Table 12.2 CDS spreads and other relevant outputs for JPM and MS

T	DF	CDS Sprd (%)		Survival Prob		Default Leg		Annuity Leg	
		JPM	MS	JPM	MS	JPM	MS	JPM	MS
1y	0.9941	0.45	1.10	0.9925	0.9818	0.0045	0.0109	0.9924	0.9857
2y	0.9755	0.49	1.19	0.9836	0.9611	0.0097	0.0231	1.9632	1.9388
3y	0.9466	0.50	1.24	0.9753	0.9397	0.0145	0.0354	2.9006	2.8469
4y	0.9121	0.54	1.29	0.9644	0.9173	0.0206	0.0479	3.7971	3.7036
5y	0.8749	0.59	1.34	0.9515	0.8937	0.0274	0.0604	4.6474	4.5061
6y	0.8374	0.60	1.35	0.9414	0.8732	0.0326	0.0709	5.4519	5.2559
7y	0.8002	0.60	1.35	0.9320	0.8539	0.0372	0.0803	6.2135	5.9570
8y	0.7642	0.60	1.33	0.9228	0.8373	0.0415	0.0881	6.9338	6.6127
9y	0.7297	0.60	1.31	0.9137	0.8217	0.0455	0.0950	7.6148	7.2272
10y	0.6961	0.60	1.30	0.9046	0.8064	0.0494	0.1015	8.2583	7.8028

In Figure 12.3, we show the calibrated jump intensities. We see that for the specific choice of the jump size, the model with ENJs implies higher intensity than the one with DNJs because, with small equity volatility, more than one jump is expected before the barrier crossing. For JPM the term structure of the CDS spread is relatively flat, so that the model intensity is also flat. For MS, the term structure of the CDS spread is inverted, so that the model intensity is decreasing with time.

In Figure 12.4, we show the implied density of the calibrated driver $x(T)$ for maturities of $1y$, $5y$, and $10y$ for JPM and MS. We see that even for short-times the model implies a right tail close to the default barrier, which introduces the possibility of default in the short term. We observe no noticeable differences between the model with DNJs and ENJs given that both are calibrated to the same set of market data.

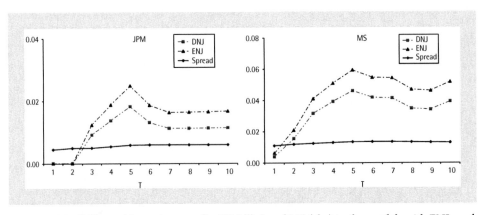

FIGURE 12.3 Calibrated intensity rates for JPM (lhs) and MS (rhs) in the models with ENJs and DNJs, respectively.

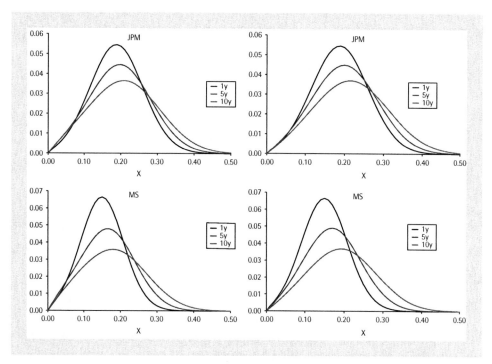

FIGURE 12.4 PDF of the driver $x(T)$ for JPM in the model with DNJs (top lhs) and ENJs (top rhs) and for MS in the model with DNJs (bottom lhs) and ENJs (bottom rhs). $T = 1y$, $5y$, and $10\ y$.

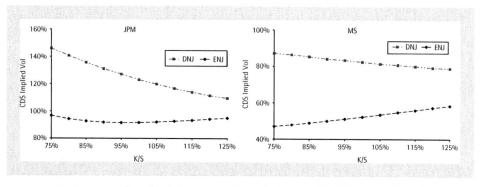

FIGURE 12.5 Lognormal credit default swaption volatility implied from model with $T_e = 1y$, $T_t = 5y$ as a function of the inverse moneyness $K/\bar{c}\ (T_e, T_e + T_t)$.

In Figure 12.5, we show the lognormal CDSO volatility for one-year payer option on five-year CDS contract ($T_e = 1y$, $T_t = 5y$), which is calculated by using the model-implied option price. The price is converted into volatility via Black's futures formula (Black 1976; Hull and White 2003; Schönbucher 2003), which assumes that the forward spread $c(T_e, T_e + T_t)$ has lognormal volatility σ. We plot the model implied volatility as a function of inverse moneyness, $K/\bar{c}(T_e, T_e + T_t)$, where $\bar{c}(T_e, T_e + T_t)$ is the CDS spread at option expiry. We observe that the model implied lognormal volatility σ exhibits a positive skew. This effect is in line with market observations because the CDS spread volatility is expected to increase when the CDS spread increases, so that option market makers charge an extra premium for out-of-the-money CDSOs. Comparing models with different jump distributions, we see that the model with DNJs implies higher spread volatility than the one with ENJs.

In Figure 12.6, we convert the model implied values for put options with maturity of $6m$ into implied volatility skew via the Black-Scholes formula. We see that the model implies a pronounced skew in line with the skew observed in the market. The implied equity skew appears to be less sensitive to the choice of the jump size distribution than the CDSO skew.

In Figure 12.7, we present the spread term structure for the CDS contract referencing MS, which should be paid by a risk-free PB to JPM as PS. This spread is determined in such a way that the present value of CDS for PB is zero at the contract inception. Similarly, we present the spread term structure for the CDS contract referencing MS, which should be received by a risk-free PS from JPM as PB. We use the calibrated model with DNJs and five choices of the model correlation parameter: $\rho = 0.90, 0.45, 0.0, -0.45, -0.90$. Spreads are expressed in basis points. We also present results for MS as counterparty and JPM as RN. We observe the same effects as before. Importantly, we see that CVA is not symmetric. As expected, riskier counterparty quality implies smaller equilibrium spread for PB and higher equilibrium spread for PS.

Figure 12.7 illustrates the following effects. First, high positive correlation between RN and PS implies low equilibrium spread for a risk-free PB, because, given PS default, the loss of protection is expected be high. Second, high negative correlation between RN and PB implies high equilibrium spread for a risk-free PS, because, given PB default, the corresponding annuity loss is high. In general, for a risk-free PB, we observe noticeable differences between the risk-free and equilibrium spreads, while for a risk-free PS, these differences are relatively small.

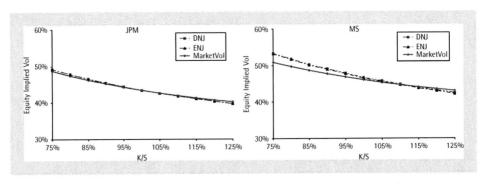

FIGURE 12.6 Lognormal equity volatility implied by the model as a function of inverse moneyness K/s for put options with $T = 0.5y$.

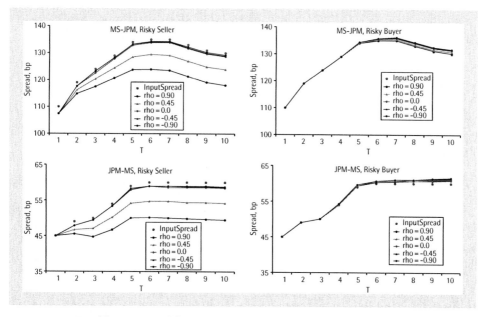

FIGURE 12.7 Equilibrium spread for a PB (top lhs) and PS (top rhs) of a CDS on MS with JPM as the counterparty; same for a CDS on JPM with MS as the counterparty (bottom rhs) and (bottom lhs). In both cases input spread is the fair spread for non-risky counterparties.

8 CONCLUSION

We have presented a multi-dimensional extension of Merton's model (Merton 1974), where the joint dynamics of the firm's values are driven by a multi-dimensional jump-diffusion process. Applying the FFT and FD methods, we have developed a forward induction procedure for calibrating the model, and a backward induction procedure for valuing credit derivatives in 1D and 2D.

We have considered jump size distributions of two types, namely, DNJs and ENJs, and showed that for joint bivariate dynamics, the model with ENJs produces a noticeably lower implied Gaussian correlation than the one produced by the model with DNJs, although for both jump specifications the corresponding marginal dynamics fit the market data adequately. Based on these observations, and given the high level of the default correlation among financial institutions (above 50%), the model with DNJs, albeit simple, seems to provide a more realistic description of default correlations and, thus, the counterparty risk, than a more sophisticated model with ENJs.

We have proposed an innovative approach to CVA estimation in the structural framework. We have found empirically that, to leading order, CVA is determined by the correlation between RN and PS (or PB), the higher the correlation the higher the charge; the second influential factor is their CDS spread volatilities. Thus, by accounting for both the correlation and volatility, our model provides a robust estimation of the counterparty risk.

References

Abate, J., Choudhury, G., and Whitt, W. (1999). 'An introduction to numerical inversion and its application to probability models'. In W. Grassman (ed.), *Computational Probability*. Boston: Kluwer, 257–323.

Albanese, C., and Chen, O. (2005). 'Discrete credit barrier models'. *Quantitative Finance*, 5: 247–56.

Andersen, L., and Andreasen, J. (2000). 'Jump-diffusion processes: volatility smile fitting and numerical methods for option pricing'. *Review of Derivatives Research*, 4: 231–62.

Avellaneda, M., and Zhou, J. (2001). 'Distance to default'. *Risk Magazine* 14: 125–29.

Bielecki, T., and Rutkowski, M. (2002). *Credit Risk: Modeling, Valuation and Hedging*. Berlin: Springer.

Black, F. (1976). 'The pricing of commodity contacts'. *Journal of Financial Economics*, 3: 167–79.

—— and Cox, J. (1976). 'Valuing corporate securities: some effects of bond indenture provisions'. *Journal of Finance*, 31: 351–67.

Blanchet-Scalliet, C. and Patras, F. (2008). 'Counterparty risk valuation for CDS'. Preprint.

Boyarchenko, M., and Levendorski, S. (2008). 'Refined and enhanced Fast Fourier Transform techniques, with an application to the pricing of barrier options'. Preprint.

Brigo, D., and Chourdakis, K. (2008). 'Counterparty risk for credit default swaps: impact of spread volatility and default correlation'. FitchSolutions Research Paper.

Broadie, M., and Yamamoto, Y. (2003). 'Application of the fast Gauss transform to option pricing'. *Management Science*, 49/8: 1071–88.

Cariboni, J., and Schoutens, W. (2007). 'Pricing credit default swaps under Levy models'. *Journal of Computational Finance*, 10/4: 71–91.

Carr, P., and Madan, D. (1999). 'Option valuation using the Fast Fourier Transform'. *Journal of Computational Finance*, 2/4: 61–73.

—— and Mayo, A. (2007). 'On the numerical valuation of option prices in jump diffusion processes'. *European Journal of Finance*, 13/4: 353–72.

Craig, I., and Sneyd, A. (1988). 'An alternating-direction implicit scheme for parabolic equations with mixed derivatives'. *Computers and Mathematics with Applications*, 16/4: 341–50.

Cont, R., and Tankov, P. (2004). *Financial Modelling with Jump Processes*. Boca Raton IL: Chapman & Hall.

—— and Voltchkova, E. (2005). 'A finite difference scheme for option pricing in jump diffusion and exponential Levy models'. *SIAM Numerical Mathematics* 43: 1596–1626.

Clift, S., and Forsyth, P. (2008). 'Numerical solution of two asset jump diffusion models for option valuation'. *Applied Numerical Mathematics*, 58: 743–82.

Davidson, C. (2008). 'Speed tests'. *Risk Magazine*, 21/10: 50–52.

d'Halluin, Y., Forsyth, P., and Vetzal, K. (2005). 'Robust numerical methods for contingent claims under jump diffusion processes'. *IMA Journal of Numerical Analysis*, 25: 87–112.

Duffie, D., and Singleton, K. (1997). 'Econometric model of the term structure of interest-rate swap yields'. *Journal of Finance*, 52/1: 1287–321.

Fang, F., and Oosterlee, K. (2008). 'Pricing early-exercise and discrete barrier options by Fourier-Cosine series expansions'. Delft University of Technology Research Paper.

Feng, L., and Linetsky, V. (2008). 'Pricing discretely monitored barrier options and defaultable bonds in Levy process models: a fast Hilbert transform approach'. *Mathematical Finance*, 18/3: 337–84.

Finger, C., Finkelstein, V., Pan, G., Lardy, J., Ta, T., and Tierney, J. (2002). 'CreditGrades Technical Document'. RiskMetrics Group.

Haworth, H. (2006). 'Structural models of credit with default contagion'. D.Phil. thesis. University of Oxford

—— Reisinger, C., and Shaw, W. (2006). 'Modelling Bonds and credit default swaps using a structural model with contagion'. University of Oxford working paper.

Hyer, T., Lipton, A., Pugachevsky, D., and Qui, S. (1998). 'A hidden-variable model for risky bonds'. Bankers Trust working paper.

He, H., Keirstead, W. P., and Rebholz, J. (1998). 'Double lookbacks'. *Mathematical Finance*, 8: 201–28.

Hilberink, B., and Rogers, L.C.G. (2002). 'Optimal capital structure and endogenous default'. *Finance and Stochastics*, 6: 237–263

Hull, J., Nelken, I., and White, A. (2004/5). 'Merton's model, credit risk, and volatility skews'. *Journal of Credit Risk*, 1/1: 3–27.

—— and White, A. (2000). 'Valuing credit default swaps I: no counterparty default risk'. *Journal of Derivatives*, 8/1: 29–40.

—— —— (2001). 'Valuing credit default swaps II: modeling default correlations'. *Journal of Derivatives*, 8/3: 12–22.

—— —— (2003). 'The valuation of credit default swap options'. *Journal of Derivatives*, 10/3: 40–50.

—— —— (2004). 'Valuation of a CDO and nth to default CDS without Monte Carlo simulation'. *Journal of Derivatives*, 12/2: 8–23.

Jackson, K., Jaimungal, S., and Surkov, V. (2007). 'Option pricing with regime switching Levy processes using Fourier space time-stepping'. *Proceedings of the 4th IASTED International Conference on Financial Engineering and Applications*: 92–7.

Jarrow, R., and Turnbull, T. (1995). 'Pricing derivatives on financial securities subject to credit risk'. *Journal of Finance*, 50/1: 53–85.

—— and Yu, J. (2001). 'Counterparty risk and the pricing of defaultable securities'. *Journal of Finance*, 56/5: 1765–800.

Kim, J., Ramaswamy, K., and Sundaresan, S. (1993). 'Does default risk in coupons affect the valuation of corporate bonds? A contingent claim model'. *Financial Management*, 22: 117–31.

Kiesel, R., and Scherer, M. (2007). 'Dynamic credit portfolio modelling in structural models with jumps'. Working Paper.

Lando, D. (1998). 'On Cox processes and credit risky securities'. *Review of Derivatives Research*, 2: 99–120.

Leland, H. (1994). 'Risky debt, bond covenants and optimal capital structure'. *Journal of Finance* 49: 1213–52.

—— and Toft, K. (1996). 'Optimal capital structure, endogenous bankruptcy, and the term structure of credit spreads'. *Journal of Finance*, 51: 987–1019.

Leung, S., and Kwok, Y. (2005). 'Credit default swap valuation with counterparty risk'. *Kyoto Economic Review*, 74/1: 25–45.

Lewis, A. (2001). 'A simple option formula for general jump-diffusion and other exponential Levy processes'. Working Paper.

Li, D. (2000). 'On default correlation: a copula approach'. *Journal of Fixed Income*, 9: 43–54.

Lipton, A. (2001). *Mathematical Methods for Foreign Exchange: A Financial Engineer's Approach*. Singapore: World Scientific.

—— (2002a). 'The vol smile problem'. *Risk Magazine*, 15/2: 81–85.

—— (2002b). 'Assets with jumps'. *Risk Magazine* 15/9: 149–53.

—— (2003). 'Evaluating the latest structural and hybrid models for credit risk'. Presentation at Global Derivatives, Barcelona.

—— (2008). 'Jump-diffusions and credit modelling: theoretical models and practical implications'. Presentation at 2nd SIAM Conference in Financial Mathematics, Rutgers University, New Brunswick, New J.

—— and Sepp, A. (2009). 'Credit value adjustment for credit default swaps via the structural default model'. *Journal of Credit Risk*, 5/2: 123–46.

—— Song, J., and Lee, S. (2007). 'Systems and methods for modeling credit risks of publicly traded companies'. Patent US 2007/0027786 A1.

Longstaff, F., and Schwartz, E. (1995). 'A simple approach to valuing risky fixed and floating rate debt'. *Journal of Finance*, 50: 789–819.

Lord, R., Fang, F., Bervoets, F., and Oosterlee, C. (2008). 'A fast and accurate FFT-based method for pricing early-exercise options under Levy processes'. *SIAM Journal of Scientific Computing*, 30: 1678–705.

Marshall, A. W., and Olkin, I. (1967). 'A multivariate exponential distribution'. *Journal of the American Statistical Association*, 2: 84–98.

Merton, R. (1974). 'On the pricing of corporate debt: the risk structure of interest rates'. Journal of Finance, 29: 449–70.

Misirpashaev, T. (2008). 'CDS and tranche with counterparty risk'. Merrill Lynch research paper.

Nielsen, L., Saa-Requejo, J., and Santa-Clara, P. (1993). 'Default risk and interest rate risk: the term structure of default spreads'. INSEAD working paper.

Pugachevsky, D. (2005). 'Pricing counterparty risk in unfunded synthetic CDO tranches'. In M. Pykhtin (ed.) *Counterparty Credit Risk Modeling*. London: Risk Books, 371–94.

Pykhtin, M., and Zhu, S. (2005). 'Measuring counterparty credit risk for trading products under Basel II'. In M. Ong (ed.), *Basel II Handbook* . London: Risk Books.

Rubinstein, M. (1983). 'Displaced diffusion option pricing'. *Journal of Finance*, 38/1: 213–17.

Sato, K. (1999). *Lévy processes and infinitely divisible distributions*. Cambridge: Cambridge University Press.

Schönbucher, P. (2003). 'A measure of survival'. *Risk Magazine*, 16/8: 79–85.

Sepp, A. (2004). 'Analytical pricing of double-barrier options under a double-exponential jump diffusion process: applications of Laplace transform'. *International Journal of Theoretical and Applied Finance*, 2: 151–75.

—— (2006). 'Extended CreditGrades model with stochastic volatility and jumps'. *Wilmott Magazine*, 50–62.

Stamicar, R., and Finger, C. (2006). 'Incorporating equity derivatives into the CreditGrades model'. *Journal of Credit Risk*, 2/1: 1–20.

Toivanen, J. (2008). 'Numerical valuation of European and American options under Kou's jump-diffusion Model'. *SIAM Journal on Scientific Computing*, 30/4: 1949–70.

Turnbull, S. (2005). 'The pricing implications of counterparty risk for non-linear credit products'. *Journal of Credit Risk*, 4/1: 117–33.

Uhrig-Homburg, M. (2002). 'Valuation of defaultable claims: a survey'. *Schmalenbach Business Review*, 54/1: 24–57.

Valužis, M. (2008). 'On the probabilities of correlated defaults: a first passage time approach'. *Nonlinear Analysis Modelling and Control*, 13/1: 117–33.

Zhou, C. (2001a). 'The term structure of credit spreads with jump risk'. *Journal of Banking and Finance*, 25: 2015–40.

——(2001b). 'An analysis of default correlations and multiple defaults'. *Review of Financial Studies*, 14/2: 555–76.

PART IV

BEYOND NORMALITY

CHAPTER 13

A NEW PHILOSOPHY
OF THE MARKET

ÉLIE AYACHE

1 THE SIGNIFICANCE OF THE CONVERTIBLE BOND

THE chapter on the convertible bond, in a book dedicated to credit derivatives, in the middle of what some already call the worst financial crisis since 1929, cannot but be symbolic and significant.[1] As its name indicates, the convertible bond is the conversion into equity of the bond binding creditor and debtor. There is a massive dissymmetry inherent in credit: eventually the debtor turns insolvent and the creditor resorts to the procedure of liquidation of the debtor's assets.

By contrast, equity means fairness, equality of chances and symmetry. It is the symmetry between the partners of a common venture, also called a *company*. Shareholders share equally (not necessarily quantitatively, but qualitatively) the risks of the enterprise, as well as its profits and losses, eventually its demise.

The convertible bond is an *invitation* issued by the entrepreneur to the investor to come and join his company instead of repayment of the debt. It is a very generous invitation, perhaps the most equitable. It is inviting the creditor to come and live in his house, in his company.

The invitation is: 'Although I have the means to repay you—since my company is presumably growing and doing well—and dismiss you, never to hear from you again, I invite you to take part in my project and future activity. In a word, I invite you to my future action, to my *future.*'

The future is the origin of the value, not the past. Hence conversion is, first and foremost, the conversion of the passivity of the debt into the activity of the share, the conversion of the past into the future.

[1] An expansion of this chapter has appeared as the concluding part of my book Ayache (2010) *The Black Swan: The End of Probability* London: John Wiley & Sons, drawing mainly on Gilles Deleuze's philosophy of creation and ontogenesis.

The word for share in French (and Dutch) is *action*. For this reason, the convertible bond may appear as an even more generous invitation, an invitation of higher order: the invitation to abandon the ethics and the logic and bindings of debt and credit (the bond, the box, the book), and altogether move to the symmetry and future of equity, to move from liquidation to liquidity.

2 GENESIS OF THE MARKET

Conversion from credit to equity is the history of the market. It is not just the historical date that chronologically marked the creation of the first stock exchange (this took place in 1602 in Amsterdam with the creation of the Dutch Company of East India Ferguson (2008)), but the *story* of the genesis of the market: the story we must repeat every time we think of the meaning of the price and of the exchange, every time we wonder what a market is, even when no equity or equity derivatives are involved. What we are saying is that the *meaning of price* lies in the process of conversion of credit into equity: the *meaning*, not the history, and *price* as a general category, not specifically the equity price. Two philosophical extrapolations are at work here.

We shall concentrate on equity, for the purpose of deducing this formidable result, and we shall unearth, in the conversion, that which imposes the necessity of the exchange or even better (as there are no transcendent entities ruling this necessity) that which materially, *immanently*, unfolds as an exchange in the conversion.

3 THE MOMENT OF THE CONVERSION

Let us not think of two individuals (exchanging) or of the stock exchange (the fluctuating Brownian movement) just yet. For the moment, let us stick with the prime moment of the conversion. B (Bond) becomes S (Share, Stake, Stock), or rather ΔS (a certain ratio, or number of shares). Credit doesn't transform into equity and suddenly disappear. The share is differential: it is risk, it is differentiation; however, it has itself to be exchanged against money. Surely, the share could become the only numeraire and the exchange would then amount to exchanging shares of this company against shares of another company. This is saying that owing and indebtedness may disappear, that credit (in this sense) may disappear and get replaced by equity; however, what cannot disappear is the Bank, or the credit line.

The conversion is the transformation of the absolute value of credit and of obligation, whose other side is bankruptcy, into the differentiating value of the stock (soon to be exchanged) and the concomitant transformation of the Bond into the Bank. We may no longer need credit, as it is being replaced by equity, but we still need the money account or the Bank. The sign of the successful conversion, witnessed by the Dutch in

1602 is that the Bank started accepting shares of the Company as collateral for loans, while at the same time loaning money to investors so they could invest in the shares.[2] The conversion from credit to equity is the transformation of the Bond (and passivity, and past) into the combination $B + \Delta S$ (money account + share).

You recognize what this is. This is the replicating portfolio of a *contingent claim*, or *derivative payoff* (although the two, as we will see later, are not philosophically and ontogenetically equivalent). This is trading. This is dynamic, as in *dynamic replication*.

Every derivative payoff is a summary of a trading strategy. To say so, however, seems to be presupposing the dynamic underlying process and the ensuing dynamic replication. Let us pretend this is not the case. Let us suppose there is no exchange, no exchanging partners, and no dynamic underlying price process yet. Astounding as it may seem, let us assume that there is no chronological time yet in which a temporal stochastic process may unfold as a series of realizations of possibilities.

Let us assume that time and possibility are not given yet. All we have instead is the *moment* of the conversion, or $B + \Delta S$. All we have is the genesis of the contingent claim: contingency, not possibility (on this crucial distinction, more to follow). Let us not call our picture static either. Indeed, the dynamics I will be investigating are the *dynamics of genesis*: the process of creation of the market as a whole (or at least, its reconstruction), the unfolding of the contingent claim and of the marketplace (as the place of pricing of the contingent claim) in one and the same movement of conversion. I call this picture dynamic because of the process of morphogenesis. By contrast, what we traditionally think is the dynamic picture of a reified market—prices that fluctuate randomly in time for no other reason than a so-called 'essence' of the market as a random generator which makes them so fluctuate—is a static essentialist view.

4 CONTINGENT CLAIM VS. PROJECTED POSSIBILITY

We have to see $B + \Delta S$ as the contingent claim and to see its contingency as caused by nothing else but the conversion, before we see it as the dynamic replication, within a temporal process of possibility, *of* the contingent claim. Soon, the problem of evaluation of the contingent claim will be upon us. However, we won't be able to evaluate the contingent claim as we do debt, by discounting and by contemplating the past as our only hope (the redemption of the debt) and death or default as our only contingency: as our only future. We have to evaluate the contingent claim looking forward, in a creative differentiating process. We have to evaluate it in a process of differentiation

[2] 'Company, bourse and bank provided the triangular foundation for a new kind of economy,' writes Niall Ferguson (2008: 132).

not in a process of redemption (or collapse) and identity.[3] Here, the important notice is that the traditional way of evaluating contingent claims is backward looking (it rolls backward in a tree of possibilities) because this procedure reflects in fact what Deleuze would call a 'process of resemblance'. No wonder it will replicate the contingent claim and make it redundant.

The process of resemblance and replication thinks it has the present spot price of the underlying as only real. From it, it projects possibilities, the future prices of the underlying, and it thinks that what it will get is the *realization* of those possibilities, the prices the underlying will actually trade at. Another possibility that it thinks is later open to it is the perspective of actually trading the underlying through the realizations of the possibilities of its price. From there, it becomes irresistible to replicate the payoff of the contingent claim with a self-financing strategy, thus making it redundant.

In reality, the real was already there from the start. It is not something more we get on top of possibilities as if fulfilling them. From the start, we had the underlying as a trading capacity (not just as a price possibility) and the contingent claim as something supposed to make a difference. So how could it end up redundant, replicable and identical? From the start, both underlying and derivative were here to trade. It is not that the reality of trading was later added to the projection of the possibilities of their prices.

The only thing that can evaluate the contingent claim in a forward-looking fashion is the market. The market is the sole debtor of this new form of credit, known as equity. It is the only debtor who can look forward (the only one who can 'give me money' against my share and my risk, the only one who can value my claim and 'redeem' it). The market is the only debtor whose bond (and bounds) is the future.

5 PRICING VS. EVALUATION

The market (that is to say, pricing, not evaluation) is what we get as soon as we get the contingent claim, and the contingent claim is what we get as soon as we get the conversion. There is a single and univocal unfolding (the conversion *is* the contingent claim *is* the market), as real and concrete and material as the historical circumstance that engendered the market. Instead of going through the abstract stages that invent a future after the contingent claim, then possibilities, then the realization of possibilities, then expectation, then value, and that finally circle back to price, perhaps we should consider that *conversion-contingency-price* is one and the same thing, something not mediated by possibility or perhaps even by chronological time. It is the contingent claim made present, or rather, made price, immediately (as this is what the market transmits and mediates). It is the *realization* of contingency: not in the sense in which

---

[3] In all that follows, I will use the verb 'to differentiate' in the intransitive sense. To differentiate, for an organism, is to undergo the process whereby it grows and develops differentiated features and organs. It is a creative process.

we speak of the realization of a possibility, this utter abstraction, but in the sense of a very concrete realization; as if we had forgotten how real contingency was (how solid and pressing and existent this may be that a thing is something and, at the same time, that it *can* be or *could* have been something else) and the market was here to remind us of that, to make us realize it again, through price.

Price is not the present value of future possibilities; it is not an equation or a closed identity. Price is a difference; it is the *same* difference as the contingent claim, where the word 'same' is different from the 'identical'. Price is the realization, the repetition in the present, in a medium we can immerse ourselves in immediately, without the future possibility and without abstraction, of a thing which is otherwise hardly imaginable and hardly representable: contingency.

Thus we are contrasting two things, two very general forms: the dogma of possibility, whose representative is debt and which is based on the *identity* of fixed states of the world and backward convergence towards them, and the reality of contingency, which is based on the process of *differentiation*. Identity against difference. Passivity against activity. Convergence (or collapse) against creation. Conversion is then the metamorphosis that converts one form into the other, together with their philosophical implications.

6 PRICE AND STOCHASTIC PROCESS

Price is not just a number; it is a cipher, a multiplicity. It doesn't just follow an explicit stochastic process, of which we wonder why it must follow *from* the exchange. To see how price is incompatible with stochastic process, let us try and confuse the two for a while.

Price as a stochastic process is the premiss of the derivative valuation problem. Price as the reflection of a trading capacity and the mapping of the possible by the stochastic process lead inexorably to the dynamic replication of derivatives and their redundant fate. This happens when derivatives are envisaged as contracts that select possibilities. In reality, derivatives are contingent claims, not *possible* claims. Their true domain is not the state space of pre-assigned and pre-charted possibilities. They were written prior to this, as possibility is only a copy and a replica.[4] They are the real. They are the reality of contingency before possibility was even conceived. They were invented in order to see what difference it makes today that a difference should occur later. Do you see possibility in this? This is a short cut between 'today' and 'later' that doesn't

---

[4] This follows from a doctrine of Bergson's, of whom Deleuze is a follower. The notion of the possible, Bergson holds in *Creative Evolution* (Bergson 1998), is derived from a false problem that confuses the 'more' with the 'less'; there is not less but more in the idea of the possible than in the real. When we think of the possible as somehow 'pre-existing' the real, we think of the real, then we add to it the negation of its existence, and then we project the 'image' of the possible into the past. We then reverse the procedure and think of the real as something more than the possible, that is, as the possible with existence added to it. We then say that the possible has been 'realized' in the real.

travel across the bridge of possibility. It crosses over something else: the *market*. Let us define the market as that *other* bridge or short cut to contingency.

We must stop seeing the market as a process unfolding in time, as a stochastic process that will guide us through time to go and see what difference the contingent claim will make. Following this path, we find there is nothing new in the difference, or price, that the contingent claim will make today—nothing newer than the difference it will make later. Price and payoff collapse into one, following the path of possibility, as dynamic replication makes them collapse into each other. Dynamic replication makes it look as if the contingent claim is expiring today.

The relation between price and payoff, between difference today and difference tomorrow should be something else than replica and a process of identity. The market is the medium of that relation. Yes, price is the contingent claim; it is the difference the contingent claim will make in the future translated today, yet price *cannot be* that, following the process of identity and replication brought about by dynamic replication. Price is the contingent claim through a process of *translation*. In translation, something is truly moved from one place to another (from the future place to the marketplace). Writing is the medium of translation; possibility is not.

Derivative valuation theory circumvented this process; it flew directly to the result, only misplacing it in possibility, and it started out with the underlying stochastic process. For a moment, the habitation of the market by market makers ignored the exchange as a translation of contingency and became absorbed by the necessity to enforce the dynamic replication, following only possibility and the stochastic process. Sooner or later, the market had to emerge again and the gravity once contained in the exchange as the place of contingency had to reappear in some other place. It reappeared in the volatility smile. This was precipitated by the October 1987 market crash.

In the technology leading to the 1987 crash, the exchange, or the meaning of the market, or the translation of contingency into price, was forgotten. The question of the genetic link between the price process and the exchange was forgotten. This is the question of why the exchange should result in a stochastic process at all, and the question of the self-differentiating nature of price itself: a nature that is not of such a 'nature' as to lend itself to the pure serialization of number and to the stochastic process.

Still, what has to be shown first is the birth of the contingent claim and of the exchange itself. What is the genesis of the contingent claim?

Just as the 1987 crash will make us relearn the place of the exchange in the price process and the priority of contingency over possibility, the 2008 credit crisis will make us relearn why this is so. Why exchange in the first place? Why is the market?

7 DEBT, DEATH, AND CONTINGENCY

I will start with debt.

The one owes the other something. Debt is a bond; it links two but it aims at one; it aims at redemption and at making-whole the creditor from whom the debtor has taken a (body) part, a lump sum of money (*The Merchant of Venice*). It is not a process of differentiation and creation but of identity and resemblance (and soon, death and collapse); it is attracted by the wrong abyss; it aims at bringing together again what was once separated. 'Pay me back my money, let the original event binding us disappear, as if it never happened; let us rewind history and fuse again in that originating moment. And this means we can go our separate ways again: we never met.' The individual degenerates into an identical individual again: he didn't evolve into a differentiated organism, a body, a corporation, a company.

This process, which looks only 'forward to the past' and which is inexorably attracted to the past, knows death as the only contingency.

Think of contingency as the engine of differentiation. Now, because the process of debt cannot differentiate and evolve as organism, because contingency cannot penetrate it and make it evolve (there is no *morphogenesis* of debt), it can only kill it. Bankruptcy and ruin and collapse and liquidation are the other face of the process of identity known as debt. They are the other face of the act of making-whole and of redeeming. They are its other face, the face marked with destiny and with the irreversibility of time. Nothing would have happened or could have happened if there had been no debt, but now that there is debt, the way back to identity cannot but be marked by the edge of collapse.

8 THE MORPHING OF DEBT INTO EQUITY

Equity is not a differentiation of debt (or its natural evolution); it is a *conversion*, a morphing of the face of debt. It takes place in an altogether different world. There is a leap of faith, literally a conversion, between credit and equity, so we cannot 'process' and analyse what goes on in between. There is no causality, no narrative other than history (the history of the Dutch), that can link the two. The only link follows the logic of *conversion*: all we can do is look at the 'elements' and 'traits' of credit and see how they get converted into the 'elements' and 'traits' of equity. We can be descriptive (and at best, speculative) about this morphing process, not analyse its internal mechanism. This is the deep mystery that is harboured by the convertible bond.

We can retrace the movement of conversion from credit to equity by saying the following.

As the *two* of debt were converted into the *one* of company and the 'process of identity'[5] was converted into a process of differentiation, *two*, which could not disappear, had to reappear somewhere else. The abyss separating the *two* of debt and around which they circled, either to end up redeeming the debt or to collapse into the abyss of liquidation, this abyss had to escape from their common circle and go outside.

---

[5] A process of resemblance and mimetism, which later degenerated into violence at the hands of John Law (1720) and his attempt to replicate the Company of the Dutch.

While the *two* of debt were becoming the *one* of company, the *two* (as such) had to be propelled outside. And what could be more 'outside' than the exchange?

The abyss could no longer be handled by the *two* becoming *one* and thus it had to out. Equity could no longer 'turn over' to be redeemed like debt and made-whole like debt and to extract its value from the value of the bond (an ethical value, that is: the value of obligation), so *it had to turn over to somebody else, outside*. Value could no longer flow from the obligation: it had to flow, or rather to diffuse, to extend, to burst, to fly, in the market.

9 COMPANY OF THE FUTURE

Conversion of debt into equity thus produces directly the contingent claim. It doesn't produce share, or equity, as such, because share or equity is insufficient in itself. The potential energy, the tension of the bond (the backward risk of redemption staring at the abyss), would remain missing if the conversion and the fusing together of the *two* of bond into the *one* of company were to stop at the share. The share is only half the story, because we wonder: what is it the share of? Much as it was clear that the bond was the bond holding debtor and creditor tightly together, now we wonder: what exactly is this share holding? It is the share *of* a company, sure enough. Sure enough, it holds a company (together?). But the company does not *hold*. It is open-ended; the company is only half the story. The company is one and therefore it is *single*. So we wonder: what is it the company *of*? In *whose* company is it? If all the shareholders are equal, in whose company can we say they find themselves? We feel like answering: they find themselves *in the company of the future*. The share is the share *of* the future, that is to say, of contingency. The contingent claim is the complete story of the conversion of credit into equity.

10 PRICE AS THE 'VALUE' OF THE CONTINGENT CLAIM

In the company, the shareholders are equal: they are all at once debtor and creditor. Or rather, the logic here is no longer one of owing and redeeming, because it is no longer tied up with the past. If anything, the company *is owed/owes* the future. This cannot stop and can never be made whole. On the contrary, it differentiates indefinitely. The *parties* are no longer debtor and creditor (as these two have merged in the same company) but they are now the two legs of the contingent claim (the two segments of its kinked payoff). Debtor and creditor convert into shareholders. Owing and redeeming disappear as notions associated with the past, and the notion of 'owing the future' (to nobody in particular, as this notion is single: it has no mate) *becomes the contingent claim*. Instead of waiting for redemption (for an obligation—what one *ought* to do—whose other side is default), now we wait and see *what can happen* (contingency).

Price is the immanent translation of the contingent claim. It *is* the contingent claim (if we think of being as immanent becoming, as in Deleuze's philosophy of immanence). Price is not the value of the contingent claim in the sense of valuation, because valuation is not immanent: it stems from transcendent principles; for instance, valuation requires the category of possibility in derivative valuation theory.

Through the conversion, the pair formed by debtor and creditor becomes company, the bond becomes contingent claim and the face value (value in the ethical sense of redeeming the face and making it whole again) becomes price.

Writing is the sign of the exchange. There is a void, an abyss, in any act of exchange and the exchanging partners stretch writing across it.[6] The written contract is what guarantees that my partner will not forget the terms of the exchange and, as it were, never repay me or never hand me what I desire in exchange of what I have given to him. Writing was the symptom of the exchange inherent in debt: it assumed the form of a bond and admitted of value. Now writing is also the symptom of the exchange inherent in company, only it is now writing in the sense of the contingent claim.

The contingent claim is written; it is essentially a writing because it expresses a difference (if A, pay x(A); else if B, pay x(B), etc.) and difference is writing. Difference has to be marked, scratched on a surface (the option strike). As writing and difference already, the contingent claim has no partner to exchange with but the future. Instead of value, it admits of *price*.

Price is the ethical obligation of the future. It is the 'value' binding the future, that is to say, the 'value' of the contingent claim. The contingent claim admits of no bound (and no binding) other than the market (the market is the future made partner of the exchange). This is an immanent binding, which depends on no transcendent principle of valuation.

11 HOW DOES PRICE DIFFERENTIATE?

I keep saying that price is the translation of the contingent claim, yet so far I haven't spoken of the price of the underlying equity itself, or of a price process of any kind (Brownian or otherwise). For one thing, the underlying equity is a special case of a

---

[6] Roland Barthes (2002: 292) writes: 'Writing, therefore, is the exchange. When I face the dangerous interval in which I let go on one side and seize on the other, writing constitutes the way of preserving myself against the risk of a lethal gap: if writing didn't exist, I would find myself *without anything*: having already let go, not having seized yet: in a state of infinite fall' (my translation).

contingent claim. *But I guess the whole purpose of deducing the contingent claim right from the miraculous (and unexplained) event of the conversion, then of deducing the market (or price) from the contingent claim, in that order, is really to overturn the traditional order of presentation where the market is first postulated as an underlying stochastic process (Brownian motion or other), a process based on possibility (not contingency), and where, second, the contingent claim is valued under the dogma of identity.*

Witness how the contingent claim is valued going backwards, in the traditional valuation theory: it is bound by identity, the same way as debt, by the identity and tautology of the process of possibility which we seem to be projecting forward but which is in reality only a copy, a retro-jection. This, as we know, ultimately erases the contingent claim as it makes it redundant. (It doesn't erase it in the same way as debtor and creditor dream of erasing debt, but in a *corresponding* way: the way the process of identity inherent in possibility—which brings nothing new—corresponds to the process of identity inherent in the tension of debt.) Not to mention that contingent claims appear totally superfluous and facultative when they are considered after the stochastic process of the underlying.

If the whole idea is to have a nice data-generating process and a nice stochastic description of the series it generates in terms of perfectly partitioned states of the world of the underlying and a probability distribution, why write a contingent claim on top of that? Where did this contingent claim come from? Do we just write it for the fun of distinguishing some states of the world in our mind (with the faculty of our thought, that is to say, *facultatively*) as opposed to others, or is our intention to trade it the real reason why we write it?

In the schema of possibility, the contingent claim is spurious and redundant even before its valuation algorithm is put in place. When the latter is developed, it will only confirm this inherent superfluity and redundancy. No matter: let us stick to our guns; let us write the contingent claim and delight in its perfect replication.[7] Then what? The next thing we are told is that we must price the contingent claim using 'implied volatility'. Where did *that* come from? From the market, we are told. But what is the market? How does it fit in our closed-circuit schema of stochastic process and replication?

So to go back to the question: 'But will price differentiate?', the answer is to try to *deduce* that. What would the price process of the underlying look like, now that we have derived the contingent claim directly from the conversion, and price from the contingent claim? It sounds, listening to our deduction, as if the conversion had led us right to the doorstep of the market and that there was only one thing we could envision next: the emanation of the ribbon of price as the Brownian motion (or some

---

[7] Or its optimal replication—it hardly matters which, since pricing within the schema of possibility is already replication, independently of whether the numerical payoff will be compensated by the numerical proceeds of the replication strategy. It is pricing 'identically', without change and without risk: I mean, without model risk and rupture in the pricing procedure and rationale. Optimal replication is fated to become perfect, anyway, by its own lights, as soon as we add instruments in the replicating procedure.

other, more complex process) that we are so familiar with and are expecting so much. However, this would be opening the wrong door and releasing the market in the wrong direction again. Yes, we do expect the price to differentiate, as it is the concentrate and end result of this whole process of morphogenesis we have been describing (the process of the debt made contingent claim by the conversion and of the contingent claim made price by the market), but it will differentiate differently than expected.

12 THE A-TEMPORAL PIT OF PRICE

Price differentiates in its own *pit*, as is, independently of the dimension of chronological time. From my deduction, price comes out accelerated by the conversion in the direction of contingency and exchange, not in the direction of possibility and chronological time. It comes out accelerated in the direction orthogonal to chronological time and possibility and that is the direction of space, or rather, of *spot*, of the market as marketplace, of the exchange as absolute beginning, that is to say, as eternal return and repetition. It is not so much a price that must follow the previous price in a time series as it is the price we must always return to as reference, and invert our valuation formulas against. It is price as the repetition of the world and market situation, as the return of the same yet not of the identical: repetition in difference.

Price as pit and as exchange is precisely the number (which is in fact a multiplicity) such that, whatever we do and no matter what pricing technology we devise in order to derive that number (as in derivative pricing by trees and by possibility) and consider it as a result, as an output of our algorithm, as something enclosed by representation, the number inverts at once into an input and acts as the reference against which to invert now our formula and to recalibrate our partitions of states of the world (the range of possibility) and our probability distributions (the stochastic process).

At the outcome of the morphogenetic process unfolding in conversion-contingent claim-price, the price process differentiates in *intensive time*, not in chronological, extensive time. With the notions of intensive and extensive we come upon a distinction that is crucial to understanding Deleuze's philosophy of difference and creation. Extensive differences, such as length, area, or volume, are intrinsically divisible. Intensive differences, by contrast, are 'the differences in temperature, pressure, speed, chemical concentration, which are key to the scientific explanation of the genesis of the form of inorganic crystals, or of the forms of organic plants and animals,' writes Manuel DeLanda (2002: 6). Elsewhere: 'The differences [Deleuze] has in mind are not external *differences between things* that are part and parcel of classificatory practices, but productive differences perhaps best illustrated by *intensive differences*, differences in temperature, pressure, etc., within one and the same system, which are marked by thresholds of intensity determining phase transitions' (DeLanda 2002: 54 n 60).

13 THE SINGLE DICE-THROW

The market or the pit is the *aleatory point* (yet another of Deleuze's key terms[8]) or the Event which distributes all of change and perpetually redistributes the probability distributions. The market maker is the player who emits the Nietzschean throw of the dice; he doesn't try to calculate probability; he doesn't live in any of the actual probability distributions or stochastic processes. He doesn't live in the 'space of time'. Rather, he affirms all of chance through the price he makes. François Zourabichvili, one of Deleuze's commentators, calls it a game of *absolute chance,*

a game where chance would be affirmed in its entirety at each throw of the dice, where each throw would create its own rules... To the rule of the single throw, where chance would be given initially and relatively and accepted 'once and for all,' we must oppose an indefinite succession of throws which reaffirm the entirety of chance at each time, and which thus appear as the fragments of one and the same Throw 'for all times.' This unique Throw... is the affirmation of absolute chance, or of becoming: a future-tensed affirmation, which is inseparable from repetition because it has as condition both the reaffirmation of absolute chance at each throw and a selective repetition which doesn't bring back what was only affirmed once and for all. The affirmation of becoming implies that the whole of chance be given all over again at each throw: thus it excludes finality, as well as causality and probability, for the benefit of *non causal correspondences* [my emphasis] between events. This, in substance (if we may say so), is Deleuze's interpretation of the theme of Nietzschean eternal return. (Zourabichvili 2004: 74)

Zourabichvili's turn of phrase might sound a bit confusing, but in it lies the most cogent summary of all I've been trying to say about the market and recalibration. What Zourabichvili calls the 'rule of the single throw' where chance is relative (i.e. not absolute) yet accepted 'once and for all', is the static probability distribution that is characteristic of the system of possibility and of stochastic process. This is the view in which the market is represented by a single stochastic process or random generator, where states of the world and probability are given once and for all, and where contingent claims end up being redundant. To this static distribution, Zourabichvili opposes a unique absolute Throw which holds 'for all times'. This throw is intensive; it is not quantifiable in terms of actual probability distributions. This is what I call the 'market', the 'pit'.

---

[8] Deleuze (1990: 56) writes: '[H]ow are we to characterize the paradoxical element which runs through the series, makes them resonate, communicate, and branch out, and which exercises command over all the repetitions, transformations, and redistributions? This element must itself be defined as the locus of a question. ... [T]he *question* is determined by an *aleatory point* corresponding to the empty square or mobile element. The metamorphoses or redistributions of singularities form a history; each combination and each distribution is an event. But the paradoxical instance is the Event in which all events communicate and are distributed. It is the Unique event, and all other events are its bits and pieces.'

To stand in the pit, to make the market, is to throw that single Throw 'for all times'. It is to affirm that absolute chance. Moreover, the market allows the image of the dice and of the redistribution of probability to stick, literally. This is due to the conjunction of the fact that the given pricing algorithm (that is to say, relative chance, chance that is given once and for all) makes the contingent claims redundant with the fact that the market, to which the contingent claims are destined and which is the single Throw of absolute chance, requires them never to be redundant. Thus we come to understand that the process of differentiation of the market and of the price (the process snaking in the intensive dimension of time, through the pit, through the single Throw, through the eternal return) is incompatible with causality or probability, because *it takes place at infinite speed in a space of meta-probability*. Now we perceive the non-causal correspondences Zourabichvili is talking about.

14 THE EXCHANGE PLACE

The quant revolution I am calling for might simply reside in recognizing that the market (that is to say, the *pricing of contingent claims*, not derivatives valuation theory) is itself, directly, *quantitative finance*. Quantitative finance of the immanent kind, without the passage through the media and the unnecessary arsenal of probability theory and stochastic processes that the quants have entrenched us in.

The market is not a generator of prices unfolding in time, but the a-temporal medium that is conductive of contingent claims and that transmits them as prices. And what is this conductivity made of? What is the elementary (molecular) property of the market medium that makes it conductive of contingent claims in the form of prices?

We don't want the market to be conductive of time and to be a medium where prices unfold in a temporal stochastic process; so what is the property that makes it conductive in the direction transversal to time: in the direction following which the contingent claims are all intensively priced and are never redundant? What is the property that makes the market so appropriate to materializing the single dice-throw? In a word, what is the particle, the molecule, that the market medium is made of?

It is the exchange.

People think that the exchange is down to the number of people exchanging, that it oscillates between one agent and another, or that it hovers above the whole crowd: that it is equivocal. So how can it be conceived of as a 'molecule', as univocal, in order at least to be conductive of the contingent claim? (In conductivity, there is a notion of univocity.)

I say the exchange has nothing to do with a pair of traders exchanging, let alone with the crowd. The nature of the exchange is already all inscribed in what it is designed for. *The market is the place of exchange only insofar as it is the place where contingent claims admit of prices*: the place where they are translated; the place where they go and where we let go of them. The way in which contingent claims admit of prices (instead of possibilities), this differential (as opposed to identical) translation of contingency, is the other face of the reason why contingent claims are exchanged and why the exchange is written all over them. Or rather, it is the same face. The exchange and the contingent claims are in 'mutual presupposition' of each other as Deleuze would say. *Contingent claims are written in order to be traded.*

The exchange can be derived and even defined from the prior definition of the *exchange place*; and the exchange place can be defined in turn from the prior definition of the *place of translation of contingent claims*: the place where we have no choice but to let go of them.

There is a place where we let go of the contingent claim we are holding because we have to take our distance from it, because we want to see what difference it makes, and this cannot happen unless we separate it from our circle of identity. In other words, we wish to 'value' the contingent claim; only this won't be value in the sense of convergence towards face. We don't face the contingent claim the way we face debt: the way we stare at redemption or contemplate the abyss. Precisely, we can let go of the contingent claim because we are not inexorably pulled toward its face. *We let go of it because it is contingent and, as such, written and because, as so written, it has its own destiny written for it: a difference it has to make without us and without our circle.*

Yet we want it to return. It escapes our identity circle; it escapes our valuation; yet we want to deal with it; we want it to return to us with the difference it makes. This can happen only if this can *take place* and if place can cut into the return: that is to say, only if we trade our identity circle (the detached, un-anchored and un-placeable circle or mirror where creditor and debtor interlock and where value circles back to them) against place.

What place? The exchange place.

And so the sequence is the following. The contingent claim creates its place; this place 'differentiates' into the exchange place, that is to say, it creates the exchange place. We don't know what exchange means at this stage, or whom to exchange with. Following our customary inversion style, the 'exchange-place' is defined and differentiated as a single expression *before* the 'exchange' or the 'place' are singled out from it. It is only later that the 'exchange-place' creates the exchange in the sense that we are exchanged with that place, that we perform an about-face with value, that value returns to us from the *other* and not from our *doppelgänger* in the debt.

15 REACTIVATING THE CONVERSION

Conversion has to be constantly reactivated in the category of price lest we never understand anything and risk losing everything (this is what is happening in today's crisis). Conversion must be constantly reactivated lest possibility quickly interferes and reopens a room in which the speed of transmission of the medium of the market will be defused and lost.

Retrieving the memory of the conversion (reactivating it) is what enables us to sustain the inversion that is characteristic of the univocity of the market and of contingency. When I say 'inversion', this is by opposition to the traditional way of going about contingency. What we traditionally think is the 'right' way, going from the spot price *S* to the stochastic process, to the contingent claim, brings nothing and introduces nothing. It only adds question over question. It doesn't answer the question of why contingent claims should be priced and why their price should serve as reference and 'inverter' for the derivative pricing formula rather than the opposite.

Conversion has to be constantly reactivated in order to remind us that *the contingent claim and the market price come before possibility and metaphysical time and that they should, therefore, always be returned to as the initial place.* Whenever we forget the conversion (the very genesis and meaning of the market), we get attracted down the fatal abyss of debt and default. We get attracted to the degenerative face of identity and we are no longer traversed by the current of univocity. We pause in a room where we think we can evaluate things, reflect them in a mirror, duplicate them and represent them. And as we stop, we fall.

John Law wasn't driven by univocity when he tried to duplicate in eighteenth-century France what the Dutch had achieved. How can you *duplicate* contingency or, what's even more difficult, the genesis of contingency: the conversion? How can you do that when contingency, or the market, is what lends itself the least to representation and fictionalization; what lends itself the least to the opening of the room of possibility, which is indispensable to fiction and duplication; what even lends itself the least to the mere intention of copying and understanding? John Law's *Grande Banqueroute* of 1720 wasn't a credit crisis. It eventually unfolded as a credit crisis but what it was, originally, was a conversion crisis. John Law's error was his misinterpretation of the genesis of the market as well as of the company and of the contingent claim: a misinterpretation of the *marketplace.*

Place can't be abstracted and transported and re-placed and reconstructed. *Place* is irreplaceable. Yet John Law thought he could reconstruct the place that the Dutch had historically, univocally, inimitably, converted out of the circle of debt: the market. No wonder John Law's contingency degenerated into a series of arbitrary decisions and readjustments that he could only enforce by the credit of the Regent (eventually corrupting that credit). John Law replaced the volatility of the market, or action, with the volatility of his reactions and decrees (Ferguson 2008).

Crisis is inherently a time of abandonment; it is a time when the moment of genesis is forgotten together with meaning. Alternatively, crisis could reveal itself a propitious occasion to retrieve the genesis and to recall it.

Price, we have said, is the unmediated translation of the contingent claim; it is an event, an interface, the meaning of the contingent claim. It doesn't occur in time but as a writing process: it is what allows the market maker to insert himself in the transversal direction and to pre-scribe the event instead of predicting it. It is a genesis, a creation. The October 1987 crash made us recall and reactivate the event character of price and of the exchange: as such, irreducible to possibility. October 1987 was an *exchange crisis* (as a matter of fact, the exchange almost didn't open the day following the crash); it was the discovery that the exchange is the line of redistribution of probability, the line that precedes the distribution of probability and metrical time. The result of the 1987 crisis was that we all learnt that the formulas of possibility should always get inverted against price. This was the discovery of the implied *volatility smile*.

1987, we may say, was the rediscovery of the exchange facet of what we may call the *conversion-contingency-price complex*, the facet that says that price is the translation of the contingent claim *as exchanged* (as shot through with the exchange). As for 2008, it is a crisis that goes back even farther that this; it goes back to the *creation* of price and not just to its event. In the conversion-contingency-price complex, 2008 retrieves the most archaic facet: the moment of creation, the genesis of the contingent claim and of the market in the same unfolding movement, the movement of escaping as far away as we can from the circle of debt.

For this reason, 2008 is not a credit crisis either. It is a conversion crisis just like John Law's and since conversion is a meta-philosophical operator, we can say that 2008 is a philosophical crisis.

1987 was a good crisis in the sense that it hit a population already equipped with the means to surmount it. It hit options traders who were immersed in the market, actively engaging in dynamic replication, already testing the limit of the whole category of possibility on which their pricing tool was based. They quickly relearned the meaning of the conversion and the genesis of the contingent claim by inverting their formula. They gave back to contingency its precedence, no longer pricing the contingent claim from the automatic and impassive replication strategy that was formulated only in possibility, but started now implying volatility from the market price of the contingent claim in order to compute the replication strategy, as this was the only way they could reaffirm their position as dynamic traders, despite the apparent abuse and misuse of the model that this meant, literally.

Conversion is not just the transformation of debt into equity; more generally, it is the conversion of the principle of identity and convergence inherent in debt and possibility into the principle of differentiation inherent in the contingent claim. Its morphological or topological expression is the conversion of the face/abyss of debt into the cut/cross of the contingent claim, or the conversion of the time-to-expiry of debt (or, equivalently, of the backward procedure of evaluation in possibility) into the open place, the exchange place where the ex-partner of the debt, formerly detached in the non-place of his bond, now becomes an active trader.

He now becomes the partner of the future, no longer of the past; he is so to speak 'crucified' to the floor, turned into a *local*, into the resident of the place where the other, the exchanging partner, may now cross, and where the *corresponding* other, the contingent claim, may now be priced.

16 POSSIBILITY IS ONLY A TOOL

A conversion crisis occurs every time this eternal return to place (which is the face of contingency) is forgotten and replaced by the space of possibility and its fixed states of the world. A crisis occurs every time the process of differentiation of price, *which needs possibility only as a tool, only to the extent* that it shall constantly depart from it and vary from it, thus truly weaving its fabric, is supplanted by a possibility that no longer differentiates and remains identical.

$B + \Delta S$ was the outcome of the conversion and we recognized it as the contingent claim only insofar as it prefigured dynamic trading, that is to say, the market, or what would later be known as the replication strategy *of* the contingent claim, once possibility and stochastic process had been created. From the first moment of genesis of the contingent claim and the market, and although the notions of possibility, probability, and dynamic replication were not yet available, the *conversion* (or what we have defined as the very movement away from the dead abyss of identity onto the creative abyss of differentiation) thus involved the term ΔS, or the trading of the underlying. The very movement away from the collapse and degeneration of identity, away from debt, away from dogma, away from 'dead probability' where death is just waiting to happen, thus seemed to want to pass via the trading floor, as if there were no differential meaning to be had for contingency (that is to say, no sense it would make) except via the cross of the eXchange and the eXchange place.

To anticipate, it is as if a constitutive part of the contingent claim, and therefore a signal of a successful conversion away from identity and collapse, was the *later* possibility of dynamically replicating the contingent claim (this is what $B + \Delta S$ means). *Derivatives that you cannot dynamically replicate are not contingent claims in our morphogenetic sense of the word*; therefore they can only precipitate a conversion crisis—thus, the Collateralized Debt Obligation (CDO). They are created, not from the conversion of debt into equity (where 'debt' and 'equity' are no longer to be taken literally but to be understood now in the generic sense of identity and differentiation respectively), not from the genesis that enfolds the market in one and the same productive difference, but from a later *degeneration* of the category of possibility, which, in our schema, is only a copy of the real and as such incapable of withstanding the real.

These degenerate derivatives derive from a category, possibility, which is itself but a derivative product, a later and minor episode of the representation of the market and of valuation theory. As such, their destiny was never linked to the market and to the process of differentiation that the market is all about. *They could never be priced, only valued*; that is to say, they could only make sense under the dogma of identity, either by being valued under the dogmatic postulation of a probability distribution, never to be questioned and differentiated and recalibrated by the market, or even, before that, by seeming to admit of a market that was in reality only a fad, or a bubble. Their market was only a trend that had no other foundation than imitation and make-believe or, in other words, the very reproduction of the mimetic and speculative and ultimately lethal process that is at work in debt (speculative in the bad sense of *speculum*: the sense of the fateful mirror image and doubling of the one).

2008 can be called a credit crisis not because the CDO has credit as underlying but because of our higher-level interpretation of *credit* as the domain where dogma and the metaphysics of possibility have taken over factual speculation and contingency (Meillassoux 2008). As a matter of fact, the 2008 crisis is not even technically a credit crisis. Single-name credit derivatives, such as the credit default swap (CDS), would never have posed a problem had they not been bundled in CDOs, whose valuation then crucially depended on the *correlation* between individual defaults.

Default correlation is a probabilistic object that is notoriously difficult to model, let alone to hedge or to infer from the market. Correlation is the big culprit; and the true crisis I am talking about, the one where the conversion of the principle of identity into the principle of differentiation was forgotten, is the consequence of having based the valuation of the most complex of derivatives, the so-called correlation products, on possibility and not on contingency, on a pure probabilistic model and not on the market.

Correlation products were valued in possibility from start to finish, without a market maker who would stand in the middle and use possibility merely as an intermediate tool to insert himself in the dynamics of the market, and then *to take and make the market beyond possibility*, that is to say, to make it where it belongs, in contingency. Replication is crucially needed only insofar as it will be overstepped by trading. While the lesson from the conversion was ultimately to replace the category of probability with the category of price, thus affirming the market as the sole medium of contingency, correlation products went absolutely the opposite way. They ignored the market and built a castle on pure probability theory instead, on the metaphysical replica of the real. Instead of the unique Throw 'for all times', they adopted the single throw 'once and for all'.

It is true that we would be better off with absolutely no credit and only equity. It is true that the genesis of the contingent claim and, correlatively, of the market have been described as taking place at absolutely the opposite end of the spectrum to debt. It is true I may have sounded as if I wanted to suppress debt completely, but this was only my reconstruction of the genesis of the market. Because of the equivalence between the market and the contingent claim on the one hand and the absolute opposition between the contingent claim and debt on the other, now that the market is created and well in place, *any product that is traded in the market will ipso facto become a contingent claim and consequently escape the circle of debt/death/identity*. The condition, of course, is that the market endures and does not disappear as a consequence of us forgetting its own genesis.

Thus, all contingent claims are not the product of the conversion of debt into equity, contrary to what our account of their morphogenesis may have suggested. You find options trading on currencies, for instance, and they certainly rank as contingent claims. But again, these contingent claims are, to our mind, already all imbued with their equivalence with the market, and as such, they are the signal that currency value has also been 'converted' into price, that it has moved away from the dogma of, say, the currency peg. To understand how currency options are contingent claims, despite the fact that they are not equity derivatives, is to understand that they are the signal of an underlying currency market, as opposed to an underlying currency stochastic process, and that, as such, they also signal a move away from the category of possibility.

Conversion of debt into equity is only needed to engender the market in our reconstruction and to make us all remember that the market is, in essence, repulsion from the metaphysical dogma of possibility. *Conversion is a conceptual engine whose goal, ultimately, is to give a new orientation to our thought of the market. Enough to say that it enables this thought to break free from possibility.*

When the time came and possibility and the stochastic process were finally created, the first crisis, the October 1987 crash, hit those who had 'forgotten' the necessity of re-calibration and differentiation and had locked themselves in the dogma of probability, namely the population of option traders on the floor using BSM (Black-Scholes-Merton).[9] However, it turned out that they were best equipped to take the lesson and get over the crisis because their very presence and raison d'être on the floor, pricing and trading options at variance with the replication plan, was in itself the very engine of contingency and of the surpassing of possibility. If anything, they confirmed the movement of conversion as a liberation from the shackles of identity and identical states of the world. In their hands, and following the 1987 crash, dynamic replication was no longer the instruction to tie up the option price to what the dynamic programming dictated; rather, it became *their* way of remaining afloat on the floor, of remaining inserted between the two price processes of option *and* underlying, in order to trade the option all the more freely, that is to say, to trade it *in contingency*, in the market, in reality, away from the edict of possibility and metaphysics.

All that 1987 did was to reverse the trend that, from the mere sight of $B + \Delta S$ as the outcome of the conversion and as genesis of the market, had fled into possibility and the stochastic process all too quickly. The 1987 market crash brought the market maker (the 'partner of the future in equity') back to contingency, using $B + \Delta S$ precisely as pivot point and lever: 'You will remain on the floor, actively inserted in the price process of the contingent claim (and this includes both underlying and derivative), actively trading, actively "replicating" the contingent claim, holding on $B + \Delta S$ as tightly as you can; only this replication will no longer take place in the retired possibility for the reason that you will be inverting the formulas of possibility against the market and recalibrating them following a differentiation process that can no longer resemble a stochastic process: following a process that will not take place in the possible but in what Deleuze calls the *virtual* (see Appendix).[10] And it is your grip on $B + \Delta S$ that precisely entitles you to calibrate and recalibrate.'

[9] They had forgotten it in our reconstruction of the market genesis, not in chronological history. In history, they had never heard of recalibration, of course. They were to learn it precisely through experiencing the crash.

[10] In *The Deleuze Dictionary* (Parr 2005: 296–97), we read the following under the entry 'Virtual/Virtuality': 'In Deleuze's ontology, the virtual and the actual are two mutually exclusive, yet jointly sufficient, characterizations of the real. The actual/real are states of affairs, bodies, bodily mixtures and individuals. The virtual/real are incorporeal events and singularities on a plane of consistency, belonging to the pure past—the past that can never be fully present. ... That the virtual is

How 2008 differs from this happy reversal of fortune is that, in 2008, $B + \Delta S$ was no longer here. The extremities that the category of possibility had gone to (multi-name correlation) and the amounts involved were such that, when the wake-up call of contingency finally sounded, there was no floor left, no $B + \Delta S$ to use as the pivot. There were no market makers or creators to discern between possibility and contingency. (We're not even sure there ever was a market to begin with.) If anything, the crisis had sapped the genesis itself, as the ban on short-selling had effectively prevented $B + \Delta S$ from *taking place*, that is to say, it had undermined the very instrument of differentiation and left us with nothing but the abyss to stare at.

17 THE PRICING TOOL

The conversion has to be constantly reactivated, the genesis of price constantly remembered, the immediacy and un-mediation between the price and the contingent claim constantly repeated (eternal return, univocity), and this should lead to the *pricing tool* in the same movement.

I talk of a pricing tool not of a valuation model or valuation principle. As a *pricing* tool, the tool must sustain all the inversions that are characteristic of my reconstruction of the market. It must be a tool in harmony with the line of transmission of *prices*—of prices as the immanent translation of contingent claims; of prices as the interface, as the face and destiny of contingent claims, once the latter have been shot through with the exchange and with the *divergence of place*.

Here, *place* means the place of arrival and crossing of the other: the same sense in which we speak of the other branch crossing and cutting in the contingent claim—*place*, as opposed to the *non-place* of debt. Debt has no 'place' other than abyss and death sentence and deadline.

The pricing tool must be a tool that accompanies the sequence of prices, or the 'price process', in the sense of the a-temporal sequence of generation of payoffs of increasing complexity, not in the sense of the variation of the underlying price in time and of generation of data by a random generator. This tool must be the result of the working through of the notion of implied volatility, of pushing it to its conse-

the Bergsonian *durée* and *élan vital* stems from the basic agreement between Deleuze and Bergson regarding the structure of temporality. Any actual present passes only because all presents are constituted both as present and as past. In all past presents the entire past is conserved in itself, and this includes the past that has never been present (the virtual).' In our interpretation, the 'past that has never been present' is the liquidity of the market. The past of a contingent claim is not the path of past prices that the stochastic process governing its underlying will have actualized in chronological time but the deeper observation that if the market were constituted of this stochastic process then the contingent claim would become redundant and would no longer admit a market of its own. So the real past is the *differentiation* that sneaks in behind the curtain of chronological time and the presentation of the stochastic process and *repeats*: 'The stochastic process should have been different.' *This* repeated change is real—it holds the key to the market—yet it was never part of an actual present, for it is always what counter-actualizes it.

quences (Ayache 2006). It is a *pricing* tool (the tool of the market) in the sense that neither the contingent claim nor its market price should ever turn spurious or become questionable. It should sustain recalibration, and the market maker should be able to virtually calibrate it against any contingent claim.

I have reasons to believe that the regime-switching model can answer this requirement (Ayache 2007). See the Appendix for its mathematical elaboration and interpretation.

Briefly, regimes of regimes are also regimes; this is why a regime-switching model made stochastic (that is to say, recalibrated) is still a regime-switching model that can be diagrammed again under the traits of the initial one. It is self-differentiating in this sense and while any one of its actualizations reproduces a traditional stochastic process in extensive time, the process of its self-differentiation unfolds in the virtual dimension, which is here crucial for creative time, or market making.

18 THE MARKET AS ALTERNATIVE TO PROBABILITY

The present crisis is an opportunity to *replace* the whole concept of probability. We are supposed to get out of the crisis, to understand what happened. But who understands the market in the first place? We are all either stuck in the dogmatism of randomness and speculation or in the dogmatism supposed to rid us of speculation. This is the dogmatism of possibility. Only if we cross in the other direction, the direction of the virtual and of price and of writing, the direction of the immanence of prices as immediate translations of contingent claims (i.e. without the mediation of possibility), only then will we be able to understand the market and no longer risk losing it, either by its own collapse, or by a political decision of some kind.

So if we want to understand the market, perhaps we should no longer try to apply probability to it and wonder what the probabilities, there, are the probabilities of: the objective probability of the next price being such and such, or alternatively the subjective probability of the exchanging partners. Maybe the question of what kind of chance set-up the market is, what kind of probability machine it is, is the wrong question to ask altogether. Instead of arguing that physical systems are producers of probability (they stage probability; they show probability), or even of chaos when they are complex enough: particles of quantum physics, dice, roulette, lottery, three-body problem, etc.; instead of arguing that non-physical (biological, social) complex systems are producers of even stranger probability, of probability that may not even get assigned, in other words, of essential uncertainty; instead of wondering what kind of producer of probability the market is, perhaps the question should be posed at the higher level and we should wonder whether the market may not be a *complete alternative to the notion of possibility and probability taken as a whole.*

Instead of conceiving of the market as a *case of* probability, instead of thinking of probability as the general category and of the market as the special case, perhaps we should generalize the market to the level of a category, such that it ends up competing with probability. Maybe the concrete market, the financial market we all know and think about, is only the numerical instance or illustration of a much more general type of medium for the transmission of events.

In the concrete market, everything eventually translates into price and price movements, i.e. numbers and number dynamics; this is why it is so irresistible to apply probability and stochastic calculus to it. However, this 'coincidence' may provide, by the same token, the best laboratory wherein to test the shift I am talking about, from probability to that other general category. A category I would like to call, for lack of a better word, the category of 'price'.

What I am pointing to is that, just as the category of probability is generally applied to events in the traditional sense of realizations of possibility in metrical time and just as it is vulnerable to contingency as a result, just so, *the general category of price might have to be applied to events in the realm of virtuality and intensive time*: to events in the true sense of contingency and unpredictability (to events unmediated by the parasitic notion of possibility). According to my proposition, prices are no longer the numbers produced in the market we all know; they become more general than that. Only in the market we know do prices turn out to be numbers, and hence are we tempted to apply probability to them instead of simply applying them to themselves.

19 SUPPRESSING POSSIBILITY

Consider: there are no possibilities or probabilities in the market (and the market is what's real) but only contingent claims and prices. What happens in the market, events, are not the realizations of possibilities (the draws from the random generator or stochastic process), but the process of writing of payoffs of contingent claims. Likewise, there are no possibilities or probabilities in the world (in History): only contingent events take place and all genuine events are unpredictable. Now, if an event is by definition a 'Black Swan' (Taleb 2007), an occurrence that simply was not part of the previous range of possibilities and that can be explained, for this reason, only after the fact, only through the backward narrative, only after the event has taught us what new range of possibilities to adopt and what possibilities *will have led* to the event; if the event is, by definition, what so upsets and exceeds possibility, then why should we rest content and adopt that as the definition of the event? Should we insist on defining the event as being always an exception? Since there are only events and there is no possibility, since history is filled with events, why keep possibility at all? What could be the use of defining something very real and very material (the event) as the systematic exception to a domain that doesn't even exist? Really, what would the world (or, for our present purposes, the market) look like if there were no possibility and no probability?

This proposition of mine might sound inconceivable as it might lead to thinking that there will therefore only be necessity or impossibility. No! Necessity and impossibility are *correlative* to possibility (necessity is the sum of all possibilities, and impossibility is their absence), so they are abstractions just like possibility and they go if it goes. Still, my proposition might sound inconceivable as I seem to be suppressing prediction when I suppress possibility and probability. 'Just how could prediction be suppressed?' asks my objector. Well, can it be maintained? We all agree that events are unpredictable, so if there are events, why keep prediction? After *The Black Swan*, I predict the writing of *The Blank Swan*.

20 THINKING OF CONTINGENCY INSTEAD

Possibility can only be substantiated by the mechanism of backward narrative, so the only reason we keep it, ahead of the event, is the *anticipation of the backward narrative*: we remember our past 'successes' in explaining the event after the fact and for this reason we project an abstract domain, not yet necessarily differentiated into specific individual possibilities—as these will be singled out after the event. We project a potential domain, the possibility of possibility, so to speak. However, if possibility is, in practice, always numerically useless because possibilities become distinct and recognizable only after the event, why even keep possibility as category? Possibility comes after the real (it is a copy—Bergson, Deleuze); the real is made of contingency.

We should be able to think of contingency without thinking of possibility. This is very difficult, because the two tend to be confused. A real Gestalt switch is needed here. We cannot separate the two 'at rest'. Thinking of contingency at rest is automatically inviting possibility, as possibility is the representation of contingency and presents itself to mind automatically as soon as we think of contingency. So maybe we should think of contingency *without thinking*; or rather, we should think it in a state, not of rest, but of entrainment, or in a state of motion (or infinite speed, as Deleuze would say). What we should do is start with the contingent claim, try and confuse the difference it makes with the triggering of its payoff in possibility (as we usually do), project a stochastic process, value the contingent claim by replication, realize it turns redundant, and only then, at the moment when we recall in a flash that the contingent claim *wasn't* immersed in that medium (the market) and in that time line (which is just history) to end up redundant, get a glimpse of the way in which contingency is different from possibility and the market is precisely this transversal medium.

How to best think of contingency without thinking of possibility might eventually come down to thinking of the market and of market prices. Simply make that leap. Here the medium, the transmission, is faster than thought. We don't need to think: we simply leap inside the market.

Why do we need possibility in the end? In a way, we always need it in order to roll back to the present. Standing in the present spot, we consider different possibilities, we weigh them up. Implicit in every thought of possibility is an evaluation: the assigning of probability and the computation of an expectation of some kind. Possibilities are cast from the real and they are 'reeled back' to the real. Since contingency is real and is always with us, why do we need this movement of unreeling and reeling back? Probably our fear is that, if contingency is really with us at infinite speed, we will always be 'too late' unless we have possibility to lean on. We need the *room* of possibility (with the projection screen on which we visualize different possibilities) in order to take a break and pause, in order to *consider* contingency and somehow slow it down. For one thing, we need to put numbers on contingency: we need the probability. How indeed could we have numbers and probability if we just withdrew possibility?

The answer is that we do not need any mediation of contingency other that the 'immediate and immanent' medium of the market and we do not need any numbers other than prices. To repeat, we already have contingent claims, we already have prices and we already have the market; so why ask for anything else? That it is a complete blunder to superimpose possibility on *this* reality should be evident from the fact that every attempt to price contingent claims in possibility (i.e. through the stochastic process and dynamic replication) inevitably results in recalibration and in defeating the model. When prices of contingent claims are interpreted as the original events that they are, they will always diverge from the prediction of any replicating algorithm that may have valued them of late, literally producing a Black Swan event for the domain of possibility underlying this valuation. From the point of view of possibility, the market line is a continuous series of Black Swan events. From the point of view of the market, possibility is only a pretext to precisely *write what exceeds it*: to replicate the contingent claims in order to trade them. That is to say, *possibility is only here to introduce us to contingency*; that is why we need it and why we need derivative valuation theory and models. However, we shall never pause to predict or to expect to be *right*; we shall always *write*.

21 CONCLUSION

We have attempted to genetically deduce the market from the historical event of the conversion of debt into equity. This event can be related, historically, to the year 1602 when the Dutch created the East India Company, the first joint stock company whose shares almost simultaneously started being exchanged in the 'street', subsequently necessitating the creation of the first stock exchange.

As such, the morphogenetic process engendering the market is not mediated by the category of probability or possibility. One of the strangest results of our deduction of the market is that we don't come up, as expected, with equity (or stock) as the consequence of the conversion of debt into equity but directly with the contingent claim.

In the logic of our deduction, the contingent claim precedes the notion of exchange and market, and precedes the notion of price. It precedes them only just, because the exchange and the market and the price will also be deduced in one and the same movement. The idea is that, *insofar as* the contingent claim is the direct result of the conversion, it cannot but get carried along by its own momentum and subsequently produce the market and become translated into price. *Insofar as it results from the conversion of debt, the contingent claim is the exchange is the market.*

One of the main benefits of this direct deduction is to short-circuit the category of possibility and of the stochastic process and to build a notion of the contingent claim (and thus of contingency) and of its 'future' price that will be *independent of possibility* and even of time. Possibility and chronological time come after contingency and are only incidental on it. This will come as a shock to all the theoreticians of derivative valuation, who cannot formulate their problem except within probability and temporal processes.

The other benefit is that the contingency-market-price complex is obtained in one stroke, following the conversion. Contingent claim, exchange place and price are facets of one and the same concept. Thus the market and speculation are not detachable parts of the conversion, and one cannot desire the conversion (as one most definitely should, since one most definitely wishes to escape the degenerate notion of debt and the dogmatism attached to it) without getting the market and speculation in the same stroke.

A APPENDIX

We have identified the *pricing tool* as a tool that must make use of possibility or the stochastic process as one of its working parts, never as its ultimate frame. As a matter of fact, it must flee the metaphysics of possibility as surely as the conversion flees the petrified dogma of credit. As pricing tool, it must deal with the *prices* of contingent claims, not with the *values* of derivatives, in as much as contingency is always original and never derivative, as it is precisely what exceeds possibility and always upsets it—what can never be replicated and made redundant by the algorithm of possibility.

$B + \Delta S$ was the outcome of the conversion. This, we recognized as the 'future' dynamic replication strategy of the contingent claim. However, we did not advance in that direction and we stood still at the crossroads where possibility and chronological time were not yet open and would not yet deploy the algorithm of dynamic replication.

On the contrary, we read $B + \Delta S$ as a material sign not as a conceptual project, the sign that the market maker had to remain rooted to the floor, inserted between the market price processes of both underlying *and* contingent claim. He must use replication as the best way to step *outside* possibility into sheer contingency and not as the surest way to lock himself up inside possibility and redundancy. Only because the market maker holds tightly on $B + \Delta S$ is he able to invert the model, or the formulas of possibility, against the market, thus calibrating and recalibrating the model.

Recalibration is the real market process, and it cannot evolve in possibility or be modelled as a stochastic process. It parallels the process of differentiation whereby payoffs of increasing complexity keep being generated, not the process of generation of data by a random generator. Recalibration is the sign of contingency; it is the insurance that the market will never be completed and that the contingent claims will never turn redundant.

Recalibration means that any valuation model will virtually become stochastic and that the market price of any contingent claim, no matter how exotic or complex, will virtually act as a calibration input to the model. This imposes, as pricing tool, a structure that must be at once open and invariant. We believe the regime-switching model is one such.

Moreover, once we ascend to the domain of meta-probability and interpret the conversion (or the lesson from the genesis of the market and the contingent claim) as an appeal to embrace the mathematics of price and recalibration instead of the mathematics of probability and fixed states of the world, it will no longer matter that credit should still be around as a matter of fact and that we didn't manage to get rid of it.

So long as credit is priced in the market and our pricing tool is calibrated and recalibrated against it, our trading and pricing process will assume the right kind of differentiation and will never get petrified in a degenerative fantasy like the CDO. Pending the total abolition of credit, a market (for credit) remains the best way of avoiding the degenerative metaphysics of credit and collapse. (This shouldn't stop us from recounting the genesis of the market as the total transmutation of credit into equity, like we did in this article.) Hence, our regime-switching model, the pricing tool supposed to espouse the mathematics of price and to handle contingency instead of possibility, must include calibration to credit default swaps as an integral part of its logic and must be deployed in a general equity-to-credit framework.

In the following sections, we give a general description of the equity-to-credit regime-switching model and we explain how to value general contingent claims, including credit default swaps (CDS). The mathematics and the financial theory of the following framework have been charted and developed by Philippe Henrotte, professor of Finance at HEC Paris and head of financial theory at ITO 33.

A.1 Description of the regime-switching model

We first describe the main assumptions underlying our model. We start with the description of the regimes, we then briefly turn to the risk free yield curve and conclude with a precise description of the dividends that we consider. Finally we describe the probability distribution between regimes through time.

A.1.1 *Regimes*

There exists K volatility regimes, indexed from 1 to K, and one default regime, indexed by d. We assume the regimes are observable and known at any time. By convention, regime 1 can be set as the present regime when we use the model, either to value contingent claims or to calibrate the model against their market prices. We let the discrete variable u_t describe the current regime at time t. The dynamic of the regime is driven by a continuous time Markov process with a finite number of states or regimes. The important correlation between the stock price and the volatility is captured by a possible jump on the stock price as a regime switch occurs. We chose to model jumps here by a very simple fixed percentage size jump, it would of course be possible to generalize to a density of jumps.

- $\hat{\lambda}_{k \to l}$ is the (risk-neutral) intensity of going from regime k to regime l. This occurs with a percentage jump $y_{k \to l}$ on the stock price.
- $\hat{\lambda}_{k \to d}$ is the (risk-neutral) intensity of going from regime k to default. The corresponding jump on the stock price is $y_{k \to d}$. When $y_{k \to d} = -1$, the stock goes to zero upon default.
- We let Λ be the vector of default intensities, with $\Lambda_k = \hat{\lambda}_{k \to d}$ for k between 1 and K.

- We let v_k and v_d be the volatility in regime k and in default respectively. The jumps indexed from $i = K$ to J correspond to stock price jumps inside a regime, which may be the default regime. Both the size and the intensity of the jumps depend on the regime.
- In every regime, we index the jumps in the following way. For i between 1 and $(K - 1)$, the jump corresponds to a regime switch, which is also denoted $y_{k \to l}$ if the current regime is k and if the jump goes into regime l. For i between K and J, the jump is a pure stock price jump within a regime. For $i = (J + 1)$ the jump corresponds to default, also denoted $y_{k \to d}$ if the current regime is k.
- There is no recovery from the default regime so that $\hat{\lambda}_{d \to k} = 0$. There may however be jumps on the stock price within the default regime.
- We let A be the $K \times K$ matrix (in general non symmetric) given, for k and l between 1 and K, by:

$$A_{k,l} = \hat{\lambda}_{l \to k} \qquad\qquad \text{for } k \neq l,$$

$$A_{k,k} = -\sum_{l \neq k} \hat{\lambda}_{k \to l} - \hat{\lambda}_{k \to d} \qquad\qquad \text{when } k = l.$$

- We let τ be the stopping time describing the time of default, that is the time when we reach the default regime.

A.1.2 Risk-free yield curve

For simplicity, we consider a non-stochastic risk-free term structure and we denote r_t the deterministic instantaneous forward rate at time t. The value at time t of the risk-free zero coupon bond with maturity T and nominal 1 is given by $\exp(-\int_t^T r_s ds)$. We consider the most general setting with both continuous and discrete time dividends, although both are usually not present at the same time. r_t^f is the non-stochastic continuous dividend rate at time t (this notation stems from the foreign exchange market).

A.1.3 Regime probability

- For $0 \leq t \leq T$, we let $\hat{\pi}(t, u_t; T, k)$ be the (risk-neutral) probability to be in the non-default regime k at time T, knowing that we are in the non-default regime u_t at time t. We collect these K conditional probabilities in the vector $\hat{\pi}(t, u_t; T)$ with $\hat{\pi}(t, u_t; T)_k$ given by $\hat{\pi}(t, u_t; T, k)$.
- We let $\hat{\pi}(t, u_t; T, d)$ be the (risk-neutral) probability to be in default at time T, knowing that we are in non-default regime u_t at time t. Because no recovery from default is possible, it is also the probability to have fallen in default anytime between t and T, that is the probability that $\tau \leq T$, knowing that the regime at time t is u_t.
- For every maturity T we have

$$\hat{\pi}(t, u_t; T, d) = 1 - \sum_{k=1}^{K} \hat{\pi}(t, u_t; T, k),$$

and for $T = t$ we have $\hat{\pi}(t, u_t; t, u_t) = 1$, $\hat{\pi}(t, u_t; t, d) = 0$, and $\hat{\pi}(t, u_t; t, k) = 0$ for $k \neq u_t$.
- The vector $\hat{\pi}(t, u_t; T)$ solves the following forward ODE with constant coefficients

$$\frac{\partial \hat{\pi}}{\partial T} = A \hat{\pi}(t, u_t; T).$$

- Since no recovery from default is possible, we obtain at the limit that $\hat{\pi}(t, u_t; +\infty) = 0$ and $\hat{\pi}(t, u_t; +\infty, d) = 1$.

- Because of the time homogeneity of our model, we remark that

$$\hat{\pi}(t, u_t; T) = \hat{\pi}(0, u_t; T - t).$$

- We also remark that $\Lambda' \hat{\pi}(t, u_t; T)$ is the intensity of falling into default at time T, knowing that the regime at time t is u_t.

A.2 general backward equations

We consider a general derivative instrument with value $F(t, S_t, u_t)$ at time t when the stock price is S_t and the current regime is u_t. We have the following partial decoupling between the non-default regimes and the default one.

- The value $F(t, S_t, d)$ in the default regime can be computed on a stand-alone basis, without knowledge of F in the non-default regimes.
- The value of F in the non-default regimes gives rise to K coupled equations, which involve in general the value of F in the default regime, unless the derivative is a call and the stock goes to zero upon default.

A.2.1 Stand-alone default regime

We start by evaluating the value of the general derivative F in the default regime. It is given by the following stand-alone equation, which does not depend on the value of F in the non-default regimes.

$$\frac{\partial F}{\partial t} + \frac{1}{2} v_d^2 S_t^2 \frac{\partial^2 F}{\partial S_t^2} + \left(r - r^f - \sum_{j=K}^{J} \hat{\lambda}_j y_j \right) S_t \frac{\partial F}{\partial S_t}$$

$$+ \sum_{j=K}^{J} \hat{\lambda}_j \left(F(t, S_t(1 + y_j), d) - F(t, S_t, d) \right) = r F, \quad (1)$$

with appropriate boundary conditions. The sums $\sum_{j=K}^{J} \hat{\lambda}_j y_j$ and $\sum_{j=K}^{J} \hat{\lambda}_j \Delta F$ correspond to stock price jumps inside the default regime.

A.2.2 Coupled non-default regimes

For every non-default regime u_t,

$$\frac{\partial F}{\partial t} + \frac{1}{2} v_{u_t}^2 S_t^2 \frac{\partial^2 F}{\partial S_t^2} + \left(r - r^f - \sum_{j=1}^{J+1} \hat{\lambda}_j y_j \right) S_t \frac{\partial F}{\partial S_t}$$

$$+ \sum_{j=K}^{J} \hat{\lambda}_j \left(F(t, S_t(1 + y_j), u_t) - F(t, S_t, u_t) \right)$$

$$+ \sum_{l \neq u_t} \hat{\lambda}_{u_t \to l} \left(F(t, S_t(1 + y_{u_t \to l}), l) - F(t, S_t, u_t) \right)$$

$$+ \hat{\lambda}_{u_t \to d} \left(F(t, S_t(1 + y_{u_t \to d}), d) - F(t, S_t, u_t) \right) = r F, \quad (2)$$

again with appropriate boundary conditions. A few remarks concerning this equation:

- We check that in the general case we need here the value of F in the default regime. In the special case where F is the value of a call and the stock price goes to zero upon default with $y_{u_t \to d} = -1$, since the value of the call is zero when the stock price is zero, we derive that $F(t, S_t(1 + y_{u_t \to d}), d) = F(t, 0, d) = 0$ and the default regime is not needed.
- The sum $\sum_{j=1}^{J+1} \hat{\lambda}_j y_j$ corresponds to a sum on all stock price jumps that may occur from the current regime u_t, both inside the regime and from the regime u_t to another one, including default. Although the notation is not explicit, the terms of this sum depend on the current regime u_t.
- The sum $\sum_{j=K}^{J} \hat{\lambda}_j \Delta F$ corresponds to the the stock price jumps inside the current regime u_t.
- The sum $\sum_{l \neq u_t} \hat{\lambda}_{u_t \to l} \Delta F$ corresponds to the changes in regime, from the current regime u_t to the other non-default regimes indexed by l.
- The last term $\hat{\lambda}_{u_t \to d} \Delta F$ corresponds to a jump from the current regime u_t to default.

A.2.3 Dividends

In absence of arbitrage, the derivative must be continuous across the payment of dividends. At a time t_i when a fixed dividend $d_i(S_{t_i-})$ is paid by the company, we have,

$$F(t_i-, S_{t_i-}, u_{t_i}) = F(t_i, S_{t_i}, u_{t_i}) = F(t_i, S_{t_i-} - d_i(S_{t_i-}), u_{t_i}),$$

where u_{t_i} can be any regime, including default.

The same reasoning applies for proportional dividends. At a time t_j when a proportional dividend $\delta_j S_{t_j-}$ is paid by the company, we have,

$$F(t_j-, S_{t_j-}, u_{t_j}) = F(t_j, S_{t_j}, u_{t_j}) = F(t_j, (1 - \delta_j)S_{t_j-}, u_{t_j}),$$

where again u_{t_j} can be any regime, including default.

A.3 Credit default swaps

A.3.1 Definitions

We describe the contingent cash flows of the CDS, when the current time is t and the current non-default regime is u_t.

- The nominal of the CDS is 1.
- The payment frequency of the premium is Δt, a fraction of a year, which can be 1 for one year, $1/2$ for a semester, $1/4$ for a quarter, or $1/12$ for one month.
- We let $N \geq 1$ be the number of remaining premium payments, assuming no default up to maturity of the CDS.
- The first premium payment occurs at time t_1, with the constraint that $0 < (t_1 - t) \leq \Delta t$.
- The remaining premium payments occur after t_1 with a constant interval Δt, which means that the dates of premium payments write $t_i = t_1 + (i-1)\Delta t$ for i between 1 and N.
- The maturity T of the CDS is the last premium payment, that is $T = t_N = t_1 + (N-1)\Delta t$.
- We define $t_0 = t_1 - \Delta t$, which is either the date of the last premium payment before t, or the issue date of the CDS.
- S is the premium of the CDS paid until default with the payment frequency Δt after the first payment date t_1. If default occurs at time τ and the last premium payment was at time t_i, then the buyer of insurance still owes the accrued premium, defined as the linear fraction of the next premium payment, that is $S(\tau - t_i)/\Delta t$.

- We let R be the recovery, between zero and one. Upon default, the party insured receives $(1 - R)$ at the time τ of default, if default occurs before maturity T, and nothing otherwise.
- For a time t and a regime u_t, we let $F^{CDS}(t, u_t; t_1, \Delta t, N, S, R)$ be the value at time t when the regime is u_t of the CDS with premium S and recovery R, whose sequence of premium payment dates are described by t_1, the date of the first one, Δt the constant time between two premium payments after the first one, and N the total number of premium payments. Its maturity is $T = t_1 + (N - 1)\Delta t$. This value assumes the point of view of the party who seeks the default insurance and who pays the streams of premia in exchange for a compensation in case of default. When $u_t = d$, we assume that default occurred at time t exactly, and $F^{CDS}(t, d; t_1, \Delta t, N, S, R)$ values the benefit of the insurance upon default. At a time t_i of premium payment, we assume that $F^{CDS}(t_i, u_t; t_1, \Delta t, N, S, R)$ corresponds to the value ex premium payment, that is just after payment of the premium S. When $(t_1, \Delta t, N)$, the maturity T, the premium S, and the recovery R are understood, we simply write $F^{CDS}(t, u_t)$.

A.3.2 Value in default

We let $F^{CDS}(t, d)$ be the value of the CDS at time t assuming that default has occurred at time t. It is the difference between the compensation immediately received and the accrued premium still owed,

$$F^{CDS}(t, d) = 1 - R - S \frac{(t - [t])}{\Delta t}. \tag{3}$$

A.3.3 Backward equation

We derive a backward equation for the value $F^{CDS}(t, u_t)$ of the CDS. At maturity T and for every non-default regime k we have,

$$F^{CDS}(T, k) = 0,$$

$$F^{CDS}(T-, k) = -S,$$

since maturity T corresponds to the last premium payment. At a time t different from any premium payment date and for every non-default regime k we have

$$\frac{\partial F^{CDS}}{\partial t}(t, k) + \sum_{l \neq k} \hat{\lambda}_{k \to l} \left(F^{CDS}(t, l) - F^{CDS}(t, k) \right)$$

$$+ \hat{\lambda}_{k \to d} \left(F^{CDS}(t, d) - F^{CDS}(t, k) \right) = r F^{CDS}(t, k),$$

where the value in default $F^{CDS}(t, d)$ has been derived in equation (3). At a time $t_i = t_1 + (i - 1)\Delta t$ where the premium S is paid, we have

$$F^{CDS}(t_i-, k) = F^{CDS}(t_i, k) - S,$$

which means that the value of the CDS increases by S after each premium payment. This yields a system of K coupled backward equations.

A.4 Calibration

A spread curve of CDS at time $t = 0$ is a series of premia S and recovery rates R for various CDS maturities. Usually, the initial premium payment date t_1 and the interval Δt are fixed, and the maturity increases together with the number N of premium payments, following $T = t_1 + (N - 1)\Delta t$. The calibration of the model to the CDS yield curve is done by stating that the initial value of every CDS is zero, which means that $F^{CDS}(0, u_0; t_1, \Delta t, N, S, R) = 0$.

A 'volatility surface' at time $t = 0$ is a scatter of market prices of vanilla equity options of different strikes and maturity dates. The calibration of the model to the volatility surface is done by searching for the model parameters (i.e. all of v_k, v_d, $\hat{\lambda}_{k \to l}$, $y_{k \to l}$, $\hat{\lambda}_{k \to d}$, $y_{k \to d}$) such that option values and CDS values, as computed by the model, match as closely as possible the present market prices of these instruments (which are zero, for the CDS). The search is accomplished by least squares minimization, where the instruments can be weighted differently if need be.

A typical implementation of the regime-switching model is one with three regimes, with no jumps occurring within a regime (i.e. jumps can only trigger regime switching), and with a single jump taking us from any regime to the other (including default). Also, typically $y_{k \to d} = -1$, and everything stops after default with the stock price absorbed at zero.

It is certainly possible to be even more parsimonious and to limit the model to only two regimes; however, we won't be able, in that case, to match term-structures of volatility or CDS spreads that are 'humped' (not monotonous).

In this typical three-regime implementation, we end up with 18 parameters:

- v_1, v_2, v_3, the Brownian volatility coeffcients in each of the three regimes.
- $\hat{\lambda}_{1 \to d}$, $\hat{\lambda}_{2 \to d}$, $\hat{\lambda}_{3 \to d}$, the default intensities in each of the three regimes.
- $\hat{\lambda}_{1 \to 2}$, $\hat{\lambda}_{1 \to 3}$, $\hat{\lambda}_{2 \to 1}$, $\hat{\lambda}_{2 \to 3}$, $\hat{\lambda}_{3 \to 1}$, $\hat{\lambda}_{3 \to 2}$, each of the intensities of switching from one non-default regime to the other.
- $y_{1 \to 2}$, $y_{1 \to 3}$, $y_{2 \to 1}$, $y_{2 \to 3}$, $y_{3 \to 1}$, $y_{3 \to 2}$, the corresponding jump sizes.

A.5 Recalibration

Recalibration, we have said, is the real (or virtual) market process. It certainly cannot be modelled as a stochastic process for then this process would itself be prone to recalibration and to stochastic change. As a matter of fact, recalibration, or the market process, does not even take place in chronological time! It unfolds in intensive time, what we have called the 'pit'. Recalibration is the process of differentiation whereby no contingent claim shall ever be redundant.

Any instance of the regime-switching model, for example our three-regime implementation above, is only a 'diagram', a stage where we momentarily pause in order to draw and diagram the infinitely fracturing fractal. Why so? Because this instantiation is an actual stochastic process which actually freezes the market and withdraws it from the intensity of the pit. Indeed, no matter how many regimes and jumps our diagram may include, no matter how incomplete the market that it represents may be, there will definitely come a stage of the continually creative process of differentiation of payoffs of contingent claims where every subsequent payoff will turn out to be dynamically perfectly replicable by a combination of payoffs created before that stage. In other words, there will come a stage where all the subsequent contingent claims become redundant and the market is denied.

Another way of pressing the point is to remark that the parameters of any instance of the regime-switching model (for example, the 18 parameters above) are 'instantaneously' made stochastic and do not have to wait to be recalibrated over time to that end, because the intention (or intension) of any pricing model is to price *and* trade contingent claims and because to be pricing contingent claims with the intention of trading them is to be assuming, from the beginning, that they will trade at variance with the theoretical value one is computing for them. For example, any trader using the Black-Scholes-Merton model to price vanilla options is *ipso facto* assuming that implied volatility shall be (as a matter of fact, is already) stochastic. For this reason, regime-switching can appear as the 'virtualization' or the making sense of BSM. It pursues the *implications* of BSM in the way of the market and the virtual. By contrast, models that have traditionally succeeded to BSM in the literature of derivative pricing are just *complications* of it in the way of possibility.

Imagine that we recalibrate our three-regime switching model in time. Imagine a calibration, followed by a recalibration the next day. Calibration against the surface of vanilla options and the CDS curve cannot in fact guarantee the unicity of the set of parameters. The minimization problem admits of multiple local minima and the indetermination can only be lifted by adding *other* payoff structures, or exotics, in the calibration procedure. The multiple local minima thus become a single global minimum. The current saying is that different smile models can very well agree on the same volatility smile and same CDS curve yet disagree on the smile dynamics, or equivalently, that they disagree on the pricing of exotics (such as barrier options, or forward starting options). Only if we calibrate the smile model to the relevant exotics simultaneously with the vanillas are we guaranteed to discriminate between the different smile dynamics.

So imagine that we calibrate our three-regime switching model, not just against the vanillas and the CDS curve, but against what it takes of exotic options for the calibration to admit of a unique solution. The price of any other imaginable exotic is now imposed, as we have no further leeway and our information set is complete. As soon as we notice, however, that the parameters do change the following day because of recalibration, we come to the conclusion that the 'real' model wasn't in fact a three-regime switching model, but a larger model which switches between the two three-regime instantiations of day 1 and day 2, in other words, a six-regime switching model.

The corollary is that our calibration wasn't actually uniquely determined from the start, because a six-regime switching model actually needs to be calibrated against exotics in greater number and of even higher degree of complexity than before, in order to admit of a unique set of parameters. This means that the prices of the 'other imaginable exotics' weren't in fact imposed. As a matter of fact, if such prices had been available in the market, they would have helped us *reduce* the indetermination of the calibration of the six-regime switching model, etc.

Now, the whole trick of moving from the actual to the virtual while remaining in the real is to think that the six-regime switching model *is* in reality our model from the beginning, only we have 'diagrammed' it under three regimes. (Indeed, there is no way to tell whether each of the initial three regimes isn't in reality a superposition of two identical regimes waiting to get differentiated.) And why stop there? As we have said, any pricing model virtually becomes stochastic; so not only six, but a twelve-regime switching model is in reality our model from the beginning; and why not twenty-four regimes, an infinity of regimes, etc.?

The whole idea is to stop thinking that this infinity of regimes is progressively revealed *over time*, as a consequence of the recalibration making any previous model stochastic, and to start thinking that this infinity is *virtually* present from the beginning. It is 'progressively' revealed only to the extent that we *practically* limit our progress at the beginning and *practically* limit our calibration to the vanillas, the CDS, and a few exotics.

Recalibration, in a word, is not a process of recalibration over time, but the instantaneous process of 'mentally' defeating any calibration we may have actually performed, and of thinking that we could have virtually calibrated, instead, against a larger set of exotics of higher degree of complexity, if only their prices had been actually available.

But does it really matter if they're not? For this is the market we are standing in, not a stochastic process, and the market is at once virtual and real. What the market really means is that all the prices of all sorts of contingent claims are virtually present *and* are not redundant. All we need, consequently, in order to solve the problem of recalibration, is a model that we can *virtually* calibrate against any kind of exotic payoff of any degree of complexity and that we can virtually expand to any number of regimes, even if it means that this expansion will be retro-jected in the past by a backward narrative.

The fractal is *already* infinitely fractured, it is already past, even if it means that the diagrams of increasing fracturing and differentation are actually only visible in the future of our drawing.

REFERENCES

Ayache, E. (2006). 'What is implied by implied volatility?' *Wilmott* (Jan.), 28–35.

—— (2007). 'Nassim Taleb author of the blank swan'. *Wilmott* (Sept.), 44–53.

—— (2010). *The Blank Swan: The End of Probability*. London: Wiley & Sons.

Barthes, R. (2002). *Œuvres complètes*, Vol. 4. Paris: Éditions du Seuil.

Bergson, H. (1998). *Creative Evolution*. New York: Dover Publications.

DeLanda, M. (2002). *Intensive Science and Virtual Philosophy*. London and New York: Continuum.

Deleuze, G. (1990). *The Logic of Sense*, trans. M. Lester. New York: Columbia University Press.

—— (1994). *Difference and Repetition*, trans. P. Patton. New York: Columbia University Press.

Ferguson, N. (2008). *The Ascent of Money: A Financial History of the World*. London: Allen Lane.

Meillassoux, Q. (2008). *After Finitude: An Essay on the Necessity of Contingency*, trans. Ray Brassier. London and New York: Continuum.

Parr, A., (ed.) (2005). *The Deleuze Dictionary*. New York: Columbia University Press.

Taleb, N. N. (2007). *The Black Swan: The Impact of the Highly Impossible*. New York: Random House.

Zourabichvili, F. (2004). *La Philosophie de Deleuze*. Paris: Presses Universitaires de France. Chapter 'Deleuze: une philosophie de l'événement'.

CHAPTER 14

AN EVT PRIMER
FOR CREDIT RISK

VALÉRIE CHAVEZ-DEMOULIN AND
PAUL EMBRECHTS

1 INTRODUCTION

IT is 30 September 2008, 9.00 a.m. CET. Our pen touches paper for writing a first
version of this introduction, just at the moment that European markets are to open
after the US Congress in a first round defeated the bill for a USD 700 Bio fund in aid of
the financial industry. The industrialized world is going through the worst economic
crisis since the Great Depression of the 1930s. It is definitely *not* our aim to give a
historic overview of the events leading up to this calamity, others are much more
competent for doing so; see for instance Crouhy, Jarrow and Turnbull (2008) and
Acharya and Richardson (2009). Nor will we update the events, now possible in real
time, of how this crisis evolves. When this chapter is in print, the world of finance will
have moved on. Wall Street as well as Main Street will have taken the consequences.
The whole story started with a credit crisis linked to the American housing market.
The so-called sub-prime crisis was no doubt the trigger, the real cause however lies
much deeper in the system and does worry the public much, much more. Only these
couple of lines should justify our contribution as indeed two words implicitly jump
out of every public communication on the subject: *extreme* and *credit*. The former
may appear in the popular press under the guise of a *Black Swan* (Taleb 2007) or a *1 in
1,000 year event*, or even as the *unthinkable*. The latter presents itself as a *liquidity
squeeze*, or a *drying up of interbank lending*, or indeed the *sub-prime crisis*. Looming
above the whole crisis is the fear for a systemic risk (which should not be confused
with systematic risk) of the world's financial system; the failure of one institution

The authors take pleasure in thanking the editors and David Hoaglin for several comments to an
earlier version of the chapter.

implies, like a domino effect, the downfall of others around the globe. In many ways the worldwide regulatory framework in use, referred to as the Basel Capital Accord, was not able to stem such a systemic risk, though early warnings were available; see Daníelsson et al. (2005). So what went wrong? And more importantly, how can we start fixing the system. Some of the above references give a first summary of proposals.

It should by now be abundantly clear to anyone only vaguely familiar with some of the technicalities underlying modern financial markets, that answering these questions is a very tough call indeed. Any solution that aims at bringing stability and healthy, sustainable growth back into the world economy can only be achieved by very many efforts from all sides of society. Our chapter will review only one very small method-ological piece of this global jigsaw-puzzle, Extreme Value Theory (EVT). None of the tools, techniques, regulatory guidelines, or political decisions currently put forward will be *the* panacea ready to cure all the diseases of the financial system. As scientists, we do however have to be much more forthcoming in stating why certain tools are more useful than others, and also why some are definitely ready for the wastepaper basket. Let us mention one story here to make a point. One of us, in September 2007, gave a talk at a conference attended by several practitioners on the topic of the weaknesses of Value-at-Risk based risk management. In the ensuing round table discussion, a regulator voiced humbleness saying that, after that critical talk against VaR, one should perhaps rethink some aspects of the regulatory framework. To which the Chief Risk Officer of a bigger financial institution sitting next to him whispered 'No, no, you are doing just fine.' It is this 'stick your head in the sand' kind of behaviour we as scientists *have* the mandate to fight against.

So this chapter aims at providing the basics any risk manager should know on the modelling of extremal events, and this from a past-present-future research perspec-tive. Such events are often also referred to as low probability events or rare events, a language we will use interchangeably throughout this chapter. The choice of topics and material discussed are rooted in finance, and especially in credit risk. In section 2 we start with an overview of the credit risk specific issues within Quantitative Risk Management (QRM) and show where relevant EVT related questions are being asked. Section 3 presents the one-dimensional theory of extremes, whereas section 4 is con-cerned with the multivariate case. In section 5 we discuss particular applications and give an outlook on current research in the field. We conclude in section 6.

Though this chapter has a review character, we stay close to an advice once given to us by Benoit Mandelbrot: 'Never allow more than ten references to a paper.' We will not be able to fully adhere to this principle, but we will try. As a consequence, we guide the reader to some basic references which best suit the purpose of the chapter, and more importantly, that of its authors. Some references we allow to be mentioned from the start. Whenever we refer to QRM, the reader is expected to have McNeil, Frey, and Embrechts (2005) (referred to throughout as MFE) close at hand for further results, extra references, notation, and background material. Similarly, an overview of one-dimensional EVT relevant for us is Embrechts, Klüppelberg, and Mikosch (1997) (EKM). For general background on credit risk, we suggest Bluhm and Overbeck (2007) and the relevant chapters in Crouhy, Galai, and Mark (2001). The latter text also provides a more applied overview of financial risk management.

2 EXTREMAL EVENTS AND CREDIT RISK

Credit risk is presumably the oldest risk type facing a bank: it is the risk that the originator of a financial product (a mortgage, say) faces as a function of the (in)capability of the obligor to honour an agreed stream of payments over a given period of time. The reason we recall the above definition is that, over the recent years, credit risk has become rather difficult to put one's finger on. In a meeting several years ago, a banker asked us, 'Where is all the credit risk hiding?'... If only one had taken this question more seriously at the time. Modern product development, and the way credit derivatives and structured products are traded on OTC markets, have driven credit risk partly into the underground of financial markets. One way of describing 'underground' for banks no doubt is 'off-balance sheet'. Also regulators are becoming increasingly aware of the need for a combined view on market and credit risk. A most recent manifestation of this fact is the new regulatory guideline (within the Basel II and III framework) for an incremental risk charge (IRC) for all positions in the trading book with migration/default risk. Also, regulatory arbitrage drove the creativity of (mainly) investment banks to singular heights trying to repackage credit risk in such a way that the bank could get away with a minimal amount of risk capital. Finally, excessive leverage allowed to increase the balance sheet beyond any acceptable level, leading to extreme losses when markets turned and liquidity dried up.

For the purpose of this chapter, below we give examples of (in some cases, comments on) credit risk related questions where EVT technology plays (can/should play) a role. At this point we like to stress that, though we very much resent the silo thinking still found in risk management, we will mainly restrict ourselves to credit risk related issues. Most of the techniques presented do however have a much wider range of applicability; indeed, several of the results basically come to life at the level of risk aggregation and the holistic view on risk.

Example 1. Estimation of default probabilities (DP). Typically, the DP of a credit (institution) over a given time period $[0, T]$, say, is the probability that at time T, the value of the institution, $V(T)$, falls below the (properly defined) value of debt $D(T)$, hence for institution i, $PD_i(T) = P(V_i(T) < D_i(T))$. For good credits, these probabilities are typically very small, hence the events $\{V_i(T) < D_i(T)\}$ are *rare* or *extreme*. In credit rating agency language (in this example, Moody's), for instance for $T = 1$ year, $PD_A(1) = 0.4\%$, $PD_B(1) = 4.9\%$, $PD_{Aa}(1) = 0.0\%$, $PD_{Ba}(1) = 1.1\%$. No doubt recent events will have changed these numbers, but the message is clear: for good quality credits, default was deemed very small. This leads to possible applications of one-dimensional EVT. A next step would involve the estimation of the so-called

LGD, loss given default. This is typically an expected value of a financial instrument (a corporate bond, say) given that the rare event of default has taken place. This naturally leads to threshold or exceedance models; see section 4, around (29).

Example 2. In portfolio models, several credit risky securities are combined. In these cases one is not only interested in estimating the marginal default probabilities $P D_i(T)$, $i = 1, \ldots, d$, but much more importantly *the joint default probabilities*, for $I \subset \mathbf{d} = \{1, \ldots, d\}$

$$P D_{\mathbf{d}}^I(T) = P \left(\{V_i(T) < D_i(T), i \in I\} \cap \{V_j(T) \geq D_j(T), j \in \mathbf{d}\backslash I\}\right). \quad (1)$$

For these kind of problems *multivariate* EVT (MEVT) presents itself as a possible tool.

Example 3. Based on models for (1), structured products like ABSs, CDOs, CDSs, MBSs, CLOs, credit baskets etc. can (hopefully) be priced and (even more hopefully) hedged. In all of these examples, the interdependence (or more specifically, the *copula*) between the underlying random events plays a crucial role. Hence we need a better understanding of the dependence between extreme (default) events. Copula methodology in general has been (mis)used extensively in this area. A critical view on the use of correlation is paramount here.

Example 4. Instruments and portfolios briefly sketched above are then aggregated at the global bank level, their risk is measured and the resulting numbers enter eventually into the Basel II and III capital adequacy ratio of the bank. If we abstract from the precise application, one is typically confronted with r risk measures $RM_1, \ldots, RM_r$, each of which aims at estimating a rare event like $RM_i = \mathrm{VaR}_{i,99.9}(T = 1)$, the 1-year, 99.9% Value-at-Risk for position i. Besides the statistical estimation (and proper understanding!) of such risk measures, the question arises how to combine r risk measures into one number (given that this would make sense) and how to take possible diversification and concentration effects into account. For a better understanding of the underlying problems, (M)EVT enters here in a fundamental way. Related problems involve scaling, both in the confidence level as well as the time horizon underlying the specific risk measure. Finally, backtesting the statistical adequacy of the risk measure used is of key importance. Overall, academic worries on how wise it is to keep on using VaR-like risk measures ought to be taken more seriously.

Example 5. Simulation methodology. Very few structured products in credit can be priced and hedged analytically. That is, numerical as well as simulation/Monte Carlo tools are called for. The latter lead to the important field of rare event simulation and resampling of extremal events. Under resampling schemes we think for instance of the bootstrap, the jackknife, and cross-validation. Though these techniques do not typically belong to standard (M)EVT, knowing about their strengths and limitations, especially for credit risk analysis, is extremely important. A more in-depth knowledge of EVT helps in better understanding the properties of such simulation tools. We return to this topic later in section 5.

Example 6. In recent crises, as with LTCM and the sub-prime crisis, larger losses often occurred because of the sudden widening of credit spreads, or the simultaneous increase in correlations between different assets; a typical diversification breakdown. Hence one needs to investigate the influence of extremal events on credit spreads and measures of dependence, like correlation. This calls for a time dynamic theory, i.e. (multivariate) extreme value theory for stochastic processes.

Example 7. (Taking Risk to Extremes). This is the title of an article by Mara Der Hovanesian in *Business Week* of 23 May 2005(!). It was written in the wake of big hedge fund losses due to betting against GM stock while piling up on GM debt. The subtitle of the article reads 'Will derivatives cause a major blowup in the world's credit markets?' By now we (unfortunately) know that they did! Several quotes from the above article early on warned about possible (very) extreme events just around the corner:

- '... a possible meltdown in credit derivatives if investors all tried to run for the exit at the same time.' (IMF)
- '... the rapid proliferation of derivatives products inevitably means that some will not have been adequately tested by market stress.' (Alan Greenspan)
- 'It doesn't need a 20% default rate across the corporate universe to set off a selling spree. One or two defaults can be very destructive.' (Anton Pil)
- 'Any apparently minor problem, such as a flurry of downgrades, could quickly engulf the financial system by sending markets into a tailspin, wiping out hedge funds, and dragging down banks that lent them money.' (*Bloomberg Business Week*)
- 'Any unravelling of CDOs has the potential to be extremely messy. There's just no way to measure what's at stake.' (Peter J. Petas)

The paper was about a potential credit tsunami and the way banks were using such derivatives products not as risk management tools, but rather as profit machines. All of the above disaster prophecies came true and much worse; extremes ran havoc. It will take many years to restore the (financial) system and bring it to the level of credibility a healthy economy needs.

Example 8. (A comment on 'Who's to blame'). Besides the widespread view about 'The secret formula that destroyed Wall Street' (see also section 5, in particular (31)), putting the blame for the current crisis in the lap of the financial engineers, academic economists also have to ask themselves some soul-searching questions. Some even speak of 'A systemic failure of academic economics'. Concerning mathematical finance having to take the blame, we side more with Roger Guesnerie (Collège de France) who said 'For this crisis, mathematicians are innocent ... and this in both meanings of the word.' Having said that, mathematicians have to take a closer look at practice and communicate much more vigorously the conditions under which their models are derived; see also the quotes in Example 10. The resulting *Model Uncertainty* for us is the key quantitative problem going forward; more on this later in the paper. See also the April 2009 publication 'Supervisory guidance for assessing banks' financial instrument fair value practices' by the Basel Committee on Banking Supervision. In it, it is stressed that 'While qualitative assessments are a useful starting point, it is desirable that banks develop methodologies that provide, to the extent possible, *quantitative* assessments (for valuation uncertainty).'

Example 9. (A comment on 'Early warning'). Of course, as one would expect just by the Law of Large Numbers, there were warnings early on. We all recall Warren Buffett's famous reference to (credit) derivatives as 'Financial weapons of mass destruction'. On the other hand, warnings like Example 7. and similar ones were largely ignored. What worries us as academics however much more is that seriously researched and carefully written documents addressed at the relevant regulatory or political authorities often met with total indifference or even silence. For the current credit crisis, a particularly worrying case is the 7 November 2005 report by Harry Markopolos mailed to the SEC referring to Madoff Investment Securities, LLC, as 'The world's largest hedge fund is a fraud'. Indeed, in a very detailed analysis, the author shows that Madoff's investment strategy is a Ponzi scheme, and this already in 2005! Three and a half years later and for some, several billion dollars poorer, we all learned unfortunately the hard and unpleasant way. More than anything else, the Markopolos Report clearly proves the need for quantitative skills on Wall Street: *read it*! During the Congressional hearings on Madoff, Markopolos referred to the SEC as being 'over-lawyered'. From our personal experience, we need to mention Daníelsson et al. (2005). This critical report was written as an official response to the, by then, new Basel II guidelines and was addressed to the Basel Committee on Banking Supervision. In it, some very critical comments were made on the over-use of VaR-technology and how the new guidelines 'taken altogether, will enhance both the procyclicality of regulation and the susceptibility of the financial system to systemic crises, thus negating the central purpose of the whole exercise. *Reconsider before it is too late.*' Unfortunately, this report also met with total silence, and most unfortunately, it was dead right with its warnings!

Example 10. (The Turner Review). It is interesting to see that in the recent Turner Review, 'A regulatory response to the global banking crisis', published in March 2009 by the FSA, among many more things, the bad handling of extreme events and the problems underlying VaR-based risk management were highlighted. Some relevant quotes are:

- *'Misplaced reliance on sophisticated maths.* The increasing scale and complexity of the securitised credit market was obvious to individual participants, to regulators and to academic observers. But the predominant assumption was that increased complexity had been matched by the evolution of mathematically sophisticated and effective techniques for measuring and managing the resulting risks. Central to many of the techniques was the concept of Value-at-Risk (VAR), enabling inferences about forward-looking risk to be drawn from the observation of past patterns of price movement. This technique, developed in the early 1990s, was not only accepted as standard across the industry, but adopted by regulators as the basis for calculating trading risk and required capital, (being incorporated for instance within the European Capital Adequacy Directive). There are, however, fundamental questions about the validity of VAR as a measure of risk . . .' (Indeed, see Danielsson et al. (2005)).

- 'The use of VAR to measure risk and to guide trading strategies was, however, only one factor among many which created the dangers of strongly procyclical market interactions. More generally the shift to an increasingly securitised form of credit intermediation and the increased complexity of securitised credit relied upon market practices which, while rational from the point of view of individual participants, increased the extent to which procyclicality was hard-wired into the system' (This point was a key issue in Danielsson et al. (2005)).

- '*Non-normal distributions.* However, even if much longer time periods (e.g. ten years) had been used, it is likely that estimates would have failed to identify the scale of risks being taken. Price movements during the crisis have often been of a size whose probability was calculated by models (even using longer term inputs) to be almost infinitesimally small. This suggests that the models systematically underestimated the chances of small probability high impact events. . . . it is possible that financial market movements are inherently characterized by fat-tail distributions. VAR models need to be buttressed by the application of stress test techniques which consider the impact of extreme movements beyond those which the model suggests are at all probable.' (This point is raised over and over again in Danielsson et al. (2005) and is one of the main reasons for writing the present chapter.)

We have decided to include these quotes in full as academia and (regulatory) practice will have to start to collaborate more in earnest. We have to improve the channels of communication and start taking the other side's worries more seriously. The added references to Danielsson et al. (2005) are ours, they do not appear in the Turner Review, nor does any reference to serious warnings for many years made by financial mathematicians of the miserable properties of VaR. Part of 'the going forward' is an in-depth analysis on how and why such early and well-documented criticisms by academia were not taken more seriously. On voicing such criticism early on, we too often faced the 'that is academic'-response. We personally have no problem in stating a *Mea Culpa* on some of the developments made in mathematical finance (or as some say, *Mea Copula* in case of Example 3.), but with respect to some of the critical statements made in the Turner Review, we side with Chris Rogers:

The problem is not that mathematics *was used* by the banking industry, the problem was that it was *abused* by the banking industry. Quants were instructed to build (credit) models which fitted the market prices. Now if the market prices were way out of line, the calibrated models would just faithfully reproduce those whacky values, and the bad prices get reinforced by an overlay of scientific respectability! The standard models which were used for a long time before being rightfully discredited by academics and the more thoughtful practitioners were from the start a complete fudge; so you had garbage prices being underpinned by garbage modelling.

Or indeed as Mark Davis put it: 'The whole industry was stuck in a classic positive feedback loop which no one party could walk away from.' Perhaps changing 'could' to 'wanted to' comes even closer to the truth. We ourselves can only hope that the Turner Review will not be abused for 'away with mathematics on Wall Street'; with an 'away with the garbage modelling' we totally agree.

3 EVT: THE ONE-DIMENSIONAL CASE

Over the recent years, we have been asked by practitioners on numerous occasions to lecture on EVT highlighting the underlying *assumptions*. The latter is relevant for understanding model uncertainty when estimating rare or extreme events. With this in mind, in the following sections, we will concentrate on those aspects of EVT which, from experience, we find need special attention.

The basic (data) set-up is that $X_1, X_2, \ldots$ are independent and identically distributed (i.i.d.) random variables (rvs) with distribution function (df) F. For the moment, we have *no* extra assumptions on F, but that will have to change rather soon. Do however note the very strong iid assumption. Denote the sample extremes as

$$M_1 = X_1, \quad M_n = \max(X_1, \ldots, X_n), \quad n \geq 2.$$

As the right endpoint of F we define

$$x_F = \sup\{x \in \mathbb{R} : F(x) < 1\} \leq +\infty;$$

also throughout we denote $\overline{F} = 1 - F$, the tail df of F.

Trivial results are that

(i) $P(M_n \leq x) = F^n(x), x \in \mathbb{R}$, and
(ii) $M_n \to x_F$ almost surely, $n \to \infty$.

Similar to the Central Limit Theorem for sums $S_n = X_1 + \cdots + X_n$, or averages $\overline{X}_n = S_n/n$, we can ask whether norming constants $c_n > 0, d_n \in \mathbb{R}$ exist so that

$$\frac{M_n - d_n}{c_n} \xrightarrow{d} H, \quad n \to \infty, \tag{2}$$

for some non-degenerate df H and $\xrightarrow{d}$ stands for convergence in distribution (also referred to as weak convergence). Hence (2) is equivalent with

$$\forall x \in \mathbb{R} : \lim_{n \to \infty} P(M_n \leq c_n x + d_n) = H(x), \tag{3}$$

which, for $u_n = u_n(x) = c_n x + d_n$ and $x \in \mathbb{R}$ fixed, can be rewritten as

$$\lim_{n \to \infty} P(M_n \leq u_n) = \lim_{n \to \infty} F^n(u_n) = H(x). \tag{4}$$

(We will make a comment later about '$\forall x \in \mathbb{R}$' above). When one studies extremes, point processes in general (see the title of Resnick 1987) and Poisson processes in particular are never far off. For instance, note that by the i.i.d. assumption,

$$B_n := \sum_{i=1}^{n} I_{\{X_i > u_n\}} \sim \text{BIN}\left(n, \overline{F}(u_n)\right);$$

here BIN stands for the binomial distribution. Poisson's Theorem of Rare Events yields that the following statements are equivalent:

(i) $B_n \xrightarrow{d} B_\infty \sim \text{POIS}(\lambda)$, $0 < \lambda < \infty$, and
(ii) $\lim_{n \to \infty} n\overline{F}(u_n) = \lambda \in (0, \infty)$.

As a consequence of either (i) or (ii) we obtain that, for $n \to \infty$,

$$P(M_n \leq u_n) = P(B_n = 0) \longrightarrow P(B_\infty = 0) = e^{-\lambda}$$

and hence we arrive at (4) with $\lambda = -\log H(x)$. Of course, the equivalence between (i) and (ii) above yields much more, in particular

$$P(B_n = k) \longrightarrow P(B_\infty = k) = e^{-\lambda}\frac{\lambda^k}{k!}, \quad n \to \infty, \quad k \in \mathbb{N}_0.$$

This result is used in EKM (Theorem 4.2.3) in order to obtain limit probabilities for upper order statistics $X_{k,n}$ defined as

$$X_{n,n} = \min(X_1, \ldots, X_n) \leq X_{n-1,n} \leq \cdots \leq X_{2,n} \leq X_{1,n} = M_n;$$

indeed, $\{B_n = k\} = \{X_{k,n} > u_n, X_{k+1,n} \leq u_n\}$. Figure 14.1 gives an example of B_n and suggests the obvious interpretation of B_n as *the number of exceedances above the (typically high) threshold u_n*.

Time to return to (2): can we solve for (c_n, d_n, H) for *every* underlying model (df) F? In the CLT we can; for instance for rvs with finite variance we know that for *all* F (discrete, continuous, ...)

$$\frac{S_n - n\mu}{\sqrt{n}\sigma} \xrightarrow{d} Z \sim N(0, 1) \text{ as } n \to \infty.$$

The situation for EVT, i.e. for (2) to hold, is much more subtle. For instance, a necessary condition for the existence of a solution to (2) is that

$$\lim_{x \uparrow x_F} \frac{\overline{F}(x)}{\overline{F}(x-)} = 1. \tag{5}$$

Here $F(t-) = \lim_{s \uparrow t} F(s)$, the left limit of F in t. In the case of discrete rvs, (5) reduces to

$$\lim_{n \to \infty} \frac{\overline{F}(n)}{\overline{F}(n-1)} = 1.$$

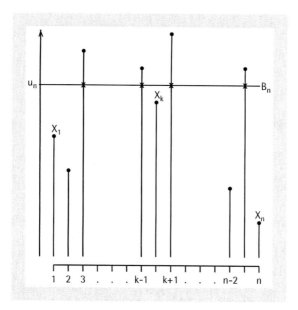

FIGURE 14.1 Realization of B_n, the number of exceedances in $X_1, X_2, \ldots, X_n$ above the threshold u_n.

The latter condition does *not* hold for models like the Poisson, geometric, or negative binomial; see EKM, Examples 3.14–16. In such cases, one has to develop a special EVT. Note that (5) does not provide a sufficient condition, i.e. there are continuous dfs F for which classical EVT, in the sense of (2), does *not* apply. More on this later. At this point it is important to realize that solving (2) imposes some non-trivial conditions on the underlying model (data).

The solution to (2) forms the content of the next theorem. We first recall that two rvs X and Y (or their dfs F_X, F_Y) are of the same *type* if there exist constants $a \in \mathbb{R}$, $b > 0$ so that for all $x \in \mathbb{R}$, $F_X(x) = F_Y\left(\frac{x-a}{b}\right)$, i.e. $X \stackrel{d}{=} bY + a$.

Theorem 1. (Fisher-Tippett). *Suppose that $X_1, X_2, \ldots$ are i.i.d. rvs with df F. If there exist norming constants $c_n > 0$, $d_n \in \mathbb{R}$ and a non-degenerate df H so that (2) holds, then H must be of the following type:*

$$H_\xi(x) = \begin{cases} \exp\left\{-(1 + \xi x)^{-1/\xi}\right\} & \text{if } \xi \neq 0, \\ \exp\{-\exp(-x)\} & \text{if } \xi = 0, \end{cases} \qquad (6)$$

where $1 + \xi x > 0$. □

Remarks

(i) The dfs H_ξ, $\xi \in \mathbb{R}$, are referred to as the *(generalized) extreme value distributions* (GEV). For $\xi > 0$ we have the *Fréchet* df, for $\xi < 0$ the *Weibull*, and for $\xi = 0$ the *Gumbel* or *double exponential*. For applications to finance, insurance, and risk management, the Fréchet case ($\xi > 0$) is the important one.

(ii) The main theorems from probability theory underlying the mathematics of EVT are (1) The Convergence to Types Theorem (EKM, Theorem A1.5), yielding the functional forms of the GEV in (6); (2) Vervaat's Lemma (EKM, Proposition A1.7) allowing the construction of norming sequences (c_n, d_n) through the weak convergence of quantile (inverse) functions, and finally (3) Karamata's Theory of Regular Variation (EKM, Section A3) which lies at the heart of many (weak) limit results in probability theory, including Gnedenko's Theorem ((13)) below.

(iii) Note that all H_ξ's are continuous explaining why we can write '$\forall x \in \mathbb{R}$' in (3).

(iv) When (2) holds with $H = H_\xi$ as in (6), then we say that the data (the model F) belong(s) to *the maximal domain of attraction* of the df H_ξ, denoted as $F \in \mathrm{MDA}(H_\xi)$.

(v) Most known models with continuous df F belong to some $\mathrm{MDA}(H_\xi)$. Some examples in shorthand are:

- {Pareto, student-t, loggamma, g-and-$h(h > 0)$, ...} $\subset \mathrm{MDA}(H_\xi, \xi > 0)$;
- {normal, lognormal, exponential, gamma, ...} $\subset \mathrm{MDA}(H_0)$, and
- {uniform, beta, ...} $\subset \mathrm{MDA}(H_\xi, \xi < 0)$.
- The so-called log-Pareto dfs $\overline{F}(x) \sim \frac{1}{(\log x)^k}$, $x \to \infty$, do not belong to any of the MDAs. These dfs are useful for the modelling of very heavy-tailed events like earthquakes or internet traffic data. A further useful example of a continuous df not belonging to any of the MDAs is

$$\overline{F}(x) \sim x^{-1/\xi}\{1 + a \sin(2\pi \log x)\},$$

where $\xi > 0$ and a sufficiently small.

The g-and-h df referred to above corresponds to the df of a rv $X = \frac{e^{gZ}-1}{g} e^{\frac{1}{2}hZ^2}$ for $Z \sim N(0, 1)$; it has been used to model operational risk.

(vi) Contrary to the CLT, the norming constants have no easy interpretation in general; see EKM, Table 3.4.2 and our discussion on MDA (H_ξ) for $\xi > 0$ below. It is useful to know that for statistical estimation of rare events, their precise analytic form is of less importance. For instance, for $F \sim \mathrm{EXP}(1)$, $c_n \equiv 1$, $d_n = \log n$, whereas for $F \sim N(0, 1)$, $c_n = (2 \log n)^{-1/2}$, $d_n = \sqrt{2 \log n} - \frac{\log(4\pi)+\log\log n}{2(2 \log n)^{1/2}}$. Both examples correspond to the Gumbel case $\xi = 0$. For $F \sim \mathrm{UNIF}(0, 1)$, one finds $c_n = n^{-1}$, $d_n \equiv 1$ leading to the Weibull case. The for our purposes very important Fréchet case ($\xi > 0$) is discussed more in detail below; see (13) and further.

(vii) For later notational reasons, we define the affine transformations

$$\gamma^n : \mathbb{R} \to \mathbb{R}$$

$$x \mapsto c_n x + d_n, \quad c_n > 0, \quad d_n \in \mathbb{R},$$

so that (2) is equivalent with

$$(\gamma^n)^{-1}(M_n) \xrightarrow{d} H, \quad n \to \infty. \tag{7}$$

Although based on Theorem 1. one can work out a statistical procedure (the block-maxima method) for rare event estimation, for applications to risk management an equivalent formulation turns out to be more useful. The so-called *Peaks Over Theshold* (POT) method concerns the asymptotic approximation of the *excess* df

$$F_u(x) = P(X - u \leq x \mid X > u), \quad 0 \leq x < x_F - u. \tag{8}$$

The key Theorem 2. below involves a new class of dfs, the *Generalized Pareto dfs* (GPDs):

$$G_\xi(x) = \begin{cases} 1 - (1 + \xi x)^{-1/\xi} & \text{if } \xi \neq 0, \\ 1 - e^{-x} & \text{if } \xi = 0, \end{cases} \tag{9}$$

where $x \geq 0$ if $\xi \geq 0$ and $0 \leq x \leq -1/\xi$ if $\xi < 0$. We also denote $G_{\xi,\beta}(x) := G_\xi(x/\beta)$ for $\beta > 0$.

Theorem 2. (Pickands-Balkema-de Haan). *Suppose that $X_1, X_2, \ldots$ are i.i.d. with df F. Then equivalent are:*

(i) *$F \in MDA\left(H_\xi\right)$, $\xi \in \mathbb{R}$, and*

(ii) *There exists a measurable function $\beta(\cdot)$ so that:*

$$\lim_{u \to x_F} \sup_{0 \leq x < x_F - u} \left| F_u(x) - G_{\xi,\beta(u)}(x) \right| = 0. \tag{10}$$

□

The practical importance of this theorem should be clear: it allows for the statistical modelling of losses X_i in excess of high thresholds u; see also Figure 14.1. Very early on (mid-nineties), we tried to convince risk managers that it is absolutely important to model $F_u(x)$ and not just estimate $u = \text{VaR}_\alpha$ or $E S_\alpha = E(X \mid X > \text{VaR}_\alpha)$. Though always quoting VaR_α *and* ES_α would already be much better than today's practice of just quoting VaR. As explained in MFE, Chapter 6, Theorem 2. forms the basis of the POT-method for the estimation of high-quantile events in risk management data. The latter method is based on the following trivial identity:

$$\overline{F}(x) = \overline{F}(u)\overline{F}_u(x - u), \quad x \geq u.$$

Together with the obvious statistical (empirical) estimator $\overline{F}_n(u)$, for $\overline{F}(x)$ far in the upper tail, i.e. for $x \geq u$, we obtain the natural (semi-parametric) EVT-based estimator:

$$\left(\overline{F}\right)^\wedge_n (x) = \frac{N(u)}{n} \left(1 + \widehat{\xi} \, \frac{x - u}{\widehat{\beta}}\right)^{-1/\widehat{\xi}}. \tag{11}$$

Here $\left(\widehat{\beta}, \widehat{\xi}\right)$ are the Maximum Likelihood Estimators (MLEs) based on the excesses $(X_i - u)^+, i = 1, \ldots, n$, estimated within the GPD model (9). One can show that MLE in this case is regular for $\xi > -1/2$; note that examples relevant for QRM typically have $\xi > 0$. Denoting $\text{VaR}_\alpha(F) = F^\leftarrow(a)$, the $a100\%$ quantile of F, we obtain by inversion of (11), the estimator

$$(\mathrm{VaR}_a(F))_n^{\wedge} = u + \frac{\widehat{\beta}}{\widehat{\xi}}\left(\left(\frac{(1-a)n}{N(u)}\right)^{-\widehat{\xi}} - 1\right). \tag{12}$$

Here, $N(u) = \#\{1 \le i \le n : X_i > u\}$ ($= B_n$ in Figure 14.1), the number of exceedances above u.

In Figure 14.2 we have plotted the daily opening prices (top) and the negative log-returns (bottom) of Google for the period 19/8/2004–25/3/2009. We will apply the POT method to these data for the estimation of the VaR at 99%, as well as the expected shortfall $ES_a = E(X \mid X > \mathrm{VaR}_a)$. It is well known that (log-)return equity data are close to uncorrelated but are dependent (GARCH or stochastic volatility effects). We will however not enter into these details but apply EVT directly to the data in Figure 14.2; see MFE, chapter 4 for further refinements of the POT method in this case. Figure 14.3 contains the so-called (extended) Hill plot:

$$\left\{\left(k, \widehat{\xi}_{n,k}\right) : k \in K \subset \{1, \ldots, n\}\right\},$$

for some appropriate range K of k-values; see also (19). It always shows higher variation to the left (small k values, u high) and bias to the right (large k values, u low). The optimal choice of k-values(s) for which $\widehat{\xi}_{n,k}$ yields a 'good' estimator for ξ is difficult; again see MFE and the references therein for details

Figure 14.4 shows the POT tail-fit for the loss-tail where a threshold $u = 0.024$ was chosen, corresponding to (approximately) a 90% quantile. As point estimates we find $\widehat{\mathrm{VaR}}_{99\%} = 0.068(0.061, 0.079)$ and $\widehat{ES}_{99\%} = 0.088(0.076, 0.119)$ where the values in

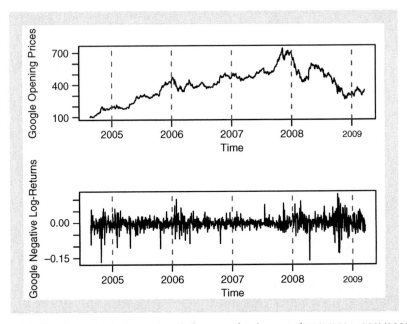

FIGURE 14.2 Google equity data: opening daily prices for the period 19/8/2004–25/3/2009 (top) with the negative log-returns below.

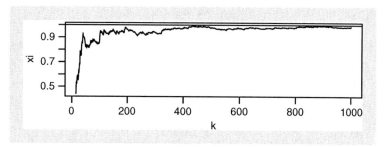

FIGURE 14.3 Hill-plot for the Google-data using the POT method.

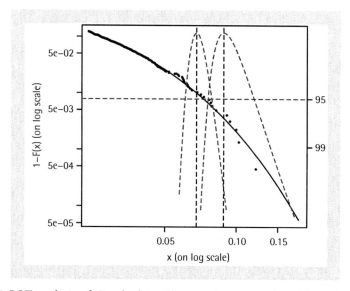

FIGURE 14.4 POT analysis of Google-data. The negative return data (black dots) on a log-log scale, above the threshold $u = 0.024$. The solid line is the POT fitted model to the tail. The parabolic type (dashed) curves are the profile likelihoods around $VaR_{99\%}$ and $ES_{99\%}$ with corresponding confidence intervals cut off at the 95% (dashed) line.

parenthesis yield 95% confidence intervals. These can be read off from the horizontal line through 95% intersecting the parabolic-like profile likelihood curves. Note how 'well' the POT-based GPD-fit curves through the extreme data points. As stressed before, this is just the first (static!) step in an EVT analysis, much more (in particular dynamic) modelling is called for at this stage. For the purpose of this chapter we refrain from entering into these details here.

One of the key technical issues currently facing QRM is *Model Uncertainty* (MU); we deliberately refrain from using the term 'model risk'. The distinction is akin to Frank H. Knight's famous distinction, formulated in 1921, between risk and uncertainty. In Knight's interpretation, *risk* refers to situations where the decision maker can assign mathematical probabilities to the randomness he/she is faced with. In contrast,

Knight's *uncertainty* refers to situations when this randomness cannot be expressed in terms of specific mathematical probabilities. John M. Keynes (1937) very much took up this issue. The distinction enters the current debate around QRM and is occasionally referred to as 'The known, the unknown, and the unknowable'; see Diebold et al. (2010). Stuart Turnbull (personal communication) also refers to *dark risk*, the risk we know exists, but we cannot model. Consider the case $\xi > 0$ in Theorem 2. Besides the crucial assumption '$X_1, X_2, \ldots$ are i.i.d. with df F', before we can use (10) (and hence (11) and (12)), we have to understand the precise meaning of $F \in \text{MDA}\left(H_\xi\right)$. Any condition with the df F in it, is a model assumption, and may lead to model uncertainty. It follows from Gnedenko's Theorem (Theorem 3.3.7 in EKM) that for $\xi > 0$, $F \in \text{MDA}\left(H_\xi\right)$ is equivalent to

$$\overline{F}(x) = x^{-1/\xi} L(x) \tag{13}$$

where L is a *slowly varying* function in Karamata's sense, i.e. $L : (0, \infty) \to (0, \infty)$ measurable satisfies

$$\forall x > 0 : \lim_{t \to \infty} \frac{L(tx)}{L(t)} = 1. \tag{14}$$

Basic notation is $L \in \text{SV} := \text{RV}_0$, whereas (13) is written as $\overline{F} \in \text{RV}_{-1/\xi}$, $\overline{F}$ is *regularly varying* with (tail) index $-1/\xi$. A similar result holds for $\xi < 0$. The case $\xi = 0$ is much more involved. Note that in the literature on EVT there is *no* overall common definition of the index ξ; readers should also be careful when one refers to the *tail-index*. The latter can either be ξ, or $1/\xi$, or indeed any sign change of these two. Hence always check the notation used. The innocuous function L has a considerable model uncertainty hidden in its definition! In a somewhat superficial and suggestive-provocative way, we would even say

$$\text{MU(EVT)} = \{L\}, \tag{15}$$

with L as in (13); note that the real (slowly varying) property of L is only revealed at infinity. The fundamental model assumption fully embodies the notion of power-like behaviour, also referred to as Pareto-type. A basic model uncertainty in any application of EVT is the slowly varying function L. In more complicated problems concerning rare event estimation, as one typically finds in credit risk, the function L may be hidden deep down in the underlying model assumptions. For instance, the reason why EVT works well for Student-t data but not so well for g-and-h data (which corresponds to (13) with $h = \xi$) is entirely due to the properties of the underlying slowly varying function L. See also Remark (iv) below. Practitioners (at the quant level in banks) and many EVT-users seem to be totally unaware of this fact.

Just as the CLT can be used for statistical estimation related to 'average events', likewise Theorem 1. can readily be turned into a statistical technique for estimating 'rare/extreme events'. For this to work, one possible approach is to divide the sample of size n into $k(= k(n))$ blocks $D_1, \ldots, D_k$ each of length $[n/k]$. For each of these data-blocks D_i of length $[n/k]$, the maximum is denoted by $M_{[n/k],i}$ leading to the k maxima observations

$$\mathcal{M}_{[n/k]} = \{M_{[n/k],i}, i = 1, \ldots, k\}.$$

We then apply Theorem 1. to the data $\mathcal{M}_{[n/k]}$ assuming that (or designing the blocking so that) the necessary i.i.d. assumption is fulfilled. We need the blocksize $[n/k]$ to be sufficiently large (i.e. k small) in order to have a reasonable approximation to the df of the $M_{[n/k],i}$, $i = 1, \ldots, k$ through Theorem 1.; this reduces bias. On the other hand, we need sufficiently many maximum observations (i.e. k large) in order to have accurate statistical estimates for the GEV parameters; this reduces variance. The resulting tradeoff between variance and bias is typical for all EVT estimation procedures; see also Figure 14.3. The choice of $k = k(n)$ crucially depends on L; see EKM, section 7.1.4, and Remark (iv) and Interludium 1 below for details.

In order to stress (15) further, we need to understand how important the condition (13) really is. Gnedenko's Theorem tells us that (13) is equivalent with $F \in \text{MDA}(H_\xi)$, $\xi > 0$, i.e.

$$\forall x > 0 : \lim_{t\to\infty} \frac{\overline{F}(tx)}{\overline{F}(t)} = x^{-1/\xi}. \tag{16}$$

This is a remarkable result in its generality, it is exactly the weak asymptotic condition of Karamata's slow variation in (14) that mathematically characterizes, though (13), the heavy-tailed ($\xi > 0$) models which can be handled, through EVT, for rare event estimation. Why is this? From section 3 we learn that the following statements are equivalent:

(i) There exist $c_n > 0$, $d_n \in \mathbb{R} : \lim_{n\to\infty} P\left(\frac{M_n - d_n}{c_n} \le x\right) = H_\xi(x)$, $x \in \mathbb{R}$, and

(ii) $\lim_{n\to\infty} n\overline{F}(c_n x + d_n) = -\log H_\xi(x)$, $x \in \mathbb{R}$.

For ease of notation (this is just a change within the same type) assume that $-\log H_\xi(x) = x^{-1/\xi}$, $x > 0$. Also assume for the moment that $d_n \equiv 0$ in (ii). Then (ii) with $c_n = (1/\overline{F})^{\leftarrow}(n)$ implies that, for $x > 0$,

$$\lim_{n\to\infty} \frac{\overline{F}(c_n x)}{\overline{F}(c_n)} = x^{-1/\xi},$$

which is (16) along a subsequence $c_n \to \infty$. A further argument is needed to replace the sequence (c_n) by a continuous parameter t in (16). Somewhat more care needs to be taken when $d_n \neq 0$. So $\overline{F} \in \text{RV}_{-1/\xi}$ is really fundamental. Also something we learned is that the norming $c_n = (1/\overline{F})^{\leftarrow}(n)$; here, and above, we denote for any monotone function $h : \mathbb{R} \to \mathbb{R}$, the generalized inverse of h as

$$h^{\leftarrow}(t) = \inf\{x \in \mathbb{R} : h(x) \ge t\}.$$

Therefore, c_n can be interpreted as a quantile

$$P(X_1 > c_n) = \overline{F}(c_n) \sim \frac{1}{n}.$$

In numerous articles and textbooks, the use and potential misuse of the EVT formulas have been discussed; see MFE for references or visit <www.math.ethz.ch/~embrechts>

for a series of re-/preprints on the topic. In the remarks below and in Interludium 2, we briefly comment on some of the QRM-relevant pitfalls in using EVT, but more importantly, in asking questions of the type 'calculate a 99.9%, 1 year capital charge', i.e. 'estimate a 1 in 1000 year event'.

Remarks

(i) EVT applies to all kinds of data: heavy-tailed ($\xi > 0$), medium to short-tailed ($\xi = 0$), bounded rvs, i.e. ultra short-tailed ($\xi < 0$).

(ii) As a statistical (MLE-based) technique, EVT yields (typically wide) confidence intervals for VaR-estimates like in (12). The same holds for PD estimates. See the Google-data POT analysis, in particular Figure 14.4, for an example.

(iii) There is no agreed way to choose the 'optimal' threshold u in the POT method (or equivalently k on putting $u = X_{k,n}$, see (19) below). At high quantiles, one should refrain from using automated procedures and also bring *judgement* into the picture. We very much realize that this is much more easily said than done, but that is the nature of the 'low probability event' problem.

(iv) The formulas (11) and (12) are based on the asymptotic result (10) as $u \to x_F$ where $x_F = \infty$ in the $\xi > 0$ case, i.e. (13). Typical for EVT, and this contrary to the CLT, the rate of convergence in (10) very much depends on the second-order properties of the underlying data model F. For instance, in the case of the Student-t, the rate of convergence in (10) is $O\left(\frac{1}{u^2}\right)$, whereas for the lognormal it is $O\left(\frac{1}{\log u}\right)$ and for the g-and-h the terribly slow $O\left(\frac{1}{\sqrt{\log u}}\right)$. The precise reason for this (e.g. in the $\xi > 0$ case) depends entirely on the second-order behaviour of the slowly varying function L in (13), hence our summary statement on model uncertainty in (15). Indeed, in the case of the Student-t, $L(x)$ behaves asymptotically as a constant. For the g-and-h case, $L(x)$ is asymptotic to $\exp\left\{(\log x)^{1/2}\right\}/(\log x)^{1/2}$. As discussed in the Block-Maxima Ansatz above (choice of $k = k(n)$) and the rate of convergence (as a function of u) in the POT method, the asymptotic properties of L are crucial. In Interludium 1 below we highlight this point in a (hopefully) pedagogically readable way: the EVT end-user is very much encouraged to try to follow the gist of the argument. Its conclusions hold true far beyond the example discussed.

(v) Beware of the *Hill-horror plots* (Hhp); see EKM figures 4.1.13, 6.4.11, and 5.5.4. The key messages behind these figures are: (1) the L function can have an important influence on the EVT estimation of ξ (see also the previous remark); (2) the EVT estimators for ξ can always be calculated, check relevance first, and (3) check for dependence in the data before applying EVT. In Interludium 2 below we discuss these examples in somewhat more detail. Note that in figure 4.1.13 of EKM, the ordinate should read as $\widehat{a}_n$.

(vi) We recently came across the so-called *Taleb distribution* (no doubt motivated by Taleb (2007)). It was defined as a probability distribution in which there is a high probability of a small gain, and a small probability of a very large loss, which more than outweighs the gains. Of course, these dfs are standard within EVT and are part of the GEV-family; see for instance EKM, section 8.2. This is once more an example where it pays to have a more careful look at existing, well-established theory (EVT in this case) rather than going for the newest, vaguely formulated fad.

Interludium 1 ($L \in SV$ matters!). As already stated above, conditions of the type (13) are absolutey crucial in all rare event estimations using EVT. In the present interludium we will highlight this issue based on the Hill estimator for $\xi (> 0)$ in (13). Let us start with the 'easiest' case and suppose that $X_1, \ldots, X_n$ are iid with df $\overline{F}(x) = x^{-1/\xi}$, $x \geq 1$. From this it follows that the rvs $Y_i = \log X_i$, $i = 1, \ldots, n$, are i.i.d. with df $P(Y_i > y) = e^{-y/\xi}$, $y \geq 0$; i.e. $Y_i \sim EXP(1/\xi)$ so that $E(Y_1) = \xi$. As MLE for ξ we immediately obtain:

$$\widehat{\xi}_n = \overline{Y}_n = \frac{1}{n} \sum_{i=1}^{n} \log X_i = \frac{1}{n} \sum_{i=1}^{n} \left(\log X_{i,n} - \log 1 \right) \tag{17}$$

where the pedagogic reason for rewriting $\widehat{\xi}_n$ as in the last equality will become clear below. Now suppose that we move from the exact Pareto case (with $L \equiv 1$) to the general case (13); a natural estimator for ξ can be obtained via Karamata's Theorem (EKM, theorem A3.6) which implies that, assuming (13), we have

$$\lim_{t \to \infty} \frac{1}{\overline{F}(t)} \int_t^\infty (\log x - \log t) \, dF(x) = \xi. \tag{18}$$

(To see this, just use $L \equiv 1$ and accept that in the end, the SV-property of L allows for the same limit. These asymptotic integration properties lie at the heart of Karamata's theory of regular variation.) Replace F in (18) by its empirical estimator $\widehat{F}_n(x) = \frac{1}{n} \# \{i \leq n : X_i \leq x\}$ and put $t = X_{k,n}$, the kth order statistic, for some $k = k(n) \to \infty$, this yields in a natural way the famous Hill estimator for the shape parameter $\xi (> 0)$ in (13):

$$\widehat{\xi}_{n,k}^{(H)} = \frac{1}{k-1} \sum_{i=1}^{k-1} \left(\log X_{i,n} - \log X_{k,n} \right). \tag{19}$$

(Compare this estimator with (17) in the case where $L \equiv 1$.) In order to find out how well EVT-estimation does, we need to investigate the statistical properties of $\widehat{\xi}_{n,k}^{(H)}$ for $n \to \infty$. Before discussing this point, note the form of the estimator: we average sufficiently many log-differences of the ordered data above some high enough threshold value $X_{k,n}$, the k-th largest observation. In order to understand now where the problem lies, denote by $E_1, \ldots, E_{n+1}$ i.i.d. rvs with EXP(1) df, and for $k \leq n + 1$ set $\Gamma_k = E_1 + \cdots + E_k$. Then using the so-called Rényi Representation (EKM, examples 4.1.10–12) we obtain:

$$\widehat{\xi}_{n,k}^{(H)} \overset{d}{=} \xi \frac{1}{k-1} \sum_{i=1}^{k-1} E_i + \frac{1}{k-1} \sum_{i=1}^{k-1} \log \left\{ \frac{L\left(\Gamma_{n+1}/\left(\Gamma_{n+1} - \Gamma_{n-i+1}\right)\right)}{L\left(\Gamma_{n+1}/\left(\Gamma_{n+1} - \Gamma_{n-k+1}\right)\right)} \right\} \qquad (20)$$

$$\equiv \beta_n^{(1)} + \beta_n^{(2)}.$$

(Here $\overset{d}{=}$ denotes 'is equal in distribution'). In order to handle $\beta_n^{(1)}$ we just need $k = k(n) \to \infty$ and use the WLLN, the SLLN, and the CLT to obtain all properties one wants (this corresponds to the $L \equiv 1$ case above). All the difficulties come from $\beta_n^{(2)}$ where L appears explicitly. If L is close to a constant (the Student-t case for instance) then $\beta_n^{(2)}$ will go to zero fast and $\widehat{\xi}_{n,k}^{(H)}$ inherits the very nice properties of the term $\beta_n^{(1)}$. If however L is far away from a constant (like for the loggamma or g-and-h ($h > 0$)) then $\beta_n^{(2)}$ may tend to zero arbitrarily slowly! For instance, for $L(x) = \log x$, one can show that $\beta_n^{(2)} = O((\log n)^{-1})$. Also, in the analysis of $\beta_n^{(2)}$ the various second-order properties of $k = k(n)$ enter. This has as a consequence that setting a sufficiently high threshold $u = X_{k,n}$ either in the Block-Maxima (choice of k) or POT method (choice of u) which is optimal in some sense is very difficult. Any threshold choice depends on the second-order properties of L! Also note that the model (13) is semi-parametric in nature: besides the parametric part ξ, there is the important non-parametric part L.

Interludium 2 (Hill-horror plots).The Hhp-phrase mentioned in Remark (v) above was coined by Sid Resnick and aims at highlighting the difficulties in estimating the shape-parameter in a model of type (13). The conclusions hold in general when estimating rare (low probability) events. In Figure 14.5 we have highlighted the

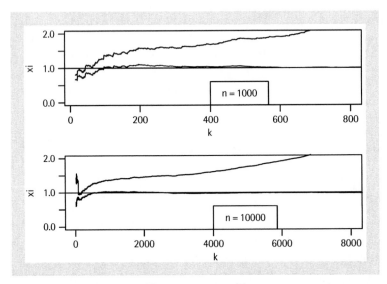

FIGURE 14.5 Hill-estimator (19) for $\overline{F}_1(x) = x^{-1}$ and $\overline{F}_2(x) = (x \log x)^{-1}$ (top for $n = 1000$, bottom for $n = 10000$). Each plot contains the Hill-plot for the model $\overline{F}_1$, bottom curve, $\overline{F}_2$, top curve.

above problem for the two models $\overline{F}_1(x) = x^{-1}$ (lower curve in each panel) and $\overline{F}_2(x) = (x \log x)^{-1}$, x sufficiently large, (top curve in each panel). Note that for F_2 (i.e. changing from $L_1 \equiv 1$ to $L_2 = (\log x)^{-1}$) interpretation of the Hill-plot is less clear and indeed makes the analysis much more complicated. In Figure 14.6 we stress the obvious: apply specific EVT estimators to data which clearly show the characteristics for which that estimator was designed! For instance, lognormal data correspond to $\xi = 0$ and hence the Hill estimator (19) should never be used in this case as it is designed for the (admittedly important) case $\xi > 0$. Of course, one can easily use methods that hold for all $\xi \in \mathbb{R}$, like the POT method. The final Hhp in Figure 14.7 is more serious: beware of dependence! Even if EVT can be applied for some dependent data (like in this AR(1) case), convergence will typically be much slower than in the corresponding iid case. In Figure 14.7 we show this for an AR(1) process

$$X_t = \varphi X_{t-1} + Z_t, \quad t \geq 1, \tag{21}$$

where Z_t are i.i.d., with df $P\,(Z_1 > t) = x^{-10}$, $x \geq 1$, hence $\xi = 0.1$. One can show that the stationary solution to (21) has as tail behaviour

$$P\,(X_1 > t) \sim c x^{-10}, \quad x \to \infty,$$

hence also $\xi = 0.1$. We can now estimate ξ both using the i.i.d. data (Z_t) and the dependent data (X_t), and this for increasing parameter φ, corresponding to increasing dependence. The conclusion from Figure 14.7 is obvious.

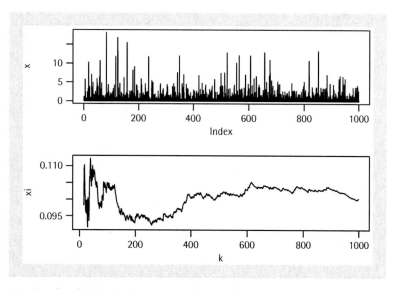

FIGURE 14.6 Simulated LN(0,1) data (top) with the Hill-plot bottom; note that LN-data correspond to $\xi = 0$, whereas the (wrongly used!) Hill estimator (19) yields a value of around 0.1, say.

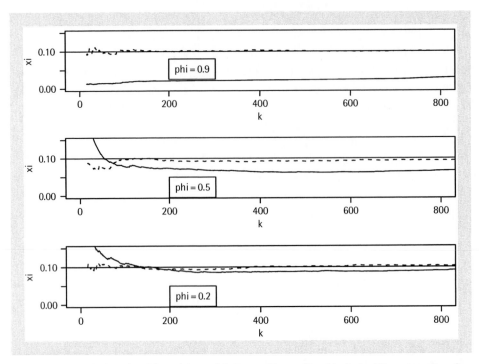

FIGURE 14.7 Hill-plots for the AR(1)-model $X_t = \varphi X_{t-1} + Z_t$ with dashed line corresponding to the Hill estimator from the Z-data, whereas the full line corresponds to the Hill estimator from the X-data, and this for three different values of φ : 0.9, 0.5, 0.2, top to bottom; $n = 1000$.

4 MEVT: MULTIVARIATE EXTREME VALUE THEORY

As explained in section 3, classical one-dimensional extreme value theory (EVT) allows for the estimation of rare events, such as VaR_α for $\alpha \approx 1$, but this under very precise model assumptions. In practice these have to be verified as much as possible. For a discussion on some practical tools for this, see chapter 6 in EKM and chapter 7 in MFE. A critical view on the possibility for accurate rare event estimation may safeguard the end-user for excessive model uncertainty (see (15)).

Moving from dimension $d = 1$ to $d \geq 2$ immediately implies that one needs a clear definition of ordering and what kind of events are termed 'extreme'. Several theories exist and are often tailored to specific applications. So consider n d-variate iid random vectors (rvs) in $\mathbb{R}^d$, $d \geq 2$, $\mathbb{X}_1, \ldots, \mathbb{X}_n$ with components $\mathbb{X}_i = \left(X_{ij} \right)_{j=1,\ldots,d}$, $i = 1, \ldots, n$. Define the component-wise maxima

$$M_j^n = \max \left\{ X_{1j}, X_{2j}, \ldots, X_{nj} \right\}, \quad j = 1, \ldots, d,$$

resulting in the vector

$$\mathbb{M}^n = \left(M_1^n, \ldots, M_d^n\right)'.$$

Of course, a realization $\mathbf{m} = \mathbb{M}^n(\omega)$ need *not* be an element of the original data $\mathbb{X}_1(\omega), \ldots, \mathbb{X}_n(\omega)$! The component-wise version of MEVT now asks for the existence of affine transformations $\gamma_1^n, \ldots, \gamma_d^n$ and a non-degenerate random vector $\mathbb{H}$, so that

$$(\boldsymbol{\gamma}^n)^{-1}(\mathbb{M}^n) := \left(\left(\gamma_1^n\right)^{-1}\left(M_1^n\right), \ldots, \left(\gamma_d^n\right)^{-1}\left(M_d^n\right)\right)' \overset{d}{\to} \mathbb{H}, \quad n \to \infty; \qquad (22)$$

see also (7) for the notation used. An immediate consequence from (22) is that the d marginal components converge, i.e. for all $j = 1, \ldots, d$,

$$\left(\gamma_j^n\right)^{-1}\left(M_j^n\right) \overset{d}{\to} H_j, \quad \text{non-degenerate}, \quad n \to \infty,$$

and hence, because of Theorem 1., $H_1, \ldots, H_d$ are GEVs. In order to characterize the full df of the vector $\mathbb{H}$ we need its d-dimensional (i.e. joint) distribution.

There are several ways in which a characterization of $\mathbb{H}$ can be achieved; they all centre around the fact that one only needs to find all possible dependence functions linking the marginal GEV dfs $H_1, \ldots, H_d$ to the d-dimensional joint df $\mathbb{H}$. As the GEV dfs are continuous, one knows, through Sklar's Theorem (MFE, theorem 5.3), that there exists a unique df C on $[0, 1]^d$, with uniform-$[0, 1]$ marginals, so that for $\mathbf{x} = (x_1, \ldots, x_d)' \in \mathbb{R}^d$,

$$\mathbb{H}(\mathbf{x}) = C\left(H_1(x_1), \ldots, H_d(x_d)\right). \qquad (23)$$

The function C is referred to as an *extreme value* (EV) *copula*; its so-called Pickands Representation is given in MFE, theorem 7.45 and Theorem 1. below. Equivalent representations use as terminology the *spectral measure*, the *Pickands dependence function*, or the *exponent measure*. Most representations are easier to write down if, without loss of generality, one first transforms the marginal dfs of the data to the unit-Fréchet case. Whereas copulas have become very fashionable for describing dependence (through the representation (23)), the deeper mathematical theory, for instance using point process theory, concentrates on spectral and exponent measures. Their estimation eventually allows for the analysis of joint extremal tail events, a topic of key importance in (credit) risk analysis. Unfortunately, modern MEVT is not an easy subject to become acquainted with, as a brief browsing through some of the recent textbooks on the topic clearly reveals; see for instance de Haan and Ferreira (2006), Resnick (2007) or the somewhat more accessible Beirlant et al. (2005) and Coles (2001). These books have excellent chapters on MEVT. Some of the technicalities we discussed briefly for the one-dimensional case compound exponentially in higher dimensions.

In our discussion below, we like to highlight the appearance of, and link between, the various concepts like copula and spectral measure. In order to make the notation easier, as stated above, we concentrate on models with unit-Fréchet marginals, i.e. for $i = 1, \ldots, n$,

$$P\left(X_{ij} \le x_j\right) = \exp\left\{-x_j^{-1}\right\}, \quad j = 1, \ldots, d, \quad x_j > 0.$$

The following result is often referred to as the *Pickands Representation*:

Theorem 1. *Under the assumptions above, $\mathbb{H}$ in (22) can be written as*

$$\mathbb{H}(\mathbf{x}) = \exp\{-V(\mathbf{x})\}, \quad \mathbf{x} \in \mathbb{R}^d, \tag{24}$$

where

$$V(\mathbf{x}) = \int_{\mathcal{S}^d} \max_{i=1,\ldots,d} \left(\frac{w_i}{x_i}\right) dS(\mathbf{w})$$

and S, the so-called spectral measure, *is a finite measure on the d-dimensional simplex*

$$\mathcal{S}^d = \left\{\mathbf{x} \in \mathbb{R}^d : \mathbf{x} \ge \mathbf{0}, \quad ||\mathbf{x}|| = 1\right\}$$

satisfying

$$\int_{\mathcal{S}^d} w_j \, dS(\mathbf{w}) = 1, \quad j = 1, \ldots, d,$$

where $|| \cdot ||$ denotes any norm on $\mathbb{R}^d$.   □

The link to the EVT-copula in (23) goes as follows:

$$C(\mathbf{u}) = \exp\left\{-V\left(-\frac{1}{\log \mathbf{u}}\right)\right\}, \quad \mathbf{u} \in [0, 1]^d. \tag{25}$$

As a consequence, the function V contains all the information on the dependence between the d component-wise (limit) maxima in the data. An alternative representation is, for $\mathbf{x} \in \mathbb{R}^d$,

$$V(\mathbf{x}) = d \int_{\mathcal{B}^{d-1}} \max\left(\frac{w_1}{x_1}, \ldots, \frac{w_{d-1}}{x_{d-1}}, \frac{1 - \sum_{i=1}^{d-1} w_i}{x_d}\right) dH(\mathbf{w}), \tag{26}$$

where H is a df on $\mathcal{B}^{d-1} = \left\{\mathbf{x} \in \mathbb{R}^{d-1} : \mathbf{x} \ge \mathbf{0}, ||\mathbf{x}|| \le 1\right\}$, and we have the following norming

$$\forall i = 1, \ldots, d - 1 : \int_{\mathcal{B}^{d-1}} w_i \, dH(\mathbf{w}) = \frac{1}{d}.$$

Again, H above is referred to as the *spectral measure*. In order to get a better feeling of its interpretation, consider the above representation for $d = 2$, hence $\mathcal{B}^1 = [0, 1]$ and the norming constraint becomes:

$$\int_0^1 w \, dH(w) = \frac{1}{2}.$$

Hence (24) and (26) reduce to

$$\mathbb{H}(x_1, x_2) = \exp\left\{-2 \int_0^1 \max\left(\frac{w}{x_1}, \frac{1 - w}{x_2}\right) dH(w)\right\}. \tag{27}$$

Recall that through (24), (26) represents all non-degenerate limit laws for affinely transformed component-wise maxima of iid data with unit-Fréchet marginals. The corresponding copula in (23) takes the form ($d = 2, 0 \le u_1, u_2 \le 1$):

$$C(u_1, u_2) = \exp\left\{-2\int_0^1 \max\left(-w\log u_1, -(1-w)\log u_2\right)dH(w)\right\}. \qquad (28)$$

The interpretation of the spectral measure H becomes somewhat clearer through some examples:

(i) If H gives probability $\frac{1}{2}$ to 0 and 1, then (27) becomes

$$\mathbb{H}(x_1, x_2) = \exp\left\{-\left(x_1^{-1} + x_2^{-1}\right)\right\}$$
$$= \exp\left\{-x_1^{-1}\right\}\exp\left\{-x_2^{-1}\right\},$$

the *independent* case. This is also reflected in the corresponding copula C in (28):

$$C(u_1, u_2) = \exp\left\{-2\left(-\frac{1}{2}\log u_1 - \frac{1}{2}\log u_2\right)\right\}$$
$$= u_1 u_2,$$

the *independence copula*.

(ii) If H is degenerate in 0.5, i.e. gives probability 1 to 0.5, then we become

$$\mathbb{H}(x_1, x_2) = \exp\left\{-\max\left(x_1^{-1}, x_2^{-1}\right)\right\}$$
$$C(u_1, u_2) = \exp\left\{\max\left(\log u_1, \log u_2\right)\right\}$$
$$= \max(u_1, u_2),$$

the *comonotonic* case.

(iii) When H is 'spread out' between these two extreme cases, i.e. if H has a density, say, a whole suite of dependence models can be found. Note however that EV-copulas (in (23)) always have to satisfy the following scaling property:

$$\forall t > 0, \quad \forall \mathbf{u} \in [0, 1]^d : C\left(\mathbf{u}^t\right) = C(\mathbf{u})^t.$$

Typical examples include the Gumbel and the Galambos copulas.

(iv) For $d \ge 2$, essentially the same representations exist (see (26)) and it is the distribution of the mass of the spectral measure H on the set $\mathcal{B}^{d-1}$ that tells the modeller where in $\mathbb{R}^d$ clusters of extremes take place.

So far we have only discussed useful representations of the limit $\mathbb{H}$ in (22). The next, more delicate question concerns the domain of attraction problem, like (13) for instance in the case $d = 1, \xi > 0$. It is to be expected that some form of (multivariate) regular variation will enter in a fundamental way, together with convergence results on (multivariate) Poisson point processes; this is true and very much forms the content of Resnick (2007). In section 3 we already stressed that regular variation is the key modelling assumption underlying EVT estimation for $d = 1$. The same is true for

$d \geq 2$; most of the basic results concerning clustering of extremes, tail dependence, spillover probabilities, or contagion are based on the concept of multivariate regular variation. Below we just give the definition in order to indicate where the important model assumptions for MEVT applications come from. It should also prepare the reader for the fact that methodologically 'life at the multivariate edge' is not so simple!

Definition (Multivariate Regular Variation). *A random vector* $\mathbb{X} = (X_1, \ldots, X_d)'$ *in* $\mathbb{R}^d$ *is regularly varying with index* $1/\xi > 0$ *if there exists a random vector* Θ *with values in the sphere* $\mathbb{S}^{d-1}$ *such that for any* $t > 0$ *and any Borel set* $S \subset \mathbb{S}^{d-1}$ *with* $P(\Theta \in \partial S) = 0$ *(a more technical assumption;* ∂ *denotes the topological boundary),*

$$\lim_{x \to \infty} \frac{P\left(||\mathbb{X}|| > tx, \; \mathbb{X}/||\mathbb{X}|| \in S\right)}{P\left(||\mathbb{X}|| > x\right)} = t^{-1/\xi} P(\Theta \in S).$$

The distribution of Θ *is called the* spectral measure *of* $\mathbb{X}$*. Here* $||\cdot||$ *is any norm on* $\mathbb{R}^d$*.*   □

One can show that the above holds if and only if

(i) $\lim_{x \to \infty} \frac{P(||\mathbb{X}||>tx)}{P(||\mathbb{X}||>x)} = t^{-1/\xi}$, $t > 0$, and

(ii) $\lim_{x \to \infty} P\left(\mathbb{X}/||\mathbb{X}|| \in S \mid ||\mathbb{X}|| > x\right) = P(\Theta \in S)$.

From these conditions the meaning of multivariate RV becomes clear: the radial part of the data, $||\mathbb{X}||$, decays in distribution like a power (heavy-tailedness), whereas given a high value of the radial part, the 'angle' $\mathbb{X}/||\mathbb{X}||$ is distributed like Θ. The distribution of Θ tells us where extremes in the underlying model (data) tend to cluster. For further details on this, and how this concept links up with the statistics of multivariate extremes, see for instance Mikosch (2004) and references therein. Note however that warnings, similar to the one-dimensional case, also apply here. It is fair to say that actual statistical applications of MEVT are often restricted to lower dimensions, $d \leq 3$, say; besides Beirlant et al. (2005), see also Coles (2001) for a very readable introduction to the statistical analysis of multivariate extremes. Finally, the statement 'Here $||\cdot||$ is any norm in $\mathbb{R}^{d}$' is *very* useful for QRM. Indeed, $||\mathbb{X}||$ can take several meanings depending on the norm chosen.

One group of results we have not yet discussed so far concerns the d-dimensional generalization(s) of Theorem 2. Again, there are numerous ways in which one can model high-level exceedances in $\mathbb{R}^d$. Clearly, the geometric shape of the exceedance-region must play a role. Within the component-wise version of MEVT discussed above, natural regions are complements of boxes centred at the origin, i.e. $([0, a_1] \times \cdots \times [0, a_d])^c$ in $\mathbb{R}_+^d$. This then quickly leads to (for credit risk) natural questions like *spillover* and *contagion*; we return to some of these problems in the next section. The reader interested in pursuing the various approaches to conditional extreme value problems for $d \geq 2$ can consult Part IV in Balkema and Embrechts (2007) or look for the concept of *hidden regular variation*; on the latter, the work of Sid Resnick is an excellent place to start. In Balkema and Embrechts (2007), the set-up is as follows: suppose $\mathbb{X} = (X_1, \ldots, X_d)'$ is a general d-dimensional random vector of risks taking values in $\mathbb{R}^d$. What are possible non-degenerate limit laws for the conditional df of the affinely scaled vector:

$$P\left(\boldsymbol{\beta}^{-1}(\mathbb{X}) \leq \mathbf{x} \mid \mathbb{X} \in \mathbf{H}_a\right), \quad \mathbf{H}_a \subset \mathbb{R}^d, \quad \mathbf{x} \in \mathbb{R}^d, \tag{29}$$

where $P\left(\mathbb{X} \in \mathbf{H}_a\right) \to 0$ for $a \uparrow 1$ and $\boldsymbol{\beta}$ is a vector of component-wise affine transformations? Hence $\mathbf{H}_a$ is a remote subset of $\mathbb{R}^d$ and consequently, $\{\mathbb{X} \in \mathbf{H}_a\}$ is a rare (or extreme) event on which one conditions. If $\mathbf{H}_a = \left\{\mathbf{x} \in \mathbb{R}^d : \mathbf{w}'\mathbf{x} > q_a\right\}$ for some $\mathbf{w} \in \mathbb{R}^d \backslash \{\mathbf{0}\}$ (portfolio weights) fixed, and q_a a high quantile level, then (29) yields a natural generalization of Theorem 2. Part IV in Balkema and Embrechts (2007) compares (29) with other approaches to multivariate threshold models for rare events.

5 MEVT: RETURN TO CREDIT RISK

At present (April 2009), it is impossible to talk about low probability events, extremes, and credit risk, without reflecting on the occasionally very harsh comments made in the (popular) press against *financial engineering* (FE). For some, FE or even mathematics is the ultimate culprit for the current economic crisis. As an example, here are some quotes from the rather misleading, pamphlet like 'The secret formula that destroyed Wall Street' by Felix Salmon on the Market Movers financial blog at Portfolio.com:

- 'How one simple equation ($P = \Phi(A, B, \gamma)$) made billions for bankers—and nuked your 401(k) (US pension scheme).'
- '"Quants" methods for minting money worked brilliantly ... until one of them devastated the global economy.'
- 'People got excited by the formula's elegance, but the thing never worked. Anything that relies on correlation is charlatanism.'(Quoted from N. Taleb).
- Etc. . . .

Unfortunately, the pamphlet-like tone is taken over by more serious sources like the *Financial Times*; see 'Of couples and copulas' by Sam Jones in its 24 April 2009 edition. Academia was very well aware of the construction's Achilles heel and communicated this on very many occasions. Even in the since 1999 available paper Embrechts, McNeil, and Straumann (2002) we gave in Figure 1 a Li-model type simulation example showing that the Gaussian copula will always underestimate joint extremal events. This point was then taken up further in the paper giving a mathematical proof of this fact; see section 4.4 in that paper. This result was published much earlier and well known to anyone working in EVT; see Sibuya (1959). Note that with respect to this fundamental paper there is some confusion concerning the publication date: 1959 versus 1960. It should indeed be 1959 (Professor Shibuya, personal communication). This definitely answers Jones's question: 'Why did no one notice the formula's Achilles heel?' The far more important question is 'Why did no one on Wall Street listen?'

The equation referred to above is Li's Gaussian copula model (see (31)), it also lies at the basis for the harsh comments in Example 7. Whereas the correlation mentioned enters through the Gauss, i.e. multivariate normal distribution, in memory of the great Carl Friedrich Gauss, it would be better to refer to it plainly as the *normal copula*, i.e. the copula imbedded in the multivariate normal df. This is also the way David Li referred to it in his original scientific papers on the pricing of CDOs. The basic idea goes back to the fairly straightforward formula (23). It is formulas like (23) applied to credit risk which form the basis of Chris Rogers's comments in Example 10. when he talks of 'garbage prices being underpinned by garbage modelling'. For some mysterious reason, after the 'formula' caught the eyes of Wall Street, many thought (even think today; see quotes above) that a complete new paradigm was born. Though we have stated the comments below on several occasions before, the current mis-use of copula-technology together with superficial and misleading statements like in Salmon's blog, prompt us to repeat the main messages again. As basic background, we refer to Embrechts (2009) and Chavez-Demoulin and Embrechts (2009) where further references and examples can be found. We refrain from precise references for the various statements made below; consult the above papers for more details and further reading, and in particular Donnelly and Embrechts (2010).

First of all, the copula concept in (23) is a trivial (though canonical) way for linking the joint df $\mathbb{H}$ with the marginal dfs $H_1, \ldots, H_d$ of the d underlying risks $X_1, \ldots, X_d$. Its use, we have always stressed, is important for *three* reasons: *pedagogic, pedagogic, stress-testing*. Note that we do *not* include pricing and hedging! We emphasize 'peda-gogic' as the copula concept is very useful in understanding the inherent weaknesses in using the concept of (linear) correlation in finance (as well as beyond). For instance, if $\mathbb{H}$ is multivariate normal $\mathbb{H} \sim N_d(\boldsymbol{\mu}, \Sigma)$, with correlations $\rho_{ij} < 1$, then for every pair of risks (X_i, X_j) we have that

$$P\left(X_j > F_j^{-1}(\alpha) \mid X_i > F_i^{-1}(\alpha)\right) \to 0, \quad \alpha \uparrow 1, \tag{30}$$

so that X_i and X_j are so-called *asymptotically* ($\alpha \uparrow 1$) *independent*. Of course, one could interpret the high quantiles $F^{-1}(\alpha)$ as VaR_α. As a consequence, the multivariate normal is totally unsuited for modelling joint extremes. More importantly, this asymp-totic independence is inherited by the Gaussian copula C_Σ^{Ga} underlying $N_d(\boldsymbol{\mu}, \Sigma)$. As a consequence, every model (including the Li model) of the type

$$\mathbb{H}_\Sigma^{\text{Ga}} = C_\Sigma^{\text{Ga}}(H_1, \ldots, H_d) \tag{31}$$

is *not* able to model joint extremes (think of joint defaults for credit risks) effectively and this whatever form the marginals $H_1, \ldots, H_d$ take. It is exactly so-called *meta-models* of the type (31) that have to be handled with great care and be avoided for pric-ing. For stress-testing static (i.e. non-time-dependent) risks they can be useful. Recall that in the original Li-model, $H_1, \ldots, H_d$ were gamma distributed time-to-default of credit risks and the covariance parameters Σ were estimated for instance through market data on Credit Default Swaps (CDS). Upon hearing this construction and calibration, Guus Balkema (personal communication) reacted by saying that 'This has a large component of Baron Münchhausen in it'; recall the way in which the famous baron 'bootstrapped' himself and his horse out of a swamp by pulling his own hair.

Also note that, in general, there is no standard time-dynamic stochastic process model linked to the copula construction (23) (or (31)) so that time dependence in formulas like (31) typically enters through inserting (so-called implied) time-dependent parameters. As the latter are mainly correlations, we again fall in the Münchhausen caveat that correlation input is used to bypass the weakness of using correlations for modelling joint extremal behaviour. We will not discuss here the rather special cases of Lévy-copulas or dynamic copula constructions for special Markov processes. For the moment it is wise to consider copula techniques, for all practical purposes, essentially as static.

Interludium 3 (Meta-models) We briefly want to come back to property (30) and the copula construction (23). One of the 'fudge models' too much in use in credit risk, as well as insurance risk, concerns so-called meta-models. Take any (for ease of discussion) continuous marginal risk dfs $F_1, \ldots, F_d$, and any copula C, then

$$\mathbb{F}(\mathbf{x}) = C\left(F_1(x_1), \ldots, F_d(x_d)\right) \tag{32}$$

always yields a proper df with marginals $F_1, \ldots, F_d$. By construction, C 'codes' the dependence properties between the marginal rvs $X_i(\sim F_i)$, $i = 1, \ldots, d$. When the copula C and the marginals F_i 'fit together' somehow, then one obtains well-studied models with many interesting properties. For instance, if $F_1 = \cdots = F_d = N(0, 1)$ and C is the normal copula with covariance matrix Σ, then $\mathbb{F}$ is a multivariate normal model. Similarly, if one starts with $F_1 = \cdots = F_d = t_\nu$ a Student-t distribution on ν degrees of freedom (df) and C is a t-copula on ν df and covariance matrix Σ, then $\mathbb{F}$ is a multivariate Student-t distribution. As models they are elliptical with many useful properties, for instance, all linear combinations are of the same (normal, t) type, respectively. The normal model shows no (asymptotic) tail dependence (see (30)), whereas the t-model shows tail dependence, leading to a non-zero limit in (30). On the other hand, because of elliptical symmetry, upper (NE) as well as lower (SW) clustering of extremes are the same. These models have a straightforward generalization to multivariate processes, the multivariate normal distribution leading to Brownian motion, the t-model to the theory of Lévy processes. If, however, C and $F_1, \ldots, F_d$ in (32) do not fit together within a well-understood joint model, as was indeed the case with the Li-model used for pricing CDOs, then one runs the danger of ending up with so-called meta-models which, with respect to extremes, behave in a rather degenerate way. A detailed discussion of this issue is to be found in Balkema, Embrechts and Lysenko (2010). In the language of MFE, the Li-model is a meta-Gaussian model. Putting a t-copula on arbitrary marginals yields a meta-t model exhibiting both upper as well as lower tail dependence. For upper tail dependence, one can use for instance the Gumbel copula whereas the Clayton copula exhibits lower tail dependence. A *crucial question* however remains 'which copula to use?' and more importantly 'Should one use a copula construction like (32) at all?' So-called copula-engineering allows for the construction of copulas C which exhibit any kind of dependence/clustering/shape of the sample clouds in any part of $[0, 1]^d$, *however* very few of such models have anything sensible to say on the deeper stochastic nature of the data under study. We therefore strongly advise *against* using models of the type (32) for any purpose beyond stress-testing or fairly straightforward calculations of joint or conditional probabilities. Any serious statistical analysis will have to go beyond (32). If one wants to understand clustering of extremes (in a non-dynamic way) one has to learn MEVT and the underlying multivariate theory of regular variation: *there is no easy road to the land of multivariate extremism!*

We were recently asked by a journalist: 'Is there then an EVT-based pricing formula available or around the corner for credit risk?' Our clear answer is definitely 'No!' (M)EVT offers the correct methodology for describing and more importantly under- standing (joint) extremal risks, so far it does *not* yield a sufficiently rich dynamic theory for handling complicated (i.e. high-dimensional) credit-based structured products. A better understanding of (M)EVT will no doubt contribute towards a curtailing of overcomplicated FE-products for the simple reason that they are far too complex to be priced and hedged in times of stress. The theory referred to in this chapter is absolutely crucial for understanding these limitations of Financial Engineering. It helps in a fundamental way the understanding of the inherent Model Uncertainty (MU again) underlying modern finance and insurance. As a consequence one has to accept that in the complicated risk landscape created by modern finance, one is well advised to sail a bit less close to the (risk-)wind. Too many (very costly) mistakes were made by believing that modern FE would allow for a better understanding and capability of handling complicated credit products based on rare events, like for instance the AAA rated senior CDO tranches.

An area of risk management where (M)EVT in general, and copulas more in particular, can be used in a very constructive way is the field of *risk aggregation, concentration,* and *diversification.* We look at the problem from the point of view of the regulator: let $X_1, \ldots, X_d$ be d one-period risks so that, given a confidence level a, under the Basel II and III framework, one needs to estimate $\mathrm{VaR}_a (X_1 + \cdots + X_d)$ and compare this to $\mathrm{VaR}_a (X_1) + \cdots + \mathrm{VaR}_a (X_d)$. The following measures are considered:

$$(\text{M1}) \quad D(a) = \mathrm{VaR}_a \left(\sum_{k=1}^d X_k \right) - \sum_{k=1}^d \mathrm{VaR}_a (X_k), \text{ and}$$

$$(\text{M2}) \quad C(a) = \frac{\mathrm{VaR}_a \left(\sum_{k=1}^d X_k \right)}{\sum_{k=1}^d \mathrm{VaR}_a (X_k)}.$$

Diversification effects are typically measured using $D(a)$ leading to the important question of sub-versus superadditivity. When $C(a) \leq 1$ (coherence!), then $C(a)100\%$ is often referred to as a measure of concentration. In the case of operational risk, it typ- ically takes values in the range 70–90%. Of course, both quantities $D(a)$ and $C(a)$ are equivalent and enter fundamentally when discussing risk aggregation, or indeed risk allocation. These concepts are not restricted to Value-at-Risk (VaR) as a risk measure, but they enter the current regulatory (Basel II and III) guidelines based on VaR.

A careful analysis of $D(a)$ as well as $C(a)$ now involves all (M)EVT tools discussed above. Starting from applications of one-dimensional EVT, for estimating the individual $\text{VaR}_a\,(X_k)$-factors or transform marginals to a unit-Fréchet scale, to the use of (M)EVT in order to understand the model uncertainty in the calculation of $\text{VaR}_a\left(\sum_{k=1}^{d} X_k\right)$. Indeed, the latter can only be calculated/estimated if one has sufficient information on the joint df $\mathbb{F}$ of the underlying risk factors $X_1, \ldots, X_d$. In the absence of the latter, only bounds can be given, coding somehow the MU in the calculation of $D(a)$ and $C(a)$. Numerous papers exist on this topic; as a start, check the website of the second author for joint papers with Giovanni Puccetti.

So far, we have restricted attention to what one could refer to as classical (M)EVT, even if several of the developments (like Balkema and Embrechts (2007)) are fairly recent. Non-classical approaches which are worth investigating further are more to be found on the statistical/computational front. We expect for the years to come to see further important developments on *Bayesian* analysis for extreme event estimation and also on various applications of methods from *robust statistics*, though the latter may sound somewhat counter-intuitive. In the optimization literature, methodology known under the name of *robust optimization* will no doubt become useful. Most of these newer techniques address in one way or another the key MU issue. A possible paper to start is Arbenz, Embrechts, and Puccetti (2010). On the computational side, for the calculation of rare event probabilities, several numerical integration techniques may be used, including so-called *low-discrepancy sequences* also known as *Quasi Monte Carlo* methods. Tools which have already been applied in the realm of credit risk modelling are standard Monte Carlo and especially *importance sampling* techniques. More broadly, *rare event simulation* is becoming a field on its own with applications well beyond finance and insurance.

Suppose $\mathbb{X}, \mathbb{X}_1, \ldots, \mathbb{X}_n$ are i.i.d., d-dimensional random vectors with df $\mathbb{F}$ and density $\mathbf{f}$. For some measurable set $\mathbf{A}$ which is to be interpreted as rare or remote, one wants to calculate

$$P(\mathbb{X} \in \mathbf{A}) = \int_A \mathbf{f}(\mathbf{x})\, d\mathbf{x} \tag{33}$$

or more generally, for some measurable function $\mathbf{h}$,

$$E\,(\mathbf{h}(\mathbb{X})) = \int_{\mathbb{R}^d} \mathbf{h}(\mathbf{x})\, \mathbf{f}(\mathbf{x})\, d\mathbf{x}.$$

The rareness of $\mathbf{A}$ in (33) translates into $P(\mathbb{X} \in \mathbf{A})$ is sufficiently small, so that standard Monte Carlo techniques become highly inefficient. One of the standard tools in use throughout credit risk management is that of importance sampling; we explain the main idea for $d = 1$ (and this just for ease of notation); we follow section 8.5 in MFE.

Suppose $\theta = E\,(h(X)) = \int_{-\infty}^{+\infty} h(x) f(x)dx$, then the Monte Carlo estimator becomes

$$\hat{\theta}_n^{\text{MC}} = \frac{1}{n} \sum_{i=1}^{n} h\,(X_i). \tag{34}$$

For the importance sampling estimator, one looks for an appropriate density function g so that for $r = f/g$,

$$\theta = \int_{-\infty}^{+\infty} h(x)\, r(x)\, g(x)\, dx = E_g(h(X)\, r(X)),$$

from which one obtains

$$\hat{\theta}_n^{IS} = \frac{1}{n} \sum_{i=1}^{n} h(X_i)\, r(X_i), \tag{35}$$

based on a sample from the g-distribution. The key task now concerns finding an optimal *importance-sampling density* g so that

$$\mathrm{var}\left(\hat{\theta}_n^{IS}\right) \ll \mathrm{var}\left(\hat{\theta}_n^{MC}\right).$$

In the case of light-tailed densities f, the standard technique used is known under the name *exponential tilting*. For some $t \in \mathbb{R}$, one defines

$$g_t(x) = e^{tx}\, f(x)/M_X(t)$$

where the moment-generating function

$$M_X(t) = E\left(e^{tX}\right) = \int_{-\infty}^{+\infty} e^{tx}\, f(x)\, dx \tag{36}$$

is assumed to exist (light-tailedness!). The key aim of using g_t is that it makes the rare event, for instance $\{X \geq c\}$, 'less rare' under the new density g_t. Solving for the optimal density (tilt) corresponds to solving a *saddle-point equation*. In the case of heavy-tailed dfs F, the moment-generating function $M_X(t)$ typically is not analytic in $t = 0$ so that exponential tilting through g_t does not work. At this point EVT becomes useful as indeed g may be chosen from the family of GEVs; see for instance McLeish (2008) for a discussion. The latter paper contains also the g-and-h and skew-normal dfs as examples relevant for risk management. See also Asmussen and Glynn (2007) for a textbook discussion.

We often are confronted by remarks of the type 'why bother about theory as one can just bootstrap for such rare events'. Here a word of warning is in order: the standard situation where the usual bootstrap fails (i.e. delivers inconsistent estimators) is exactly in the realm of very heavy-tailed dfs, maxima, or extreme quantiles. Ways to remedy this deficiency have been found but need to be handled with care (the catchword is *m*-out-of-*n* bootstrap). For a start on this problem, see for instance Angus (1993) and Chernick (2007). Not surprisingly, the theory of regular variation also plays a crucial role here; see section 6.4 in Resnick (2007), it has the telling title 'Why bootstrapping heavy-tailed phenomena is difficult'. In using simulation technology or numerical integration techniques (as there are quadrature formulae or quasi Monte Carlo), one should always be aware of the essential difference between light-tailed and heavy-tailed dfs. For instance, in the case of large deviation methodology (which is also relevant for the above problems) this translates into the standard theory where Cramér's condition *is* satisfied (see (36)) and the theory where Cramér's condition does *not* hold, often translated into a regular variation condition of the type (13). Not being aware of this fundamental difference may result in faulty applications of existing theory.

6 CONCLUSION

Modern risk management in general, and credit risk management more in particular is confronted with serious challenges which bring the analysis of rare events to the forefront. In our chapter, we discuss some of these developments with the current financial crisis as an overall background. Besides giving an overview of some of the basic results in EVT and MEVT, we also address the wider issue of the use, or as some say, misuse, of mathematics and its role in the current crisis. We stress that a trivial reduction of the crisis to a 'too much use of mathematics' is misleading at best and dangerous at worst. Risk management is concerned with technical questions, answers to which in part(!) will have to rely on quantitative tools. In order to avoid a renewed abuse of mathematics, as it was no doubt the case in the credit crisis, end-users will have to understand better the conditions, strengths, and weaknesses of the methodology they are working with. We as mathematicians *must* do better in communicating our findings to the wider public. Or in the words of Ian Stewart: 'It is becoming increasingly necessary, and important, for mathematicians to engage with the general public ... Our subject is widely misunderstood, and its vital role in today's society goes mostly unobserved ... Many mathematicians are now convinced that writing about mathematics is at least as valuable as writing new mathematics ... In fact, many of us feel that it is pointless to invent new theorems unless the public gets to hear of them.' The current economic crisis puts this quote in a rather special perspective.

REFERENCES

Acharya, V. V., and Richarson, M. (eds.) (2009). *Restoring Financial Stability: How to Repair a Failed System*. New York: Wiley.

Angus, J. E. (1993). 'Asymptotic theory for bootstrapping the extremes'. *Communications in Statistics-Theory and Methods*, 22: 15–30.

Arbenz, P., Embrechts, P., and Puccetti, G. (2010). 'The AEP algorithm for the fast computation of the distribution of the sum of dependent random variables.' *Bernoulli* (forthcoming).

Asmussen, S., and Glynn, P. W. (2007). *Stochastic Simulation: Algorithms and Analysis*. New York: Springer.

Balkema, G., and Embrechts, P. (2007). *High Risk Scenarios and Extremes: A Geometric Approach*. Zurich Lectures in Advanced Mathematics, European Mathematical Society Publishing House.

————and Nolde, N. (2010). 'Meta densities and the shape of their sample clouds'. *Journal of Multivariate Analysis*, 101: 1738–54.

Beirlant, J., Goegebeur, Y., Segers, J., and Teugels, J. (2005). *Statistics of Extremes: Theory and Applications*. New York: Wiley.

Bluhm, C., and Overbeck, L. (2007). *Structured Credit Portfolio Analysis, Baskets & CDOs*. London: Chapman & Hall/CRC.

Chavez-Demoulin, V., and Embrechts, P. (2009). 'Revisiting the edge, ten years on.' *Communications in Statistics-Theory and Methods*, 39: 1674–88.

Chernick, M. R. (2007). *Bootstrap Methods: A Guide for Practitioners and Researchers*, 2nd edn. New York: Wiley.

Coles, S. (2001). *An Introduction to Statistical Modeling of Extreme Values*. New York: Springer.

Crouhy, M. G., Galai, D. and Mark, R. (2001). *Risk Management*. New York: McGraw Hill.

——Jarrow, R. A., and Turnbull, S. M. (2008). 'Insights and analysis of current events: the subprime credit crisis of 2007'. *Journal of Derivatives*, 16/1: 81–110.

Daníelsson, J., Embrechts, P., Goodheart, C., Keating, C., Muennich, F., Renault, O., and Shin, H. S. (2005). 'An academic response to Basel II'. Special Paper No 130, Financial Markets Group, LSE.

de Haan, L., and Ferreira, A. (2006). *Extreme Value Theory: An Introduction*. New York: Springer.

Diebold, F. X., Doherty, N. A., and Herriny, R. J. (2010). *The Known, the Unknown, and the Unknowable in Financial Risk Management: Measurement and Theory Advancing Practice*. Princeton: Princeton University Press.

Donnelly, C., and Embrechts, P. (2010). 'The devil is in the tails: actuarial mathematics and the subprime mortgage crisis'. *Astin Bulletin*, 40/1: 1–33.

Embrechts, P. (2009). 'Copulas: a personal view'. *Journal of Risk and Insurance*, 76: 639–50.

——Klüppelberg, C., and Mikosch, T. (1997). *Modelling Extremal Events for Insurance and Finance*. New York: Springer.

——McNeil, A., and Straumann, D. (2002). 'Correlation and dependence in risk management: properties and pitfalls'. In M. Dempster (ed.), *Risk Management: Value at Risk and Beyond*. Cambridge: Cambridge University Press, 176–223.

Keynes, J. M. (1937). 'The general theory'. *Quarterly Journal of Economics*. Rept. in D. Moggridge (ed.), *The collected Writing of John Maynard Keynes*, vol. 14. London: Macmillan, 1973

McLeish, D. (2010). 'Bounded relative error importance sampling and rare event simulation'. *Astin Bulletin*, 40/1: 377–98.

McNeil, A. J., Frey, R., and Embrechts, P. (2005). *Quantitative Risk Management: Concepts, Techniques, Tools*. Princeton: Princeton University Press.

Mikosch, T. (2004). 'Modeling dependence and tails of financial time series'. In B. Finkenstädt and H. Rootzén (eds.), *Extreme Values in Finance, Telecommunications, and the Environment*. London: Chapman & Hall/CRC, 185–286.

Resnick, S. I. (1987). *Extreme Values, Regular Variation, and Point Processes*. New York: Springer.

——(2007). *Heavy-Tail Phenomena: Probabilistic and Statistical Modeling*. New York: Springer.

Sibuya, M. (1959). 'Bivariate extreme statistics'. *Annals of the Institute of Statistical Mathematics*, 11: 195–210.

Taleb, N. N. (2007). *The Black Swan: The Impact of the Highly Improbable*. Harmondsworth: Penguin Books.

CHAPTER 15

··

SADDLEPOINT METHODS
IN PORTFOLIO THEORY

··

RICHARD J. MARTIN

1 INTRODUCTION

··

PROBLEMS in quantitative finance can, in the main, be put into one of two compartments: ascribing probabilities to events and calculating expectations. The first class of problems is essentially what modelling is about, whether in derivatives pricing or in portfolio or risk management; the second is of course fundamental to their practical application. The distinction between the two compartments is worth making. On the one hand there are some computational techniques such as the binomial or trinomial tree that are applicable to many different models and asset classes (provided the underlying dynamics are diffusive). Conversely, there are some models that can be calculated using many different techniques, such as for example synthetic CDO models which can be tackled by numerical grid techniques, analytical approximations or Monte Carlo, or as a second example the emerging application of Lévy processes in derivatives theory, which give rise to models that can be calculated using Fourier transforms, Laplace transforms, or Monte Carlo. Divorcing the model from its calculation is, therefore, quite a useful idea; as for one thing, when something goes wrong, as frequently happens in the credit world, one needs to know whether it is the model or the calculation of it that was at fault. In my experience, it is generally the former, as usually what has happened is that the modellers have overlooked an important source of risk and implicitly ascribed far too low a probability to it. That said, accurate and fast calculation is important, and that is what I shall be talking about here.

I have benefited greatly from interacting with other practitioners in the last ten years. Two deserve a special mention: Tom Wilde for his perceptive observations and depth of understanding in credit portfolio modelling, and Fer Koch for his particular talent in building analytics and systems and understanding how best to develop and apply the results in the rigours of a live trading environment.

The construction of the distribution of losses, or of profit-and-loss, of a portfolio of assets is a well-established problem, whether in structuring multi-asset derivatives or running part of a trading operation, an investment portfolio, or a bank. It can take many guises, according to whether one is concerned with risk on a buy-and-hold view, or whether it is mark-to-market that is of more importance.

In this chapter we shall give the first complete exposition of the *saddlepoint method* to the calculation and management of portfolio losses, in an environment that is quite general and therefore applicable to many asset classes and many models. The methods described here apply equally well in the buy-and-hold and the mark-to-market contexts, and have been applied successfully in both arenas. Their most natural application is in credit, as through the collateralized debt obligation (CDO) market, and investment banks' exposure to bonds and loans, there has been an impetus to understand the losses that can be incurred by portfolios of credit assets. Portfolios of hedge fund exposures or derivatives of other types could also be analysed in the same framework. What makes credit particularly demanding of advanced analytics is that in general the losses that come from it are highly asymmetrical, with the long-credit investor generally receiving a small premium for bearing credit risk and occasionally suffering a very much larger loss when he chooses a 'bad apple'. This asymmetry has also given rise to the exploration of risk measures other than the conventional standard deviation, with the Value-at-Risk (VaR) and expected shortfall (also known as conditional-VaR or CVaR). Another offshoot of the presence of credit portfolios has been the discussion of correlation in its various guises, and indeed in the form of CDO tranches one can actually trade correlation as an asset class. This has led to a standardization of approach, with the conditional-independence approach now being almost universally used in the specification and implementation of portfolio models (the CDO world's brief flirtation with copulas being little more than another way of dressing up a fairly basic concept). The principle behind conditional independence is that the assets are independent conditionally on the outcome of some random variable often called a *risk factor*. By specifying the correlation this way, one has a clear interpretation of the behaviour of large-scale portfolios (which has led to the ASRF model of Gordy 2003) and the joint distribution of all assets is specified reasonably parsimoniously.

The technique described here is called the saddlepoint approximation and comes from asymptotic analysis and complex variable theory. Although common in statistics and mathematical physics, its first application in portfolio theory seems to have been 1998 (Arvanitis et al. 1998), when the present author applied it to the calculation of distributions arising from simple credit loss models; since then the method has been applied and improved by various authors (Gordy 1998; Glasserman and Ruiz-Mata 2006; Wang and Oosterlee 2007).

This chapter naturally divides into two parts. First, we have the construction of the distribution of losses, which is an essential ingredient of valuing CDO tranches and calculating risk measures at different levels of confidence. Secondly, we want to understand where the risk is coming from, by which more formally we mean the sensitivity of risk to asset allocation, an idea that is fundamental to portfolio theory and risk management and is at the heart of the Capital Asset Pricing Model (CAPM). The two parts are closely connected, as we shall see that in obtaining the loss distribution, much information about the risk contributions is already apparent and needs only a few simple computations to extract it. In the theory of risk contributions, we shall identify some problems with the sensitivity of VaR to asset allocation, and show that, somewhat paradoxically, analytical *approximations* to VaR contribution are actually more useful than the 'correct' answer. We will also re-establish the fact that shortfall does not have these technical difficulties, and give a complete derivation of the sensitivity theory in both first and second order. The second-order behaviour will be shown to be 'well-behaved' by which we mean that the saddlepoint approximation preserves the convexity and therefore is a reliable platform for portfolio optimization (unlike VaR).

2 APPROXIMATION OF LOSS DISTRIBUTIONS

2.1 Characteristic functions

Portfolio analytics can, in the main, be understood by reference to the characteristic function (CF) of the portfolio's distribution. The characteristic function of the random variable Y, which from now on will denote the loss (or P&L) of the portfolio in question, is defined as the following function of the complex[1] variable ω:

$$C_Y(\omega) = \mathbf{E}[e^{i\omega Y}].$$

The density of Y can be recovered from it by the inverse Fourier integral

$$f_Y(x) = \frac{1}{2\pi} \int_{-\infty}^{\infty} C_Y(\omega) e^{-i\omega x}\, d\omega. \tag{1}$$

If the distribution of Y is discrete then the convergence is delicate and the result has to be interpreted using delta-functions: $\frac{1}{2\pi} \int_{-\infty}^{\infty} e^{i\omega(y-x)}\, d\omega = \delta(y - x)$.

Obviously we have to be able to efficiently compute C_Y. The ingredients are: (i) the characteristic function of independent random variables is the product of their characteristic functions, and (ii) the characteristic function is an expectation, so one can do the usual trick of conditioning on a risk factor and then integrating out. This construction is universal in portfolio problems, so we can review a few examples now.

2.1.1 *Example: CreditRisk+*

Consider first a default/no-default model. Let the jth asset have a loss net of recovery a_j and a conditional default probability $p_j(V)$, where V is the risk factor. Then

$$C_Y(\omega) = \mathbf{E}\left[\prod_j \left(1 - p_j(V) + p_j(V)e^{i\omega a_j}\right)\right]$$

[1] As usual i denotes $\sqrt{-1}$.

Make the assumption that the default probabilities are quite small, so that

$$C_Y(\omega) \approx \mathrm{E}\left[e^{\sum_j p_j(V)(e^{i\omega a_j}-1)}\right],$$

(the Poisson approximation), and then impose the following model of the conditional default probability: $p_j(V) = \overline{p}_j \cdot V$, so that the action of the risk factor is to scale the default probabilities in proportion to each other. Of course the risk-factor has to be non-negative with probability 1. Then

$$C_Y(\omega) \approx \mathrm{E}\left[e^{\sum_j \overline{p}_j(e^{i\omega a_j}-1)V}\right] = M_V\left(\sum_j \overline{p}_j(e^{i\omega a_j} - 1)\right)$$

where $M_V(s) = \mathrm{E}[e^{sV}]$ denotes the moment-generating function (MGF) of V. It is then a matter of choosing a distribution for V (apart from positivity, it needs to have a MGF that is known in closed form, so the Gamma and inverse Gaussian distributions are obvious candidates). Incidentally CreditRisk+ is configured to have exposures that are integer multiples of some quantum, and this enables the loss distribution to be obtained recursively.[2] □

2.1.2 Example: Extended CreditRisk+; Gaussian copula

Sometimes $C_{Y|V}$ is known in closed form but C_Y is not. Here are two examples.

An objection to the basic CreditRisk+ model as just described is that assets can default more than once, which for low-grade assets is a problem. In that case we cannot use the Poisson approximation, and instead have to calculate the CF numerically. One therefore has

$$C_Y(\omega) = \int_{-\infty}^{\infty} \prod_j \left(1 - p_j(v) + p_j(v)e^{i\omega a_j}\right) f(v)\, dv \tag{2}$$

with $p_j(v) = \min(\overline{p}_j v, 1)$ and $f(v)$ denoting the density of V (which is zero for $v < 0$).

The Gaussian copula model requires the same treatment. In that case (2) can still be used, but with different ingredients: $p_j(V) = \Phi\left(\dfrac{\Phi^{-1}(\overline{p}_j)-\beta_j V}{\sqrt{1-\beta_j^2}}\right)$ and $V \sim N(0, 1)$ for the risk factor.

It is apparent that in this framework any model can be handled, once the distribution of V and the 'coupling function' $p_j(V)$ are specified. In fact, it is worth noting in passing that specifying a model this way leads to overspecification, as replacing V by $h(V)$ (with h some invertible function) and p_j by $p_j \circ h^{-1}$ leaves the model unaffected. One can therefore standardize all one-factor models to have a Normally distributed risk factor, which simplifies the implementation somewhat. □

---

[2] Which imposes further restrictions on the distribution of V; see Gundlach and Lehrbass (2004) for a full discussion of the Panjer recursion.

2.1.3 Example: Merton model

There are also situations in which even $C_{Y|V}$ is not known in closed form, though to find examples we have to go beyond the simple default/no-default model. A detailed exposition of mark-to-market (MTM) models would take us outside the scope of this chapter, but here is the basic idea. We adopt the Merton approach, in which the holder of debt is short a put option on the firm's assets. The put value relates to the firm value through the Black-Scholes put formula (for a simple model, at least), and the values of differerent firms' debt may be correlated by correlating their asset levels. If the firms' asset returns Z_j are distributed as N(0, 1) after suitable normalization, then a simple Gaussian model is the obvious choice:

$$Z_j = \beta_j V + \sqrt{1 - \beta_j^2}\, U_j,$$

where V is the common part and U_j the idiosyncratic part. Let the value of the debt be some function $g_j(Z_j)$ say. Then, conditioning on V and integrating out the idiosyncratic return U_j, we have

$$C_{X_j|V}(\omega) = \int_{-\infty}^{\infty} \exp\left(i\omega g_j\left(\beta_j V + \sqrt{1 - \beta_j^2}\, u\right)\right) \frac{e^{-u^2/2}}{\sqrt{2\pi}}\, du$$

and the integral has to be done numerically. On top of that, the outer integral over V has to be done. This can be viewed as a continuum analogue of 'credit migration' (the more common discrete version having been discussed by Barco (2004)). The simple model above with Normal distributions is not to be recommended for serious use because the probability of large spread movements is too low, but one can build more complex models in which jump processes are used and from the point of view of risk aggregation the same principles apply. □

2.2 Inversion

Having arrived at the characteristic function, we now wish to recover the density, tail probability, or whatever. The density of the random variable Y can be recovered from (1) which can, for conditional independence models, be written in two equivalent forms:

$$f_Y(x) = \frac{1}{2\pi} \int_{-\infty}^{\infty} E[C_{Y|V}(\omega)] e^{-i\omega x}\, d\omega \tag{3}$$

$$f_Y(x) = E\left[\frac{1}{2\pi} \int_{-\infty}^{\infty} C_{Y|V}(\omega) e^{-i\omega x}\, d\omega\right] \tag{4}$$

(i.e. the 'outer integration' over V can be done inside the inversion integral, or outside). Other expressions such as the tail probability and expected shortfall can be dealt with similarly.

In simple cases, such as default/no-default with equal loss amounts, the most direct route is to assemble the loss distribution on a grid (see e.g. Burtschell, Gregory, and Laurent 2005). The distribution of independent losses is found recursively, building the portfolio up asset by asset, and for conditionally independent losses one follows the usual 'condition, find distribution, integrate-out' route: this is, in essence, eq. (4). When the loss amounts are not identical, this procedure can still be followed as long as one is prepared to bucket the losses so that they do end up on a grid. Note that for very large portfolios this method is very inefficient because the computation time is proportional to the square of the portfolio size. The method is also unsuited to continuous distributions.

For the aggregation of arbitrary distributions the Fast Fourier Transform, essentially a numerical integration of the Fourier transform, is a useful tool. As the inversion integral is a linear function of the characteristic function, it does not matter which of (3, 4) is followed, though the former requires fewer calls to the FFT routine and is therefore preferable. A few things should be borne in mind about FFTs: first, the FFT is a grid method and the use of distributions that are not precisely represented on a grid can cause artefacts; secondly, although the inversion is fast, the evaluation of the characteristic functions at each gridpoint is not always, and this is where most of the computation time is spent.

Finally we have analytical approximations e.g. Central Limit Theorem (CLT), Edgeworth, Saddlepoint. In their classical form these are large portfolio approximations for sums of independent random variables, and they have an obvious advantage over numerical techniques on large portfolios: numerical methods spend an inordinately long time computing a distribution that the CLT would approximate very well knowing only the mean and variance (which are trivial to compute). These methods are non-linear in the CF and so (3) and (4) give *different* results.

When the analytical approximation is done inside the expectation, as in (4), it is said to be *indirect*. If outside, as in (3), so that the unconditional CF is being handled, it is *direct*. It is argued in Martin and Ordovás (2006) that the indirect method is 'safer', because it is still being applied to independent variables, with the outer integration having essentially no bearing on the accuracy of the approximation: by contrast, the direct method is more like a 'black box'. We concentrate on the indirect method that we shall be using throughout this chapter, with only a short section on the direct method. (In any case, the formulas for the direct methods will be obvious from the indirect ones.)

2.3 Saddlepoint approximation: concepts and approximation to density

We need to introduce some more notation, in the shape of the moment-generating function (MGF), $M_Y(s) = E[e^{sY}]$, and when doing so we understand that it is to be evaluated for values of s that might not be purely imaginary. As $M_Y(s) = C_Y(\omega)$ when $s = i\omega$, and $C_Y(\omega)$ exists for all $\omega \in \mathbb{R}$ regardless of the distribution of Y, it must hold that $M_Y(s)$ exists for all pure imaginary s. However, when using the notation M_Y we will take it as read that $M_Y(s)$ exists for values of s off the imaginary axis (more precisely, in some band $s_- < \text{Re}(s) < s_+$ with $s_- < 0 < s_+$. This imposes the restriction that the distribution of Y decay at an appropriate rate in the tails (exponential decay is sufficient). Note that in many examples for credit risk (portfolios of bonds, CDS, CDOs, etc.) the maximum loss is finite and so this condition is automatically satisfied. It is also satisfied for anything Normally distributed. The term cumulant-generating function (KGF) is used for $K_Y(s) = \log M_Y(s)$.

The most well-known results for the approximation of the distribution of a sum of independent random variables

$$Y = \sum_{i=1}^{n} X_j, \qquad (X_j) \text{ i.i.d.,}$$

are the Central Limit (CLT) and Edgeworth expansions, but they are found not to approximate the tail well: they give best accuracy in the middle of the distribution. So a neat idea is to change measure by 'tilting' so that the region of interest becomes near the mean. A convenient approach is to use an exponential multiplier:

$$\tilde{f}_Y(y) = \frac{e^{\lambda y} f_Y(y)}{M_Y(\lambda)}$$

where the denominator is chosen so as to make the 'tilted' distribution integrate to unity. It is easily verified that under the tilted measure ($\tilde{P}$) the mean and variance of Y are $K_Y'(\lambda)$ and $K_Y''(\lambda)$, where $K_Y = \log M_Y$. By choosing $K_Y'(\lambda) = y$, we have in effect shifted the middle of the distribution to y. We then argue that if Y is very roughly Normal under P, and hence also under $\tilde{P}$, then its probability density at its mean must be about $1/\sqrt{2\pi\tilde{\sigma}^2}$ where $\tilde{\sigma}^2$ is its variance under $\tilde{P}$. Then

$$f_Y(y) = e^{K_Y(\lambda)-\lambda y}\tilde{f}_Y(y) \approx \frac{e^{K_Y(\lambda)-\lambda y}}{\sqrt{2\pi K_Y''(\lambda)}}$$

which is the saddlepoint approximation to the density of Y. The '$1/\sqrt{2\pi\tilde{\sigma}^2}$' approximation is a lot better than appearances might suggest. For example, with an exponential distribution (density e^{-x}) the true density at the mean is e^{-1} and the approximation is $1/\sqrt{2\pi}$, which is about 8% too high: this in spite of the fact the exponential and Normal distributions have very different shape. Note that, when applied to the saddlepoint approximation, this 8% error is observed uniformly across the distribution (because an exponential distribution remains exponential under tilting).

This method, known as the *Esscher tilt*, is a recurring theme in more advanced work, particularly on risk contributions (Martin, Thompson, and Browne 2001b), which we shall develop later in this chapter, and in importance sampling (Glasserman and Li 2005) where it is used to steer the bulk of the sampling to the point of interest on the distribution (usually a long way out in the tail where there would otherwise be very few samples). One of the vital ingredients is the uniqueness of the tilting factor. This follows from the convexity of K_Y, which in turn follows by consideration of the quadratic $q(t) = \mathbf{E}[(1 + tY)^2 e^{sY}]$. As q is non-negative its discriminant ('$b^2 - -4ac$') must be ≤ 0, and so $\left(\mathbf{E}[Ye^{sY}]\right)^2 \leq \mathbf{E}[e^{sY}]\mathbf{E}[Y^2 e^{sY}]$, which on rearrangement gives $(\log M_Y)'' \geq 0$, as required. We shall encounter the same method of proving convexity later on, in conjunction with the expected shortfall risk measure.

Although the Esscher tilt is neat, our preferred approach uses contour integration, and explains where the term 'saddlepoint' comes from. The reader is directed to Bender and Orszag (1978) for a fuller discussion of the asymptotic calculus. Assume first that Y is the sum of independent and identically distributed random variables, so that $K_Y = nK_X$ with $K_X(s) = \mathbf{E}[e^{sX}]$. Expressing the density as a contour integral, distorting the path of integration $\mathcal{C}$ until it lies along the path of steepest descent— which is why the MGF must exist for s off the imaginary axis—and then applying Watson's lemma gives:

$$f_Y(y) = \frac{1}{2\pi i} \int_{\mathcal{C}} e^{n(K_X(s) - sy/n)} \, ds \tag{5}$$

$$\sim \frac{e^{n(K_X(\hat{s}) - \hat{s}y/n)}}{\sqrt{2\pi n K_X''(\hat{s})}} \left[1 + \frac{1}{n}\left(\frac{K_X''''(\hat{s})}{8K_X''(\hat{s})^2} - \frac{5K_X'''(\hat{s})^2}{24K_X''(\hat{s})^3}\right) + O(n^{-2})\right]$$

where $\hat{s}$ is the value of s that makes $K_Y(s) - sy$ stationary, that is,

$$K_Y'(\hat{s}) = y, \tag{6}$$

from which we see that $\hat{s}$ is interchangeable with λ. We prefer this method of proof on the grounds that it is more upfront about the nature of the approximation, and is more useful when singular integrands such as the tail probability and shortfall are being examined. The term *saddlepoint* refers to the nature of $K_Y(s) - sy$ at its stationary point: it has a local minimum when approached along the real axis, but a maximum when approached in the orthogonal direction, which is the path of integration here. A three-dimensional plot of the function would therefore reveal it to be in the shape of a saddle. By deforming the contour of integration so as to pass along the path of steepest descent, one avoids the problem of approximating a Fourier integral that is generally oscillatory (Figures 15.1, 15.2).

A fundamental point is that the result can be written entirely in terms of K_Y as

$$f_Y(y) \sim \frac{e^{K_Y(\hat{s}) - \hat{s}y}}{\sqrt{2\pi K_Y''(\hat{s})}} \left[1 + \left(\frac{K_Y''''(\hat{s})}{8K_Y''(\hat{s})^2} - \frac{5K_Y'''(\hat{s})^2}{24K_Y''(\hat{s})^3}\right) + O(K_Y^{-2})\right]. \tag{7}$$

Rather than being in descending powers of n, this approximation is in 'descending powers of K_Y'. One can therefore in principle use it in situations where Y is not the sum of i.i.d. random variables. It can thus be applied to sums of variables that are

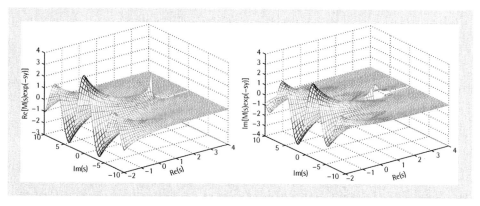

FIGURE 15.1 Real and imaginary parts of the inversion integrand $M(s)e^{-sy}$ where $M(s)$ = $(1 - \beta s)^{-\alpha}$ (the Gamma distribution), with $\alpha = 1$, $\beta = 0.5$, $y = 1$. There is a branch point at $s = 1/\beta$ and the plane is cut from there to $+\infty$. The integrand is oscillatory for contours parallel to the imaginary axis.

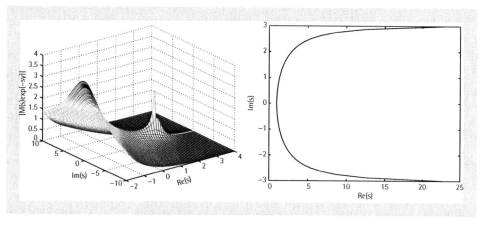

FIGURE 15.2 Absolute value of the same inversion integrand $M(s)e^{-sy}$ as Figure 15.1, and path of steepest descent. The contour runs in a horseshoe from $\infty - \pi i$, through 1 (the saddlepoint), round to $\infty + \pi i$.

independent *but not identically distributed*, and this is one of the most important developments and insights in the theory and application. Common sense dictates, however, that the further away one gets from the non-identically distributed case, the less reliable the approximation is likely to be. For example, if there is a large exposure to one very non-Gaussian instrument in the portfolio, a poorer approximation should be expected (and indeed the correction term is considerable in that case).

2.4 Tail probability

The probability density function is not particularly useful in practice: the density function for a discrete model of losses consists of spikes and the fine structure of these is not especially important; one usually wants to know how likely it is for losses to exceed a certain level without having to integrate the density; and the approximated density does not exactly integrate to unity. We therefore derive the tail probability and related quantities as integrals and approximate them.

The tail probability integral is in MGF form[3]

$$\mathbf{P}[Y \gtrdot y] = \frac{1}{2\pi i} \int_{\mathcal{I}+} e^{K_Y(s)-sy} \frac{ds}{s}. \tag{8}$$

The symbol $\gtrdot$ is to be interpreted thus:

$$\mathbf{P}[Y \gtrdot y] \equiv \mathbf{P}[Y > y] + \tfrac{1}{2}\mathbf{P}[Y = y].$$

The reason for the $\frac{1}{2}\mathbf{P}[Y = y]$ term is that if Y contains probability mass at y then $M_Y(s)e^{-sy}$ contains a constant term of strength $\mathbf{P}[Y = y]$, and now the interpretation of (8) is rather delicate: the basic idea is to subtract out the divergent part of the integral and observe that the 'principal value' of $\frac{1}{2\pi i}\int_{-i\infty}^{i\infty} ds/s$ is $\frac{1}{2}$. Notice therefore that if the true distribution of Y is discrete then a naive comparison[4] of $\mathbf{P}[Y > y]$ with (8) (or any continuum approximation to (8)) produces appreciable errors, but these have little to do with the quality of the analytical approximation because they arise from the continuity correction. In our examples, when we plot the tail probability, it will be $\mathbf{P}[Y \gtrdot y]$ vs y.

Daniels (1987) points out that although the two methods of deriving the saddlepoint expansion for the density (Edgeworth using Esscher tilt, or steepest descent using Watson's lemma) give the same result, they give different results for the tail probability. In essence this problem arises because of the singularity at $s = 0$.

The method of Lugannani and Rice, which is preferable and will be used in several places in this chapter, removes the singularity by splitting out a singular part that can be integrated exactly. The saddlepoint expansion is then performed on the remaining portion. We refer to Daniels (1987) for a fuller exposition, but here is the idea. It is convenient when performing the asymptotic approximation for the term in the exponential to be exactly quadratic rather than only approximately so. This can be effected by changing variable from s to z according to

$$\tfrac{1}{2}(z - \hat{z})^2 = \big(K_Y(s) - sy\big) - \big(K_Y(\hat{s}) - \hat{s}y\big)$$
$$-\tfrac{1}{2}\hat{z}^2 = K_Y(\hat{s}) - \hat{s}y$$

---

[3] $\mathcal{I}$ denotes the imaginary axis in an upward direction; the + sign indicates that the contour is deformed to the right at the origin to avoid the singularity there (so it passes round the origin in an anticlockwise, or positive, direction).

[4] As, for example, in a discussion by Merino and Nyfeler in Gundlach and Lehrbass (2004), ch. 17.

which ensures that $s = 0 \Leftrightarrow z = 0$ and also $s = \hat{s} \Leftrightarrow z = \hat{z}$. Then the integral can be split into a singular part that can be done exactly and a regular part to which the usual saddlepoint treatment can be applied. The result is

$$\mathbf{P}[Y > y] \sim \Phi(-\hat{z}) + \phi(\hat{z}) \left\{ \frac{1}{\hat{s}\sqrt{K_Y''(\hat{s})}} - \frac{1}{\hat{z}} + \cdots \right\}, \tag{9}$$

the celebrated *Lugannani-Rice formula*. As pointed out by Barndorff-Nielsen (1991), this has the flavour of a Taylor series expansion of the function $\Phi(-\hat{z} + \cdots)$, which does look more like a tail probability than (9) does; after doing the necessary algebra the result is

$$\mathbf{P}[Y > y] \sim \Phi\left(-\hat{z} + \frac{1}{\hat{z}} \ln \frac{\hat{z}}{\hat{s}\sqrt{K_Y''(\hat{s})}} + \cdots \right). \tag{10}$$

Note that both expressions are regular at $\hat{s} = 0$ but need careful numerical treatment near there: the preferred method is to expand in a Taylor series in $\hat{s}$, and one obtains

$$\mathbf{P}[Y > y] \sim \Phi\left(-\frac{K_Y'''(0)}{6K_Y''(0)^{3/2}} + \cdots \right).$$

An interesting consequence of the Lugannani-Rice formula is that, in the saddlepoint approximation,

$$\frac{\partial^2}{\partial y^2} \ln \mathbf{P}[Y > y] < 0; \tag{11}$$

we say that the resulting distribution is *log-concave*. Hence the graph of $\mathbf{P}[Y > y]$ vs y on a logarithmic scale, as we often plot, will always 'bend downwards'. Not all distributions are log-concave; for example the exponential distribution clearly is, and more generally so is the Gamma distribution with shape parameter ≥ 1, and the Normal distribution is too (by virtue of the inequality $\mathbf{E}[(Z - x)\mathbf{1}[Z > x]] > 0$); but the Student-t is not. To prove the result, note from log-concavity of the Normal distribution that

$$\hat{z}\Phi(-\hat{z}) - \phi(\hat{z}) < 0.$$

After some minor manipulations this can be recast as

$$\frac{\hat{s}\phi(\hat{z})}{\sqrt{K_Y''(\hat{s})}} \left(\Phi(-\hat{z}) + \frac{\phi(\hat{z})}{\hat{s}\sqrt{K_Y''(\hat{s})}} - \frac{\phi(\hat{z})}{\hat{z}} \right) < \left(\frac{\phi(\hat{z})}{\sqrt{K_Y''(\hat{s})}} \right)^2.$$

By (9) this can be written, with $\mathbf{P}[Y > y]$ abbreviated to $P(y)$,

$$P''(y)P(y) < P'(y)^2,$$

from[5] which (11) is immediate.

---

[5] Differentiation w.r.t. y slots in a factor of $(-\hat{s})$, so the first term on the LHS is $-1\times$ the derivative of the density.

2.5 Tranche payoffs and expected shortfall (ESF)

We are now in a position to deal with the ESF, which is defined by $S^+[Y] = E[Y \mid Y > y]$ or $S^-[Y] = E[Y \mid Y < y]$ (according as Y denotes portfolio loss or portfolio value) where y is the VaR at the chosen tail probability.[6] The integral representation of the ESF is

$$E[Y1[Y \gtrless y]] = \frac{1}{2\pi i} \int_{\mathcal{I}\pm} K_Y'(s)e^{K_Y(s)-sy}\frac{ds}{s}.$$

By following the methods that we applied to the tail probability, we write the singularity in the integrand as the sum of a regular part and an analytically tractable singular part near $s = 0$:

$$\frac{K_Y'(s)}{s} = \frac{\mu_Y}{s} + \frac{K_Y'(s) - \mu_Y}{s} + O(s)$$

with μ_Y the mean of Y. The singular part then gives rise to the same integral as the tail probability, calculated earlier, and the regular part can be given the usual saddlepoint treatment. We have

$$E[Y1[Y \gtrless y]] \sim \mu_Y P[Y \gtrless y] \pm \frac{y - \mu_Y}{\hat{s}} f_Y(y), \tag{12}$$

which is easily evaluated using the expressions for the density and the tail probability. Division by the tail probability then gives the ESF. As usual the formula is exact if Y is Normally distributed, as can be verified longhand.

There is a close link to tranche payoffs (calls and puts on the loss distribution), as follows. When computing the payoff in a tranche it is necessary to find the difference between two call payoffs, where the call strikes (denoted y in what follows) are the attachment and detachment points of the tranche. The 'call' and 'put' payoffs are $C_y^+ \equiv E[(Y - y)^+]$ and $C_y^- \equiv E[(y - Y)^+]$ which have integral representation

$$C_y^\pm = \frac{1}{2\pi i} \int_{\mathcal{I}\pm} M_Y(s)e^{-sy}\frac{ds}{s^2}$$

(incidentally the put-call parity formula $C_y^+ - C_y^- = \mu_Y - y$ can be inferred by combining the two paths, which collapse to a loop round the origin, where the residue is $M_Y'(0) - y = \mu_Y - y$). Integration by parts reduces the double pole to a single pole:

$$C_y^\pm = \frac{1}{2\pi i} \int_{\mathcal{I}\pm} (K_Y'(s) - y)e^{K_Y(s)-sy}\frac{ds}{s},$$

---

[6] From now on we shall assume that the distributions in question are continuous, so we shall be less careful about distinguishing > from >. This avoids the complication of defining VaR and ESF for discontinuous distributions (see Acerbi and Tasche (2002) for the generalization).

clearly a close relative of the ESF integral. (This can also be arrived at by noting that $E[(Y - y)^+] = E[(Y - y)\mathbf{1}[Y > y]]$, which is what we did above for ESF.) Following the same route as with ESF we obtain

$$C_y^{\pm} \sim (\mu - y)P[Y \gtrless y] + \frac{y - \mu}{\hat{s}} f_Y(y).$$

2.6 Examples 1 (Independence)

It is now time for some numerical examples. We take a default/no-default model for ease of exposition. In each case we obtain the true distribution by inverting the Fourier integral numerically (by the FFT (Press et al. 2002)), the saddlepoint approximation and the Central Limit Theorem(CLT). This allows the analytical approximations to be verified. Different portfolio sizes and different default probabilities are assumed, as follows.

- Figure 15.3: 10 assets, exposure 10, default probability 1%. Apart from the obvious problem of trying to approximate a discrete distribution with a continuous one, the saddlepoint accuracy is reasonably uniform across the distribution.
- Figure 15.4: 100 assets, exposure 4, default probability 1%. This portfolio is more fine-grained, but note that even with 1,000 assets the CLT is appreciably in error for higher quantiles.
- Figure 15.5: 100 assets, unequal exposures (median 5, highest 50), default probabilities variable (typically 0.1–4%; lower for the assets with higher exposure). Again the saddlepoint approximation works well and accuracy is roughly uniform across the distribution.
- Figure 15.6: 100 assets, a couple of very large exposures (median 1, highest 150), default probabilities variable (typically 0.04–4%; lower for the assets with higher exposure).

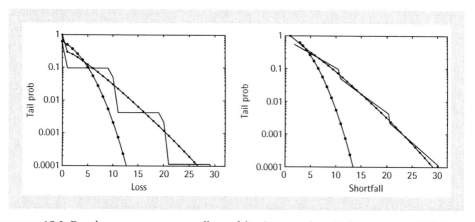

FIGURE 15.3 Equal exposures, very small portfolio (10 assets). ●=Saddlepoint, ○=CLT. Exact result (which is 'steppy') shown by unmarked line.

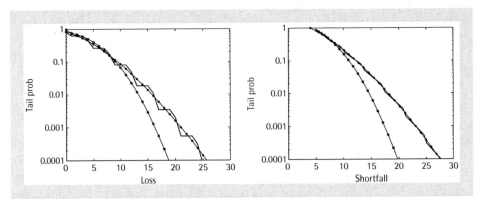

FIGURE 15.4 As Figure 15.3 but for larger portfolio (100 assets).

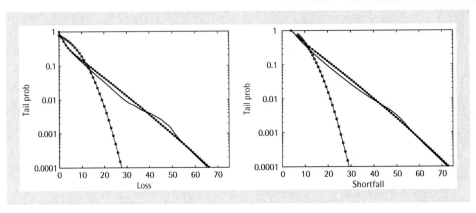

FIGURE 15.5 Inhomogeneous portfolio (100 assets). The largest exposure is 10× median.

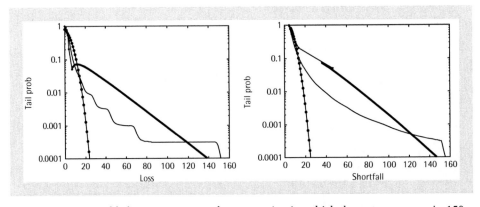

FIGURE 15.6 An unlikely case: extreme heterogeneity in which largest exposure is 150×
median. The true distribution has a step in it at loss=150, which the saddlepoint approximation
attempts to smooth out, thereby overestimating risk at lower levels.

The last case is extreme and has a few features that make it difficult to deal with: a large step in the loss distribution caused by the very binary nature of the portfolio (if the biggest asset defaults, a huge loss is incurred; otherwise the losses are of little importance). In mark-to-market models there is a continuum of possible losses so this situation does not arise. Furthermore, even if a situation like this does crop up, the approximation is erring on the side of being conservative about the risk. Given that the period of the current 'Credit Crunch' has witnessed many allegedly 'very low probability' events, this form of approximation error is unlikely to result in bad risk management decisions. In the context of a portfolio optimization, the method would immediately start by chopping back such large exposures—and once it had done that, the approximation error would decrease anyway.

Later on (Figure 15.15) in discussing risk contributions we shall give another example of a smallish inhomogeneous portfolio, showing that the approximation works well. Other examples are given in Martin, Thompson, and Browne (2001a) and Martin (2004), the latter showing the results of applying the method to assets that are Gamma distributed (a continuous distribution).

2.7 Accuracy and asymptoticity of saddlepoint approximation

To understand why the saddlepoint approximation is accurate it is necessary first to understand in what sense the asymptotic expansion is being taken: the method is asymptotic for a large number of independent random variables being added, though as we have just seen, the number need not be very large in practice. Typically the relative accuracy *when the method is used only for addition of independent random variables* is roughly uniform across the whole distribution (Kolassa 1994) rather than just being a 'tail approximation'.

For small portfolios, one can easily develop direct computations for establishing the loss distribution, essentially by considering all possible combinations of events. Asymptotic expansions work for portfolios that have a large number of assets. Why do we regard asymptotic methods as more useful? Essentially because there are more large numbers than there are small ones!

We have said that a 'large number' of random variables have to be added, and to understand what 'large' means in practice we can look at the first correction term (5). Clearly the smaller the higher cumulants the smaller the error. However, certain non-Gaussian distributions give very small errors: for example the error vanishes altogether for the inverse Gaussian distribution, while for the Gamma distribution with shape parameter a it is $-1/(12na)$ which is small when the shape parameter of Y, which is na, is large. (If Y is exponentially distributed then the correction term can be calculated easily from (7) and it works out as $-\frac{1}{12}$, for all s; this almost exactly cancels the aforementioned 8% error in the leading-order term. Jensen (1995) has a more complete discussion.)

Being more adventurous, one could even forget about independence and then use the saddlepoint approximation as a black box, as suggested in Martin, Thompson, and Browne (2001a). This is the 'direct approach'; we shall return to it later.

2.8 Conditionally independent variables

By inserting the outer integration over the risk factor we obtain all the results for conditionally independent variables. This means that $\hat{s}$, μ, and the density and tail probability are all factor dependent. Treating things this way, we divorce the question of the saddlepoint approximation's accuracy from the choice of correlation model, as the approximation is only being applied to the distribution of a sum of *independent* variables. This is important, because the subject of correlation is a vast one and one could never hope to check the method's accuracy for 'all possible correlation models'. Making the choice of correlation model irrelevant is therefore a useful step.

For the density, one has

$$f_Y(y) \approx \mathbf{E}\left[\frac{e^{K_{Y|V}(\hat{s}_V) - \hat{s}_V y}}{\sqrt{2\pi K''_{Y|V}(\hat{s}_V)}} \left(1 + \left(\frac{K''''_{Y|V}(\hat{s}_V)}{8 K''_{Y|V}(\hat{s}_V)^2} - \frac{5 K'''_{Y|V}(\hat{s}_V)^2}{24 K''_{Y|V}(\hat{s}_V)^3} \right) + \cdots \right) \right], \quad (13)$$

and for the tail probability,

$$\mathbf{P}[Y > y] \approx \mathbf{E}\left[\Phi\left(-\hat{z}_V + \frac{1}{\hat{z}_V} \ln \frac{\hat{z}_V}{\hat{s}_V \sqrt{K''_{Y|V}(\hat{s}_V)}} + \cdots \right) \right], \quad (14)$$

while for the shortfall,

$$S_y^{\pm}[Y] \approx \frac{1}{P^{\pm}} \mathbf{E}\left[\mu_{Y|V} \mathbf{P}[Y \gtrless y \mid V] \pm \frac{y - \mu_{Y|V}}{\hat{s}_V} f_{Y|V}(y) \right] \quad (15)$$

with P^+, P^- the upper and lower tail probability (subscripts V and $|V$ denote the dependence on V). Incidentally the Central Limit Theorem would give the following, which is obtained by taking $\hat{s}_V \to 0$:

$$S_y^{\pm}[Y] = \frac{1}{P^{\pm}} \mathbf{E}\left[\mu_{Y|V} \Phi\left(\frac{\mu_{Y|V} - y}{\sigma_{Y|V}} \right) \pm \sigma_{Y|V} \phi\left(\frac{\mu_{Y|V} - y}{\sigma_{Y|V}} \right) \right], \quad (16)$$

with $\mu_{Y|V}$ and $\sigma^2_{Y|V}$ denoting the mean and variance of the portfolio conditional on the risk factor; this can be obtained directly.

It is worth mentioning at this point the *granularity adjustment* which gives a formula for VaR when a *small* amount of unsystematic risk is added to the portfolio. This can be derived from the above equations. Now if we wish to incorporate the effects of unsystematic risk we can model the loss as $Y = Y_\infty + U$, with $Y_\infty = \mathbf{E}[Y \mid V]$ (the loss of the putative 'infinitely granular portfolio', which need not exist in reality) and U denoting an independent Gaussian residual of variance σ^2 which can depend on Y_∞.

The difference between the upper P-quantiles of Y_∞ and Y is given by the granularity adjustment (GA) formula (Martin and Wilde 2002 and references therein):

$$\mathrm{VaR}_P[Y] \sim \mathrm{VaR}_P[Y_\infty] - \frac{1}{2f(x)}\frac{d}{dx}\sigma^2(x)f(x)\bigg|_{x=\mathrm{VaR}_P[Y_\infty]}, \qquad (17)$$

where f is the density of Y_∞. The shortfall-GA is

$$\mathbf{S}_P[Y] \sim \mathbf{S}_P[Y_\infty] + \frac{1}{2P}\sigma^2(x)f(x)\bigg|_{x=\mathrm{VaR}_P[Y_\infty]}. \qquad (18)$$

Note that the correction to shortfall is always positive (and analytically neater), whereas the correction to VaR is not; we will be discussing this issue in more detail later, and essentially it follows from non-coherence of the VaR risk measure (Artzner et al. 1999; Acerbi and Tasche 2002).

The equation (15) and its simpler Central Limit analogue are the sum of two pieces and it is attractive to interpret them as, respectively, the contributions of systematic and specific risk to the portfolio ESF. This is because the first term is related to the variation of the conditional mean of the portfolio ($\mu_{Y|V}$) with the risk factor and the second term is related to the residual variance ($\sigma^2_{Y|V}$) not explained by the risk factor. Roughly, the first term is proportional to the interasset correlations (R-squared in KMV (Kealhofer-McQueen-Vasteek)terminology or β^2 in CAPM) and the second to the reciprocal of the portfolio size. It turns out that this decomposition is analogous to the well-known result for the standard deviation,

$$\mathbf{V}[Y] = \mathbf{V}\big[\mathbf{E}[Y \mid V]\big] + \mathbf{E}\big[\mathbf{V}[Y \mid V]\big].$$

This and related issues are discussed in Martin and Tasche (2007).

Note that the log-concavity property derived earlier is destroyed by the mixing operation, so in the conditionally independent case it is only the V-*conditional* distributions that are log-concave; the unconditional distribution may well not be.

2.9 Computational issues

It is worth mentioning some of the computational issues needed to implement a workable calculator. A large proportion of the computation time is spent in the root-searching for $\hat{s}$: the equation $K'_{Y|V}(s_V) = y$ has to be solved for each V, and if one is finding the VaR for some given tail probability, the loss level (y) will have to be adjusted in some outer loop. Consequently, it is worth devoting some effort to optimizing the root searching. The first thing to note is that the saddlepoint is roughly given by $\hat{s} \approx (y - K'(0))/K''(0)$, as a development of $K(s)$ around $s = 0$ gives $K(s) = K'(0)s + \frac{1}{2}K''(0)s^2 + \cdots$ (which would be exact for a Normal distribution). The value $K''(0)^{-1/2}$, which is the reciprocal of the standard deviation, is a convenient 'unit of measurement' that tells us how rapidly things vary in the s-plane: note that s has dimensions reciprocal to Y, so if typical losses are of the order 10^6 USD, then typical values of $\hat{s}$ will be of order 10^{-6}USD^{-1}. Secondly, as K' is an analytic function, it makes sense to solve $K'(s) = y$ by Newton-Raphson, but higher-order variants (i.e. formulas that take into account the convexity of K') generally converge much more quickly and have a wider basin of convergence. This means that $K'''(s)$ will need to be known for any s. It follows that the routine that evaluates $K_{Y|V}(s)$ had better calculate *three s*-derivatives. (Recall also that $K'''(0)$ is explicitly used in a special case of the tail probability calculation when $\hat{s} = 0$.) A well-optimized root-searching routine should be able to find $\hat{s}$ to machine precision in about three trials.

2.10 Examples 2 (Conditional independence)

As an example of correlated assets we take a default/no-default model under the one-factor Gaussian copula. (To remind: this means that the conditional default probability of an asset is $p(V) = \Phi\left(\frac{\Phi^{-1}(\overline{p}) - \beta V}{\sqrt{1-\beta^2}}\right)$, where $V \sim N(0, 1)$ is the risk-factor, $\overline{p}$ is the expected default frequency and β is its correlation.) The characteristics are: 50 assets, exposures net of recovery mainly 1–5 units, with one or two larger ones; $\overline{p}$ 0.2%–3%; β's equal. Figures 15.7–15.10 show the results, comparing with Monte Carlo with 1 million simulations. Four different values of β are considered to show the full range of correlations that might reasonably be applied in practice. It is not surprising that the accuracy is good, as all that is happening (in essence) is that results analogous to those displayed previously are being mixed together for different values of the risk factor.

2.11 The direct saddlepoint approximation

So far our exposition of analytical approximations has been confined to sums of independent random variables, and extension to conditionally independent variables

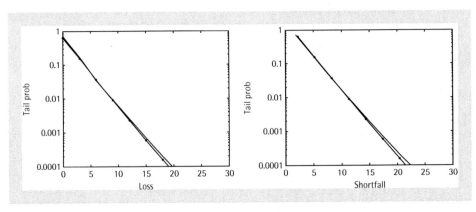

FIGURE 15.7 Correlated test portfolio in Example 2: $\beta = 0.3$.

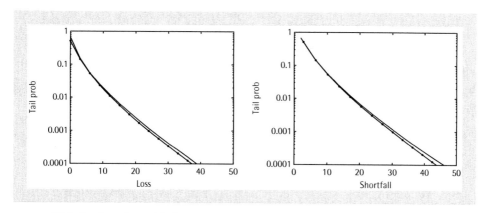

FIGURE 15.8 As above but with $\beta = 0.5$.

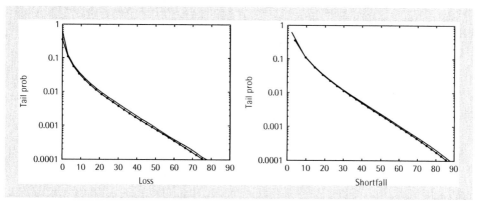

FIGURE 15.9 As above but with $\beta = 0.7$.

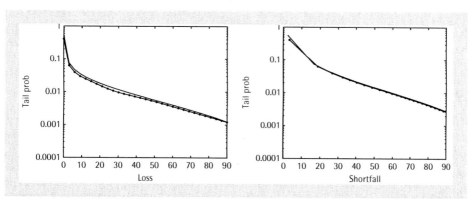

FIGURE 15.10 As above but with $\beta = 0.9$.

has been trivial (condition on risk factor, find distribution, integrate out)—which is the intuitively obvious way of doing it. Experience shows however that the direct approach (3), where the saddlepoint method is applied to the unconditional MGF, can also be quite effective. The main attraction of the direct approach is that if $C_Y(\omega) = \mathbf{E}[C_{Y|V}(\omega)]$ is known in closed form, there is no subsequent integration over V to be done; and the saddlepoint no longer depends on the risk factor, which makes for simple computation. (The formulas are obvious, as one simply uses the unconditional MGF in the cases derived for independence.) The direct approach also has the mathematical elegance of being a natural extension of mean-variance theory, which is recovered in the limit $\hat{s} \to 0$ (see Martin, Thompson, and Browne 2001a, 2001b); the indirect approach does not do this, because the saddlepoint is a function of the risk factor. But how justifiable is the direct approach?

Suppose, for the purposes of illustration, that it is the *exposures* rather than the default probabilities that depend on the risk factor (so that correlated exposures are being modelled, as perhaps in a model of counterparty risk in OTC derivatives). Let us also assume the risk factor to be lognormally distributed and that each counterparty's exposure is a constant multiple of that factor. Now focus on what happens when the factor integration is done. In the indirect approach it is the conditional tail density, probability, etc., that is being integrated over the risk factor, which causes no problems. But in the direct approach, it is the conditional MGF that is being integrated prior to the saddlepoint approximation being done: and that integral doesn't exist, because the lognormal distribution is too fat-tailed: the integral is

$$M_Y(s) = \mathbf{E}[e^{sY} \mid V] = \int_0^\infty \prod_j \left(1 - p_j + p_j e^{s\bar{a}_j\alpha}\right)\psi(\alpha)\,d\alpha$$

where p_j are the default probabilities and $\bar{a}_j$ the average exposures, and ψ denotes the lognormal density. So in this sort of situation the direct approach cannot possibly work. Therefore the indirect approach is prima facie more generally applicable.

On the other hand the direct method does work very well for some models:

- Feuerverger and Wong (2000) used it to approximate the distribution of a quadratically transformed multivariate Gaussian variable, which they used as a general tool for market risk problems.
- Gordy (1998) used it on the CreditRisk+ model, which we have described: the loss distribution is a Poisson distribution whose mean is stochastic and Gamma distributed.
- Previously to both, (Martin 1998; see also Jensen 1995) used it to approximate a Gamma distribution integrated over a Poisson, as a prototypical insurance or reliability problem. Explicitly: events occur as a Poisson process and each time an event occurs a loss is generated. The distribution of total loss over some time period is required. In other words the distribution of $\sum_{i=1}^{N} X_i$ is required, where X_i are i.i.d. Gamma(α, β) and N is Poisson(θ). By conditioning on N and integrating out, we find the MGF to be

$$M_Y(s) = \sum_{r=0}^{\infty} \frac{e^{-\theta}\theta^r}{r!}(1 - \beta s)^{-r\alpha} = \exp\big(\theta\big((1 - \beta s)^{-\alpha} - 1\big)\big)$$

and, rather conveniently, the equation $K_Y'(\hat{s}) = y$ can be solved for $\hat{s}$ algebraically. As a check, the loss distribution can also be calculated directly as an infinite series of incomplete Gamma functions.

The first problem can be boiled down to the sum of independent Gamma-distributed variables, and in the other two, the distributions at hand are from exponential families that are known to be well approximated by the saddlepoint method. By 'exponential family' one means a distribution in which $\nu K(s)$ is a valid KGF for all real $\nu > 0$. Such distributions are then infinitely divisible.[7] It is therefore not surprising that the direct saddlepoint approximation worked well. However, there is no uniform convergence result as for a sum of independent random variables.

This is a difficult area to make general comments about. We suggest that the direct method be applied only to exponential families. This includes what is mentioned above, or for example portfolio problems in which the joint distribution of assets is multivariate Normal Inverse Gaussian or similar.

3 RISK CONTRIBUTIONS

The objective behind risk contributions is to understand how risk depends on asset allocation. Often, the precise risk number for a portfolio is not the most important issue, as for one thing that is critically dependent on the parameters such as default probabilities or spread volatilities and distributions, default or spread correlations, and the like. It is therefore more important to use the risk measure comparatively, i.e. compare two portfolios or one portfolio over time. In other words, the real issue is: what makes the risk change? This means that we wish to calculate derivatives of VaR and ESF with respect to the asset allocations in the portfolio. It turns out that these quantities provide an explicit answer to the following fundamental question: given that I lose more than a certain amount, which assets, positions or scenarios are likely to have been responsible? We shall see that these so-called 'contributions' sum to give the portfolio risk. From the point of view of the portfolio manager, this information is easily presented as a list, in decreasing order, of the biggest contributions, or, if you like, the biggest 'headaches'. Once these have been identified, it is clear how to improve the efficiency of the portfolio: one identifies the riskiest positions and, if these are not generating a commensurate expected return, one hedges them or chops them down.

In the context of a credit portfolio, which instruments generate the most risk? Clearly large unhedged exposures to high-yield names will be the biggest, but there is more to it than that. For one thing, the more correlated a name is with the portfolio, the

---

[7] Which connects them to Lévy processes, an issue which the reader may wish to pursue separately (Saito 2002).

more risk it will contribute. Secondly, what is the tradeoff between credit quality and exposure? It is common sense that banks will lend more to so-called 'less-risky' names than riskier ones, usually based on credit rating. But should one lend twice as much to an AA as to a BB, or twenty times? The answer to that depends on the risk measure. For tail-based measures such as VaR and ESF, poor-quality assets are not penalized as much as they are with the standard deviation measure. This is because the worst that can happen to any credit is that it defaults, regardless of credit rating; so with VaR at 100% confidence, the risk contribution is just the exposure (net of recovery). So a VaR- or shortfall-based optimization will produce a portfolio with a lower proportion of so-called high-grade credits than a standard-deviation-based one, preferring to invest more in genuinely risk-free assets such as government bonds or in 'rubbish' such as high-yield CDO equity that has a small downside simply because the market is already pricing in the event of almost-certain wipeout. To give a quick demonstration of this, Figure 15.11 compares standard deviation contribution with shortfall contribution in the tail for a default/no-default model. Tail risks and 'standard deviation risks' are not equivalent.

In the context of a trading book, the considerations are different. Books are not generally conceived as portfolios, particularly on the sell-side, and positions may be turned over rapidly (potentially within a day). Given this, there is no interpretation of any position having an expected return, which would make an optimization seemingly pointless. However, the concept of risk contribution is still important, even if risk is now to be defined as a *mark-to-market* variation at a much shorter time horizon such as a couple of weeks; default is still included, as a particularly large move in value, but

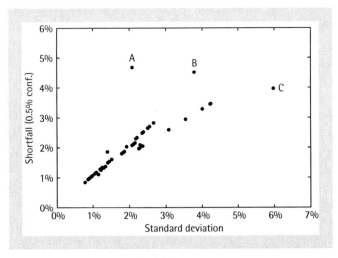

FIGURE 15.11 VaR and shortfall contributions, as % of portfolio risk, compared in a default/no-default model. 'A' and 'B' are tail risks (large exposures to high-grade assets) and 'C' is the opposite: a smallish exposure to a very low-grade credit. In a standard deviation-based optimization, C generates most risk, with A being of little importance; in a tail-based one, A contributes most risk.

for most credits will generally be too unlikely to show up on the 'risk radar'. The risk contribution is to be interpreted as a way of determining positions that contribute far too much risk in relation to the profit that they might conceivably generate, such as levered positions on so-called 'safe' names.

One would expect that, given (almost-) closed-form expressions for tail probability and shortfall, it should be relatively simple to obtain derivatives either by direct differentiation of the approximated tail probability and shortfall, or alternatively by performing the saddlepoint approximation on the derivatives. It turns out that the second route gives slightly neater results and that is the one that we shall pursue here. Following option-pricing parlance, we refer to the first and second derivatives of risk measures w.r.t. their asset allocations as their 'delta' and 'gamma'.

We start by developing the VaR contribution as a conditional expectation. It turns out that there are some fundamental conceptual difficulties with VaR contribution, notably for discrete-loss models such as CreditRisk+. Paradoxically, the exact contribution is an ill-posed problem and analytical approximations are considerably more useful in practice. The shortfall contribution suffers less from these problems. For the shortfall it is known that the measure is convex, and it turns out that the saddlepoint approximation preserves that convexity. This is an important result because it shows that use of the saddlepoint-ESF will give a unique optimal portfolio in an optimization. We will show examples along the way.

3.1 VaR

Our starting point is the expression for the upper tail probability[8]

$$P^+ \equiv \mathbf{P}[Y > y] = \frac{1}{2\pi i} \int_{\mathcal{R}+} C_Y(\omega) e^{-i\omega y} \frac{d\omega}{\omega} \tag{19}$$

and we now wish to perturb the VaR ($= y$) while keeping the tail probability constant. This gives

$$0 = \frac{\partial P^+}{\partial a_j} = \frac{1}{2\pi i} \int_{\mathcal{R}} \left(\frac{\partial C_Y}{\partial a_j} - i\omega \frac{\partial y}{\partial a_j} C_Y(\omega) \right) e^{-i\omega y} \frac{d\omega}{\omega}$$

(the integrand is regular, so the contour can go through the origin). As

$$\frac{\partial C_Y}{\partial a_j} = \frac{\partial}{\partial a_j} \mathbf{E}[e^{i\omega \sum_j a_j X_j}] = i\omega \mathbf{E}[X_j e^{i\omega Y}] \tag{20}$$

we have

$$\frac{\partial y}{\partial a_j} = \frac{\mathbf{E}[X_j \delta(Y - y)]}{\mathbf{E}[\delta(Y - y)]} = \mathbf{E}[X_j \mid Y = y] \tag{21}$$

---

[8] $\mathcal{R}$ denotes the real axis, with + indicating that the contour is indented so as to pass anticlockwise at the origin, and − clockwise.

which is the well-known result. From 1-homogeneity of VaR we should have $\sum_j a_j \partial y / \partial a_j = y$, which is clear from the above equation. The VaR contribution is (21) multiplied by a_j, so the VaR contributions add to the VaR.

Before pressing on with the theory let us consider some practical implications of this result. First, as the VaR contribution requires one to condition on a precise level of portfolio loss, it is quite difficult to estimate by Monte Carlo simulation. Two approaches that have been applied are kernel estimation, which uses information from simulations where the portfolio loss is close to the desired level, and importance sampling, in which the 'region of interest' is preferentially sampled by changing measure. A strength of the analytical approaches is that they are free of Monte Carlo noise.

A second issue is not so well known but fundamentally more worrying: even if it were easily computable, the exact VaR contribution might not be a very sensible construction. The problem occurs with discrete distributions, for example in grid-based models such as CreditRisk+ (Gundlach and Lehrbass 2004), or CDO pricing algorithms (Andersen, Sidenius, and Basu 2003; Burtschell, Gregory, and Laurent 2005) and in Monte Carlo simulation of any model. The following example is quite illuminating: with a default/no-default model of portfolio loss, let the exposures net of recovery be

$$9, 8, 18, 9, 8, 20, 17, 16, 12, 12.$$

The following assertions may come as a surprise:

- At portfolio loss=40, the VaR contribution of the first asset is zero (regardless of the default probabilities or correlation model). It is possible for a loss of 40 to occur (16+12+12, 8+20+12, etc.) but none of the relevant combinations includes a loss of 9.
- However, the VaR contribution increases if the exposure is *decreased* by 1 unit (assuming that the VaR does not change thereby): 8+20+12=40. So VaR contribution is not a 'sensible' function of exposure.
- Also, the first asset does contribute if the loss level is 38 (9+9+20, etc.) or 41 (9+20+12, etc.). So VaR contribution is not a 'sensible' function of attachment point either.
- As a consequence of the previous point, the position changes markedly if another asset is added: for example, addition of another asset will in general cause the VaR contribution of the first asset to become non-zero (e.g. an additional exposure of 1 gives 9 + 20 + 12 + 1 = 40).

Figure 15.12 illustrates the problems for this portfolio. For simplicity we have assumed independence of the losses and given each asset a default probability of 10%. The exact VaR deltas can be computed by direct calculation of the Fourier integral above, using the Fast Fourier Transform Algorithm. The figure shows the VaR delta for the first asset, for different loss levels. The most striking thing is that the graph is, to put it colloquially, all over the place. The delta is not even defined at some loss levels because those losses cannot occur (e.g. loss of 11). By way of motivation, let us

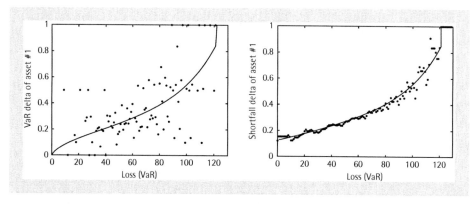

FIGURE 15.12 VaR and shortfall contributions of one particular asset as a function of VaR. Dots show the exact result; the curve is the saddlepoint result.

point in Figure 15.12 to some more results that we shall derive presently. First, we have plotted the saddlepoint VaR delta for asset 1 as a function of loss level, and observe that the graph is nice and smooth, appearing to steer some sort of median course— and indeed, a polynomial fit to the exact VaR delta is quite close. The adjacent plot shows the shortfall deltas, which are much less 'random', and again the saddlepoint approximation picks up the important feature of the graph very well. We have also plotted VaR and shortfall as functions of tail probability to compare the saddlepoint approximation with the exact answer, and find them to be very close, despite the small size (10 names) and inhomogeneity of the portfolio.

Intriguingly, working with the VaR of a continuum model of a portfolio distribution actually works much better in practice. This leads us to the saddlepoint approximation.

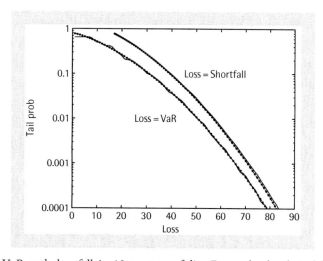

FIGURE 15.13 VaR and shortfall in 10-asset portfolio. For each, the dotted line shows the approximation, and the solid one shows the exact result.

Incidentally Thompson and co-workers (Thompson and Ordovás 2003a) arrive at essentially the same equations through an application of the statistical physics concept of an ensemble, in which one looks at an average of many independent copies of the portfolio. We recast (19) using the MGF, writing the V-expectation outside the inversion integral (i.e. following the 'indirect' route):

$$P^+ = E\left[\frac{1}{2\pi i}\int_{\mathcal{I}+} e^{K_{Y|V}(s)-sy}\,\frac{ds}{s}\right]. \tag{22}$$

Differentiating w.r.t. the asset allocations gives

$$0 = \frac{\partial P^+}{\partial a_j} = E\left[\frac{1}{2\pi i}\int_{\mathcal{I}}\left(\frac{\partial K_{Y|V}}{\partial a_j} - s\frac{\partial y}{\partial a_j}\right)e^{K_{Y|V}(s)-sy}\,\frac{ds}{s}\right]$$

(note that the integrand is now regular at the origin). Performing the saddlepoint approximation, we arrive at

$$\frac{\partial y}{\partial a_j} \sim \frac{1}{f_Y(y)}E\left[\frac{1}{\hat{s}_V}\frac{\partial K_{Y|V}}{\partial a_j}f_{Y|V}(y)\right]. \tag{23}$$

If we define the tilted conditional expectation $\widehat{E}_V[\cdot]$ by

$$\widehat{E}_V[Z] = \frac{E[Ze^{sY}\mid V]}{E[e^{sY}\mid V]}\bigg|_{s=\hat{s}_V} \tag{24}$$

(note, when $\hat{s}_V = 0$ we have $\widehat{E}_V \equiv E_V$) then we have

$$\frac{1}{\hat{s}_V}\frac{\partial K_{Y|V}}{\partial a_j} \equiv \widehat{E}_V[X_j].$$

From (21), (23), and Bayes' theorem we can associate the conditional loss with the saddlepoint approximation,

$$E[X_j\mid Y = y, V] \sim \widehat{E}_V[X_j]. \tag{25}$$

Of course, it is also possible to derive this directly, i.e. without recourse to VaR, simply by writing down the integral representation of $E[X_j\delta(Y - y)]$ and performing the saddlepoint approximation.

As a specific example, in the case of a default/no-default model with independence[9] we have the contribution of the jth asset as

$$\tilde{p}_j a_j, \qquad \tilde{p}_j \equiv \frac{p_j e^{a_j \hat{s}}}{1 - p_j + p_j e^{a_j \hat{s}}}$$

which is its expected loss in the exponentially tilted probability measure with tilting factor $a_j\hat{s}$. It is important to note that the default probability is thereby weighted with a loading that *increases exponentially with loss*, making large loss events show up on the 'risk radar' even if they have low probability. The same idea is used in importance sampling (Glasserman and Li 2005), in which tilting the probabilities to

---

[9] p_j, a_j are as before the default probabilities and losses.

increase them allows the point of interest in the loss distribution to be preferentially sampled. Indeed, the change of measure thereby performed is that which moves the expected loss of the distribution to the desired value while keeping the distribution's entropy as high as possible (another concept that links to statistical physics). When correlation is introduced the situation is not much different, as is apparent from (23), for one is only averaging a similar expression over different states of the risk factor.

It is worth noting that, for each value of the risk factor, the saddlepoint VaR 'delta' $\widehat{E}_V[X_j]$ is an increasing function of the threshold y (because $K_{Y|V}(s) = \sum_j K_{X_j|V}(a_j s)$ in that case and $K'_{X_j|V}$ is an increasing function). But this is a property of saddlepoint approximations, not a general result: as we already know from Figure 15.12, where for simplicity the losses are independent, the exact VaR contribution is not necessarily an increasing function of the threshold. So the saddlepoint approximation is doing some sort of desirable 'smoothing'. For positively correlated losses the saddlepoint approximation will again give monotonicity, but if they are negatively correlated then this will no longer be so: an asset negatively correlated with the portfolio will on average have a lower value when the portfolio value is high, and vice versa. (The reason for the non-monotonicity is that $f_{Y|V}(y)/f_Y(y)$ is not necessarily an increasing function of y; for the case of independence though, it is always unity.)

A final advantage of the saddlepoint approximation is its computational efficiency. Surprisingly perhaps, the calculation of saddlepoint risk contributions requires no more work than calculating the risk in the first place. The reason for this is that, by conditional independence,

$$K_{Y|V}(s) = \sum_j K_{X_j|V}(a_j s)$$

and so

$$\frac{1}{\hat{s}_V} \frac{\partial K_{Y|V}}{\partial a_j}(\hat{s}_V) = K'_{X_j|V}(\hat{s}_V).$$

Now, when $K'_{Y|V}(\hat{s}_V) = y$ was solved for $\hat{s}_V$, the derivatives of $K_{X_j|V}$ were calculated (the first derivative is of course essential; second- and higher-order ones are used for Newton-Raphson iterative schemes). One only has to cache these derivatives (for each j and V) during the root-searching routine and recall them when it is desired to calculate the VaR contribution. The same remark applies to both derivatives shortfall, when we derive them. This compares favourably with other methods in which differentiation must be carried out for each asset in the portfolio (Takano and Hashiba 2008).

To round this section off we show the special case where $\hat{s}_V \to 0$, which generates the CLT. If the portfolio loss distribution conditional on V is Normal (with mean $\mu_{Y|V}$ and variance $\sigma^2_{Y|V}$), then the conditional density and distribution function are, respectively,

$$f_{Y|V} = E[\sigma_{Y|V}^{-1}\phi(z_V)], \qquad P[Y < y] = E[\Phi(z_V)],$$

with

$$z_V \equiv \frac{y - \mu_{Y|V}}{\sigma_{Y|V}}.$$

(note that this *is* actually the same z as we used in conjunction with the Lugannani-Rice formula earlier). It is then readily established, and also verifiable from first principles, that

$$\frac{\partial y}{\partial a_j} = \frac{1}{f_Y(y)} \mathbf{E}\left[\left(\frac{\partial \mu_{Y|V}}{\partial a_j} + z_V \frac{\partial \sigma_{Y|V}}{\partial a_j}\right)\frac{1}{\sigma_{Y|V}}\phi(z_V)\right]. \tag{26}$$

3.2 Shortfall

3.2.1 First derivative

The starting point is the Fourier representation of $\mathbf{S}^{\pm}[Y]$:

$$\mathbf{E}[Y \mid Y \gtrless y] = y \mp \frac{1}{2\pi P^{\pm}}\int_{\mathcal{R}\pm} C_Y(\omega)e^{-i\omega y}\frac{d\omega}{\omega^2} \tag{27}$$

From this we obtain derivative information via the obvious route of differentiating w.r.t. a_j at constant tail probability. Note that because the tail probability is being held fixed, y will depend on the (a_j); however, we know all about that from the VaR derivations, and conveniently some cancellation occurs en route. This gives

$$\frac{\partial \mathbf{S}^{\pm}[Y]}{\partial a_j} = \mp\frac{1}{2\pi P^{\pm}}\int_{\mathcal{R}\pm}\frac{\partial C_Y}{\partial a_j}e^{-i\omega y}\frac{d\omega}{\omega^2}.$$

Using (20) we obtain

$$\frac{\partial \mathbf{S}^{\pm}[Y]}{\partial a_j} = \frac{\pm 1}{2\pi i P^{\pm}}\int_{\mathcal{R}\pm}\mathbf{E}[X_j e^{i\omega Y}]e^{-i\omega y}\frac{d\omega}{\omega}$$

$$= \frac{1}{P^{\pm}}\mathbf{E}[X_j \mathbf{1}[Y \gtrless y]] = \mathbf{E}[X_j \mid Y \gtrless y]. \tag{28}$$

It is clear that the homogeneity result is obeyed: $\sum_j a_j \partial \mathbf{S}^{\pm}[Y]/\partial a_j = \mathbf{S}^{\pm}[Y]$.

We said when discussing the problems of VaR contribution for discrete distributions that ESF is smoother than VaR, and in fact it is one order of differentiability smoother. This means that the first derivative of ESF is a continuous function of asset allocation, but, as we shall see later, the second derivative of ESF is as 'bad' as first derivative of VaR (so it is discontinuous). So we still want to work everything through for the analytical approximations, which is what we do next.

The saddlepoint analogue of the equations is

$$\frac{\partial \mathbf{S}^{\pm}[Y]}{\partial a_j} = \frac{\pm 1}{2\pi i P^{\pm}}\mathbf{E}\left[\int_{\mathcal{I}\pm}\frac{\partial K_{Y|V}}{\partial a_j}e^{K_{Y|V}(s) - sy}\frac{ds}{s^2}\right] \tag{29}$$

(and the integrand now has only a *simple* pole at the origin). Following Martin (2006) we split out a singular part that can be integrated exactly and leave a regular part to be saddlepoint approximated. The result then follows:[10]

$$
\begin{aligned}
\frac{\partial S^{\pm}[Y]}{\partial a_j} &= \frac{1}{2\pi i P^{\pm}} \mathbf{E}\left[\pm \mu_{X_j|V} \int_{\mathcal{I}\pm} e^{K_{Y|V}(s)-sy} \frac{ds}{s} \right. \\
&\quad \left. \pm \int_{\mathcal{I}\pm} \frac{1}{s}\left(\frac{1}{s}\frac{\partial K_{Y|V}}{\partial a_j} - \mu_{X_j|V}\right) e^{K_{Y|V}(s)-sy}\, ds \right] \\
&= \frac{1}{P^{\pm}} \mathbf{E}\left[\mu_{X_j|V} \mathbf{P}[Y \gtrless y \mid V] \pm \frac{1}{\hat{s}_V}\left(\frac{1}{\hat{s}_V}\frac{\partial K_{Y|V}}{\partial a_j} - \mu_{X_j|V}\right) f_{Y|V}(y)\right]
\end{aligned}
$$

$$(30)$$

To obtain the conditional-Normal result, we can either let $\hat{s}_V \to 0$ or derive from first principles. As

$$
S^{\pm}[Y] = \frac{1}{P^{\pm}} \mathbf{E}\left[\mu_{Y|V}\Phi(\mp z_V) \pm \sigma_{Y|V}\phi(z_V)\right] \tag{31}
$$

we have[11]

$$
\frac{\partial S^{\pm}[Y]}{\partial a_j} = \frac{1}{P^{\pm}} \mathbf{E}\left[\frac{\partial \mu_{Y|V}}{\partial a_j}\Phi(\mp z_V) \pm \frac{\partial \sigma_{Y|V}}{\partial a_j}\phi(z_V)\right]. \tag{32}
$$

As we pointed out earlier in the context of the shortfall at portfolio level (and in Martin 2006; Martin and Tasche 2007), shortfall expressions naturally fall into two parts, the first being systematic risk and the second unsystematic. We can see that the same holds true for the deltas, in (32) and (30). The systematic part can be written

$$
\mathbf{E}[\mathbf{E}_V[X_j] \mid Y \gtrless y]];
$$

expressed in ungainly fashion, it is the expectation of the conditional-on-the-risk-factor-expectation of an asset, conditionally on the portfolio losing more than the VaR. The discussion surrounding Figure 15.15 later will show this in practice: cor-related assets or events contribute strongly to the first part, which roughly speaking is proportional to the asset's 'beta', and uncorrelated ones mainly to the second.

Note also that the contribution to unsystematic risk *must be positive*, for both approximations, and for the exact result too, because conditionally on V the assets are independent and so any increase in allocation to an asset must cause the conditional variance (= unsystematic risk) to increase. This is exactly what we would like to conclude (see Martin and Tasche 2007 for a fuller discussion). VaR does not have this property, which means that one could in principle be in the awkward position

---

[10] $\mu_{X_j|V}$ denotes the conditional expectation of the jth asset.

[11] It may appear that some of the terms have gone missing, on account of z_V depending on the asset allocations; however, these terms cancel. A nice thing about working with ESF is that much of the algebra does come out cleanly.

of increasing the exposure to an uncorrelated asset, keeping the others fixed, and watching the VaR *decrease*.

3.2.2 *Second derivative*

One of the main things that we shall prove here is that the saddlepoint approximation preserves the convexity of the shortfall. The convexity arises in the first place because the Hessian matrix (second derivative) of the shortfall can be written as a conditional covariance, so we show that first.

Differentiating (27) again gives

$$\frac{\partial^2 S^{\pm}[Y]}{\partial a_j \partial a_k} = \frac{\mp 1}{2\pi P^{\pm}} \left[\int_{\mathcal{R}^{\pm}} \frac{\partial^2 C_Y}{\partial a_j \partial a_k} e^{-i\omega y} \frac{d\omega}{\omega^2} + \frac{\partial y}{\partial a_k} \int_{\mathcal{R}^{\pm}} \frac{\partial C_Y}{\partial a_j} e^{-i\omega y} \frac{d\omega}{i\omega} \right]$$

and the second integral is already known to us because we dealt with it when doing the VaR delta. As

$$\frac{\partial^2 C_Y}{\partial a_j \partial a_k} = -\omega^2 \mathrm{E}[X_j X_k e^{i\omega Y}],$$

we can tidy things up to arrive at

$$\frac{\partial^2 S^{\pm}[Y]}{\partial a_j \partial a_k} = \frac{\pm f_Y(y)}{P^{\pm}} \left(\mathrm{E}[X_j X_k \mid Y = y] - \mathrm{E}[X_j \mid Y = y] \mathrm{E}[X_k \mid Y = y] \right)$$

$$= \frac{\pm f_Y(y)}{P^{\pm}} \mathrm{V}[X_j, X_k \mid Y = y] \tag{33}$$

where V[] denotes covariance. Hence the second derivative of ESF is (up to a factor) the conditional covariance of the pair of assets in question, conditionally on the portfolio value being *equal to* the VaR. As any covariance matrix is positive semidefinite the ESF is a convex function of the asset allocations. It is also clear that

$$\sum_{j,k} a_j a_k \frac{\partial^2 S^{\pm}[Y]}{\partial a_j \partial a_k} = 0, \tag{34}$$

as the LHS is, up to a factor,

$$\sum_{j,k} a_j a_k \mathrm{V}[X_j, X_k \mid Y = y] = \mathrm{V}[Y, Y \mid Y = y] = 0.$$

This is as expected: if the risk measure is 1-homogeneous then scaling all the asset allocations by some factor causes the risk to increase linearly (so the second derivative iz zero) and so the vector of asset allocations must be a null eigenvector of the Hessian matrix. Incidentally, because the conditioning is *on* a particular portfolio value or loss, the estimation of second derivative of ESF is as troublesome as that of the first derivative of VaR for discrete portfolio models or Monte Carlo.

We now turn to the saddlepoint approximation, which as we shall see contains a trap for the unwary. The second derivative of ESF has (after using (23) to tidy it up) the following integral representation:

$$\frac{\partial^2 \mathbf{S}^{\pm}[Y]}{\partial a_j \partial a_k} = \frac{\pm 1}{P^{\pm}} \left\{ \mathbf{E}\left[\frac{1}{2\pi i} \int_{\mathcal{I}\pm} \left(\frac{\partial^2 K_{Y|V}}{\partial a_j \partial a_k} + \frac{\partial K_{Y|V}}{\partial a_j} \frac{\partial K_{Y|V}}{\partial a_k} \right) e^{K_{Y|V}(s) - sy} \frac{ds}{s^2} \right] \right.$$

$$\left. - \frac{\partial y}{\partial a_j} \frac{\partial y}{\partial a_k} f_Y(y) \right\} \tag{35}$$

As the integrand is regular at the origin, it looks obvious to approximate the integral as

$$\left(\frac{1}{s^2} \frac{\partial^2 K_{Y|V}}{\partial a_j \partial a_k} + \frac{1}{s} \frac{\partial K_{Y|V}}{\partial a_j} \cdot \frac{1}{s} \frac{\partial K_{Y|V}}{\partial a_k} \right)_{s = \hat{s}_V} f_{Y|V}(y).$$

This expression is incorrect and if it is used, one ends up violating (34) and producing expressions for the conditional asset covariances that do not make sense. [From now on, we abbreviate $K_{Y|V}(s)$ to K.]

The problem is that we have been careless about the size of the terms neglected in the asymptotic expansion and ended up by omitting a term that is of the *same* order as shown above. In recalling that the saddlepoint expansion is asymptotic as $K \to \infty$, the error becomes clear: $(\partial K / \partial a_j)(\partial K / \partial a_k)$ is order K^2, and therefore needs a higher-order treatment at the saddlepoint to make the neglected terms of consistent order. Suffice it to say that the correct expression for the integral is[12]

$$\left\{ \frac{1}{s^2} \frac{\partial^2 K}{\partial a_j \partial a_k} + \frac{1}{s} \frac{\partial K}{\partial a_j} \cdot \frac{1}{s} \frac{\partial K}{\partial a_k} - \frac{1}{K''(s)} \left(\frac{\partial}{\partial s} \frac{1}{s} \frac{\partial K}{\partial a_j} \right) \left(\frac{\partial}{\partial s} \frac{1}{s} \frac{\partial K}{\partial a_k} \right) \right\}_{s = \hat{s}_V} f_{Y|V}(y).$$

On collecting terms we arrive at an expression that naturally divides into two parts:

$$\frac{\partial^2 \mathbf{S}^{\pm}[Y]}{\partial a_j \partial a_k} \sim \frac{\pm 1}{P^{\pm}} \mathbf{E}\left[\left(H_{jk}^S + H_{jk}^U \right) f_{Y|V}(y) \right],$$

or equivalently, by (33),

$$\mathbf{V}[X_j, X_k \mid Y = y] \sim \frac{1}{f_Y(y)} \mathbf{E}\left[\left(H_{jk}^S + H_{jk}^U \right) f_{Y|V}(y) \right],$$

with

$$H_{jk}^S = \left(\frac{1}{\hat{s}_V} \frac{\partial K}{\partial a_j} - \frac{\partial y}{\partial a_j} \right) \left(\frac{1}{\hat{s}_V} \frac{\partial K}{\partial a_k} - \frac{\partial y}{\partial a_k} \right) \tag{36}$$

$$H_{jk}^U = \frac{1}{\hat{s}_V^2} \frac{\partial^2 K}{\partial a_j \partial a_k} - \frac{1}{K''(\hat{s}_V)} \left(\frac{\partial}{\partial s} \frac{1}{s} \frac{\partial K}{\partial a_j} \right)_{s = \hat{s}_V} \left(\frac{\partial}{\partial s} \frac{1}{s} \frac{\partial K}{\partial a_k} \right)_{s = \hat{s}_V}$$

It is clear that H^S is a positive semidefinite matrix (because it is of the form $v_j v_k$); also $\sum_{j,k} a_j a_k H_{jk}^S = 0$ by (23).

---

[12] Actually a term is still missing from this as there are two terms of the form $(\partial / \partial s)^2 (s^{-1} \partial K / \partial a_j) \times s^{-1} \partial K / \partial a_k$. However, omission of these does not violate (34), and they also vanish for the Normal case.

By homogeneity properties of K (it depends on a_j and s only through their product),

$$\frac{\partial^2 K}{\partial s^2} = \sum_j a_j \frac{\partial}{\partial s} \frac{1}{s} \frac{\partial K}{\partial a_j} = \sum_{j,k} a_j a_k \frac{1}{s^2} \frac{\partial^2 K}{\partial a_j \partial a_k}$$

so $\sum_{j,k} a_j a_k H_{jk}^U = 0$ too, and (34) is satisfied. The only thing to settle now is whether H^U is positive semidefinite, and this is basically the Cauchy-Schwarz inequality. Indeed, defining the quadratic

$$q(t) = \widehat{\mathbf{E}} \left[\left((Y - \widehat{\mathbf{E}}[Y]) + t\, u \cdot (X - \widehat{\mathbf{E}}[X]) \right)^2 \right]$$

(we drop the v suffix for convenience), where X is the vector of asset values and u is some arbitrary vector, we find the coefficients of $1, t, t^2$ in $q(t)$ to be:

$$1 : \widehat{\mathbf{E}} \left[(Y - \widehat{\mathbf{E}}[Y])^2 \right] \qquad\qquad = \frac{\partial^2 K}{\partial s^2}$$

$$t : 2\widehat{\mathbf{E}} \left[u \cdot (X - \widehat{\mathbf{E}}[X])(Y - \widehat{\mathbf{E}}[Y]) \right] = 2 \sum_j u_j \frac{\partial}{\partial s} \frac{1}{s} \frac{\partial K}{\partial a_j}$$

$$t^2 : \widehat{\mathbf{E}} \left[\left(u \cdot (X - \widehat{\mathbf{E}}[X]) \right)^2 \right] \qquad = \sum_{j,k} \frac{u_j u_k}{s^2} \frac{\partial^2 K}{\partial a_j \partial a_k}$$

As q can never be negative its discriminant must be ≤ 0, so

$$\frac{\partial^2 K}{\partial s^2} \sum_{j,k} \frac{u_j u_k}{s^2} \frac{\partial^2 K}{\partial a_j \partial a_k} \geq \left[\sum_j u_j \frac{\partial}{\partial s} \frac{1}{s} \frac{\partial K}{\partial a_j} \right]^2$$

which amounts to $\sum_{j,k} u_j u_k H_{jk}^U \geq 0$, as required. We conclude that the saddlepoint approximation has preserved the convexity.

In the conditional-Normal framework, we have a rather simpler expression. In the same notation as before:

$$\frac{\partial^2 S^\pm[Y]}{\partial a_j \partial a_k} = \frac{\pm 1}{P^\pm} \mathbf{E} \left[\left(\sigma_{Y|V}^2 \frac{\partial z_V}{\partial a_j} \frac{\partial z_V}{\partial a_k} + \sigma_{Y|V} \frac{\partial^2 \sigma_{Y|V}}{\partial a_j \partial a_k} \right) \sigma_{Y|V}^{-1} \phi(z_V) \right] \qquad (37)$$

Predictably, we can identify the first term as a convexity contribution to systematic risk and the second to the unsystematic risk. As we can expect from the saddlepoint derivation, *both* terms are positive semidefinite matrices: the first is of the form $v_j v_k$ with $v_j = \sigma_{Y|V} \partial z_V / \partial a_j$, while the second is the Hessian of the standard deviation (a convex risk measure). As the mixture weights $\sigma_{Y|V}^{-1} \phi(z_V)$ are non-negative—they are the V-conditional density of Y—the LHS must also be semidefinite.

3.2.3 Conditional covariance

There are some interesting issues surrounding the covariance of two assets conditional on the portfolio loss being some level which, as we have seen, is the second derivative of shortfall. We earlier found the approximation to the expectation of an asset conditionally on the portfolio value (again we drop the $_V$), as a tilted expectation:

$$E[X_j \mid Y = y] \sim \widehat{E}[X_j], \qquad \widehat{E}[Z] = \frac{E[Ze^{sY}]}{E[e^{sY}]}\bigg|_{s=\hat{s}}.$$

It is superficially attractive, but incorrect, to extend this to higher-order expressions, thereby surmising

$$E[X_j X_k \mid Y = y] \overset{??}{\sim} \widehat{E}[X_j X_k]$$

and (defining the tilted variance in the obvious way, i.e. as the tilted expectation of the product minus the product of the tilted expectations)

$$V[X_j, X_k \mid Y = y] \overset{??}{\sim} \widehat{V}[X_j, X_k].$$

The problem with this is that if one multiplies by $a_j a_k$ and sums over both suffices one ends up with

$$V[Y, Y \mid Y = y] \overset{??}{\sim} \widehat{V}[Y, Y].$$

The LHS must be zero, of course (it is the variance of something that is not being allowed to vary), but the RHS is $\partial^2 K_Y / \partial s^2 \neq 0$. In other words, the homogeneity relation is wrong.

The reason for the error is that terms have gone missing in the derivation, and those terms are the ones alluded to in the saddlepoint derivation above.[13] The quadratic (covariance) expression should read

$$V[X_j, X_k \mid Y = y] \sim \widehat{V}[X_j, X_k] - \frac{\widehat{V}[X_j, Y]\widehat{V}[X_k, Y]}{\widehat{V}[Y, Y]}.$$

In effect, the extra term corrects the homogeneity relation by subtracting the unwanted convexity along the line of the asset allocations, exactly as in the following method of killing eigenvalues in a symmetric matrix Ω:

$$\Omega^* = \Omega - \frac{\Omega a \otimes \Omega a}{a'\Omega a}.$$

If Ω is positive semidefinite then so is Ω^* (by Cauchy-Schwarz); and as $\Omega^* a = 0$, Ω^* has one more zero eigenvalue than Ω.

3.3 Examples

We conclude with some examples of the theory in action.

We revisit the example of Figures 15.7–15.10 of a default/no-default model under the one-factor Gaussian copula, where now we mix up the β's, so that some assets have

---

[13] The error occurs in Thompson and Ordovàs (2003b), where higher-order generalizations were also stated without proof. Correcting these seems to require a fair amount of reworking of their theory.

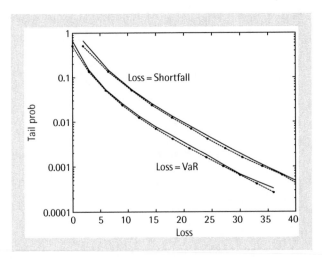

FIGURE 15.14 VaR and shortfall in 50-asset portfolio. For each, the dotted line shows the approximation, and the solid one shows the result obtained by Monte Carlo.

$\beta = 0.3$, some 0.5, and some 0.7. Figure 15.15 shows the systematic and unsystematic ESF contributions (30) of all the assets, in a scatter graph. The asset at the far top-left of the graph (coordinates (0.27, 0.56)) is the largest exposure and is to a name with low default probability, i.e. a tail risk; those on the bottom right have higher correlation and higher default probability, though generally lower exposure. The interpretation of Figure 15.13 for the purposes of portfolio management is that the assets in the top left need single-name hedges and those in the bottom-right can largely be dealt with using baskets or bespoke index protection.

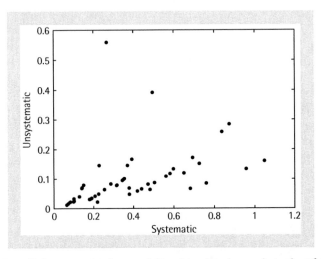

FIGURE 15.15 For all the assets in the portfolio, this plot shows their shortfall contribution divided into systematic and unsystematic parts. Correlated assets sit on the bottom right, large single-name exposures on the top left. Assets in the bottom left contribute little risk.

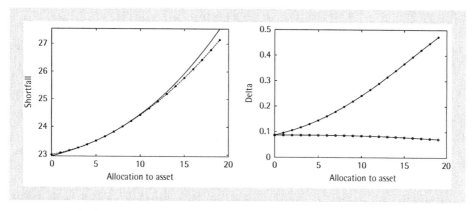

FIGURE 15.16 [Left] Shortfall (solid line) vs quadratic approximation (dotted), as asset allocation is varied. The approximation requires only the shortfall, delta, and gamma in the 'base case', whereas the exact computation requires a full calculation at each point. [Right] Again for varying that particular asset allocation, this shows the delta of the asset and the systematic delta. The systematic delta remains roughly constant so the inference is that more unsystematic risk is being added to the portfolio.

Next we consider what happens when one particular exposure is varied. Figure 15.16 shows the performance surface (risk vs allocation), and also shows a quadratic approximation based on the first and second derivatives estimated using (30, 36). The importance of this is that the derivatives can be easily calculated along with the risk in one go, after which the quadratic approximant is easily drawn, whereas tracing the exact line requires the portfolio to be re-analysed for each desired asset allocation.

4 CONCLUSIONS

We have given a reasonably complete overview of the theory of risk aggregation and disaggregation of distributions that are not necessarily Normal. The results from Fourier transformation are completely general; the saddlepoint ones assume the existence of the moment-generating function, and are thereby suited to semi-heavy-tailed distributions. This assumption is sufficiently restrictive to allow useful and interesting results to be derived, particularly in the subject of risk contributions; and it is sufficiently general to allow application to real-world problems. The subject has developed over the last ten years and is now gaining general acceptance. In general we prefer to operate with shortfall rather than VaR and routinely use the formulas here for the risk contributions and the like.

It is worth emphasizing however that, no matter how clever the techniques of calculation, the results are only as good as the model assumptions used to provide the input. In the 'credit crunch' these have generally been found to be woefully inadequate. However, the methods described here to perform fast aggregation and disaggregation of risk are an important part of the backbone of credit risk management systems and are to be recommended.

A SUMMARY OF RESULTS

To help the reader navigate the formulas, the following summarizes where the results can be found. First, the basic results for the risk measures and related quantities:

	Eqn
Density	(7/13)
Tail probability	(10/14)
Shortfall	(12/15)

Secondly, for the derivatives:

	1st			2nd		
	Exact	CLT	SPt	Exact	CLT	SPt
VaR	(21)	(26)	(23)	–	–	–
Shortfall	(28)	(32)	(30)	(33)	(37)	(36)

REFERENCES

Acerbi, C., and Tasche, D. (2002). 'On the coherence of Expected Shortfall'. *Journal of Banking and Finance*, 26/7: 1487–503.

Andersen, L., Sidenius, J., and Basu, S. (2003). 'All your hedges in one basket'. *Risk*, 16/11: 67–72.

Artzner, P., Delbaen, F., Eber, J. M., and Heath, D. (1999). 'Coherent measures of risk'. *Mathematical Finance*, 9: 203–28.

Arvanitis, A., Browne, C., Gregory, J., and Martin, R. (1998). 'A credit risk toolbox'. *Risk*, 11/12: 50–5.

Barco, M. (2004). 'Bringing credit portfolio modelling to maturity'. *Risk*, 17/1: 86–90.

Barndorff-Nielsen, O. E. (1991). 'Modified signed log likelihood ratio'. *Biometrika*, 78: 557–63.

Bender, C. M., and Orszag, S. A. (1978). '*Advanced Mathematical Methods for Scientists and Engineers*'. New York: McGraw-Hill.

Burtschell, X., Gregory, J., and Laurent, J.-P. (2005). 'A comparative analysis of CDO pricing models'. <www.defaultrisk.com>

Daniels, H. E. (1987). 'Tail probability approximations'. *International Statistical Review*, 55/1: 37–48.

Feuerverger, A., and Wong, A. C. M. (2000). 'Computation of value-at-risk for nonlinear portfolios'. *Journal of Risk*, 3/1: 37–55.

Glasserman, P., and Li, J. (2005). 'Importance sampling for portfolio credit risk'. *Management Science*, 51/11: 1643–56.

—— and Ruiz-Mata, J. (2006). 'Computing the credit loss distribution in the gaussian copula model: a comparison of methods'. *Journal of Credit Risk*, 2/4.

Gordy, M. B. (1998). 'Saddlepoint approximation of CreditRisk+'. *Journal of Banking and Finance*, 26/7: 1337–55.

—— 'A risk-factor model foundation for ratings-based bank capital rules'. *Journal of Financial Intermediation*, 12/3: 199–232.

Gundlach, M., and Lehrbass, F.(eds.) (2004). *CreditRisk+ in the Banking Industry*. New York: Springer.

Jensen, J. L. (1995). *Saddlepoint Approximations*. Oxford: Clarendon Press.

Kolassa, J. E. (1994). *Series Approximation Methods in Statistics*. New York: Springer.

Martin, R. J. (1998). 'System failure statistics: some asymptotic formulae'. *GEC Journal of Technology*, 15/1: 10–15.

—— (2004). *Credit Portfolio Modeling Handbook*. London: Credit Suisse First Boston.

—— (2006). 'The saddlepoint method and portfolio optionalities'. *Risk*, 19/12: 93–5.

—— and Ordovàs, R. (2006). 'An indirect view from the saddle'. *Risk*, 19/10: 94–9.

—— and Tasche, D. (2007). 'Shortfall: a tail of two parts'. *Risk*, 20/2: 84–9.

—— Thompson, K. E., and Browne, C. J. (2001a). 'Taking to the saddle'. *Risk*, 14/6: 91–4.

—— —— —— (2001b). 'VaR: who contributes and how much?' *Risk*, 14/8: 99–102.

—— and Wilde, T. S. (2002). 'Unsystematic credit risk'. *Risk*, 15/11: 123–8.

Press, W. H., Flannery, B. P., Teukolsky, S. A., and Vetterling, W. T. (2002). *Numerical Recipes in C++*. Cambridge: Cambridge University Press.

Saito, K.-I. (2002). *Lévy Processes and Infinitely Divisible Distributions*. Cambridge: Cambridge University Press.

Takano, Y., and Hashiba, J. (2008). 'A novel methodology for credit portfolio analysis: numerical approximation approach'. <www.defaultrisk.com>

Thompson, K. E., and Ordovàs, R. (2003a). 'Credit ensembles'. *Risk*, 16/4: 67–72.

—— —— (2003b). 'The road to partition'. *Risk*, 16/5: 93–7.

Wang, X., and Oosterlee, C. (2007). 'Computation of VaR and VaR contribution in the Vasicek portfolio credit loss model: a comparative study'. *Journal of Credit Risk*, 3/3.

PART V

SECURITIZATION

CHAPTER 16

QUANTITATIVE ASPECTS OF THE COLLAPSE OF THE PARALLEL BANKING SYSTEM

ALEXANDER BATCHVAROV

1 PARALLEL BANKING SYSTEM, ECONOMIC GROWTH, AND CREDIT RISK

1.1 The parallel banking system defined

ONE way to define the parallel banking system is as the opposite of the traditional banking system, but in reality the two systems have much more in common than is generally admitted. Traditional banks have developed over the years as a utility transforming retail and corporate sectors' savings deposits into loans to those same retail and corporate clients. The inherent mismatch between short-term savings deposits and long-term loans against those deposits is the fault-line in the traditional banking system, which has many times prompted tremors in the form of 'run on the bank' when depositors withdraw their deposits as fears that a bank may be insolvent surface, and the bank cannot collect on its outstanding longer-term loans fast enough to satisfy the withdrawal demands. A way of addressing such flaws in the banking system is to replace the 'faith and credit of the bank' with the 'faith and credit of the government' via a government deposit guarantee scheme and/or via a mechanism to provide liquidity directly to the banks to address the deposit withdrawal requests. In such a way the unavoidable asset-liability mismatch flaw of the traditional banks is addressed through the intervention of the government.

With the fall in the deposit base due to declining savings rates, the development of savings products with higher yields than savings deposits and the decline of interest rates on savings deposits banks needed another source of funds to replace shrinking deposits and continue their lending activities. One such source would come from the capital markets, where banks could raise funds either directly—via bank debentures, or indirectly—by debentures backed by bank assets. Packaging and selling bank assets via securitization became a source of funding for the banks in the course of the 1990s. As the securitization market developed in size and scope, it became clear that non-banks could also use it to raise new funds for lending by packaging and selling bundles of loans they had already originated. That gave an opportunity to the finance companies (i.e. non-bank banks) to increase substantially their participation in lending to the consumer (mortgages, auto-loans, credit cards, student loans) and corporate (leases, franchise loans, floor-plan loans, commercial real estate), and funds to extend financing to the LBO market (leveraged loans, mezzanine finance).

A new type of lender emerged—the conduit with a sole purpose to originate residential or commercial mortgage loans against a revolving lending facility provided by a bank (a warehousing facility), repackage them in a bond format, and distribute the bonds to investors. These practices were eventually embraced by fund managers who could raise equity funding and then obtain a warehousing facility from a bank to acquire leveraged loans, corporate bonds, or structured finance bonds to build a portfolio, and then repay the warehousing loan by repackaging the loan or bond portfolio via a CDO (collateralized debt obligation) placed on the structured finance markets.

The most recent stage of securitization market development was associated with the development of the credit default swap (CDS) markets and synthetic structures, with the emergence of the so-called synthetic securitization and risk transfer. Synthetic securitizations were embraced by the banks as a risk-transfer mechanism and by fund managers as a way to build and manage credit portfolios of credit default swaps with low initial cash outlay. The CDS market also provided the mechanism (imperfect as it was later proven) for hedging corporate and, less so, consumer exposures. Correlation trading was meant in part to hedge managed or static CDS portfolios, customized single-tranche exposures, corporate loan and bond portfolios, etc. CDS spread to the ABS (asset-backed securities) sector and related portfolio CDS boosted the negative correlation trade, which eventually led to the collapse of the monoline insurers. In short, the expansion of the parallel banking system and the growth in its credit creation were supported by the parallel growth and expansion of the CDS markets.

1.2 Securitization models

Securitization[1] in its different permutations emerged as a main funding mechanism for the parallel banking system. The securitization models that evolved in Europe, the

---

[1] For a detailed discussion of the evolution of the structured finance markets, please see Fabozzi (2006); De Servigny and Jobst (2007); Jeffrey (2006).

US, and other developed securitization markets can be broadly classified as 'private sector', 'public sector', and 'covered bond' models The underwriting of loans with the intention of securitizing them, i.e. lending against financing via securitization, by banks, non-bank banks, fund managers, and conduits became known as the 'originate-to-distribute' model of the parallel banking system in contrast to the 'originate-to-hold' model that was associated with the traditional banking system and the covered bonds model. Banks were actually in the nexus of all three models.

The 'private sector' model can be described as a direct securitization executed by banks and finance companies. In this case the respective banks and finance companies originated assets on their balance sheets which they subsequently securitized for the purposes of obtaining financing to continue their core lending activities and/or for the purposes of risk management and regulatory capital relief. Private sector securitizations embraced a wide range of assets associated mainly with bank lending activities; a smaller portion of the market was associated with the fund management business.

The 'public sector' model can be described as a securitization of consumer products (mortgages, student loans) executed with the direct support of government agencies (explicitly or implicitly supported by the respective sovereign) whereby the securitization involves assets originated by the banks in line with specific predetermined eligibility criteria and subject to credit protection provided by the respective agencies. The purpose of such securitization is the provision of liquidity to the private sector, so that it can continue lending in crucial consumer finance areas, such as mortgages and student loans.

The 'covered bond' model is associated with the issuance of senior bank debt secured by legally or structurally ring fenced asset pools. Depending on whether the ring-fencing of the assets is achieved by following the provisions of a dedicated covered bond law or via structures contractually tailored under existing laws (often using the securitization laws and structures to achieve asset ring fencing), covered bonds evolved along the lines of 'traditional (specific-law-based) covered bonds' and 'structured (general-law) covered bonds'. As more countries are adopting specific laws for covered bonds, the convergence is towards a more 'traditional' type of covered bond markets. Covered bonds are issued by public and private banks and are based on asset pools ('cover pools') comprising mainly residential mortgage loans and commercial real estate loans ('mortgage covered bonds') or municipal debt obligations ('public sector covered bonds'), and to a much lesser degree on shipping loans and aircraft loans.

The 'private sector' securitization is generally associated with the 'originate-to-distribute' model, while the 'covered bond' securitization is associated with the 'originate-to-hold' model. Another way to differentiate the two models is to define the latter as 'on balance sheet securitization' and the former as 'off balance sheet securitization'. The 'public sector' model is effectively a hybrid between 'originate-to-distribute' and 'originate-to-hold', given the fact that the loans originated by the private sector are passed on to the public sector which retains them on its 'balance sheet' and funds them by issuing bonds, which it guarantees.

Nearly all developed securitization markets are dominated by residential mortgage loans–RMBS and mortgage covered bonds. This closely corresponds with the composition of the respective banks' assets books. Securitization and covered bonds are—above all—bank financing tools, so it is natural that they are applied to the dominant part of the banks' balance sheets. Subsequently, securitization embraced other assets, such as credit cards, consumer loans, auto loans, small and medium size enterprise loans, equipment leases, commercial real estate loans and leases, and corporate (leveraged) loans. Once the securitization and covered bond technologies were well established the need and the temptation arose to apply them to new areas—ship finance, commercial real estate loans, corporate bonds, project finance, royalties, future flows from export receivables and remittances, etc.

At the more recent stages of market development, securitization techniques were also applied to credit default swaps and synthetic risk transfers. These are known as 'synthetic securitizations' and were initially meant to allow for credit risk transfer from holders of credit exposures (corporate loans, ABS) to a third party, willing to take the credit risk of such portfolios for a fee—similar to writing an insurance policy. Going beyond the credit risk transfer/hedging by banks, the use of credit derivatives allowed investors to build large (on a notional basis) credit portfolios without equally large initial cash outlays. The 'credit insurance' providers were insurance companies (general and monoline insurers), specialist credit derivatives companies, and investors of all other types via credit-linked notes. The credit default swap market, the hedging and transfer of exposures indirectly and somewhat surreptitiously contributed to the expansion of the parallel banking system well beyond its visible cash quantifiable volume.

1.3 The parallel banking system and its fault-line

The traditional banking system intermediates short-term deposits and long-term lending, and through government support bridges the asset-liability gap. On the face of it, the parallel banking system finances long-term lending with capital markets instruments of similar maturity (a securitization bond is repaid by the cash flows of the underlying asset pool), i.e. securitization facilitates match funding of assets. However, a more careful look into how the securitization bond purchases are funded by the ultimate investors reveals a fault-line one step removed from the direct asset funding.[2]

Securitization bond investors were dominated by:

- banks—funding via deposits, repos, and short-term borrowing, along longer-term bonds, loans, and equity,
- commercial paper conduits—funded through the issuance of commercial paper of one-to-three-month maturity and regularly rolled over,

---

[2] Batchvarov et al. (2007).

- structured investment vehicles (SIVs)—funded by repos, commercial paper of one-to-three-month-maturity, and medium-term notes of one-to three-year maturity,
- hedge funds—often relying on repos and prime broker financing for gearing,
- insurance companies and pension funds, to a much lesser degree.

In summary, the majority of securitization investors relied predominantly on short-term funding in order to invest in longer maturity securitization paper, which leads us to conclude that the parallel banking system replicated in a different format an asset-liability mismatch similar to the one inherent in the traditional banking system. Furthermore, the parallel banking system had a limited backstop support in case of funding disruption, i.e. the equivalent of the run on a traditional bank. The backstop where it existed was provided by the banks: liquidity facilities for commercial paper conduits and to a lesser degree to structured investment vehicles. When such liquidity facilities were drawn, the result was effectively a transfer of the respective assets from the parallel banking system onto the books of the traditional banking system. That also happened not by obligation, but as a result of banks' reputation considerations—many of the affected investors in the parallel banking system were good clients of the traditional banks. Hence, upon the disruption of the commercial paper (CP) funding market (i.e. the capital markets equivalent of a run on the parallel banking system), the traditional banking system subsumed the assets of the parallel banking system.

To illustrate the role of the short-term markets in funding the growth of the parallel banking system, in general, and securitization in particular, we highlight in Tables 16.1–16.2 and Figure 16.1 the growth of the CP market and its share of the overall CP market in Europe and the US. At its peak years 2006–7, the asset-backed commercial paper (ABCP) market reached an outstanding volume of circa USD1.5trl in total, and represented 56% (with 333 ABCP programmes) and 36% (86 ABCP programmes) of the total CP market in US and Europe, respectively.

Table 16.1 US and European ABCP number of programmes outstanding and share (%) of the respective CP markets

	2000	2001	2002	2003	2004	2005	2006	2007	2008	3Q 2009
US ABCP # Programs o/s	271	292	260	249	248	272	333	295	148	130
US ABCP % of total US CP	39	52	54	54	50	52	56	46	42	41
Europe ABCP # Programs o/s	n/a	n/a	n/a	73	71	77	86	76	42	44
Europe ABCP % of total Europe CP	9	12	16	21	24	31	36	21	10	8

Source: BofA Merrill Lynch Global Research, Moody's Investor Service.

Table 16.2 US and European CP markets' composition

	2000	2001	2002	2003	2004	2005	2006	2007	2008	3/31 2009
					USCP Market					
Direct Placement	308	271	224	213	188	209	237	132	81	46
Corporates & Banks	652	424	393	358	527	591	644	842	854	640
ABCP	624	740	715	665	704	858	1127	814	664	484
Total	1584	1435	1332	1236	1419	1658	2008	1788	1599	1169
					ECP Market					
Euro Unsecured	212	233	264	338	387	331	406	566	602	600
EA BCP	20	31	52	89	122	149	225	153	67	53
Total	232	264	316	427	509	480	631	719	669	653

Source: BofA Merrill Lynch Global Research.

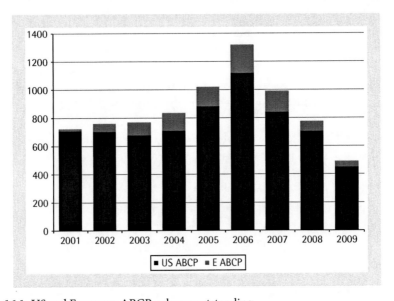

FIGURE 16.1 US and European ABCP volume outstanding.

Source: BofA Merrill Lynch Global Research.

1.4 The parallel banking system and the decoupling of the product chain

Under the framework of the traditional banking system a loan product was controlled by the bank throughout its entire life—from sourcing through underwriting to servicing and full repayment or work out. By contrast, in the parallel banking system, in the name of efficiency and volume, the product chain was cut into separate autonomous functions often performed by agents—independent and often uncoordinated entities such as brokers, packagers, appraisers, underwriters, sponsors, investors—each with its own economic imperatives and motivation. The conflicting interests may have ulti-mately weakened the entire system of loan underwriting and servicing, and deprived the creditors (actually, the ultimate bond investors) of control over the loan products. It may have further reduced the flexibility to work out loans if and when they deteri-orate under idiosyncratic borrower or general economic conditions. Furthermore, it created a wide range of products meant to address the interests of a specific borrower or the above-mentioned agents.

Securitization bonds are nothing more than a derivative of the loan pool, on the basis of which they are structured. The securitization itself can only magnify or mute that pool's performance through its embedded leverage, structural features, man-ager or servicer actions, etc. Given that the performance of a securitization bond is directly related to the performance of the underlying asset pool, it is difficult to see how securitization itself can contribute to a weaker pool performance, unless one takes into account the effects of the decoupling of the product chain securitization contributed to.

The lax underwriting and documentation criteria prompted by the 'chopping' of the product chain, to which securitization may have contributed indirectly, led to the weak performance of securitization markets first in the US sub-prime mortgage sector, and eventually was among the main reasons for the collapse of the parallel banking system. The consequences will be expressed quantitatively in higher default/repossession and high severity of loss levels.

1.5 The economic impact of the parallel banking system

Gradually over time, the parallel banking system captured an ever-increasing share of lending to consumer and corporate borrowers. The rapid growth in consumer lending was supported by financing through traditional securitization and covered bond markets. In our estimates:

- in some countries up to 50% of new origination of residential mortgage and con-sumer credit was funded through residential mortgage-backed securities (RMBS) and/or covered bonds
- large portions of the leverage loan new issuance was syndicated into the capital markets through securitization
- the share of commercial real estate loans that were securitized in some countries exceeded 60% of the newly originated loan volumes.

The high participation of capital markets financing in the consumer, corporate, and mortgage lending effectively transfers the capital markets (securitization and whole-sale financing) prices into the pricing of the final products to the consumer and the corporate sector. The capital markets can provide these sectors with adequate funding when the pricing between the sectors is realigned as was the case during the boom of 2002–7, but cease to provide it when there is a discrepancy between the pricing

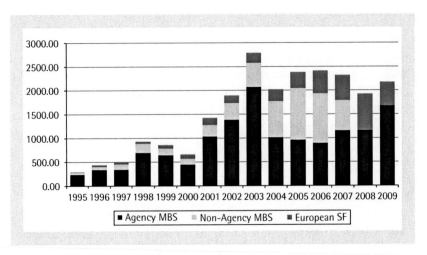

FIGURE 16.2 Securitization issuance: US and Europe.

Source: BofA Merrill Lynch Global Research.

of the lending and the pricing demanded by the capital markets during the crisis of 2008–9. In the latter period, loans were originated at lower spreads than the spreads demanded by the capital markets to fund them. In other words, the way banks intend to fund their lending should have an impact on the way they price their lending— with the seizure of the securitization markets, the cheap finance for the consumer and corporate sectors slowed to a trickle and so did the related lending. During the market collapse the funding availability and cost superseded borrowers' credit quality in the loan pricing equation.

The decline in deposits in many developed economies relates to the decline in savings rates and use of savings/investment instruments (mutual funds, hedge funds, pension funds) as alternatives to deposits has brought the banking system to the acute need for wholesale funding. Capital markets and securitization provided that for a long period of time. Securitization and covered bonds allowed the flow of loans to the final borrower and indirectly affected the economic growth potential of the respective countries. Figure 16.2 shows the volume of new issuance of securitization. The new issue volume which was fully placed on the markets peaked in 2006. The new issuance in 2008 found investors predominantly in government purchase programmes or government repo facilities, and the new issuance in 2009—significantly down on previous years—was further propped up by such existing or new dedicated government support programmes (e.g. US TALF, ECB purchase programme for covered bonds).[3]

The decline in securitization and covered bond funding, which was experienced by the developed economies in the 2008–9 period will likely affect mid-to-long-term economic growth unless it is offset by increased bank lending based on deposits or by

---

[3] Batchvarov et al. (2009).

government lending. This is unlikely to happen quickly enough, if at all, to offset the seizure in the capital markets. The government involvement has its limits. Therefore, the collapse of the parallel banking system will have long-term consequences for the lending volume and potentially induce a below-trend economic growth of the respective economies for a period of time.

To illustrate our argument we look at three sets of data:

- growth of overall securitization (Figure 16.2) and European covered bond markets (Figure 16.3)

We note the relationship between the growth of the securitization issuance in Europe and the US and the growth of the European and US ABCP volumes outstanding (Tables 16.1 and 16.2). This co-temporal growth supports our view of the importance of the short-term financing in the placement of securitization and the related growth of the parallel banking system.[4] The jumbo covered bond market also experienced a tremendous growth after year 2000 and recorded its growth peak in the same period as the securitization markets (years 2006–2007) (Figure 16.3).

- substantial portion of new residential mortgage advances in Europe financed via the structured finance markets (Table 16.3)

The data supports our view of the importance of securitization for the financing of consumer credit, particularly mortgage credit. The role of securitization markets increased

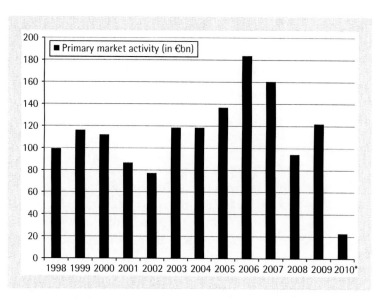

FIGURE 16.3 European jumbo covered bond new issuance.

Source: BofA Merrill Lynch Global Research.
*The 2010 figure includes Jumbo primary market activity from 1 January 2010 until 15 January 2010.

---

[4] Batchvarov et al. (2008a).

Table 16.3 Covered bond (CB) and RMBS new issuance as % of new gross residential loans

	2001			2006		
	CB	RMBS	Both	CB	RMBS	Both
Germany	61.9	0.9	62.8	50.7	2.3	51.9
Spain	14.6	6.3	20.8	41.5	23.1	64.6
France	13.1	3.9	17.1	12.7	0.2	12.9
Italy	0	18.1	18.1	4.7	19.6	23.3
UK	0	9.9	9.9	4	26.9	31

Source: European Mortgage Federation National Experts, National Central Banks, National Statistics Offices, BofA Merrill Lynch Global Research.

between years 2001 and 2006 significantly in Spain and in the UK and maintained very high presence in Germany (Table 16.3). The seizure of the public capital markets prompted government intervention. The collapse of the parallel banking system and subsequent effects on mortgage lending could not be fully offset by the increased participation of the agency (quasi-government) sector as evidenced by the volumes of US agency vs. non-agency MBS, but the former certainly provided some support for a continuous mortgage lending in the US. In Europe, the strong issuance volume of ABS and MBS can be almost fully attributed to the ECB repo facilities, without which the MBS and covered bonds new issue volume and related consumer lending would have completely collapsed. The data in Figures 16.2 and 16.3 supports our view that the vacuum due to the collapse of the parallel banking system in Europe and the US was partially or fully filled by the respective governments.[5]

- the 'true' US GDP growth, discounting the effect of the mortgage withdrawals on GDP growth

Table 16.4 presents a difficult and controversial recalculation of US GDP growth including and excluding mortgage equity withdrawals, i.e. the use of the housing unit as a source of savings deposits by the borrower. With high appreciation of housing prices in the US, it became all too attractive for borrowers to cash in on such appreciation and increase consumption. The result was buoyant consumption, on one the hand, and widespread negative equity in the following correction of house prices. While the exact contribution of house equity withdrawals and the boom in mortgage financing to GDP growth may be difficult to quantify, the contribution of the parallel banking system which made them possible cannot be doubted.

[5] Batchvarov et al. (2008a); Batchvarov, Liang, and Winkler (2009).

Table 16.4 US GDP growth with and without Mortgage Equity Withdrawals (MEW)

	US GDP growth with MEW (%)	US GDP growth w/out MEW (%)
2000	3.7	2.5
2001	0.8	−0.8
2002	1.6	−0.8
2003	2.6	0.3
2004	4.2	0.8
2005	3.9	0.7
2006	3.2	1.2

Source: As reported by John Mauldin, Thoughts, Frontline Weekly Newsletter, March 2009

2 THE PARALLEL BANKING SYSTEM AND THE DISRUPTION OF HISTORICAL TIME SERIES

2.1 Unreliability of historical data series and the collapse of the SF bond markets

Structured finance and associated quantitative models depend on historical data series of defaults, delinquencies, recoveries, and other data inputs in order to determine probability and timing of default, establish credit enhancement, or to price structured finance bonds. In addition to those variables, other inputs include ratings and estimates of rating stability, counterparty risk, correlation of default, liquidity factors, and so on. Pricing should ultimately integrate all of the above inputs and combine them with qualitative understanding of investor base changes, regulatory capital considerations, rating agencies behaviour, etc.

While it would be virtually impossible to assign quantitative values to all the different factors that play a role in the credit analysis and pricing of structured finance instruments, it is also questionable as to how readily quantifiable certain quantitative—on their face value—factors really are. We are referring here to the basic quantitative inputs such as default, timing of default, recovery, and correlation. The existence of historical time series may actually confuse rather than clarify matters:

- in the consumer sector, the period 2000–7 saw an unprecedented increase in the availability of consumer credit at historically low cost and consequently led to a jump in consumer leverage across all income brackets, first time availability on a large scale of credit to low income and low creditworthy consumers, and to a massive increase in consumer loan product diversity and complexity.

- in the corporate sector, the period 2002–7 experienced a dramatic rise in lending to the high-yield corporate sector with a particularly steep growth in leveraged finance, accompanied by a similar to the consumer credit sector relaxation of underwriting standards, highest by historical standards leverage, shift of creditor base away from the usually-hold-to-maturity banks and towards trading-oriented institutional investors and CDO managers.
- in the commercial real estate sector, the entry of the conduits may have led to relaxation of underwriting criteria and dispersion of ownership among multiple creditors on an unprecedented scale; it made available financing to lower-quality borrowers as well, as the competition for loans and the limited share of high-quality property and borrowers to lend to forced relaxation of underwriting criteria.
- a persistently low interest rate and low inflation environment forced investors to look for higher yield to meet investment targets by compounding leverage during the period 2004–7. That leverage took the form of securitization and related tranching, or the form of investing long term by funding short term. In other words, the leverage was either imbedded in the structures of the bonds or was achieved by borrowing to invest in longer-term bonds. Leverage was achieved also via the credit derivatives markets. The resulting overall compounded leverage is without precedent in the history of the bond markets.

All of the above changes happened simultaneously with the growth of 'originate-to-distribute' models in consumer and corporate finance and the decoupling of the product chain, i.e. with reduced underwriting scrutiny and impaired credit standards, and related reduced ability to work out troubled loans.

Such radical changes in consumer and corporate lending patterns and in consumer credit paradigms make historical data about consumer and corporate credit performance unreliable, irrelevant, or simply non-existent. The clearest evidence of that is the deterioration of consumer credit performance to a degree without precedent in previous cycles. Another expression is the massive wave of downgrades-structured finance credit experienced in 2008–9: the performance of the securitization asset pools was much worse than initial expectations, based on primary historical data series or on subjectively stressed historical evidence. We highlight rating transition changes in Tables 16.5 and 16.6.

2.2 The birth and death of extreme leverage

The parallel banking system led to a massive unprecedented increase in leverage across the capital markets and their agents. The concept of leverage evolved. While historically leverage was associated with borrowing money, i.e. debt, and was calculated in the context of debt-to-equity and debt-service ratios for individual loans and corporates, in the framework of the parallel banking system new aspects of leverage emerged: structural leverage, maturity mismatch leverage, layering of leverage, synthetic leverage:

- we associate structural leverage with tranching of structured finance instruments—in fact, the definition of securitization suggests prioritization of cash flows when senior tranches received principal and interest payments first and junior tranches last—and the cash flow prioritization may change depending on the credit health of the underlying asset pool expressed in the breach of covenants and triggers.
- tranching can be applied at a second stage, where the pools consisting of tranched exposures are securitized and further tranched.
- alternatively, tranched exposure can be purchased via borrowed money or repoed. It was common during the boom times of 2005–7 for hedge funds to acquire leverage to the tune of 20 times, which collapsed to the 2–4 times range in 2008–9.
- leverage could be achieved without investing borrowed money by selling protection on a given name or a tranche of a given portfolio; the majority of such transactions were executed on a proprietary basis.
- another variation in leverage could be the purchase of long-term tranches with high risk of maturity extension, using short-term borrowed money, whose continued availability depends on the lender's willingness to roll the maturing loan until an uncertain maturity.
- an extreme example would be investing highly geared short-term borrowed money in a junior/equity tranche of a CDO squared based on senior/mezzanine tranches of high loan-to-value (LTV) negative-amortization mortgage loan portfolios!

The effect of leverage, while positive on the upside—magnifying returns in good times—is pernicious on the downside. This has been well known for centuries and has been demonstrated in all previous bubble bursts in history (take the tulip mania or any real estate boom and bust), but leverage has never been so extreme on the brink of any of the preceding crises.

The unwinding of such leverage leads to unprecedented losses and to the demise of whole sectors and ranges of products or financing instruments:

- individual loans, such as high LTV mortgage loans, negative amortization mortgages
- financing instruments, such as CDO squared, CDO of ABS
- sectors, such as hedge funds dedicated to specific high-leverage strategies, ABCP conduits.

The existence of such leverage through products and agents magnified both price movements and loss levels accompanying the collapse of the parallel banking system. The pricing effects can be tracked on Figure 16.4 for European ABS and on Figures 16.5–16.8 for US CMBX and Figures 16.9–16.11 for US ABX. A comparison between the spread movements of triple-A structured finance bonds and corporate bond index is rather telling regarding the degree of impact of the collapse of the parallel

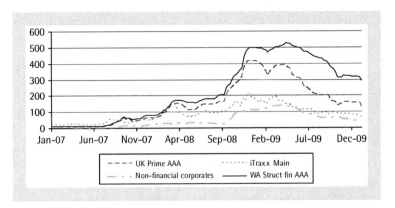

FIGURE 16.4 AAA SF Spreads in comparison with corporate spread.

Source: BofA Merrill Lynch Global Research.

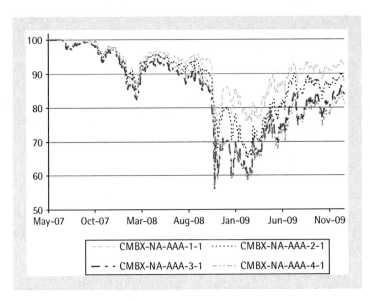

FIGURE 16.5 CMBX—AAA.

Source: BofA Merrill Lynch Global Research.

banking system and external leverage; the minor spread differential between them before the crisis widened to more than 400bps.

The price of a bond when purchased with leverage is different from the price of the same bond when purchased without leverage. The elimination of the leverage effect on pricing is best tracked in the price and spread behaviour of triple-A bonds, under the simplifying assumption that triple-A bonds are likely to repay interest and principal in full. The reapplication of leverage through government support (e.g. US TALF) led to significant spread tightening in the sectors directly affected. This point is demonstrated through the upward price movements of the AAA CMBX index following the announcement about the commercial mortgage-backed securities (CMBS) inclusion

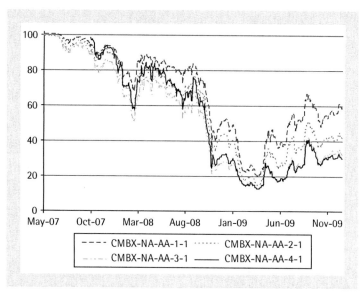

FIGURE 16.6 CMBX—AA.

Source: BofA Merrill Lynch Global Research.

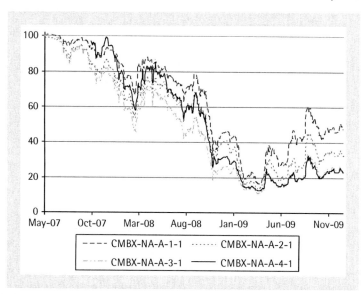

FIGURE 16.7 CMBX—A.

Source: BofA Merrill Lynch Global Research.

in TALF in early May 2009 and the first CMBS TALF subscription in mid-July 2009. By contrast, no such uplift can be observed in AAA ABX as it was initially unclear as to whether TALF would be applied to the subprime mortgage sector.

A similar and greater fall occurred as the parallel banking system collapsed—a significant portion of the senior and mezzanine ABS at the peak of new issuance were

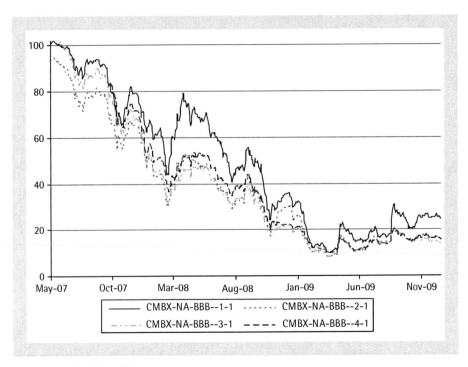

FIGURE 16.8 CMBX—BBB.

Source: BofA Merrill Lynch Global Research.

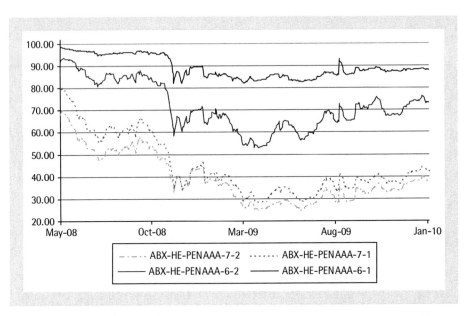

FIGURE 16.9 ABX—AAA.

Source: BofA Merrill Lynch Global Research.

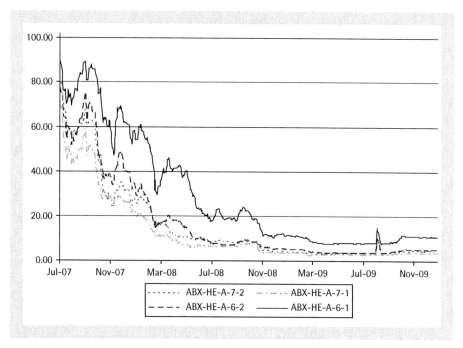

FIGURE 16.10 ABX—A.

Source: BofA Merrill Lynch Global Research.

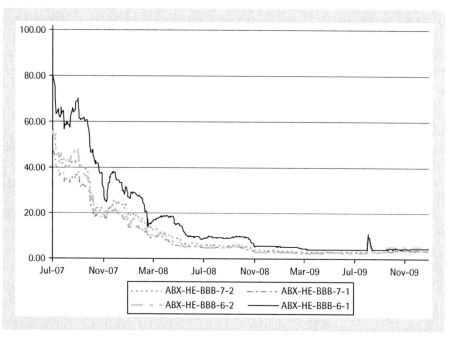

FIGURE 16.11 ABX—BBB.

Source: BofA Merrill Lynch Global Research.

funded by CDO of ABS, i.e. through structural leverage, and the senior tranches of the CDO of ABS were acquired by the ABCP funded conduits, i.e. through maturity mismatch leverage.

Another interesting observation from Figures 16.5–16.8 is the pricing behaviour of the different tranches, i.e. positions in the capital structure with different leverage. While the price of the most senior tranches (low credit risk) appears to be affected by the availability of external leverage, the price of the junior tranches (high credit risk) is a reflection of the structural leverage and credit deterioration—the two junior mezzanine tranches are effectively pricing a loss of principal and a finite stream of interest payments.

The quantitative consequences of these developments now form part of the new historical data series, especially when it comes to liquidity and the liquidity effects on default and severity of loss. These new data series serve as the new benchmark for assessing deal, portfolio, market, credit, and other risks in the future; a future when such instruments or conditions may not exist and the entire banking system and capital markets may be radically different, as we discuss later.

2.3 The modified rating stability view of structured finance instruments

Tables 16.5 and 16.6 show the global rating transitions for US structured finance bonds by Fitch for the periods 1991–2006 and 1991–2008 and for structured finance bonds and for corporate bonds by Moody's for the periods 1984–2006 and 1984–2008.[6] Without going into much detail here are several conclusions, which we believe will have a long-term effect on the structured finance market future ratings and on the construction of structured finance portfolios:

- the rating transitions have accelerated and the rating stability of structured finance bonds has deteriorated—the deterioration is more pronounced for the mezzanine tranches than for the most senior tranche.
- the decline in rating stability can be attributed to RMBS (subprime) and to CDOs; however, the periods we review do not include the full impact of the 2008–9 credit and economic crisis unleashed by the collapse of the shadow banking system and the subsequent changes in rating agencies' methodologies, which may have a further negative effects on the ratings of Collateralized loan obligations (CLOs) and CMBS, thus compounding the effects already observed in the area of RMBS and CDOs.
- the comparison of the rating stability between global structured finance and global corporates is in favour of global structured finance bonds until 2006, but as of

---

[6] Tables 16.5 and 16.6 and our conclusions about structured finance rating transitions are based on the information provided in the following rating agencies' publications: Moody's Investor Service (2007, 2009); Fitch Ratings (2009); Fitch Ratings (2007).

Table 16.5 Fitch US Structured Finance Transition Matrices: 1991–2008 vs. 1991–2006 Average three-year (%)

	1991–2008								
	Aaa	Aa	A	BBB	BB	B	CCC	CC & below	TOTAL
Aaa	96.22	1.24	0.76	0.57	0.41	0.39	0.26	0.15	100
Aa	23.04	68.89	2.5	1.79	1.25	0.96	0.68	0.9	100
A	12.55	11.85	61.92	4.57	2.44	2.09	1.57	3	100
BBB	5.45	6.6	9.43	56.14	5.58	4.33	2.11	10.36	100
BB	1.82	3.23	6.66	13.9	55.36	4.95	2.28	11.79	100
B	0.59	0.8	2.35	5.38	11.66	56.36	4.44	18.43	100
CCC	0	0.12	0.12	0.12	1.16	4.87	25.87	67.75	100

	1991–2006								
	Aaa	Aa	A	BBB	BB	B	CCC	CC & below	TOTAL
Aaa	97.22	1.21	0.51	0.33	0.23	0.24	0.11	0.16	100
Aa	26.12	69.28	1.52	1.01	0.54	0.55	0.21	0.76	100
A	13.88	13.27	65.36	2.74	1.1	1.19	0.58	1.9	100
BBB	6.04	7.92	10.45	61.97	3.57	2.77	1.22	6.06	100
BB	2.14	3.98	7.35	14.46	58.08	3.43	1.65	8.92	100
B	0.63	1.02	3.1	6.31	12.46	55.92	3.76	16.8	100
CCC	0	0	0	0.18	1.05	2.63	26.27	69.88	100

Source: Fitch

2008 structured finance bonds demonstrate higher rating stability than corporate bonds only in the top and the bottom ratings: significantly better for triple-As and marginally better for single-Bs.

In summary, global structured finance bonds retain their rating stability advantage over corporates at triple-A level according to Moody's, but lose that advantage for other investment grade categories. The current advantage at AAA level is likely to diminish once the full effects of the economic and credit crisis and of the rating methodology changes transpire.

The full effect on the ratings of structured finance instruments expressed in rating stability and rating transitions will not be fully known until after the crisis is over and the market embarks on its next expansionary stage. While the trends can already be observed in the data and we summarized them above, their full impact will not be quantitatively known until probably 2012.

The quantitative results for rating transitions and stability will be further influenced by three 'event risks':

- radical changes in rating methodologies—radical to the point where the definitions of ratings are revamped
- radical involvement of the governments—radical to the point where private contracts are revamped and overruled (for example, massive government

Table 16.6 Moody's global Structured finance Rating Transitions Matrices 1984–2006 vs. 1984–2008

Moody's global Structured Finance Rating Transition Matrices 1984–2008 averages over 12 month horizon (%)

	Aaa	Aa	A	Baa	Ba	B	Caa & below
Aaa	97.79	0.76	0.53	0.37	0.19	0.14	0.21
Aa	5.27	87.19	2.14	1.12	0.8	1.72	1.77
A	1.1	3.26	85.61	3.28	1.39	2.02	3.34
Baa	0.37	0.47	2.46	83.17	3.46	2.92	7.14
Ba	0.15	0.07	0.45	2.46	82.33	3.56	10.98
B	0.07	0.04	0.08	0.34	1.95	83.63	13.89
Caa and below	0.03			0.07	0.08	0.51	99.3

Moody's global Structured Finance Rating Transition Matrices: 1984–2006 averages over 12-month horizon (%)

	Aaa	Aa	A	Baa	Ba	B	Caa & below
Aaa	98.95	0.7	0.2	0.06	0.03	0.02	0.03
Aa	5.74	91.56	1.79	0.56	0.13	0.08	0.13
A	1.28	3.59	92.38	1.78	0.52	0.21	0.24
Baa	0.35	0.57	3.04	91.66	2.37	1.01	1
Ba	0.1	0.09	0.55	3.17	88.74	3.23	4.11
B	0.06	0.04	0.11	0.41	2.22	87.39	9.78
Caa and below	0.02			0.04	0.09	0.38	99.47

Moody's global Corporate Finance Rating Transition Matrices: 1984–2008 averages over 12-month horizon (%)

	Aaa	**Aa**	A	Baa	Ba	B	Caa & below
Aaa	92.76	6.97	0.26		0.02		
Aa	1.26	91.45	6.95	0.27	0.05	0.02	0.01
A	0.07	3.01	90.91	5.3	0.55	0.11	0.04
Baa	0.05	0.21	5.37	88.33	4.53	1	0.51
Ba	0.01	0.06	0.43	6.48	81.47	9.56	2
B	0.01	0.05	0.18	0.4	6.16	81.72	11.47
Caa and below		0.03	0.04	0.19	0.67	11.44	87.63

Moody's global Corporate Finance Rating Transition Matrices: 1984–2006 averages over 12-month horizon (%)

	Aaa	Aa	A	Baa	Ba	B	Caa & below
Aaa	92.76	6.92	0.29		0.02	0	
Aa	0.88	91.86	6.9	0.29	0.05	0.02	0.01
A	0.06	2.59	91.45	5.18	0.57	0.12	0.04
Baa	0.05	0.24	5.21	88.52	4.47	1	0.52
Ba	0.01	0.07	0.54	6.08	82.4	8.88	2.02
B	0.01	0.05	0.19	0.42	6.01	82.04	11.27
Caa and below		0.03	0.04	0.21	0.67	9.45	89.59

Source: Moody's Investor Service.

programmes to support mortgage borrowers through mortgage loan modification and refinancing)

- new understanding and requirement for liquidity—this is associated with both public and private sector liquidity availability, which in turn affects default risk and default correlation.

2.4 The role of rating stability in future ratings

The question of rating stability of structured finance ratings is as old as the structured finance instruments themselves. The environment of elevated collateral loss expectations following the collapse of the shadow banking system brought up the issue of initial and subsequent evaluation of loss severity and loss probability. In light of the experience of 2007–9 investors would want to see a different level of credit enhancement for structured finance bonds (higher and based on a broader distribution of loss scenarios, as well as larger tranche sizes with tranche sizes becoming much more central than in the past to tranche behaviour evaluation). These questions need to be addressed also in the context of how stable a structured finance rating should be.[7]

Rating agencies can always make the AAA-rating of a tranche of a structured finance deal (self-liquidating pool) more resilient to downgrades by requiring higher credit enhancement, while for other types of ratings rating agencies attempt to address both downward and upward rating stability (through-the-cycle rating for a going concern).

While higher credit enhancement will bring extra protection for investors, in practice there will be a ceiling on credit enhancement levels, imposed by the economic efficiency of a transaction. Let's take a simplified example of a leveraged loan CLO (100 single-B loans) to see what level of credit enhancement would be necessary to guarantee the triple-A rating to be retained under the worst scenario observed in the past (Table 16.7).

For single-B corporates, the worst ten years of defaults are 1984–93, according to Moody's data. The worst average annual recovery on secured bank loans was 47.25% observed in 1993. With these assumptions, we look at the portfolio one year on, assuming a certain proportion of downgrades in the remainder of the portfolio, and run a rating model—S&P CDO Evaluator. We ignore cash-flow modelling and look only at SLR (standard loss rate) rates as a proxy for required subordination. We obtain a proxy for required subordination for the new portfolio which has fewer loans and worse credit quality (but shorter remaining life) at the end of each year. Comparing it to the actual AAA subordination each year (and taking into account de-levering due to prepayments of 20% and/or over collateralization breaches), we determine that for AAA to remain AAA under this scenario the subordination level at inception needs to be at least 51%.

---

[7] Batchvarov et al. (2008b).

Table 16.7 CLO subordination*

End of year	0	1	2	3	4	5	6	7	8	9	10
Default Scenario		7.0%	8.0%	12.0%	6.0%	7.0%	9.0%	16.0%	15.0%	9.0%	6.0%
# loans	100	93	85	76	74	72	65	52	41	36	34
Portfolio par	100	93.5	86.0	79.2	78.2	77.9	73.3	61.5	52.3	47.6	44.7
Downgrade scenario for the remainder of the portfolio		30% by 1 notch	60% by 1 notch	100% by 1 notch	50/50% by 1/2 notches	100% by 2 notches	100% by 2 notches	100% by 2 notches	100% by 2 notches	n/a	n/a
Required subordination	31.5%	34.6%	36.0	37.48%	40.63%	44.69%	43.82%	43.62%	42.46%	n/a	n/a
AAA tranche par	49.0	48.1	45.9	44.4	42.8	41.3	39.9	29.3	20.4	n/a	n/a
AAA actual subordination	51%	48.56%	46.64%	43.87%	44.99%	46.50%	44.96%	45.41%	49.23%	n/a	n/a

*Note: 47.25% recovery, assume recoveries are realized after 2 years since default,
Source: Banc of America Securities–Merrill Lynch.

If we take a more extreme scenario of 19.7% annual default rate, i.e. the worst annual default rate experienced by single-B corporates, the minimum initial subordination level would need to be 60% for AAA rating to survive the above scenario without a downgrade. Thus, to get a 100% stable AAA CLO rating, the structure would need to have nearly double the subordination level currently observed in CLOs. This will likely remain only a theoretical possibility, however, given that the economics of a CLO may no longer be achieved.

At present, securitization ratings address the risk of losses (first dollar loss or expected loss). But if structured finance ratings are to address rating stability as well, a number of additional questions must be answered:

- what scenarios should a triple-A rating withstand?
- should that be the historical worst scenario, so that there is no principal loss or should it be the historical worst scenarios, so that there is no downgrade?
- should it be a scenario worse than the historical worst in order to ensure no principal loss (or downgrade) in case the future performance is worse than the past, and by how much worse.

Answers to the above questions will lead to a different approach to sizing credit enhancement and assigning ratings, and ultimately will affect the very existence of the individual structured finance products and sector securitizations.

2.5 Credit transformation and the effects of correlation

The majority of securitization and structured finance transactions is based on a pool of assets and multiple obligations by participating parties. The range is very wide. Examples include: a lower-rated bond guaranteed by a highly rated entity (monoline-insured bond–monoline risk);—a repackaged bond, where an existing bond is repacked with a currency swap and a new bond is issued in a different currency (counterparty risk);—a pool of thousands of mortgage or SME (Small and medium enterprises) loans, funded through a tranched securitization in the same as or a different currency from the one in which the loans are denominated (systemic risk); two or three real estate loan exposures packaged into a structured finance bond tranched in three or four levels (large concentration risk or large single-exposure risk).

In any case, the key transformation mechanism is that two or more exposures/obligations of different credit quality support a new single bond of higher credit quality or a new bond with at least several tranches of much higher credit quality than the one(s) of the underlying exposures/obligations.

That transformation relies on the key assumption that not all exposures/obligations will default simultaneously. While the analysis may be somewhat different whether it is applied to a set of two obligations (the so-called 'two-party pay' analysis) or to a pool of multiple obligations (a copula function-based analysis), the crux of the transformation

Table 16.8 Implied rating of a two–party pay structure of two A1 rated obligations

Correlation	High	Medium	Low
Implied rating	Aa3	Aa1	Aaa

Source: Moody's Investor Service.

Table 16.9 Implied rating stability of a two–party pay structure–volatility of underlying obligations' ratings

Correlation	High	Medium	Low
Implied rating	A1–Baa3	Aa1–A1	Aaa–Baa2

Source: Moody's Investor Service.

is the quantification of the joint probability of default, the degree of independence among the exposures/obligors.

An important work that laid the foundation for the above analysis in the context of credit ratings was done by Douglas Lucas.[8] The joint probability of default of two entities A and B is quantified as follows:

$$P(A \text{ and } B) = P(A)^*P(B) + Corr(A, B)^* [P(A)^*(1 - P(A))]1/2^* [P(B)^*(1 - P(B))]1/2$$

where P(E) is the probability of an event occurring and Corr (E) is the correlation between the two outcomes.

Further analysis of the two-party pay approach application in the rating process is provided by Jerome Fons.[9] From here the analysis can be extended to include multiple obligations and their joint probability of default, i.e. correlation.

Assuming that the P(E) of the exposures is derived on the basis of historical default studies of obligations of similar credit quality, the key input in the above formulas is the Corr (A,B), which in turn is not observable in practice and its qualification and quantification may be highly subjective in nature. Furthermore, P(E) is also subject to change as the credit quality of an obligation may deteriorate or improve, and such change may affect Corr (A,B). Lastly, the correlation may change for reasons other than the creditworthiness of the underlying obligations.

To illustrate we use Moody's matrices for joint support ratings[10] and track the evolution of the implied joint support rating in a two-party pay structure based on assumed level of correlation between two A1 rated parties (Tables 16.8, 16.9, and 16.10).

If the rating of one of the parties is to change, in order not to affect the implied joint support rating, that change must be within a range as in Table 16.9.

[8] Lucas (1995).   [9] Fons (1997).   [10] Ibid.

Table 16.10 Moody's Implied Joint Support Ratings for Different Correlation Cases

Implied Joint Support Rating for High Correlation Case

	Aaa	Aa1	Aa2	Aa3	A1	A2	A3	Baa1	Baa2	Baa3	Ba1	Ba2	Ba3	B1	B2	B3	Caa
Aaa	Aaa																
Aa1	Aaa	Aaa															
Aa2	Aaa	Aaa	Aa1														
Aa3	Aaa	Aaa	Aa1	Aa2													
A1	Aaa	Aaa	Aa1	Aa2	Aa3												
A2	Aaa	Aaa	Aa1	Aa2	Aa3	A1											
A3	Aaa	Aaa	Aa1	Aa2	Aa3	A1	A2										
Baa1	Aaa	Aaa	Aa1	Aa2	Aa3	A1	A2	A3									
Baa2	Aaa	Aaa	Aa1	Aa2	Aa3	A1	A2	A3	Baa1								
Baa3	Aaa	Aaa	Aa1	Aa2	Aa3	A1	A2	A3	Baa1	Baa2							
Ba1	Aaa	Aa1	Aa2	Aa3	A1	A2	A3	Baa1	Baa2	Baa3	Ba1						
Ba2	Aaa	Aa1	Aa2	Aa3	A1	A2	A3	Baa1	Baa2	Baa3	Ba1	Ba2					
Ba3	Aaa	Aa1	Aa2	Aa3	A1	A2	A3	Baa1	Baa2	Baa3	Ba1	Ba2	Ba3				
B1	Aaa	Aa1	Aa2	Aa3	A1	A2	A3	Baa1	Baa2	Baa3	Ba1	Ba2	Ba3	B1			
B2	Aaa	Aa1	Aa2	Aa3	A1	A2	A3	Baa1	Baa2	Baa3	Ba1	Ba2	Ba3	B1	B2		
B3	Aaa	Aa1	Aa2	Aa3	A1	A2	A3	Baa1	Baa2	Baa3	Ba1	Ba2	Ba3	B1	B2	B3	
Caa	Aaa	Aa1	Aa2	Aa3	A1	A2	A3	Baa1	Baa2	Baa3	Ba1	Ba2	Ba3	B1	B2	B3	Caa

Implied Joint Support Rating for Medium Correlation Case

	Aaa	Aa1	Aa2	Aa3	A1	A2	A3	Baa1	Baa2	Baa3	Ba1	Ba2	Ba3	B1	B2	B3	Caa
Aaa	Aaa																
Aa1	Aaa	Aaa															
Aa2	Aaa	Aaa	Aa1														
Aa3	Aaa	Aaa	Aa1	Aa1													
A1	Aaa	Aaa	Aa1	Aa1	Aa1												
A2	Aaa	Aaa	Aa1	Aa1	Aa2	Aa2											
A3	Aaa	Aaa	Aa1	Aa1	Aa2	Aa2	Aa3										
Baa1	Aaa	Aaa	Aa1	Aa1	Aa2	Aa3	A1	A2									
Baa2	Aaa	Aaa	Aa1	Aa1	Aa2	Aa3	A1	A2	A3								
Baa3	Aaa	Aaa	Aa1	Aa1	Aa2	Aa3	A1	A2	A3	Baa2							
Ba1	Aaa	Aa1	Aa1	Aa2	Aa3	A1	A2	A3	Baa1	Baa2	Baa3						
Ba2	Aaa	Aa1	Aa1	Aa2	Aa3	A1	A2	A3	Baa1	Baa2	Ba1	Ba1					
Ba3	Aaa	Aa1	Aa1	Aa2	Aa3	A1	A2	A3	Baa1	Baa3	Ba1	Ba1	Ba2				
B1	Aaa	Aa1	Aa2	Aa3	A1	A2	A3	Baa1	Baa2	Baa3	Ba1	Ba2	Ba3	B1			
B2	Aaa	Aa1	Aa2	Aa3	A1	A2	A3	Baa1	Baa2	Baa3	Ba1	Ba2	Ba3	B1	B2		
B3	Aaa	Aa1	Aa2	Aa3	A1	A2	A3	Baa1	Baa2	Baa3	Ba1	Ba2	Ba3	B1	B2	B3	
Caa	Aaa	Aa1	Aa2	Aa3	A1	A2	A3	Baa1	Baa2	Baa3	Ba1	Ba2	Ba3	B1	B2	B3	Caa

Implied Joint Support Rating for Low Correlation Case

	Aaa	Aa1	Aa2	Aa3	A1	A2	A3	Baa1	Baa2	Baa3	Ba1	Ba2	Ba3	B1	B2	B3	Caa
Aaa	Aaa																
Aa1	Aaa	Aaa															
Aa2	Aaa	Aaa	Aaa														
Aa3	Aaa	Aaa	Aaa	Aaa													
A1	Aaa	Aaa	Aaa	Aaa	Aaa												

(continued)

Table 16.10 Continued

A2	Aaa	Aaa	Aaa	Aaa	Aaa	Aa1											
A3	Aaa	Aaa	Aaa	Aaa	Aaa	Aa1	Aa2										
Baa1	Aaa	Aaa	Aaa	Aaa	Aaa	Aa1	Aa3	Aa3									
Baa2	Aaa	Aaa	Aaa	Aaa	Aaa	Aa1	Aa3	A1	A1								
Baa3	Aaa	Aaa	Aaa	Aaa	Aa1	Aa1	Aa3	A1	A1	Baa1							
Ba1	Aaa	Aaa	Aaa	Aa1	Aa1	Aa2	A1	A1	A2	Baa1	Baa3						
Ba2	Aaa	Aaa	Aa1	Aa1	Aa1	Aa2	A1	A1	A2	Baa2	Baa3	Ba1					
Ba3	Aaa	Aaa	Aa1	Aa1	Aa2	Aa3	A1	A2	A3	Baa2	Baa3	Ba1	Ba2				
B1	Aaa	Aa1	Aa1	Aa2	Aa3	Aa3	A1	A3	Baa1	Baa2	Ba1	Ba1	Ba2	Ba3			
B2	Aaa	Aa1	Aa2	Aa2	Aa3	A1	A2	A3	Baa1	Baa3	Ba1	Ba1	Ba3	Ba3	B1		
B3	Aaa	Aa1	Aa2	Aa3	A1	A1	A3	Baa1	Baa2	Baa3	Ba1	Ba2	Ba3	B1	B1	B3	
Caa	Aaa	Aa1	Aa2	Aa3	A1	A2	A3	Baa1	Baa2	Baa3	Ba1	Ba2	Ba3	B1	B2	B3	Caa

Source: Moody's Investor Service.

The above analysis becomes more complex and potentially misleading if the rating of one or both of the obligations is derived from the analysis of a pool of obligations, where correlation of default of the underlying obligors plays again a key role. One need go no further than reviewing the effects of the monolines' and Lehman's debacles on the structured finance market in order to see the consequences of correlation analysis and assumptions gone wrong. Tables 16.8 and 16.9 answer in the affirmative the basic question as to whether two inferior in rating quality entities/obligations can jointly support a superior in rating quality entity/obligation. This is the starting assumption whose corollary is the massive CDO market of 2005–7, in particular, and the whole securitization bonds' edifice, in general.

While the goal of the rating analysis is assigning a rating, i.e. sizing a probability of default or a level of expected loss or default probability and the correlation input plays an important role in the rating process, those same correlation inputs also play an important role in building investment portfolios and are often reflected through the concept of portfolio diversification. We explore this point further in the discussion of systemic and idiosyncratic risks. This analysis might not have been used as a basis for the development of correlation assumptions for CDO of ABS, or it might have been used under the assumption that systemic risk probabilities are extremely low. Either of these approaches could have led to the creation of different forms of leverage which we discussed earlier.

2.6 Modified views on systemic and idiosyncratic risks, and correlation

Defining the multiple aspects of correlation in the ABS world is difficult; assigning correct values to correlation is even more difficult. In the course of the rise and fall of the securitization market and the parallel banking system it supported, several dimensions of securitization came to be re-evaluated. Here we explore the angle of the contribution of ABS to the diversification of an existing portfolio. The same issue can be formulated from the angle of diversification in a portfolio of ABS, i.e. re-securitization, and CDO squared. We first explored this issue in 2005.[11]

The less correlated a new asset is with an existing portfolio, the more it could contribute to its diversification, and vice versa: if a new asset is not correlated or has a low correlation to the assets in a given portfolio, when added to the portfolio it brings risks different from the ones already there—the risk of an individual asset is referred to as idiosyncratic risk. As more assets come into the portfolio, and the levels of correlation within that portfolio increase, the more the collective behaviour of the portfolio components strays away from the idiosyncratic risk of the individual assets and assumes systemic risk characteristics. As the number of assets in a portfolio increases, the risk profile of the portfolio improves rapidly (diversification effect) up to a point, beyond which the marginal contribution of each new asset to the pool's diversification becomes marginal—the portfolio has reached the state of non-diversifiable, systemic risk profile.

Generally, ABS is structured on the basis of a pool of assets, which may exhibit different degrees of correlation. While in the case of corporate assets, such correlation is perceived as easier to quantify and finds its expression in diversity scores or other forms of measurement, its quantification in the case of retail assets is viewed as more difficult, not to say irrelevant due to the small concentration of individual exposures. Alternatively, the view that high correlation within a highly granular portfolio occurs as an expression of systemic risk only may have tempted many market participants to disregard it or to assign a low probability of systemic risk (i.e. high correlation) scenario. Nonetheless, that an asset pool of an ABS structure is diversified to some degree, depending on its composition, is still widely accepted.

The diversification argument (quantified or not explicitly as a correlation factor) is what allows a pool of low credit quality assets to back up an obligation of a higher credit quality (than that of the assets in the pool, individually or on average). This is the same argument we made in the previous section on jointly supported obligations. To take a step further: the diversification benefits are redistributed within the capital structure of ABS—the senior tranches will be immune to the risks of individual exposures in the pool, while the more junior a tranche is, the more sensitive it is to individual credit exposures risk. This is related to how ABS credit enhancement level is established, all else being equal; a better diversified asset pool or a pool in which assets have lower correlation among themselves will require lower credit enhancement to achieve higher rating. Hence, diversification and correlation is related to tranche size and tranche thickness.

In line with the preceding discussion, it becomes evident that the senior tranches are carriers of predominantly systemic risk, while the junior tranches represent more idiosyncratic risk associated with the assets in the pool.

[11] Batchvarov and Davletova (2005).

Having defined the risk characteristics of the different tranches along those lines, we can now determine the characteristics of their correlation with the portfolio, to which they are added:

- senior ABS tranches will contribute primarily systemic risk—that is, their contribution to the risk profile of a well-diversified portfolio should be to 'increase' its systemic risk. On that basis, they should be viewed as highly correlated with that portfolio. Highly correlated assets behave like a single asset with binary outcome—default and loss, or no default and gain. A default of all or a large number of assets may suggest systemic risk. (For example, the collapse of the US housing market and subsequent default of sub-prime mortgages led to default of sub-prime RMBS at all rating levels, which in turn led to the default of highly rated CDO of ABS).
- junior ABS tranches, due to the more idiosyncratic nature of their risk, should contribute to the diversification of the portfolio—marginally, if the portfolio is already well diversified, or significantly, if the correlation of the assets in the ABS pool with those in the portfolio to which the tranche is added is low. Low correlation among assets in the total portfolio means a more 'normal' distribution of the losses in that pool in the case of assets' default. Yet, in the case of performance deterioration, the junior tranches suffer first.
- mezzanine tranches, as a consequence of the above, will fall somewhere in-between in the continuum. So, they will be introducing a different combination of systemic and idiosyncratic risk to the portfolio they are added to. One could expect a varying degree of correlation of the mezzanine tranches with the portfolio.

When determining the correlation of an ABS tranche with a given portfolio or with another ABS tranche, several aspects need to be considered:

- the composition of the portfolio in question.

The assumption we made about the high level of diversification in that portfolio may be incorrect to a different degree, meaning that the ABS tranche at any level may or may not be contributing to its diversification and may have a correlation with the portfolio anywhere between zero and one. From that angle, the definition of 'systemic' is elusive.

- ABS pool performance may be dependent not only on the quality of the asset pool, but also on third parties, such as a servicer, swap counterparty, guarantor, thus adding additional correlation/diversification aspects. The best example is the effect of Lehman Brothers collapse on the performance of multiple ABS transactions.
- The cumulative nature of some exposures or exposure overlap—a given exposure may be present in the combined portfolio in several different ways: as part of the ABS pool, as a stand-alone investment, as a supporting party of an ABS transaction (servicer, swap provider, liquidity provider, guarantor).
- Tranche size is linked to assumed credit risk and diversification in the underlying pool, and tranche performance is thus linked to tranche size.

If the above analysis is correct, then a portfolio of senior triple-A tranches should not be considered diversified, i.e. the pool correlation will be very high, in comparison to a portfolio of junior ABS tranches, whose level of diversification should be higher, i.e. the pool correlation factor would be lower. To take this one step further, if the pool correlation factor is inversely related to the size of the credit enhancement, then a portfolio of AAA ABS would require higher credit enhancement to support a triple-A tranche than a portfolio of mezzanine ABS, all else being equal. The assumption of 'caeteris paribus' may not be that far-fetched—the probability of default which by definition should be lower for triple-A ABS and higher for mezzanine SF (structured finance) tranches may in reality be similar due to a common factor in the underlying pools, i.e. systemic risk, as it turned out to be the case for ABS backed by US sub-prime mortgage pools. Another example could be the almost simultaneous default of different mezzanine tranches of the same ABS due to the combination of systemic risk unfolding and very thin mezzanine tranches. The tradeoff between default and corre-lation of default becomes increasingly tenuous when working off common underlying risks and tranched exposures in ABS.

The widely accepted approach assumes that the mezzanine ABS tranches are inde-pendent of each other and disregards the relationships between the assets in their underlying pools and in assessing the risks of triple-A ABS tranches such an approach assumes low correlation and emphasizes low-default frequency. However, in the dom-inant case where the underlying assets are newly originated sub-prime mortgage loans, the diversification argument becomes a mute point. This is the point which the securi-tizations markets and investors failed to see in the period 2005–7 and which ultimately led to the collapse of the parallel banking system. It was further exacerbated by the element of correlation in bond and loan behaviour introduced by liquidity or lack thereof. The correlation effects of liquidity merit a detailed study in its own right.

2.7 The unreliability of the new historical time series and stifling of the future SF bond markets

The new historical data series, i.e. the ones that incorporate the period 2008–10, which is the period of the collapse of the shadow banking system, the reregulation of the banks and the re-intermediation of the credit (mainly consumer) market, will be the ones which reflect the consequences of the unprecedented increase in credit, leverage, underwriting laxity, and product diversity discussed above, i.e. all the processes asso-ciated with the effects of the parallel banking system. All in, the new historical time series will reflect higher default rate, higher correlation of default, lower recoveries and longer period to recovery, and more severe rating transitions.

These time series will become the new reference point for future analysis of the credit and structured finance markets, and will present a benchmark for establishing credit enhancement for structured finance bond. The new credit enhancement levels will be much higher than in the preceding period.

How much higher they will be also depends on the expectation for rating stability. For example, in a simplified form, the expected loss (EL), which translates into a credit enhancement for a structured finance bond is a weighted average of the ELs for the base, worst, and best case scenario. While the best case scenario has not changed, the worst case scenario post 2008–10 period is significantly worse than in any preceding period. The integration of the 2008–10 data into the historical data series will change the base case scenario, if that is to reflect the historical averages, now that the new historical time series incorporate actual events much worse than many experienced before 2008. So the credit enhancement for structured finance bonds will rise: even if P(worst), P(base), and P(best) remain the same in

$$P(worst) + P(base) + P(best) = P = 100\%,$$

the EL(worst), EL(base), and EL(best) will change, increasing the EL(new) (i.e. post-2008) to EL(old) (i.e. pre-2008), so EL (new) > EL (old). It is likely, however, that P(worst) will rise as well, increasing further the EL(new).

In addition, the demand for rating stability will lead to either increase of the weight of P(worst) in P, or in the extreme it will lead to P(worst) = 100%, hence using EL(worst) for sizing credit enhancement for structured finance bonds. The tolerance to rating downgrades will determine the weights of P(worst), P(best), and P (base) in P=100%. Similarly, the rating transition time series post-2010 will reflect a significant increase in rating downgrades in 2007–10 period in sharp contrast to the rating transition statistics of the preceding fifteen-year period.

The new (post-2010) rating transitions statistics and ELs to be used to size credit risk will be applied to a market and systemic environment materially different from the one in which these time series were derived, in the same way the historical time series used to quantify credit risk during the 2004–8 period (the apogee of the parallel banking system) were derived from the preceding period, when the parallel banking system was underdeveloped or not developed at all.

How materially different will the new environment post-2010 be from the environment of the preceding period? While that is difficult to fully anticipate, the main principles of the new financial system can be defined as follows: limit on leverage for banks and large financial institutions, differentiation between utility (low risk, systemically important) banks and other financial institutions, more stringent regulation for all financial institutions, stricter supervisions by domestic and international regulators, countercyclical provisioning by banks and other regulated financial institutions, regulatory and central banks' focus on systemic risk and asset values in addition to monetary policy, lower leverage for consumer and corporates and related elimination of a whole range of credit products, reduction or complete elimination of off balance sheet vehicles and exposures, significant reduction in internal and external leverage in the structured finance markets, etc.

In other words, at least in the medium term, the credit risks in the financial system and on the credit markets will be substantially reduced, but the reference points for quantifying such risks will be based to some degree or entirely on historical data incorporating conditions which will not exist and are unlikely to be replicated for a long period in the future.

The reliance on historical data fuelled the growth of the parallel banking system and the economy by underestimating risks in securitization and many aspects of risk management. The collapse of the parallel banking system and the integration of its consequences in the new historical data series may be equally detrimental to the securitization market, the economy and risk management by overestimating the risks in securitization and portfolio behaviour.

REFERENCES

Batchvarov, A., and Davletova, A. (2005). *Synthetic CDO Guidebook.* Merrill Lynch.

——Liang, J., and Winkler, S. (2009). *Global SF in Laissez-Faire Countries.* BofA Merrill Lynch Global Research.

——Davletova, A., Martin, J., Gakwaya, N., Cook, C., and Rusconi, F. M. (2007). *The Illiquid Cash.* New York: Merrill Lynch.

——Clement, L., Cook, C., Davletova, A., Gakwaya, N., Martin, J., and Winkler, S. (2008a). *European SF markets 2008–2009 (part 1).* Merrill Lynch.

——Davletova, A., Dickstein, A., Gakwaya, N., Kidwai, F., Lynch, K., Winkler, S. (2007b). *Ratings and Rating Notations,* Merrill Lynch.

——Liang, J., and Winkler, S. (2009). *Global SF Bonds: Value in Laissez-Faire Countries.* BofA Merrill Lynch Global Research.

De Servigny, A., and Jobst, N., (2007). *The Handbook of Structured Finance.* New York: McGraw-Hill.

Fabozzi, F. J. (2006). *The Handbook of Mortgage-Backed Securities,* 6th edn. New York: McGraw-Hill.

Fitch Ratings (2007). *1991–2006 US Structured Finance Transition Study.* London: Fitch Ratings Ltd.

——(2009). *Global Structured Finance 2008 Transition and Default Study.* London: Fitch Ratings Ltd,

Fons, J. (1997). *Approach to Jointly Supported Obligations.* Moody's Investor Service.

Jeffrey, P. (2006). *A Practitioner's Guide to Securitisation* Woking: City & Financial Publishing.

Lucas, D. (1995). 'Default correlation and credit analysis'. *Journal of Fixed Income.* (Mar.)

Moody's Investor service (2007). *Structured Finance Rating Transitions: 1983–2006.*

——(2009). *Structured Finance Rating Transitions: 1983–2008.*

CHAPTER 17

....

HOME PRICE DERIVATIVES AND MODELLING

....

ALEXANDER LEVIN

THE recent financial crisis in the US was triggered, in large part, by a housing price bubble followed by its collapse. Unsound mortgage programmes offered to borrowers in the first half of the 2000s caused massive delinquencies and losses to investors— once cash-constrained homeowners who betted on refinancing or selling homes at a profit became unable to do so. Hence, it is not an overstatement to view the value of residential properties as an enormously important economic indicator. Introducing the concept of Credit OAS for MBS valuation, Levin and Davidson (2008) propose using interest rates and home prices as two major factors.

Already in 2004–5, leading economists generally agreed that the growth of home prices outpaced household income and rent. R. Shiller (2005, 2008) expressed concerns that the country's mindset 'over-encouraged' homeownership and warned of an upcoming collapse. Interestingly enough, his prediction, while correct principally and directionally, was not correct on the timing of when this would happen. Similarly, unlike many others on Wall Street, K. Weaver (2007) overall correctly predicted the decline of home prices between mid-2007 and mid-2008. However, her main argument—the ratio of mortgage payments to household income exceeded its historical equilibrium—could be made in the 1970s and 1980s when a severe lack of affordability had not led to a housing market decline.

I am grateful to a number of individuals who supported this work and contributed to it. Andrew Davidson has been providing me with support and constructive feedback over the years of our joint research. Stefano Risa contributed to the concept of HPI equilibrium and compiled the 25-MSA index using the FHFA home purchase data. Peter Carr inspired the risk-neutral modelling approach demonstrated in this chapter. Will Searle, Daniel Swanson, and Ming Zheng helped integrate and use the model in a practical business regimen. Nathan Salwen corrected errors in an earlier version and validated production code. I also wish to thank Taryn Arthur for providing details on RPX indexing and trading, and Fritz Siebel of TFS for the CME/CS market data and comments, and Laura Gridley and Simone Davis for their editorial efforts.

One lesson we learned from these examples is that one should regard home prices as random processes; their construction is the first main goal of this chapter. In fact, there are similarities (and dissimilarities) to other assets as we discuss further. Home prices have been volatile, and the realized volatility has a unique pattern and carries important information.

Home price modelling can use a purely empirical rationale, but can be also tied to traded financial contracts thereby becoming 'risk neutral'. In the US, such contracts became available to both risk management and speculation in 2006 (Chicago Mercantile Exchange) and 2007 (ICAP trading platform). Taking a bet on the direction of home prices does not require buying or selling residential properties anymore. One can simply take a long or a short position in an index in the form of a futures contract (even an option) or an over-the-counter forward contract. Their use in risk-neutral home price modelling represents the second main goal of this chapter. Hence, this chapter serves a dual purpose, and its flow alternates modelling of home prices and related financial instruments.

1 HOME PRICE INDICES AND DERIVATIVES: AN OVERVIEW

Home prices are measured by indices, some of which are 'traded', i.e. used to define the payoff of certain financial contracts. The four major families of US home price indices (HPI) are those compiled and published by Federal Housing Finance Agency (FHFA), S&P/Case-Shiller (CS), Radar Logic (RPX), and the National Association of Realtors (NAR). The Appendix contains a brief description of these indices including methodology and geographical coverage. The FHFA indices and the NAR indices are widely cited, but they do not trigger any market transactions, unlike the Case-Shiller indices and the Radar Logic indices.

1.1 The CME Case-Shiller Futures

The Chicago Mercantile Exchange (CME) market started trading Case-Shiller futures in May of 2006. It engages the same exchange mechanics as all other futures markets and removes the counter-party risk, i.e. the risk that a party facing an adverse market development will stop honouring its liability. Futures expirations are set in February, May, August, and November; contracts are reset daily and therefore have zero value at any point in time.

Each participant has an account that is continuously credited or debited as the futures price moves. As in other futures markets, futures price is a martingale. At maturity of the contract, futures last value is set to be equal to the published underlying, a Case-Shiller home price index. Note that HPI futures are priced by publication date, not the measurement reference date. A November contract expires on the last Tuesday when the Case-Shiller index is published (this publication refers to the September measurement).

The Case-Shiller futures are traded in ten geographical segments (Boston, Chicago, Denver, Las Vegas, Los Angeles, Miami, New York City, San Diego, San Francisco, and Washington, DC), in addition to the composite index containing all ten cities. The offered product line includes up to five-year expiration, but only a few indices actually trade that far. In addition to futures, CME offers options on futures, but most actually traded option contracts, calls, and puts, have been so far limited to one year. CME also offers over-the-counter custom-tailored contracts. The market is brokered by major Wall Street dealers as well as facilitated by inter-broker traded platforms, for example, TFS. The CME CS market is described in detail on the CME website, <www.cme.com>.

1.2 The RPX forwards

Another market utilizing the twenty-eight-day version of the RPX index family started trading in September of 2007. At inception, it offered two types of over-the-counter contracts, a total return swap (TRS) and a simple forward agreement. TRS involved a periodic cash flow exchange with the floating leg receiver getting paid market return on the index. Since September of 2008 the market has been quoted solely in terms of forward contracts.

The RPX forwards are settled at each year-end based on the Radar Logic index published for five preceding consecutive business days. Much like in the case of the CME CS market, it is the publication date that matters, not the period of measured real estate transactions. The RPX market does not currently offer options; it has just a few geographical segments traded (New York, Los Angeles, Miami, and Phoenix at the time of writing), along with the 25-city Composite. The Composite index is traded up to five years forward whereas forward contracts for geographical indices don't extend beyond three years. The market is brokered by major Wall Street dealers as well as facilitated by inter-broker traded platforms, for example, ICAP. The market's quotes can be found on the Radar Logic website, <http://www.radarlogic.com/RPX_fixing.html>.

The HPI derivatives markets are currently small in both traded volume and instrument selection. For example, the total volume of RPX trades in 2008 was about $1B per calendar quarter and the bid-ask spread reaches two or more percentage points. Therefore, government agencies or large loan insurers cannot hedge out their credit exposure simply due to lack of market size. However, some MBS investors or home builders can hedge their risk. The market can be also used by speculators who are willing to take directional bets. The HPI derivatives markets are currently dominated by credit protection buyers and include a large risk premium. Hence, forward prices inferred from the CS futures or the RPX forwards are likely to be lower than real-world ('physical') expectations.

Although forward and futures prices cannot be used in lieu of real-world expectations, they have been correctly predicting a home price decline since inception. For example, the CMI CS futures pointed to home price depreciating at the time when the real estate fever was still strong and even many Street analysts expected a 'soft landing' rather than a decline.

2 HISTORICAL PROPERTIES OF HPI AND HPA

2.1 The diffusion and white noise pattern of the HPA

If we take an HPI index, compute periodic returns and annualize them, we will obtain the Home Price Appreciation (HPA) measure. The FHFA US HPA rate readjusted for seasonality is shown in Figure 17.1 going back to 1975. Along with HPA, Figure 17.1 depicts the behaviour of the MBS current coupon rate.

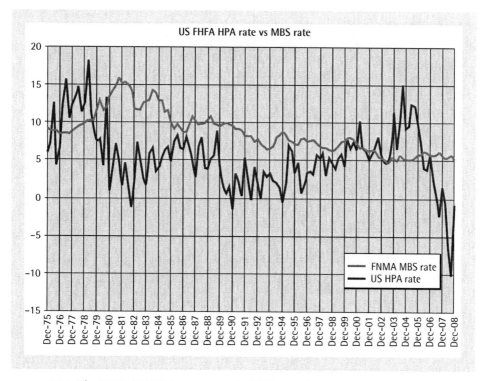

FIGURE 17.1 The FHFA US HPA rate versus the MBS rate since 1975.

The purpose of showing both indices on the same plot is twofold: to assess a visual correlation (if any), and to compare the two distinctly different types of dynamics. It is clear that the MBS rate is continuous whereas the HPA rate is not. The latter seems to contain random 'jumps' or 'shocks' that occur around otherwise continuously changing mean levels. A diffusion + white noise pattern seems to resemble the dynamics of the HPA rate reasonably well. We can prove this fact by measuring an empirical standard deviation function of horizon and an autocorrelation function of lag (Figure 17.2).

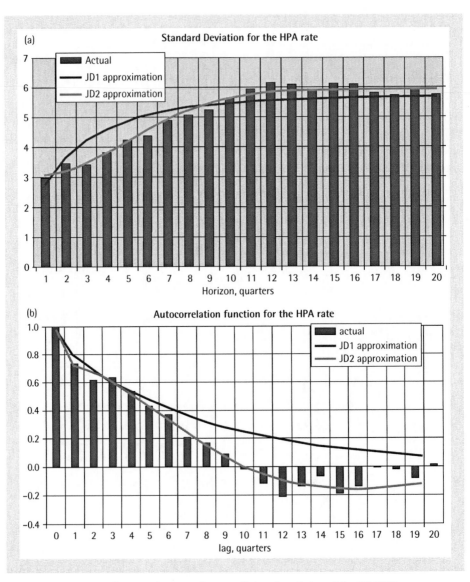

FIGURE 17.2 Empirical versus theoretical unconditional statistics of the US HPA.

Bars in Figure 17.2 are taken from the empirical data; we compute these statistics for generally overlapping intervals, but with an adjustment for actual degrees of freedom. Had HPA(t) been a continuous random process, both statistics would have been continuous functions. In reality, without them, an apparent discontinuity exists between t = 0 and t = 1 that lets us statistically assess the size of random shocks. Without the jumps, it would not be possible to explain a sizeable short uncertainty in the HPA (t = 1) and the drop in the autocorrelation function.

Lines in Figure 17.2 reflect the theoretical combination of white noise (normal 'jumps' when observed in discrete time) and a first-order mean reverting diffusion (JD1, darker line) or a second-order mean reverting diffusion (JD2, lighter line). Let σ_d and σ_w be the volatility of the HPA diffusion and the magnitude of the white noise, respectively, and a be the diffusion's mean reversion. Then, theoretical statistics for the JD1 pattern depicted in Figure 17.2 as function of $t > 0$ are

$$stdev[HPA(t)] = \left[\sigma_d^2 \frac{1 - e^{-2at}}{2a} + \sigma_W^2 \right]^{\frac{1}{2}}$$

$$Corr[HPA(T), HPA(t + T)] \underset{T \to \infty}{\longrightarrow} e^{-at} \frac{1}{1 + 2a\sigma_w^2/\sigma_d^2}$$

Similarly, let the second-order diffusion have a pair of complex eigenvalues, $a \pm i\beta$ with a negative a. Then, the theoretical statistics for the JD2 pattern will be

$$stdev[HPA(t)] = \left\{ \frac{\sigma_d^2}{4\beta^2} \left[\frac{e^{2at} - 1}{a} - \frac{a(e^{2at}\cos 2\beta t - 1) + \beta e^{2at} sin 2\beta t}{a^2 + \beta^2} \right] + \sigma_w^2 \right\}^{\frac{1}{2}}$$

$$Corr[HPA(T), HPA(t + T)] \underset{T \to \infty}{\longrightarrow} \frac{e^{at}(cos\beta t - \frac{a}{\beta}sin\beta t)}{1 - 4a(a^2 + \beta^2)\sigma_w^2/\sigma_d^2}$$

As demonstrated by Figure 17.2, the JD2 model with optimally selected parameters approximates empirical standard deviation and autocorrelation well. Note that the empirical data exhibits an oscillatory behaviour well matched by a second-order oscillator, but not feasible in the first-order model. For example, the empirical autocorrelation function turns negative for remote time lags suggesting an 'overshooting' when responding to a disturbance in the initial condition. This cannot be observed in the JD1 model, the autocorrelation function of which is always positive. In the next two subsections, we attempt to explain the causes for the diffusion and white noise pattern and the oscillatory behaviour.

2.2 Home prices versus dynamic assets

The existence of immediate shocks in the HPA series should not be unexpected although seems to have eluded many researchers who tend to treat an HPA as a continuous process, a forecast of which can start from the last observation. Indeed, an HPA is the return rate of an HPI index. Recall that, in the real world, the log-price X of a volatile asset would follow the stochastic differential equation (SDE),

$$dX = \mu dt + \sigma dz \tag{1}$$

where σ is volatility, μ is drift, and z is the Brownian motion. The latter is the integral of white noise (w), a mathematical limit for normally distributed, uncorrelated shocks. Let us denote the annualized return on X as $x = dX/dt$. Then,

$$x = \mu + \sigma w \tag{2}$$

or 'diffusion + white noise'. The first term in (2) determines the expected return. The white noise is the source of the immediate randomness. Therefore, if the HPI's time series represents values of an asset or an index, its return rate (the HPA) must be compliant with the 'diffusion + white noise' form. This proves that our modelling guess was a good one, and, when looking at Figure 17.1, our vision does not malfunction. It is now clear why the MBS rates shown in Figure 17.1 are continuous: they represent *expected* (not actual) returns on an MBS and are, therefore, chiefly diffusive.

We borrowed the dynamic asset's pricing set-up to explain the discontinuous nature of an HPA. It does not mean that we must treat an HPI as a traded index nor the risk-neutral μ must be equal to the risk-free rate. In fact, we cannot trade a storable asset for an HPI value, a point that will be further explored in section 6.

2.3 The oscillator property

Why do stochastic properties of historical HPA resemble those of an oscillator? Here is a rather simple economic postulate: home prices cannot drift (lead or lag) away from other economic indicators forever. Hence, the direction of HPA depends on whether HPI is too high or too low. Therefore, the first derivative of HPA should depend on the attained value of HPI (HPA's integral) thereby making the (HPA, HPI) system akin to the mechanical spring-and-mass oscillator $dx = \cdots - k(X - Xeq)dt$ with $dX = xdt$. In this relationship, log-HPI (X) is a 'coordinate' whereas HPA (x) is 'speed'. Without dampening and random terms, X will perpetually oscillate around its 'equilibrium' (Xeq).

The best-fit JD2 model depicted in Figure 17.2 has a pair of $-0.38 \pm 0.77i$ (1/yr) eigenvalues pointing to an 8.1-year periodicity with a 2.6-year time decay. It should be understood, however, that once we specify the dynamics and role of the explicit economic factors (such as income and interest rates), the optimal parameters change.

The oscillatory behaviour model we advocate is rather different from the popular concept of 'business cycles' that have haunted many economists. A practically stable two-dimensional system with complex eigen-roots has dampening forces (frictions); also we cannot predict its phase without the knowledge of external forces. We do not at all suggest that peaks and troughs of an HPI can be predicted by cycles.

3 INFLATION, INTEREST RATES, AND THE CONCEPT OF 'SOFT' EQUILIBRIUM

How do interest rates affect home prices? This question seems to be a puzzling one and has been answered differently by different researchers. First, let us start with an objective statistical measure, a cross-correlation function between the logarithm of total mortgage payment rate and the FHFA HPA rate measured as a function of time lag (Figure 17.3).

The correlation is apparently negative for the near term and turns positive for the long run. Here is our possible explanation of this dynamic: a decline in MBS rate improves housing affordability, but reduces the inflation and the long-term HPA.

Note that Figure 17.3 depicts two lines for two non-overlapping historical intervals. The strength of correlation has apparently changed historically. Recall that the correlation is a measure of *linear* relationship for *stationary* processes. With the changing relationship, the long-term correlation can be artificially low. Had we depicted the 1975–2008 cross-correlations, we would have witnessed a misleadingly low level that could have discouraged some analysts to look any further at the HPA dependence on interest rates. In fact, this relationship exists and, *when stationary*, exhibits a steady pattern proven by Figure 17.3.

Let us elaborate on the assumption that, over a long run, home prices cannot lead or lag other economic indicators, most importantly, household income. Historical data seems to confirm this statement. During the thirty-three-year period (1975–2008), the FHFA HPI grew at the average annual rate of 5.33% whereas the national household income grew only at a 4.37% rate. However, with declined mortgage rates,

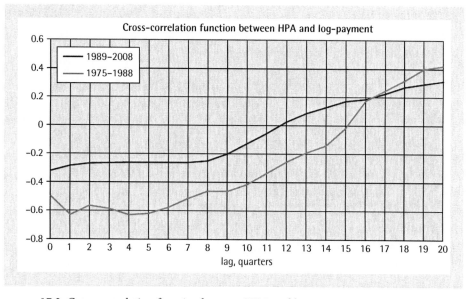

FIGURE 17.3 Cross-correlation function between HPA and log-payment.

the standard mortgage payments grew at a pace of only 4.11% per year, i.e. close to income. Postulating that the loan payment should constitute a constant part of the household income, we derive an equilibrium level of HPI (denoted by HPIeq) as

$$\text{(in logarithms) HPIeq} = \text{Income} - \text{Payment Rate} + \text{const} \tag{3}$$

As we argue a little further, we may not need to know the constant to build a decent model. Let us subtract Income from HPIeq and call this difference 'real HPI equilibrium'. Relationship (3) suggests that the derivative of this measure with respect to time must offset the derivative of Payment Rate. This introduces the explicit relationship between the logarithm of real equilibrium and the mortgage rate; it is nearly linear within a limited region of MBS rates. For example, with the base loan rate of 5% to 6%, a 1% shift causes approximately an 11% shock to the equilibrium. The relationship weakens somewhat as the loan rate gets higher.

How can HPIeq affect HPI? It is unlikely that the equilibrium, being a function of mortgage rates, can be directly additive to HPI. Had it been this way, historical volatility of HPI would have been much higher. A more plausible assumption is that a change in mortgage rate immediately affects the HPI equilibrium, but not the immediate HPI. This disturbance will affect HPI gradually, after some transient process, similarly to other disturbing forces. When a mortgage rate stays constant, the real HPI equilibrium won't change.

Having postulated the existence of equilibrium, we face the challenge of determining it. How much of its disposable income should an average US household allocate for mortgage payments? Californians pay more than the rest of the country, and mortgage originators use a higher underwriting threshold. While the right guess can very well be 30%, 35%, or 40%, this uncertainty itself points to a dramatic dispersion of HPI equilibrium effectively invalidating an otherwise well-designed HPI model. In what we we show in the next section, one can 'soften' the concept of equilibrium by accounting only for its dependence on changing interest rates, but not the knowledge of a constant shown in formula (3). To put this simply, we will formulate a model that measures and employs only $dHPIeq/dt$ and not $HPIeq$ itself.

4 THE HPA STOCHASTIC SIMULATOR

In this section, we formally describe our model's construct intended for physical modelling of HPA. We also review the necessary statistical technique. The next section discusses forecasts the model generates.

4.1 The model equations

As before, we denote $x(t)$ the HPA rate, $X(t)$ the log-HPI, $w(t)$ the white noise that produces normally distributed, serially uncorrelated, shocks in discrete time. We represent the HPA as a sum of continuous diffusion, white noise and income inflation (*iinf*).

$$x(t) = x_1(t) + \sigma_w w(t) + iinf(t) \tag{4}$$

where $x_1(t)$ follows a second-order linear system of differential equations:

$$\dot{x}_1 = x_2 + k_1 \dot{X}_{eq} \tag{5.1}$$

$$\dot{x}_2 = -ax_2 - bx_1 + k_3 \dot{X}_{eq} + \sigma_d w_d \tag{5.2}$$

For brevity, equations (5) are written in 'engineering' notations, with the dot denoting time derivatives. The HPA diffusion is disturbed by another white noise w_d (independent of w, interest rate and income) and the derivative of log-HPI equilibrium that is measured via the mortgage payment rate. The pair of SDEs (5) describes a stable process if $a > 0$, $b > 0$ and becomes an oscillator when $a^2 < 4b$.

Changes in the HPI equilibriums affect diffusion's first and second derivatives via coefficients k's. With a non-zero k_1, a change in mortgage rate results in an immediate change in x_1, hence, the HPA. Aside from the above stated inequalities, coefficients should be bound by one equality condition. To show this, let us assume that there are no random forces and the mortgage rate drifts very weakly, at a constant pace that is much slower than the transients of the model (5). In this case, we expect the HPA diffusion to converge to $\dot{X}_{eq}$ as $t \to \infty$ so that the HPI eventually follows HPIeq. This consideration imposes another constraint on the model's parameters: $ak_1 + k_3 = b$.

The interest rates enter the HPA model via two terms: the income inflation and the time derivative of X_{eq}. We often refer to $x_1(\dot{X}_{eq})$ as the 'affordability effect'; it can be generated by setting both white noises to zero. In contrast, the $x_1(w_d)$ term generated without $\dot{X}_{eq}$ is sometimes referred to as 'HPA diffusion'. This term is due to economic forces other than inflation and interest rates and is independent of them. General economic conditions, unemployment not reflected in the household income, or prevailing speculation can cause large HPI deviations from the equilibrium. Figure 17.4 presents the HPA modelling process as a flowchart.

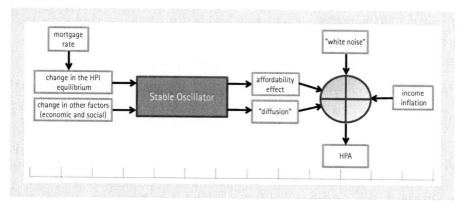

FIGURE 17.4 The flowchart of the HPA model.

In the complete absence of random forces and change of equilibrium, our HPA will follow a second-order ODE (ordinary differential equation). In particular, it will be continuously differentiable, i.e. bound not only to the previous value, but to its derivative too. Such a model can maintain momentum and explain why HPA may continue to grow or decline after the HPI equilibrium has passed. This particularly useful feature lets us properly initialize a forecast using historical series.

4.2 The dataset and adjustments

Unless we state otherwise, most of the modelling observations and results will refer to a quarterly FHFA 25-MSA composite index that we computed ourselves. We use the MSAs and the weights published by Radar Logic and apply them to the FHFA historical purchase-only HPI. At the time of writing, FHFA did not have purchase-only HPI series for all MSAs, so we interpolated them by combining the available purchase-only state series and the total-transaction series published at both state and MSA levels. This approach presents advantages over using the FHFA US index or the RPX25 index for the modelling purposes outright. The RPX index family itself, while informative, does not extend deep into history. The FHFA US index is not representative for MBS analytical purposes because it under-weighs regions with an un-proportionally modest volume of conforming loans (e.g. California).

The other adjustment we made was to recognize the proliferation of 'affordable' loan programmes such as Option ARMs (adjustable rate mortgages) and IO (interest only) ARMs giving the borrowers a dubious privilege of making small payments and not amortizing the balance. Coupled with the compromised underwriting of sub-prime and Alt-A loans when borrowers were not required to pay for the credit risk fairly, these practices effectively lowered the available financing rate. Although the resultant rate is difficult to assess, it is safe to assume that, in 2002–6, many Americans were not paying a traditional mortgage rate. This assumption can be backed by a geographical comparison: while 40–50% of Californians had been lured into 'affordable' products, most Ohioans borrowed conventionally. Coincidentally, California, but not Ohio, experienced a pronounced bubble followed by a housing market collapse. Hence, we have to consider two interest rate factors: the usual conventional rate and the suppressed one that existed in 2002–6 which we depict in some figures to follow.

4.3 Statistical technique and the use of Kalman filtration

Let us rewrite the system of differential equations (4)–(5) in an approximate discrete vector-matrix form (h is a time step):

$$X_k = F X_{k-1} + W_k + u_k \tag{6}$$

$$x_k = H X_k + v_k + iinf_k \tag{7}$$

where, for our two-dimensional diffusion, X, w, u are vectors of state variables, disturbance and external forces, respectively, F is a square matrix, and H is a row-vector:

$$X = \begin{bmatrix} x_1 \\ x_2 \end{bmatrix}, w = \begin{bmatrix} 0 \\ \sigma_d w_d \sqrt{h} \end{bmatrix}, u \begin{bmatrix} hk_1 \dot{X}_{eq} \\ hk_3 \dot{X}_{eq} \end{bmatrix}, F = \begin{bmatrix} 1 & h \\ -bh & 1-ah \end{bmatrix}, H = \begin{bmatrix} 1 & 0 \end{bmatrix}$$

We observe the HPA rate x_k subject to unobservable random shocks $v_k = \sigma_w w_k \sqrt{h}$ and observable income inflation $iinf_k$. If the time step h is small, the discrete system (6)–(7) approximates the continuous system (4)–(5) well. If the time step is not small, parameters a, b, etc. of the discrete model may have to be somewhat different from those of the continuous model.

Before we attempt to optimize the model to best-fit historical data, we need to recognize the existence of two unobservable random forces, w and w_d. Even if we knew all of the model's parameters, determining historical $w(t)$ and $w_d(t)$ would remain an ambiguous task. In essence, we want to split one process into two, a problem that can be solved by the linear Kalman filter. Under the assumption that the coefficients in equations (6)–(7) are known, the filter maximizes the conditional log-likelihood function with respect to discrete realization of w and w_d. For each time period, it is done in two steps.

<u>Predict.</u> We first forecast the diffusion vector $\hat{X}_{k|k-1}$ using the $(k-1)$th estimate $\hat{X}_{k-1|k-1}$, available interest rates and setting $w_{dk} = 0$:

$$\hat{X}_{k|k-1} = F\hat{X}_{k-1|k-1} + u_k$$

We also update the error covariance matrix (estimating accuracy of state variables):

$$P_{k|k-1} = FP_{k-1|k-1}F^T + Q$$

Where Q is the covariance matrix of w, i.e. $Q = \begin{bmatrix} 0 & 0 \\ 0 & h\sigma_d^2 \end{bmatrix}$

<u>Update.</u> Using actual HPA observation x_k, we can update our estimates of the state vector X and the covariance matrix P:

$$\hat{y}_k = x_k - H\hat{X}_{k|k-1} - iinf_k \text{ (residual's measurement)}$$

$$S_k = HP_{k|k-1}H^T + h\sigma_w^2 \text{ (residual's covariance)}$$

$$K_k = P_{k|k-1}H/S_k \text{ (optimal gain)}$$

$$\hat{X}_{k|k} = \hat{X}_{k|k-1} + K_k\hat{y}_k \text{ (updated state estimate)}$$

$$P_{k|k} = (I - K_kH)P_{k|k-1} \text{ (updated estimate covariance)}$$

The above Predict-Update Kalman algorithm is well known and cited here following a Wikipedia article. A good reference is the D Simon (2006) book. It is proven to minimize the Euclidean error norm: $E\|X_k - \hat{X}_{k|k}\|^2$. At each step, one can back the shocks $\hat{w}_k$ and $\hat{w}_{dk}$ from the values of estimated state variables.

The Kalman filter possesses another, less known, useful practical feature: it allows predicting variances-covariances of all variables involved in the process theoretically. For example, the variance of $\hat{w}_k$ and $\hat{w}_{dk}$ coming out of the Kalman filtration won't be equal to 1, but can be expressed via other statistics. If the process (x_k, X_k) indeed follows equation (6), (7), then the empirical statistics will asymptotically converge to theoretical ones listed below:

$$E(h\sigma_d^2 \hat{w}_d^2) \rightarrow K_{2k}^2(P_{11k|k-1} + h\sigma_w^2)$$

$$E(h\sigma_w^2 \hat{w}^2) \rightarrow (1 - K_{1k})^2(P_{11k|k-1} + h\sigma_w^2)$$

These conditions can be complemented by a variety of other trivial requirements such as zero correlation between $\hat{w}_k$ and $\hat{w}_{k-i}$ for various $i > 0$ or their independence from the interest rate and inflation terms. Using these properties one can optimize the model by forcing these important theoretical statistics to match their respective empirically computed values. Therefore, we employ Kalman filtering both as a signal observer and as a model estimator.

If we apply the Kalman filtering to a stable linear dynamic system with constant coefficients, the elements of matrix P, vector K, and scalar S get gradually stabilized and stop changing between time steps. Since we normally do not have reliable initial conditions for the state estimates, it makes sense to start the filtration process ahead of the model's estimation window. Figure 17.5 depicts outputs of the filtering process with optimized parameters. Filtration starts with the somewhat frivolous initial condition $\hat{X}_{0/0}$ in 1984, but only the 1989–2008 dataset is used for estimation.

The white horse process (panel B) exhibits apparent heteroskedasticity. The rate-related HPA factor's bubble (panel A) owes its existence to the artificially inflated affordability during the 2002–6 period that we discussed above. Once borrowers stopped getting access to option ARMs etc., the HPI equilibrium fell, dragging HPA deeply negative. Hence, our model links both the formation of the housing bubble and, especially, its subsequent collapse to the birth and death of 'affordable' lending.

5 HPI FORECASTS, BUBBLE, AND DECLINE

A good model validation test should include a comparison of retrospective forecasts to actual data. Note that 'forecasting' for statistical models usually means computing mathematically expected values. Since the HPA to HPI transformation is non-linear, it is easier for us to compute the median path that does not need to be adjusted for convexity. The following three exhibits depict the forecasts that we would have made had we been using the model on December 2008, December 2005, and December 2002, respectively. For example, observing the index up to December 2008 we would have predicted its further decline by 17% with the trough reached in September of 2011 (Figure 17.6). When forming these forecasts, we turned both w and w_d to zero, set the

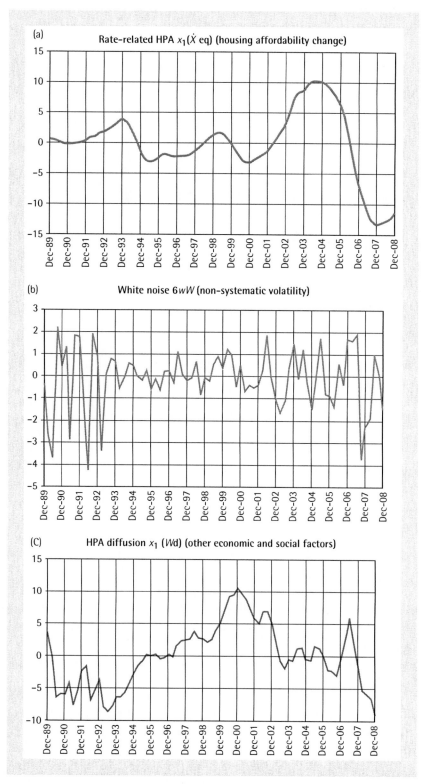

FIGURE 17.5 Composition of the 25-MSA HPA (results of Kalman filtering, 1989–2008).

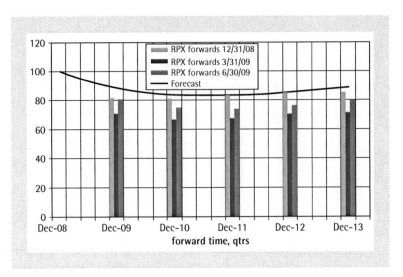

FIGURE 17.6 FHFA-25MSA HPI forecast from 2008–end.

MBS rate to its December 2008 level and assumed that inflation will slowly grow from 1% per year to 4% per year. The initial conditions for x_1, x_2 were given by the Kalman filter.

We compare the forecast to the RPX forward market quotes observed on 31 December 2008, 31 March 2009, and 30 June 2009, for each year-end settlement (bars). Apparently, the market views change from better to worse and back. As we should have expected, our forecast is more optimistic than the forward market. First, we are using a physical model whereas forward quotes reflect the price of risk. Second, our modelling object—the FHFA composite—should look better than the corresponding RPX. The FHFA HPI data is compiled using transactions backed by conforming loans and exclude foreclosed sales. In contrast, the RPX HPI includes properties backed by sub-prime loans and distressed sales; it therefore declines deeper.

Was the model forecasting the HPI decline? Figure 17.7 suggests that, had the model used the thirty-year MBS conforming rate as the financing basis, it would have expected housing prices to continue to grow, albeit at a slower pace (dashed line). This would be the 'soft landing' scenario that many economists anticipated. It is only if we consider that many borrowers were lured into cheap financing or were granted compromised underwriting short cuts during the prior years that we can explain what happened. Assuming that the solid line represents the effective financing rate, artificially lowered in 2002–5 and suddenly brought up to reality in 2006, we sent the model a signal of the substantial affordability decline. The model accepts this signal, keeps HPA momentum for a while, but shifts its gears downward (solid line). This HPI(t) path the model predicted matches well to what would really have happened (bars in Figure 17.7), perhaps not without some luck as we compare a median path to the reality, i.e. a unique realization of randomness.

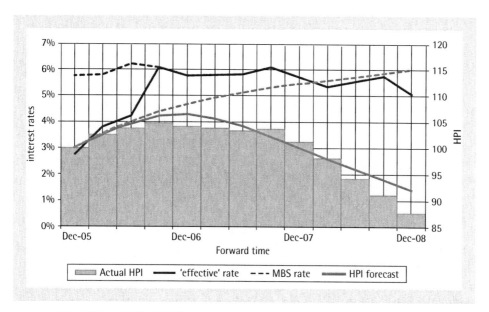

FIGURE 17.7 FHFA-25MSA HPI forecast vs actual from 2005–end.

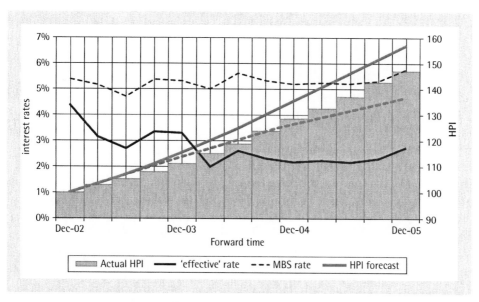

FIGURE 17.8 FHFA-25MSA HPI forecast versus actual from 2002–end.

Figure 17.8 continues our exploration into historical forecasting by depicting two lines the model could be producing at 2002-end. It predicted a relatively fast HPI growth of 37% in three years even if the MBS rate was the true indicative of lending (punctured lines). With 'affordable' lending, the effective rate was as much as 3% lower, and the model forecast a 57% HPI growth in 2002–5 (the HPI had actually grown by 47%). The ratio of these two HPI forecasts is $1.57/1.37 = 1.15$; hence, the model attributes 15% of the HPI to the proliferation of affordable lending.

Our modelling work suggests that the catalyst of the housing crisis was not the bubble alone. The interest rate door slammed into the face of existing and potentially new Option ARM, IO ARM, and sub-prime borrowers drastically reduced the affordability-based HPI equilibrium.

6 RISK-NEUTRAL MODELLING, FORWARDS, AND FUTURES

Risk-neutral conditions should be defined with respect to some set of other assets ('basis') along with permissible trading strategies. If an asset can be traded both long and short continuously at a spot market (can be stored), its risk-neutral return is known to be equal to the risk-free rate. Furthermore, if the same asset is also traded at a forward or futures market, there will exist a well-known trivial relationship between its spot price and its forward price. Both statements become invalid when a spot market does not exist, it is not continuous, or the asset cannot be stored.

An HPI is not a price for a traded asset itself. Although an HPI can be thought of as an average home price backed by actual purchases, its replication via a large number of individual trades is known to be impractical. During the decline of the housing market in the US, quotes on forward or futures contracts were found noticeably below published spot HPI values, with no way to explore this 'arbitrage'. If so, where can the risk-neutral conditions come from? As we show below, if $X(t)$ is the spot value of an HPI, its risk-neutral evolution has to be tied to the forward or futures price process. The method we demonstrate in this section is akin to that of the HJM (Heath-Jarrow-Morton).

6.1 Derivation of a risk-neutral spot HPI process

Let us assume that an HPI is continuously traded forward and that the HPI forward price $F(t, T)$ observed at time t for exercise at $T \geq t$ is a single-factor diffusion:

$$\frac{dF(t, T)}{F(t, T)} = \mu(t, T)dt + \sigma(t, T)dz(t) \tag{8}$$

Denote $f(t, T) \equiv lnF(t, T)$, then, by Ito's Lemma,

$$df(t, T) = \left[\mu(t, T) - \frac{1}{2}\sigma^2(t, T)\right]dt + \sigma(t, T)dz(t), \; f(0, T) = lnF(0, T) \tag{9}$$

and its solution

$$f(t, T) = lnF(0, T) + \int_0^t \left[\mu(\tau, T) - \frac{1}{2}\sigma^2(\tau, T) \right] d\tau + \int_0^t \sigma(\tau, T)dz(\tau) \qquad (10)$$

Therefore,

$$F(t, T) = F(0, T)exp\left\{ \int_0^t \left[\mu(\tau, T) - \frac{1}{2}\sigma^2(\tau, T) \right] d\tau + \int_0^t \sigma(\tau, T)dz(\tau) \right\}$$

By definition, the spot value $S(t) \equiv F(t, t)$, hence,

$$S(t) = F(0, t)exp\left\{ \int_0^t \left[\mu(\tau, t) - \frac{1}{2}\sigma^2(\tau, t) \right] d\tau + \int_0^t \sigma(\tau, t)dz(\tau) \right\} \equiv exp[f(t, t)]$$

Let us write down the SDE followed by the spot-value return rate $f(t, t)$. Note that it will differ from (9) not only by notation (t instead of T), but also by the fact that this second argument t is a variable. Hence, $df(t, t)$ will include all the terms from (9) plus the differential of the right-hand side of (10) taken with respect to the second argument T and evaluated at $T = t$:

$$df(t, t) = \left[\mu(t, t) - \frac{1}{2}\sigma^2(t, t) \right] dt + \sigma(t, t)dz(t)$$

$$+ \left\{ \frac{F_t'(0, t)}{F(0, t)} + \int_0^t [\mu_t'(\tau, t) - \sigma(\tau, t)\sigma_t'(\tau, t)]d\tau + \int_0^t \sigma_t'(\tau, t)dz(\tau) \right\} dt$$

Now, $S(t) = F(t, t) = exp[f(t, t)]$, via Ito's Lemma we obtain the SDE for the spot value:

$$\frac{dS(t)}{S(t)} = M(t)dt + \Sigma(t)dz(t) \qquad (11)$$

where volatility function $\Sigma(t)$ and the drift $M(t)$ are equal to

$$\Sigma(t) = \sigma(t, t) \qquad (12)$$

$$M(t) = \frac{F_t'(0, t)}{F(0, t)} + \mu(t, t) + \int_0^t [\mu_t'(\tau, t) - \sigma(\tau, t)\sigma_t'(\tau, t)]d\tau + \int_0^t \sigma_t'(\tau, t)dz(\tau) \qquad (13)$$

We now clearly see that volatility of the spot-value process is that of the forward price computed at $T = t$. In general, the drift of the spot-value process is random and non-Markov even if the forward-price volatility function $\sigma(t, T)$ is a deterministic function of t and T. It depends on the entire history of $z(\tau)$, $0 \leq \tau \leq t$ via the last term in (13). Note that the risk-neutral drift only depends on random factors that enter the forward-price process. In particular, if the forward-price HPI process does not depend on income inflation, MBS rate, and the diffusion's shocks $w(t)$, then the risk-neutral process $S(t)$ will not depend on them either even if our physical process does.

To clarify the importance of this remark, let us consider the case when $F(t, T)$ represents HPI futures price of continuously traded futures contracts. It is known that

$F(t, T)$ must be a zero-drift martingale, i.e. $\mu(t, T) = 0$. Let us further assume that our volatility function $\sigma(t, T)$ depends only on t, and not on T. This assumption means that the entire curve of futures prices $F(t, T)$ moves at the same rate independent of T. Then, we will have a dramatic simplification of (13):

$$M(t) = F'_t(0, t)/F(0, t)$$

meaning that the risk-neutral HPI value $S(t)$ must have a deterministic drift along the initial forward curve.

6.2 A mean-reverting Markov case

In the absence of traded options, the critical forward volatility function $\sigma(t, T)$ can be estimated using historical quotes for $F(t, T)$. For example, having reviewed the daily trading quotes of the RPX-25 index for the second half of 2008, we estimate the annualized volatility at 6.6% for the 2008-end settlement, 11.9% (2009-end), 12.7% (2010-end), 12.0% (2011-end), and 12.5% (2012-end). Other historical periods exhibit different levels, but a similar pattern: the nearest contract is the least volatile one and the long-term volatility structure almost saturates at the second-year contract. These observations suggest a mean-reverting pattern in T so that $\sigma(t, T)$ starts from $\sigma_0(t)$ when $T = t$ (i.e. the spot-volatility level) and converges to $\sigma_\infty(t)$ with $T \to \infty$; both levels can be random or deterministic in t. Let us assume that $\sigma(t, T)$ follows a simple linear ODE in T,

$$\sigma'_T(t, T) = a_\sigma[\sigma_\infty(t) - \sigma(t, T)] \text{ initialized at } \sigma(t, t) = \sigma_0(t),$$

so that, with changing T, $\sigma(t, T)$ indeed changes exponentially between $\sigma_0(t)$ and $\sigma_\infty(t)$. Now, the last term in (13) becomes a state variable $N(t) \equiv \int_0^t \sigma'_t(\tau, t)dz(\tau)$ subject to an SDE:

$$dN(t) = -a_\sigma N(t)dt + a_\sigma[\sigma_\infty(t) - \sigma_0(t)]dz(t), \quad N(0) = 0 \quad (14)$$

and, with the zero-drift of the futures price, the risk-neutral drift for spot HPI becomes

$$M(t) = \frac{F'_t(0, t)}{F(0, t)} - \int_0^t \sigma(\tau, t)\sigma'_t(\tau, t)d\tau + N(t)$$

This result can be further simplified when $\sigma_0(t)$ and $\sigma_\infty(t)$ are constants. In this case, function $\sigma(t, T) = (\sigma_0 - \sigma_\infty)\exp[-a_\sigma(T - t)] + \sigma_\infty$ will be stationary, i.e. depends only on $\tau = T - t$. We will denote it σ_τ, in a way consistent with the already introduced notations σ_0 and σ_∞. Since $\sigma'_t(\tau, t) = -\sigma'_\tau(\tau, t)$, we can explicitly integrate

$$M(t) = \frac{F'_t(0, t)}{F(0, t)} - \int_0^t \sigma(\tau, t)\sigma'_t(\tau, t)d\tau + N(t) = \frac{F'_t(0, t)}{F(0, t)} + \frac{\sigma_0^2}{2} - \frac{\sigma_t^2}{2} + N(t)$$

Recall that $M(t)$ is the drift rate of our spot-HPI process, $S(t)$. The HPA rate, denoted $x(t)$ for physical modelling, was defined as $x(t) \equiv dX(t)/dt \equiv d\ln S(t)/dt$, hence, its continuous part will be equal to $M(t) - \frac{1}{2}\Sigma^2(t)$, i.e. the drift of HPI reduced by Ito's convexity of logarithm. According to (12), $\Sigma(t) = \sigma(t, t) = \sigma_0$, therefore, the total risk-neutral HPA rate will be equal to

$$HPA(t) = \frac{F_t'(0, t)}{F(0, t)} - \frac{\sigma_t^2}{2} + N(t) + \sigma_0 w(t) \tag{15}$$

Interestingly, this risk-neutral HPA appears in the form 'white noise plus mean-reverting diffusion' because the first two terms in (15) are deterministic and $N(t)$ reverts to zero in the absence of random forces. The essential difference from our physical model is that, in (15), the diffusion $N(t)$ is disturbed by the same noise $w(t)$ that forms the immediate shocks.

6.3 Forwards, futures, and convexity adjustment

The forward-price process $F(t, T)$ will have a zero drift if it is quoted by forward contracts (rather than futures), but independent of random interest rates. Otherwise, $F(t, T)$ will drift at a non-zero rate derived in this section.

A forward contract is a non-dividend traded asset, the value of which $V(t, T)$ has to drift at a risk-free rate $r(t)$ in the risk-neutral model. On the other hand, it is equal to the product of a discount bond's price $B(t, T)$ and $F(t, T)$: $V(t, T) = B(t, T)F(t, T)$. Combining the SDE (8) for the forward price and a similarly written SDE for $B(t, T)$ disturbed by forward rate's increments $\sigma_f(t, T)dz_f(t)$ and drifting at the risk-free rate we can derive the SDE for $V(t, T)$. Skipping these derivations, we present the result as

$$\frac{dV(t, T)}{V(t, T)} = \left(r(t) + \mu(t, T) - \rho\sigma(t, T) \int_0^T \sigma_f(t, \tau)d\tau \right) dt + \sigma(t, T)dz(t)$$

$$- \left(\int_t^T \sigma_f(t, \tau)d\tau \right) dz_f(t)$$

where ρ denotes a correlation between $dz_f(t)$ and $dz(t)$. Equating the drift term to the risk-free rate $r(t)$, we obtain the required drift for the forward-price process:

$$\mu(t, T) = \rho\sigma(t, T) \int_0^T \sigma_f(t, \tau)d\tau \tag{16}$$

Hence, if forward price $F(t, T)$ is independent of interest rates ($\rho = 0$), it will be a zero-drift martingale. With a positive (negative) correlation to interest rates, it must drift upwards (downwards). Naturally, the drift of forward price must offset the drift of discount bond's value, i.e. compensate for convexity of the product of two. For this reason, the forward-price drift is sometimes called 'convexity adjustment'. At expiration of the forward and futures contract, $S(T) = F(T, T)$, i.e. spot, forward, and futures prices are identical. Since the forwards and futures have differing drifts, we conclude that they must differ prior to expiration. In particular a discount bond's forward price must be above its futures price when $t < T$ because the bond's value negatively correlates to the forward rate.

Although our physical HPI model included the interest rate effect, we attributed it to the drift term, not the local volatility 'jumps'. Hence, under the assumptions used throughout this section, there should be no difference between HPI forwards and HPI futures. However, if the forward-price process depends on the interest rate increments $dz_f(t)$, correlated to $dz(t)$, then so will the risk-neutral spot value.

7 AVERAGE VOLATILITY

7.1 Conditional versus unconditional measures

We complete this chapter with a comparison between empirically assessed realized volatility and the one implied by the model. Our focus, however, will not be on testing the local volatility, but rather the average volatility measured between t and $t + \tau$ as a function of τ. Namely, we will compute the HPI's τ-long logarithmic increments as long as observations exist. The standard deviation of this measure divided by the square root of τ has the same meaning as the average (Black) volatility between t and $t + \tau$:

$$\sigma_{avg}(\tau) = stdev\left\{\ln\frac{HPI(t + \tau)}{HPI(t)}\right\}/\sqrt{\tau} \tag{17}$$

This measure can be computed both analytically (using the HPI model's equations) and empirically. In the latter case, we deal with an unconditional standard deviation in (17) whereas in the former case, one can compute both unconditional and conditional (given an initial point) statistics. In order to explain how it can be accomplished analytically, let us consider the discrete system (6), (7), and find the covariance matrix:

$$E[X_k X_k^T] = E[(FX_{k-1} + w_k + u_k)(X_{k-1}^T F^T + w_k^T + u_k^T)]$$
$$= FE[X_{k-1}X_{k-1}^T]F^T + E[w_k w_k^T] + E[u_k u_k^T] \tag{18}$$

In deriving this relationship, we accounted for mutual independence of X_{k-1}, u_k, w_k. Therefore, the covariance matrix can be computed iteratively, starting from $k = 1$ without simulations. In (18), matrices $E[w_k w_k^T]$ and $E[u_k u_k^T]$ serve as 'inputs' to the process, they are:

$$E[w_k w_k^T] = h\sigma_w^2\begin{bmatrix} 0 & 0 \\ 0 & 1 \end{bmatrix}, \; E[u_k u_k^T] = h\sigma_{pmt}^2\begin{bmatrix} k_1 k_1 & k_3 k_1 \\ k_1 k_3 & k_3 k_3 \end{bmatrix}$$

where σ_{pmt} is proportional volatility of the loan payment due to volatility of the financing rate. We can extend the method to compute variances of HPA (x_k) and log-HPI (X_k). Note that the income inflation may be negatively correlated to the change in financing rate.

Conditional statistics. The iterative process (18) must start with some initial condition for $E[X_0 X_0^T]$. If we surely observe today's vector X_0, it has a zero variance. This case corresponds to computing the conditional average volatility. We can even consider the uncertainty in X_0 estimated by the Kalman filter and stored in matrix P_{00}.

Unconditional statistics. In order to apply this method to computing the unconditional volatility, we assume that we deal with a stationary random process, so that $E[X_0 X_0^T]$ is the same as unconditional $E[X_k X_k^T]$ measured for large k. Our point of interest becomes not the variance for log-HPI (i.e. X_k), but rather for $X_k - X_0$.

Figures 17.9a and 17.9b depict a family of measures computed using the model's equations. We show the jump, diffusion, and interest rate related components (due to affordability, inflation, and the total) separately as well as the Pythagorean sum. Figure 17.9b also shows the empirical (1989–2008) measure.

Naturally, the unconditional average volatility is larger than the conditional one, for any horizon. The difference between these two is particularly sizeable for shorter horizons. When we know the initial conditions surely, the short-term uncertainty is mainly due to jumps. Over a longer term, jumps lose importance. However, with the unconditional statistics, jumps contribute weakly even for the one-quarter period. Indeed, the unconditional uncertainty of $HPI(t + 1)/HPI(t)$ is the same as the unconditional uncertainly of HPA (just over 3% annualized, revisit Figure 17.2), which far exceeds the jump effect (just over 1% annualized).

It is evident that, for longer-term horizons, the HPA diffusion term dominates. To some extent, the effects of income inflation and housing affordability partially offset each other, thereby mitigating the entire dependence on interest rates. When computing model-implied statistics in Figure 17.9, we assumed a 75% correlation between the inflation rate and mortgage financing rate. Empirically, these two rates show a much lower correlation when measured over a short period as generally do the short rate and long rates. However, mortgage rates correlate with a longer-term expectation of inflation and the level we used may be justified. At times, housing financing rates may depart from income inflation as happened in 2002–5 when the housing market went into a bubble. When this happens, interest rates may become a greater factor of risk and a much greater contributor to the HPI volatility than Figure 17.9 depicts.

How can we relate these volatility measures to valuation of HPI options? In the previous section, we demonstrated that the local volatility structure $\sigma(t, T)$ of forward prices dictates volatility $\sigma(t, t)$ of the risk-neutral spot HPI process. Hence, if we could continuously trade in forwards or futures, the HPI options would have very low volatility limited to jumps. In reality, according to TFS, a traded platform for CS futures and options, in January of 2009, dealers offered one-year options on the ten-city CS Composite index at a 9% implied volatility. This level is comparable with the empirical $\sigma(t, T)$ estimate in the 6–12% range that we cited in section 6. One explanation we can give here is that the assumption of continuous trading we made for the purpose of

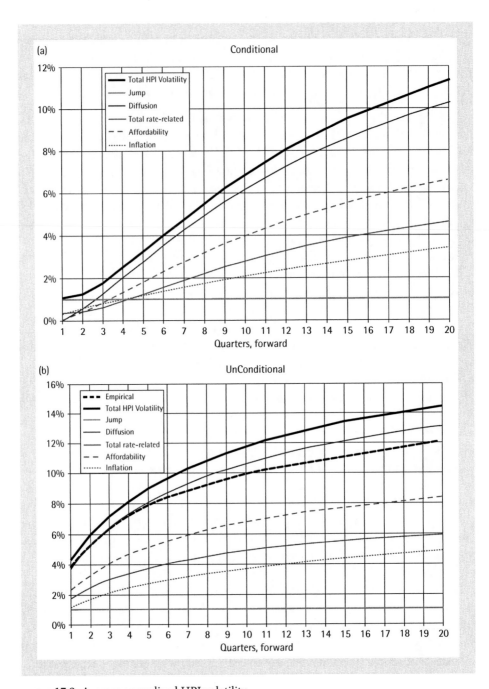

FIGURE 17.9 Average annualized HPI volatility.

risk-neutral derivations in section 6 is practically unrealistic for residential derivatives. With a low liquidity and an intimidating bid-ask spread, market participants cannot take full advantage of the known HPI drift. Therefore, the drift's uncertainty must also be reflected in the risk-neutral model.

7.2 The geographical angle

If our views of the home price evolution are valid, we expect them to stay valid across geographical regions, states, and metropolitan statistical areas (MSAs). Figure 17.10 depicts unconditional average volatility measured for the US, New York, California's large cities, and Cleveland, OH.

We can make a few interesting observations:

1. Densely populated urban areas are the leading source of the US housing market volatility. Compare the 25-MSA Composite to the FHFA US average, for example. Volatility ranges drastically across regions and indices, from 2% to nearly 20%.

2. The Case-Shiller indices are somewhat more volatile than the region-matching FHFA indices. As we explain in the Appendix, the CS family accounts for distressed sales (foreclosures), and includes transactions backed by sub-prime loans with borrowers unable or unwilling to maintain homes (Leventus 2008).

How does our model explain the super-low realized volatility of Cleveland in comparison to the much higher theoretical levels shown earlier in Figure 17.9? One explanation comes from the fact that, with lower or non-existing jumps and diffusion components, and local income inflation partially offsetting mortgage rates, the interest rate part of the HPI can have relatively low volatility too. Another explanation is that cities like Cleveland and Pittsburgh borrowed mostly conventionally and never experienced a bubble. Hence, the interest rate related HPI could actually differ in volatility across the US.

APPENDIX

A BRIEF DESCRIPTION OF US HPI INDICES

A.1 FHFA (OFHEO) indices

FHFA formerly known as the Office of Federal Housing Enterprise Oversight (OFHEO) compiles a family of HPIs going back to 1975. These indices are traditionally computed using the repeat-sale method and published quarterly. Due to its method, the index computation requires that a property be sold twice; the index is recomputed retroactively (e.g. a property sold in 1980 and then in 2000 affects the index value for the entire historical period between the sales). The index is published with (approximately) a two-month lag, and covers the US, its nine Census Bureau divisions, each of fifty states, and 292 Metropolitan Statistical Areas (MSAs).

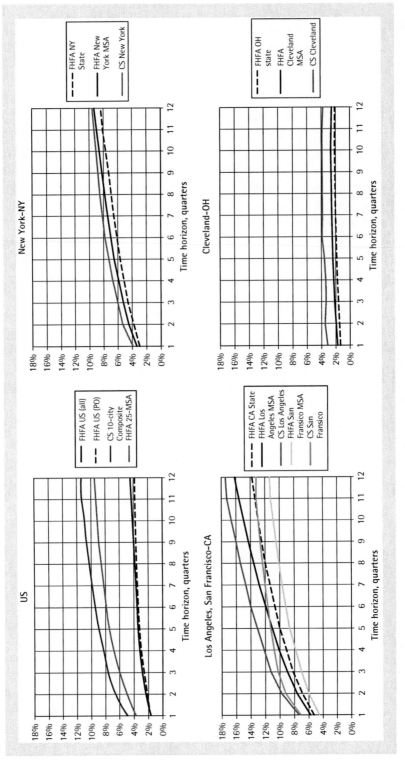

FIGURE 17.10 Empirical unconditional volatility: indices and geography.

FHFA derives its family of HPIs by the virtue of being the regulator of Fannie Mae and Freddie Mac, the US mortgage agencies (nationalized in October of 2008). Therefore, FHFA HPIs are based on home sales and appraisals secured by conforming loans only and exclude most foreclosures. For these reasons, the FHFA indices are the least volatile among the HPIs and may understate home price decline at the time of crises.

Along with traditionally published quarterly data, FHFA now produces monthly estimates as well. It publishes both all-transaction indices and purchase-only indices, with and without seasonal adjustments.

A.2 The Case-Shiller indices

The repeat sales methodology we mentioned above belongs to Karl Case and Robert Shiller. Standard & Poor's computes HPI for twenty metropolitan regions across the US along with two composites. Indices are published on the last Tuesday of each month with a two-month lag, using a three-month moving average. In addition, a broader US composite index is computed and published quarterly. The Case-Shiller indices include distressed sales (fore-closures), but filter out outliers that may point to a physical change of property. They go back to January of 1987 (albeit not for all regions); all CS indices are set to 100 on January 2000.

The Case-Shiller repeat-sales method is also employed by Fiserv, a company that computes and maintains the CS indices covering thousands of zip codes and metro areas, but not all. However, it is the S&P ten-city family of Case-Shiller indices that is traded at the CME.

A.3 The Radar Logic indices (RPX)

While the Case-Shiller method controls the quality of traded homes by using a pair of sales for the same property, Radar Logic does this differently: it computes and publishes indices as a price per square foot. Radar Logic publishes its indices daily, with a 63-day lag. Along with daily indices, the RPX family includes a 7-day and a 28-day version that aggregates transactions. The geographic coverage is limited to 25 MSAs and a composite plus a number of Manhattan Condominium indices; it includes all transactions and is not seasonally adjusted.

The RPX family of indices (the 28-day version) is employed for the residential derivative market inter-brokered by ICAP and some other trading platforms.

A.4 The National Association of Realtors (NAR) indices

NAR publishes indices that are comprised of all transactions gathered from Multiple Listing Services (not listed transactions are excluded). The index is published monthly at the national and census region levels and quarterly for more than 150 metropolitan areas. The day of publication—around the the 25th of the next month—makes NAR indices the timeliest information about housing market conditions available.

NAR indices are expressed via the median dollar figures, but do not provide an adequate home quality control, e.g. a change in size of homes sold next month from the previous month will send a false signal of change in the HPI.

References

Arthur, T., and Kagarlis, M. (2008). 'The RPX residential house price index', In S. Perrucci (ed.), *Mortgage Real Estate Finance*. London: Risk Books.

Benaben, B., and Saragoussi, J. (2008). 'Real estate indexes and property derivative markets'. In S. Perrucci (ed.), *Mortgage Real Estate Finance*. London: Risk Books.

Leventus, A. (2008). 'Real estate futures prices as predictors of price trends'. OFHEO working paper 08–01, Jan.

—— (2008). 'Recent trends in home prices: differences across mortgage and borrower characteristics', OFHEO, (Aug.).

Levin, A., and Davidson, A. (2008). The concept of credit OAS in the valuation of MBS'. *Journal of Portfolio Management* (Spring), 41–55.

Risa, S. et al. (2007). *Home Price Appreciation for Mortgage Pricing*. Lehman Brothers. (Feb.)

Shiller, R. (2005). *Irrational Exuberance*, (2nd edn.), New York: Random House.

—— (2008). *The Subprime Solution*. Princeton: Princeton University Press.

Simon, D. (2006). *Optimal State Estimation: Kalman, H Infinity, and Nonlinear Approaches*. Hoboken, NJ: John Wiley & Sons.

Weaver, K. et al. (2007). *The Outlook for U.S. Home Prices, DB's Nationwide and MSA Level Forecasts for 2007–2009*. Deutsche Bank (June).

CHAPTER 18

A VALUATION MODEL FOR ABS CDOS

JULIAN MANZANO, VLADIMIR
KAMOTSKI, UMBERTO PESAVENTO
AND ALEXANDER LIPTON

1 INTRODUCTION

ABS CDOs are complex securities. In a few words they are tranches receiving principal and interest payments (following certain allocation rules, so-called 'waterfall' structure) coming from a collateral pool that is managed and composed by cash, ABS cash notes, ABS CDSs, and ABS CDOs. By the mere fact that ABS CDOs are managed (dynamic collateral) and that their collateral pool can include more ABS CDOs, their level of complexity can grow unchecked.[1]

To clarify the language from now on we will use the name ABS (asset-backed securities) generically (for CDOs (collateralized debt obligations), CDSs (credit default swaps), cash, and synthetic structures) and will reserve the name *ABS deal* to refer to securities whose collateral is given by mortgage pools without further structure (first securitization). Hence an ABS deal can be fully funded (cash) or synthetic but cannot have other ABSs as part of its collateral.

In order to illustrate the collateral structure of a typical ABS CDO Figure 18.1 shows dependencies down two levels deep.

On top of the complexity observed in the collateral structure, each ABS CDO allocates collateral cash flows to each of its notes (tranches) following a complex set of rules (waterfall). These rules are described in lengthy prospectuses (typically 300

We very much appreciate discussions with Andrew Rennie and Vickram Mangalgiri. We also appreciate the help provided by Enping Zhao and Arkady Krutkovich on the usage of INTEX subroutines.

[1] Including cases where the top most CDO is included as collateral of itself.

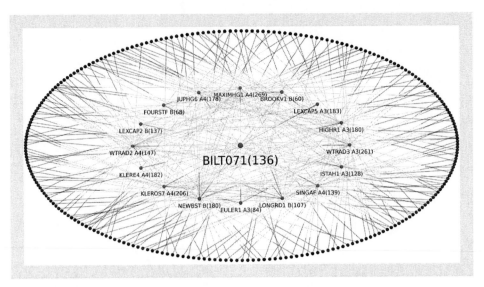

FIGURE 18.1 Graph showing two levels of the collateral dependence for Biltmore CDO 2007–1 (represented in the centre of the graph). The collateral of this CDO is currently composed of 136 ABS deals (cash and synthetic) and 16 ABS CDOs ('inner circle' in the graph). These 16 CDOs in turn depend on 256 CDOs ('outer circle') and 2025 ABS deals. The number of ABS deals directly below each CDO is indicated between parenthesis. For obvious reasons, only two levels of collateral are depicted.

pages long) and take into account several performance indicators (delinquency levels, loss levels, agency ratings, and other miscellaneous events) not freely available in an organized way. These idiosyncrasies make an attempt to translate waterfalls into algorithmic descriptions a non-trivial task. Nevertheless this task has been undertaken by INTEX Inc. (<www.intex.com/main/>) a professional analytics provider used de facto by market practitioners in the mortgage backed securities business.

INTEX releases subroutines that model waterfall rules applied to prepayment, delinquency, loss, and interest rate (IR) scenarios specified by the user. The user interface (API) is provided in the C language, and the subroutine libraries together with the relevant data files can be installed by the user in his local system.

Due to the complexity of the collateral structure, running even a single scenario through INTEX can take unlimited computer resources if simplifications are not made. The most obvious (and necessary simplification) can be guessed by inspecting of Figure 18.1. From this picture it is clear that as we go deeper in the collateral description the number of ABSs grows significantly. Nevertheless as we go deeper the importance of cash flows coming from ABS CDOs becomes negligible. Therefore in our methodology we will replace cash flows produced by ABS CDOs L_c levels deep by zero cash flows.[2] For example $L_c = 0$ would mean that cash flows for the top level ABS CDO are zero and $L_c = 1$ would mean that all ABS deals immediately below the top

[2] This simulates complete write-down of the CDO. If the CDO is synthetic total write-down is translated into the corresponding negative principal cash flow.

level CDO are run but the cash flows for the CDOs immediately below the top level CDO are set to zero. The numerical results presented here have been obtained running INTEX at $L_c = 2$.

Even with this simplification running a single scenario to price a single ABS CDO at $L_c = 2$ can take several minutes in a single machine. Because of this we run underlying ABS deals in parallel in a grid of ten machines (four cores each) carefully selecting a low number of representative scenarios. Finally, those scenarios are given probability weights calibrated against available quotes of ABS deals. This calibration is performed using a maximum entropy regularizer in order to obtain a single probability distribution with a sensible balance between calibration accuracy and predictive power.

The rest of the article is organized as follows: in the next section we present a brief historical overview of the sub-prime market. Section 3 provides the core technical description of the scenario generator. After the stochastic model is established, in section 4, we present the calibration procedure and finally in the last two sections we discuss results and conclusions.

2 BRIEF HISTORICAL OVERVIEW

Since the beginning of the credit crisis in July 2007 pools of mortgages of different asset types and vintages have exhibited a significant degree of performance deterioration.

In Figure 18.2 we show the historical prices of all ABX indices (see in References under Markit ABX.HE). Each ABX index references a portfolio of twenty ABS deals with sub-prime collateral. Indices tracking the same vintage (indicated by the last two digits in the index name) reference different tranches with the same underlying pool of mortgages. Note how AA 2007 vintages that were priced above par in February 2007 are trading below 6% since January 2009. How can we explain the market deterioration observed in Figure 18.2? One way to understand it is to go back to the time when the US house bubble was in full swing. In 2004 Morgan Stanley published a thorough research report about the Home Equity Loan Market (Morgan Stanley 2004). In this report we find two interesting pieces of information:

1. The capital structure of a representative HEL (home equity loan) transaction is given by: A NIM[3] security sized 6.95% of the collateral balance, then 2% over-collateralization followed by the BBB securities getting 5.75%, the A securities getting 5%, the AA securities getting 6.5%, and finally the AAA securities getting 80.75% of the collateral balance.
2. The typical historical cumulative loss at that time was given by a curve starting at 0 and flattening out around 5% in 96 months.

---

[3] NIM: Net Interest Margin Security. This security gets paid only the excess interest cash flow (no principal).

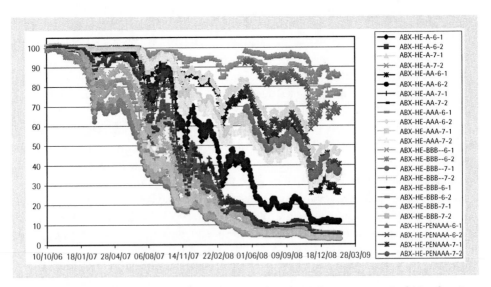

FIGURE 18.2 Historical prices of ABX indices. Each index references a pool of 20 sub-prime ABS deals. There are 4 different vintages corresponding to the first and second halves of 2006 and 2007. For each vintage there are 6 indices referencing different tranches of the same securitization.

Without entering into the details of particular securitizations it is clear from these two points that investors in 2004 who did not expect significant deviations from their historical experience would feel confident that ABS securities with ratings from A to AAA were safe investment vehicles. This perception changed dramatically in 2007 when the market agreed that the housing bubble was over and the refinancing cycle which was the main factor keeping losses at bay would vanish.

Besides the obvious drop in ABS prices attributed to the deterioration of the underlying collateral another factor that accelerated the demise of highly rated securities was the high effective correlation stored in their collateral pools. An example of this effect is seen in ABS CDOs backed by thin tranches of sub-prime collateral (TABX indices (see in References under Markit TABX.HE) are good examples). Because the tranches forming the collateral of those CDOs were thin BBB or A tranches they could either all survive in a benign environment or all be wiped out under a severe but not necessarily catastrophic event. Therefore the risk differentiation offered by the new tranches created on top was marginal and did not justify their assigned ratings.

The purpose of this historical overview is not to expose past pricing as overoptimistic (which is obvious only in hindsight) but to show that the risk involved in certain structures could have been asserted with proper modelling. In that spirit the rest of the article will deal with a model that is calibrated using current market prices and therefore does not take into account any macro-view about the future. In other words the task of the model is to produce prices consistent with the market and more importantly serve as a risk management tool.

3 SCENARIO GENERATOR

In order to price ABSs backed by mortgage pools we create scenarios where different mortgage pools will experience different levels of CPR (Constant Prepayment Rate), CDR (Constant Default Rate), and Severity S (100% minus the price at liquidation as a percentage of the loan balance). In principle one can specify these parameters with a term structure but in our model we restricted ourselves to constant levels of CDR, CPR, and Severity. Moreover, the INTEX interface also accepts the specification of a future delinquency level that in our model has been fixed to the one observed at the valuation date.

Our scenario set is produced using a Mersenne twister random number generator producing as many scenarios as desired. A given scenario will produce a triplet of CPR, CDR, and Severity values for a given ABS deal (identified by a cusip). This triplet will be expressed as percentages and denoted

$$\left(CPR_i^c, CDR_i^c, S_i^c\right),$$

where i is the scenario index ($i = 0, 1, \ldots$) and c is the cusip index. In order to describe the mapping $(i, c) \rightarrow \left(CPR_i^c, CDR_i^c, S_i^c\right)$ we introduce the following notation

$T(c)$	Settlement time of cusip c
$V(c)$	Vintage of cusip c
$Q(c)$	Collateral type for cusip c (Prime, Commercial, ALT-A, Sub-prime, Second Lien)

where $V(c)$ takes the values

$$
\begin{aligned}
&V(c) = 0 \text{ for } T(c) \leq 31 \text{ Dec. 2004},\\
&V(c) = 1 \text{ for } T(c) \text{ in 2005},\\
&V(c) = 2 \text{ for } T(c) \text{ in 2006},\\
&V(c) = 3 \text{ for } T(c) \geq 1 \text{ Jan. 2007},
\end{aligned}
\tag{1}
$$

and the collateral type $Q(c)$ takes the following values depending on the collateral backing cusip c:

$$
\begin{aligned}
&Q(c) = 0 \text{ for Prime},\\
&Q(c) = 1 \text{ for Commercial},\\
&Q(c) = 2 \text{ for ALT-A},\\
&Q(c) = 3 \text{ for Sub-prime},\\
&Q(c) = 4 \text{ for Second Lien},
\end{aligned}
\tag{2}
$$

with $Q(c) = 3$ (as sub-prime) for any other collateral type not given in the list.

To obtain the $\left(CPR_i^c, CDR_i^c, S_i^c\right)$ vector we will use correlated random variables with marginal distributions given by mixtures of beta and uniform[4] distributions. To fix the notation, given parameters a and β, we define

$$B\left(x, a, \beta\right) := \frac{\Gamma(a + \beta)}{\Gamma(a)\,\Gamma(\beta)} x^{a-1} \left(1 - x\right)^{\beta-1},$$

$$h^{a,\phi}\left(x, m\right) := \phi + (1 - \phi) \times B\left(x, \frac{m}{\sigma^2}, \frac{1 - m}{\sigma^2}\right),$$

$$H^{a,\phi}\left(y, m\right) := \int_0^y h^{a,\phi}\left(x, m\right) dx := p,$$

$$H_{Inv}^{a,\phi}\left(p, m\right) := y,$$

with the properties

$$\int_0^1 x h^{a,\phi}\left(x, m\right) dx = \phi \times \frac{1}{2} + (1 - \phi) \times m,$$

$$\int_0^1 x^2 h^{a,\phi}\left(x, m\right) dx - \left(\int_0^1 x h^{a,\phi}\left(x, m\right) dx\right)^2 = \frac{\phi}{12} + (1 - \phi)\frac{\sigma^2 m (1 - m)}{1 + \sigma^2}$$

$$+ \phi(1 - \phi)\left(m - \frac{1}{2}\right)^2.$$

For each scenario i we generate $5 \times 4 \times 3 = 60$ uniform correlated random numbers (5 collateral types $\times$ 4 vintages $\times$ 3 pool performance parameters[5]). These uniforms are correlated using a 60-dimensional Gaussian copula with correlation matrix described below. We denote these correlated uniforms u_j^i where $i = 0, 1, \dots$ is the scenario index and $j = 0, 1, \dots 59$ is the model parameter index. In order to define the correlation matrix (C) for the uniforms $\{u_j^i, j = 0, 1, \dots 59\}$ we introduce the following mappings for the model parameter index j

$$p(j) := \mathrm{mod}(j, 3) \qquad\qquad p(j) = 0, 1, 2$$

$$v(j) := \mathrm{mod}\left(\frac{j - p(j)}{3}, 4\right) \quad v(j) = 0, 1, 2, 3 \qquad\qquad (3)$$

$$q(j) := \frac{j - 3 \times v(j) - p(j)}{4 \times 3} \quad q(j) = 0, 1, 2, 3, 4$$

and the inverse mapping

$$j = q(j) \times 4 \times 3 + v(j) \times 3 + p(j), \qquad j = 0, 1, \dots 59,$$

---

[4] The uniform component is added to create 'fat' tails.
[5] These performance parameters are uniform random numbers acting as drivers of the CDR, CPR, and Severity parameters for a given scenario, collateral type and vintage (see eq. (7)).

where $p(j)$ is a pool performance index, $v(j)$ is a vintage index (same convention as $V(c)$ in eq. (1)) and $q(j)$ is a collateral type index (same convention as $Q(c)$ in eq. (2)). Hence the correlation matrix C coupling u_j^i with u_k^i is defined as

$$C_{j,k} = \cos\left(\frac{\pi}{2}\min\left(1, a \times |v(j) - v(k)|\right)\right)$$
$$\times \left(\rho + (1-\rho) \times \delta_{q(j),q(k)}\right) \times \delta_{p(j),p(k)}, \tag{4}$$

where all entries are constrained by $|C_{j,k}| \le 1$ and by C being positive semi-definite (all eigenvalues non-negative). In practice we use the three-parameter positive semi-definite matrix determined by

$$a = 10\%, \tag{5}$$
$$\rho = 95\%.$$

Note that from eq. (4) it is clear that correlations get smaller as the corresponding vintages get further away and as the corresponding collateral types become different. Note also that C becomes the identity matrix when $a = 100\%$ and $\rho = 0\%$.

Given the correlated uniforms $\{u_j^i, j = 0, 1, \ldots 59\}$, in order to compute the scenarios, we have to introduce some auxiliary quantities. For each cusip c these quantities are given as follows:

The bucketing index b_c given by

$$b_c = Q(c) \times 4 \times 3 + V(c) \times 3. \tag{6}$$

and for each index b_c the 3 pool performance parameters given by the uniform random numbers

$$u_{b_c+0}^i, \; u_{b_c+1}^i, \; u_{b_c+2}^i. \tag{7}$$

The first two performance parameters drive the prepayment fraction PF_i^c (introduced to guarantee $CDR_i^c + CPR_i^c < 100$) and the Home Price Ratio R_i^c given by

$$PF_i^c = H_{Inv}^{\sigma_{PF},\phi_{PF}}\left(u_{b_c+0}^i, \frac{PF_{Q(c),V(c)}^{Base}}{100}\right), \tag{8}$$

$$R_i^c = H_{Inv}^{\sigma_S,\phi_S}\left(u_{b_c+1}^i, \frac{R_{Q(c),V(c)}^{Base}}{100}\right), \tag{9}$$

where the parameters $PF_{Q(c),V(c)}^{Base}$ and $R_{Q(c),V(c)}^{Base}$, depending on collateral type $Q(c)$ and vintage $V(c)$, control the expected values of PF_i^c and R_i^c and the parameters σ_{PF}, ϕ_{PF}, σ_S, ϕ_S control their dispersions. The concrete values of these parameters are given below in eqs. (14) and (15).

Given the Home Price Ratio R_i^c and following the seasoning procedure given in the next subsection we define the scenario severity as

$$S_i^c = 100 \times \left(1 - R_i^c \frac{\sum_{l=1}^{Nsp(c)} \frac{B_l^c(t_0)}{LTV_l^c} \frac{I_{G_l(c)}(t_{peak})}{I_{G_l(c)}(T_l(c))}}{\sum_{l=1}^{Nsp(c)} B_l^c(t_0)} \right). \tag{10}$$

In order to link the expected CDR value to the scenario severity we introduce the stochastic quantity

$$m_{c,i}^{CDR} = \max \left(0, \frac{CDR_{Q(c),V(c)}^{Base}}{100} + \left(1 - \frac{CDR_{Q(c),V(c)}^{Base}}{100} \right) \times \frac{S_i^c}{100} \right), \tag{11}$$

where $CDR_{Q(c),V(c)}^{Base}$ is given below (see eq. (14)). Note that $m_{c,i}^{CDR}$ lies in the interval $\left[\frac{CDR_{Q(c),V(c)}^{Base}}{100}, 1 \right]$ and is positively correlated to S_i^c. Given $m_{c,i}^{CDR}$ we define CDR_i^c and CPR_i^c as

$$CDR_i^c = 100 \times H_{Inv}^{\sigma_{CDR},\phi_{CDR}} \left(u_{b_c+2}^i, m_{c,i}^{CDR} \right), \tag{12}$$

$$CPR_i^c = PF_i^c \times \left(100 - CDR_i^c \right), \tag{13}$$

where it is clear that CDR is, by construction, positively correlated to severity and that $CDR_i^c + CPR_i^c < 100$.

The various constants controlling expected values in eqs. (8), (9), and (11), are given by

$$\left(PF_{0,v}^{Base}, CDR_{0,v}^{Base}, R_{0,v}^{Base} \right) = (10, 00, 50)$$

$$\left(PF_{1,v}^{Base}, CDR_{1,v}^{Base}, R_{1,v}^{Base} \right) = (05, 05, 40)$$

$$\left(PF_{2,v}^{Base}, CDR_{2,v}^{Base}, R_{2,v}^{Base} \right) = (05, 05, 30) \tag{14}$$

$$\left(PF_{3,v}^{Base}, CDR_{3,v}^{Base}, R_{3,v}^{Base} \right) = (05, 10, 20)$$

$$\left(PF_{4,v}^{Base}, CDR_{4,v}^{Base}, R_{4v}^{Base} \right) = (05, 10, 10)$$

where, for simplicity, we have chosen to use a flat vintage structure. The constants controlling dispersions in eqs. (8), (9) and (11), are given by

$$\begin{aligned} \sigma_{PF} &= 40\%, & \phi_{PF} &= 10\%, \\ \sigma_S &= 40\%, & \phi_S &= 10\%, \\ \sigma_{CDR} &= 10\%, & \phi_{CDR} &= 0\%, \end{aligned} \tag{15}$$

where the dispersion parameters for CDR have been chosen smaller than the rest because CDR is already picking a contribution to its variance coming from its dependence on Severity through eq. (11).

Finally, the last point to mention is that for all Government Agency Securities (e.g. sponsored by Fannie Mae or Freddie Mac) we assume full US guaranty and because

INTEX does not specify the collateral type in this case we also assume that the collateral is Prime with the following changes in the performance parameters

$$CPR_i^c \rightarrow CPR_i^c + CDR_i^c,$$

$$CDR_i^c \rightarrow 0.$$

In the next section we explain the rationale behind the seasoned severity given by eq. (10).

3.1 Severity seasoning

In order to understand the severity formulas given by eqs. (9) and (10) we have to introduce the following concepts: given the l-th loan in the collateral pool of cusip c define the time-dependent home price ratio $R_l^c(t)$ as

$$R_l^c(t) = \frac{p_l^c(t)}{p_l^c(t_{peak})}, \qquad (16)$$

where $p_l^c(t)$ is the price of the associated property at time t and t_{peak} is the time corresponding to the peak of the market. As a proxy for the market we use the S&P Case-Shiller Home Price Indices (see References) (see Figure 18.3).

Standard & Poor publishes the Case-Shiller (CS) Home Price indices for different representative cities in the US (e.g. Miami, San Francisco, etc.). We use those indices to

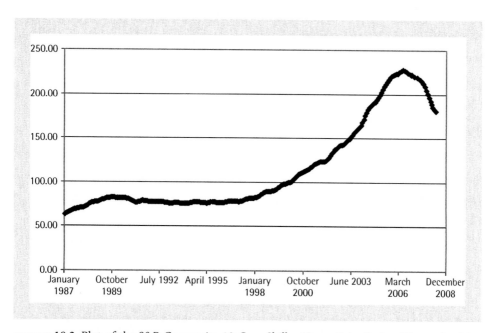

FIGURE 18.3 Plot of the S&P Composite-10 Case-Shiller Home Price Index. The peak of the index occurred at July 2006.

represent the average price on the corresponding states. For those states where we have more than one CS index (e.g. California has CS indices for Los Angeles, San Diego, and San Francisco) we take the average and for those states where there is no representative index we use the Composite-10 one. Introducing the following quantities

$G_l(c)$	Geographical location (US state) for the l-th loan in the collateral pool of cusip c
$T_l(c)$	Origination time for the l-th loan in the collateral pool of cusip c
$B_l^c(t)$	Balance at time t for the l-th loan in the collateral pool of cusip c
LTV_l^c	Loan To Value ratio for the l-th loan in the collateral pool of cusip c

for each state $G_l(c)$ we associate a CS index (or average) that at time t has value $I_{G_l(c)}(t)$. We use linear interpolation if t is inside the range covered by the available data and constant extrapolation otherwise.

Then using the index $I_{G_l(c)}(t)$ as the proxy for the value of the property associated to the l-th loan we immediately obtain

$$p_l^c(t_{peak}) = \frac{B_l^c(T_l(c))}{LTV_l^c} \frac{I_{G_l(c)}(t_{peak})}{I_{G_l(c)}(T_l(c))}. \tag{17}$$

Moreover defining $S^{c,l}$ as the severity of the l-th loan we have

$$\frac{S^{c,l}}{100} = 1 - \frac{p_l^c(t_{liq})}{B_l^c(t_{liq})}. \tag{18}$$

Hence from eqs. (16), (17), and (18) we obtain

$$\frac{S^{c,l}}{100} = 1 - R(t_{liq}) \frac{p_l^c(t_{peak})}{B_l^c(t_{liq})}$$

$$= 1 - \frac{R(t_{liq})}{LTV_l^c} \frac{B_l^c(T_l(c))}{B_l^c(t_{liq})} \frac{I_{G_l(c)}(t_{peak})}{I_{G_l(c)}(T_l(c))}.$$

In order to get a seasoning rule such that severity remains constant here we will make the simplification

$$\frac{R(t_{liq})}{B_l^c(t_{liq})} = \frac{R_i^c}{B_l^c(t_0)}, \tag{19}$$

where t_0 is the current time and R_i^c is a time-independent random variable that in our model is given by eq. (9). With this simplification we get the scenario dependent severity $S_i^{c,l}$ given by

$$S_i^{c,l} = 100 \times \left(1 - \frac{R_i^c}{LTV_l^c} \frac{B_l^c(T_l(c))}{B_l^c(t_0)} \frac{I_{G_l(c)}(t_{peak})}{I_{G_l(c)}(T_l(c))} \right). \tag{20}$$

Note that $S_i^{c,l}$ picks idiosyncratic dependencies on the loan geographical location, origination time, principal payment history, and LTV value. Eq. (20) gives us the seasoned severity at the loan level, however INTEX provides information about loans grouped in pools of similar characteristics. Therefore in order to adapt Eq. (20) to the information actually available in INTEX we have to interpret the index l as a sub-pool (of loans) index. Hence the l-th sub-pool will have associated geographical location $G_l(c)$, origination time $T_l(c)$, balance $B_l^c(t)$, number of loans $N_{c,l}^{Loans}(t)$ and average LTV_l^c. Taking this into account when we reinterpret the index l as a sub-pool index we have to replace

$$B_l^c(t) \rightarrow \frac{B_l^c(t)}{N_{c,l}^{Loans}(t)}.$$

and therefore the scenario dependent severity $\hat{S}_i^{c,l}$ corresponding to the l-th sub-pool will given by

$$\hat{S}_i^{c,l} = 100 \times \left(1 - \frac{R_i^c}{LTV_l^c} \frac{B_l^c(T_l(c))}{B_l^c(t_0)} \frac{N_{c,l}^{Loans}(t_0)}{N_{c,l}^{Loans}(T_l(c))} \frac{I_{G_l(c)}(t_{peak})}{I_{G_l(c)}(T_l(c))} \right). \tag{21}$$

However at the time of this writing $N_{c,l}^{Loans}(T_l(c))$ was not available in INTEX so we decided that as a working approximation we will take

$$\frac{B_l^c(T_l(c))}{N_{c,l}^{Loans}(T_l(c))} = \frac{B_l^c(t_0)}{N_{c,l}^{Loans}(t_0)}. \tag{22}$$

Finally, in order to get a seasoned severity at the cusip level we take a weighted average (using current balances as weighs) over sub-pools obtaining

$$S_i^c = \frac{\sum_{l=1}^{Nsp(c)} B_l^c(t_0) \times \hat{S}_i^{c,l}}{\sum_{l=1}^{Nsp(c)} B_l^c(t_0)}, \tag{23}$$

where $Nsp(c)$ is the number of sub-pools in the collateral pool of cusip c. Hence from eqs. (21), (22), and (23) we obtain the seasoned scenario dependent severity S_i^c given by

$$S_i^c = 100 \times \left(1 - R_i^c \frac{\sum_{l=1}^{Nsp(c)} \frac{B_l^c(t_0)}{LTV_l^c} \frac{I_{G_l(c)}(t_{peak})}{I_{G_l(c)}(T_l(c))}}{\sum_{l=1}^{Nsp(c)} B_l^c(t_0)} \right). \tag{24}$$

Finally we have to add two more points:

In the case of pools of second-lien mortgages the argument used above is not applicable because in case of liquidation only the remaining proceeds after paying the first lien are available for the second lien. Because of this and as a good proxy, for second lien pools we still use eq. (24) but setting LTV to 100%, that is

$$LTV_l^c = 1, \qquad \text{if } Q(c) = 4.$$

The last point to mention is that for some pools the LTV information is not available in INTEX, in that case we use the following default values $LTV_l^{c,def}$ calculated using averages using 1000 ABS deals per asset type

$$LTV_l^{c,def} = 69\% \text{ for } Q(c) = 0 \text{ (Prime)}$$
$$LTV_l^{c,def} = 69\% \text{ for } Q(c) = 1 \text{ (Commercial)}$$
$$LTV_l^{c,def} = 74\% \text{ for } Q(c) = 2 \text{ (ALT-A)}$$
$$LTV_l^{c,def} = 80\% \text{ for } Q(c) = 3 \text{ (Subprime)}$$

4 PROBABILITY MEASURE CALIBRATION

Once our scenario set is established we want to calibrate a risk-neutral probability measure using available market quotes. Let us now introduce some notation to describe the calibration procedure. Given N scenarios we want to calibrate the probability weights p_k for $k = 1, \ldots, N$ subject to the constraints

$$0 \le p_k \le 1, \quad \sum_{k=1}^{N} p_k = 1. \tag{25}$$

We define q_j^{market} as the market quote for the j-th calibration instrument and $q_{j,k}^{model}$ as its model price calculated using INTEX under the k-th scenario. We also define the model price for the j-th calibration instrument as

$$q_j^{model} = \sum_{k=1}^{N} p_k \times q_{j,k}^{model},$$

and the entropy E of the distribution as

$$E = -\frac{1}{\ln(N)} \sum_{k=1}^{N} p_k \ln\left(\frac{p_k}{h_k}\right).$$

where h_k are prior probabilities (typically flat). Then the calibration methodology minimizes (over the p_k satisfying eq. (25)) the objective function O given by

$$O = \frac{1}{2} \sum_{j=1}^{M} w_j \left(q_j^{market} - q_j^{model}\right)^2 - \alpha \times E, \tag{26}$$

where M is the number of quotes, w_j is the calibration weight for the j-th quote and $\alpha \ge 0$ is the entropy weight. The entropy weight α is chosen small enough to allow for good approximation of market quotes and big enough to avoid over-fitting (and therefore losing out-of-the-sample robustness). In calibration tests we found that $a \sim 4 \times 10^{-3}$ give us a good compromise.

One can easily see that the objective function given by eq. (26) is a convex function of p_k and that the constraints (25) define a convex set. Therefore from convex programming theory (Rockafellar 1970; Boyd and Vandenberghe 2004) it immediately follows that there is a unique solution to the minimization problem. This uniqueness property is very important as it guarantees the stability of the pricing methodology in a production environment. The details of the calibration algorithm are given in Appendix A.1.

Another important point of the methodology is that it allows for fast and exact calculation of price sensitivities. Once the model has been calibrated the computation of the derivatives of the probability measure with respect to the market quotes becomes a trivial linear algebra problem (see Appendix A.2 for details). And once the derivatives of the probability measure are known, computing the sensitivities of any ABS priced using the model becomes a trivial linear operation.

To illustrate the speed of the methodology let us mention that our implementation of the minimizer is able to calibrate hundreds of instruments using thousands of scenarios in seconds. The exact sensitivities with respect to all market quotes are obtained in sub-second times.

5 RESULTS

Here we will present our main results. In the first subsection we will analyse the model's calibration accuracy and generalization power. In the second subsection we will analyse the pricing and sensitivity analysis of a representative ABS CDO.

5.1 Calibration and robustness

To calibrate the model we use 852 cusips spanning all collateral types given in eq. (2). Market prices presented here correspond to 20 November 2008 and have been obtained using a pool of quotes coming from dealers inside and outside Merrill Lynch. Here it is important to remark that these market prices represent averages of quotes for illiquid assets and therefore they suffer from significant uncertainty. We do not have access to this market uncertainty for our calibration set but we do have individual dealer quotes for sub-prime cusips publicly available in Markit. These quotes and their uncertainty are plotted in Figure 18.4. In this plot we also show how the calibrated model typically stays inside the error bars. The conclusion obtained from inspecting Figure 18.4 is that the market uncertainty for these illiquid assets is significant, in some cases quotes for the same asset can have dispersions of up to 40%.

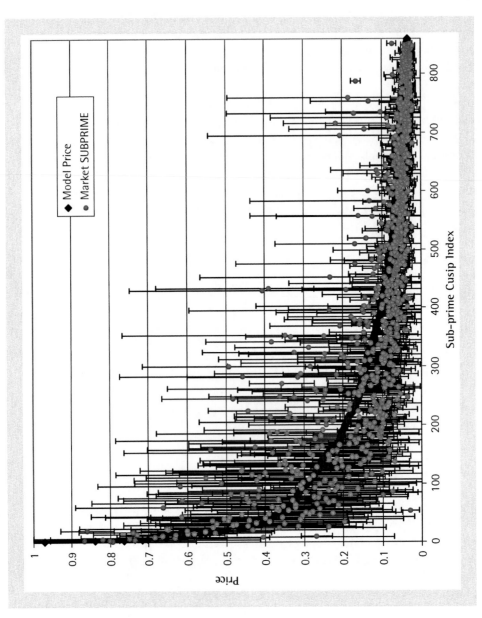

FIGURE 18.4 Markit quotes and model quotes for ABS deals with sub-prime collateral. The y-axis is the price given as percentage of current notional and the x-axis is the cusip index (where cusips are ordered by model quote). Each Markit quote is the average of the quotes contributed by several dealers. Error bars are given by the standard deviation of those quotes and illustrate the market uncertainty.

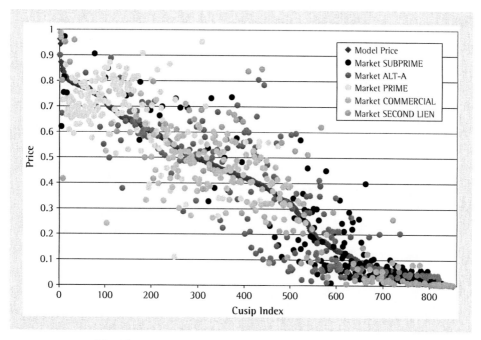

FIGURE 18.5 Model and market quotes for the 852 cusips used for calibration. These cusips represent ABS deals spanning different collateral types and vintages.

The calibration shown in Figure 18.4 was obtained using cusips with sub-prime collateral. In Figure 18.5 we show the calibration accuracy of the model after a joint calibration of 852 cusips with different collateral classes. Note that the calibration errors observed in Figure 18.5 are consistent with the market uncertainty observed in Figure 18.4.

In Figure 18.6 we plot the calibrated cumulative probability for the scenarios ordered with decreasing probability weight. Note how the probability distribution becomes smoother as we increase the entropy weight. However, the most important role of the entropy weight is to control the robustness or extrapolation ability of the calibrated model.

In order to illustrate the model robustness, in Figure 18.7 we show the pricing errors as a function of the entropy weight for calibration and out-of-the-sample sets of cusips. To be precise Figure 18.7 was constructed as follows:

1. We took a set of 1,452 cusips comprising all collateral classes (this is an extension of the 852 set used for calibration in Fig. 18.5)
2. This set was divided into two sets of 726 cusips with similar weighting across asset classes and vintages. Let's name these sets set 1 and set 2.
3. The model was calibrated using set 1 only and set 2 only for different levels of the entropy weight. The error was computed as the square root of the average square error. The curve plotted using circles shows the average of the two calibration errors as a function of entropy weight.

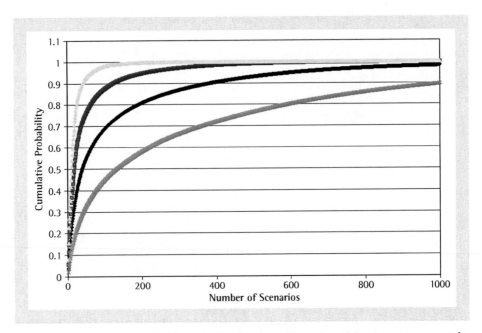

FIGURE 18.6 Cumulative probability profiles for the calibrated model using entropy weights $a = 1 \times 10^{-3}$, $a = 2 \times 10^{-3}$, $a = 4 \times 10^{-3}$ and $a = 1 \times 10^{-2}$. Out of 3,000 scenarios and in order to account for 99% probability the model required 2,307 scenarios for $a = 1 \times 10^{-2}$, 1,249 scenarios for $a = 4 \times 10^{-3}$, 470 scenarios for $a = 2 \times 10^{-3}$, and only 135 scenarios for $a = 1 \times 10^{-3}$.

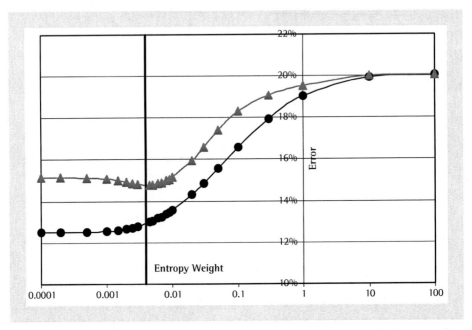

FIGURE 18.7 Behaviour of calibration (circles) and out-of-the-sample (triangles) average errors as a function of the entropy weight a. The optimal entropy weight ($a = 4 \times 10^{-3}$) is indicated by the vertical line.

4. The out-of-the-sample error curve (triangles) was constructed computing the error observed in set 2 using the model calibrated against set 1 averaged with the error observed in set 1 using the model calibrated against set 2.

Note how, as expected, the calibration error is a monotonically increasing function of the entropy weight. Note also how the out-of-the-sample error is larger than the calibration error, converges to the calibration error for a large entropy weight, and exhibits a minimum for an optimal entropy weight. This minimum (located at $\alpha = 4 \times 10^{-3}$) is understood noting that for a large entropy weight the model decouples from the market (probabilities converge to the prior regardless of the quotes) and for a very low entropy weight the model over-fits the calibration set.

The out-of-the-sample error provides a clear measure of the model capability to extrapolate outside the calibration set. From Fig. 18.5 it is clear that picking α around the optimal value (4×10^{-3}) produces average out-of-the-sample errors in the level of 15% which are compatible with the market uncertainty observed in Fig. 18.4.

5.2 CDO pricing and sensitivity analysis

In order to illustrate the pricing and, most importantly, the price sensitivity of an ABS CDO, we have chosen a representative security such that most of the ABS deals composing its collateral had market quotes available to us. As of 20 November 2008, the ABS CDO Biltmore CDO 2007-1 (see Fig. 18.1) had 136 ABS deals in its first layer and 2,025 ABS deals in its second layer. We had quotes for all the ABS deals in the first layer and for 33% of the ABS deals in the second layer. In total we have selected 800 cusips for calibration, all of the ABS deals of the first layer, and 664 of the second layer. The calibration accuracy, which can be observed in Fig. 18.8, is in line with the calibration accuracy observed for other calibration sets (see Figs. 18.4 and 18.5)

The pricing of all tranches (notes) of Biltmore CDO 2007-1 is given in Table 18.1.

Note that the price of the two most junior tranches is 0. This is because the remaining collateral is not enough to generate any positive cash flow for these tranches. We double-checked these points running only optimistic scenarios with 0 Severity, 0 CDR and CPR in the range (0,100%) and for all those scenarios the cash flows allocated to D and E tranches were strictly 0.

To illustrate the pricing sensitivity (see the Appendix for formulas) we pick the most senior tranche (A1) and compute its price sensitivities as

$$\theta_{A1}^{(s)} = \frac{\partial p_{A1}}{\partial q_s}, \qquad s = 1, \ldots, 800.$$

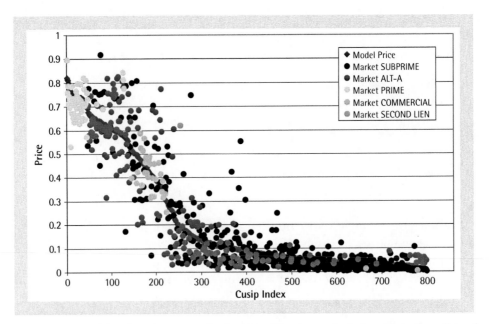

FIGURE 18.8 Model and market quotes for the 800 calibration cusips belonging to the collateral of Biltmore CDO 2007-1. All the ABS deals present in the first collateral layer (136 deals) are calibrated and 664 of the ones in the second layer are also included in the calibration set.

Table 18.1 Prices of 20 November 2008 for all tranches of Biltmore CDO 2007-1

Class	Price
A1	21.5%
A2	5.2%
A3	11.4%
A4	10.7%
B	9.4%
C	9.9%
D	0.0%
E	0.0%

where p_{A1} is the price of the tranche and q_s ($s = 1, \ldots, 800$) are the prices of the 800 cusips used for calibration. Fig. 18.9 shows the sensitivities $\theta_{A1}^{(s)}$ aggregated by asset type and vintage. Note how, mainly due to the collateral composition, most of the sensitivity is located in the Sub-prime and ALT-A sectors and recent vintages.

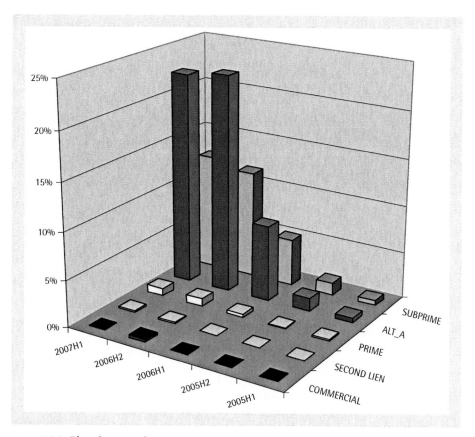

FIGURE 18.9 Plot showing the sensitivity of the A1 tranche of Biltmore CDO 2007-1 to the prices of the calibration ABS deals aggregated by asset type and vintage.

6 CONCLUSIONS

In this chapter we presented a Monte Carlo based framework for valuation of ABS CDOs. The model generates a rich set of scenarios for the prepayment and loss behaviour of different types of mortgage collateral. These scenarios are used to compute cash flows for ABS securities using the INTEX libraries. The scenario weights are calibrated, using a maximum entropy regularizer, against available market quotes. We found that the calibration errors and the out-of-the sample accuracy are consistent with the market uncertainty. We presented a full description of the scenario generator, the calibration algorithm and the sensitivity calculation. We concluded by pricing the full capital structure of a typical ABS CDO and showing the sensitivity profile for one of its tranches.

One possible improvement to our model is to provide a term structure for the Severity, CDR, and CPR parameters. This would make the model more realistic, for example, by lifting the simplification given by eq. (19) and by allowing the variance of all parameters to increase with time.

The last point that we would like to make is that even though the model was calibrated against observable market prices, it can still be used in a completely illiquid market. In this case the model is still a useful tool for investigating relative value and assessing risk. For example the model can be used assuming certain scenarios with a distribution given by a non-trivial prior or the user can express a view by pricing certain ABS deals that are later used as the calibration set.

A APPENDIX

Here we present the details and derivation of the calibration algorithm and sensitivity calculation.

A.1 Probability calibration

We have M cusips with market quotes q_i $(i = 1, \ldots, M)$ and N scenarios with probabilities p_j $(j = 1, \ldots, N)$. The calibrated p_j minimize the objective

$$
O = \frac{1}{2} \sum_{i=1}^{M} w_i \left(\sum_{j=1}^{N} A_{ij} p_j - q_i \right)^2 + \hat{a} \sum_{j=1}^{N} p_j \ln \left(\frac{p_j}{h_j} \right),
$$

$$
\hat{a} = \frac{a}{\ln(N)},
$$

where w_i are scenario weights, A_{ij} model quotes for cusip i and scenario j and h_j a prior probability for scenario j. The probabilities p_j are subject to the constraint

$$
\sum_{j=1}^{N} p_j = 1.
$$

We add the normalization constraint to the objective using a Lagrange multiplier γ obtaining

$$
\tilde{O} = \frac{1}{2} \sum_{i=1}^{M} w_i \left(\sum_{j=1}^{N} A_{ij} p_j - q_i \right)^2 + \hat{a} \sum_{j=1}^{N} p_j \ln \left(\frac{p_j}{h_j} \right) + \gamma \left(\sum_{j=1}^{N} p_j - 1 \right),
$$

Hence the equations for the p solving the optimization problem are given by

$$
\sum_{i=1}^{M} A_{ik} w_i \left(\sum_{j=1}^{N} A_{ij} p_j - q_i \right) + \hat{a} \ln \left(\frac{p_k}{h_k} \right) + \hat{a} + \gamma = 0, \tag{27}
$$

$$
\sum_{j=1}^{N} p_j = 1. \tag{28}
$$

We will solve these equations iteratively. Defining

$$p_j = \exp\left(y_j\right) = \exp\left(y_j^0 + \varepsilon_j\right) = p_j^0 \left(1 + \varepsilon_j\right),$$

$$\gamma = \gamma^0 + \varepsilon, \qquad \sum_{j=1}^{N} p_j^0 = 1,$$

we have

$$\sum_{i=1}^{M} \sum_{j=1}^{N} A_{ik} w_i A_{ij} p_j^0 \varepsilon_j + \hat{a}\varepsilon_k + \varepsilon = -\sum_{i=1}^{M} A_{ik} w_i \left(\sum_{j=1}^{N} A_{ij} p_j^0 - q_i\right)$$

$$-\hat{a} \ln\left(\frac{p_k^0}{h_k}\right) - \hat{a} - \gamma^0,$$

$$\sum_{j=1}^{N} p_j^0 \varepsilon_j = 0,$$

or defining

$$\varepsilon_j = \chi_j - 1,$$

$$\varepsilon = \xi - \gamma^0,$$

we obtain

$$\sum_{i=1}^{M} \sum_{j=1}^{N} A_{ik} w_i A_{ij} p_j^0 \chi_j + \hat{a}\chi_k + \xi = \sum_{i=1}^{M} w_i q_i A_{ik} - \hat{a} \ln\left(\frac{p_k^0}{h_k}\right), \tag{29}$$

$$\sum_{j=1}^{N} p_j^0 \chi_j = 1. \tag{30}$$

That is, defining the $N + 1$ dimensional vectors x, b and the $(N + 1) \times (N + 1)$ matrix Q as

$$x_j = \begin{cases} \chi_j & \text{if } j < N, \\ \xi & \text{if } j = N, \end{cases}$$

$$b_k = \begin{cases} p_k^0 w_i q_i A_{ik} - \hat{a} p_k^0 \ln\left(\frac{p_k^0}{h_k}\right) & \text{if } k < N, \\ 1 & \text{if } k = N, \end{cases}$$

$$Q_{kj} = \begin{cases} \hat{a} p_k^0 \delta_{kj} + \sum_{i=1}^{M} p_k^0 A_{ik} w_i A_{ij} p_j^0 & \text{if } j < N, \quad k < N, \\ p_k^0 & \text{if } j = N, \quad k < N, \\ p_j^0 & \text{if } j < N, \quad k = N, \\ 0 & \text{if } j = N, \quad k = N, \end{cases}$$

we can write the linear system

$$Q \cdot x = b.$$

The next step is to get an approximate solution to this linear system using a few iterations of a conjugate gradient method. Setting the initial variables

$$x_0 = 1,$$

$$r_0 = b - Q \cdot x_0,$$

$$\beta_0 = 0,$$

the algorithm is given by the following recursion starting with $k = 0$

$$w_k = -r_k + \beta_k w_k,$$

$$z_k = Q \cdot w_k,$$

$$v_k = \frac{r_k \cdot z_k}{w_k \cdot z_k},$$

$$x_{k+1} = x_k + v_k w_k,$$

$$r_{k+1} = r_k - v_k z_k,$$

$$\beta_{k+1} = \frac{r_{k+1} \cdot z_k}{w_k \cdot z_k}.$$

A.2 Sensitivities

Taking derivatives with respect to q_s in eqs. (27, 28) (and remembering the Lagrange multiplier dependence on q_s) we obtain

$$\sum_{i=1}^{M} \sum_{j=1}^{N} A_{ik} w_i A_{ij} \frac{\partial p_j}{\partial q_s} - A_{sk} w_s + \hat{a} \frac{1}{p_k} \frac{\partial p_k}{\partial q_s} + \frac{\partial \gamma}{\partial q_s} = 0, \tag{31}$$

$$\sum_{j=1}^{N} \frac{\partial p_j}{\partial q_s} = 0. \tag{32}$$

Defining

$$\theta_k^{(s)} = \frac{\partial p_k}{\partial q_s},$$

$$\sigma^{(s)} = \frac{\partial \gamma}{\partial q_s},$$

and multiplying by p_k in eq. (31) we obtain

$$\sum_{i=1}^{M} \sum_{j=1}^{N} p_k A_{ik} w_i A_{ij} \theta_j^{(s)} + \hat{a} \theta_k^{(s)} = p_k A_{sk} w_s - p_k \sigma^{(s)}, \tag{33}$$

$$\sum_{j=1}^{N} \theta_j^{(s)} = 0. \tag{34}$$

If $N \leq M$ we solve the primal problem defining

$$\theta_j^{(s)} = p_j v_j^{(s)},$$

$$H_{kj} = \hat{a} p_k \delta_{kj} + \sum_{i=1}^{M} p_k A_{ik} w_i A_{ij} p_j,$$

$$b_k^{(s)} = p_k A_{sk} w_s,$$

$$g_k = p_k,$$

$$r^{(s)} = H^{-1} b^{(s)},$$

$$z = H^{-1} g,$$

we have

$$\sigma^{(s)} = \frac{\sum_{j=1}^{N} p_j r_j^{(s)}}{\sum_{j=1}^{N} p_j z_j},$$

$$v^{(s)} = r^{(s)} - \sigma^{(s)} z.$$

If $N > M$ we solve the dual problem defining

$$h_i^{(s)} = \sum_{l=1}^{N} A_{il} \theta_l^{(s)} - \delta_{si}, \tag{35}$$

and substituting it in eq. (33) we immediately obtain

$$\sum_{i=1}^{M} p_k A_{ik} w_i h_i^{(s)} + \hat{a} \theta_k^{(s)} = -p_k \sigma^{(s)}, \tag{36}$$

and then multiplying by $w_j A_{jk}$ and summing over k we obtain

$$\sum_{i=1}^{M} \left(\sum_{k=1}^{N} w_j A_{jk} p_k A_{ik} w_i + \hat{a} w_j \delta_{ij} \right) h_i^{(s)} = -\hat{a} w_j \delta_{sj} - \sigma^{(s)} \sum_{k=1}^{N} w_j A_{jk} p_k. \tag{37}$$

Hence defining

$$H_{ij} = \hat{a} w_j \delta_{ij} + \sum_{k=1}^{N} w_j A_{jk} p_k A_{ik} w_i,$$

$$g_j = \sum_{k=1}^{N} w_j A_{jk} p_k,$$

$$r_i^{(s)} = \left(H^{-1} \right)_{is} w_s,$$

$$z_i = H^{-1} g = \sum_{l=1}^{M} \left(H^{-1} \right)_{il} \sum_{j=1}^{N} w_l A_{lj} p_j,$$

we obtain

$$h^{(s)} = -\hat{a}r^{(s)} - \sigma^{(s)}z, \tag{38}$$

but from eqs. (36) and (38) we also have,

$$\theta_k^{(s)} = \frac{1}{\hat{a}}\left(-p_k\sigma^{(s)} - \sum_{i=1}^{M} p_k A_{ik}w_i h_i^{(s)}\right)$$

$$= \sum_{i=1}^{M} p_k A_{ik}w_i \left(H^{-1}\right)_{is} w_s + \frac{\sigma^{(s)}}{\hat{a}} p_k \left(\sum_{i=1}^{M} A_{ik}w_i z_i - 1\right).$$

So defining

$$\xi_k^{(s)} = \sum_{i=1}^{M} w_s \left(H^{-1}\right)_{si} w_i A_{ik} p_k, \tag{39}$$

we obtain

$$\theta_k^{(s)} = \xi_k^{(s)} + \frac{\sigma^{(s)}}{\hat{a}} p_k \left(\sum_{i=1}^{M} A_{ik}w_i z_i - 1\right)$$

$$= \xi_k^{(s)} + \frac{\sigma^{(s)}}{\hat{a}}\left(\sum_{l=1}^{M}\sum_{j=1}^{N}\sum_{i=1}^{M} p_k A_{ik}w_i \left(H^{-1}\right)_{il} w_l A_{lj} p_j - p_k\right)$$

$$= \xi_k^{(s)} + \frac{\sigma^{(s)}}{\hat{a}}\left(\sum_{l=1}^{M}\sum_{j=1}^{N} \xi_k^{(l)} A_{lj} p_j - p_k\right), \tag{40}$$

Hence plugging eq. (40) into eq. (34) we find

$$\frac{\sigma^{(s)}}{\hat{a}} = \frac{\sum_{k=1}^{N} \xi_k^{(s)}}{1 - \sum_{k=1}^{N} \xi_k^{(l)} \sum_{l=1}^{M}\sum_{j=1}^{N} A_{lj} p_j}. \tag{41}$$

Finally substituting eq. (41) into eq. (40) we obtain the solution

$$\theta_k^{(s)} = \xi_k^{(s)} + \left(\sum_{l=1}^{M}\sum_{j=1}^{N} \xi_k^{(l)} A_{lj} p_j - p_k\right)\frac{\sum_{i=1}^{N} \xi_i^{(s)}}{1 - \sum_{i=1}^{N} \xi_i^{(l)} \sum_{l=1}^{M}\sum_{j=1}^{N} A_{lj} p_j}. \tag{42}$$

A.3 Dual approach

Starting from probabilities p_k^0 satisfying

$$\sum_{k=1}^{N} p_k^0 = 1,$$

we define the primal variables χ_j and the duals h_i as

$$p_j = p_j^0 \exp(\chi_j - 1),\tag{43}$$

$$h_i = \sum_{j=1}^{N} A_{ij} p_j - q_i.\tag{44}$$

Then expanding eqs. (27) and (28) around $\chi_j = 1$ we obtain the first-order equations

$$\sum_{i=1}^{M} A_{ik} w_i \left(\sum_{j=1}^{N} A_{ij} p_j^0 \chi_j - q_i \right) + \hat{a}\chi_k + \gamma = -\hat{a} \ln \left(\frac{p_k^0}{h_k} \right),\tag{45}$$

$$\sum_{j=1}^{N} p_j^0 \chi_j = 1,\tag{46}$$

or using the dual variables

$$\sum_{i=1}^{M} A_{ik} w_i h_i + \hat{a}\chi_k + \gamma = -\hat{a} \ln \left(\frac{p_k^0}{h_k} \right),\tag{47}$$

$$\sum_{j=1}^{N} p_j^0 \chi_j = 1.$$

Multiplying eq. (47) by $w_j A_{jk} p_k^0$ and summing over k we obtain

$$\sum_{i=1}^{M} \left(\sum_{k=1}^{N} w A_{jk} p_k^0 A_{ik} w_i + \hat{a} w_j \delta_{ij} \right) h_i = -\gamma \sum_{k=1}^{N} w_j A_{jk} p_k^0$$

$$-\hat{a} \sum_{k=1}^{N} w_j \left(q_j + A_{jk} p_k^0 \ln \left(\frac{p_k^0}{h_k} \right) \right).$$

Therefore defining

$$H_{ij} = \hat{a} w_j \delta_{ij} + \sum_{k=1}^{N} w_j A_{jk} p_k A_{ik} w_i,$$

$$g_j = \sum_{k=1}^{N} w_j A_{jk} p_k^0,$$

$$b_j = \sum_{k=1}^{N} w_j \left(q_j + A_{jk} p_k^0 \ln \left(\frac{p_k^0}{h_k} \right) \right),$$

$$z = H^{-1} g,$$

$$r = H^{-1} b,$$

we obtain

$$h = -\gamma z - \hat{a} r,$$

but from eq. (47) we have

$$
\chi_k = -\ln\left(\frac{p_k^0}{h_k}\right) - \frac{\gamma}{\hat{a}} - \frac{1}{\hat{a}}\sum_{i=1}^{M} h_i w_i A_{ik}
$$

$$
= \sum_{i=1}^{M} r_i w_i A_{ik} - \ln\left(\frac{p_k^0}{h_k}\right) + \frac{\gamma}{\hat{a}}\left(-1 + \sum_{i=1}^{M} z_i w_i A_{ik}\right), \tag{48}
$$

so plugging eq. (48) into eq. (46) we obtain

$$
1 = \sum_{i=1}^{M}\sum_{k=1}^{N} p_k^0 A_{ik} w_i r_i - \sum_{k=1}^{N} p_k^0 \ln\left(\frac{p_k^0}{h_k}\right) + \frac{\gamma}{\hat{a}}\left(-1 + \sum_{i=1}^{M}\sum_{k=1}^{N} z_i w_i A_{ik} p_k^0\right)
$$

$$
= \sum_{i=1}^{M} g_i r_i - \sum_{k=1}^{N} p_k^0 \ln\left(\frac{p_k^0}{h_k}\right) + \frac{\gamma}{\hat{a}}\left(-1 + \sum_{i=1}^{M} z_i g_i\right)
$$

or

$$
\frac{\gamma}{\hat{a}} = -\frac{1 + \sum_{k=1}^{N} p_k^0 \ln\left(\frac{p_k^0}{h_k}\right) - \sum_{i=1}^{M} g_i r_i}{1 - \sum_{i=1}^{M} z_i g_i}. \tag{49}
$$

Hence replacing eq. (49) into eq. (48) we obtain

$$
\chi_k = \sum_{i=1}^{M} r_i w_i A_{ik} - \ln\left(\frac{p_k^0}{h_k}\right)
$$

$$
+ \frac{1 + \sum_{k=1}^{N} p_k^0 \ln\left(\frac{p_k^0}{h_k}\right) - \sum_{i=1}^{M} g_i r_i}{1 - \sum_{i=1}^{M} z_i g_i}\left(1 - \sum_{i=1}^{M} z_i w_i A_{ik}\right). \tag{50}
$$

Once the solution for χ_k is found, we plug it into Eq. (43) and renormalize the p_k to account for non-linear corrections. The process is repeated until we observe convergence.

REFERENCES

Boyd, S., and Vandenberghe, L. (2004). *Convex Optimization.* Cambridge: Cambridge University Press.

Markit ABX.HE, <http://www.markit.com/en/products/data/indices/structured-finance-indices/abx/abx.page>.

Markit TABX.HE, <http://www.markit.com/en/products/data/indices/structured-finance-indices/tabx/tabx.page>.

Morgan Stanley (2004). *Home Equity Handbook,* Morgan Stanley, Fixed Income Research.

Rockafellar, R. T. (1970). *Convex Analysis.* Princeton: Princeton University Press.

S&P Composite-10 Case-Shiller Home Price Index, <http://www2.standardandpoors.com/portal/site/sp/en/us/page.topic/indices_csmahp>.

Name Index

SUBJECT INDEX